SHYNESS AND LOVE:
Causes, Consequences, and Treatment

By Dr. Brian G. Gilmartin

UNIVERSITY
PRESS OF
AMERICA

Lanham • New York • London

Copyright © 1987 by

University Press of America,® Inc.

4720 Boston Way
Lanham, MD 20706

3 Henrietta Street
London WC2E 8LU England

Printed in the United States of America

British Cataloging in Publication Information Available

Library of Congress Cataloging-in-Publication Data

Gilmartin, Brian G.
  Shyness and love.

  Bibliography: p.
  Includes index.
  1. Single men—Psychology.   2. Bashfulness.
3. Love.   4. Interpersonal relations.   I. Title.
HQ800.3.G55   1987   305'.90652   86-33658
ISBN 0-8191-6102-0 (alk. paper)

All University Press of America books are produced on acid-free
paper which exceeds the minimum standards set by the National
Historical Publication and Records Commission.

This book is dedicated to the promotion of responsible free choice and self-determination—something to which all human beings everywhere ought to be fully entitled.

This book is dedicated to three people:

(1) To Ms. (soon to be Dr.) Allegra Patten, a more breathtakingly spectacular and totally unforgettable "natural wonder" than Machu Picchu. Dedicated to Allegra with all of my deepest and most eternal love.

(2) To Mr. Taras "the Gnome" Fortuna of Bradford, West Yorkshire, England, my favorite male friend.

(3) To Mr. George V. Gilmartin, my father, without whose help this project would never have been possible.

Acknowledgements

No project of this size and scope could be brought to a successful conclusion without the help, emotional support and encouragement of a great many people. It was most heartening to me to find that many people are deeply interested in the love-shyness problem and in helping to find ways of effectively solving it. And it is my most sincere hope that this book will serve to strongly stimulate a burgeoning in research efforts on love-shyness and on ways of painlessly remediating the problem for those who are most severely afflicted with it.

First I'd like to thank Dr. Murray Adams, professor and chairperson of the sociology department at Auburn University, for his help in getting me the grant which permitted this project to be launched in the first place. In addition, I shall always be very grateful to Dr. John P. Garrison and Dr. David Clavier of the speech communication department at Auburn for their encouragement and for their never-ending flow of stimulating ideas.

I also owe a debt of gratitude to my current colleagues at Westfield State College in Massachusetts. In particular, Dr. Mostafa Noury, Dr. Larry Levitt, and Dr. David Miller of the sociology department, Dr. Joseph Tobia of Media Studies, and Dr. Joseph Connolly of the psychology department, have all been sources of valuable encouragement and creative ideas.

And I shall always remain grateful to Professor Hallowell Pope of the University of Iowa, and to Professor Ira L. Reiss of the University of Minnesota (under whose direction I took my Ph.D. a decade ago), for the endless supply of stimulating ideas, support and encouragement they have been able to provide. Special thanks are also due to my long-time friend Dr. Roger W. Libby of the University of Massachusetts at Amherst, for his many stimulating and provocative conversations. And I want to thank Dr. Robert Leik of the University of Minnesota for the interest and encouragement he showed towards this project during its early stages.

My "California connection" has also been of considerable importance to me throughout the duration of this study. And I would particularly like to thank Dr. Paul Leon Mastarakos, Dr. Hazel Hampton, Dr.
Frankie Mitchell, Dr. Henry Anderson, Dr. James Carroll, Dr. Franz
Adler, and Dr. William Larson, for their helpful support. And in the
U.K. there is Mr. Taras "Gnome" Fortuna, who has supplied me with
a steady flow of inspiration along with the chance to derive some further
quite useful stimulation from "the birds of Blackpool."

Further, even though there is much about their approaches to the
subject of love-shyness with which I disagree, I owe a debt of gratitude
to Dr. Philip Zimbardo of Stanford University, and to Dr. Letitia Anne
Peplau of University of California at Los Angeles, for giving me a much
needed "intellectual shot in the arm." Their work as well as the work
of Dr. Hal Arkowitz, Dr. Andrew Christensen, Dr. Paul Pilkonis, Dr.
William Martinson, Dr. Craig Twentyman, and Dr. Joseph Melnick, did
much to stimulate my thinking. Without their work and the invaluable
scholarly contributions of Dr. Hans Eysenck, Dr. Alexander Thomas,
Dr. Thomas J. Bouchard, Jr., and Dr. Jerome Kagan, this book would
not have been possible.

Finally (*and most importantly*), I wish to thank the 500 men who so
willingly opened up their lives to me so that this book could be written
in a meaningful manner. Assurances of anonymity render it impossible
for me to mention any names. However, I shall always be enormously
grateful to the many people who so generously gave of their time and
who bestowed upon me and upon the "love-shyness project" a very
great deal of personal trust and support. This book is dedicated to these
men. Simply put, the 500 interviewees were more instrumental than
anybody in assuring the successful completion of this book. I learned a
very great deal from them, and I feel very confident that each and every
reader of this book will do so as well.

DR. BRIAN G. GILMARTIN

Department of Sociology,
Westfield State College,
Westfield, MA 01086
January 27, 1985

Table of Contents

Acknowledgments vii

List of Figures xix

Preface xxi

Chapter 1:   INTRODUCTION 1
             What is Love-Shyness? 4
             The Gender Factor 4
             Enlightened Self-Control versus Shyness 7
             Love-Shyness is a Serious Problem 8
                 The Christopher Jencks Study 9
                 Studies in the Employment Sector 9
                 On Remedying Social Skill Deficits 11
                 Early Marriage versus Professional Success . . 11
                 Dating and General Happiness 12
                 Love as a Powerful Elixir 13
                 Premarital Virginity and Adjustment 15
             Viewing Someone to Love as a Cure-All 17
             Normative Timetables of Self-Revelation 19
             Why This Book? 21
             Love-Shyness Costs Society Money 27
             Summary 30
             Plan of the Book 31

Chapter 2:   LOVE-SHYNESS AND THE NATURE VERSUS
             NURTURE DEBATE 35
             The Phenomenon of Inborn Temperament 38
             The Work of Hans J. Eysenck 40
             Love-Shyness and the Inborn Anxiety
             Threshold 43
             The Importance of Social Stimulus Value 45
             The Work of Alexander Thomas 47

The Jerome Kagan Work .50
　　Heart Rate Patterns 52
　　Long-Separated Identical Twins 55
The Importance of Enzymes. 56
　　Enzyme Activity and Propitious Fetal
Growth 57
　　Painful Anxiety and Enzyme Neutralization   59
Some Related Work on Depression 60
Suicide. 64
Anxiety Disease. 67
Schizophrenia 74
Obsessive-Compulsive Disorders 75
Conclusions 78
Chapter 3:　SOCIETAL REACTIONS AND ELASTIC LIMITS 81
The "Wish Bone Effect". 83
The Sociological Perspective. 88
Every Group Needs a Deviant. 88
The Mentally Retarded as Analogous to the
Shy 90
The Jane Elliott Study 92
　　The Taking Over of a Role 95
　　Dark Crayons and Drab Drawings 97
The "Apperceptive Mass" Concept 98
Conclusions 102
Chapter 4:　ASTROLOGY AND REINCARNATION 103
Astrological Factors 103
　　How Astrology Is Believed to Work. 105
　　The Present Research. 106
Reincarnation. 109
Psychodormia 110
Chapter 5:　HOW THE INFORMATION WAS OBTAINED. . .115
Who Is "Love-Shy"?. 117
Why Study Men Only? .118
The "Felt Deprivation" Concept 119
Distinguishing Heterosexuals from
Homosexuals 120
The "Closet Heterosexual" Concept. 123
The "Male Lesbian" Concept 125
Three Samples Were Studied 127
　　Sample Heterogeneity 129
　　Reliability 130

The Prevalence of Love-Shyness 131
How the Respondents Were Obtained 132
    The Younger Love-Shy Men 132
    The Socially Self-Confident Non-Shy Men . . .134
    The SHI Inventory 137
    The Older Love-Shy Group 138
    The Commercial Dating Service 139
The Importance of LOVE-Shyness 140
Summary 141

Chapter 6: LOVE-SHYNESS: ITS INTRAUTERINE
                BEGINNINGS 143
The East German Research 143
    Blood Testosterone 143
    Relevant American Research Efforts 144
My Own Findings 146
    Miscarriages and Stillbirths 147
    The Infant Mortality Issue 148
    The Pains of Giving Birth 149
    Premature Births and Caesarean Sections 150
    Painful Menopause 150
Love-Shys as Quiet Babies 151
Mothers' Personalities 152
    Maternal Bashfulness During Pregnancy 154
    Mothers' Employment .155
    Employment Among Mothers of Teenagers . . .156
The Issue of Prevention 157

Chapter 7: FAMILY COMPOSITION 161
Brothers and Sisters 161
The Mode of Standardization 162
    Interactions vis-a-vis Married People 164
    Implications for Prevention 165
The Only Child 166
Kinship Relationships 168
Quality of Parents' Marriages 169
Conclusions 170

Chapter 8: PARENTS AS A CAUSE OF LOVE-SHYNESS . . .173
Family Atmosphere 175
    Extent of Family Emotional Supportiveness . .176
    The Komarovsky Study 178
Family Democracy 179
Mutual Sensitivity to Needs and Feelings 180

"Milk" versus "Honey" 182
Seriousness............................185
Paternal "Sex Anxiety" 187
Appearance of the Home 190
Parental Overprotectiveness..................191
Negative Comparisons........................191
Forcing the Summer Camp Experience on
Children 193
    Summer Camps as Torture Prisons 195
    Homesickness 198
Parents and Inheritance......................199
"Get Me a Goose!" 205

Chapter 9:   THE FAMILY AS A HOTBED OF RAGE AND
             BELITTLEMENT 211
Temper and Rage 212
Spankings, Beatings, and Physical Abuse......213
    When People "Stop Behaving" 218
    Corporal Punishment's Negative
Consequences 218
Persistent Belittlement and Ego Deflation......220
Argument Initiation 223
Doesn't All of This Contradict the Genetic
Perspective? 223

Chapter 10: LOVE-SHYNESS AND THE ALL-MALE PEER
             GROUP 225
The Key Importance for Dating of Friendship
Networks 227
The Harlow Research......................228
The Polish Peasant 229
Bullying...................................230
Frailness of Body Build 231
Inauspicious Introductions to the All-Male Peer
Group 232
Masculine Toys 235
The Baseball, Basketball, and Football
Syndrome 237
    The "National Pastime"....................238
    Basketball 239
    The "Left Out" Syndrome 240
Most People Know What Is In Their Best
Interests...................................241

The Solution 243
   Use of School Letters 251
   Football: Should It Be Made Illegal? 256
The Current Peer Group Interaction 256
   Discrepancy Between the Actual Self and the
Ideal Self 257
   Implications for Therapy 259
   "Society's Goal" 261
   Friendship Networks and Happy Marriages   262
Chapter 11: THE POWERFUL IMPACT OF PREADOLES-
           CENT INFATUATIONS 265
The Paradox 266
Social Supports 268
The Field of Roses Metaphor 271
"Oh, Leave Him Alone; He's Still Got Plenty of
Time!" 272
The "Male Lesbian" State of Mind 273
The Preadolescent Love Experience 273
Beautiful, Driving Obsessions 280
A Preadolescent's Preference for a Sister 285
The Principle of the Superordinate Goal 286
Love in the Middle Childhood Years 286
Self-Disclosure Inhibitions 288
Media Inspired Love Infatuations 292
Chapter 12: BEAUTY AND THE LOVE-SHY 299
The Need for Beauty 300
The Love-Shys' Own Esthetic Attributes 306
Beauty and the Older Love-Shys 309
Clothing 310
Cloning as a Future Option 311
Hypnosis 318
Accentuating the Positive .319
Summary 320
Chapter 13: THE SEXUAL LIVES OF THE LOVE-SHY 323
Masturbation 323
Love-Shyness and Sexual Desire 324
Felt Deprivation Creates Preoccupation 326
Degree of Satisfaction with Sex Life 326
Sexual Values and Attitudes 327
Moral Liberality versus Conservatism 329
Unusual Sexual Directionality 331

Fending Off Unwanted Overtures 334
Being Misperceived as Homosexual 335
Being Misperceived by Homosexuals 336
On Envying Homosexuals 337
Chapter 14: LOVE-SHYNESS AND THE CRIMINAL MIND . .343
Violent Fantasies 344
Bullying 345
Similarity to Child Abusers 346
Psychopathy 347
Shoplifting 348
Marijuana Use 349
Alcohol Use 350
Staring and Following 353
The Hinkley Case 360
Difficulties Concentrating 361
Chapter 15: MEDICAL SYMPTOMS AND LOVE-SHYNESS . .363
Headaches 364
Backaches and Back Trouble 364
Bedwetting 364
Weight Problems 365
Constipation and Diarrhea 365
Problems of the Nose 365
Allergies 371
Dry Mouth 371
The Common Cold 372
Reactive Hypoglycemia 375
Other Hypoglycemia Symptoms 379
Halitosis 379
Hyperactive Salivary Glands 380
Hyperprespiration 381
Depression 383
Throat Clearing and Coughing 384
Gas 385
Eyeglasses 385
Shortness of Stature 387
Acne 387
Insomnia 389
Stuttering 390
Buck Teeth 390
Hypochondria 390
Psychotherapy 391
Chapter Postscript 391

Chapter 16: LOVE-SHYNESS AND THE INNATE SENSITIVI-
            TIES ISSUE.............................393
            Bodily Itches.............................394
            Climate 395
            Bright Sunlight 397
            Wool......................................398
            Physical Pain 398
            Miscellaneous Sensitivities 402
            Annoyance at Petty Stimuli 404
            Eye Color and Hair Strand Width...........406
Chapter 17: SOME PSYCHOLOGICAL CHARACTERISTICS
            OF THE LOVE-SHY...........................409
            Being Friendly Requires Nerve 409
            Extreme Self-Consciousness 410
            Telephones 411
            Assertion Phobia..........................412
            A Life-Threatening Scenario...............413
            Items Clearly Earmarking the Love-Shy 414
            Sense of Humor 417
            Control Over the Good and Bad 418
            Loneliness................................419
            Loneliness and Experimental Social Psychology 423
            Envy of Female Privilege..................427
            Chapter Postscript 429
Chapter 18: PARENTHOOD ASPIRATIONS 431
            Fear of Discipline 434
            Recycled Fathers 436
            Selecting the Gender of One's Future Children 436
                Pre-Selecting a Baby's Sex............437
                The Eugen Jonas Method 438
            Shyness and Contracepting 439
Chapter 19: CAREER, MONEY, EDUCATION, AND THE
            LOVE-SHY 441
            Level of Attained Education...............442
            Unemployment and Underemployment 442
            Annual Incomes 443
            Places of Abode...........................443
            Childhood Socioeconomic Status 443
            Implications of Money for Love-Shyness ...444
            Shyness in the Job Search.................445
                The Unadvertised Job 447
                Shyness on the Job....................449

Employment Attitudes......................450
Some Positive Recommendations 451
On Selling an Employment Interviewer 455
The Importance of Being in Demand........456
Alleged "Frills" in Education 457
Higher Education as a Mode of Compensation 459
Moving During the Formative Years 461
Chapter 20: POLITICS, RELIGION, AND THE LOVE-SHY ...463
Religion 464
Amenability to Religious Participation.......467
A Rejoinder to Ponder....................469
Spiritualism 470
Chapter 21: MOVIES, MUSIC, AND THE LOVE-SHY 473
The Love-Shys' Prime Film Experiences 479
Music 486
Chapter 22: PRACTICE-DATING THERAPY 491
Behavior Therapy Approaches.................491
The "Practice-Dating" Model 493
Screening 498
Dealing with the Love and Beauty Problem..499
The Alcoholics Anonymous Model of Mutual
Caring and Concern.......................501
Visualization and Mental Rehearsal 502
The "Second Plateau" 504
When a Practice-Dating Participant Fails to
Show Up....................................506
"Going Outside" 508
Waiting Lists 508
Practice-Dating Therapy for High Schoolers..509
The Termination of Therapy 511
Psychodrama and Role Playing 512
No Time Limit 513
Exceptionally Stubborn Cases 515
Conclusions and Recommendations..........517
Practice-Dating and the University Campus..521
Some Militancy Needs to be Displayed......522
Chapter 23: SOME THERAPEUTIC ADJUNCTS 525
The Nude Jacuzzi Experience.................525
Therapy Employing Sexual Surrogates 527
Use of Audio-Cassette Programs..............532
Bibliotherapy 533
Meditation 534

Why Not Simply Use Commercial Dating
Services? 539
    The Gender Ratio Problem 539
    Commercial Vested Interests 542
    Barriers Posed by the Love-Shys' Psycho-
emotional Handicaps 543
    A Corroborating Study 545
    Attractiveness and Education.............546
Self-Image Psychology as a Therapeutic
Adjunct 548
    The Key Principles 548
    Blending Self-Image Psychology with the
Biological Perspective......................551
Self-Image Therapy........................555
    Affirmation-Making and Self-Talk..........555
    Visualization...........................558
    The Self-Fulfilling Prophecy 560
Some Rejoinders for Traditional
Psychotherapists 561
    The Symptom Displacement/Symptom Need
Argument 561
    Insight 561
    Encouraging Dependency and Low Self-
Sufficiency 562
    The Love-Shys' Need for Structure and their
Fear of Social Ambiguity....................563
    The "Responsibility" Argument 564
    The "It's Too Mechanistic" Argument 565
    Postscript to Chapter 23 566
Chapter 24: SOME RECOMMENDATIONS CONCERNING
            PREVENTION 567
Research on Gene Splicing 567
Bullying.................................568
    The Perils of Competition 571
    A Non-Punitive Antidote for Bullying 572
The Cruelest Bully of All....................574
Cowardice...............................579
Corporal Punishment Needs to be Outlawed ..580
Some Recommendations Concerning Dogs 582
Coeducational Dormitories: Their Limitations ..585
The "Harrad" Dormitory Option.............586
The Psychic Healing of Important Enzymes....589

The Effect of Increasing Social Interaction 591
The High School Curriculum 593
　　Foreign Languages 593
　　History and Civics 593
　　Literature Courses 594
Ballroom Dancing 596
Religion 598
Encounter Groups..........................598
Might Fraternity Membership Help? 601
　　Use of Sorority Girls.....................604
　　What Can Be Done.....................606
　　A System of Coed Room Mates............606
　　The Courtship System versus Marriage and
　　the Family................................607
Use of Autistic Adolescent Girls 608
Changing the Norms 609
Chapter 25: SOME FINAL THOUGHTS 613
A Different Philosophy 615
What Is Needed 616
Interpersonal Skills versus Interpersonal
Anxiety 622
Some Final Thoughts on Prevention 624
　　The Family Structure Factor 626
　　The Abuse Factor 627
Judging a Person By His Actions 629
Misreading Actions and Inactions............630
Postscript 632
BIBLIOGRAPHY 654
Appendix I: THE SURVEY OF HETEROSEXUAL
　　INTERACTIONS 659
Appendix II: THE GILMARTIN LOVE-SHYNESS SCALE 665
Appendix III: Summary of Mean Scores on Eysenck Personality
　　Questionnaire 673

Name Index 675

Subject Index 681

LIST OF FIGURES

Figure 1:   EYSENCK CROSS OF INBORN TEMPERAMENT 41
Figure 2:   THE WISH BONE EFFECT.................... 84
Figure 3:   A CAUSAL MODEL OF HOW SEVERE LOVE-
             SHYNESS DEVELOPS......................107
Figure 4:   IMAGES OF PREADOLESCENT ROMANTIC
             LOVE.....................................280
Figure 5:   LIST OF ALL FILMS WHICH RECEIVED MEN-
             TION BY THE LOVE-SHY MEN AS HAVING
             BEEN SEEN INSIDE A THEATRE AT LEAST
             FIVE OR MORE TIMES......................477
Figure 6:   LIST OF ALL FILMS WHICH RECEIVED MEN-
             TION BY THE SELF-CONFIDENT NON-SHYS
             AS HAVING BEEN SEEN INSIDE A THEATRE
             AT LEAST FIVE OR MORE TIMES...........478

Preface

During the past twenty years a tremendous number of books and magazine articles have been written about the so-called sexual revolution. However, virtually no attention at all has ever been accorded a class of people whom the sexual revolution has totally bypassed. This book will allow the reader to learn about a very fascinating segment of the population which can best be described as *"love-shy."* The love-shy include fully grown men in their late 30s and 40s who are not only as "virginal" as it is possible for anyone to be, but who can also be accurately described as less experienced in ordinary dating, courting, and elementary kissing than the typical, contemporary 12-year old youngster. The love-shy also include 19 to 24 year old university students who are similarly incapable of getting started with the opposite sex, quite in spite of their very strong desires for a close, loving heterosexual relationship.

No, these are not homosexual men by a long shot. In fact, this book is devoted exclusively to men with very strong and very normal heterosexual urges. Indeed, it is devoted to men who would like nothing better than to be able to marry and to have children, but who are not moving towards these goals because of severe bashfulness, shyness and social timidity.

Love-shyness is a life-crippling condition. Victims of love-shyness cannot marry. They cannot have children, and they cannot participate in the normal adolescent and young adult activities of dating and courtship. The love-shy are often misperceived as "homosexual." And they are often made to pay the price for being "homosexual" without being accorded access to the rewards that go with a homosexual identity. Because love-shy people are *not* homosexual they cannot join up with any of the many "gay rights" organizations or homosexual support groups.

And as very few love-shy people are alcoholic, Alcoholics Anonymous is similarly "off limits" to them. *Zero percent* of the love-shy ever take part in any form of gambling or risk-taking, social *or* financial. So Gamblers Anonymous is also "off limits" to them. And so are all of the various substance abuse and drug addict support groups. With very few exceptions, the love-shy do not take drugs. In fact, they do not allow themselves to become involved in *anything* or in *any activity*, wholesome or otherwise, for which there is any kind of existent social support group.

That is the whole trouble. The love-shy do not have anybody to relate to as a friend or to count on for emotional support. They deeply crave heterosexual love and romance. Most of them would like to have children. And yet all of these normal life activities and rewards are blocked to them. In fact, they are about as severely cut off from these normal social gratifications as they would be if they were serving a life sentence in a federal or state prison.

So how did the love-shy get to be the way they are? Can they be cured? And if so, how might this be accomplished? These are just some of the questions with which this book will deal. Every day love-shyness creates enormous pain and suffering for some 1.7 million American males whose normal desires for self-determination and self-expression are thwarted by their condition. And yet up until quite recently this quite sizable proportion of the population has been almost totally ignored by authors, journalists, scholarly reserachers, the clergy, and members of the helping professions. This book is, in point of fact, the very first of its kind ever to be published either here in the United States or anyplace else in the world.

Moreover, this book does far more than merely address the problem of love-shyness. Fully 300 love-shy males, ranging in age from 19 to 50, were extensively interviewed and studied for this book. Their lifestyles, personal histories and thought processes were carefully scrutinized and compared to those of 200 non-shy men. And this book contains the results of this research, all of which is presented here in the language of the layperson.

In addition, various therapeutic and preventive approaches for dealing with love-shyness are reviewed in this volume. And those which up to now have shown the greatest promise are highlighted. To be specific, even the most severely love-shy man *can now be cured* (and comparatively painlessly), although the process requires some amount of time and resources. The how, why and wherefore of therapeutic and preventive measures *which work* will be both detailed and explained in this book.

This book was written with the victims of love-shyness constantly in mind. And as author of this book I sincerely hope that it reaches as many afflicted people as possible. One of the major lessons which almost a decade of researching love-shyness has taught me is that the love-shy need to band together both as a social/political force *and* as social networks providing needed friendship and social support. As of now, there is no *"Shys Anonymous."* I strongly hope that one of the fruits of this book will be the development of such a nationwide organization, and of other support organizations such as *"Coed Scouts,"* and "practice-dating" support groups. As a socio-political force the love-shy can and should begin making themselves visible; they can begin now to make their needs known to the "powers that be." And, most importantly, they can begin getting their most basic human rights honored *and their needs met.*

This book is intended for interested laypersons, therapists, and scholarly researchers. Love-shyness is a surprisingly fascinating topic. And I believe that a key reason for its inherent interest and fascination is that most people can learn a surprisingly great deal about themselves from studying the underlying causes of behavioral inhibitions. Love-shyness is a form of *deviance*. It is a form of *behavioral nonconformity*. Deviance (nonconformity) is the *opposite side of the same coin as conformity and "normality."*

Of course, love-shyness is *not* a freely chosen form of behavioral nonconformity. And that is why the love-shy are often regarded as "sick," "neurotic," "unfriendly," etc. Freely selected nonconformist life-styles are usually quite healthy. Every society needs some amount of freely selected behavioral nonconformity. Without it a society would begin to stagnate. Nonconformists who deliberately and rationally choose their behavioral style often accord their society and local communities a great deal of useful "fresh air" and creativity.

But for the love-shy free choice and self-determination are unknown and unsavored experiences. In short, the underlying roots of both personal and societal health can be better appreciated through a careful and systematic study of those persons who do not have such health, and who do not enjoy the free choice and self-determination which most of us take for granted each day.

So if you want to understand how human beings come to be and feel "free," or if you simply want to help yourself or a loved one who may be suffering the throes of love-shyness, read on. I can guarantee you a host of new and useful insights both about yourself *and* about those who, despite their strong heterosexual/romantic needs, cannot obtain or experience the emotionally meaningful love and companionship of someone of the opposite sex.

DR. BRIAN G. GILMARTIN

Department of Sociology,
Westfield State College,
Westfield, MA 01086
January 27, 1985

Also by Dr. Brian G. Gilmartin:
    THE GILMARTIN REPORT: INSIDE SWINGING FAMILIES (1978).
    PREMARITAL BIRTH CONTROL (1988).

Chapter 1

Introduction

Only about 5.5 percent of the male population in America never marries. Approximately 50 percent of this group is believed to be composed of homosexuals who have chosen not to marry. And about one-half of what remains is composed of heterosexual men who for a variety of personal reasons have similarly *chosen* on a voluntary basis not to marry.

This book is about heterosexual, "single, never married" men who *have never voluntarily chosen* to remain "single, never married", but who have been constrained to remain that way because of severe shyness in informal social situations involving women. This form of chronic, severe shyness can best be labeled *"love-shyness"*. And it afflicts approximately 1.5 percent of all American males. More succinctly, love-shyness will effectively prevent about 1.7 million males currently residing in the United States from ever marrying and from ever experiencing any form of intimate sexual contact with a woman.

Today many young women complain about what they perceive to be a serious shortage of eligible heterosexual men who are desirous of a permanent, intimate, committed relationship with a woman. As this book will make quite clear, the love-shy constitute a rich and long neglected supply of such men.

Until quite recently the problem of shyness was ignored by social scientists. Yet few if any personal problems are associated with greater suffering for the individual victim or pose a greater potential danger for society. Shyness inhibits and very often obviates free choice and responsible self-determination. This poses a very serious dilemma because American society was founded upon the principle of rational self-direction and self-determination. Indeed, the principle of free choice underlies the very philosophy upon which our legal and political way of life rests.

The American way of life is also in very large measure dependent upon the ability and willingness of all citizens to speak out, to voice their ideas, and to contribute to the common good commensurate with

1

their strengths and abilities. It is further dependent upon each person being able to constructively deal with and satisfy his or her own needs. No person who is prevented from effectively contributing and receiving in line with his or her own assets and abilities can be happy. No person who is prevented from playing meaningful roles in or from being an integral part of his or her society can be stable. Unfulfilled and unhappy people tend to create problems both for themselves and for society.

To be shy is to have one's actions (or lack of them) misunderstood, misinterpreted and misread by others. An extreme fear of the pain of anxiety prevents the shy person from taking the kinds of action that are in accordance with his or her values, wishes, knowledge and rational judgment. More simply put, shyness inhibits people from assuming a sense of responsibility for their behavior. It makes them feel and truly believe that they are not in the "driver's seat" of their own lives and destinies. Shy people disclaim responsibility for their inaction and for their seemingly (to others) unfriendly, detached attitude. This inability to effectively deal with the interpersonal anxiety which for them accompanies normal social intercourse makes them feel that they are not "in charge of" or responsible for their own lives and for the behavior which they manifest to others.

The fact that shys can seldom perform up to the level of their potential is a further problem as it gives rise to a tremendous waste of human resources and talent. Shys' extreme fear of interpersonal anxiety and of rejection prevents them from taking prudent risks and from developing necessary social skills. This leads to a vicious circle of ever increasing shyness, social withdrawal, and low social self-confidence.

The Webster dictionary defines shyness as being "uncomfortable in the presence of others." The Oxford English Dictionary indicates that the word's earliest recorded use was in an Anglo-Saxon poem written around 1000 AD, in which it meant "easily frightened." They define shyness as being "wary in speech or action, shrinking from self-assertion; sensitively timid; retiring or reserved from diffidence, and cautiously averse in encountering or having to do with some specified person or group."

Most definitions stress that shyness pertains to *social* fears and anxieties. Accordingly this book views shyness as:

> A state of behavioral inaction or avoidance in *social* situations that is out of harmony with a person's conscious wants, needs and values, and which is precipitated by a real or imagined social situation clashing with that person's low interpersonal anxiety threshold and unusually strong fear of anxiety.

Social situations can be classified into two basic categories: (1) the impersonal, and (2) the purely sociable. Many social situations entail no essential purpose apart from pure, unadulterated sociability. These are fundamentally ambiguous situations in which there is no clear script, and in which there is no role to play. On the other hand, many people are shy in certain kinds of *impersonal* social situations. This is particularly true with regard to situations calling for such public performance as speech making in front of a large audience, singing and acting in public, piano playing, etc.

This book will concern itself with victims of the first type of shyness. It is perfectly possible for a person to go through life quite happy and content, and yet never get over his/her fears of public performance, public speechmaking, etc. In contrast, it is downright unfathomable for a person to go through life incapable of comfortably interacting in *informal* social situations, and still remain happy and content. Simply put, shyness in purely informal social situations has a far more deleterious, damaging impact upon a person's mental health and happiness than any other kind of shyness. And this is why such shyness warrents careful study and scrutiny.

Of course, people who are very shy in purely friendly, social situations are quite often *also* shy in impersonal situations as well. Yet it is almost always much easier to cure shyness in impersonal situations than it is to cure shyness in purely informal social situations. In order to function effectively in any impersonal situation all a person needs to do is (1) learn a "script" or "role" as well as he/she can, and (2) gain sufficient self-confidence to go public with it.

In purely informal social situations, on the other hand, there is no "script" or "role" to learn. Purely sociable situations are *inherently ambiguous* by nature. They call for the participants to *be themselves*, and to be able to spontaneously improvise their performance as they go along. In American society many people (especially males) have developed a trained incapacity for "being themselves". They cannot "be themselves" because they do not really know who they actually are! People *become themselves*— develop a firm sense of identity—only through informal interaction from early childhood onward in informal friendship and kinship groups. For reasons this book will make clear, a significant minority of American boys grow up friendless, as *social isolates*.

Since a person cannot learn a "script" or "role" in preparation for effective performance in purely friendly, sociable situations (which are in many ways inherently ambiguous), there is no easy way a person can gain the self-confidence he needs in order to test himself out. In doing the research necessary for delivering a stimulating public lecture, a person will inevitably gain quite a bit of self-confidence. At the outset he might be "scared shitless" about talking for an hour before a large audience about some subject. But the more he learns, the more he wants to share, and the faster and smoother his "script" manages to get put together.

The same thing applies to rehearsals in preparation for putting on a stage play or musical. At the outset some of the performers may be quite frightened about "going on" before a large, paying audience. Yet as regular, disciplined rehearsals effectively hone up the players' roles to the point of perfection, most of the initial stage fright subsides, and each player begins looking forward to opening night. Yes, even fine actors and actresses will have some stage fright as the overture blares away on opening night. But as the curtain goes up these jitters are almost always forgotten. The actors and actresses *take command* because they know their roles and are very comfortable with them. The chance that anything unpredictable will happen on stage as the performance unfolds is almost nil.

Purely sociable situations do not allow for any such beforehand preparation. To most readers of this book "being friendly" in purely sociable situations seems to be "the most natural thing in the world". To a severely shy man, on the other hand, it represents a far more frightening prospect than does assuming responsibility for any public lecture or public performance.

What is Love-Shyness?

This book is interested in a particular kind of shyness which prevails in *coeducational* or *man/woman* situations wherein there is no purpose apart from pure, unadulterated friendliness and sociability. This type of shyness can best be termed *"love-shyness"*, and it is the most painful and life-crippling of all kinds of shyness. Just as shyness in purely sociable situations is far more painful than shyness in impersonal business or performance situations, shyness vis-a-vis the opposite sex for virtually all of its victims is far more painful than any other kind of shyness. According to the best evidence at our disposal, love-shyness has a more disastrous impact upon the lives of its victims than any other kind of shyness. And that is why this book will confine its attention exclusively to *love-shyness*, its causes, consequences, and remedies (both preventive and therapeutic).

The Gender Factor

Love-shyness can be found among people of all ages and of both sexes. However, research evidence indicates that the problem impacts far more severely upon males than it does upon females. Women who remain love-shy throughout lengthy periods of their lives usually adapt very well and often quite happily to their situations. Spinsters, for example, often become highly successful career women. The never-married woman typically goes through life with *fewer* mental and physical health problems than her *married* sister of the same age. In stark contrast, the never-married, heterosexually inactive man has long been known to be vulnerable to all manner of quite serious and often bizarre pathologies.

Data recently obtained by Stanford University researcher Paul Pilkonis strongly suggests that shy women are no more likely to be neurotic than non-shy women. This same study, on the other hand, found shy men to be far more likely than non-shy men to be suffering from very severe neurotic conditions. In American society some degree of shyness is considered tolerable and even quite socially acceptable in females. In *males* of all ages from kindergarten through all the years of adulthood, in contrast, shyness is widely viewed as very deviant and highly undesirable. Moreover, shyness in males inspires bullying, hazing, disparaging labeling, discrimination, etc. In females shyness is often looked upon as being "pleasantly feminine" and "nice".

The biggest and most consequential difference in the way shyness impacts upon the two genders has to do with the strong social requirement prescribing that *males must assume the assertive role* in all manner of social situations. This same norm *proscribes* males from assuming the passive role. Today most women have the option of being either assertive or passive. And whereas the normally assertive woman has been found by researchers to stand a better chance at happiness and adjustment than the chronically passive one, the occasional display of passivity rarely causes a woman to suffer highly disparaging or punitive reactions from others.

Hence, shyness in women is very rarely found to be coterminus with *love-shyness*. In other words, extremely few shy women are *also* love-shy. The best available evidence clearly indicates that *shy women are just as likely as non-shy women* to date, to get married, and to have children.

In short, shyness does not force women to remain against their wills in the "single, never married" category, as it often does with men. In essence, because love-shyness (*not* shyness itself) is very rare among women, this book and the research it incorporates will focus exclusively upon men.

In order to avoid misunderstanding I want to stress the fact that both sexes do suffer from *general shyness* about equally. Moreover, there are many different kinds of situations in which shyness is a real problem for some women. However, a young woman's shyness vis-a-vis the opposite sex is permitted by our cultural norms to dissipate and fade away. Because women are not required *to initiate* informal conversations with men, or even with members of their own sex, their future prospects and chances in terms of dating, courtship and marriage are in no way hampered by any psychoemotional inability (shyness) on their part to initiate informal conversations with men. Further, the fact that a woman's success with her all-female peer group is far less dependent upon competitive effectiveness than is a young man's success with *his* all-male peer group, assures most women (including very passive ones) of meaningful friendships and of some opportunities for meeting eligible men through female friends.

Many studies have convincingly documented the point that men are far more susceptible than women to severe and intractable love-shyness. For example, in a 1983 study which incorporated a large sample of university students, sociologists David Knox and Kenneth Wilson obtained strong support for the view that love-shyness is primarily a male problem. Fully 20 percent of the male students surveyed complained of painful feelings of shyness vis-a-vis the opposite sex in informal social situations. Less than 5 percent of the women students had a similar complaint. And very few of this small minority of women students suffered emotionally from their shyness vis-a-vis the opposite sex to the debilitating extent to which the male love-shys suffered from their shyness.

A seldom mentioned factor which I believe serves to increase the shyness (and diminish the self-confidence) of young men as compared to that of young women is the fact that *women* do the lion's share of the rejecting in male/female relationships. Within marriage, 90 percent of all divorces are sought by wives and not by husbands. And among courting couples at least two-thirds of all of the break-ups which occur are precipitated by the *female* partner, *not* by the male partner. In a well-known 1976 study by sociologists Charles Hill, Letitia Peplau, and Zick Rubin, most of the terminated "steady dating" relationships had been terminated by the girl, *not* by the boy.

Even normally self-confident men have been found to suffer far more than women when courtship relationships are terminated. Yet most young men are forced to suffer far more such relationship break-ups than women. Such broken relationships very often take a severe emotional toll upon many of the men who suffer them. It is often forgotten that males are human beings with feelings too, every bit as much as females. Yet the relationship terminations which men are forced to endure often create large-scale and often dangerous emotional upheavals; and some victims of such persistent rejection eventually become so emotionally scarred and calloused that they become incapable of expressing their feelings, even to themselves. Women often complain that men cannot express their feelings in a meaningful way; yet the steady stream of rejections which some men suffer at the hands of women often creates a *trained incapacity* for the expression of inner feelings.

It is also important to note that even normally adjusted young men experience significantly *fewer* serious man/woman relationships before marriage than (even *very average*) young women do. And I think this too bespeaks some of the serious shortcomings in contemporary courtship norms. Human beings do not like to be rejected. It can be extremely painful when a person is rejected by an opposite-sexed stranger upon asking for a date. And it can be profoundly devastating to the emotions when a man is rejected by a woman with whom he has maintained a relationship over several months or longer. Why does the American culture persist in requiring the *male* (not the female) to withstand the lion's share of such emotional devastation?! I would suggest that the severe emotional scars endemic in severe and intractable love-shyness very often reflect a history of such rejection. In essence, the risk-taking involved in starting new relationships must be shared equally by women and men alike.

Enlightened Self-Control versus Shyness

Unfortunately, there are many influential people around who do not think love-shyness is a very important problem. In fact, some people even view shyness as a good thing. For example, some view love-shyness as a kind of healthy yoke, tying teenagers and young adults down to the everyday rigors of homework and study. Some people even view love-shyness as a blessing in disguise. They believe that if love-shyness can help to keep young people serious about preparing well for their futures, studying hard, and not getting prematurely pregnant, etc., then this "alleged problem" is really much more of an asset than a liability. Particularly in today's increasingly free sexual atmosphere, many parents and teachers wish that love-shyness would become a great deal more commonplace than it now is.

In essence, many people fear *freedom* and *choice*. Indeed, many people believe that humanity is not sufficiently evolved as yet for its members to be able to responsibly handle very much freedom of choice— hence, the proliferation in the popularity of very strict, fundamentalistic religious organizations.

What such parents and teachers fail to realize is that there is a very big difference between enlightened self-discipline and love-shyness. In fact, love-shyness is the very opposite of self-control. The shy person cannot make choices. The shy person *lacks* the self-discipline and self control necessary for commanding his/her performance in accordance with his/her internalized values and wishes. Again, the shy person lacks free choice and self-determination. He or she is not in the driver's seat of his or her own life.

Simply put, declining to participate in certain kinds of heterosexual activity because one deliberately and rationally *chooses* not to partake in them is perfectly healthy. The making of rational, well-planned decisions is a healthy sign in any person or age group. Choosing to behave in accordance with one's rationally internalized value system is also a healthy sign.

On the other hand, problems of a very serious nature inevitably arise for those who do not feel that they have any choice in the behavior that they pursue. This is certainly the case for love-shys who avoid many behaviors *not* because they have chosen to avoid them, but because the fear of experiencing painful anxiety has effectively blocked them from making and pursuing rational choices about their lives. It is certainly highly desirable for a person to establish values and goals. But for the severely love-shy person, the retaining of values and goals is often little more than an intellectual exercise. Again, the love-shy person is incapable of behaving in accordance with many of his own chosen values and goals because the mere thought of behaving in accordance with them arouses excruciatingly painful feelings of anxiety. This is why in dealing with very shy people it is not possible to correctly infer values and attitudes from observations of behavior.

Love-Shyness Is a Serious Problem

One of the most highly inaccurate misconceptions people have about love-shyness is that it is a problem with little or no bearing upon a person's ultimate life chances. Many people sincerely believe that love-shyness is "just a stage" through which many adolescents quite naturally pass. Unfortunately, the evidence at hand very strongly suggests that most love-shyness victims *do not* "just naturally" or spontaneously "outgrow" the problem.

For most of its victims, love-shyness persists year after year and profoundly affects ultimate life chances. It does this in two ways: First, love-shyness has a major bearing upon the development of interpersonal skills that are of crucial importance for career and personal success. And secondly, love-shyness prevents its victims from developing the networks of informal friendships which are extremely important for the promotion of career effectiveness, community involvement, marriage partner selection, and even for the avoiding of involvement in deviant or self-destructive behavior patterns.

The Christopher Jencks Study

Love-shyness and, indeed, the very fact of being without the companionship of a woman has been found to be related to a large host of negative outcomes. For example, Harvard University sociologist Christopher Jencks followed up a large sample of Indiana high school students for ten years—until they were 28 years of age. Among many other things, he compared men and women who had not dated at all while they were in high school with those who had dated. And his findings revealed that the non-daters were far less successful than the daters (1) financially, (2) career-wise, and (3) adjustment-wise, ten years after their high school graduation. Indeed, the more socially active a person had been during his/her high school years, the more successful and happy he/she was likely to be ten years later. Moreover, those young people who had been involved in steady dating relationships while in high school tended to be *best off* ten years later in terms of economic and career success.

Not surprisingly, these findings were all much stronger for the *men* than they were for the women. The socially active women were also better off ten years later than were the women who had been socially inactive while in high school. However, the differences between the socially active and inactive individuals were *far greater for the males than for the females*. In other words, the 28-year old men who had not dated at all in high school were found by Jencks and his associates to be the least successful, least happy, least well adjusted individuals.

Informal boy-girl interaction tends to be a highly effective facilitator for the development of interpersonal skills *and social self-confidence*— attributes which are extremely valuable from the standpoint of career success in today's business world. The frequent daters, for example, had all been actively involved in same-sexed peer networks. Simply put, high school dating both (1) reflects reasonably effective interpersonal skills, and (2) helps to build increasingly higher levels of interpersonal competence and self-confidence. And interpersonal competence is the single, most important correlate of occupational and career success today. In fact, we are beginning to learn that interpersonal skills together with friendship networks represent the single, most effective ticket towards the initial winning and keeping of the best job opportunities.

Studies in the Employment Sector

Social scientists have learned that better than ninety percent of all employment terminations from white-collar jobs are caused by deficits in interpersonal skills, and *not* by technical shortcomings. In fact, among white-collar people who lose their jobs only about one in twelve is terminated for reasons of technical incompetence. The other eleven are "let go" because they are not good team players, because they are less than adequately competent at partaking in the small talk that prevails during coffee breaks, lunch hours, and in the rest rooms. And a very large number of them are "let go" because their supervisors and/or work colleagues feel less than comfortable about having a work mate who withdraws too much or who is not adequately relaxed and naturally sociable.

Another little-known fact is that about 70 percent of the *best job and career opportunities* are obtained "under the table" *through informal social networks*. Quite in spite of "Affirmative Action" and "Equal Opportunity Employment", only about 30 percent of the better job opportunities are obtained through such traditional sources as newspaper job ads, personnel offices, employment agencies, etc. Moreover, recent studies have shown that compared to jobs obtained the regular ways, jobs obtained through informal social networks (1) pay significantly better, (2) provide far better growth opportunities, (3) are about three times more likely to provide high levels of career satisfaction, and (4) are about five times more likely to be retained by the incumbent for ten or more years.

Research evidence also shows that among people of approximately the same education and technical training, employers are most likely to be disarmed by the warm, relaxed, naturally sociable job applicant. The incumbent of any position who has an easy-going, natural command of strong interpersonal skills and finesse is the one who is (1) likely to be promoted the fastest, and (2) who is least likely to be laid off when things get tough.

In addition, several studies have shown that deficits in actual job performance are a good deal more likely to be overlooked and forgiven in socially effective people. In essence, the person with strong social skills and social self-confidence (non-shyness) is accorded many more chances to prove himself than is the shy, retiring person who commonly avoids informal social intercourse. Indeed, the latter type person often makes work mates feel uncomfortable. And a technical error that would easily be overlooked or forgiven in the friendly, highly sociable employee is often viewed as cause for termination in the shy and retiring employee.

In order for a person to belong to informal social networks he must be a relaxed, easy-to-get-to-know, sociable person. Further, he must be a person of at least average interpersonal skills relative to his chronological age and education/economic status group. The experience of dating has long been known to be instrumental in promoting these social skills and personal qualities. Moreover, very rare indeed is the young man who is popular with women but unpopular among members of his own gender. Indeed, the all-male peer group has long been known to be extremely important in terms of introducing its members to suitable female partners and in terms of promoting informal dating and courtship activities.

Finally, ours is a *coeducational world*. To an increasing extent women are successfully permeating all sectors of the work force, and this trend can be expected to continue unabated. A male who has not learned to feel at home with women can surely anticipate encountering a never-ending array of anxiety-provoking situations whenever he is involved either within the world of employment or in the process of obtaining same.

On Remedying Social Skill Deficits

It is a well established fact that deficits in interpersonal skills are much, much more difficult for a person to remedy in later life than are deficits in intellectual/technical skills. A person can successfully accumulate book learning at *any* time of life once he or she has made the commitment. In contrast, the correction of deficits in interpersonal skills is extremely difficult to bring about, no matter how dedicated the commitment to learning might be. This is why at the elementary school level and beyond, the cultivation of socioemotional interpersonal skills is of far greater importance from the standpoint of ultimate success and happiness than is the cultivation of intellectual skills. At *any* age any person of normal intelligence can develop technical or intellectual competence from exposure to books and classroom instruction. Sadly, the cultivation of expressive social skills *cannot* be effected through book learning, nor can it be accomplished like intellectual learning at just any time of life.

Early Marriage versus Professional Success

Columbia University sociologist Ely Ginzberg published a related study in which he had followed up for some fifteen years a large group of medical school graduates. Over that period of time all of the doctors studied had achieved a considerable amount of professional success. But Ginzberg found that one of the strongest *and least expected* predictors of career success was the age at which a doctor had married. Most Americans have long operated under the ascetic assumption that one of the sacrifices a person must make in order to become a medical doctor is that of *delayed marriage*. NOT SO, according to Ginzberg's findings.

Ginzberg divided the doctors up into thirds in terms of how successful they were fifteen years after graduation from medical school. There was the most successful one-third, the least successful one-third, and the third that was in the middle in terms of career success. In a nutshell, the most successful one-third had married *earliest in life*, whereas the least successful one-third had married *latest*. Indeed, several of the least successful one-third had not married at all, whereas none of the *most* successful one-third had remained unmarried. Moreover, a majority of the most successful doctors had married while they were still in their junior or senior year of undergraduate work, or while they were in their first two years of medical school training.

Of course, early marriage does not assure strong interpersonal skills. However, the evidence from the research of Jencks, Ginzberg, and many others, strongly suggests that early, successful heterosexual interaction does lead to the kind of social skills and social self-confidence that is as valuable in the world of employment as it is within the context of an individual's personal life.

Dating and General Happiness

The love-shy male of any age can usually think of little else apart from the mental-emotional prison which blocks him from making meaningful contact with that which he most sorely wants and needs—*girls*! This fact was driven home to me several years ago in a study I conducted on the campus of the University of Utah in Salt Lake City. This study dealt with the relationship between personality traits and all aspects of student behavior. A representative sample of over 300 students was taken, and thousands of correlation figures were obtained. A correlation coefficient is simply a barometer as to how strongly or closely two factors are associated with each other. Of the thousands of correlation coefficients my study produced, the strongest one of all was the one relating the following two variables:

a. Degree of personal satisfaction and contentment with the amount of informal boy/girl interaction engaged in of late.

b. General happiness with life.

Simply put, *nothing* in the entire study correlated more strongly with happiness and general sense of well-being than did extent of satisfaction with amount of informal boy/girl interaction. The correlation between these two factors was $+.65$ for the young men and $+.32$ for the young women. A related correlation coefficient dealt with the relationship between *general happiness* and *number of dates* averaged per month with the opposite sex. And this correlation figure was similarly far above average by social science standards: it was $+.49$ for male students and $+.16$ for the female students. Thus we have another clear indication of the fact that girls are far more important to men than men are to girls.

It is commonplace for moralists to disparage happiness as something which is "overemphasized" in America, and as something which is alleged to be not a very important end goal. To be sure, happiness cannot successfully be sought directly. Happiness is, in essence, a natural byproduct of (1) making effective progress within the sorts of socially valued activities that are most germane to a person's prime goals in life, and (2) active involvement in networks of meaningful (*love* and *work*) roles and relationships.

More succinctly, happiness is *very important* in a whole host of ways about which ascetic moralists are invariably blind. Research evidence has shown that (1) happiness is a prerequisite for self-love, and that (2) self-love is a prerequisite for a loving, caring attitude towards others. Unhappy people are in a very poor position to be of genuine service to their fellow man. And there is a kind of vicious circle here because it is only through service to humanity that a person can achieve maximum happiness and contentment. However, a person's own cup must be adequately filled before he can begin to share the contents of his cup with other people. The cup of a love-shy male quite typically has very little in it. And as this book will clearly demonstrate, love-shy males of all ages are often profoundly unhappy.

Why is the happiness and contentment of males so much more strongly influenced by successful heterosexual interaction than that of females? Most researchers today believe that the answer rests on the fact that women tend to be capable of finding emotionally intimate companionship vis-a-vis their own sex whereas men are able to satisfy their needs for emotional intimacy only in the company of women. Furthermore, non-dating females can normally manage to develop and maintain their socioemotional social skills and social self-confidence in their all-female peer groups. In contrast, non-dating males are usually isolated from social networks involving same-sexed peers.

Love as a Powerful Elixir

Further testimony as to the highly deleterious consequences of love-shyness can be seen in work that has come out of the U.C.L.A. "love laboratory". It seems that there is a very big difference (*especially for men*) between being involved in a love relationship wherein there is actual interaction between the man and the woman and the two people love each other about equally, and the sort of *unrequited* "love" situation where either (1) the boy loves the girl and she is not even aware of his existence, or (2) the boy loves the girl a great deal more than she loves him. The latter situation might best be described as *infatuation*, rather

than "love". And it has been found to be especially commonplace among
the ranks of love-shy males of all ages.

Such romantic infatuation in the absence of real interaction and
sharing tends to be associated with such classic symptomology as loss
of appetite, insomnia, inability to concentrate on work or studies, behavioral instability, a sharp dropping off in grades at school, inefficiency,
uncooperativeness, the need to walk or run around the town aimlessly,
and the need to walk (or run) around all day long in a stuporous world
of daydreams and fantasy. This is the type of symptomology which
poets down through the ages have associated with "being in love"—a
fact which suggests that many classic poets may well have been seriously
love-shy themselves. Indeed, poets very often are "dreamers" rather
than "doers", and chronic dreaming about the same theme is normally
a reflection of wish-fulfillment—of a way of coping with a problematical
void in everyday living.

In stark contrast, the U.C.L.A. love researchers found *mutual* love
relationships to be associated with a dramatically different kind of symptomology. Young men who were actively involved in *mutual* love relationships (wherein the girl interacted with and loved the young man in
return) tended to be fired up with an intense vibrancy, exuberance, and
"aliveness" that even the best adjusted among them had never known
before. This vibrancy and natural enthusiasm was associated with (1) *better*
grades in school, (2) an increased capacity to deeply concentrate when
they did sit down to study, (3) better and more efficient use of time,
(4) *increased* participation in social activities with *their own* gender, (5) an
improved appetite, (6) an increased ability to sleep soundly when they
did go to bed, (7) an ability to remain effective with less sleep than they
had required prior to falling in love, (8) better health, (9) increased atten-
tiveness to all facets of personal appearance and grooming, and (10) an
outward appearance and general ambiance that made their friends and
acquaintances view them as looking better, more alive and vibrant, than
they had formerly known them to be.

One of the most important findings to emerge from this "love
laboratory" research was that (1) men who were involved in a geniunely
reciprocated love relationship tended to have an extremely bright, very
strong Kirlian aura, whereas (2) men who were involved in unreciprocated *infatuations* tended to have a very weak, "sick" kind of Kirlian aura
of a type commonplace among severe neurotics, hypoglycemics, and
some schizophrenics.

Dr. Thelma Moss is one of America's most respected psi researchers. Specializing in Kirlian Photography, which is a form of electrical
photography which permits the photographing of the human aura

(sometimes called the *etheric* or *bioplasmic body*), Dr. Moss had her laboratory in the same U.C.L.A. building as that which contained the "love laboratory". And she took full advantage of the opportunity to photograph the Kirlian auras of (1) those in reciprocated love, (2) those not in love, and (3) those involved in unrequited, unreciprocated infatuations.

Involvement in a reciprocal love relationship was found to benefit women in much the same ways that it benefitted men. And this included the Kirlian aura. However, the findings were substantially weaker for the women than they were for the men. Certainly the experience of being in love did not harm any of the women studied. But being in love tended to have a much more nearly neutral impact upon the women subjects than it had upon the male subjects. On the other hand, in one significant respect the women studied were better off than the men: In particular, women were found to be substantially less vulnerable than men towards becoming involved in nonproductive, non-reciprocal romantic infatuations of the sort which the researchers found to give rise to the first quite negative set of symptoms.

Finally, when women did become involved in unreciprocated romantic infatuations, the effect upon their Kirlian aura was minimal. In other words, unrequited love tended to very adversely affect the corona of a young man's Kirlian aura; the effect of unrequited love feelings upon a woman's aura tended to be minimal. On the other hand, being involved in a *real* love relationship tended to galvanize a young man's Kirlian corona into a brilliant, full-bodied glow. The effect of such a love relationship upon a young woman's Kirlian aura was also noticeably positive. But the effect was substantially less dramatic than what had obtained for the men.

In sum, becoming involved in a *genuine* love relationship appears to constitute an extremely beneficial, life-enhancing medicine for young men. The love experience is at once a kind of elixir of life, a sort of fountain of youth and of vibrant aliveness and of masculine effectiveness. It might also be seen as representing the richest form of fertilizer for the cultivation of social self-confidence and expressive interpersonal skills. Besides being immediately life-enhancing, such positive outcomes are bound to exert a positive impact upon a man's lifetime productivity and general effectiveness.

Premarital Virginity and Adjustment

Premarital virginity in males over the age of 20 is often a reflection of severe love-shyness and of interpersonal skill deficits. And this is exactly what sociologist Mirra Komarovsky found in her sample of

Columbia University men. For example, she found that fully 77 percent of the virginal university men fell *below* the 50th percentile on national *self-confidence* norms. In contrast, this was true for only 34 percent of the sexually experienced men. Fully 78 percent of her non-virginal men scored above the 50th percentile (national norms) on *leadership capacity*, compared to only 47 percent of the virgins. On *sociability* 71 percent of the sexually experienced men scored above the 50th percentile on national norms, compared to only 27 percent of the virginal men. And on *self-acceptance* only a mere 2 percent of her non-virginal Columbia University men scored below the 50th percentile on national norms. In stark contrast, fully 47 percent of the virginal men scored below the 50th percentile on self-acceptance.

Now to be sure, premarital sex (monogamous *or* promiscuous) does not *cause* a person to become self-confident, self-accepting, sociable, etc. The cause of these findings rests upon the *goodness of fit* between (1) a person's behavior, and (2) how that person thinks and feels about his/her behavior. For example, twenty-five years ago most studies showed a *negative* relationship for single women between non-virginity and self-esteem. In other words, the sexually experienced ones usually did not think as highly of themselves as did those who had managed to preserve their virginity. Today, on the other hand, most studies are showing that for single women as well as men (beyond the age of 19), there is a *positive* relationship between monogamous premarital sexual experience and level of self-esteem. This positive relationship is usually found to be a good deal stronger for single males than for single females—because sexual experience is usually a good deal more important to the emotional needs and to the value systems of single men than it is to single women. However, the statistical association between self-esteem and sexual experience has become positive nowadays for both genders.

Parenthetically, young women (and even men) who are very casual and "loose" in their premarital sexual activity usually have poorer self-images than those whose premarital sex is kept monogamous and faithful. In other words, monogamous, loving, contraceptively protected premarital sexual activity is usually found in today's research studies to be associated with the most favorable results as far as self-esteem in both sexes is concerned. However, even the more promiscuous young men have usually been found to enjoy higher overall levels of self-esteem than young men who remain quite socially inactive (as well as virginal) as far as informal man/woman interaction is concerned.

I think the major reason for these findings is that virtually all heterosexually oriented young men *want* to have someone of the opposite sex to love. Those young men who continue much beyond the age of 20 shy of this goal (which is important to them from the standpoint of their own stated *values and goals*) are bound to develop increasingly poorer self-images and increasingly lower levels of self-esteem. Premarital sexmaking itself is of considerably less importance than it is commonly made out to be. I have become convinced that premarital sexmaking (including coitus) is a natural byproduct and concomitant of being enmeshed in the right man/woman love relationship. Hence, those without premarital coital experience are less likely than people with such experience to have ever savored the joy of being involved in what for a time at least had been "the right relationship".

I fully realize that there are young men and women "out there" whose value systems prohibit premarital sexual activity. This comparatively small minority of young people will be able to sustain strong, healthy self-images without premarital sex *if and only if they too manage to experience the joy of being involved in what for them is "the right man/woman relationship"*. In short, the sense of personal freedom (non-shyness) necessary for obtaining a love relationship is every bit as important to the emotional well-being of religiously conservative young people as it is to that of religiously more moderate to liberal ones. The latter will incorporate premarital sex into their love relationships; the former will be less likely to do so. However, *both* types of young people (especially *males*) need to be able to relax and to enjoy informal, friendly interaction with the opposite sex.

Viewing Someone to Love as a Cure-all

Love-shy males are often accused of thinking that if they only had a girl to love all of their problems would be solved. I believe that this sort of viewpoint deserves comment early on in this book. Clinical psychologists and counselors often feel that the love-shy have not taken the time to properly assess the nature of their situation. My own work with the love-shy has convinced me that most shy people are, if anything, far *too introspective*. They are constantly thinking and worrying about all conceivable facets of their situation. And this represents a significant aspect of their difficulties. In essence, shy people think too much about the wrong things, and always with negative mental imagery and negative affirmations. Since they lack informal support (friendship) groups and since they are almost constantly alone, there is nothing in their social field to provide positive feedback and to distract their negative thought and imagery towards positive directions.

On the basis of the evidence thus far cited, it should be clear that meaningful female companionship and love *IS ITSELF A POWERFUL CAUSAL AGENT*. It is, in a word, a kind of *medicine* even for healthy men, much less for disordered ones! The conclusion seems inescapable that many of the personal problems from which love-shy men suffer are due *at least in part* to the leading of isolated, loveless lives.

Moralists perceive female companionship for men strictly in terms of its being *AN EFFECT or reward* for "taking the bull by the horns" and thus expurgating whatever problems that might have been suffered. In essence, moralistic psychotherapists do not recognize love as a *CAUSE—* as a *prime mover.* And in another less obvious sense this moralistic viewpoint is ridiculous: *Everybody* has at least some problems to contend with every day of their lives. When a person stops having problems he/she is dead!

At the outset I would insist that it is *inconceivable* that involvement in a meaningful love relationship with a woman would not benefit a love-shy man, even to the point of ridding him of a significant portion of his many problems. As the data presented in this book will make clear, *almost all* of a love-shy man's problems are a direct result of love-shyness. LOVE IS A *CAUSE* AS WELL AS A CONSEQUENCE. Down through human history there has nearly always been a woman behind virtually every successful man. Indeed, this is so true that it has become a popular cliche.

As the reader wends his/her way through the chapters which follow he/she will observe that in almost every instance the *older* love-shy men are worse off in their many problems than the younger ones. Having been without the meaningful love/compassion of a woman for a significantly greater length of time, it logically follows that they would be worse off. Heterosexual love is a great medicine and healing elixir. And this is why I believe that it would greatly benefit society to pull out the stops (1) in getting its love-shy members healed of their love-shyness, and (2) in getting all people involved in meaningful social networks. Love-shyness represents a horrendous waste of valuable human resources.

Of course, anyone who would jump precipitously into marriage under the assumption that marriage would solve all of his problems would obviously be headed for trouble. However, as this book will make clear, love-shy men have a considerably below average susceptibility towards taking overly hasty actions. Indeed, if anything they are vulnerable towards acting *far too slowly* for their own good!

For many years now family sociologists have been advising the public that courtships of less than 24-months duration are much more likely to eventuate in unsuccessful marriages than those which last for more than 24 months. Today neither the love-shy nor the non-shy need to actually be married in order to enjoy intimate and thoroughgoing involvement in all facets of their loved one's life. They can "go steady" and/or they can premaritally cohabit as opposite sexed roommates and lovers. Therapists who tell their love-shy clients that marriage won't solve all their problems need to remain cognizant of the fact that court-ship *precedes* marriage and serves as a *screening device* for same.

In sum, the "going steady" and the premarital cohabitation can and should serve as a testing ground that is preliminary to marriage. It should assure (1) that when lovers do make the final leap into marriage they are taking the right step. Finally (2), such courtship processes should clearly indicate to a person just exactly what problems are likely to be healed or alleviated by active involvement in a love relationship, and just exactly what personal problems may not be healed or affected by participation in a meaningful love relationship.

Is having someone to love a cure-all? Obviously not! Indeed, noth-ing can ever be viewed as a panacea for all of life's problems. However, for the love-shy I would suggest that the obtaining of someone to love comes closer than anything else ever could to representing a potential near-panacea.

Remember that *the law of the Lord is love—and compassion!* This is the single most important message of the Christian Bible. And it is the one idea promulgated by organized religion to which we would all do well to pay heed—even though religionists seem to be as likely as anyone to forget this enormously important message. *Love is the great healer.* Defined in terms of a deep and sincere caring and concern for the needs and the feelings of others, *LOVE* can heal almost any wound and it can solve virtually any and all personal and social problems.

Accordingly, I would say that it is both *insensitive* and *unloving* for a therapist to continually remind his/her love-shy client that "a love relationship won't solve all of a person's problems", and that "love is not a panacea". Such reminders constitute superfluous tautologies; and they have the effect of placing the love-shy client on the defensive. In other words, such reminders represent formidable roadblocks to com-munication and to therapy.

The most sensible and viable programs for both *remediating* and *preventing* love-shyness are those which are focused specifically upon the goal of getting and assuring *all* people of the love that they need. When this goal is ultimately achieved, we shall all enjoy the benefit of living in a far better, safer, healthier and more secure world than the one which we currently have available to us.

Normative Timetables of Self-Revelation

In America as in all western societies there are unwritten rules governing how early in a heterosexual love relationship each party may reveal himself/herself to the other. Early in a relationship a person (*if* he/she is to ultimately be successful in winning the partner) must be both willing and able to *wear a mask*, metaphorically speaking—to *play act*, and to assiduously try to "be" something other than what he/she truly is. Both partners will try to impress the other. The man will try to present himself vis-a-vis his girl as a masculine "he-man" who is a "regular guy", into sports, athletics, body-building, and the other endeavors which inside America accompany the prototypical masculine stereotype. The girl partner will similarly try to present herself as a prototypical female with all the "normal" attributes of the "ideal" female stereotype.

It requires quite a bit of *"work"* and *effort* in order to be able to do this. Moreover, since it involves play acting (of a sort towards which the participants are scarcely even aware), it is *less than honest*. The person is not presenting his/her *real self* vis-a-vis the partner. The norms prevent this completely honest and open presentation of self until the relationship has reached a certain point of maturity. Among college/university aged young people, it usually requires around six months of "steady dating" of the love-partner before this point is reached. Among high school students more than a year would be required; among junior high schoolers the amount of time required could well be over two years. Divorcees in their thirties have an advantage here inasmuch as these very strong and demanding (unwritten rules/norms) permit older daters to "remove their masks" and to present their *real* selves vis-a-vis each other as early as the second, third, or fourth date.

Now, love-shy men are *extremely* romantic and sentimental. This sort of play-acting (which is *absolutely required* by our courtship system) represents an abomination to them. They want to find someone who will accept and love them *as they are*. And when they spot someone with the appropriate (and much desired) long hair and pretty face, they strongly desire to intimate their very strong interest in marriage vis-a-vis that person as early in the relationship as possible. In short, they don't want to beat around the bush. Dating and courtship for love-shy men hold no special allure. Most love-shy men would love to completely bypass the *"game"* of dating and courtship, and get right into a permanent, binding relationship with their romantic image of the girl with the "long hair and pretty face".

Needless to say, such outright candor early in a relationship enormously scares and frightens away most women—particularly the attractive ones who are likely to be very much used to the *"game"* of dating. The love-shy man is thus viewed as "weird" for verbalizing himself and his true desires and fantasies too early in a relationship. (And usually he does this through letter-writing rather than through talk. Again, letter-writing is far easier for the love-shy man to handle. But this too is likely to be regarded by the woman as "weird"—especially if she is but a local telephone call away from the love-shy man.)

Further, love-shys usually renounce aspects of the masculine sex-role stereotype. Love-shy men hate football, baseball, basketball, weight-lifting, beer-drinking, swearing and carousing with same-sexed associates, etc. They are far more likely to be interested in "settling down", and in the sorts of things women are likely to be interested in. Again, such honest and open self-revelation frightens women away when it occurs early on in a relationship. Moreover, expressed disinterest in and hostility towards prototypically "masculine" sex-role stereotypical activities and interests is also quite likely to be regarded by an attractive young woman as "weird" and strange. A less-than-attractive woman might be charmed by this approach—because she too hasn't got many same-sexed friends and thus similarly lacks a full awareness of what the rules of the dating "game" are. But as I have documented in chapter 12, love-shy men (because they are deeply and unshakably romantic) are extremely *visual*; they do not permit themselves to become involved in conversations with women who are less than very attractive and who do not possess the "long hair and pretty face".

Of course, *awareness* of the dating game rules and *acceptance* of same are two entirely different things. Many love-shys are aware of the rules, but their unadulterated romanticism disallows them from accepting such rules and acting upon them. Again, love-shy men value complete honesty. They want to remove the play-acting "mask" immediately, as soon as they find themselves engaged in a conversation with a pretty girl. They crave and aspire to immediate acceptance and love *as they are*—no false "fronts" presented.

Why This Book?

Shy people tend to be very quiet. This is why they are often labeled "wall-flowers". And it represents a key reason why they have been accorded very little attention by research scholars, by popular journalists, and by people in general. Shy people are simply not noticed, and this fact applies as much to the love-shy as it does to any other kind of shy person.

Up to now only one popular, research-based account has been published on shyness. And this was Philip Zimbardo's (1977) book titled SHYNESS: WHAT IT IS AND WHAT TO DO ABOUT IT. Dr. Zimbardo's book remains worth reading. However, its usefulness is severely limited by four basic shortcomings.

(1) General Shyness

First, Zimbardo's work dealt with *generic* shyness. Further, he dealt with shyness in a very *general* kind of way, painting a picture of the problem for us in very broad strokes. As I pointed out in the preceding section, *love*-shyness is the most emotionally debilitating and painful of all the different forms of shyness. And because of the requirement in male/female situations that the *male partner* must always be the one to make the first move (1) in initiating social contacts, (2) in the risk-taking of asking for first dates, and (3) in initiating physical expressions of affection, I determined that *love-shyness* is a problem that is suffered primarily and almost exclusively by the male sex. After many years of studying the shyness problems of women, it became clear to me that *love*-shyness was very seldom among them, and that it would be most fruitful to focus upon love-shyness in the male sex only.

Hence, this book focuses entirely and exclusively upon *love*-shyness, and it deals exclusively with *male* victims of the problem. Throughout all the pages of his book Dr. Zimbardo scarcely even mentions shyness in informal male/female situations. Hence, his book would have to be considered of very limited value from the standpoint of the needs of those with an interest in this most life-debilitating of all forms of shyness.

(2) *Sampling*

Dr. Zimbardo simply asked each of his respondents: "Do you consider yourself to be a shy person?" And slightly better than 40 percent of his respondents said "yes", whereas the other 60 percent said "no". And in looking for the causal antecedents of the shyness problem he simply compared the social and family backgrounds of the "shy" 40 percent with those of the "non-shy" 60 percent. Not surprisingly, he came up with next to nothing. In short, the family and social backgrounds of the "shys" were essentially the same in nature as those of the "non-shys". "Shy people" could be found in varying proportions among all demographic categories, and in every geographic area. And it was found to be most commonplace in Japan, and least commonplace in Israel.

The conclusion to be drawn from all of this was obvious: *shyness is learned*. Nobody is ever born shy. And another inevitable conclusion was: teach people (1) that shyness is learned, and (2) how to go about unlearning (extinguishing) it. These conclusions were, in essence, all too pat and frought with holes.

First, 40 percent represents a huge fraction of the population. Virtually any statistician will agree that if you compare 40 percent of the population with the other 60 percent *on ANY variable*, you will get no significant difference between the two groups for that variable. In other words, the family backgrounds (including socialization practices, disciline, etc.) of *ANY* 40 percent of the population will not differ appreciably from those of the other 60 percent. It makes no difference whether you choose shyness, degree of religiosity, political liberality versus conservatism, etc. The chance that statistically meaningful differences will obtain between groups that are so large is virtually nil.

In order for real differences to be obtained between two groups, and in order for the actual causes of shyness to be isolated, the term "shyness" would need to be much more carefully defined and delimited. It is not surprising that 40 percent of the American population feels "shy" from time to time. In fact, Dr. Zimbardo tells us that fully 85 percent of Americans admit to having been "shy" *at some point* in their lives. And that too is far from surprising. What needs to be stressed, however, is that very few of this huge number of people have a life-debilitating form of shyness. Very few of them suffer from the sort of chronic shyness that is so painful that free choice and self-determination are effectively blocked. For example, 40 percent of the male population does not remain involuntarily unmarried throughout their lives on account of severe shyness!

This book is concerned with just that very life-debilitating, severely painful form of shyness. What is more, it is concerned with a specific form of severe shyness that prevents a person from partaking in the normal round of dating, courtship, marriage and family activities. In short, this book is concerned with a form of shyness that is so strong that it serves to *prevent* a normally heterosexual person from ever having sex and getting married, and from ever being able to savor the joys and satisfactions of membership inside a family of his own making.

Defined in these terms, we are certainly not talking about 40 percent of the population! We are talking about roughly 1.5 percent of the American male population, or about 1,670,000 American males. When 1.5 percent of the male population is compared against a healthy group without this love-shyness problem, significant differences do show up in great abundance. Moreover, many of these differences have a strong bearing upon the question of what *causes* love-shyness. Further, that quite sizable chunk of the American population with less severe and debilitating forms of love-shyness should be permitted by the findings delineated in this book to gain considerable valuable insight into themselves and their problems. In addition, everyone who reads this book will become much better equipped than they had been to effectively *prevent all* degrees of shyness (both mild and severe) from ever developing in the lives of their loved ones.

(3) *Nature versus Nurture*

Dr. Zimbardo is a learning psychologist. And like most psychologists whose careers have focused almost exclusively upon learning processes and upon laboratory experimentation, Dr. Zimbardo has remained abysmally unaware and unaffected by the burgeoning research literature on the biological basis of shyness. This literature includes material on genetics, congenital factors, human physiology, and human biochemistry. And in recent years the message of this literature has become strong and consistent. In essence, shyness itself is indeed learned; but severe and chronic forms of it are learned primarily as a direct result of two dimensions of temperament called *inhibition* and *emotionality* (low anxiety threshold) which *ARE INBORN* and genetically rooted.

As author of this book I have an extensive knowledge and understanding of BOTH kinds of research literature: (1) that which has focused upon learning, *AND* (2) that which has focused upon inborn, biologically based considerations. The extensive bibliography that is provided at the end of this book should provide the reader with some idea of the *balanced perspective* which this book has endeavored to represent. I firmly believe that therapists with a one-sided perspective cannot and will not succeed in remedying any but the most mild cases of shyness. Zimbardo himself admits that he helps only 50 percent of the people who seek help at his "shyness clinic". Such a therapeutic success record is not very impressive (1) because a 50 percent cure rate could be obtained by pure chance, and (2) because with very few exceptions the young men and women who seek help at his clinic suffer from only very mild degrees of shyness.[1]

Unlike Dr. Zimbardo's book, this book will endeavor to provide the reader with a truly balanced perspective on the causal antecedents of shyness. My approach will in no way underestimate the prime importance of social learning—particularly that which goes on inside the contexts of the family and the peer group. However, I will similarly not underestimate what I consider to be the even greater importance of *inborn* factors. The inborn factors constitute a set of *elastic limits*. They set the stage for and limit that which can be learned. And even though there is no shyness gene, those born with the *"inhibition/emotionality gene"* are far more likely, as this book will show, to develop and learn love-shyness—here within the context of the United States of America.

Finally, there is a third class of variables falling outside the purview of *both* "nature" *and* "nurture" which up to now Zimbardo and most other psychologists have totally ignored. These variables might best be termed *occult*. And a balanced perspective on shyness *must* take these into account along with variables pertinent to learning and to biological, inborn considerations. As this book will show, not all "occult" variables are non-amenable to empirical analysis. In essence, many occult factors have been studied through the use of the five physical senses. And this book will discuss these variables and the important implications which they may entail for the development of love-shyness.

Man is far more than merely a physical body. The physical body is merely the *vehicle* for man's immortal spirit at the earth (incarnate) level of energy vibration. Severe love-shyness can be seen as a byproduct of a synergistic interaction between and among (1) inborn factors, (2) learning factors, and (3) spiritual/occult factors.

(4) *Advice to the Shy*

Lacking a balanced perspective on how shyness develops, Zimbardo's book is less than understanding or insightful in the way it doles out advice and recommendations to victims of the problem. In essence, it tells people without any "bootstraps" to go out and "pick themselves up by their own bootstraps." Most of the love-shy men I interviewed who had read Zimbardo's book had emerged quite depressed and exasperated by the experience. The book was allegedly the first to be written about *their* problem. And yet the love-shy men I talked to could not relate to Zimbardo's therapeutic and preventive recommendations. Indeed, they saw his "therapeutic" recommendations, in particular, as being a *sham* as well as highly insensitive.

A major purpose of this book is to provide recommendations for both therapy and prevention which are realistic and meaningful to those afflicted with severe love-shyness problems. Perhaps more than anything else (other than a suitable lover), the love-shy need a *spokesman*. Further, they need support groups with some political influence and power—groups which will effectively move them towards their goals of marriage and a satisfying family life.

This book is based upon extensive interviews with 300 severely love-shy men. Each of these 300 men represents a case of genuine, life-debilitating shyness. All have been effectively prevented from dating, marrying, having sex, informally interacting with women, etc., by their love-shyness problem. And all have been bogged down by shyness throughout the entirety of their respective life spans. The recommendations that are made in this book are to the maximum extent possible sensitive to the needs, wishes and very real human feelings of these men. Furthermore, this book contains no recommendations or pieces of advice that are out of harmony with what has been learned about the inborn, biologically based attributes of the love-shy.

In fact, readers who are love-shy should feel heartened to learn that there are plenty of attractive female partners around who would be quite amenable to loving a love-shy man. This book will present a therapeutic approach which can be engineered *now*, which is already available in diluted form on certain university campuses, and which can and will assure each and every love-shy man of a female lover. This is an approach which can and will accomplish this goal *without* requiring the love-shy to perform any anxiety-provoking "homework" exercises, such as *starting conversations with strangers*. Zimbardo's approach requires the love-shy to confront and deal with excruciatingly painful anxiety feelings. This book, in contrast, recognizes that it is unreasonable to require anyone to "walk on fire" in order to be healed. In essence, this book does not prescribe any anxiety-provoking exercises for the love-shy, nor does it recommend any costly and exasperating "talking cure" based upon insight or so-called unconscious motivation. No love-shy man was ever cured as a result of talking to a psychotherapist over months and years of time!

A further problem with Zimbardo's approach to therapy is that he endeavors to treat people with all manner of different kinds and degrees of shyness. And this represents a key reason why love-shy men cannot relate to much of what Zimbardo has to say. For example, it has long been known that alcoholics cannot be helped through participating in therapy groups that are composed of people suffering from a wide variety of different sorts of psychoemotional problems. On the other hand, as soon as they are introduced to Alcoholics Anonymous groups most alcoholics begin deriving significant benefits almost immediately. I believe that the love-shy are similar to alcoholics in this regard. They need and require therapy groups that are focused specifically and exclusively upon heterosexual love-shyness.

Most love-shy men feel very different from the majority of clients who partake in Zimbardo's "shyness clinic" therapy programs. Most love-shy men don't really much care if they *never* become capable of starting conversations with strangers, or delivering informal talks before large groups of people, etc. *All they really want is a girl*! And all else is nothing more than an abrasively irritating distraction which they would much prefer to do without. To be sure, *after* they have found a girl most love-shy men might well be expected to become tolerant and patient enough to recognize the desirability of working on *other* shyness-related problems. But unless and until they have found their girl, these other shyness-related problems have just about as much significance to love-shy men as the falling of a leaf in a distant forest. They are simply not interested in other shyness-related difficulties.

Finally, Zimbardo's attitude towards shy people is quite moralistic. In this book I take pains to avoid intimating any moralistic or judgmental attitudes towards the love-shy. It has been my experience that a moralistic attitude tends to cause the erection of strong defenses and to foster feelings of alienation between the shy person and his therapist. Love-shy men tend to be bogged down with feelings of helplessness and hopelessness about their problem. And a moralistic (gung ho for rugged individualism) attitude together with unreasonable expectations regarding "homework exercises" only serves to render the attainment of therapeutic goals patently impossible.

Zimbardo's attitude towards therapy vis-a-vis shy clients is by his own admission one of *"take it or leave it"*—*"do the homework exercises I'm requiring or don't come back"*. His attitude is "if the therapeutic approach does not work, there must be something wrong with the SHY CLIENT, *not* with the therapeutic approach itself".

This book takes the exact opposite position. In short, I do not believe that *square pegs can be forced into round holes* without causing an exacerbation of the problem. This book is aimed at effectively remedying severe love-shyness for *all* of its victims. And it is dedicated to the proper engineering of therapeutic modalities that *fit the client*. Therapeutic and preventive approaches must be made to fit the client in lieu of the traditional approach (which almost always fails) of trying to make the client fit some therapeutic approach that had been worked out in some moralistic ivory tower somewhere.

Love-Shyness Costs Society Money

One of the key reasons why the public needs to become concerned about love-shyness is that the problem does cost state and federal governments a great deal of money. During the past twenty years a great deal of research has been conducted on the relationship between *social support systems* and medical well-being. In general, social support has to do with the extent to which a person is integrated into family and friendship networks. The results of this research have been quite consistent and remarkable. A list of some of the most representative findings follows:

1. Hospital patients who are married and who have friends who sincerely care about them recuperate from their diseases, surgical procedures, etc., significantly faster, and with fewer complications, than do those who are not married and/or do not have meaningful friendships.

2. People who have many disruptive changes happening in their lives tend to be far more vulnerable to all manner of medical and psychiatric disorders than those whose lives are not afflicted by disruptive changes. *However*, even among people with an enormous amount of disruptive change in their lives, medical and psychiatric symptoms are exceedingly rare among those

who are well integrated into loving family and friendship networks which deeply and sincerely care about them. In other words, deficits in social and emotional support wield effects upon a person's health that are much more dangerous and damaging even than severe life stress and change.

3. Elderly people whose rate of social interaction with friends is high, tend to (1) live significantly longer, and (2) enjoy significantly better health, than do those elderly who do not enjoy meaningful friendships.

4. Pregnant women are far more likely to suffer birth complications if they are not well integrated into a caring family and friendship support system. In one study of women with many significant life changes occurring over a short period of time, 91 percent of those whose family and friendship support was inadequate suffered birth complications, compared to only 33 percent of women (with similar high life change scores) who had the friendly support of family and friends.

5. Alcoholics who try to stop drinking on their own are less than *one-twentieth* as likely to succeed as are those alcoholics who are well integrated into supportive family and friendship networks, such as Alcoholics Anonymous groups.

6. Asthmatics who are poorly integrated into family and friendship support systems typically have to take as much as *four times as much medication* as those who enjoy the benefit of integration into such systems.

7. In a random sample of women who had suffered a severe event or major difficulty in their lives, only 4 percent of those *with* a close confidante came down with a depressive psychiatric disorder, compared to 38 percent of those who did *not* have a confidante. In effect, those without a meaningful friendship were almost *ten times* more vulnerable to serious psychiatric problems as were those *with* a close friendship.

8. In a large sample of blue-collar men who had lost their jobs, extent of social support was found to be very strongly associated with high blood pressure, heart disease, and arthritis symptoms. For example, only 4 percent of the men who were well integrated into kinship and friendship support systems had two or more swollen joints. In contrast, 41 percent of the men classified as "low" in social/emotional support had two more more swollen joints.

9. Unemployed people without a supportive friendship network evidence significantly higher elevations and greater changes in measures of serum cholesterol, illness symptoms and depressed

behavior, than do unemployed people with a supportive family and friendship network.

10. Low social/emotional support is strongly associated with all manner of serious crime and psychopathology. In fact, the more serious and violent a person's crime is, the more thoroughgoing the extent of alienation from supportive friendship and family networks that one can expect to find in the life of the perpetrator.

11. Social support increases coping ability, which is the etiological gateway to health and well-being. Social-emotional support short-circuits the illness responses to stress.

12. A low sense of social-emotional support exacerbates life stress. And for most people it is a major stressor *in and of itself*.

Fifteen years ago sociologist Derek Phillips found that social participation was the single, most important correlate of human happiness. Working with a much larger, nationwide sample, psychologist Jonathan Freedman published essentially the same finding in 1978. During the 1970s decade many different sociologists and psychologists explored the causes of human happiness. And virtually all of these researchers concured with the conclusion of Phillips and Freedman that frequent social involvement with other people is the most important of all factors giving rise to feelings of happiness and well-being. The second most important factor, by the way, is the feeling that one is in charge—in the "driver's seat"—of one's own life. And this too is a feeling which tends to be virtually nonexistent among the ranks of the severely love-shy.

Scores of additional research findings similar to the foregoing could be cited. The message of all of this work is clear: love relationships and friendship support systems help people to cope better with the stresses and strains of everyday living. The very fact of having an intimate confidante mollifies and greatly reduces the effects of stress upon both the mind and the body. Hence, medical and psychiatric symptomology tends to be significantly less for people who are well integrated into family and peer group support systems. Further, when illness does strike, those with love relationships and friends manage to recuperate significantly faster than those lacking in such social-emotional support systems.

In essence, people with families and close friends make significantly fewer demands upon medical care delivery systems than do those without close ties to family or to friends. The same can be said in regard to psychiatric services. The lonely and the isolated constitute the major consumers of psychiatric services; and this includes services which are geared towards the remediation of alcohol and drug addiction. Indeed, this fact is well symbolized in the title of a psychiatric book that was popular approximately ten years ago. Its title was PSYCHOTHERAPY: THE PURCHASE OF FRIENDSHIP.

Fortunately, most people know how to make friends and to give each other the needed social and emotional support. Similarly, most people are able to marry and to partake in the full range of normal social activities pertinent to family formation. People such as the love-shy who lack these abilities need to be systematically educated and trained so that they too can be effectively shielded against many of the stresses and strains of everyday living. It is obviously in society's best interest to provide such education and training. Any expenditures that are made in the interests of such training will eventually be repaid to society more than one-hundredfold in the form of healthier, better adjusted citizens. In short, if every person has both a lover and a confidante, the incidence of medical and psychiatric pathologies will be far less than what prevails today. The savings in both money and in human suffering will be extremely formidable.

Summary

There is strong empirical evidence that love relationships *when they are reciprocal* tend to promote psychoemotional growth as well as social, financial, and career effectiveness. Many studies also support the view that it is the most interpersonally skilled people who are most likely to enjoy mutual, reciprocated love relationships early in life. Moreover, young men who are involved in such heterosexual love relationships have been found to be far more likely than those not so involved to be enmeshed in networks of rewarding *male* friendships. Young men who throughout their high school and college years continue to experience trouble meeting members of the opposite sex almost invariably tend to be characterized by a dearth of male friendships as well. And their social ineffectiveness here can normally be counted upon to greatly undermine their ultimate life chances for success and happiness in the world of work.

Love-shy men are usually highly self-conscious; and this impedes their performance academically, socially, and in the world of employment. In lacking normal degrees of assertiveness, the love-shy are often passed over and ignored by those who could provide significant rewards. And in lacking normal levels of sociability and social self-confidence they make other people around them feel uncomfortable, insecure, and in time somewhat hostile.

One of the most important reasons why love-shyness is a serious problem is that it prevents its victims from participating in self-confidence building experiences. There are very few if any experiences that build the sense of self-confidence and self-esteem of a young man more surely and thoroughly than that of winning the companionship and emotional support of an attractive girl. Furthermore, the self-confidence that eminates from successful heterosexual interaction is scarcely ever limited to that sphere of human activity alone. It *transfers* to virtually all spheres of human activity in which a person happens to be involved.[2]

Plan of the Book

This book represents the first scientific study ever published on the subject of love-shyness. The book has five essential purposes: (1) to create a compassionate awareness and understanding of a long neglected and ignored segment of the American male population; (2) to help the public better understand and constructively deal with the love-shy; (3) to help the love-shy better understand themselves and to clearly see that they are not alone—and that they need to unite as a social and political force on behalf of their own interests; (4) to delineate as fully and comprehensively as possible *all* of the causal antecedents of love-shyness; and (5) to delineate and explain the most promising modalities for both the treatment and the prevention of love-shyness.

The remaining chapters of this book are organized into *three sections*. The chapters in the first section (*Part One*) are concerned with the biological underpinnings of severe shyness. This book endeavors to be quite thoroughgoing in its approach to the subject of inborn factors. There are more myths and falsehoods floating about pertinent to the relationship between biology and shyness than there are about any other shyness-related issue. These myths must be arrested and corrected if the love-shy are ever to be properly understood and successfully helped. In the absence of a valid understanding of the biological basis of shyness, there is no way severe and chronic love-shyness can ever be prevented or successfully treated.

The chapters contained in *Part Two* of this book are based upon an original investigation of 300 love-shy men, 200 of whom were between the ages of 19 and 24 when the data were obtained, and 100 of whom were between the ages of 35 and 50. This study also incorporated a comparison group of 200 *non-shy* men, all of whom were between the ages of 19 and 24, when the data were obtained from them.

The chapters contained under *Part Two* systematically compare the love-shys with the non-shys on such important matters as (1) past family life with the mother and father, (2) family composition, (3) peer group life throughout the formative years of childhood and adolescence, (4) the development of early boy-girl romantic interests, (5) current sex life and sexual attitudes/values, (6) current social and demographic characteristics, (7) current life styles, (8) employment effectiveness, (9) medical symptoms, (10) physical characteristics, (11) the need for physical beauty in a lover, (12) loneliness, (13) parenthood aspirations, (14) social-political attitudes and values, and (15) artistic and recreational interests and predilections.

The many comparisons that are made between the love-shy and non-shy men provide a host of very useful insights as to what the key factors are which cause and sustain pathological love-shyness. Each of the chapters in this section provides a unique constellation of insights which should ultimately prove very useful in both preventive and therapeutic work.

The chapters contained in *Part Three* deal with therapy and prevention. The chapter on "practice-dating therapy" introduces a therapeutic approach which will effectively cure 95 to 100 percent of even the most severe and intractable cases of love-shyness. This is perhaps the most important chapter in this book because it contains a detailed discussion of all the important aspects of a procedure which can ultimately emancipate the love-shy to the point where they are able to experience the love relationships to which they are eminently entitled. Hopefully this chapter will serve as an inspiration to all who work with the love-shy.

Prevention is similarly a very important subject. In a whole host of ways contemporary American society both creates and assures a certain amount of pathological love-shyness. The chapter on prevention provides a discussion of some thought-provoking, innovative ways of engineering our society so that painfully severe forms of shyness are effectively prevented from ever developing in the first place. Without inconveniencing the lives of the non-shy and without spending a great deal of money, there is a very great deal that can be done right now which could totally obviate the development of any new cases of severe love-shyness.

Finally, a summary chapter is provided which highlights the major points of the book as a whole. An overview is provided in this last chapter of some of the major recommendations towards which my research conclusions seem to point.

In sum, love-shyness is *not* the mild little developmental problem that some people think it is. Love-shyness is a potentially very serious problem that is in society's best interests to prevent and to cure. It is my hope that this book will serve to effectively point the way toward that end.[3]

Notes

1. As incisive testimony to the inadequacy of Dr. Zimbardo's approach, Zimbardo's own *"shyness clinic"* at Stanford University had to be disbanded because its therapeutic approach was simply not working. In fact, it was making many of its clients worse off than they had been when they had first sought aid.

2. As per WPIX (New York Channel 11) evening news (broadcast 11/23/84), *ten percent* of the letters which nationally syndicated advice columnist Ann Landers has received of late have been *complaints about shyness*. According to Landers, the proportion of her letters containing complaints about shyness has increased noticeably over the past several years. The so-called "sexual revolution" has provided no relief for those afflicted with shyness-related problems.

3. Shyness among university males is by no means rare. In 1967, Ellis and Lane found that 25 percent of all university males surveyed were quite socially inactive due to shyness. They further found that 8 percent of all graduating seniors of heterosexual orientation had yet to experience their very first date with a girl. A study published in 1973 by Landis and Landis, further revealed that better than half of all college students experience at least occasional severe shyness symptoms vis-a-vis the opposite sex in informal social situations; and 25 percent of them were found to be victims of such severe shyness that they seldom or never dated. Only 23 percent of those surveyed were found to be always or nearly always comfortable in informal interaction with opposite sexed age mates.

Part One

THE BIOLOGICAL UNDERPINNINGS OF LOVE-SHYNESS

Chapter 2

Love-Shyness and the Nature Versus Nurture Debate

In discussing their problems the love-shy often say that they feel as though they had been "born shy", or that shyness has always been a part of their fundamental underlying nature. And in taking this position about themselves and their problems the love-shy typically receive little compassion or understanding from the major power sources of contemporary psychology. Such major figures as Philip Zimbardo and Albert Ellis continue to insist that *shyness is learned*, and that until shy people recognize and accept that alleged "fact" they will not be amenable to help.

A major purpose behind this book is to show that two quite crucial, dominating components of shyness *are inborn*. Nevertheless, much of shyness behavior is a byproduct of a certain *process* of learning—a process that is dependent upon inborn attributes and society's reactions to them.

A key source of the confusion over this issue rests upon the fact that researchers in the behavioral and social sciences seldom if ever interact socially with the scholarly researchers of other disciplines. And as a result they often have little idea as to what is going on in fields other than their own. Research findings are constantly coming to the fore in such fields as human physiology, genetics, biochemistry, human anatomy, pharmocology, and microbiology, which have profound implications for the types of human problems with which clinical psychologists and sociologists deal. Yet with all their Ph.D.s and extensive learning in their own narrow areas of specialization, extremely few clinical psychologists or sociologists have any awareness at all of research findings of profound importance which have been arrived at by biologically and physiologically oriented research scholars. Even more tragically, they are often unaware of and refuse to consider the biologically oriented work of their own colleagues.

Academic people are often perceived by the public as constituting prime models of open-mindedness and of non-prejudiced attitudes. Indeed, a primary element of the philosophy of science has long been that any and all hypotheses are worth considering and researching until such time as those hypotheses have been disproved. Yet almost all clinical psychologists quite blythly reject the notion that there could possibly be anything "inborn" about shyness. And they are often quite callous and abrupt with colleagues who challenge "sacred" assumptions and long-standing theoretical ideology.

Genuine progress towards the prevention and cure of love-shyness can never be effected as long as scholars and researchers insist upon remaining rigidly married to their ideological and "therapeutic" belief systems. Progress towards the prevention and cure of this and of countless other forms of human suffering can only (and will only) be made through the concerted efforts of research scholars from the *full range* of disciplines.

The Phenomenon of Inborn Temperament

Since the end of World War II, a small number of scientists in various parts of the world have been working on the issue of inborn components to personality. And a very great deal of progress has been made on this subject. Specifically, *temperament* can be defined as those elements of personality that are *inborn*, whereas *personality* can be defined as representing those comparatively stable elements of our behavior patterns that are learned.

Up to now, the five most important researchers on this subject have been (1) Hans J. Eysenck of the University of London, (2) Alexander Thomas of New York University, (3) Jerome Kagan of Harvard University, (4) Thomas J. Bouchard's University of Minnesota study on identical twins reared apart, and (5) David V. Sheehan's work on *"anxiety disease"*. This chapter will endeavor to present the prime essence of their findings. I believe that their work holds indispensable significance for any truly valid and meaningful understanding of love-shyness. In the absence of an understanding of inborn temperament or of the genetic/biological basis of human personality differences, one cannot pretend to any reasoned understanding as to how love-shyness (or any other kind of shyness) develops. Without an accurate understanding as to how shyness develops, there can be no hope of effectively preventing the phenomenon from developing in the first place. And there can be no truly viable means of therapy.

Puppies and Babies

For many generations obstetrical nurses and midwives have known that all people are not born alike in terms of personality. A person can observe a large number of newborn babies, all of which are *of the same gender*. And he or she will quickly notice that some of the infants cry a great deal more than others do. Some are exceedingly noisy whereas others tend to be remarkably quiet. Some infants wriggle around a very great deal and are quite restless. Others, on the other hand, tend to remain near motionless over long periods of time.

These and myriad other differences in behavioral reactions cannot be attributed to differences in quality of mothering, cleanliness care, medical attention, feeding, or gender. Environmental and learning-related factors have been carefully controlled by many different researchers. Yet no matter how carefully the various extraneous factors are controlled, male babies of the same very young age behave very differently from one another. And indeed the same applies to female babies of the same very young age. The important point is that these quite substantial differences in behavioral reactions have been observed in healthy, well-loved and cared for infants *long before* any differential learning could possibly have taken place.

Psychologists, despite the widespread unwillingness among them to recognize the phenomena of inborn temperament in humans, often raise strains of white rats and mice for high aggression or low aggression, friendliness or seclusiveness, high versus low intelligence, etc. Psychologists' rat experiments often call for rats with a certain type of inborn temperament. Animals with the sort of native temperament appropos to experimental requirements are often bread; this can be accomplished rather easily in view of the comparatively short lifespan that characterizes the rat.

Doubtless many readers of this book have a strong interest in dogs. And whereas there is a variety of differences in modal temperament among the 125 A.K.C. recognized canine breeds, a person can take any one of these breeds and find highly substantial differences in temperament among the puppies of a newly born litter. For example, take a litter of newly born golden retrievers. Right at the outset some of the dogs will behave more assertively than others. Some will behave more sociably and fearlessly than others. Generally speaking the more assertive animals will get more food. And so after a comparatively brief period of time they will appear larger and healthier than their same-sexed litter mates.

Most dog manuals recommend that dog purchasers deliberately select the largest, most highly assertive, sociable animal from within a litter. It is believed that such a puppy has a head start towards developing into a happy, healthy animal—an animal that will adapt well to life among humans. In psychological terms it can be said that the highly sociable member of the litter has a strongly positive *social stimulus value* vis-a-vis the educated humans who are trying to make a decision as to which member to purchase of the seven or eight member litter. This concept of *social stimulus value* is of enormous importance from the standpoint of enabling us to correctly understand the development of chronic love-shyness in humans. And I shall return to this matter shortly.

The Work of Hans J. Eysenck

Prior to the onset of World War II, Eysenck fled his native Germany. He ended up in London where he successfully completed *both* a Ph.D. in psychology and an M.D. (doctor of medicine) degree as well. In short, Eysenck became one of the truly rare psychologists to develop a firm grounding in the biochemical and physiological nature of man.

Shortly after the war was over, Eysenck commenced an extensive research investigation, parts of which he is still pursuing even today. Much of his work entailed the recording of chemical and physiological attributes in humans. He has followed up thousands of people over twenty and even thirty years in some cases. And he has found that these physiological and biochemical indicators *change very little* in the same person over the years and even over decades of time. More importantly, several of these biochemical and physiological indicators have a strong bearing upon the native, *inborn* differences in personality which we now call *temperament*. These are the *same* inborn behavioral differences which (1) cause some very young dogs to behave more assertively and sociably than others in their litter, and (2) which cause the temperamental differences in newborn human babies that have been observed by nurses and obstetricians down through the ages.

After some 35 years of research in both human physiology and in psychology, Eysenck has been able to conclude that there are but *three* statistically independent, genetically rooted dimensions of inborn temperament: (1) extroversion-introversion or *inhibition*; (2) *emotionality* or "high versus low anxiety threshold"; and (3) psychoticism. Curiously, the first two dimensions had been isolated by the ancient Greeks more than 2,500 years ago. Inasmuch as psychoticism is not related to the subject of love-shyness it will not be dealt with in this book. *Figure 1* graphically illustrates what has come to be known as the *Eysenck Cross of Inborn Temperament*. And it is no accident that people who suffer from

Figure One
Eysenck Cross of Inborn Temperament

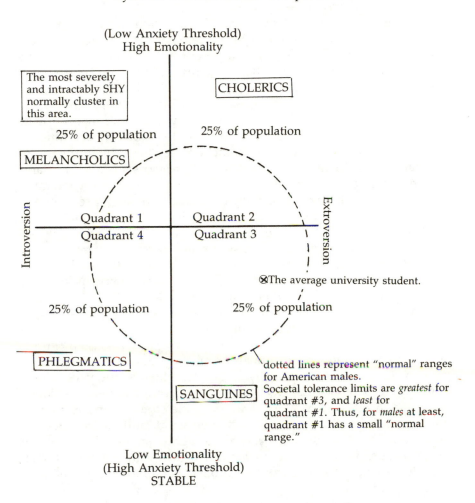

(Low Anxiety Threshold)
High Emotionality

The most severely
and intractably SHY
normally cluster in
this area.

CHOLERICS

25% of population   25% of population

MELANCHOLICS

Introversion   Extroversion

Quadrant 1 | Quadrant 2
Quadrant 4 | Quadrant 3

⊗The average university student.

25% of population   25% of population

PHLEGMATICS

dotted lines represent "normal" ranges
for American males.

SANGUINES

Societal tolerance limits are *greatest* for
quadrant #3, and *least* for
quadrant #1. Thus, for *males* at least,
quadrant #1 has a small "normal
range."

Low Emotionality
(High Anxiety Threshold)
STABLE

chronic, intractable cases of love-shyness ALL (with no exceptions) possess native temperaments which place them high up in the *first quadrant* (*melancholic quadrant*) of the cross.[1]

Eysenck has concluded that inborn introversion is a natural byproduct of high native arousal levels in the cerebral cortex, and that these high arousal levels are caused by an overactive ascending reticular formation (*lower brain*) which bombards the higher brain and central nervous system when social or other stimuli (perceived as threatening) are presented. This inborn hyperarousability of introverts accounts (1) for their forming conditioned patterns of anxiety and other inappropriate emotional responses all too easily; and (2) for the much greater difficulty in extinguishing maladaptive conditioned responses in introverts as compared to extroverts and ambiverts. (*Ambiverts* include the large majority of the population who are "in between" the extrovert and introvert extremes.) These facts partially account for the high prevalence of introverts among the ranks of neurotics and the love-shy. However, as I shall attempt to demonstrate shortly, *even an extreme introvert need not develop chronic, intractable love-shyness or any other form of neurosis.*

In stark contrast to the foregoing, Eysenck found that highly extroverted people tend to have *underaroused* brains and nervous systems. Simply put, they are stimulus hungry. This is why they are always craving and seeking excitement of one kind or another, and why they must constantly have people around them.

Emotionality (high versus low anxiety threshold) is also a byproduct of inborn differences in human physiology, and particularly in the autonomic nervous system and lymbic system. Simply put, various reactions of the body such as heartbeat, rapid breathing, the cessation of digestion to make blood flow away from the stomach and to prepare the organism for flight or fight, tend to be significantly more labile and easily aroused (*and less easily stopped*) in highly emotional (*low* anxiety threshold) people. Emotional reactions are regulated by the visceral brain, and herein lies the locus of the inborn personality dimension of emotionality.[2]

Studies employing the electroencephalograph have similarly revealed large differences between introverts and extroverts that are apparent from early infancy and which persist on a consistent basis throughout life. Introverts, for example, tend to have low amplitude and high frequency alpha waves, typical of high arousal, whereas extroverts tend to have high amplitude and low frequency alpha waves; and this is indicative of *low* arousal. Of course, most people are ambiverts; and that means that most of us have patterns which fall somewhere *in between* these two extremes. Many laboratory studies of conditioning, sensory thresholds, vigilence, reactions to emotion-producing stimuli, etc., have further revealed often dramatic differences between people high on the emotionality dimension and those low on it. And longitudinal studies have revealed that these inborn patterns tend to remain quite stable over many years and decades of time.

Love-Shyness and the Inborn Anxiety Threshold

In order to clarify the foregoing, let me present two itemized lists. The first list is composed of *attributes of inborn temperament*; the second list contains a partial summary of *learned* personality traits which entail strong implications for the development and maintenance of love-shyness. Indeed, one of the items on the second list *is love-shyness*.

ATTRIBUTES OF INBORN TEMPERAMENT:

1. Extroversion
2. Introversion/Inhibition
3. Emotionality
4. High Anxiety Threshold
5. Low Anxiety Threshold**
6. Pain Threshold
7. Activity Level
8. Aggressiveness.

PARTIAL LIST OF LEARNED PERSONALITY TRAITS:

1. Love-Shyness
2. Self-Image/Self-Esteem
3. Self-Confidence
4. Sociability
5. Positive Mental Attitude
6. Negative Mental Attitude
7. Interpersonal Skills
8. Social Spontaneity and Natural Casualness
9. Neurotic Behavior Patterns.

A person with a *low* anxiety threshold experiences anxiety (1) much more frequently, and (2) much more intensely and *painfully* than a person who is blessed with a *high* or *normal* anxiety threshold. Further (3), he is likely to begin experiencing the painful anxiety *more quickly* upon the

**Certain antidepressant drugs such as the MAO Inhibitors have been found to *raise* this threshold.

initial presentation of whatever stimulus he had learned to associate with anxiety. People with *high* native anxiety thresholds are often said to be "thick skinned" inasmuch as it usually requires a great deal to unruffle them. Corollatively, the person with a very *low* native anxiety threshold is often said to be "thin skinned". Unlike the "thick skinned" and "normal" persons, it takes very little to unruffle the "thin skinned" person. To reiterate, he experiences anxiety more frequently, more painfully, more intensely, and in response to a wider range of different stimuli, than does the person with a normally high native anxiety threshold.

Before a person can ever become love-shy he must first learn to associate the thought of informal, unstructured heterosexual interaction with the experience of strong and painful anxiety feelings. The low anxiety threshold (high inborn emotionality) must be there *before* this can be accomplished to any "pathological" extent. People with middle-range to high anxiety thresholds occasionally do experience brief periods of love-shyness in their lives. In fact, transitory love-shyness is a quite commonplace accompaniment of adolescence here in American society— although not in all societies. However, these transitory periods are *exactly that*. In essence, for most teenagers they are transitory and brief. They last perhaps two or three weeks at the most. And then the person gets over the love-shyness to the point wherein he or she can interact reasonably comfortably vis-a-vis the opposite sex.

Moreover, even during periods when temporary, short-term love-shyness is suffered, moderate-to-high anxiety threshold teenagers typically continue interacting successfully with their same-sexed buddies. Their low anxiety threshold peers, in stark contrast, usually interact (*if they are males*) little if at all with their same-sexed peers. In short, by the mid-teens the very low anxiety threshold male has usually developed a generalized *people-phobia*. He withdraws from same-sexed age mates just as he withdraws from opposite sexed age mates. And in not having the benefit of membership in a social network of same-sexed peers, no one feels any need to introduce him to potential girl friends. It is well known that in America most people of *both* sexes meet their future spouses through social networks comprised of same-sexed peers.

Now the really crucial point which must be understood by the reader before we move onward is that a person can learn to associate *ANY STIMULUS* with strong, painful feelings of anxiety. In this book we are concerned with love-shyness. But a person can become extremely fearful of (and avoid) dogs or snakes or high elevations or automobiles or dentists or *ANY* type of social experience *OR* any substance which you, the reader, might wish to name. The inborn anxiety threshold does not determine (AND *CANNOT* DETERMINE) specifically *what* will arouse the anxiety feelings and cause avoidance behavior. THIS MUST ALWAYS BE LEARNED.

In the case of love-shyness the victim *learns* over time to associate the thought of interacting with an attractive woman with feelings of extremely painful anxiety. The love-shyness itself is *learned*; the anxiety threshold, on the other hand, is *INBORN*. If the native anxiety threshold is very low, the person will condition maladaptive anxiety patterns altogether too rapidly and easily. If the inborn anxiety threshold is *high* or *moderate*, the person will not easily condition chronic anxiety patterns. And through the help of his family and friendship networks he will be able to get over any shyness patterns which temporarily do develop. This is the essence of what I meant when in the second paragraph of the first page of this chapter I stated that two very major *components* of shyness *are inborn*, but that *shyness itself is learned*.

In sum, there are *two inborn components*: one is the high emotionality (low anxiety threshold); the second component is inhibition/introversion. When a person is *very high* on *both* emotionality *and* introversion (the *MELANCHOLIC* quadrant of the Eysenck Cross of Inborn Temperament), the chances are exceedingly good within the context of American society that he will develop into a chronically love-shy individual. Let us now examine *why* this is so, understanding at the outset that it is true for males but *not* for females. (The reasons why it is *not* true for females will be dealt with in due course.)

The Importance of Social Stimulus Value

Social stimulus value can be defined as simply representing the extent to which any given person or object is viewed as being attractive, desirable and worthwhile. Everything has a social stimulus value which will vary somewhat from one social/cultural context to another. In this book we are concerned with people rather than with objects. Every person has a social stimulus value right from the moment he or she is born. This social stimulus value is heavily determined by the values of a particular society and culture. A person with a positive social stimulus value in Culture "*A*" may have a negative social stimulus value in Culture "*B*". And most importantly, a specific behavioral manifestation that has neutral-to-positive social stimulus value when it is displayed by *females* in a particular culture may wield a strongly negative or adverse social stimulus value when it is displayed by *males* in that same culture.

As a case in point, being frightened away by "rough and tumble" play is a behavior that carries little or no adverse social stimulus value when it is displayed by little girls. But that *same frightened behavior* tends to carry very negative social stimulus value when it is displayed by little boys. And as a result, little boys are often punished for behavior patterns which yield rewards (or at least an absence of punishment) for little girls.

There are *four* personal characteristics entailing social stimulus value which are of preeminent importance: (1) native temperament; (2) physical attractiveness; (3) native aptitudes and intelligence; and (4) inborn health characteristics/limitations. And of these four, there is no doubt in my mind that native temperament is the most important, with level of physical attractiveness following closely behind in second place.

The overall social stimulus value exuded by a person (small child) is determined primarily by five key factors:

1. The *gender* of the child who is being evaluated;
2. The internalized values and normative expectations, feelings, etc., of the father, mother, and other significant family members;
3. The normative values, expectations, and feelings of the same-sexed peer group;
4. Norms and values of school officials and policy makers;
5. Norms and values of the community and nation.

A child's developing self-image and the likelihood of his developing a case of pathological shyness will be a direct function of the *goodness of fit* of these five factors with his (1) native temperament, (2) physical appearance, (3) aptitudes & intelligence, and (4) health.

Let me illustrate with some insights derived from findings reported in various parts of this book. In American society there is an irrational albeit near ubiquitous *learned* tendency on the part of most young adults to associate the very thought of "boy" with the thought of a natural, inborn enthusiasm for baseball, football, and basketball. Thus my findings clearly show that those boys who best fit this stereotyped expectation quickly come to possess the strongest interpersonal skills and the lowest incidence of love-shyness. On the other hand, my data also show that those boys who fit this stereotype least well include among their members the highest incidence of intractable love-shyness combined with a history of inadequate socialization for interpersonal skills and social self-confidence. Girls without a natural enthusiasm for such rough, contact sports do not suffer negative outcomes as a result. A liking for such sports is considered (at best) *optional* for them, and it is not normatively prescribed as it is for boys.

It is through the cumulative tenor of the responses of others, *particularly parents and peers*, that a child decides whether it is intelligent or stupid, attractive or homely, lovable or unlovable, competent or incompetent, worthy of social companionship or worthless in this regard. If a male child is born in America with an innate temperament that places him high up in the *melancholic quadrant* (quadrant #1) of the Eysenck Cross, and if this native temperament with its concomitants of very low pain and anxiety thresholds, nervousness and inhibition/introversion, cause him to constantly avoid the rough and tumble play of the all-male peer group (and not physically defend himself against its assaults), that child is highly likely to develop a very low social self-image along with a case of intractable shyness.

Such a development is *NEVER* a *necessary* consequence of such an inborn temperament. There is nothing intrinsically "unhealthy" about being an emotional introvert *per se*. But insofar as *within the American social context* such a temperament is likely to serve as a stimulus for consistent and continual bullying, ignoring and rejection on the part of the peer group and expressed disappointment and disapproval on the part of parents (especially fathers), shyness together with a low self-esteem, a "people-phobia", and poor interpersonal skills are all highly likely to develop.

The Work of Alexander Thomas

The extensive research on inborn temperament by Alexander Thomas and his associates at New York University is of especial relevance to a complete understanding of how severe love-shyness develops. Like Hans Eysenck. Dr. Thomas has been able to show that the traits of inborn temperament (such as introversion-extroversion, activity level, emotionality-withdrawal, etc.) persist from very early childhood over long periods of time. However, he has also been able to demonstrate how *NO* attribute of native temperament can ever *by itself* be indicative of "sickness" or of "neurosis". After having followed up some 146 children for sixteen years after their respective births, he found that whether or not a child developed neurotic behavior patterns as a result of an "undesirable" trait of native temperament was *entirely determined* by the way in which that child had been treated by parents and peers.

Thomas was especially interested in the etiology of behavior disorders in children. And his research data clearly proved that behavior disorders are the result of a *poorness of fit* between (1) a child's native temperament on the one hand, and (2) internalized norms, values and expectations of parents, peers and teachers, on the other hand. To the extent that a child enjoys *a reasonably good fit* between these two factors, to that extent chronic behavior disorders (such as shyness and neuroses) will never develop in that child. The poorer the fit, on the other hand, the greater the likelihood that a child will develop problems.

In his book entitled TEMPERAMENT AND BEHAVIOR DISOR-DERS IN CHILDREN, Dr. Thomas talks at considerable length about what he calls the "*slow-to-warm-up child*". And he presents an impressive amount of research evidence showing how this type of seemingly "difficult" child can eventually become indistinguishable in adjustment from the other seemingly "easy", naturally sociable children when (1) copious opportunity is accorded for informal play amidst an *accepting* peer group that is engaged in enjoyable, non-anxiety-provoking activities, and (2) when patient, kindly and accepting attitudes are held by parents and teachers.

Simply put, when a child is *accepted as he is* he becomes free to grow, to mature, to change in a positive direction, and to become his true self. When a child is accorded caring and respect for his feelings and emotional needs, he inevitably becomes a caring and respecting person who gradually comes to "fit in" remarkably well. But when that same "slow-to-warm-up" child is forced to conform to parental or teacher expectations and to play amidst a physically aggressive, highly competitive peer group which he finds frightening and anxiety-provoking, he tends to withdraw. Indeed, he tends to regress and to become progressively less mature by comparison with the other children in his age cohort.

In essence, the more rigid and uncompromising the parental expectations are, the more time the "slow-to-warm-up" child will take to adjust, to mature, and to "fit in". Simply put, it is counterproductive to try to standardize human personality because the raw materials (including native temperament) differ for each child within each of the two sexes.

As Thomas has argued, there is a long-standing tradition in American society of trying to force square pegs into round holes—of endeavoring to do whatever seems feasible to make the behavior, feelings and interests of a child *fit* prevailing norms and expectations. Thomas' findings show that there is a costly price to be paid for our callous insistence upon trying to standardize human personalities. A far more socially beneficial approach, as Thomas' research data have shown, is to modify the expectations of parents, peers and teachers to fit the native temperament of the child. When *this tact* is followed, the child flourishes, grows, matures, and is ultimately as normal in his behavior patterns as the bulk of his peers.

Modifying parental and peer expectations can be effectively accomplished through (1) education of the parents and teachers as to the nature and limits posed by native temperament; (2) the creation of *support groups* for parents of shy, inhibited, "slow-to-warm-up" children; and (3) providing the seemingly "difficult" child with a *choice* of peer groups and of peer group activities. In regard to this last point, one child's medicine is another child's poison. The *typical* male child flourishes in the all-boy peer group that is engaged in "rough and tumble" play. In contrast, the introverted, inhibited, "slow-to-warm-up" child flourishes best in the small sized, *coeducational* peer group that engages in more gently competitive activities such as volleyball, bowling, hide and seek, miniature golf, swimming, shuffle board, horseshoes, croquet, ping pong, etc.

To be sure, militant physical education enthusiasts have quibbled that these more gentle sports and games do not provide the exercise that male children need. (This objection is ludicrous inasmuch as the "gentle" sport of swimming, for example, exercises more bodily muscles than does football, basketball and baseball. Moreover, all male children *are not alike* in their exercise needs!) As Thomas' research data have shown, the traditional tact of insisting that *all* male children take part in the *same* "rough and tumble" activity has eventuated in two consequences that are very deleterious from the standpoint of *both* the individual *and* the wider society:

(1) The melancholic child (1st quadrant, page 41) *withdraws* from play and consequently does not get any outdoor physical exercise *at all*. In short, very few melancholic male children subordinate themselves to the rigid requirement they they *must* play "rough and tumble" games. They simply withdraw; and as a result they get little or nothing of the physical exercise which the physical education enthusiasts deem so extremely important. The point here is that *something is always better than nothing!*

(2) The melancholic child fails to develop the interpersonal skills and the social self-confidence that are so necessary for success, happiness and adjustment in this or in any other society. Since he is mistreated, bullied, abused, and/or ignored by the peers society tells him he *must* play with, he quickly develops a "people-phobia". In essence, he learns to associate being around age-mates with feelings of anxiety, pain, and strong displeasure. More succinctly, whereas most people learn to associate feelings of pleasure and happiness with the idea of "friends", the melancholic boy learns to associate feelings of pain and anxiety with the idea of "friends". For him peers cause *pain*, NOT pleasure!

This latter point is of enormous importance. Active involvement in enjoyable childhood play has long been known to be an indispensable prerequisite (in both humans and monkeys) to competent, effective adulthood. Indeed, social and psychoemotional adjustment in adulthood *absolutely requires and necessitates* a long-term history of happy involvement in play throughout the years of childhood. Play is not the sort of frivolous activity some people think it is. Play represents an indispensable component of the classroom of life—much more indispensable, in fact, than the "3 Rs" that are learned in the indoor classroom. Research has shown that people can pick up the "3 Rs" and other intellectual/ technical skills *at any age*. Unfortunately, socioemotional and interpersonal skills that are not picked up at the normal times during the course of childhood play cannot normally be picked up for the first time in later life. More succinctly, it is vastly more difficult for an adult to pick up interpersonal skills and social self-confidence *for the first time*, than it is for him to pick up intellectual/technical skills or knowledge for the first time.

People can cultivate and expand their intellects at any age. Unfortunately, the nature of man is such that deficits in the interpersonal/ socioemotional areas cannot easily be rectified in adulthood or late adolescence. This is why education in these areas is so important throughout the years of early and middle childhood. And it is the peer group, *NOT* parents or teachers, who provide this indispensable education. And this is why we shall never successfully prevent chronic love-shyness in males unless and until we make sure that *ALL* little boys have ready access at all times throughout their formative years to a peer group and to play activities which they can truly enjoy and to which they can always look forward with positive emotional feelings of happiness and enthusiasm.

The Jerome Kagan Work

Jerome Kagan is an eminent Harvard University psychologist. And his represents the third of the five major research efforts leading towards an understanding and appreciation of the innate biological underpinnings of human personality and behavior.

During the early 1960s Dr. Kagan carefully examined nearly two dozen classes of behavior in a large group of children composed of hundreds of two and three-year-olds. These classes of behavior included such traits as dependency, aggression, dominance, competitiveness, passivity, etc. These children were all followed up over a substantial number of years. And only one of these traits turned out to have a substantial bearing upon later behavior. And that trait was *inhibition*. In his initial work Dr. Kagan called this trait "passivity". Now he simply designates it as "inhibition".

The difference between inhibited and uninhibited infants is best seen when an unfamiliar event occurs. Inhibited youngsters stop whatever they are doing, as though they were trying to understand the puzzling event. The uninhibited children seem to note the event, but then go on to other matters.

In a Fels Institute study there were seven boys who were noteworthy for being extremely inhibited and easily frightened during their first three years—the period during which they were observed and studied. These children were all healthy and came from good families. The key point is that they behaved in a consistently *inhibited* way. Dr. Kagan followed up these boys until they became adults. And he found their temperaments in adulthood to be conspicuously different from those of other adults in his study. All were heterosexual, but all were still very inhibited and "shy" in their informal interactions with others—particularly in the sort of ambiguous social situations wherein there is no role to play or script to follow.

As adults all seven of these men were found to be particularly vulnerable to anxiety attacks and to various sorts of internal conflicts. Interesting too is the fact that none of them had pursued any sports or athletic activities, and none had pursued traditional masculine occupations. For example, two of the men had become music teachers and one had become a psychologist. None had entered the world of engineering or business. (All of these men would doubtless fall in the "melancholic" *first quadrant* of the Eysenck Cross. See *Figure One* on page 41.)

Dr. Kagan has found evidence that what most people describe as fearfulness may be accompanied by such positive intellectual qualities as curiosity and creativity, which can have a major impact on later mental development and career choice. As I shall document in this book, loveshy men do indeed appear to be more intellectually oriented than the majority of the population. And, in general, they do seem to acquire rather extensive educations despite their social/emotional difficulties. On the other hand, the low emotional resilence ("thin skinned") and low competitiveness which characterizes love-shy men causes the majority of them to fail to use their educations propitiously. Being too shy to compete for the best jobs, they are commonly shunted to positions which are sharply below their levels of attained education. *Education alone does not confer social self-confidence!*

One of Christopher Jencks' findings which I reported in Chapter 1 is also of relevance here. Non-daters had devoted a great deal more of their time to studying during their high school years than did those who had been actively involved in dating and partying. And more of the non-daters managed to go on to college and to actually get through college. But by age 28, those who had dated and partied in high school were found to be earning significantly greater amounts of money than the non-daters. Again, the daters and party-goers (1) had gained interpersonal skills and social self-confidence crucial for effectiveness in the world of employment, and (2) the self-same competitive drive and emotional resilence necessary for involvement in dating (for males at least) appeared to have been quite useful for success in the cold, hard business world of jobs and careers.

Several studies in which Kagan had followed inhibited boys up through the school years towards adulthood clearly indicated that the ones who had been inhibited as three-year olds tended throughout their school years to: (1) avoid dangerous activities, (2) show exceedingly little physical or verbal aggression, (3) display substantial timidity in social situations, (4) tended to avoid sports and other masculine activities throughout their childhood and adolescence, and (5) tended to conform more than most children to their parents' wishes.

Heart Rate Patterns

One of the most puzzling of Dr. Kagan's findings was that as adults the heart-rate patterns of the inhibited boys showed an absence of sinus arrhythmia. Sinus arrhythmia refers to the fact that normally the heart rate increases when a person takes a breath, and it decreases when he/she exhales. But in an experimental session when males high on *inhibition* ("melancholia") listened to tape recorded discussions involving a very high aggression and/or sexuality content, much of their sinus arrhythmia, or variability in heart rate, disappeared. In essence, their heart rates became *stable* during these periods.

In 1970 Dr. Kagan and a team of researchers were conducting a study on the effects of day care on Chinese and Caucasian children residing in the Boston area. The Chinese-American infants showed more stable heart rates and were more inhibited in unfamiliar social situations than the Caucasian children. This pattern of differences tended to hold up irrespective of whether the children studied were in attendance at day care facilities or had been reared strictly at home. And in a study of three-year olds which was recently published in a book entitled THE SECOND YEAR, Dr. Kagan found that *shy* children showed the same heart anomaly whenever they were confronted with the unfamiliar.

When Kagan and his staff placed the inhibited children with an unfamiliar adult or child or took them to an unfamiliar day care center, they were initially very anxiety-ridden and behaved in an exceedingly reserved and inhibited fashion. To use Alexander Thomas' terminology, they were exceedingly "slow to warm up". When the mothers of these children left them alone in a room, they became much more distressed than the other children in the study.

In a related study of Chinese and Caucasian newborns, Daniel Freedman similarly found that the Chinese infants had a higher *inhibition mean* (average) than did the Caucasian infants. For example, in one of his tests when he covered the baby's nose, a Caucasian baby would *typically* squirm and flail about more than would a *typical* Chinese baby. Taking his cue from this research effort by Freedman, Dr. Kagan decided to look at another sample composed exclusively of Caucasian children, and see whether there was any connection between the tendency towards behavioral inhibition to the unfamiliar during the first and second years of life, and a *stable heart rate* while studying discrepant information. In brief, he again found that this expected relationship *did obtain*. And he realized at this time that he had a replication which strongly suggested that he was looking at a reliable phenomenon.

This relationship between heart rate and behavioral inhibition makes theoretical sense. And Dr. Kagan began to suspect that this relationship constitutes a key portion of the physiological underpinnings of the inborn temperamental trait of behavioral inhibition (shyness). There are several mechanisms which could lead to a loss of variability in heart rate. And one of the more reasonable of these involves the balance between the sympathetic and the parasympathetic nervous systems. When a person inspires, the discharge of the sympathetic system leads to an increase in heart rate. And when a person breathes out, the action of the para-sympathetic nervous system, through the vagus nerve, leads to a decrease in the heart rate. It is important to realize, of course, that it is the sympathetic nervous system that causes the heart to pound when we are afraid. And it is the parasympathetic nervous system that slows the heart beat back down again.

If a discharge from the sympathetic nervous system blocked the vagus nerve, the heart rate would not decrease with expiration. Indeed, it would stabilize or become less variable. Moreover, if this is a correct interpretation, then perhaps inhibited children and adults have a special tendency to become sympathetically aroused by psychologically unfa-miliar or ambiguous stimuli. In essence, they are unusually apprehensive.

To use Eysenck's terminology, perhaps the ambiguous and unfa-miliar in a social situation arouses their low inborn anxiety threshold; and they withdraw—thus assuring that they will be perceived by most others as "slow to warm up". And since society (male peer group in particular) seems to want a certain number of deviants, it uses these "slow to warm up", easily frightened, "shell-shock prone" tendencies as a major criterion for recruiting some children and adults for the deviant role in life. And these "slow to warm up", easily frightened tendencies become publicly labeled, internalized by the victim, and reinforced (strengthened). Simply put, nurture (social learning) strengthens and enhances nature (inborn tendencies). And this applies to *both* "good" and "bad" inborn tendencies.

In late 1979, Dr. Kagan conducted another confirmatory study. Several hundred Caucasian children, all of whom were just under two years of age, were carefully screened; 117 of these children were put through a series of episodes that included unfamiliar people, a robot, and separation from the mother. Dr. Kagan and his associate for this study (Dr. Cynthia Garcia-Coll) then selected thirty consistently inhibited youngsters and thirty consistently uninhibited youngsters. And they recorded the heart rates and respirations of all of these children during a series of stimulus episodes.

One month later Dr. Garcia-Coll retested all of these children. The inhibited children had higher and more stable heart rates when they were confronted with information that was difficult for them to assimilate. In essence, her findings continued to support Dr. Kagan's premise that there is a strong relationship between (a) inhibited behavior when a person is exposed to unfamiliar people or social contexts, and (b) heart-rate patterns in response to unfamiliar stimuli.

Ten months subsequent to this research effort Dr. Garcia-Coll visited forty of the children in their homes. And she also brought them into the laboratory for a special test. In the laboratory environment each child was confined with and asked to play with an unfamiliar child of the *opposite* behavioral style. The inhibited children quickly became highly apprehensive in this situation. And all were *dominated* by the uninhibited children.[3] The inhibited ones retreated to their mothers and became very quiet. In addition, they continued to show a more stable heart rate in response to discrepant information than did the uninhibited children.

Finally, Dr. Kagan's writings point out that a good many behavioral geneticists (such as Plomin and Rowe) have found that when one identical twin is extremely inhibited or uninhibited vis-a-vis strangers, the other identical twin tends to behave quite similarly. That concordance does not usually exist between fraternal twins.

In fact, recent studies at the University of Minnesota have shown that genetically identical twins are far more likely to share shyness than are fraternal twins. In fact, identical twins reared apart in totally different households are far more likely to be alike on shyness than are fraternal twins who grow up in the same household with the same parents. Identical twins, of course, have the same genetic constitution, whereas fraternal twins (even when they are of the same gender) do not inasmuch as their bodies grew from different zygotes.

Long-Separated Identical Twins

In looking over the available literature on long-separated identical twins, it is quite clear that something very strange and uncanny is going on. Scores of cases are now on record regarding identical twins who had been separated shortly after birth and given to different pairs of adopting parents. In several of these instances the identical twins did not even know that they had an identical twin brother or sister until as an adult they bumped into him or her quite by accident.

Even though many of these twins never see their twin for as much as thirty or more years after birth and grow up virtually hundreds of miles apart, when they do *first meet* they often find that (1) they have married women/men of the same first name, physical description, career and education; (2) they themselves have pursued the same education and career; (3) they drive the same make and model of motor vehicle; (4) they have the same breed of dog and use the same name for their dogs; (5) their children are of the same ages and genders and had been assigned the same first names; and (6) their personality traits, behavioral dispositions and predilections are all found to be exactly the same.

A multidisciplinary organization of researchers at the University of Minnesota, Minneapolis, (headed by Thomas J. Bouchard, Jr.), is presently engaged in an exhaustive study of identical twins, with especial emphasis upon those who had been separated at birth and who had grown up without any contact of any sort with each other. The range of similarities among these pairs has been found to be absolutely astounding, and is in fact greater even than the range of similarities usually found for identical twins reared together in the same household.

Obviously this material has a substantial bearing upon the love-shyness issue, and upon the whole matter of *"elastic limits"* and of human destiny and purpose. This subject has a further bearing upon the limits of free choice and the extent to which some aspects of "choice" may be illusory, and *may* be a function of karmic destiny and astrology. In essence, the available research data on identical twins provides one of the strongest sets of evidence supporting the position that love-shyness is rooted to a large extent in a very strong biological base.[4]

In sum, Dr. Kagan believes that socialization experiences in the family and with peers can cause children (*particularly boys*) with inborn inhibition to become even more inhibited as well as extremely fearful. As Alexander Thomas has pointed out, a "slow to warm up" little boy can and will develop a strong, positive self-image plus fine sociable tendencies *if* he is accorded appropriate levels of emotional support and tolerance from parents and peers—*if* he is accepted, respected and liked for *what* he is *as* he is.

Unfortunately in contemporary American society this is highly unlikely to happen. Behavioral inhibition and reserve is viewed as highly undesirable in boys. Simply put, such behavior does not *fit* traditional gender role expectations for boys. And even though the women's liberation movement has created a great deal of new role flexibility for little girls, such role flexibility has not as yet even begun to extend to little boys. In fact, the pressure on boys to participate in rough, contact sports is even greater today than it had been in the past.

As Hans Eysenck's data have shown, people with inborn inhibition tend to learn things far more deeply and thoroughly than uninhibited people do. And they corollatively find it far more difficult than uninhibited people to forget things. Thus malevolent experiences in the all-male peer group and/or in the home will have a much more deleterious impact upon those with inborn inhibition than upon those with more propitious inborn characteristics. In this sense *nurture* (experience/social learning) tends to interact in a synergistic way with nature (inborn temperament). And as a result of disparaging labeling and other forms of punishment or reward, social experience tends to reinforce and render increasingly intractable that which we call nature (inborn temperament).

The Importance of Enzymes

Perhaps even more intriguing from the standpoint of leading us toward an understanding of chronic love-shyness is the work of biochemistry professor Dr. Justa Smith, of Rosary Hill College, in Buffalo, New York. Dr. Smith believes that the *first or initial cause* of severe and intractable love-shyness is a *malfunctioning enzyme*. Enzymes are functionally indispensable to the normal growth and development of all living organisms. Without normally functioning enzymes the hormones cannot and will not do their job, even if they (the hormones) are present throughout the bloodstream in appropriate abundance. For example, elementary school aged boys and girls have about the same ratio of estrogens to androgens throughout their respective blood streams. The secondary sex characteristics are prevented from developing in children this young because the appropriate enzymes have not as yet been released. The pituitary gland along with possibly the pineal gland serve to govern the time clock that determines for each person when the appropriate enzymes will be released. Again, it is only when a healthy, appropriate and well-functioning enzyme is released into the blood that appropriate growth changes can occur. The hormones are necessary for the promotion of these growth changes. But hormones will not operate in the absence of the appropriate enzymes to metabolize them.

Enzyme Activity and Propitious Fetal Growth

Dr. Justa Smith together with an ever increasing number of other biochemists and microbiologists believe that a number of different enzymes crucial to the development of "culture-appropriate" masculine assertiveness, competitiveness and drive, are released sometime during the second trimester of pregnancy—*if the fetus is male*. These enzymes permit the testosterones and androgens to work on various sections of the brain which nature has programmed to be responsive to these male hormones. In other words, assuming healthy enzymes, the male hormones will work to masculinize the brain. If one or another enzyme is for any reason malfunctioning, then the part of the brain that is specific to that enzyme will not permit the male hormones to do their job. And that part of the boy fetus' brain will not be suitably or sufficiently masculinized.

If the brain of a fetus is left alone. it will develop into a *female brain* regardless of whether or not it is exposed to feminizing hormones. In essence, this is one of the myriad reasons why the male is a more delicate organism than the female. Many more things can go wrong in male fetal development than in female fetal development. Unless the male fetus is exposed to masculinizing hormones *plus* the enzymes which permit each of these hormones to work on various sections of the brain, that male fetus will develop a brain that is in at least some ways *feminine*. The number of ways in which it will be feminine will be determined by the number of sections of the developing brain that had been deprived of the appropriate masculinizing enzymes. Again, the enzymes permit the male hormones to do their masculinizing job.

Now, as I point out in a later chapter, maternal depression, stress, nervousness and irascibility of temperament, have been found to impact adversely upon the masculinizing enzymes and hormones. This is why tense, nervous, depressed, high strung women are far more likely than calm, happy-go-lucky, relaxed women to give birth to children who are passive, shy, and noncompetitive. Of course, if such a woman's fetus is female there is no chance that any harm will be done. But if the fetus is male, harm quite typically is done as a result of important enzymes being neutralized or enfeebled by the psychosomatic, biochemical processes caused by the pregnant woman's irascibility, depression, tense nervousness, etc.

There are different sections of the fetal brain that need to be masculinized. And each of these sections calls for the propitious operation of a *different* enzyme. Some sections of the brain have to do with sexual/romantic directionality. When these brain sections are inadequately masculinized, the person stands a good chance of becoming a pre-homosexual or a pre-bisexual little boy. Other brain sections have to do with effeminacy. When these are not masculinized, the person becomes an effeminate little boy. And contrary to popular impression, most effeminate men are NOT homosexual. Because of a specific enzyme deficiency during their prenatal period, they become effeminate heterosexuals. And most of them, like heterosexuals generally, will marry and become fathers. But because of rigid and often uncompromising gender role expectations for males, they will suffer much teasing and hazing throughout their formative years as a result of their effeminacy.

Now, another section of the brain has to do with social assertiveness, competitiveness and drive—the opposite of "feminine" passivity. And this is the brain section which has a very strong bearing upon shyness generally, and especially upon love-shyness and the behavioral inertia that typically accompanies it. The nonassertive, unaggressive little boy will commonly develop non-masculine interest patterns. In essence, he violates traditional gender role expectations in terms of interests and preferences rather than in terms of either effeminacy or in terms of homosexuality or erotic orientation. For example, he will prefer quiet, non-physical forms of play; working with arts and crafts, music and theatre arts, dolls and figurines, etc., all of which relate in different ways to violation of gender role expectation.

To be sure, occasionally a number of different enzymes will malfunction while a child is intrautero. And in that case the child (*if male*) will develop a number of different problems. For example, he may develop BOTH effeminacy AND homosexuality. Or he may develop BOTH effeminacy and chronic shyness. Or he may develop chronic shyness and homosexuality. And in a few rare cases he may develop all three of these separate problems.

The shy, passive boy is very often mislabeled "homosexual" just as the effeminate boy is perhaps even more often mislabeled "homosexual". Conservative and rigid people tend to apply the label "homosexual" to any young boy who violates traditional gender role expectations, just as these same people commonly affix such labels as "communist" and "unAmerican" to any person who espouses a political, social or religious attitude or belief with which they happen to disagree.

However, just as the person who believes in the judicious propriety of premarital cohabitation is almost never either a "communist" or "anti-American" or even "promiscuous", so the little boy who prefers gentle, quiet activities in a coeducational play group is similarly very seldom a pre-homosexual. For such a little boy, the enzyme affecting heterosexual directionality worked *properly*. Similarly, the one impacting upon masculinity of demeanor (versus effeminacy) probably also worked satisfactorily well. Only the enzyme affecting that part of the brain which is associated with masculine assertiveness and competitive drive failed to work well enough to permit the appropriate androgens and testosterones to do their brain-masculinizing work.

Painful Anxiety and Enzyme Neutralization

Just as tensions, stress and anxiety feelings in a pregnant woman have been found to cripple and slow down enzyme activity in the fetus, severe stress and anxiety in a grown man or teenager will similarly cripple or slow down enzyme activity.

The non-shy tend to suffer at any given point in time from much less internal stress and anxiety than the love-shy. And this fact *may* be associated with a healthier enzyme situation in day-to-day living than that with which the love-shy have to deal. Having a healthy constellation of enzymes *may* itself help to militate against debilitating love-shyness by enabling an individual to cope more constructively with stress. If, as many biochemists believe, all illnesses and all chronic behavioral maladjustments are due to one or more malfunctioning enzymes, then there may be a kind of vicious circle operating that looks something like this:

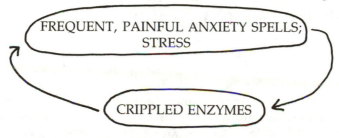

Injections of masculinizing hormones may eventually help to remedy this vicious circle to some extent. Pertinent research currently eminating from East Germany strongly suggests that some remedying of the problem may be accomplished in this way. However, so long as an individual remains highly stressed, his body cannot produce fully healthy enzymes. And without these the body cannot produce appropriate masculinizing hormones on its own. If, as commonly happens, masculinizing hormones help to reduce psychic stress, appropriately injected love-shy individuals may possibly be in a better position to manufacture their own healthy hormones.

In sum, chronic tension and stress in a pregnant woman has been found to neutralize certain enzymes that catalyze into action certain hormones that have a masculinizing effect upon parts of the male fetus' brain which are sensitive to (and which are supposed to expand in response to) male hormones. In an adult or teenager strongly painful and/or frequent anxiety feelings may similarly act to cripple or injure certain enzymes. And this process may have a further feminizing impact upon the individual in addition to undermining his defense system and lowering his resistance to certain types of germs—particularly head cold germs. This may partly explain why the love-shy tend to catch many more head colds and suffer from many more minor health problems than non-shy males do (see chapter titled "Medical Symptoms and the Love-Shy"). Thus the bodily defense system of the love-shy may not be functioning at its best because certain enzymes that are crucial to health maintenance have been effectively crippled and neutralized by frequent painful anxiety and stress.

Again, enzymes catalyze the activity of hormones and other crucial bodily chemicals. All disease may indeed be caused in the final analysis by a disordered enzyme. And this may be true for love-shyness as well. As a case in point, congenital disorders precipitated by maternal mental states may interact in a synergistic way with genetic variables to greatly increase the chances of severe love-shyness developing.

Some Related Work on Depression

Many of the chronic, psychoemotional problems from which people suffer are rooted first and foremost in *biochemical imbalances* which, in turn, are passed on genetically from one generation to the next. Because of America's long-standing tradition of rugged individualism, the tendency on the part of most people has been to attribute emotional problems to deficits of character and to an unwillingness to assume personal responsibility for one's problems. This viewpoint has been particularly prevalent regarding *males* with emotional and behavioral problems. We have always been far more tolerant with women in this respect than we have been with men.

Let me take depression as a case in point. Depression is hardly unrelated to love-shyness. In fact, 72 percent of the middle-aged love-shys I interviewed and 51 percent of the younger ones checked "frequent feelings of depression" on the medical symptom checklist I administered. In stark contrast, *none* of the non-shys I interviewed checked this symptom.

Just a few years ago there was a general feeling that depression was a personality disorder, and that conventional psychiatric techniques (such as the "talking cure") could handle it, and that with the right social impetus people could snap themselves out of it upon their own initiative. Today there is incontrovertible evidence proving beyond any reasonable doubt that *at least* ninety percent of all cases of serious, chronic depression are a byproduct of abnormalities in brain biochemistry.

The first inkling that depression was a disease and not a mood came in the 1950s. Iproniazid, which is a chemical originally designed to treat tuberculosis patients, was quite unexpectedly found to have a very strong anti-depressant effect. Further investigation revealed that depressed persons had abnormalities in the chemical make-up of their brains, and that these abnormalities could be corrected through the use of certain drugs.

Here is how medical researchers speculate that it works. Think of the brain as a mass of electrical energy. Billions of infinitesimal cells called neurons compose this mass. And each one stands alone—almost but not quite touching its neighbors. These cells make up the energy that ceaselessly flows through the brain. Consider two neurons, one of which generates an electrical impulse that it wants to send to its immediately adjacent neighbor. However, the two neurons do not touch; so the electrical impulse has to be carried across the gap by a chemical called a *neurotransmitter*. The second neuron which receives the impulse fires; and the process is repeated. Eventually these impulses become the feelings and the thoughts that are a part of human emotion.

It has been found that in depression there is something wrong with the regulation of these neurotransmitters. The drugs now available compensate for this irregularity by adjusting the flow and the amount of the neurotransmitters. Recent breakthroughs have led to the development of an array of drugs that, singly and in combination, can be aimed at specific chemical reactions in the brain. The drugs that had been used to treat depression ten years ago were crude by comparison with today's drugs; and there were too few of them. Today the choice of drugs is wide, and the possible courses of treatment are quite various.

This new understanding of the brain's chemistry has led to the ability to test for the presence of depression in a body the same way that it is possible to test for diabetes, pneumonia, and other diseases. And this is exactly what Dr. David Kupfer does. Dr. Kupfer is a pioneer in depression research; and he heads the Depression Research Clinic at Western Psychiatric Hospital in Pittsburgh. For example, in treating a 21-year old woman who had suffered chronic depression most of her life, Dr. Kupfer began with a general checkup. The purpose of this was to rule out any illness that might look like depression. Secondly, he turned to the various tests that have proven valuable for the ascertaining of depression. For example, the *blood* of a depressed person shows hormonal abnormalities, and the *urine tests* show abnormal levels of brain chemicals. And finally the young woman was given a *sleep test*; for this she was wired up to a monitor that printed out the pattern of her brain when she slept. Without fail, a depressed person's sleep has an identifiable pattern of sleep disturbances. Young people who are depressed usually sleep too much, whereas older people cannot fall asleep and/or they wake up excessively early in the morning. In both cases they wake up exhausted and severely lacking in energy—a pattern which seems to be quite prevalent among the ranks of the love-shy, and which may be due to reactive hypoglycemia as well as to biochemically-based depression.

The 21-year old woman written about by Dr. Kupfer was quite fortunate in that the first drug administered to her worked to the point of quite totally relieving her of her chronic depression. The drug used in this case was the anti-depressant called Aventyl. And in recent years hundreds of chronically depressed people have been fully and permanently relieved of their depression through its use. Dr. Kupfer merely requires patients on this drug to return to the hospital from time to time for a routeine monitoring of drug levels in the blood.

Among the things that medical functionaries are learning these days is the point that chronic depression spares no age group. Much of what we call "senility" in old people is depression. And it can be cured via the same treatment techniques that work for younger people. However, a far more remarkable discovery is the fact that the disease of chronic depression is now being found in children from toddler age through adolescence. And among this very youthful group it is being found *in the same proportion* as it is being found in the adult population; namely, *one in ten*.

Moreover, the damage is just as severe in children as it is in adults. Indeed, given the very adverse social stimulus value of a depressed ambiance in a young boy (particularly as viewed by the all-male peer group), the damage is often considerably worse for children than it is for adults—because it causes social and psychoemotional development to be launched on a very poor footing.

For example, Drs. Donald McKnew and Leon Cytryn have been engaged in a long-term study of childhood depression. And their findings thus far jibe well with the extensive work of Hans Eysenck and Alexander Thomas on inborn temperament. In 1968, McKnew and Cytryn discovered childhood depression, and today they are finding that the condition is often hereditary. In one of their papers they discuss a 21-month old baby who had long manifested all of the signs of depression including apathy, sadness, listlessness, and lack of interest in his toys. A severely depressed 17-year old boy upon whom they had been working was similarly found to have been very depressed as an infant. Having suffered chronic depression and peer bullying throughout his childhood, he had long been frustrated in his search for treatment by the lack of understanding of children's depression. As a result of appropriate drug treatment, Dr. McKnew and his staff were able to effectively and permanently cure him.

It is estimated that approximately 20 million Americans are depressed. Most go untreated or inappropriately treated because depression is too often viewed as a type of personal failure, a flaw of the self and not of the body. The damage to the lives and the families of these people cannot be calculated. For example, it is known that alcoholics and drug abusers are often really suffering from depression. And it has been estimated that 80 percent of the suicides in the United States are the result of biochemically-based depression.

An amazingly simple and accurate medical test for diagnosing certain types of depression is presently in the process of revolutionizing psychiatric diagnosis. Known as the dexamethasone suppression test (DST), it is the first biological test that pinpoints the presence of certain quite common forms of depression that are believed to afflict approximately one out of every twenty-five persons, and which are caused by biochemical imbalances in the brain. People with these forms of depression often go from feeling quite normal to feeling extremely depressed for no logical reason. And then they become better without treatment until the next episode.

The DST test can accurately identify about 70 percent of those afflicted with severe, biologically based depression, according to Dr. Michael Feinberg, a psychiatrist at the University of Michigan Mental Health Research Institute at Ann Arbor. To take the DST test, a patient simply swallows a small, yellow tablet containing dexamethasone, which is an artificial steroid. On the following day two blood samples are drawn from the patient at different times. When dexamethasone is given to people who don't have the appropriate forms of biologically based depression, for about 24 hours their bodies stop producing the hormone cortisol, which is a secretion of the adrenal glands. On the other hand, if a patient *is* afflicted with biologically based depression, taking the steroid does not shut off cortisol production. Thus some of the cortisol shows up in the blood samples.

In sum, we are beginning to find that many behavioral and psychoemotional problems are rooted in genetically based biochemical imbalances; and that these behavioral and psychoemotional problems are often severely exacerbated (1) by bullying, and (2) by the widely held assumption that the victim can and should assume responsibility for his own problems, pull himself up by his own bootstraps (even when he hasn't got any bootstraps!), and snap himself out of it. The evidence such as that which is reviewed in this book is beginning to point to the strong possibility that chronic, intractable love-shyness is similarly caused by genetically based biochemical imbalances which lead to bullying and to social avoidance.[5]

Suicide

It happens much too often: a severely depressed person, or one who has unsuccessfully tried to kill himself, is hospitalized. When doctors conclude that there is no further danger of suicide the patient is sent home. Within a few months the conclusion is proved tragically wrong.

A lab test has now been devised which may accurately differentiate patients who are potentially suicidal from those who are depressed or disturbed, but not likely to kill themselves. The key to this test is *serotonin*, which is a chemical messenger that transmits impulses from one nerve cell to another. Although serotonin bathes the surface of the brain and spinal cord, it is an elusive substance which leaves an end product only in the spinal fluid. This end product is known as "5-HIAA" (5-hydroxyindoleatic acid). And a simple laboratory test can now detect "5-HIAA" in a sample of spinal fluid.

Scientists at the National Institute of Mental Health in Bethesda, Maryland, and at the Karolinska Institute in Stockholm, working together and separately, have discovered that people whose spinal fluid contains unusually small amounts of "5-HIAA" are at especially high risk of suicide. Whereas statistics have shown that about 2 percent of all hospitalized suicide attempters eventually succeed in killing themselves, a Swedish study of 27 such patients revealed that 22 percent of patients with low "5-HIAA" levels took their lives in the year after testing. An NIMH study of 27 Navy men with low "5-HIAA" has similarly shown that 82 percent eventually attempted suicide.

In another Swedish study investigators found that 60 percent of a group of suicide attempters who later killed themselves had low "5-HIAA", whereas in a group of non-suicidal depressed patients only 20 percent had low "5-HIAA". Moreover, impulsive and aggressive men who chose violent means of suicide had especially low levels of this biochemical—which some scientists are now dubbing "the suicide factor".

By the way, 36 percent of the 300 love-shy men studied for this book had given serious consideration to taking their own lives. *Zero percent* (nobody) of the 200 non-shy men I interviewed had ever given any thought to suicide, and none had ever experienced frequent bouts of depression.

Biogenic Amines

Since the late 1970s, one of the most important conclusions to which psychiatric research has led is that certain brain chemicals called *biogenic amines* have a very strong bearing upon the control of mood. For example, in one study it was found that animals became *socially inactive* when they were given drugs that diminished the brain's ability to produce biogenic amines. In essence, the tested animals were found to manifest one of the key symptoms of depression. Animal studies as well as research with psychiatric patients have also indicated that deficiencies in biogenic amines tend to be associated with low energy level, with irritability, with *anhedonia* (a diminished ability to experience pleasure or emotion), and with strong feelings of anger (see Wender and Klein, 1981).

The biogenic amine theory of depression attributes severe cases of depression (when there is no environmentally-based reason for depressed feelings) to an underactivity of certain nerve cells. Some of these nerve cells are intimately connected with the experience of pleasure; and the neurotransmitters of these nerve cells are the biogenic amines. The theory holds that such underactivity might be due to (a) a deficient production of the neurotransmitters, or (b) excessive breakdown of the neurotransmitter before it is released, or (c) inability to release the neurotransmitter, or (d) a decreased response sensitivity of the stimulated nerve cell. This same theory holds that *mania* represents the reverse side of the coin—with *too much* of the critical biogenic amines available.

The differences in the actions of stimulants and antidepressants on both normal individuals and patients with biologically-based depression are not as yet fully understood by researchers. The antidepressant drugs will usually relieve depression in *vital depressives* (i.e., in those with biologically-based depression), but will *not* produce feelings of euphoria in persons who are not depressed (e.g., in "normal" individuals). Thus, such drugs are not abusable or habit-forming. In fact, the action of these drugs can be roughly compared to the action of aspirin—which lowers body temperature when fever is present but does not noticeably lower the body temperature of a person whose temperature is normal.

People with biologically-based depression ("vital depression") do not develop a *tolerance* to these antidepressant drugs—as they indeed would to cocaine or to amphetamines. When contemporary antidepressant drugs work, the depressed patient does not need to take increasingly larger doses in order to obtain the same effect. Hence, these new antidepressant drugs may operate to temporarily repair a defective "thermostat" in the biogenic amine metabolizing section of the brain. Such an explanation would account for these drugs' lack of effect upon normal persons and their very profound effect upon persons with depressive states.

Psychiatrists Paul Wender and Donald Klein (1981) suggest that many people with *low self-esteem* (especially in cases where feelings of low self-worth are difficult to explain on the basis of personal history) may indeed suffer from undetected biologically-based *"vital depression"*. On the positive side, the question as to whether or not they are indeed actually suffering from this may be answered through the administration of these antidepressant drugs. Simply put, if medication that usually only sedates normal persons serves to increase self-esteem in a given individual, we can be relatively certain that the feelings of low self-esteem were the result of faulty brain biochemistry rather than the learned residues of unfortunate early personal experience.

Even though traditional "talking cure" psychotherapy has never been shown to be particularly effective in the treatment of severe depression, many contemporary psychotherapists continue to be convinced (on faith) of the validity of their ideology that chronic depressed feelings are due to psychoemotional conflicts dating from infancy and childhood, and that such conflicts typically involve much guilt and hostility. The efficacy of modern antidepressant drugs in reversing depressed moods cogently and incisively calls into question the reasonableness of attributing these illnesses to psychological conflicts. In essence, a simple pharmacological treatment has been found to work quickly and effectively for depressed patients whereas the exasperating business of the patient trying to release imputed "guilt" through talking and insight usually fails.

Along with some cases of low self-esteem, recent data has suggested that cases of *separation anxiety* in children tend to be associated with the biologically-based depression syndrome. Thus, when psychiatrist Donald Klein studied patients with agoraphobias he noted that when younger they had quite typically suffered from overpowering homesickness and "school phobia". Throughout virtually all of this century such feelings in children have been explained on the basis of less than healthy family dynamics and parent-child interaction patterns. Now a very different picture is beginning to emerge as to what *actually causes* these painfully distressing feelings and behaviors in children.

When Klein discovered that separation-anxious agoraphobics responded well to antidepressant medication, he hypothesized that the younger versions of such patients (the severely homesick child and the school phobic child) might quite similarly respond favorably to treatment with that same medication. So he and his wife Rachel Gittelman-Klein (1971) designed a research study involving school-phobic children who had not responded well to the usual treatment techniques of behavior therapy, play therapy, and "talking cure" psychotherapy.

The administration of behavior therapy alone resulted in only about half of the children being able to return to school. But once back at school the children often continued to feel very distressed; and they experienced significant difficulties in being accepted by their peers. On the other hand, when the behavior therapy techniques *were combined* with antidepressant medication, the children's anxiety and depressive complaints diminished or disappeared; and the children not only returned to school but did so happily.

In essence, the antidepressant medication had greatly benefitted the children's subjective state, thus permitting an anxiety-free separation. The implication of these and related findings is that traditional psychodynamic reasoning typically advanced to explain separation anxiety in children has little to do with its basic cause—*a deficiency of biogenic amines* and a defective "thermostat" in the biogenic amine-metabolizing section of the brain.

Anxiety Disease

Some five percent (one in twenty) of all Americans suffer from a *biologically-based*, medical problem that has come to be known in medical circles as "anxiety disease". In his recent book entitled ANXIETY DISEASE, psychiatrist/physician David V. Sheehan explains that better than 90 percent of all victims can be completely cured of all symptoms by administration of a drug called "nardil". Sheehan goes on to quite clearly and incisively document how anxiety disease victims have a "different brain-chemical activity" than do unafflicted individuals. Sheehan also shows how intravenous administration of a certain drug can inside of fifteen minutes set off a severe anxiety attack in an afflicted individual (i.e., a person with the "anxiety disease" brain biochemical activity), whereas the same quantity of this same drug will have no effect at all on the 95 percent of the population that is unafflicted with this problem.

People with anxiety disease will characteristically be susceptible to having an attack at virtually any time. They typically average four attacks per week; and occasionally these will come even during sleep. Thus, a person might wake up in the middle of the night suffering from a severe attack of anxiety for no apparent reason at all. Loved ones might label such an experience a mere "nightmare" or a "bad dream". But just as a geyser might go off four times per week because that is how often the water pressure reaches the required degree of sheer force, for an anxiety disease victim that is how often the brain biochemistry reaches such a degree of imbalance as to trigger off the anxiety attack. If the victim happens to be in bed at the time, his/her attack will be attributed to a bad dream. If he/she is in a crowded store it will be attributed to *agoraphobia*. In either case, the difficulty *cannot* be successfully treated via behavior therapy alone, or via any of the "talking therapies". Simply put, appropriate pharmacological treatment is a mandatory *sine qua non* for complete and effective, permanent remission of symptoms.

Agoraphobia is one of many problems that has long been quite incorrectly viewed as stemming purely from psychoemotional causes. The tradition in the helping professions as well as in the wider society has long been to *blame the victim* instead of focusing upon genetics, brain biochemistry, or even upon difficult stresses that might be endemic in the victim's *life situation*. This moralistic approach (rooted in the ethic of "rugged individualism" and personal responsibility *for everything*) characteristically resulted in only very temporary and quite ephemoral "cures". Thus, after spending thousands of dollars on various "talking cures" the victim would still be plagued by the uncomfortably frequent manifestation of symptoms.

An interesting earmark of anxiety disease is that frequently the victim would *learn to associate* severe anxiety feelings with the *situation* in which he/she happened (often quite by chance) to be located at the time of an attack. Such learned associations are especially likely to develop in impressionable young children. Thus, severely painful and frightening anxiety feelings might become associated by a young person with being in a dark bedroom, with being in a crowded supermarket, with being in a situation far away from an exit door, with being in the presence of a dog, cat or rabbit, with involvement in some harmless activity, *or* perhaps maybe even with informal, sociable interaction vis-a-vis the opposite sex. In view of the fact that stressed feelings (i.e., feelings of stress that might accrue from sheer inexperience) can easily set off one of these anxiety attacks in a biochemically susceptible person, it is distinctly possible that severe and intractable shyness vis-a-vis the opposite sex in informal situations might be spearheaded by a synergistic combination of anxiety disease *in interaction with* normal stress resulting from behavioral inexperience.

To be sure, severely love-shy men do not appear to be agoraphobic; nor do they appear to have a history of having unprovoked "panic attacks" or unprovoked spells of anxiety. However, a great deal of the burgeoning medical/biochemical literature on anxiety disease may still be of considerable relevance to the problem of severe love-shyness.

In essence, severely love-shy men may indeed have a different genetic structure and brain/body biochemistry than the rest of us—and from those who can manage to work through their shyness problems with the aid of a few normal psychotherapeutic (talking cure) sessions. Further, it is quite possible that *in some people* anxiety disease *per se* manifests itself only in childhood and then dissipates gradually away. If such is the case, then it is distinctly possible that biologically based anxiety attacks might have in some love-shys precipitated the learned association of anxiety feelings with social assertiveness and with informal heterosexual interaction. As children, stress created by social inexperience may have triggered off this possibly learned association. Habits of social nonparticipation wrought by an above average anxiety-prone brain/body chemistry may thus underlie severe love-shyness in adult males. Such adults may not quite have "anxiety disease"; but their brain biochemistry may be all too similar to that of those who do have this medical problem.

Dr. Sheehan underscores the importance of making a conceptual distinction between *"endogenous anxiety"* and *"exogenous anxiety"*. "Endogenous" comes from a Greek word which means "to be born or produced from within". The central problem in cases of endogenous anxiety springs from some source *inside* the individual's body, rather than as a response to a situation outside the person. Thus, panic or severe anxiety attacks with no source of provocation outside of the victim's body would represent a pure and undiluted case of "endogenous anxiety".

In contrast, *exogenous anxiety* is provoked anxiety, and it represents a reaction to subjectively perceived stress outside the individual. In its pure form there is no genetic or biochemical basis underlying exogenous anxiety. Indeed, all humans suffer from exogenous anxiety from time to time; it might be construed as a quite normal reaction to stress. Because what is *seen* as stressful is a *subjective* matter and is strictly up to each individual and unique person, some people experience exogenous anxiety extremely frequently as well as extremely painfully. Other people with approximately the same sorts of stresses impacting on their lives experience relatively infrequent bouts of anxiety which they perceive as quite mild and manageable.

As useful as this conceptual distinction is in terms of helping us to better understand anxiety, it also entails some serious dangers. First, it is highly unlikely that very many anxiety cases can accurately be classsified as being either *totally* endogenous or *totally* exogenous. What we actually have here is a *continuum* with endogenous anxiety resting at one extreme and exogenous anxiety at the other. The person with completely endogenous anxiety suffers anxiety or panic spells for no apparent external reason.

Simply put, I would contend that endogenous (genetically and biochemically based) anxiety disease is *not* limited to those with such unprovoked anxiety or panic attacks, and that the key reason why some people learned to subjectively perceive certain social stimuli (e.g., intimacy with the opposite sex or participation in "rough and tumble" sports) as painfully threatening in the first place is that they have an unusually low native anxiety threshold. Further, the basis of this very low native anxiety threshold would be a very high amount of electrical activity in the *locus ceruleus* region of the brain—quite irrespective of whether or not the anxiety provoking stimulus is a much desired attractive woman or something else. Labeling love-shyness as being exclusively indicative of exogenous anxiety will inevitably result in a dearth of compassionate understanding directed toward the victim; and it will result in a grossly insufficient array of therapeutic modalities being engineered and used.

David Sheehan's work on severe anxiety has provided strong documentation suggestive of a genetic basis for the disorder. Statistical studies were done on the prevalence of the anxiety disorder among the relatives of affected people. It was found that those who had a close relative with the condition were more likely to develop it than those who did not. This finding was strong enough for it to be highly unlikely that it was due to chance alone. It also seemed that the closer the biological relationship to the affected person, the greater the likelihood of developing the anxiety disorder. Special mathematical techniques were used to analyze the family trees of affected families. The evidence suggested that the proneness to the anxiety disorder fit closely, though not perfectly, with a *dominant-gene inheritance pattern*. This inheritance pattern would allow it to be passed down by one parent, and would not require it to be inherited from both sides of the family.

Like Thomas J. Bouchard of the University of Minnesota, Dr. Sheehan (at the Harvard University Medical School) has also studied twins with the anxiety condition. Sheehan's preliminary findings suggest that there is a greater tendency for both twins to have the anxiety disease if they are identical than if they are nonidentical (fraternal) twins. Twin studies such as these are frequently used to sort out the relative contributions of environmental (stress and learning) factors from genetic factors. If a disease is learned or due to an environmental stress, then growing up at the same time in the same family, exposed to the same environment, should result in both twins having it equally, whether they are identical or not. On the other hand, if anxiety disease is mainly genetic in its basis, you would expect both of the identical twins who have an identical genetic makeup to have it together. The findings in Sheehan's twin study suggest that genetic inheritance forces tend to outweigh the effects of the enrivonment in their overall contribution to the disorder.

It is possible that such a genetic weakness could give rise to biochemical abnormalities, and that these in turn could lead to the symptoms the victim feels physically. As far as delineating what the precise, bio-chemical abnormalities of the anxiety actually are, the best guesses so far (on the basis of the extensive amount of research work that has been done) involve certain nerve endings and receptors in the central nervous system which produce and receive chemical messengers that stimulate and excite the brain. These nerve endings manufacture naturally occurring stimulants called catecholamines. It is believed that in the anxiety disease the nerve endings overfire to a profuse extent. In essence, the nerve endings tend to work too hard, and in so doing they overproduce these stimulants along with perhaps others as well.

At the same time there are nerve endings and receptors that have the opposite effect: they produce naturally occurring tranquilizers called inhibitory neurotransmitters which serve to inhibit and calm down the nerve firing of the brain. From the research knowledge we have been able to acquire so far, it appears that the neurotransmitters or the receptors may be deficient, either in quality or in quantity.

Why are they deficient? Several other substances regulate the firing of the nerves, acting like accelerators or brakes on the firing process. These substances include prostaglandins, which are local regulators, and ions, especially calcium ions, which flow across cell membranes. Enzymes regulate how fast these substances are produced and destroyed in the nerve endings. There is some evidence suggesting that all of these substances may be involved in some way in the malfunctions that produce the anxiety disease. A chain of events apparently runs from the inherited gene or genes through the cell nucleus to the cell membrane to the nerve ending and the chemicals it uses, involving some or all of the above mechanisms. As ongoing research continues to provide us with more and more answers, undoubtedly other neuropeptides and neurotransmitters will be identified that play a role in that chain.

Recent research has documented some fascinating differences in the brain blood flow between panic-attack-prone and *non*panic-attack-prone persons. A Washington University (St. Louis) medical research team examined seven individuals who had severe anxiety attacks in response to injections of lactate, three who were not lactate sensitive, and six with no history of anxiety disease. Using positron emission tomography scans, the researchers measured blood flow in seven areas of the brain that are thought to control panic and anxiety reactions. In one of these areas, the *parahippocampal gyrus*, the researchers observed a startling difference between the lactate-sensitive patients and the others.

In every lactate-sensitive patient, the blood flow on the *right side* of the gyrus was much higher than on the left side. This difference was not observed in the other two groups. There is typically a high degree of symmetry in the brain; thus, this observed difference went well beyond the normal range of that symmetry. In *every instance* the pattern of blood flow was different than normal, and the flow on the right side was higher than on the left.

It appears from further research that this brain abnormality consistently distinguishes lactate-sensitive panic sufferers from other people. Researchers indicate that it may reflect an exaggeration of the normal hemispheric specialization in part of the brain important to the expression of anxiety. Thus, the differences in blood flow between hemispheres probably is connected with differences in metabolic rate. Any changes in blood flow reflect differences in the activity of nerve cells on the two sides.

As per discussions in chapters 15 and 16 of this book, love-shy men are far more likely than unafflicted individuals to have milk allergies and sensitivities. Thus, upon drinking milk many of them develop a copious abundance of very thick, foul-tasting saliva. Milk, of course, contains a heavy amount of lactate. In this regard research is needed to determine the extent to which milk intake might influence anxiety-proneness and social avoidance in young children—especially boys.

Chapter 10 of this book will provide ample documentation of the point that most love-shy males tend to avoid strenuous forms of exercise. Interestingly, one of the main byproducts of muscle activity is *lactate* which, as indicated above, is a substance to which low anxiety threshold people tend to be highly sensitive. Thus, it is not unreasonable to suspect that this lactate sensitivity might well represent an important reason (even if a minor one) as to why love-shys as children tend to avoid "rough and tumble" play, and tend to prefer less energetic "feminine" activities.

In 1966 Dr. Ferris Pitts found that administering an intravenous infusion of sodium lactate to victims of unusually low anxiety threshold served to almost immediately bring on spells of painful anxiety and even panic, just like the victims' original symptoms. It is possible to turn the anxiety condition on simply by injecting this substance, which is produced in everyone's body in response to exercise. If you give sodium lactate to normal persons, *nothing happens*; with anxiety disease victims, turning off the lactate infusions stops the symptoms.

Recently, three families of drugs known as (1) the MAO inhibitors, including "nardil", (2) the tricyclics, and (3) alprazolam, have been found to attenuate the anxiety spells that are induced by lactate. A patient sensitive to lactate could be given a lactate infusion after treatment with any of these three drugs and *not develop the very strong and painful anxiety feelings*. Thus, these drugs change the anxiety-prone person's metabolism in such a way that they lose their abnormal sensitivity (allergy) to lactate, and hence respond once again more like normal people.

Since 1980, other drugs and food substances have been found to have the same anxiety-attack-inducing effects as lactate. These substances include isoproterenol and yohimbine. The next few years of research effort should uncover a great deal of valuable new knowledge about the drug and food substances which issue forth anxiety symptoms (or which *lower* the anxiety threshold), and those which serve to extinguish anxiety symptoms or *raise* the anxiety threshold. The best general summary as to what is now known about the genetic and biochemical basis of anxiety and its pharmacological treatment can be found in Dr. David V. Sheehan's 1984 book titled THE ANXIETY DISEASE.

Incidentally, carbon dioxide has also been found to be related to severe anxiety attacks. It appears that anxiety-prone individuals are less able than nonafflicted people to properly and effectively metabolize the carbon dioxide that they breath. This difficulty might well be due to an enzyme deficiency.

And in women, the hormone progesterone has been found to be linked to anxiety attacks. Afflicted individuals are less capable than others of metabolizing the progesterone hormone. And this problem might well be linked to the pre-menstrual stress syndrome ("PMS") from which some women suffer.

Finally, neuroscientist Dr. Eugene Redmond of Yale University, was able to conclude from his research that panic, anxiety and fear may be controlled by changes in *norepinephrine* metabolism in the *locus ceruleus* region of the brain. Locating an isolated brain area such as this (i.e., one that is vulnerable to the influences of substances in the blood *due to its lack of a protective blood-brain barrier*) provides us with potentially valuable information about the physiological roots of severe anxiety attacks, and of ultimately the fear of anxiety (anticipatory anxiety). In essence, it would appear from Redmond's studies that severe anxiety feelings may often result from a *hyperactivity* of the neurons in the *locus coeruleus* section of the brain.

Thus, Redmond implanted an electrode in the locus coeruleus section of the lower brain of a group of stumptailed monkeys. When this electrode was stimulated electrically, the monkeys behaved as if they were panicked, anxious, fearful, or in impending danger. In contrast, damaging this small brain center in the monkeys had the opposite effect: the monkeys without a functioning locus coeruleus showed an absence of emotional response to threats, and they were without apparent fear of approaching humans or dominant monkeys. *Socially, they became much more aggressive;* and they moved around in their cages much more than before and more than normal monkeys. In view of the fact that the locus coeruleus has the highest density of norepinephrine-containing neurons in the central nervous system, Redmond concluded from his work that panic and fear result from *a hyperactivity of these neurons in the brain*.

The fact that anxiety and fear could be switched on and off in this fashion conveys the idea of how *physical* the anxiety problem may well be. The site of the locus coeruleus is one of the most permeable areas of the brain, and hence it is one of the most sensitive areas to local metabolic changes. When the particular biochemical changes associated with the anxiety disease occur, this part of the brain may be the most sensitive to the changes and may be stimulated to produce its characteristic fear reactions.

Dopamine

There is considerable evidence from the work of Wender and Klein (1981) that highly emotionally sensitive introverts suffer from excessive *dopamine* activity in the brain. Dopamine is a brain chemical which in normal amounts is healthy. Too much or too little of it can and does create problems. Very inhibited, highly sensitive people have too much brain dopamine activity, and may also have brain cells that are unusually hypersensitive to this brain chemical.

Schizophrenia

Schizophrenia constitutes another psychiatric problem about which traditional psychiatric wisdom appears to have been quite false and misleading. For example, schizophrenia had long been believed to be a *learned* disorder. However, recent research has shown that certain forms of schizophrenia can be one-hundred percent cured virtually immediately through *kidney dialysis!* This finding was arrived at quite by accident. A 21-year old woman with what appeared to be a hopeless case of schizophrenia (requiring life-long mental hospitalization) came down with a kidney disease. The doctors put this mental patient on a kidney dialysis machine in order to clean her blood and treat the kidney problem. And much to their dismay they found that what had been a veritable human vegetable at the outset of the dialysis process was now a few hours later behaving remarkable normally—as though she had just awakened from a long and restful sleep!

It needs to be stressed, of course, that only certain forms of schizophrenia have been found to be treatable via kidney dialysis. However, I think the fact that *any* substantial number of cases can be *effectively and totally cured* this way is quite remarkable and extremely heartening. Less than a decade ago it had been blythly assumed by almost all psychiatrists that curing schizophrenia by "removing something bad" from the afflicted person's body was nothing more than a fairy tale delusional fantasy commonly dreamed up by psychotherapy patients who wish to avoid assuming personal responsibility for their problems. The very idea of a biochemical or surgical cure had been viewed by almost all psychiatrists as a "cop out"—as a refusal on the part of the patient to face up to his/ her emotional problems and to assume personal responsibility for overcoming them.

Anyone who has studied chronic love-shyness realizes that its victims have many strongly schizoid tendencies. Schizophrenia is simply a variety of schizoid tendencies that is so severe that the victim has lost touch with reality and can no longer go to work or attend school. The schizoid neurotic is a loner who has *not* lost contact with reality; he is a person who merely avoids informal interpersonal contact with other people. He does this (1) because he has a very low inborn anxiety threshold which, possibly due to biochemical anomalies in the brain, makes him experience anxiety much more severely, painfully and frequently than most people do, and (2) because he has *learned to associate* these painful internal feelings with being around people, rather than with being around something else.

So what is the underlying basis of a person's learning of these avoidance tendencies? This side of the picture will be covered in full detail in the next chapter. For now suffice it to say that the *same* biochemical imbalances which cause the neurotransmitters in the brain of the depressed person to malfunction, may also help to create the genetically rooted inborn temperament we call *melancholia* (figure 1, page 41) which, in turn, appears to constitute a primary antecedent of chronic love-shyness. Simply put, the love-shy man may well be a victim of many of the same brain-based biochemical imbalances that characterize to a much worse extent certain varieties of psychotic schizophrenics.

Obsessive-Compulsive Disorders

As a final example of the recently discovered fact that many psychoemotional problems have a genetically rooted and/or biochemical base, let us consider obsessive-compulsive disorders. People with *obsessions* find it very difficult to get certain useless thoughts out of their minds. In essence, they are extremely anxiety-ridden about forgetting certain objectively unimportant items which could just as well be forgotten without any adverse consequences accruing as a result.

People with *compulsions* have an extremely strong drive to engage in some form of behavior or ritual, even when that behavior or ritual does not need to be done. The compulsive person performs the needless behavior anyway because failure to do so would create too much strong anxiety. For most compulsives the energy sapped up by engaging in useless acts is *less* taxing than the anxiety he/she would have to suffer if he/she did not engage in the useless act or ritual.

Many childhood tics are essentially compulsions. And tics were especially prevalent in the childhood backgrounds of the 300 love-shy men interviewed for this study. For example, one love-shy man had had a childhood tic wherein he would repeatedly punch his chin, even to the point (sometimes) of drawing blood. Another man had had a nagging compulsion to frequently check his post card collection, even though he knew from an intellectual standpoint that all of his post cards were there, and no one could have stolen any of them. Avoiding sidewalk cracks or sidewalk dividers had been an especially prevalent compulsive tic among these love-shy men; and some of them were still affected by it even now as adults. Another love-shy man had driven his elementary school teachers "up the wall" by momentarily stooping down every ten or twelve steps he took. In other words, everytime he took a walk of any length he would be observed constantly popping up and down. Several other love-shy men had had the sort of compulsive tic which made them constantly touch corridor walls as they walked.

People with compulsions are usually afflicted with obsessions as well. Similarly, those afflicted with obsessions usually suffer from some compulsions. The point to all of this is that if ever there was a disorder that was *learned* rather than innate, obsessive-compulsive problems would appear to exemplify it.

Yet during the past five years neurologists and biochemists have uncovered strong evidence indicating that this too is a genetically and biochemically rooted disorder which may very soon be fully treatable with certain kinds of drugs. Of course, the specific substantive content of the obsession or compulsion *has to be learned*. But the drive itself to own compulsions or obsessions is biologically rooted and *not* learned.

As with depression, the interview data obtained for the research upon which this book is based indicated a far greater prevalence of compulsions and obsessions among the ranks of the love-shys than among the ranks of the non-shys. Of course, it has long been known that obsessions and compulsions dissipate to some extent with age. For example, children are generally more vulnerable than adults to tics of one sort or another. However, as children the love-shys interviewed for this book had had many more compulsive tics than the non-shys; and these compulsive tics tended to have been far more grossly apparent in the behavior of the love-shys than in that of the non-shys. The relatively few nervous tics suffered by the non-shys had been of a sort which had created relatively little public notice.

Now as adults the love-shys continue to suffer from many more obsessions and compulsions than the non-shys. Several of the interview questions employed for this research had a bearing upon the issue of obsessive-compulsive problems. For example, I asked each of my respondents for his reaction to this statement: "I frequently become very upset without outwardly showing it when people interrupt my fantasy life." Fully 81 percent of the 300 love-shy men indicated that this statement was *true* for them. In contrast, only 4 percent of the 200 non-shy men indicated that the statement had any validity for themselves.

In a related question I requested reactions to this statement: "Even when I read for pleasure, I find that I write many more notes in the margins than most people do." And again, only 4 percent of the non-shy men said "yes", compared to fully 41 percent of the love-shys. I similarly asked each respondent to give his reaction to this statement: "I can become extremely upset when I can't remember what I had been thinking about a few minutes ago before some distraction." Fully 63 percent of the love-shy men agreed with this statement compared to a mere 2 percent of the non-shy men.

Difficulty concentrating is another major symptom of affliction with useless obsessions. And 84 percent of the love-shy men agreed that they very frequently experienced serious difficulty concentrating while reading or studying. Despite their very active social lives, only 6 percent of the non-shy men indicated similar difficulties with concentration while reading or studying. *External* distractions appeared to bother the love-shy men a great deal less than *internal* ones. Many of the love-shys indicated that they could read or study despite the presence of many different kinds of noises. Their *real* problem was that of dealing with the host of uninvited thoughts and obsessions that kept constantly bombarding their conscious minds as they were trying to read or study.

The obsessions and compulsions of many of the love-shys created very real learning and study problems for them. Even though many of them claimed knowledge (from an intellectual standpoint) of speed reading techniques, their compulsion to underline and make useless notes (based upon these obsessive thoughts) obviated their using these techniques. In fact, about a third of the men advised me that they could talk faster than they could read. One man, in fact, could talk about five times faster than he could read. This man had attained a Masters degree in psychology and was considered a plodder. By his own admission he usually had to spend approximately five times more of his time in the library studying than he would have had to spend if he did not have the distracting obsessive and compulsive thought patterns. Again, highly debilitating albeit less serious obsessions and compulsions afflicted most of the love-shy men interviewed for this book. And as children many of them were seen as "underachievers" and as "under-utilizers of time" as a result.

Conclusions

The material covered in this chapter has clear implications for psychotherapeutic treatment. Even today most psychiatrists and clinical psychologists try to convince patients whose symptoms remain refractory to treatment over long periods of time that on an "unconscious" level change is not truly desired. In essence, the love-shy client is told that he is "not yet ready" to change. The implicit assumption, of course, is that the unconscious mind might eventually permit change, but that it is not yet ready to do so now. Another implicit assumption is that the wishes of the unconscious mind should be accorded priority over the wishes of the conscious, rational, goal-setting part of the mind. Despite the fact that research evidence *does not support* their view, the belief remains widespread among psychiatrists that people "need" their symptoms; and that if you "take away" a person's symptoms he/she will generate new and possibly even worse ones.

Many psychiatrists believe that if a patient remains refractory to help over long periods of time, there must be something untruthful and fallacious about that patient's consciously stated goals. In essence, the problem lies with the patient, *NOT* with the psychotherapeutic method. This attitude, which remains quite dominant among psychiatrists and clinical psychologists, assumes that the patient who is refractory to treatment has an ultra-strong set of defenses—and that in time that set of defenses might be made to crumble to the point where constructive change might become possible.

I believe this "force a square peg into a round hole" attitude represents a major barrier against the development of new, far more effective psychotherapeutic technologies. In short, if a person is not helped "because his defense system remains too strong" and *NOT* because the therapeutic methodology itself is wanting, then there need be no motive towards the development of better therapeutic modalities.

It is for this reason that virtually all chronically love-shy men who commence psychotherapy sooner or later drop out of it without having been helped by the process one wit. To be sure, not all love-shy men give up so easily as far as their hopes and fantasies pertinent to psychotherapy are concerned. One 36-year old love-shy man I interviewed had had 13 years of one-on-one psychotherapy from six different therapists. His most recent attempt had been with a behavior therapist. And after seven months of treatment that therapist came to the same conclusion to which all of the prior therapists had arrived. In essence, this severely love-shy man was told that his defense system was too strong, and that he really did not truly want to have a woman to love. And for the past nine years this love-shy man has maintained his resolve not to allow himself to get roped in on any more "psychotherapy".

Quite clearly, if chronic and intractable love-shyness is biologically rooted as the evidence presented in this chapter very strongly suggests, then none of the traditional methods of psychotherapy or of behavior therapy are going to be of any viable service. Other methods must be devised.

The purpose of this chapter has been to introduce the major evidence regarding the biological basis of inherited, fearful behavior. It was shown that all biological characteristics having *observable* concomitants entail *social consequences*. Biologically based traits and physical appearances invariably incorporate some sort of *social stimulus value*. And this social stimulus value can vary from being enormously favorable down to being enormously unfavorable.

However, all biologically based human traits are to a greater or lesser extent *elastic*, NOT rigid. All traits can and do change in response to societal reactions, positive and negative labelings, and social definitions. Much of what we perceive as "reality" is *socially constructed*. It is constructed by the ways in which significant societal agents such as parents, peers and teachers, respond and react to the biological givens of life. These biological givens contain great elasticity and potential for both favorable and unfavorable change as we shall see in the next chapter.[6]

Notes

1. According to Paul Pilkonis' analysis, fully two-thirds of the male clients treated at Philip Zimbardo's "Shyness Clinic" (Stanford University), possess native temperaments which place them *outside* the *melancholic quadrant* of the Eysenck Cross. This represents a major reason in support of my contention that very few of Zimbardo's clients are *genuinely shy*. Yet despite the mildness of their problems, fully 50 percent of Zimbardo's clients drop out of the "Shyness Clinic" program because of an inability to do the required homework exercises.

2. Thus, the nonstability-stability (high versus low emotionality) dimension appears to be governed by the innate nature of a person's *autonomic nervous system*, whereas the extroversion-introversion dimension appears to be governed by the innate nature of a person's *central nervous system*.

3. This represents a key reason why I believe inhibited and uninhibited children should not be either required or expected to play together in the same peer groups. Simply put, boys whose inborn nature is inhibited tend to flourish best when they are permitted to play in noncompetitive coeducational peer groups that are comprised of both girls and *inhibited* boys.

4. With regard to a variety of personality characteristics that are measured by widely used personality inventories, S. G. Vandenberg carried out a remarkably complete tabulation comprising 185 pairs of monozygotic twins and 908 pairs of dizygotic twins. Eleven tests measured personality traits, needs, and attitudes in factors of many kinds: for example, those labeled energetic, conformity, masculinity, femininity, dependency needs, punitive attitude, responsibility, and so forth. In all but eight of the 101 variables, the monozygotic

pairs were more alike than the dizygotic pairs. Interestingly, the kinds of variables that most often emerged in both members of identical-twin pairs seemed to measure the *degree of sociability and energy*, a concept very close to that of degree of extraversion-introversion. In another investigation of twins—79 pairs of monozygotic twins and 68 pairs of dizygotic twins—Irving Gottesman demonstrated a strong genetic component for social introversion. Further, in a longitudinal twin study that was conducted by Robert Dworkin, the traits of anxiety-proneness and dependency were found to be highly heritable. This was found by Dworkin to be the case for a sample of teenagers as well as for a sample of adults.

5. Other evidence of biological factors where none were heretofore suspected includes that of certain subgroups of children with severe separation anxiety that prevents them from going to school or camp or staying overnight with friends or relatives. According to the work of psychiatrists Paul Wender and Donald Klein, the specific response of such children to antidepressant medication has been impressive.

6. To untangle the knot between family and genetic influences, psychologists Denise Daniels and Robert Plomin published a fascinating new study in 1985. Simply put, their data provide additional very strong evidence of a *genetic* factor underlying shyness. Using several personality and temperament questionnaries, they compared 152 families who had adopted children with 120 families who were bringing up their own babies.

All of the parents rated how shy their baby had been at 12 months and at 24 months of age. They described how many unfamiliar social situations the baby might encounter at home; and they also reported on their own shy or outgoing temperament. Husbands and wives also rated each other. In addition, Daniels and Plomin asked the adopted babies' biological mothers to rate their own degree of shyness and sociability.

One of the most striking findings of this study (sponsored by the Colorado Adoption Project) was a strong resemblance between the degree of shyness of the biological mothers and their adopted-away babies at the age of 24 months (the babies had all been adopted within three months of birth). This result must be considered particularly impressive because the biological mothers' scores had been derived from self-report questionnaires completed before the birth of the infant. And the infants' scores represented ratings by the adoptive parents *over two years later*. Daniels and Plomin assert that this constitutes strong evidence of a genetic connection between the personalities of parents and their infants.

Chapter Postscript Regarding Monoamine Oxidase

On August 12, 1986, NBC televised a show titled "Nature and Nurture" which was hosted by Phil Donahue. On this program it was announced that it had indeed been found that the brain chemical *monoamine oxidase* clearly differentiates extroverts from introverts. Extroverts tend to have *very low levels* of this brain chemical. In constrast, *shy, inhibited people tend to have very high levels of monoamine oxidase in their brains*. This finding constitutes a very important new development in our efforts to understand severe and chronic shyness. Further, it is no accident that today the monoamine oxidase inhibitors ("MAO Inhibitors") constitute the "drug of choice" in the treatment of anxiety/panic attacks—a condition that may well be biochemically and neurologically related to severe shyness. Perhaps the heavy amount of electrical activity in the brains of introverts *causes* monoamine oxidase to be produced. Or perhaps the monoamine oxidase causes the unusually high electrical activity. There could be a vicious cycle in operation here.

Chapter 3

Societal Reactions and Elastic Limits

Inborn temperament constitutes a kind of limit, just as native intelligence represents a kind of limit within which a person must function throughout his/her life. Moralists and many positive mind science devotees delight in continually reminding us that virtually anything is possible—that any person can become anything he/she chooses to become. All he/she needs to do is to set his/her goal clearly in his/her mind's eye (imagination), and commence striving towards it.

Now up to a point there *is* an important element of truth to this positive mind science philosophy. But it is an element that is often misunderstood and not seen in its proper perspective. In order to illustrate this point, let us consider the issue of *learning how to play the piano*.

Theoretically, almost everyone *could* learn how to play the piano at a high level of proficiency. However, research over the years has shown that some people (a rather small minority) are born with the potential for learning how to play the piano rather quickly and easily. Others, on the other hand, remain "all thumbs" at this art over very long periods of time, no matter how long and tirelessly they endeavor to develop the requisite eye-hand coordination and finger dexterity. *Most people* are born with capacities and limits that place them somewhere "in between" these two extremes.

Now all three different kinds of people will have to expend effort and work if they wish to become accomplished pianists. And this includes the Mozarts and the Gershwins who began diddling around the piano keys at age three and with seemingly remarkable success. The key point is that the *amount of time and effort* that might have to be expended by *some* people might be so exceedingly enormous that continuing to work at the piano might logically be deemed a less than productive way for them to spend their time. More succinctly, if these same people found some other type of activity that entails a closer fit to their native talents and potentials, they would far more quickly reap the positive self-feelings that inevitably accrue from noteworthy progress toward worthwhile accomplishments.

To be sure, learning how to play the piano well may be of such enormous importance to some people that the amount of effort required for attaining mastery is simply not an issue for them. This is fine! For example, Theodore Roosevelt was a weakling as a child; yet he became adept at boxing, hunting, football, as well as at a host of other highly "masculine" activities. Of course, there is no evidence that Roosevelt had been a *melancholic* (figure 1, page 41) child as far as his native temperament had been concerned. We do know that he had been physically weak throughout much of his childhood. But physical weakness is *only sometimes* accompanied by high inborn introversion and by a low native anxiety threshold. This is because *physical weakness* is a trait that is *statistically independent* from inborn melancholia.

If the physically weak child is blessed with an advantaged inborn temperament, he will be able to develop his weak body; and he will probably enjoy the process! If, on the other hand, such a weak, physically frail child *also* happened to be born high on melancholia, then it is extremely unlikely that he will wish to work to develop his body and to become something which from a psychoemotional standpoint he is not.

And so we are dealing here with *elastic limits*. Like the limits of native intelligence, native temperament does not set hard, fast limits. There is always some degree of flexibility to the inborn limits within which all human beings must function and live. For most people with poor native aptitude for learning how to play the piano, it will *normally* be more productive for them to find something else to become good at. Their time will be put to far more constructive and efficient use if they do work at something which better fits their native, inborn potentials.

It *is* good for all people to learn the desirability of hard work and of the joys and satisfactions that accrue therefrom. But to force a person to work hard at something that is at great variance from his native temperament and inborn potentials is tantamount to causing him to continually beat his head against a brick wall. American culture is enormously rich with thousands of possible activities at which a person can become good or even great. What gain can there be from forcing square pegs into round holes?! What gain can accrue from forcing a person to spend hours working at something for little gain, when that same amount of time and effort in another equally worthwhile pursuit would have netted considerable progress, advancement, and positive self-feelings?

And so it is with the little boy who is high on inborn introversion/ inhibition and high on inborn emotionality. If left alone to the ravages of the conventional all-boy peer group he will almost certainly become love-shy and lonely without the interpersonal skills that are indispensable for effective, happy survival. If, on the other hand, that little boy is introduced to an *alternative* peer group composed of little boys *and* *girls* who are reasonably similar to himself in native temperament *and* if that little boy is introduced to games and sports that will not frighten him or inspire any sort of bullying, then the chances are exceedingly good that he will be headed for psychoemotional and social adjustment. In fact, as Alexander Thomas has shown, such a little boy's chances for success will actually be about as good as those of children who had been born with more advantaged inborn temperaments.

The "Wish Bone Effect"

There is a small figure drawing which I have found to be very helpful in explaining to people the very important concept of *adverse social stimulus value*. An adverse social stimulus value is an indispensable precondition for the development of chronic, intractable love-shyness. Simply put, no one without a negative social stimulus value could ever develop a pathological degree of love-shyness. Mild or transitory, situationally-based shyness is a problem that plagues at least half of the American population from time to time. But the really painful, highly debilitating, life-long kind of love-shyness which obviates participation in dating, courtship, sexual lovemaking, marriage and family formation, etc., absolutely requires a negative social stimulus value throughout the victim's formative years. And it is this highly debilitating type of love-shyness about which this book is concerned.

Visualize, if you will, a class of one hundred kindergarten boys, all of whom are starting kindergarten together at the age of five and on the same day. The "5" in *Figure 2* represents this starting point. Some of these children will come from better, warmer, more competent and loving homes than others will. Similarly, some of them will have had rewarding nursery school experiences, whereas others will not have had this.

Now every class of children has its "stars". These are the children who exude a very positive social stimulus value right from the very beginning. Occultists might say of such children that they possess very positive, powerful "auras". Generally speaking, the "stars" represent only a comparatively small minority of children. Of our one hundred children we might assume that fifteen are "stars". And we will let the letter "A" represent these fifteen lucky children.

Just as every class of children contains its "stars", every group similarly contains a certain number of children who exude negative social

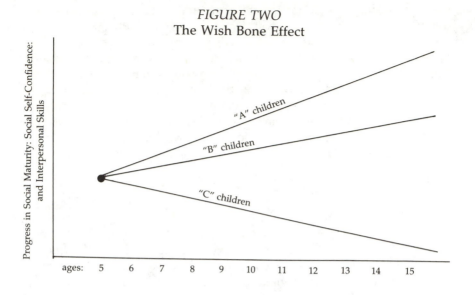

FIGURE TWO
The Wish Bone Effect

stimulus value. In the case of our "wish bone effect" drawing, let us assume that the negative social stimulus value is caused by three factors: (1) a melancholic inborn temperament represented by the first quadrant of the Eysenck Cross (figure 1, page 41); (2) low physical attractiveness: these children are not handsome or muscular; and (3) residence with parents who are less than adequately competent at dealing with children. We will further assume that these children possessing negative social stimulus value are all quite normal in the areas of both native intelligence and physical health. In other words, we will assume that their budding problems are not being caused by deficits in the intellectual or physical health areas. Let us allow the letter "C" to represent these children in the diagram. And let us assume that there are five such children in the total group of one hundred five-year olds.

The remaining 80 children are represented in our diagram by the letter "B". These children are all *average to somewhat above average* in social stimulus value. And the main point which the diagram illustrates about this majority group is that throughout the formative years of elementary school each of its members makes good, steady progress in the growth and development of interpersonal skills, social self-confidence and social maturity.

The numbers running along the bottom of *Figure 2*, represent chronological ages. Inasmuch as this is a hypothetical diagram, the ages included range from 5 through 15. All three lines, each of which commences from the *same point at age 5*, are intended to reflect progress in social/emotional growth, and in level and adequacy of interpersonal skills.

The major point of the "wish bone effect" diagram is that *the rich get richer while the poor get poorer*. This cliche is as valid in understanding the development of social self-confidence, interpersonal skills and social/emotional maturity as it is in understanding the development of financial fortunes. The three lines all start out *at the same point*. Yet with each passing year the distance between each of the three lines becomes greater and greater.

Again, please understand that *line B* people are progressing normally. They are growing and progressing at a normal, healthy pace. This is why the *"B"* line moves upward from one chronological age to the next chronological age. The ever increasing amount of distance (1) between *line A* and *line B*, and (2) between *line B* and *line C* reflects the fact that relative to the "normal" masses of children, the social stimulus value of *both* the "A" children and the "C" children is becoming stronger and stronger with each passing year.

The social stimulus value of the "A" children is becoming ever better and better compared to that of the masses. In effect, their "star" quality continues to improve to the point wherein they appear to be becoming ever brighter and brighter relative to the large bulk of their classmates. The "C" children are similarly becoming increasingly *conspicuous* with each passing year. Indeed, the distance between the "C" children and the "B" children quickly becomes and remains substantially greater than the distance between the "B" children and the "stars" or "A" children. Let us consider *how this occurs*.

The reason why the "C" boys follow the downward slope from the very beginning is that they withdraw from their fellows' invitations to take part in "rough and tumble" play. They prefer more quiet play at the craft tables with the girls, and they refuse to physically defend themselves when they are punched and bullied. In contrast to the other boys who enthusiastically pursue the "rough and tumble" play and who fight back when they are assaulted, the "C" boys either run away from the irrational boyish hostilities which they cannot understand, or they seek the teacher's protection from this hazing. The more frequently the "C" boys follow this avoidant course of action, the more conspicuous they become vis-a-vis their classmates. In essence, they develop a reputation as a good person to bully because they don't fight back and because they display their suffering and displeasure in an ever more conspicuous manner. And this serves to compound the bullying and the hazing.

Psychologist Howard Kaplan has done a good deal of experimental work on aggression. And one of the major conclusions of his many experiments is that aggression is more likely if the other person (the victim) is perceived as unwilling or unable to retaliate. And this is exactly the position of the "C" children. Physically aggressive retaliation is not in keeping with their native temperaments. They cannot understand the feelings and the motives of the "B" children; and the "B" children cannot understand them (the "C" children). Being fundamentally serious by nature, the "C" children are not really *"kids"*; it is not congruent with their temperaments to "kid around". And this is one of the things that makes adults and virtually all *male* "B" children incapable of understanding them (the "C" children).

Meanwhile these "C" children are gradually learning to run right home immediately after school, and to avoid all informal social activity. Being anywhere near peers when a supervising adult is not around to protect them is a potentially very painful and dangerous thing. And so they become isolates. They are discouraged by all different kinds of people from playing with the girls because "boys are not supposed to play with girls". And they cannot play with the boys because the boys are a source of physical pain and danger. And they cannot choose any alternative peer groups, sports and games because there are no sanctioned alternatives available. Since boys are not supposed to even want to "play gentle", no gentle sports or games are made available to them.

As the "C" boys grow older their deficits in interpersonal skills become ever greater, thus rendering them more and more adversely conspicuous vis-a-vis their normally adjusted "B" group peers. Again, the children's peer group is an indispensable socializer for interpersonal skills and social self-confidence. In being denied a peer group and in being forced to function all the time as social isolates, the "C" children are prevented from acquiring interpersonal attributes that are quite crucial for successful adult living. This is why with each passing year they become ever more adversely conspicuous vis-a-vis their peers. And the more adversely conspicuous they become, the more often they are singled out for bullying and/or for ignoring. The "B" children who do not bully simply do not care to have anything to do with the "C" children inasmuch as merely being seen with or around a "C" child could confer a negative reputation. In this sense tolerant and compassionate behavior tends to be punished and stigmatized by the all-boy peer group. Seldom is such positive behavior rewarded by male children here in American society.

Since all human beings require some sort of attention and recognition, some of the bullied and/or ignored "C" boys may become class clowns. As negative attention is almost always less painful than an absence of attention, some of them can be expected to generate a host of increasingly unhealthy defense mechanisms. These clownish behaviors will themselves serve to further alienate the "C" boys more and more from the "B" boys and from the "A" boys. And the more alienated, detached and unidentified with their age-mate peers they become, the more emotionally immature they will be perceived by others as being. Simply put, by the time they become teenagers their level of interpersonal skills and social-emotional maturity will be very, very poor by comparison with the normally adjusted "B" and "A" children in their class. And by that time many of them will be perceived as "weird" or "queer" or "gay" (homosexual).

For the "A" boys the same mechanism operates except in the reverse way. At the outset they are more handsome and muscular than most of the other boys. And this positive social stimulus value thus renders them sought after companions. Even at age 5, everyone wants to play with them because they are attractive and competent, and because they behave (due to inborn temperament) in a sociable and fearless yet friendly, nonpugnacious manner. And since everyone wants to be with them, they gradually develop a strongly positive, robust self-image and social self-confidence. Further, they swiftly come to develop a friendly, positive attitude towards most of their age-mates. They like most of their age-mates because these age-mates almost constantly honor them by selecting them first for games and for a host of other social and recreational activities.

All of this positive attention has its *cumulative impact*. These people in the "A" category come to feel so good about themselves that they experience little anxiety in asserting themselves vis-a-vis their peers as well as vis-a-vis the adult community. In essence, their social maturity and interpersonal skills grow and proliferate by leaps and bounds as the years pass. By the time they enter adolescence they are likely to be elected to important class offices, and all the girls consider them "cute" and want to go out with them. Their social presence by this time has become quite conspicuous in the *positive* sense by comparison with that of the normally adjusted "B" children.

In sum, the inborn social stimulus value created by (1) native temperament, and (2) physical attractiveness, serves to get young boys started on either the right foot or on the wrong foot relative to their peers. As *figure 2* illustrates, those who commence school at age five with an adverse social stimulus value tend to be avoided, ignored, or bullied. And as a consequence such disadvantaged children learn to avoid people; and they learn to associate the very thought of informal socializing with thoughts of mental pain and anguish. As such, their interpersonal skill deficits and their social self-confidence deficits relative to their peers become worse and worse with each passing year. In addition, their social stimulus value similarly becomes ever worse with each passing year. This is the essence of how boys become chronically love-shy adults.

Yes, the shyness itself is learned. But one cannot begin to correctly understand how this learning takes place without understanding and appreciating the fact that the inborn temperament factors represent indispensable catalysts and prerequisites for this negative learning to get under way in the first place. The learning which results in intractable love-shyness could never get started in the first place in the absence of the *twin catalysts* of (1) an inborn temperament of adverse social stimulus value, and (2) less than pleasing physical attractiveness/handsomeness.

The Sociological Perspective

For readers with some background in sociology it will be apparent that Charles Horton Cooley's *"looking-glass self"* theory is highly applicable here. The people in a child's social field represent, metaphorically speaking, a kind of looking-glass or mirror. Human beings are constantly seeing a kind of reflection of themselves in this social looking-glass—in the sorts of feedback reactions (good, bad, and indifferent) that it provides. The problem, of course, is that impressionable minds *internalize* the messages that they are constantly in the process of receiving from this social mirror. Parents, teachers and age-mate peers represent *significant others*—a salient and highly influential part of the social mirror. In essence, when the social *mirror* feeds back consistently ego disparaging, caustically unkind messages, the sense of self (self-image) rapidly becomes one with those messages. Thus, the child internalizes these consistent messages and becomes intractably welded to an inferiority complex.

Every Group Needs a Deviant

For many years now sociologists have been arguing that every group of at least five or more persons needs a deviant, and that members will be constantly on the alert for whatever criterion they can find which might permit them to recruit a particular one of their fellows for the deviant status. Seeing the deviant (noncomformist) get punished or ostracized for his behavior tends to enhance the awareness of all group members of the prevailing norms. And it tends to make each group member become more and more mindlessly and uncritically accepting of the "righteousness" of the prevailing norms.

This is certainly true for norms regarding what for male children represents inadequately "masculine" behavior. For example, some thirty years ago social psychologist Muzafer Sherif conducted what has become a classic study of 10-year old boys at a summer camp. Sherif's study dealt with a number of important group processes. And for it he recruited about 100 boys, all of whom were the "cream of the crop" back in their respective communities and elementary schools. Each boy accepted as a research subject was given a free five-week stay in a Connecticut summer camp. Boys were accepted into the study from all over the state of Connecticut. However, in order to be accepted for the study all had to be *leaders*, and at the "top of the pecking order" in the respective fifth grade classrooms from which they had just graduated. In essence, all of the boys were highly sociable, "normal", and uninhibited as far as their regular behavior back home had been concerned.

Shortly after their arrival at the camp the boys were divided up into twelve-person groups. The boys had all arrived at the camp as strangers. None of them had known any of their fellow campers before their summer camp experience had begun. Yet within just three days of the time the various groups were formed, each group of boys had begun to develop a "pecking order". For the first time in their lives some of the boys were being bullied, teased, and ostracized. One group singled out a boy for the disparaged (deviant) role because of the shape of his head—and they called him "lemon head". Another group singled out a boy because he was not considered fast enough—even though back home that boy had been faster than any of his classmates.

In short, even when all the members of a particular group are considered "ultra-normal", inside of a comparatively short time span *some criterion* will be found for creating a pecking order. Especially regarding male children in our highly competitive society, it would appear that not everybody can be "at the top". Many of the boys who had been "at the top" in both popularity and respect back in their heterogeneous fifth grade classrooms now found themselves at the middle or low end of the totum pole.

Sherif's findings have a bearing upon the "wishbone effect". If a deviant can be recruited within three days by a group of boys all of whom had been initially well adjusted and used to being well-respected leaders, it becomes all the easier for us to understand how extremely easy it can be for a group of many different kinds of school boys to recruit an inhibited, isolated classmate for the disparaged, deviant role. In short, boys along the "C" line (figure 2; page 41) tend to be highly conspicuous right from the very beginning. And they become ever more conspicuous as time passes—as they are increasingly ignored, bullied, and deprived of a chance to develop interpersonal skills and a socially confident self-image. The more conspicuous they are, the more intractably crystalized their disparaged, deviant role becomes.

Young boys tend to be more insecure than adult men. And in a highly competitive society the more insecure a boys is, the more he will revel in ostracizing and bullying his shy, inhibited classmate. The bully is thus reminded a good deal more often of what the norms are than the better adjusted, more secure boys. The bully is frequently reminded of the norms because he is almost constantly teasing, hazing and bullying the inhibited "deviant" for violating them. The tragedy, of course, is that the inhibited, isolated boy cannot help violating the masculine behavior norms. The inhibited, shy boy is only being true to his native, inborn temperament—and he is being punished for thus being himself.

The Mentally Retarded as Analogous to the Shy

Research activity on the mentally retarded can be used as an example of how (1) an *accommodating* society facilitates adjustment, and of how (2) a society with rigid norms and ideas often causes the shy—and the mentally retarded—to become lifelong problems to both themselves and to others. Some of the important lessons we have learned include the following:

1. The mentally retarded flourish best when they are permitted to play exclusively with the mentally retarded. When they are forced to play among heterogeneous groups of age-mates who are not mentally retarded they are often bullied and severely hazed. And as a consequence they regress by engaging in schizophrenic withdrawal, clownish behavior, or through just plain becoming sick.
2. We have learned that the mentally retarded flourish best, as do *all* human beings, when they are accorded genuine recognition, respect and encouragement for their accomplishments. This is the theory behind the so-called "Special Olympics" wherein the retarded are encouraged to compete with children who are like themselves, and to experience the joy of winning and of the social recognition that accrues therefrom.
3. We have learned that it is almost always best to encourage the mentally retarded to date and to marry. As is true with almost all human beings, marriage brings the best out of the mentally retarded. Encouraging the mentally retarded to procreate children represents another matter entirely. And very often this cannot be done. But we have learned that through involving

the mentally retarded in meaningful work and love roles (including marriage), they flourish and they contribute maximally to themselves and to society.

Now I believe that a useful parallel can be drawn between the mentally retarded child and the inhibited, shy child. For some reason American society has long been far more ready and willing to accommodate itself to the needs of the blind child, the mentally retarded child, the deaf mute child, the physically ill or deformed child, etc., than it has been to make reasonable accommodations to the inhibited, shy child, particularly if that child is a boy. The implicit assumption is that being born in the melancholic quadrant (figure 1, page 41) of the Eysenck Cross is a *characterological defect and flaw* rather than the trait of *inborn* temperament that it *actually* is. And the further assumption is that what the boy with inborn melancholia (low anxiety threshold/high inhibition) really needs is *a good, swift kick in the ass*!

Nobody ever seriously suggests a "kick in the ass" for the epileptic child, for the deaf mute, for the blind, or for the mentally retarded. Indeed, we do not even suggest such a course of action for the child of seemingly normal intelligence who just doesn't seem to be able to learn how to read. No! Instead we devise special classes in remedial reading, and we expend a great deal of both personnel and financial resources in order to enable such children to grow and to flourish on as normal a basis as possible.

We have always assumed that temperament is somehow different from other human traits. And we have become quite moralistic about this quite false assumption. Too many psychologists continue believing that *all* behavior and *all* elements of personality are *learned*—and because they are *all* learned they can *all* be unlearned if and when the right therapy is provided. These psychologists and the educators and parents who have been influenced by them continue to be strangely oblivious to the hundreds of scholarly papers and books that have been published over the last twenty years on the subject of inborn, biologically based temperament. And they continue to be oblivious to the fact that while certain traits, such as shyness, low self-esteem and neurosis *are* learned, they are learned as a direct byproduct of a hostile, punishing attitude that is displayed towards boys who manifest a melancholic inborn temperament.

Why, in fact, do inhibited boys usually end up as friendless isolates whereas passive, quiet girls almost always end up with at least a few friends along with satisfactory levels of interpersonal skills? The answer must be that the same inborn temperament that is punished with hazing, bullying and ignoring when it is displayed by little boys is accepted with kindly tolerance when it is displayed by little girls. The point is that this hazing, bullying and ignoring has an extremely deleterious *cumulative impact* upon a growing child over the course of his formative years.

The Jane Elliott Study

A classic study which very clearly illustrates the cumulative impact of wrongful social definitions upon people was conducted in 1968 through 1971, by Jane Elliott. Ms. Elliott was a rather unlikely candidate for the authoring of one of social science's most creative and important studies. She worked as a third grade teacher in the small northeastern Iowa town of Riceville. Up until the time of her experiment she had been a very motherly, highly respected teacher who had been well liked by all.

However, upon the assination of Dr. Martin Luther King in March 1968, she became very distressed and upset. She wanted to teach her eight and nine year old pupils the evils of racial discrimination, but did not know how to approach the problem in a way that would prove incisive and thoroughly convincing. Eight year olds cannot be lectured to in the way that university students and adults are commonly dealt with in educational settings. And aggravating the problem was the fact that most of her young pupils had never even seen a black person apart from on television or in the movies. The children were all living in a very rural part of a state which has very few black residents. Of our fifty states, only Wyoming has a smaller fraction of black residents than does Iowa.

She finally hit upon a plan which she decided to pursue with enthusiasm and conviction. She entered her classroom one morning with a large book which she claimed had been written by a very famous scientist who is extremely wise and knowledgeable. She proceeded to tell her young pupils that this scientist had determined that brown-eyed people are naturally dirty, unkempt, uncooperative, incapable of learning at a satisfactory speed, incapable of retaining knowledge, discourteous, unlikely to go far in life, etc. She proceeded to enumerate quite systematically a whole host of ways whereby brown-eyed people were alleged by the scientist to be inferior to blue-eyed people. And since her class was composed of *nine* brown-eyed children and *nine* blue-eyed children (and she herself was green-eyed), she had rather fertile soil for her experiment.

Again, Ms. Elliott had been well-liked, and there was a very strong tendency for these impressionable young minds to believe everything that she said. And as she proceeded through her twenty minute sermon about the evils of brown-eyed people and the virtues of those with blue eyes, she could see the brown-eyed children begin to slouch and to travel off into a world of daydreams. In fact, throughout the experimental day the disparaged brown-eyed children reacted primarily in one of four different ways—depending upon their individual temperaments: (1) withdrawing and going off into a world of fantasy, daydreams, or sleep; (2) crying and sulking; (3) clowning and goofing off behavior; and (4) hostile, obstreperous, inconsiderate and/or bullying behavior.

Meanwhile, as Ms. Elliott made her way through the same initial spiel, the blue-eyed children began to sit up more and more erect. They began to pay attention to what was going on in class more closely and intensely than many of them had ever done before. In essence, right from the very outset of the experiment the disparaged group (brown-eyed children) and the exalted group (blue-eyed youngsters) began to behave in dramatically and very conspicuously different ways.

After Ms. Elliott completed her twenty minute lecture she announced that since brown-eyed children are not likely to go very far in life anyway, and since they do not learn as well as other youngsters, are dirtier, less cooperative, etc., it makes good sense to accord them fewer classroom privileges than the "naturally superior" blue-eyed children should be accorded. And with that she ran down a prepared list of new rules and restrictions that would impact the brown-eyed children from that moment on. And just so that each child in the classroom could tell every other child apart on the basis of the criterion of eye color, she placed large black collars around the necks of each of the brown-eyed youngsters. Once this was accomplished everyone could easily tell whether any particular pupil had brown eyes or blue eyes.

Then she began to involve the children in their daily reading lesson. As usual each child was required to read aloud a passage from a third grade reader. When a blue-eyed child made a mistake or stumbled through a passage, Ms. Elliott helped him/her along in a kindly manner, and then praised him/her. If a blue-eyed student read a passage well, lavish praise was heaped upon him/her. And she would say: "See, that just goes to show that everything I said is really true. Blue-eyed people really are smarter; and they learn their reading lessons much better than brown-eyed children do."

On the other hand, if a brown-eyed child read his/her passage without error, Ms. Elliott rather abruptly asked the child to stop, and she immediately moved on to the next child without according the brown-eyed youngster a word of praise or recognition. If a brown-eyed youngster stumbled through a passage, she reacted with a statement similar to this: "See, that just goes to show how brown-eyed children just won't learn."

In essence, positive or disparaging remarks were systematically applied to the children throughout the day strictly on the basis of eye color. Positive behavior was ignored in the brown-eyed youngsters, whereas negative behavior was always noticed and punished with a rather coldly phrased comment such as: "I guess this is what can naturally be expected from brown-eyed youngsters."

By the end of the school day quite remarkable changes had occurred in Ms. Elliott's classroom. For example, the brown-eyed third graders had regressed to first grade reading level, whereas the blue-eyed third graders were reading *at or beyond the fifth grade level*. Arithmetic scores, vocabulary scores, spelling scores, and all other academic criteria employed to assess change in young children showed that the blue-eyed pupils were all performing (1) far beyond what would normally be expected for third graders, and (2) far beyond where they (*these very same children*) had performed just one week prior to the experiment. These same test scores similarly revealed the brown-eyed children to be functioning at a level that was (1) *far below* what would ordinarily be expected for third grade youngsters, and (2) far below the level of performance that they had displayed just one week prior to the experiment.

Academic performance was hardly the only thing to be affected by the experimental design that Ms. Elliott had imposed upon her pupils. After a mere six hours of their new experiences in Ms. Elliott's classroom the brown-eyed children had all suffered serious blows to their self-images. None of these children liked themselves anymore, and they displayed these self-disparaging attitudes in a whole host of ways. Some of the children cried and sulked. Many began to behave in a sullen and disrespectful manner. Several of the nine brown-eyed children spoke of how they didn't want to come to school anymore, and about how they would find ways to play hookey. All began to look increasingly dirty and unkempt. None revealed any interest in learning or in open, friendly socializing with their classmates.

Contrariwise, by the end of the school day the blue-eyed children had begun behaving far more maturely towards their teacher and vis-a-vis each other than they had ever behaved before. Each child displayed a conspicuously strong enthusiasm for learning and asserted himself/herself in a friendly, courteous matter, except vis-a-vis their disparaged brown-eyed classmates. And this was as true for children who just one day prior had been the class clowns, the "slow learners", and the all-round "bad boys", as it had been for the blue-eyed children who had always performed well. The posture, grooming, and attitudes towards self that were manifested by these blue-eyed children were nothing short of amazing.

It is not necessary to summarize here all of the many interesting facets of Ms. Elliott's experiment. Interested readers will find a good coverage of the study in her book entitled A CLASS DIVIDED which I have listed in the bibliography at the end of this volume. Suffice it to say that she ran the study on four different third grade classes: 1968 through 1971. And each year she reversed things on the second day of the experiment. In other words, on the second day she advised the children that she had made a mistake, and that it was *really* brown-eyed people who are "superior", and that blue-eyed people are actually the inferior ones.

It should be stressed that Ms. Elliott's findings proved equally strong each time she ran the experiment. Similarly, immediately after she turned the tables she found that the academic performance and the mental attitudes of the blue-eyed children slid downhill in an extremely dramatic and precipitous fashion; whereas the performance and the mental attitudes of the brown-eyed children shot upward quite drastically after only a very short period of time in the exalted role.

The Taking Over of a Role

Jane Elliott was interested in demonstrating to her young pupils what it feels like to be a victim of discrimination on the basis of some arbitrarily and capriciously selected criterion such as skin color. She used role playing (*psychodrama*) techniques to accomplish this. And, of course, she changed the criterion for discrimination from skin color to eye color. Both criteria are equally arbitrary inasmuch as a person can choose neither his/her eye color nor his/her skin color.

The point that needs to be stressed here is that blindness, deafness, clubfoot, *AND INBORN MELANCHOLIA* (being born high up in quadrant #1 of the Eysenck Cross depicted in figure #1 on page 41), are all factors that are above and beyond the purview of human choice. People are born with each of these various attributes. And each can be viewed as constituting a "handicap". And just as millions of Americans in past decades had been programmed by their parents through socialization to disparage and discriminate against black people, so it is that many Americans are programmed to disparage and discriminate against melancholic boys—but not melancholic girls.

The children in Jane Elliott's classroom had only to put up with their second class status for a mere seven hours. But that was enough time for a great deal of damage to be done. Riceville, Iowa, is an isolated, rural community, and Ms. Elliott's pupils had indeed led sheltered lives. So perhaps they believed her pro-discrimination rhetoric at the beginning of the school day faster and easier than older, less sheltered children would have believed it. The point, however, is that all young children are to a substantial extent *highly suggestible*. And if such enormous changes for the bad or for the good can be effected in children in a mere seven hours, we can begin to appreciate the permanent scars, the lifelong damage, which can and most probably will be done to children who cannot escape from this treatment after a mere seven hours of an experimental psychodramatic exercise! Black children who grew up in the Deep South had to live *the entirety of their formative years* amidst this sort of arbitrary and capricious discrimination and disparaging treatment. And melancholic boys (with high inborn introversion/inhibition together with high emotionality) are similarly made to pass through the entirety of *their* formative years the victims of this sort of mindless cruelty. It is no wonder that few black children had been able to cultivate a positive attitude towards the American education system—AND TOWARDS THEMSELVES. And it is similarly no wonder at all that highly introverted, low anxiety threshold males come to think very poorly of themselves. Simply put, disparaged people of all kinds develop negative self-attitudes as well as negative attitudes towards their society as a direct result of the cruel and depersonalized treatment that they are accorded throughout the entirety of their formative years.

In Ms. Elliott's study an exalted role had been superimposed over the blue-eyed youngsters. They had been defined as having all the virtues, strengths and potentials; and they believed these definitions of the situation. A disparaging role had been superimposed upon the brown-eyed youngsters. And they similarly came to *believe* what they had been told about themselves. Many sociologists today call this process the *self-fulfilling prophecy*. In short, when we come to define certain things or ideas as real (even when they are actually quite false), those things and ideas tend to become real in their consequences. Perhaps the Bible summarized the same idea in simpler terms: "As a man thinketh in his heart, so is he"; "According to your faith, so be it unto you".

As a result of Ms. Elliott's *definition of the situation*, each child came to embrace a role. And in so doing he/she incorporated a *label* into the innermost depths of his/her subconscious mind—which is like a computer memory bank that does not know the difference between what is true and what is false. For some children it was a self-disparaging role (label), and for others it was an exalted role (label). And a great moral dilemma raised by Ms. Elliott's experiment is summarized in the question: "HOW CAN WE ENGINEER A SYSTEM THAT WOULD BRING THE VERY BEST OUT OF *EVERY* BOY AND GIRL *WITHOUT* HAVING A DISPARAGED GROUP?" In studying Ms. Elliott's experiment most people pay attention *only* to what happened to the discriminated against group. But it is *equally important* for us to focus upon what happened to the exalted group—to the blue-eyed pupils who had been defined as being intrinsically superior in ability, potential, and in moral and behavioral attributes.

As a result of having been placed in an exalted role and status, the blue-eyed youngsters began performing better than they had ever performed before. And they enjoyed their school work more thoroughly than they had ever done before as well. Just one day before the experiment had begun, these blue-eyed children had been performing in all ways no differently than the brown-eyed children had been performing. But once they had been given some group of fellows to disparage, to make fun of, to haze and to bully, they started performing better than ever whereas the disparaged victims began behaving worse than ever.

This has a profound bearing upon the issue of children who bully and haze introverted and fearful children. Those who haze are made to feel better about themselves to the extent that they have someone whom they can "put down". Only the most secure human beings are normally able to rise above the temptation to poke fun at others. In essence, emotionally secure, self-loving people do not have any need to hurt others in order to feel good about themselves. What we sorely need in American society right now is a system of education that would promote this inner sense of security and peace in *all* children.

By the way, each time Ms. Elliott ran her experiment there was always a little boy who refused to go along with the procedure. He refused to accept the benefits and rewards that accrued to those having eyes of the "right" color. And he similarly refused to participate in the bullying and harassing of his less advantaged classmates. Indeed, he often helped out his less advantaged colleagues.

Each of these noncomformist boys was found to be unusually mature for his age, well adjusted and self-accepting. Each had had the benefit of well educated, highly articulate mothers and fathers who were very emotionally supportive, and who found a great deal of pleasure in reading as opposed to watching television all the time. The parents of these unusually mature and compassionate youngsters were in all cases liberal in their political and social views. And they were significantly *less religious* in a conventional sense than most parents in their local community.

Dark Crayons and Drab Drawings

Here is another example of the often very serious consequences that befall a child as a result of being enmeshed in a role from which he/she cannot extracate himself/herself. The story concerns a little boy in a fourth grade classroom comprised of about forty pupils. Several times each week all the children were encouraged to draw pictures with the crayons that the teacher provided. And after each picture-drawing session the boy would hand in a drawing that invariably was composed exclusively of dark, drab colors. All of this little boy's drawings were consistently limited to blacks, grays, dark greens, and other very drab shades. And after several months of such drawings the teacher began to become worried. She finally decided to take a large number of the boy's drawings to the school psychologist.

A few days later the psychologist called the child into his office and simply asked him why he drew all these dark, drab pictures. The child's response was that he really didn't have any choice in the matter. He didn't *want* to draw such dreary pictures. But the teacher always started the crayon box at the front of the room. And by the time the crayon box got back to him in the final seat of the rear row, the only crayons left were the blacks, the grays, the dark greens, the browns, and other less than "happy" colors.

The moral to this story is that society often creates pathology as a result of the *situations* in which it places people. Some situations are especially conducive to pathology whereas others are conducive to health, happiness and adjustment. In essence, boys with high inborn introversion and fearfulness are often required to adapt to situations which simply do not "fit" these native attributes. And because they are forced to remain in these situations they simply do not thrive; and indeed they *regress* as per the "wishbone effect" discussed earlier. Were society to place these boys in school situations that comfortably *fit* their native temperaments, they would no longer be bullied, hazed, harassed or belittled for inborn attributes over which they have no control or choice. And they would begin to thrive.

The "Apperceptive Mass" Concept

During the seventeenth century German philosopher George Herbart introduced a new concept which he called "the apperceptive mass". Herbart had been trying to explain how human beings get to be the way they are. And his many observations of people led him to become quite dissatisfied with John Locke's idea of the *tableau rasa*. Locke had believed that a blank slate (tableau rasa) represented a good metaphor for man's mind at the time of birth. Herbart disliked this metaphor for two primary reasons: (1) you can always erase a slate whereas learning experiences quite frequently tend to remain indelibly and permanently imprinted in the mind; and (2) a slate is a rock, and rocks are hard, rigid and unmaleable. In contrast, the mind of man is in most respects quite pliable. Within limits it can be shaped.

This led Herbart to suggest "a glob of clay" as representing a much more accurate metaphor for the way man's mind exists at the time of his birth. In essence, he suggested that man's mind is like a *shapeless* "glob of clay" upon the initial entrance into the incarnate world.

However, taking this one step further, Herbart began to realize that *nothing* is completely "shapeless". Every so-called "shapeless" form has a shape. For example, all clouds have shapes, even though it could accurately be argued that each cloud is actually quite "shapeless". Moreover, "shapeless" forms *vary* in their attractiveness—in what could be labeled their *social stimulus value*. One could take a large number of clouds of similar size; and some of these might be seen as being so beautiful as to cause the conjuring up of romantic images. Others might be seen as being quite ugly or unappealing.

Suppose 15,000 twenty ounce globs of clay were laid out on a huge table somewhere. Let us suppose that 15,000 elementary school art students were to be given an outing, and each of them had to select a twenty ounce glob of clay upon which to work. All of these globs of clay are essentially shapeless, and all are of approximately twenty ounces in weight.

The first thing one might observe is that some of these globs of clay are preferred over other globs of clay. Indeed, we might expect to observe many of the more aggressive children fighting with one another as to who is going to get to work with the more attractive of the twenty ounce, *shapeless* globs of clay.

Not only do some of the shapeless globs appear superficially to be more or less attractive than its neighbors, but each shapeless glob varies at least a little bit from each other glob in terms of malleability and pliability. Some of the globs of clay might be a slight bit harder in texture than others, and thus may be a little bit more difficult to mold, and less pleasant to the touch. Others, in contrast, may appear to be a modicum too soft. We can assume that the lion's share of these 15,000 globs of clay *can be successfully molded* into something attractive and worthwhile— given the attention of a reasonably dedicated artist-sculptor (parent). A small minority of the globs of clay may not be quite so easy to shape; but *all can* be molded into *something*, given the right amount of patience, dedication, knowledge and artistic skill.

Further, each glob of clay (analog of the human mind) can be construed as incorporating both a *passive* and an *active* component. During a person's formative years the *passive* component will always be far more influential than the active component. Hence, *each perception a person experiences through his/her five physical senses acts to shape and mold (ever so slightly) the glob of clay (mind)*. The glob of clay (mind) is constantly being shaped and molded because a person can never stop perceiving and experiencing things until the moment of physical death. Thus the molding (experiencing) is *always* going on. And it is always going on in a *cumulative* manner so that each change builds upon all of those which had preceeded it. Clay can usually be reshaped after clear patterns (a mold) has been established. But it is invariably far easier to set the clay into the right shape and pattern *initially*, than it is to destroy an old shape and then try to mold a new one out of the same raw material.

The impact of the artist's shaping and molding tends to be far more influential during the early stages of the work (childhood) than during the later stages. Hence, the parents establish the basic form (permitted by their clay's characteristics) of their "sculpture" during the formative years of the young child's mind. Adolescent and adult experiences simply serve to sharpen and perfect the sculptured piece into its final shape.

Just as the glob of clay is constantly being shaped and molded *and changed* with each new experience (with some experiences molding and changing it more deeply than others), the glob of clay is *simultaneously functioning in an active way*. Simply put, the *apperceptive mass* (mind) "glob of clay" *is ALSO the thing that is doing the perceiving and interpreting*. People "see" and interpret things with their MINDS, and *not* with their eyes. The eyes are merely receptors. Similarly, the ears, smell, taste and touch senses are nothing more than receptors. The sense organs do no interpreting or perceiving on their own. Perceiving and interpreting (which is an integral part of perceiving) can only be accomplished by the *mind* (apperceptive mass).

This shaping of the glob of clay (apperceptive mass) by life experience illustrates the fact that as people we are constantly changing. We do not interpret things the same way today as we interpreted them yesterday. During early childhood, changes in the structure and content of the *apperceptive mass* (perceiving and interpreting *mind*) are often quite dramatic. In a very real sense the three-year old child is in a whole host of ways a *different person* than he/she had been at the age of two. Extreme trauma, such as that which might accrue from forcing an inhibited person into wartime combat, might well be expected to drastically alter the *apperceptive mass* of an adult male and render his interpretive/experiential apparatus enormously altered. But in general, drastic changes over short periods of time are normally limited to the early childhood years. Such drastic changes can occur in perfectly healthy family environments. No trauma need be involved in rendering the five year old a quite different person from whom he had been at age four.

The gist of this discussion is that people interpret their world with and through an *apperceptive mass* (mind) whose content is constantly changing. Changes become fewer and slower as the organism grows older and matures. But people are nonetheless constantly changing in their perceptions/interpretations of social stimuli. They are constantly in the process of change from the moment of birth until the moment of death.

In sum, there is both an *active* and a *passive* component to the apperceptive mass. The apperceptive mass is constantly being shaped and molded, just like a glob of clay. But *at the same time* just as the apperceptive mass is being fed more and more *new content* with each new experience, it is also functioning in a very active way as *a perceiving and interpreting mechanism*. Thus it will see and react to things at least slightly differently today from the way in which it reacted to and perceived them yesterday. This is because its content is constantly in the process of dynamic change. Each new experience (perception) becomes dynamically amalgamated and integrated into the whole of the subconscious mind (computer tape memory/feeling bank).

"Easy children" are perceived by their parents as having attractive (*easily malleable*) minds ("globs of clay"). They are labeled by their significant adults as being "easy", and they gradually internalize all of the positive intimations that are inherent in this label. The quite total biological and psychoemotional dependency which a very young child feels for its parents virtually assures full, unquestioned, uncritical internalization into the subconscious (robot computer) mind of the mother's labels, regardless of whether these labels might be false or accurate. And in a very important respect these labels serve to enhance the initial characteristics of the seemingly shapeless "glob of clay" (mind), irrespective of whether these inborn characteristics are socially defined as desirable or undesirable.

The same process applies with regard to so-called "difficult children". Parents perceive certain aspects of their shapeless "glob of clay" as being socially undesirable. They react to and label these "undesirable" features. And in so doing they cause these attributes to become accentuated. Thus, the initial inborn traits (regardless of whether they are viewed by the parents as socially favorable or as socially unfavorable) tend to become accentuated and reinforced as a direct consequence of parental labeling. The negative label becomes deeply internalized into the robot computer of the subconscious mind. And initially shy and reserved children thus tend to become more and more shy as time goes by.

In essence, the apperceptive mass/"glob of clay" concept of George Herbart provides a useful explanatory "bridge" between the innate, inborn, genetic/biological factors on the one hand, and the learning/experiential factors on the other hand. The apperceptive mass concept illustrates in a concrete way that there is nothing contradictory or mutually exclusive between *"nature"* and *"nurture"*. They both work together in a synergistic manner to produce the human being.

Conclusions

All human beings are born with a large number of different kinds of limits. The large majority of these limits are to a greater or lesser extent *elastic* (not rigid) in nature. All human beings must learn how to function (and adapt) within the confines of their elastic limits. And rendering this task quite difficult in many societies (especially in highly competitive ones) is the fact that the nature and substance of most of these *elastic* limits varies enormously from one *male* human being to another *male* human being. The same, of course, applies to female human beings except that the consequences for deviance are usually milder and much less punitive for females than for males.

Each elastic limit (human attribute) incorporates a *social stimulus value*. Some traits (limits) are viewed as being socially positive whereas others are viewed as being socially undesirable, or neutral. In essence, significant people such as parents, peers and teachers, *react to and label* behavioral traits representing the various elastic limits which belong to an individual. Hence, societal reactions interact in a dynamic, synergistic manner with inborn, biologically based characteristics. The interaction between these societal reactions and biologically based traits *creates* in a significant minority of males that consciousness which we call *love-shyness*.

Thus, a male who had been born very high on brain monoamine oxidase would be in the context of American society *severely handicapped* from the standpoint of societal (especially all-male peer group) reactions. (Ibid., p. 80).

In America, high brain monoamine oxidase would render a male "neurotic" rather than "schizophrenic." Today it is widely recognized that schizophrenia and autism are full-fledged *brain diseases*, just like multiple sclerosis. As brain diseases they are in no way caused by faulty learning or by bad parenting. They are caused entirely by degenerative biological processes impacting the brain and limbic systems that we are only just beginning to understand.

In essence, the major point of this chapter is that societal reactions act to reinforce, accentuate and enhance inborn characteristics irrespective of whether these inborn characteristics are good or bad.

Chapter 4

Astrology and Reincarnation

Respected scientific research journals are finally beginning to publish papers on the possible causative influence of psychic and occult variables. As of the middle 1980s, no book intending to present a comprehensive overview of the most probable causes of severe love-shyness could afford to ignore such factors. Accordingly, I offer this chapter as a brief summary of the very best of what is known or suspected at this time.

Astrological Factors

The August 1978, issue of the quite reputable JOURNAL OF SOCIAL PSYCHOLOGY contained an especially thought-provoking research paper on the influence upon native temperament of astrological sun signs. James Mayo, the author of this study, had been a graduate student of Hans Eysenck at the University of London. Like most scientific scholars, Eysenck had long considered astrology as being in the category of myth and nonsense. However, one day Mayo pointed out to him that a crucial astrological hypothesis could be tested at virtually no cost.

In essence, Eysenck had available a computer tape which contained a very great deal of research data including (1) the introversion-extroversion scores, and (2) the birth dates, for 2,324 University of London students. In addition, (3) native emotionality scores were also available for all of these students. Eysenck was about to use all of these data for research purposes that had nothing to do with astrology. However, his student, James Mayo, succeeded in convincing Eysenck of the prudence of checking out certain astrology-based hypotheses "while he was at it". Again, he might just as well test these astrological hypotheses inasmuch as it would not cost any additional time, money or trouble to do so. All the necessary data were already there!

As I have stressed, introversion-extroversion is one of the factors of native temperament that is most strongly related to love-shyness. Chronically love-shy men tend to be unusually introverted and inhibited.

For the past 6,000 years, astrological theory has contended that people born under *even* numbered sun signs (i.e., Taurus, Cancer, Virgo, Scorpio, Capricorn, and Pisces) are likely to be significantly more introverted and inhibited in their approach to life than people born under the odd numbered sun signs of Aires, Gemini, Leo, Libra, Sagittarius, and Aquarius. And much to the astonishment of both Mayo and Eysenck, this is exactly what was found for the 2,324 students studied. It was further found that Taurus, Pisces, Capricorn, and Scorpio *males* (in that order) were the most introverted people of all. On the other hand, Sagittarius and Aires people (regardless of sex) were found to be the most extroverted and outgoing of all people. Simply put, these findings are exactly in accord with what astrological theory has long predicted.

Further, for thousands of years *water sign* people (i.e., Cancer, Scorpio, and Pisces) have been believed by astrologers to be highest on emotionality. And with one exception, this is exactly what Mayo found. *Only four* of the twelve sun signs scored above the mean on emotionality; and in order of strength of emotionality these were: Pisces, Aires, Cancer, and Scorpio. Of these four, only Aires was "out of place". Aires is not a water sign.

It needs to be stressed, of course, that the sun sign represents *only one* small element of a person's natal chart (horoscope). In fact, many astrologers consider the ascendant or *"rising sign"* to be of at least equal importance as the sun sign. And many other practicing astrologers believe the moon sign to be almost as crucial to accurately understanding a person as the sun and ascendant signs. (The ascendant sign is the constellation of stars that is on the horizon at the moment of a person's birth.)

For most contemporary astrologers each human being has twelve signs: one for each of the *eight planets* (not counting the Earth), the sun, the moon, the *ascendant constellation* (rising sign), and the *midheaven constellation*. Thus a professional astrologer looks at where in the heavens each one of these twelve items had been located at the moment of a person's birth. Apart from the rising sign and the midheaven, the other ten items for any given person could have been located anywhere within the 360 degree circle representing the heavens. For convenience astrologers divide the 360 degree circle representing the heavens into twelve equal slices that are known as *houses*. And each one of these twelve *houses* entails implications for a different aspect of human life.

A person's natal chart (horoscope) is nearly unique. It would require in excess of 25,000 years before another person could be born with the exact same horoscope as you, the reader. Contrary to widespread popular impression, almost all contemporary astrologers *reject* the notion that the sun, planets, and constellations of stars, *cause* differences in human behavior or personality. To be sure, the position and fullness of the sun and moon (because of their close proximity to the Earth) may have some temporary effects upon behavior just as they do upon the tides. But the essential core of astrological causation lies in the concept of *synchronicity*, a term originally coined by the late, great psychoanalyst Carl Jung, who at the beginning of his career had been one of Freud's major disciples.

How Astrology Is Believed to Work

Simply put, *synchronicity* means that at the time of a person's birth there is a unique *alignment of nature* in the heavens, and that this alignment of nature, signified by the exact position of all of the planets, sun, moon and stars, closely correlates (1) with the constellation of lessons the person must learn in this particular incarnation and "classroom of life", and (2) with the person's behavioral predispositions, inborn temperament, intelligence, aptitudes, attractiveness, adaptive capacity, and potential problem areas. According to this viewpoint astrology imposes a uniquely different set of *elastic limits* upon each person. And through studying his or her natal chart a person can arrive at a better understanding of what these elastic limits are and of what his or her life purposes are.

Astrology is *NOT deterministic* in that each person is believed by astrologers to be fully capable of exercising free will and self-determination up to the boundaries of his/her elastic limits. Of course, elastic bands *break* when they are pushed beyond their limits. And like elastic bands, each person has his/her own unique set of limits. Nevertheless, each person *chooses* what he/she *does* and *does not* do with each problem area or opportunity that arises in his/her life.

More specifically, the alignment of nature (in the heavens) at a person's birth is believed to constitute a direct reflection of that person's *karma* for this specific incarnation. In essence, life is comprised of an unlimited series of classrooms of learning. For each and every soul, some of these classrooms exist on this (the mortal) side of the veil. And some (probably many more) exist on the "other side" of the veil on innumerable etherial levels at the higher planes of vibration. The ratio of positive to negative (and/or neutral) learning experiences which a person must undergo during any given incarnation or discarnation is simply a reflection of the karma which he or she had worked up in his/her former incarnations and discarnations. The soul chooses the time, place, parents, and the circumstances of its own birth for the lessons it must learn and for the progress it wishes to make during the course of the appointed incarnation. Hence, the model posited by most contemporary astrologers for explaining love-shyness might look something like that which is indicated in *Figure 3*.

In essence, *karma* is the *first cause*; and the synchronistic operation of astrology is nothing more than a manifestation of this first cause ("karmic law"). Thus karma, with astrology as its *overt* and analyzable byproduct, gives rise to the *genes* and to the *congenital problems/advantages* (such as malfunctioning or well functioning enzymes and hormones), which in turn give rise to such key factors as native temperament, attractiveness of appearance, intelligence, gender, etc. These key factors all entail a good, bad, or indifferent social stimulus value. People respond to them in negative or in positive ways. Chronic love-shyness or its polar opposite is thus created. More succinctly, it is created as a byproduct of the person's underlying karma—the *first* cause.

Karma is believed by Spiritualists and by astrologers to follow the immutable laws of the universe which are contained within the universal cosmic intelligence or "universal God-mind" which, in turn, is contained within everything animate and inanimate.

Thus astrological theory does not contradict or disagree with the principles of social learning and of behavior modification. Instead it fills out the picture. Some people are born with a passive, withdrawn inborn temperament and/or they are born into a social group that does not react favorably to passivity and/or to the newly incarnated soul (child) in his/her physical body. Rejection by others combined with an unusually sensitive inborn temperament doubtless leads to a low self-esteem as far as functioning in purely sociable, social situations is concerned which, in turn, leads to intractable love-shyness.

The Present Research

When I first began the data collecting for the research upon which this book is based, I had every intention of studying astrological factors in a very comprehensive way. Unfortunately, most of the love-shy men studied did not know their exact birth times. In order for astrological hypotheses to have been correctly tested, I as researcher would have had to have had access to each respondent's birth time within an accuracy range of *five minutes*. Since it was not feasible to obtain this information, I had to make do with mere birth date data alone as far as most of the respondents were concerned.

Briefly stated, my own analysis corroborated that of Mayo. Hence, significantly more of my chronic love-shys had sun signs of Taurus, Pisces, and Capricorn, than would have been expected by chance. Similarly, the self-confident non-shys I studied had many more Sagittarians

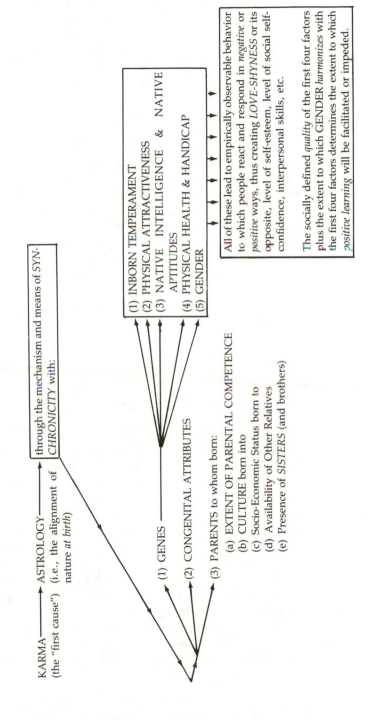

FIGURE THREE

A Causal Model of How Severe Love-Shyness Develops

and Aires people among them than would have been expected by chance. In addition, the following generalizations also appear warrented:

1. Love-shy men have a surfeit of planets located in the 4th, 5th, and 6th houses. This is interesting because in astrology this signals low self-sufficiency combined with high introversion/ inhibition.

2. The chronically love-shy are significantly more likely than self-confident men to have their natal Saturn in the 5th or 7th houses. This is interesting because in astrology Saturn is the planet of restrictions. It is often referred to as the "negative teacher". The 7th house is the house of marriage and partnerships; the 5th house is the house of sex and of children.

3. Chronically love-shy men have an overrepresentation of Mars in Cancer and in Pisces. In astrology Mars is the planet of *energy and drive*. Cancer and Pisces are regarded as the two worst signs for Mars because they are associated with inertia and with energy wastage.

4. Love-shy men tend to have significantly more fixed signs and earth signs in their horoscopes than do self-confident, non-shy men. In astrology such combinations would be associated with inhibition and with stubborn and often intractable problems such as love-shyness.

5. Love-shy men are quite likely to have a natal Saturn that is square or conjunct to the natal sun or natal moon. Many love-shys have Saturn in the same sign as either their sun, moon, or ascendant.

6. Severely love-shy men are significantly more likely than non-shys to have their natal Mars in one of the following four houses: 7th, 6th, 4th, and 3rd, in that order. Severe love-shyness seems to be associated with the natal Mars being *opposite* either the native's ascendant or the native's midheaven—give or take an orb of ten degrees.

7. Severely love-shy men show some tendency for their natal Neptunes to be at or near their midheavens. Neptune is the planet of fantasy, daydreams and illusion. Those with Neptune at or near the midheaven are believed by astrologers to be dominated (ruled) by fantasy and illusion.

8. Severely love-shy men show some preponderance of planets, sun, moon, ascendant, and midheaven, in signs ruled by Venus: i.e., Taurus and Libra. Many love-shy men have at least *two* of the three major astrological elements (sun, ascendant, and moon) in the Venus-ruled Taurus and Libra.

9. Down through the centuries it has been noticed that the severely love-shy (*men* in particular) are substantially more likely than the non-afflicted to have been born during the *May 16 to 19* period than during any other four-day period of the calendar year. The star called *Caput Algol* rules this four-day period. Traditionally this star had been called "The Evil One". And the evidence collected from scores of astrologers (including contemporary ones) indicates that this star does appear to have a detrimental impact upon a person's powers of endurance. Men, in particular, who had been born during this four-day period are highly likely to be *excessively passive*. Further, the *Caput Algol* personality is commonly perceived as being "pleasant but non-competitive" and sort of unambitious.

10. Astrologers determine a person's sign for twelve different items: the sun, the moon, the rising sign, the midheaven, the two inner planets, and the six outer planets. Each of these twelve items had been in some astrological sign at the moment of a person's birth. The severely love-shy are much more likely than the non-afflicted to have been born with *nine or more* of these twelve items in *"negative"* or *"feminine"* signs: i.e., Taurus, Cancer, Virgo, Scorpio, Capricorn, and Pisces.

11. Those born with Jupiter and Saturn *conjunct* (give or take an orb of ten degrees) have an above average vulnerability towards becoming severely love-shy. This is especially true if the conjunction occurs in the 5th or 7th houses.

Implications

Eventually *we will know for sure* whether these and other possible astrological factors correlate with severe love-shyness. If there is a real and significant association between any of these factors and the tendency to develop severe love-shyness, the astrological natal chart will provide society (including medical and education functionaries) with a conspicuous clue from the very beginning as to just exactly which children may be at risk of developing pathological degrees of love-shyness. The astrological natal chart is set at the precise moment a person is officially born into this incarnate world. Therefore, if it should turn out that there is anything really worthwhile to astrology as a diagnostic and predictive tool, it will eventually prove extremely advantageous as such a tool in helping towards the propitious engineering of home and school environments for the love-shy prone. This will serve to effectively block love-shyness symptomology from developing in the first place, as well as all of the other social and psychological factors which are known to be causal antecedents for the development of love-shyness.

Reincarnation

In 1977 the prestigious and esteemed medical JOURNAL OF NERVOUS AND MENTAL DISEASE published two research articles on the subject of reincarnation. Both were written by Dr. Ian Stevenson of the University of Virginia School of Medicine. (See especially his article titled: "The Explanatory Value of the Idea of Reincarnation".)

For the past three decades Dr. Stevenson has traveled all over the world studying cases of young children between the ages of two and six, who possess vivid memories of former incarnations. These memories often incorporate an ability to speak a language which had not been learned (*or even heard*) during the current life. This phenomenon is known as *xenoglossey*. And it is not at all unusual for such children to name names, dates, places, etc., which can be and often are checked out and verified by research teams such as the one headed by Ian Stevenson. In some of the most dramatic cases a three or four year old child will have lucid memories of his wife, sons and daughters in a previous life. Indeed, such children have been known to discuss the most intimate details of their sexual lives vis-a-vis their spouses of a past incarnation. And they articulate their ideas quite fluently and in adult vocabulary.

There are essentially two major methods of studying reincarnation. The first of these is the technique employed by Dr. Stevenson. This involves studying young children with vivid and detailed memories of former lives. The second approach is known as hypnotic age regression. And it involves placing a person into a deep trance and hypnotically regressing him/her back prior to his/her current lifetime. Hypnotic age regression is quite a bit more popular than the first approach because (1) it is far less expensive, and (2) it is easier to accomplish provided that the services of a skilled hypnotist are enlisted. As with the Stevenson approach, detailed data complete with names, dates, places, etc., often surface. Such data can be and very often are checked out and verified empirically. People often commence speaking in a foreign language once they are under a deep trance. Of course, the remarkable thing is that these languages and other information had never been learned by the person in his or her current lifetime.

So extensive is the use of age regression hypnosis today that some of its practitioners have devised a new school of psychotherapy that has come to be known as *past lives therapy*. Since 1976, several books have been published on this approach to psychotherapy, and these include at least a half-dozen that had been written primarily with the lay person in mind. (See especially the works of Netherton, Wambach, and Sutphen, all of which are listed in the bibliography.)

The essential idea behind "past lives therapy" is that pathological, highly debilitating phobias, fears, and other hang-ups are often the result of traumas that had taken place during former incarnations. Therapy proceeds by gradually bringing the patient back to the traumatic event and having him/her *relive* it through the hypnotic process. In other words, just as the conventional psychoanalyst tries to get his/her client to experience a catharsis and a highly emotional abreaction of a traumatic event of his/her *current* life, past lives therapy strives toward this same goal *via hypnosis* with regard to *a past life* or lives.

We do not know why. But past lives psychotherapists have allegedly achieved a far more impressive "cure rate" than have conventional psychoanalysts. (Again, see the writings of Netherton, Wambach, and Sutphen.) Personally, I do not believe that *"insight"* or an emotionally charged "reliving" of a traumatic event (irrespective of whether that event had occurred during the present lifetime or during a past one) could ever prove sufficient to help the severely love-shy man out of his plight. Nevertheless, a full awareness of the ultimate source of one's problem can never hurt and indeed may even help—at least a little bit.

Up to now Netherton, Wambach and Sutphen have not worked with any severely love-shy men. They have worked primarily with female clients who had been phobic or severely anxiety-prone at the time they had been treated. Of course, this does not render their highly impressive and most heartening results any less meaningful or any less important. However, it is certainly to be hoped that their techniques will soon be tried on the severely love-shy.

Implications

The highly detailed memories of past lives which Dr. Stevenson found among certain two-to-six year old children are not very commonplace. But cases do crop up from time to time all over the world, including right here in the United States and Canada. However, when such memories become conspicuously manifest in the life of a child such significant others as parents, peers and teachers feel quite "unnerved" about it and frequently take steps (often punitive in nature) to discourage the phenomena. This is why almost all children forget such memories by the time they reach the age of six. Children become so involved in the excitements and demands of their current existence that their memories of the past tend to become lost.

And so it is with people who discover detailed memories of a past life or lives through hypnotic age regression. Mrs. Ruth Simmons, the quite conventional housewife of Pueblo, Colorado, who had been permitted through hypnosis to recall vivid memories of her former life as Bridey Murphy in 18th century Cork, Ireland, found herself becoming increasingly upset by these memories—particularly because of the tremendous amount of unwanted publicity which they attracted. Like hundreds of other people, Mrs. Simmons chose to terminate her experiences with age-regression hypnosis because the publicity combined with the highly detailed memories that she had been recalling were causing her current life to become increasingly uncomfortable. Nevertheless, many of her quite detailed memories called up specific facts which were subsequently verified by research teams who went to Ireland in order to analyze what they could of 18th century Cork.

I believe that all serious research work on reincarnation entails clear implications for the study of love-shyness. It is true that comparatively few of us ever manage to remember anything of our past lives. But reincarnational memories may impact upon all people in far more *subtle* ways. In essence, *some* of our behavior may be affected by figments of memory of which we are *not consciously aware*, and which we do not think of as being associated with or indicative of past incarnations.

A good analogy here would be the way in which conventional "ESP" operates. We know that all people have extra-sensory perception to *some* extent. Very few people have it to a powerful extent; and most of those who do have it to a powerful extent enjoy this benefit for only a comparatively brief portion of their lives—much as the children in Dr. Stevenson's work managed to sustain their strong reincarnational memories only until about the age of six. Psychic healing ability works the same way. All of us have *some* psychic healing ability. But a miniscule proportion of people command very powerful and amazing abilities along these lines. The ability of most people for serving as a channel for healing energies is quite limited. And some people have even been found to be "negative healers"—sort of like the "brown thumb" person around plants. These "negative healers" unintentionally sap energy away from the sick and make them worse!

Helen Wambach of John F. Kennedy University in Orinda, California, has age-regressed thousands of quite ordinary people. And she has found that virtually everyone appears to have at least some past life memories of which they had been entirely unaware and which could be recaptured. Together with Morris Netherton and Dick Sutphen, Dr. Wambach has been able to show that these memories often impact upon predilections, interests, long-term traits of temperament, fears, career patterns, esthetic and romantic love predilections, etc., in ways that the person had never had any awareness of at all.

Again, as with "ESP" and psychic healing, very few people recall vivid thoughts and feelings or traumatic events from past lives. However, virtually everyone tested by Wambach recalled *something*. And those with serious psychoemotional adjustment problems often recalled a rich supply of memories when they were hypnotically age-regressed. Through the reliving of these memories, many people have allegedly had their present adjustment problems quite fully remedied.

In sum, if reincarnation impacts at all on human beings its influence is not likely to be limited to people such as Ruth Simmons or to four-year old children who vividly recall a life as someone's father or mother in another time and place. Such memories need not be a manifest part of everyday consciousness in order to wield an impact upon peoples' lives. Conventional empirical scientists have forgotten that man is part spirit and not all physical brain and body. If the spirit mind is indeed immortal, then subtle facets of its past experiences during former incarnations may well impact in significant and long neglected ways upon the development in the current life of such pesky problems as severe love-shyness.

Psychodormia

During the past twenty years a great deal of work has been done at leading universities on the subject of Kirlian photography. Kirlian photography is a form of electromagnetic photography which is capable of capturing on film a likeness of the electromagnetic energy body ("aura") which suffuses the human body as well as all other living things.

During the past few years a number of psychologists have begun using Kirlian photography as a diagnostic device. For example, New York City clinical psychologist Lee Steiner has found marked differences between the Kirlian auras of socially self-confident people and those of individuals who are inhibited and shy. Happy, self-confident people have auras which are vibrant and brilliantly pulsating with a full and steady glow of strong, white light. Shy and inhibited people, on the other hand, tend to have weak and uneven auras. Dr. Steiner has labeled this latter pattern as "*psychodormia*".

Numerous types of people have auras which display the psychodormia pattern. Patients with hypoglycemia, iron deficiency anemia, neurotic difficulties, excessive tiredness due to overwork or insufficient sleep, as well as shyness and inhibition, all tend to exude the very weak and uneven Kirlian aura that is indicative of psychodormia. The important point for our purposes, however, is that the Kirlian aura gradually becomes fuller and stronger to the extent that a prescribed, comprehensive therapeutic regimen is followed and the undesirable symptoms begin to dissipate. In other words, once a person is cured of psychodormia, his/her Kirlian aura manifests itself in a full, rich glow.

In sum, the condition of a person's aura (etheric or energy body) appears to be highly associated with shyness and inhibition. A person's life situation can affect his/her aura. And auric health can and does substantially influence the nature and progress of a person's life.

Part Two

THE RESEARCH STUDY AND THE DATA IT UNCOVERED

Chapter 5

How The Information Was Obtained

The purpose of this chapter is two-fold: (1) to provide a comprehensive summary of the major personal characteristics of the love-shy and the non-shy samples; and (2) to provide a clear and understandable statement as to how the research data obtained for this book were obtained. In a book of this nature there is nothing to be gained by an elaborate discussion of statistical and methodological issues or procedures. However, the reader should have an accurate awareness of the nature of the people studied. Such an awareness will render my discussion of the research results far more interesting and meaningful than it otherwise would be.

Who Is "Love-Shy"?

At the outset it is important for the reader to have a clear understanding of the nature of love-shyness and of the key characteristics shared by all the people studied for this research. In essence, a love-shy person is one who possesses *each and every one* of the following seven characteristics:

(1) He is a *virgin*; in other words, he has never had sexual intercourse.
(2) He is a person who very rarely goes out socially with women. None of the love-shys studied for this book had dated more than four times during the year prior to being interviewed.
(3) He is a person without a past history of any emotionally close, meaningful relationships of a romantic and/or sexual nature with any member of the opposite sex.
(4) He is a person who has suffered and is continuing to suffer emotionally because of a lack of meaningful female companionship. In short, he is a person *who desperately wishes* to have

a relationship with a woman, but does not have one because of shyness.

(5) He is a man who becomes extremely anxiety-ridden over so much as the mere thought of asserting himself vis-a-vis a woman in a casual, friendly way. This is the essence of "love-shyness".

(6) He is a man who is *strictly heterosexual* in his romantic and erotic orientations. In other words, he is a person who is *in no way* a homosexual.

(7) He is *male*. No female love-shys were studied for this research.

Why Study Men Only?

In regard to point #7, it is recognized that shyness afflicts women in about the same ratio and proportion as it affects men. However, it is also recognized that love-shyness is a far more deleterious condition in the male than it is in the female. In American society it is the *male* who is required to make the first move when it comes to the initiating of romantic relationships. This remains a hard, fast, absolute requirement of the male gender that has not been reduced or mitigated in any way by the social changes that have been instigated by the women's liberation movement. To be sure, contemporary norms do permit a woman to initiate contact with a man *after* a relationship has already commenced. But the norms do not permit a woman to make the first or initial contact with a man; nor do they enable a woman to feel comfortable about the idea of initiating sexual love-making with a man *even after* a love relationship has gotten started.

As a result of these norms, chronic love-shyness entails far deeper and more thoroughgoing consequences for the life of an afflicted male than it does for the life of an afflicted female. For example, most love-shy women manage to successfully pass through the various stages of dating and courtship; and they manage to do this at the normal ages. Simply put, the very shy young woman is *no less likely* to date and to marry than is the self-confident, non-shy woman. Moreover, unless she is well below average in "looks" there is evidence that she is no more likely than the typical self-confident woman to suffer deprivation of male companionship.

In essence, even very shy women marry. Love-shy men cannot and do not marry irrespective of how strong their desires might be to contract a marriage. Inasmuch as love-shyness blocks and impedes men from living a normal life *and does not do this for women*, it is clear that love-shyness is a far more momentous problem for males than it is for females. Study after study have presented irrefutable evidence to the effect that *men need women a very great deal more than women need men.* Women who for any reason remain in the single, never married category almost always manage to make an emotionally healthy adjustment. In fact, several research investigators have found spinsters to be a happier, better adjusted lot than married women! In stark contrast, the single, never married man has been found to be far more vulnerable than the married man (and the spinster) to a wide range of physical health and social adjustment problems—to say nothing of psychoemotional problems!

A key reason for my choosing to limit my research to the problem of shyness in males is the fact that male shyness is a great deal more likely than female shyness to be associated with *neuroticism*. In essence, shy women are not any more likely than non-shy women to be neurotic. In stark contrast, shy men are a very great deal more likely than non-shy men to be quite seriously neurotic.

Most single, never married men are a burden both to themselves and to society, whereas most single, never married women are not. Desperately wishing to marry but being incapable of doing so because of shyness renders the situation of the love-shy male all the more problematic and deserving of serious study. More succinctly, it is only through understanding the plight of the heterosexual man who is "single, never married" *against his most deeply felt wishes and desires* that we will be able to offer and provide constructive help.

The "Felt Deprivation" Concept

I don't believe that anyone can be correctly classified as *"love-shy"* unless he truly craves emotionally meaningful *female* companionship. Deprivation is never enough by itself to cause mental anguish, pain and suffering. A person cannot *feel* deprived of something *unless and until* he actually wants the thing of which he is being deprived. A person who truly *feels* deprived of something he very dearly wants will necessarily suffer a very great deal (1) from anxiety, and (2) from very painful and highly distracting feelings of preoccupation. He will not be able to concentrate effectively on his work or, if he is a student, on his studies. He will very likely be an underachiever because his intensely painful feelings of deprivation impede him from directing his energies towards constructive ends.

If the deprived person is accorded an opportunity to work towards the thing he so strongly desires, his energy-wasting preoccupation and distractability will rapidly dissipate. However, the love-shy man cannot do this. The love-shy man is prevented from working towards his female companionship goal by his intractable shyness and inhibition, and by the inordinately strong fears of interpersonal anxiety that accompany love-shyness and which are intrinsic to it. Simply put, the mere thought of asserting himself in a friendly way vis-a-vis a girl whom he finds attractive fills a love-shy man with overwhelmingly painful (and forbidding) anxiety feelings. Hence, he can only continue to feel preoccupied and painfully distracted.

Criterion #4 for determining who is and who is not love-shy is of crucial and indispensable importance to the research upon which this book is based. Without such a criterion there would inevitably be a good many men getting into the sample who are not personally bothered very much by the fact that they do not have any loving female companionship in their lives. It is important to realize that human beings differ in the extent of their needs for female companionship and for love. A person who is deprived *but who does not feel deprived* cannot be a problem either to himself or to his society or community. In short, deprivation on an *objective* level is not the thing to look for in understanding love-shyness and the many problems to which it gives rise. It is how a person feels on a *subjective* level that *really* matters. And this is why I made sure that no one got into the love-shy samples unless they very deeply and strongly desired the emotionally meaningful companionship of a woman.

In sum, the problem of love-shyness can be deemed to exist in a man only when that man: (1) deeply and sincerely craves the love and companionship of a woman, and (2) when the mere thought of asserting himself in a friendly way vis-a-vis a woman he finds attractive fills him with extremely painful anxiety feelings. Of course, inasmuch as this study was to concern itself strictly with love-shyness among *heterosexual* males, criteria had to be established which would accurately differentiate heterosexual research respondents from those who might be homosexual. It is to this important matter that we now turn.

Distinguishing Heterosexuals from Homosexuals

In order for my research to make any sense at all I had to be certain that my samples of love-shy men did not include any homosexuals among their ranks. This is an important issue because young men who are heterosexually inactive and who do not participate in conventional courtship activities are often viewed as being homosexual.

Today most social scientists are in agreement that the following *four* criteria accurately distinguish heterosexuals from homosexuals:

(1) In order for a person to be considered a heterosexual he must agree that throughout his life his romantic infatuations (romantic fantasies and daydreams) had always been directed towards people of the opposite sex rather than towards people of his own sex. Even during the earliest years of elementary school, homosexuals tend to have romantic daydreams about loving and being loved by attractive male classmates. In contrast, heterosexuals have romantic fantasies about pretty girl classmates.

(2) Heterosexuals always fantasy being with a female partner, *never* a male partner, whenever they masturbate. In contrast, the homosexual always fantasies being with a male partner whenever he masturbates.

(3) In order for a person to be a heterosexual he must *very strongly prefer* the idea of having sexual intercourse with a woman to the idea of having sex with a man. (All of the love-shys studied for this book were virgins; none had ever been to bed with anyone of *either* gender.)

(4) In order for a person to be a true heterosexual he must define himself (*self-image*) as a heterosexual, and not as a homosexual or bisexual.

Early in each interview questions were asked that were of pertinence to each one of the four foregoing points. If a respondent displayed any ambivalence with respect to any of the four issues the interview was terminated. In other words, respondents whose heterosexuality was in doubt were simply not used.

Interestingly, 94 percent of the love-shy men who were interviewed for this study turned out to be strong believers in homosexual rights. Yet at the same time every single man interviewed for this study indicated disgust at the mere thought of kissing or making love to another man. In this regard criterion #3 was a good deal more than satisfied. These love-shy men did not merely "prefer" the idea of making love to a woman over the idea of making love to a man. Loving and romancing a beautiful woman was the only thing many of these deprived men ever seemed to think about in their almost incessant fantasies and daydreams. And the idea of doing these things with another man was something which none of the 300 love-shy men whom I interviewed could even fathom.

With regard to points #1 and #2, social scientists have learned in recent years that *romantic* interests and fantasies crop up in most people's lives a good deal earlier than do *sexual* interests and fantasies. In fact, most Americans commence their strong *romantic* interests in members of the opposite sex some time during their elementary school years.

Moreover, these romantic interests and fantasies appear to be very heavily affected by *esthetic* considerations, whereas burgeoning sexual interests in males appear to be little affected by esthetics. For example, the nine-year old boy has fantasies about befriending and spending time with the *pretty* nine-year-old female classmate: *never* the female classmate who is "less than pretty".

Studies of the childhoods of hundreds of homosexuals have revealed that most homosexuals had begun becoming infatuated with the "pretty faces" of certain *boys* some time around the ages of ten or eleven. At such early ages sex tends to be pretty well removed from a boy's conscious awareness; this is as true for homosexual boys as it is for heterosexual boys. At such early ages most pre-homosexuals had never even heard of the word "homosexual", and had no idea as to what it meant or that they were displaying interest patterns which placed them in that social category.

An identifying feature of most of the love-shy men studied for this book was that throughout their formative years they neither enjoyed nor fantasized about either being with or playing with members of their own gender. They did not enjoy the "rough and tumble" play style of their fellow boys. And in addition to their distaste for the rougher play of the all-male peer group, a key reason for their wanting to avoid the all-male peer group was the fact that it did not contain "any pretty people".

Heterosexual love-shy males appear to develop a sense of beauty significantly earlier in life than do most people of either gender. And this predilection for the enjoying of beauty seems to become *a driving and heavily preoccupying need* for many of them. Several of the love-shys told me that even when they were third grade youngsters they could remember not being able to concentrate on what the teacher was talking about because they were off in a world of rewarding bliss wherein they were enjoying the loyal and steadfast companionship of a very pretty little girl who was one grade below them—in the second grade.

This very early need for the intense companionship of an opposite sexed age-mate is something which scholars have never found to prevail in the backgrounds of male homosexuals. Pre-homosexual little boys very often do become romantically and esthetically fixated upon other pretty little *boys*. In essence, the pre-homosexual little boy never chooses a *little girl* to daydream and fantasize about.

One of the strongest indicators of male homosexuality is that of being more interested in sex play with boys than with girls: 78 percent of adult homosexuals in one study said that they had felt this way as children, whereas 82 percent of adult heterosexuals said that they had *not* felt this way as children. In the current study upon which this book is based, *not one* love-shy man out of the 300 surveyed had had any preference at all during childhood for sex play with boys over sex play with girls. Furthermore, not a single one of the 300 love-shys had had any *actual* sex play experience during childhood or adolescence with a member of *either* gender. As children many of the men I interviewed had *wanted* to enjoy sex play with a girl. But not surprisingly they simply did not have the nerve to pull it off—or, for that matter, even to attempt pulling it off!

In short, *social withdrawal* appears to have long been the key earmark of the love-shy. Even though the love-shy are quite clearly heterosexual in their preferences and orientations, they engage in significantly less of BOTH heterosexual AND homosexual sex play during childhood and adolescence than do the non-shy. Interestingly, fully 23 percent of the 200 *non-shy* heterosexuals interviewed for this study had engaged in some homosexual sex play with their male peers as young teenagers. In contrast, *not a single one* of the 300 heterosexual love-shy men interviewed had ever done this. And not a single one had ever even *wanted* to do it. Indeed, all indicated that throughout childhood (as now) they would have been revolted at the mere thought. Then, as now, they wanted to romance a *female*, not another male.

Finally, most homosexual males become aware of their romantic-sexual attraction to other males sometime between their tenth and thirteenth years. It has been found that almost all become aware of this attraction by the time the seventeenth birthday rolls around. The 300 love-shy men and the 200 non-shy men studied for this research were all well beyond their seventeenth year in chronological age. Hence, there can be little doubt as to the true heterosexuality of all of the 500 men who were studied for this research.

The "Closet Heterosexual" Concept

The term "closet queen" or "closet homosexual" is often used in reference to the "gay" man or woman who has not as yet "come out". I believe that this concept is equally useful as a *diagnostic label* for the *heterosexual* man who does not date or informally interact with women even though he would much prefer to be able to do so. To be sure, "closet homosexuality" is only occasionally caused by shyness. Indeed, there is evidence that love-shyness is about equally prevalent among the ranks of homosexuals as it is among the ranks of heterosexuals. More succinctly, there probably is no difference between heterosexuals and homosexuals in this regard.

However, whereas *closet heterosexuality* appears to be *almost exclusively* caused by severe love-shyness, *MOST closet homosexuality* is due to the fear of being detected by potentially hostile employers, family members, heterosexual friends and acquaintances, etc. Because of the many constructive social and political changes that were wrought throughout the decades of the 1960s and 1970s, closet homosexuality appears to be a good deal less commonplace today than it formerly had been. Today most homosexuals eventually *do* "come out of the closet". And the evidence is unequivocal that homosexuals have gained enormously in mental health, personal pride and self-esteem as a result of this. As a direct consequence of their "coming out", they have become of far greater value both to themselves and to their respective communities.

The only sort of "closet heterosexual" whose lack of social involvement with women may not ordinarily be due to love-shyness is the Roman Catholic priest or brother, Buddhist monk, or other similar religious functionary who for his own religious reasons has taken vows to avoid informal heterosexual interaction with non-family members. Of course, there are some graduate students in American universities who have sold themselves a bill of goods to the effect that they are not really interested in the "distraction" posed by women. Many of these seemingly dedicated and very serious young men have a good deal in common psychologically with the religious functionary who similarly studies books a very great deal and who has taken vows of celebacy.

On the other hand, for many ultra-serious graduate students the avoidance of women for the alleged reason of improving concentration may well constitute more of a "cop out" rationalization than anything else. Research evidence has shown that for all fields of scholarly endeavor, men with a close, loving relationship with a woman earn significantly better grades than do those without the benefit of this. Moreover, after such heterosexually attached men have completed their studies they move ahead in their respective fields significantly faster than do those who had avoided female companionship while in school.

Finally, it has been found that *unattached* male university graduate students (those without girl friends or wives) have a great deal in common psychologically with men studying to become Roman Catholic priests. Using the widely employed *Minnesota Multiphasic Personality Inventory* ("MMPI"), several researchers have found that both groups evidence far below average mental and emotional health. In fact, graduate students in psychology and seminary students preparing for the priesthood have both been found to have "MMPI" profiles as bad as those of long-term residents in mental hospitals! For example, both groups tend to score far above average on "schizoid tendencies"—a diagnostic category having to do with social withdrawal and social isolation.

The "Male Lesbian" Concept

Another potentially useful diagnostic label is that of *"male lesbian"*. On the surface the whole idea appears ludicrous; everyone knows that lesbians are female homosexuals who want to "make it" vis-a-vis another woman. Yet in selecting the men to be interviewed for this research the seemingly incongruous notion of "male lesbian" kept staring me in the face again and again. For this reason, I don't think that any book pretending to be complete on the subject of chronic love-shyness *in men* can afford to ignore the "male lesbian" idea.

Specifically, a "male lesbian" is a heterosexual man who wishes that he had been born a woman, but who (even if he had been a woman) could only make love to another woman and never to a man. Unlike the transsexual, the "male lesbian" does not feel himself to be "a woman trapped inside the body of a man". Moreover, none of the love-shy men studied for this research entertained any wishes or fantasies of any kind pertinent to the idea of obtaining a sex change operation. All wanted to keep their male genitalia; all wanted to remain as males. However, all deeply envied the perogatives of the female gender and truly believed that these perogatives fitted their own inborn temperaments far more harmoniously than the pattern of behavioral expectations to which males are required to adhere. The following represent some typical comments from love-shy males:

> "From the time I was very, very young, I had always wished that I had been born a girl. I know I would have been much happier as a girl because I have always been attracted to the kinds of things that girls do. But every time I think about how great it would have been if I had been born a girl, I immediately realize that if I had been born a girl I would be a lesbian. I have always strongly disliked the idea of doing anything with my own sex. I despise men. Just thinking about making love to a man, even as a woman, makes me want to throw up! But I would also never want to play football or baseball or any of the other games boys are supposed to like playing. I never wanted to have *anything* to do with the male sex, on any level. So, like if I had been born a girl as I would have wanted, I would definitely be a lesbian because I'd be falling in love with and having sex with girls instead of with men." (40-year old heterosexual love-shy man.)

> "To be perfectly frank, I don't think I would be shy at all if it wasn't for this goddam norm that says that only the man can make the first move with a woman in asking for dates. I mean if both sexes had equal responsibility for having to suffer the indignity of having to make the first move, I just know I would have been married fourteen or maybe fifteen years ago." (35-year old love-shy man.)

"Well, I don't know if I'd actually like to be a woman. All I know is that I've always envied women because they can play the passive role and still get married. I think our society is extremely cruel to men. It treats them like second class citizens all the time while women get treated like prima donnas. When you write your book I hope you emphasize the fact that men have feelings too. I mean, men are human beings too, and they have feelings just as much as any woman does. I think it's rotten and stinking the way it's always the man who is made to suffer—like in the military, for example. Just because a person happens to be a male he has to suffer all the horrors and indignities of the military establishment and the selective slavery system. If you're a man you're not supposed to feel any pain. You're not supposed to have any feelings. You're supposed to be just like a piece of steel and press forward no matter what harm or pain comes to you. Well, I was lucky in being able to avoid the military— thank God! But when it comes to getting a woman there doesn't seem to be any way of getting around these extremely cruel social rules that insist that only the man can be allowed to make the first approach with a woman . . . . If I was writing a book on shyness I'd hollar and shout on every page that the only way to solve the problem is to change these cruel social rules. You tell your readers that we've got to change the rules. And we've got to keep telling our daughters from the time they are little that they have just as much responsibility as men for making the first move in starting romantic relationships." (38-year old love-shy man.)

Male lesbians differ from *both* transsexuals *and* homosexuals in that they cannot conceive of themselves making love to a man. For example, after sex change surgery the male transsexual almost always wants to begin making love *to a man* AS A WOMAN. The male homosexual wants to make love AS A MAN *to a man*. The *male lesbian*, on the other hand, wishes that he had been born a woman. But he always makes it clear that if he indeed had been born a woman he would be a *full-fledged lesbian*. In other words, he would want to socialize exclusively with women and he would choose female partners exclusively for love-making and for sexmaking activity. In short, a secret fantasy of many love-shy men is to be a beautiful woman who lives with and makes love with another beautiful woman.

The love-shy men studied for this book all reluctantly accepted the fact that they are males. And none of them had ever revealed any *transvestite* tendencies. Thus, none of them had ever experienced any urge to dress up as a woman or to put on lipstick or nail polish, etc. Since they could not be a woman, most of them visualized themselves *as a man* romancing a beautiful woman. And most of them had begun doing this from a much earlier age in life than had the large majority of non-shy heterosexual men.

As the later chapters of this book will clearly demonstrate, many of the love-shy men studied never liked their own gender very much. As young children most of them had avoided playmates of their own sex. And most of them had envied the girls' play groups and play activities. They had come to view conventional societal expectations as cruel and callously insensitive because they perceived the girls' peer groups and play activities as being their "natural terrain". Hence, they had often thought to themselves that if they could only find a way of gaining acceptance into the all-female peer group they would find happiness, inner peace and contentment.

From a very early age in life onward, the love-shys felt somehow "different" from their male peers. Something inside of themselves told them that they did not belong around male peers. Male peer group activities appeared foreign and often totally unappealing to them. And they tended to view males and their peer group activities with feelings of total and complete alienation and detachment. As one love-shy man expressed it, "Whenever I watched the boys in my school playing I might just as well have been watching a bunch of bear cubs play. I knew they were having a good time; but I just didn't feel that I belonged to their species. I knew that I belonged somewhere else, but I did not know how to find that someplace else." The "someplace else" referred to was, of course, an all-girl peer group.

And so the *male lesbian* (1) does not want to play with males, (2) does not want to make love to or experience sex with males, (3) does not have male recreational interests, and (4) does not even want to procreate male children. The vast majority of the love-shy men interviewed for this book confessed that if they ever did become fathers they would want to have *girl* children only—NO BOYS. In stark contrast, only one percent of the self-confident, non-shy men felt that way. In fact, the non-shy men preferred the idea of fathering male children to the idea of fathering female children by a ratio of almost three to two.

Three Samples Were Studied

Three different samples of men were obtained for this research. These three groups were as follows:

(1) 100 single, never married men, all of whom were between the ages of 35 and 50 at the time they were interviewed. Each of these men met all seven of the criteria for love-shyness that were delineated on page 117, the first page of this chapter.

(2) 200 single, never married men, all of whom were (a) full-time or part-time college or university students, and all of whom

were (b) between the ages of 19 and 24 at the time they were interviewed. Each of these men met all seven criteria for love-shyness that were delineated on page 000.

(3) 200 single, never married men, all of whom were very self-confident and *non-shy* vis-a-vis the opposite sex. These 200 men were all (a) full-time or part-time college or university students; and all of them were (b) between the ages of 19 and 24 at the time they were interviewed.

Sample #3 is known in the social sciences as a *comparison group*. The non-shy comparison group was composed of people who were very similar to the love-shys on a host of social and demographic background factors. None of the members of this comparison group had any current problems with love-shyness. In essence, none were love-shy. In fact, all 200 members of the comparison group viewed themselves as being above average in social self-confidence vis-a-vis members of the opposite sex.

Technically speaking, samples *one* and *two* are known as "*experimental groups*". Each of these two samples was composed exclusively of love-shy men. The presence of a comparison group in a research study often permits the making of educated and reasoned deductions about *causation*. In this study I was very interested in determining the causes of love-shyness and the various factors that may be associated with it. The uncovering of lines of causation is what any scientific enterprise is all about.

To the extent that we are able to arrive at an awareness of the various major causes behind a phenomenon, to that extent we are likely to be in a better position to predict, to control, to cure, and possibly even *to prevent* the phenomenon from occurring in the future. In the case of this study on love-shyness, it is possible to deduce probable *causes* that are responsible for severe shyness by comparing the data obtained for the two love-shy groups (experimental groups) with the data obtained for the comparison group of non-shy men.

Ideally it would have been desirable for me to have included a *second* comparison group. In other words, it would have been helpful to this research had it been feasible to have a group of non-shy men in the 35 to 50 year old age bracket. The major reason why I chose not to obtain such a comparison group is that the majority of non-shy heterosexual men in the 35 to 50 year age group are married. Married men are no longer involved with the various problems, trials and tribulations pertinent to dating and courtship activities. In fact, their interactional style vis-a-vis the female population is defined and delimited in very significant ways by the fact of being married. To be sure, a sample of non-shy divorced, widowed and separated men could have been drawn up for this study. But such a sample would hardly have been adequately representative of well-adjusted, non-shy men in the 35 to 50 year old age range.

Limiting the non-shy comparison group to single, never married young men in the 19 to 24 year old age range served this study well in providing the contrast that was required: By comparing and contrasting the backgrounds of the non-shys with those of the love-shys (both groups), it became feasible to arrive at meaningful conclusions as to what the *key causes* of love-shyness most probably are. In virtually every comparison that was made, the younger love-shys differed from the non-shys *in exactly the same way as the older love-shys differed from the non-shys*. And this fact can be viewed as assuring the reader that the differences which are highlighted between the non-shys and the love-shys are *real differences*. In essence, it is likely that many of these differences have a very strong bearing upon the *causes* of the love-shyness problem.

Sample Heterogeneity

The younger love-shys would be described in social science lingo as a more *heterogeneous* group of men than the older love-shys. This means that the *younger* love-shys include among their ranks men of a wider range of different prognoses than is the case for the older love-shy men. Simply put, many of the younger love-shys will eventually solve their love-shyness problem (or somehow have it solved for them). And they will consequently manage to marry and have children as per their very strong desires.

On the other hand, we may rightly suspect that very few of the *older* love-shys will ever be able to marry and have children according to their desires. United States Government statistics indicate that only about *5 percent* of men still "single, never married" after age 35, will *ever* marry. Thus it would seem to be a good guess that for the severely and chronically love-shy single, never married, the percent *ever marrying* beyond the age of 35 is most probably a good deal lower than 5!

In essence, we may speculate that the younger love-shy men include among their ranks *some* individuals who will go on to become 35 to 50 year old "single, never married" love-shys. On the other hand, it is also quite likely that at least half of these younger love-shy men will eventually work out a way of getting their love-shyness problem solved *before* becoming old enough to qualify for entrance into a group of 35 to 50 year old heterosexual love-shy virgins.

Because the younger love-shys represent a more heterogeneous group than the older love-shys do, we may reasonably expect that most facets of their backgrounds are probably less extreme than those of the older love-shys. In other words, we can expect that most of the behavioral and background differences between the non-shys and the love-shys will be *substantially less* for the younger love-shys than for the older ones. Thus when the love-shy men are compared to the non-shy men, the younger love-shys can be expected to be a lot more similar to the non-shys than the older love-shy men can be expected to be. And this is exactly what was found as will become clear to the reader as he/she makes his/her way through this book.

Hence, the younger (university) love-shy men probably include significantly fewer intractable cases. All of these younger men do indeed suffer from severe and chronic love-shyness. But for many of them it is likely that events will ultimately conspire at some future time to relieve their painful inability to obtain meaningful and rewarding female companionship. Much of the young lives of these men had already been wasted as far as their not having been able to experience or enjoy any kind of a social life was concerned. Again, for many of the younger love-shys this inability and lack might ultimately prove quite temporary; for the *older* love-shys it will ultimately prove tragically permanent.

Reliability

A key advantage behind studying two different samples of love-shy men is that an opportunity is provided for ascertaining the *reliability* of findings. The term "reliability" here means *repeatability*. Every researcher must be concerned about whether different samples of people with the same problem will reflect the same pattern of findings. If the findings obtained for one group of love-shy men turn out quite different from the findings obtained for a second group of love-shy men, there might be good reason to question the accuracy and validity of any conclusions that might be drawn. Simply put, if research findings turn out to be quite different for two groups of the *same* (*love-shy*) description, serious doubt would be cast upon the overall reliability of any of the obtained findings. On the other hand, if essentially the *same* findings accrued for two totally separate groups of love-shy men, we could be reasonably confident as to the *reliability* (repeatability) of the data. In essence, we could feel reasonably confident about obtaining basically the same research findings for *any* group of love-shy men we might choose to study, no matter where in the western world those love-shy men might reside.

However, one note of caution is in order here. It is of the utmost importance that different researchers working in different geographic areas obtain their love-shy samples using the same criteria as to what does and does not constitute love-shyness. To the extent that different researchers define "love-shyness" in different ways, quite different find-ings can quite legitimately be expected with each new study that is published.

As mentioned earlier, Philip Zimbardo employed a very loose approach for determining who is and who is not shy. He simply asked people whether or not they consider themselves to be shy. And 42 percent usually said "yes". Now 42 percent is a rather large fraction of the population. Moreover, most of the 42 percent who said "yes" did not have their day-to-day lives "cramped" or harmed to any *major* extent by their respective shyness problems.

On the other hand, when I first began the study to be dealt with in this book I realized that the lives of certain victims of shyness are *severely* harmed and encroached upon by love-shyness. After all, if a person cannot date at all, if he is deprived of any opportunities for marriage, sexual expression (apart from masturbation), and from family formation, etc., then it is quite clear that his shyness wields a continuing and very destructive, debilitating impact upon his life.

Hence, I decided that it was this highly debilitating, chronic and intractable type of shyness that was really worth studying. This is not to imply that lesser kinds of shyness are unimportant or that they are not worth studying and understanding. The point is that we need to get a good grip on the more serious varieties of the problem first because they cause the most suffering and wastage of human resources. The fact that a very high proportion of the less serious forms of shyness undergo spontaneous remission seems to further suggest that the everyday "gar-den variety" shyness may have a very different constellation of under-lying causes than the more serious forms of love-shyness that are dealt with in this book. And indeed if the causes are different, then different forms of therapy and of preventive efforts may ultimately be warrented.

The Prevalence of Love-Shyness

My own analysis has convinced me that at any given point in time about 1.5 percent of all American heterosexual males suffer from severe love-shyness. Thus chronic love-shyness among heterosexual males is probably somewhat less commonplace than is homosexuality. However, the *total number* of American males afflicted at any given point in time is actually quite high. I would place the figure at approximately 1,695,000. In other words, I think there is good reason to suspect that there are presently in excess of one-and-one-half million severely love-shy males resident in the United States. This estimate includes males of all ages. It does *not* include women, and it does not include homosexuals of either gender. Further, I think there is good reason to suspect that the large, urban centers of the United States attract more than their proportional share of the love-shy. This is particularly true for the New York, Los Angeles, San Francisco, Boston, New Orleans, Chicago, and Seattle metropolitan areas.

How the Respondents Were Obtained

In 1979, Auburn University accorded me a sizable financial grant for purposes of studying the love-shyness problem. This grant served two very important purposes: (1) it lent an ambiance of importance and respectability to the project; and (2) it enabled me to pay each cooperative respondent a small amount for his time. To be sure, $10 is not very much money for an extensive interview that often lasted in excess of three hours. Nevertheless, money talks; and even a small amount of it has a way of opening doors and assuring a high level of quality cooperation.

The Younger Love-Shy Men

The cooperation of 200 19 to 24 year old men (all with the *seven love-shyness characteristics* delineated on page 000) was obtained from the following seven campuses: (1) University of California at Los Angeles; (2) California State University at Northridge; (3) New York University; (4) City University of New York; (5) Auburn University; (6) Westfield State College; and (7) State University of New York at Stony Brook. In addition, 24 men (12 percent of the total sample) were drawn from the membership of a New York area commercial dating service. All of these men were similarly enrolled in classes at a number of area colleges.

With the exception of the 25 men interviewed on the Auburn University campus in Auburn, Alabama, all of the younger love-shys had grown up in the suburbs of major west and east coast metropolitan areas. Parenthetically, there is no evidence that the 25 Auburn love-shys were any less severely afflicted with their problem than their 175 fellow sufferers from the much more highly urbanized west and east coasts.

For the obtaining of the university respondents, announcements were placed on bulletin boards in (1) classroom buildings, (2) in dormitories, and (3) in off-campus laundermats. These announcements briefly described the nature of the study and the type of respondents that would be needed. They also indicated the $10 reward that would be accorded the appropriate individuals for participation in the study.

I had already been aware of the fact that love-shy people seldom have telephones. In fact, severely love-shy people often find it too threatening to use a telephone even for the making of impersonal, business contacts. Since love-shy men often choose to write letters in situations wherein most people would simply opt to make a telephone call, the bulletin board announcements that were used all requested that interested men contact me by mail at a clearly delineated address.

Because I was inviting responses from severely shy young men who often harbor strong inhibitions blocking self-disclosure vis-a-vis strangers, I wanted to make the announcements as (1) non-threatening, and (2) inviting, as I possibly could. I also wanted to arouse the love-shys' curiosity. I therefore pointed out that I was a licensed therapeutic counselor in the State of California, and that I was particularly interested in finding ways whereby the social system could be restructured so as to better meet the needs of love-shy men. Hence, the announcements all stated that young men who were very shy vis-a-vis women had long been totally ignored by politicians, university and college administrators, social event coordinators; and that the time had finally come for something constructive to be done to remedy this situation.

Thus, most of what little research work has been done on shyness has started off from the basic premise that shyness is the *victim's* problem, the *victim's* fault, and the *victim's* responsibility. It has started off from the premise that any ultimate remedy for the shyness problem would have to come from the *victim himself*. In contrast, the bulletin board announcements used for this study proclaimed the fact that love-shy men are human beings as worthy of dignity and respect as anyone else; and that *society* had a responsibility in the *causing* and ultimately in the *prevention and cure* of love-shyness. In addition, the announcements clearly indicated a recognition of the fact that love-shyness is by far the most painful and life-destructive of all the various forms of shyness—and that it is the form of shyness that requires the most immediate attention from the "powers that be".

Finally the bulletin board announcements briefly described the essential respondent characteristics that the study would require. For example, in order to qualify for an interview and for the $10 payment, each respondent would have to be (1) heterosexual; (2) male; (3) virginal; (4) never or very rarely dates; (5) for a very long time desperately desirous of the emotionally meaningful love and companionship of a member of the opposite sex; (6) lacking any history of emotionally meaningful involvement (other than through fantasies and daydreams) with the other sex; and (7) extremely anxiety-prone at the mere thought of friendly self-assertion vis-a-vis a person of the opposite sex.

This bulletin board method worked, although progress was slow. Over a lengthy period of time letters trickled in from interested potential respondents. And each respondent was contacted in person and screened. Some of the people who contacted me could not be used for the study because they did not fit one or more of the seven delineated criteria. However, better than eighty percent of those who wrote to me did fit all of the criteria and were eventually interviewed—in most cases within a few days of the original contact by mail.

The bulletin board announcements had requested that respondents specify the times and places that would prove convenient and comfortable for them. Of course, privacy and security from interruptions had to be assured; and these matters posed little problem. A three-hour time block had to be secured; and that similarly posed fewer problems than I had anticipated. In fact, many of the interviews ran beyond four hours. People with strong inhibitions against self-disclosure often "open up" surprisingly well when they are with somebody who shows a sincere interest in them, and who makes himself known as someone who is looking for ways of catalyzing society into taking steps towards the direct helping of love-shy people.

I, the author of this book, am the person who conducted all of the interviews for the study. I accomplished this by going to the appointed place at the appointed time as mutually agreed beforehand by letter. With some respondents two or three or even four letters prefaced the actual interview. Some respondents needed various types of assurances. And in some cases interview appointments had to be changed or confirmed.

Finally, some of the information required for this study had to be obtained by self-administered questionnaire. All such information was obtained with me (the interviewer) present in the room. This procedure proved quite helpful because (1) it enabled respondents to receive prompt and immediate answers to any questions they might have had concerning certain questionnaire items; and (2) it prevented a lot of time-consuming callbacks. Simply put, the procedure employed for the data collecting phase of this study assured that when I left a particular respondent I had in my possession all of the data that would be required from that respondent. I did not have to depend upon any respondent to mail me any data. To depend on respondents to mail information can be very frustrating because initially enthusiastic respondents often lose interest; and much of the information that the research requires never actually gets received.

The Socially Self-Confident Non-Shy Men

Like the younger love-shys, the non-shy men were similarly in the age range from 19 to 24; and there were 200 of them. Their cooperation was obtained in much the same way as it had been obtained for the love-shys, except that contact was requested by telephone rather than by letter. Non-shy individuals are usually quite averse to letter writing, and they will normally do everything within their power to avoid having to put pen to paper. Their style is always to communicate directly with people on a face-to-face basis, or by telephone.

The posted announcements for the non-shy men did not indicate that the required respondents were to comprise merely a *"comparison group"*, or that the subject of the research was love-shyness or, for that matter, any other kind of shyness. I felt that any mention of "shyness" in the posted announcements might serve to turn off potentially good respondents. On the other hand, the $10 reward was mentioned; and the subject of the research investigation was delineated as being that of young men who are socially successful with women and who engage in a great deal of informal heterosexual interaction including dating, partying, love-making, etc.

Inquiries came in from non-shy men at a much, much faster pace than they came in from the love-shys. Of course, this was to be expected, given the many anxieties and fears which love-shy males entertain regarding self-disclosure and self-assertion. The net result of this differential was that I could have easily obtained all 200 non-shy men from the same university and had the non-shy data collection phase of the research over and done with very early. However, I decided that it was not in the best interests of the study to do this, and that the best "comparison group" would be one composed of young men from the *same* seven universities as those used for obtaining the love-shys. I similarly decided that each university should contribute approximately the *same number* of respondents to each of the two categories: (1) love-shy, and (2) self-confident non-shy. This was done, and the number of men interviewed from each of the schools was as follows:

U.C.L.A.: 62 love-shys and 62 non-shys;

Cal State Northridge: 32 love-shys and 32 non-shys;

New York University: 20 love-shys and 28 non-shys;

C.U.N.Y.: 14 love-shys and 22 non-shys;

Auburn University: 25 love-shys and 25 non-shys;

Westfield State College: 14 love-shys and 14 non-shys;

S.U.N.Y. at Stony Brook: 9 love-shys and 17 non-shys;

The 24 younger love-shys who were drawn from the membership of a commercial dating service were all in attendance, full-time or part-time, at other New York area colleges.

In order for a young man to qualify for inclusion into the non-shy sample, each of the following six criteria had to be met:

(1) Each respondent had to be heterosexual;

(2) Each respondent had to be "single, never married";

(3) Each respondent had to be of the male gender;

(4) Each respondent had to consider himself happily self-confident and relaxed in informal interactions vis-a-vis the opposite sex;

(5) Each respondent had to be actively involved in a social life that included daily informal social interaction with the opposite sex;

(6) Each respondent had to be in the 19 to 24 year age range.

No minimum number of dates with women per week or per month was required for inclusion in the non-shy sample. Unlike the situation that prevailed twenty or more years ago, young people today differ quite a bit from one another in terms of how they choose to define the word "date". Moreover, 38 percent of the non-shys studied were premaritally cohabiting with a lover; and most of these men did not view themselves as being involved in "dating" at all.

Throughout the United States there continues to exist some quite thoroughly self-confident non-shy young men who CHOOSE to remain virginal because of certain deeply internalized religious values which are very important to them. The key word here is "choice". As I have reiterated at several points in this book, shyness removes "choice" from its victims, and with it a full sense of personal responsibility for both behavior and behavioral inaction. Of course, better than a score of social science investigations have revealed that for both sexes there is an inverse association between sociability (including social self-confidence) and choosing to remain virginal until marriage. In short, socially successful young people seldom choose to remain virginal. But there are individual exceptions to all statistical generalizations. And a minority of very attractive, highly sociable, socially self-confident young men and women do manage, by choice, to remain virginal until marriage.

In this particular study only 6 of the 200 self-confident non-shy men (3 percent) were virginal. Three of these came from the Auburn University sample; two came from Cal State University at Northridge, and one came from the Westfield State College sample. In short, 97 percent of the self-confident non-shys were sexually experienced. Further, a majority of this 97 percent had had a considerable amount of premarital coital experience—although most of their sexual experiences had been enjoyed on a monogamous basis. In other words, most of the

non-shy men had incorporated their premarital sex into love relationships which had been stable and constant throughout most of their
duration.

Most of the non-shys had been involved in three or four love
relationships which had incorporated sexual intercourse. And 53 percent
had cohabited with a girl for a period of at least six or more months; 38
percent of them were cohabiting at the time they were interviewed for
this study.

The SHI Inventory

I had to find some means for quickly and accurately assessing each
potential respondent with respect to criterion #4. Each non-shy respondent had to consider himself happily self-confident and relaxed in informal social interactions vis-a-vis the opposite sex. A substantial minority
of the seemingly non-shy men who contacted me appeared to be primarily interested in earning a quick $10, and in assuaging their curiosity
about the nature of the research. Thus inappropriate individuals had to
be screened out.

Towards this end I used an instrument devised during the early
1970s by psychologists Craig Twentyman and Richard McFall. This
instrument is known as the *Survey of Heterosexual Interactions*, or "SHI
Inventory". Up to now the SHI remains the only diagnostic device for
assessing the extent of love-shyness in males which has the advantage
of national norms. Thus the SHI Inventory is now a standardized test
with national norms which are based upon the scores of over 10,000
young men from all over the United States.

The SHI Inventory is composed of just twenty brief questions. Each
of the twenty items presents a scenario involving the making of a friendly,
assertive move vis-a-vis an attractive person of the opposite sex. For
each of the twenty scenarios the young man taking the test simply
indicates *on a seven point scale* just how shy or non-shy he would be
about making a friendly/assertive move vis-a-vis the girl described in
the scenario. Scores on this instrument can range from a maximum of
140 (the non-shy end) to a minimum low of 20 (the extremely love-shy
end).

The mean or average score for normally self-confident American
college and university men is 103.9. (The SHI Inventory can only be
taken by males.) I decided to establish the score of *105* as the minimum
required for acceptance into the non-shy sample. Thus the score of 105
is more than a point higher than the self-confident non-shy norm established by Twentyman and McFall.

The mean or average SHI Inventory scores for each of the three groups of men studied for this book were as follows:

Self-Confident Non-Shy Men:	114.3
Young (University) Love-Shy Men:	47.8
Older Love-Shy Men	38.6
General Mean for Healthy College Males:	103.9

The SHI Inventory is an outstanding diagnostic device. And because I am often asked about its content, for the convenience of interested readers I have provided the twenty scenarios it contains in Appendix *I* at the end of this book.

The Older Love-Shy Group

The older love-shy group was composed of 100 virginal, single, never married men in the 35 to 50 year old age category. My original intention had been to obtain 200 men for the older love-shy group. But the required data became available to me all too slowly. So I decided that it would be far better to cut the sample off at 100 men than wait the additional two to three years that would have been required for the completion of 200 interviews from appropriate people.

Each of the 100 older love-shy men possessed all of the seven love-shyness characteristics that are delineated on page 000 of this chapter. Hence, they were all quite similar to the younger (university) love-shys. Given their much older ages, however, the older love-shy men had all lived with their conditions for much longer periods of time. And the ambiance of dreamy-eyed optimism that characterized a significant minority of the younger love-shys did not appear to exist at all for these older men. In fact, most of them appeared quite pessimistic about their love-shyness problems and cynical about the world and about women in general.

The cooperation of the older love-shy men was obtained in two different ways: (1) 78 of the men were obtained via the posting of public bulletin board announcements, and (2) the cooperation of 22 of the men was obtained through the help of the owner-manager of a New York area commercial dating service.

Announcements were placed on the bulletin boards of a large number of laundermats throughout the greater Los Angeles and New York metropolitan areas. Each announcement indicated that respondents were needed for a study of severe shyness in informal man/woman situations. The announcements indicated that the study was to be concerned with men in the 35 to 50 year age range who were still "single, never married" *not out of choice* but because of chronic and severe shyness vis-a-vis appealing women in informal social situations.

As had been the case with the younger love-shys, the announcements made clear the fact that only heterosexual men were needed for the study. Interested respondents were asked to contact the researcher *by mail* with an indication of the times and places that would be convenient for the interview. The announcements advised that a mutually convenient time would be confirmed by return mail, and that $10 would be paid for each respondent's cooperation.

Finally, the announcements that were used to attract the attention of the older love-shys pointed out that a key goal of the study was to help remedy and prevent all forms of shyness which impede comfortable and relaxed heterosexual interaction. I wanted to present myself as someone who had a compassionate interest in the plight of the love-shy, and who did not subscribe to the traditional view that shyness is entirely the victim's responsibility. As with the bulletin board announcements used to attract the younger love-shys, I pointed out that I was a licensed therapeutic counselor, and that I was deeply and sincerely interested in the development of techniques that might be used to engineer the painless remission of love-shyness symptoms.

The Commercial Dating Service

Sooner or later a high proportion of severely love-shy men join commercial introduction services. This issue will be discussed at length in part three of this book. Because I had long been aware of the popularity of commercial dating services among love-shy men, I decided to contact the owner-managers of several such organizations in both the greater New York and Los Angeles metropolitan areas. I succeeded in obtaining interviews with six such owner-managers. Unfortunately, only one of these proved willing on my behalf to ask love-shy men if they would be willing to cooperate in this research investigation. This manager provided me with 62 names and addresses; and 46 of these men did meet the seven criteria for love-shyness delineated on page 000.

It turned out that 22 of the 46 men were in the 35 to 50 year age range. And these men were employed for the older love-shy sample. The other 24 men were all in the 21 to 24 year age range; and I employed them for my younger love-shy sample. (By the way, 19 and 20 year old men are not eligible for membership in most commercial dating services because there aren't any available women that young or younger to whom to assign them.)

For ethical reasons, the cooperating dating service manager mailed a notice to each of the 62 men selected. This notice was included along with each man's monthly "matches". The notice concluded by asking the recipient to contact the dating service office by a specified date if he objected to his name and address being given to me. None of these men owned telephones—a fact which is "par for the course" among the love-shy.

The Importance of LOVE-Shyness

Most of the people who have researched shyness up to now have concentrated upon *general* shyness. In interviewing hundreds of young men it became very clear to me that only one form of shyness caused severe and chronic emotional pain. Only one form of shyness created feelings of deprivation so excruciatingly painful that it severely distracted and handicapped its victims' ability to concentrate on work, school, and other important facets of their everyday lives. I decided to call this form of shyness "*love-shyness*". And it is, in essence, a painful bashfulness and behavioral inertia that effectively prevents its victims from making any kind of overtures vis-a-vis members of the opposite sex. Love-shyness is strongly associated with many of the more general forms of shyness. But since it is the most emotionally debilitating of all forms of shyness I decided that it is the form most deserving of research attention.

As a case in point, many people are too shy to start conversations with strangers. And yet everyday people with this deficit manage to go through life perfectly happy and adequately well-adjusted. In short, many men with wives and children are too inhibited to deal in an open, friendly way vis-a-vis strangers—even though most of them might very much like to be able to do so. The fact that these people have their wives and children along with usually a small circle of friends serves to effectively cushion them against long-term feelings of unhappiness and depression. Men who are too shy to interact informally with women at all do not have and are effectively blocked from obtaining this cushion.

A condition known as "*speech reticence*" represents another area of shyness that has received a good deal of research attention lately. But a person can go all the way through life without *ever* getting up to make a speech (or entertain), and still be at least satisfactorily happy if not very happy. To be sure, speech reticence can impede career advancement. In some fields of endeavor it can even obviate success. However, most careers do not require the ability to engage in public speaking. And whereas a speech professor might view serious deficits in this area as "tragic" or "intolerable", in point of fact the large apathetic "silent majority" does not appear to have its lives cramped very much by this problem.

But more importantly, a relative dearth or absence of "speech reticence" *does not assure* against love-shyness. Almost *three out of every ten love-shy men* interviewed for this study were not at all afraid to talk publicly. In fact, many of them greatly relished every opportunity they could obtain for talking or entertaining in some way before the public. These men were shy only in situations where there is no script—where there is no clearly defined, non-ambiguous role to play. Hence, many love-shys are shy only in situations where there is no purpose apart from pure, unadulterated sociability. Let this sort of person talk before a large audience and he will enjoy every minute of it. On the other hand, put this person in a coctail party situation, or worse yet in a one-on-one situation with a woman whom he finds attractive, *and he will freeze*.

Of course, in all candor I must agree that seventy percent of the love-shys I studied *were* too shy to speak publicly. However, it appears quite clear that any remedying of this deficit would in no way assure a remission of the love-shyness problem. In fact, even if a shy person could be turned into an outstanding public speaker, this would in no way assure him of what he will need to secure the affectionate female companionship that he so greatly needs and requires.

The moral here is simply that of *let's take first things first*. An inability to function in a purely social, sociable situation wherein there is no purpose apart from pure friendliness, is far more debilitating to a person's personal, social, *and business* life, than is any inability to deliver speeches or any inability to start conversations with strangers. Simply put, we will be serving the needs of mankind far better if we focus our attentions upon the alleviating and curing of love-shyness. The other forms of shyness are of far less importance and can for the most part be ignored. To the extent that a person has his love-shyness remedied, to that extent the other forms of shyness with which he may be afflicted will eventually take care of themselves.

Summary

The major purpose of this chapter has been to present an easily understandable discussion (1) of respondent characteristics, and (2) of the methods that were employed for obtaining the research information. Academic readers might feel that the discussion presented here is too brief. However, this book was written primarily with the lay reader in mind. Love-shyness is a very serious, painful problem that requires a much better understanding than presently prevails in our society. I believe that a widespread dissemination of knowledge regarding this problem is very necessary. There is no way love-shyness can be effectively remedied and prevented without such a dissemination of research knowledge. Moreover, people must be able to properly understand knowledge in order to be able to make any kind of constructive use of it.

Three different groups of men were studied for this research. Simply put, there were two love-shy groups and one *comparison group* that was composed of 200 *non-shy* individuals. The 200 non-shys were all university men between the ages of 19 and 24. Similarly, one of the love-shy groups was composed of 200 university men who were between the ages of 19 and 24. The second love-shy group was composed of 100 men in the 35 to 50 year age category. The cooperation of all three groups was obtained primarily through the aid of posted bulletin board announcements. The two 19 to 24 year old groups were both drawn primarily from seven different universities. The 100 older love-shy men were drawn entirely from the New York and Los Angeles greater metropolitan areas.

Seven criteria were used for this study in determining who is and who is not "love-shy". Briefly, all respondents in both love-shy groups possessed each and every one of these seven characteristics: (1) all were male; (2) all were strictly heterosexual; (3) all were virginal; (4) all very strongly desired a romantically intimate relationship with a woman; (5) all very rarely or never dated; (6) all lacked a personal history that incorporated any meaningful romantic and/or sexual relationships with women; and (7) all suffered strong anxiety pains at the mere thought of making an assertive move towards the initiation of a relationship with a woman.

Finally, this chapter presented a discussion on how heterosexuals could be accurately distinguished from homosexuals. This is an important issue because love-shy heterosexuals are often misperceived and publicly mislabeled "homosexual" as a result of their never being observed interacting informally with women. New diagnostic categories such as (1) the *closet heterosexual*, and (2) the *male lesbian*, were also introduced. And their key relevancy to love-shyness among heterosexual males was explained and discussed. Attention was also accorded such issues as (1) why this investigation was designed to study males only, and (2) why love-shyness was studied rather than other kinds of shyness.

NOTE: In Appendix III of this book the reader will find a table which summarizes the mean *Eysenck Personality Questionnaire* (EPQ) scores for the non-shy and the love-shy samples.

Chapter 6

Love-Shyness: Its Intrauterine Beginnings

Up to now, most of the people who have written about shyness have been of the opinion that learning accounts for all. This view holds that shyness is the natural outcome of years of negative learning, and of a negative self-image. Inasmuch as the self-image is always the cumulative byproduct of all of a person's past learnings, shyness according to this view can only be cured through a process of rational re-education and resocialization.

Learning *is* a matter of utmost importance. But as far as severe shyness is concerned it is only part of the total picture. Years of intensively studying and researching shyness have convinced me that therapists, parents, and others who attempt to cure shyness without the benefit of a *balanced perspective* will achieve only very limited results. A key problem is that the psychology of learning is an intellectual *ideology* AS WELL AS a body of empirically verifiable knowledge. Ideology by its very nature *always* creates blinders. And these blinders militate against the much needed development of a balanced perspective. In fact, a person cannot even become aware of a body of knowledge that he/she has (motivated by ideology) never even bothered to read.

The East German Research

On the surface communist East Germany would seem to be one of the least likely places to produce important research findings pertinent to the love-shyness problem. However, for many years East German officials have been endeavoring to obtain distinction for their country by getting their youth to score very highly and even to win most of the Olympic Games.

Towards this end East Germany does everything in its power to involve youth (and especially young boys) in demanding athletic activity

143

as early in their lives as possible. Their goal is to produce outstanding athletes. And boys who for whatever reasons (1) perform inadequately at physical activity, and/or (2) who display less than an enthusiastic attitude, interest, and motivation with respect to such activity, remain at the bottom of the social status and prestige ladder among their peers and vis-a-vis the adult community as well.

Because such highly masculine, strenuous activities are so important to the East Germans, they have tried to find out (1) why some boys remain uninterested in athletic, "rough and tumble" activity, and (2) whether anything can be done to successfully get disinterested boys involved in such activity. With respect to the second question the East Germans learned early in their investigative efforts that the application of psychological pressure often made matters worse rather than better. In essence, the disinterested children tended to become even more disinterested quite in spite of burgeoning social unpopularity and an ever increasing public ostracism eminating from all-make peer groups and athletic coaches.

The fact that there is a strong relationship for boys between athletic disinterest/incompetence and love-shyness will be amply documented in the chapter on the all-male peer group. The point that needs to be stressed here is the fact that the East Germans would not allow a disinterest among boys in athletic achievement to go unstudied. As they see it, not being interested in athletics is "unnatural" for boys; and this is a feeling that is widely shared among physical education teachers and parents here in American society. But in America the tendency has long been to "get into a kid's head" through extensive psychological tests and interviews. In contrast, the East Germans have long believed in commencing an investigation with a detailed probing of the nonconformist's anatomy, physiology, and body biochemistry. Simply put, the East Germans have been conditioned to look first to the medical laboratory for the answers they seek.

Blood Testosterone

The first finding to be uncovered by the East German research was that many of the boys who had been disinclined towards "rough and tumble" play had below average amounts of the male hormone *testosterone* in their blood. This was especially true for boys whose size and weight had always been quite normal, but who still sustained a disinterest in body contact sports and strenuous athletics.

One of the East Germans' first thoughts was that they had uncovered a hormonal and biochemical basis for homosexuality. Like all politically fascist states, East German leaders have long detested anything which smacks of homosexuality. Thus the scientists there fully believed that anyone who could uncover a cure for homosexuality would gain a formidable amount of professional status and prestige.

However, it turned out that very few of the low testosterone boys grew up to become homosexuals. In fact, incipient homosexuality turned out to be only very slightly more common among the low testosterone boys than among those with normal levels of blood testosterone. On the other hand, the boys who had low blood testosterone continue to remain uninterested in "rough and tumble" athletics. And as young adults they took longer than their peers in obtaining the love interest of a female partner—a fact which had created quite a bit of unhappiness for them. Obviously, this is a reflection of love-shyness.

However, the most remarkable finding to be uncovered by the East German scientists was the fact that a strong relationship was discovered between (1) a pregnant woman's personality, and (2) her male fetus' blood testosterone level. The East Germans focused upon the pregnancies of a large group of mothers. And it was found that certain personality traits of a pregnant woman had the effect of *neutralizing* either the testosterone that is released into the bloodstream of the fetus, or the enzymes which metabolize the testosterone to the point of permitting it to do its job on the various parts of the male fetus' brain that nature has programmed to respond to testosterone.

Personality traits of a pregnant woman deemed by this research to have a deleterious influence upon the propitious development of a male fetus are: (1) irascibility, (2) tenseness, (3) truculent abrasiveness, (4) irritability, (5) depression, (6) high strung and volatile, (7) petulance, and (8) cantankerousness. Most of the mothers studied retained these personality traits long after their babies were born. But the important point to be stressed here is that these traits of personality *in a pregnant mother* had the effect of neutralizing testosterone and/or related enzymes, and thus *feminizing* yet-to-be-born male offspring.

Equally important in the findings of the East German scientists was the fact that *girl fetuses* carried by tense, irascible mothers did not possess any noticeably abnormal traits. The brain of a female fetus is not programmed by nature to respond in any way to the *presence or absence* of testosterones. In fact, *unlike a boy fetus* a girl fetus is not biologically programmed by nature to have her blood stream bathed in testosterones in the first place! Thus the absence of such hormones can do no damage.

Moreover, in East Germany as in America, it is "okey" for a girl to be femine and passive, and not too enthusiastic about "rough and tumble" sports. Consequently, even if a *female fetus* were to be excessively feminized as a result of its mother's personality, there would be little in the form of *social* consequences. A passive boy owns a low social stimulus value; he is vulnerable to being either bullied or ignored. A passive girl, on the other hand, owns a neutral to positive social stimulus value. People are not likely to ignore or bully her simply because she behaves passively. More succinctly, a boy fetus is much more vulnerable than a girl fetus to things going wrong during the course of its intrauterine development.

The idea that what goes on in the mind affects what goes on in the body is not new. Indeed, the body of knowledge known as psychosomatic medicine and holistic medicine has been expanding enormously in recent years. But what has been ignored until now is the fact that what goes on in the mind of a pregnant woman affects the fetus, and it does so in a host of ways. We have learned that hormonal and enzyme imbalances in a fetus are easily created by the type of attitude, personality, and approach to life a woman normally sustains. If her normal personality is tense and irascible or depressed, she is likely to give birth to a feminized (*pre-shy*) boy baby.

Now, just as a tense, irascible, high strung or depressed woman will very likely give birth to a *pre-shy* baby (if that baby is a boy), a relaxed, fun-loving, happy-go-lucky woman who does not take life too seriously will typically give birth to a highly masculine baby. And that is exactly what the East German researchers found. More succinctly, the more relaxed, sociable and *non*-serious a pregnant woman normally is, the greater the likelihood that any male babies born to her will be highly masculine, energetic, and naturally ready to enter enthusiastically into the "rough and tumble" of boyish play. On the other hand, the further down the continuum a pregnant woman normally falls in terms of hyperseriousness, tenseness, irritability, petulance, etc., the more passive, withdrawn, *and shy* her *male children* are likely to be.

These traits in a mother's personality are, of course, also bound to affect the learning that a child does during the early years of his post partum life. Indeed, as I shall show later, some of these maternal traits may even provoke love-shyness by rendering boys fearful and distrustful of getting close to a woman. However, the thing we are most concerned about in this chapter is the fact that these maternal personality traits have a strong impact upon the native, inborn biology and physiology of a boy child. And this is true quite irrespective of genetic considerations.

Relevant American Research Efforts

Thus far little of this type of research has been conducted here in America. And most of what has been done has been conducted on animals. However, the same type of findings seem to be coming to the fore. As a case in point, two American researchers subjected pregnant rats to stress by confining them in a small cage under very bright lights. They found, in essence, that the rats' *male* offspring had low levels of testosterone, and they exhibited passive, shy, and socially withdrawn behavior.

American research has also established that neonate little girl babies react much more negatively to physical pain stimuli than do little boy babies. The love-shy males studied for this book were much more sensitive to physical pain than were the non-shy males. This finding similarly suggests that the brains of most of the love-shy men studied for this book had not been appropriately masculinized prior to their respective births.

The greater liking for sweets that has long been known to prevail among girl babies as opposed to boy babies also seems to have prevailed among the love-shy males who were interviewed for this book. For example, the much higher prevalence of reactive hypoglycemia among the love-shys (versus the non-shys) would appear to reflect this penchant for sugar among love-shy men. (See the chapter on medical symptoms for a more detailed discussion of this issue.)

My Own Findings

As a social scientist I had no legal way of testing the blood testosterone levels for each of the 500 men studied. Further, for truly incisive data it would have been necessary to obtain blood samples from each one of the men during the time when they were still fetuses yet to be born! On the other hand, my study did turn up a substantial amount of data which lend strong support to the proposition that severely love-shy males had been feminized while still in the uterus. Simply put, most of my love-shy respondents had been born to mothers with the personality syndrome characterized by tenseness, irascibility, cantankerousness, high irritability, depression, etc. Moreover, an unusually high proportion of the mothers of my love-shy respondents had had significant problems in the management of their pregnancies.

Miscarriages and Stillbirths

For example, I asked each respondent whether or not his mother had had any miscarriages either before or after he was born. Only 12 percent of the self-confident non-shy men responded in the affirmative, compared to 26 percent of the younger love-shys and 31 percent of the older love-shys. And in response to a question about whether or not the mother had ever had any babies born dead (stillbirths), fully 42 percent of the older love-shys responded in the affirmative, compared to only 5 percent of the self-confident non-shy men. The analogous figure for the younger love-shy men was 36 percent, which is itself a very high figure.

The issue of miscarriages and stillbirths is of significance to our understanding of the etiology of love-shyness in two different respects: (1) the miscarriage or stillbirth may represent a psychosomatic reflection of the possibility that deep down inside a woman does not really want to have a live and healthy child. Secondly (2), female hormones that are being taken today by an ever increasing number of pregnant women have been found to cause mild degrees of hermaphroditism in growing fetuses.

The second point may be one of considerable importance. For many years now female hormones have been prescribed as a means of *preventing miscarriages and stillbirths*. Of course, I had no way of finding out whether or not the love-shy's mothers had taken female hormones during the course of their respective pregnancies. However, since 31 percent of the mothers of the older love-shys had been prone to miscarriages, compared to only 12 percent of the non-shys' mothers, there is at least some possibility that a few of the love-shy men might have been feminized while intrautero by the female hormones which their mothers had taken in an effort to prevent miscarriage and stillbirths. Again, the difference between the love-shys and the non-shys had been even greater with regard to the matter of stillbirths: 42 percent of the older love-shys' mothers had had one or more stillbirths compared to just 5 percent of the mothers of the non-shys.

The Infant Mortality Issue

I also asked each man: "How many times did your mother have a baby that died within a few days or a week of when it was born?" Let us consider the percent of men who indicated *"once or more times"* in response to this question. More specifically, 47 percent of the older love-shys and 44 percent of the younger love-shys responded that it had happened *"once or more times"*. Zero percent (nobody) of the self-confident non-shy men gave me a similar response. In essence, whereas *none* of the mothers of the non-shy men had ever had this experience, *almost half* of the men in the two love-shy groups had mothers who at one time had had a baby that died within a few days of birth. These differences are extremely remarkable and noteworthy. And it is to be hoped that other researchers will soon check them out with their own samples and corroborate them.

The Pains of Giving Birth

Birth is a painful experience for most if not all women. Yet the large majority of women seldom if ever complain about the pain they had endured while giving birth. Even fewer women complain to their children about such pain. Moreover, nature seems to have a way of making most women forget the pains and discomforts which accompany the childbirth experience.

Nevertheless I asked each respondent whether his mother had complained a lot about the pain and stress she had suffered and endured while giving birth—to him. And not surprisingly, *none* of the self-confident non-shy men responded in the affirmative. On the other hand, 16 percent of the older love-shys and 12 percent of the younger love-shys replied that their mothers had complained quite a bit about the pains and stresses that had been related to giving birth to the respondent.

I then asked each man to react to the statement: "It took me a good deal longer to be born than most babies take." And 27 percent of the older love-shys together with 21 percent of the younger love-shys responded in the affirmative. In contrast, only 4 percent of the non-shy men believed that it had taken them a good deal longer to be born than most babies require.

It is interesting to note that several research studies have found obstetrical complications to increase the risk of the newborn child eventually developing a schizoid disorder (see Wender and Klein, 1981). This is especially so if the mother or father of the child happens to be carrying a schizoid-predisposing gene. (The gene *may* render the young child susceptible to being invaded by a schizoid-inducing virus.) Prolonged labor has been found to be the complication that is most consistently associated with an increased risk of developing a schizoid personality. Hence, some measure of oxygen-deprivation may be implicated here.

Schizoid personality disorders are much milder than the far more serious, psychotic condition known as schizophrenia. However, like schizophrenia the schizoidia condition is chronic; and there is strong evidence that it (or a susceptibility to it) is inherited genetically. The schizoid personality may be of considerable relevance to extreme love-shyness. Thus, schizoids tend to be quite shy and withdrawn. They are in touch with reality, and many of them tend to be quite intelligent. But they lack a normal capacity for responding warmly to others, making and keeping friends, or of evoking warm or friendly responses in other people. They are typically seen as distant, aloof, estranged and peculiar. And as with love-shy males, they grow up as friendless social isolates who are heavily bullied and hazed by age-mate peers.

Also similar to love-shy men, they do not respond well at the outset to attempts to bring them out of their shells—unless these attempts are unusually persistent and well organized. Their ability to experience pleasure is greatly below average, especially the pleasure of informal sociable interaction.

Premature Births and Caesarean Sections

I asked each respondent whether or not he had been born prematurely. *None* of the non-shy men responded in the affirmative. In contrast, 16 percent of the older love-shy men along with 13 percent of the younger love-shy men had been born prematurely. I also asked: "At your birth, were you delivered by Caesarean section?" And 14 percent of the older love-shys together with 11 percent of the younger love-shys *had been*. Zero percent (nobody) of the self-confident non-shys had been delivered by Caesarean section.

In 1968 only 5 percent of all American births were delivered by Caesarean section. In 1983, only about half as many babies are delivered per doctor as had been the case in 1968. Yet each doctor delivers *five times as many* babies by Caesarean section today, in 1983, as had been the case in 1968. Hence, if Caesarean section births are related in any way to love-shyness or to any other psychoemotional problem, the current situation does not bode well for the future. The paradox, of course, is that pregnant women are healthier today than they had been in 1968. The problem is that obstetricians don't have nearly as many babies to deliver today as they used to have. Obstetricians are the highest paid of all medical specialists; and the only way they can sustain their very high incomes is to intimidate women in labor into getting a great many quite unnecessary Caesarean sections.

Painful Menopause

The love-shys' mothers seemed to have many more psychosomatic complaints than did the mothers of the non-shys. For example, 29 percent of the older love-shys together with 23 percent of the younger love-shys recalled their mother as having had an unusually long and painful menopause. In contrast, only 4 percent of the self-confident non-shys recalled their mothers as having had difficulties with the menopause.

Briquet's Syndrome

In listening to the love-shys discuss their mothers it became apparent to me that a large fraction of these women may have suffered from a chronic, usually life-long condition known as *Briquet's syndrome*. This is an hysterical disorder in which the patient is almost always female; and it is estimated to occur in between one and two percent of all women. Basically, it entails complaining about a multitude of different physical difficulties over a period of many years. Normally unattributable to any underlying physical disease, the symptoms include headache, numbness, tingling, palpitations, shortness of breath, pain during coitus, painful joints and a host of painful abdominal complaints. Because of the host of continuing complaints, such patients often convince their exasperated physicians that genuine physical disease may lie at the root of their problems. Thus, a myriad of exploratory surgical procedures are often performed on these women. Such women typically endeavor to derive secondary gain (sympathy and a plethora of special considerations) from their families. But because their personalities are so abrasive and truculently irritable—especially vis-a-vis their love-shy sons, they seldom enjoy much success in this regard.

Love-Shys as Quite Babies

At one point in the interview I asked each man to react to the statement: "My mother used to comment from time to time that I was a rather quiet baby, and that I didn't cry very much." I decided that if the love-shys agreed with this statement to a significantly greater extent than the non-shys, it would provide further support for the view that the intrauterine stage of existence had had a feminizing effect on the love-shy men. Of course, I realized that many mothers might never have said anything, even if their children had been very quiet as infants. I also realized that many people might very easily have forgotten comments of this nature made by their mothers many years ago. Nevertheless, if the respondent had indeed been a quiet baby, it seemed to me that he would be at least somewhat likely to vaguely remember maternal comments to that effect.

Only 16 percent of the self-confident non-shy men agreed that their mothers had indeed commented from time to time about the fact that they had been quiet babies. In stark contrast, fully 86 percent of the older love-shys and 73 percent of the younger love-shys agreed that their mothers had occasionally made this comment about them.

Even with all the problems entailed by a question of this nature which places a heavy emphasis upon memory and recall, it seems highly unlikely that the love-shys would remember such a comment whereas the self-confident non-shys would not be able to remember it. Furthermore, when it is taken into account that (1) throughout their formative years the love-shys had gotten along with their mothers a good deal less well than the non-shys had gotten along with theirs, and (2) the fact that a quiet baby is considered by most people to be easier to care for than a normally noisy one, it would appear unlikely that the mothers had been lying in their comments about the love-shy child having been a quiet baby. Indeed, the love-shys' mothers had been so hypercritical that it seems highly improbable that they would cast praise upon their children for having been quiet babies—unless their children had indeed been unusually quiet at that time of life.

In sum, the love-shy men studied for this research had most probably been unusually quiet babies who had been born to tense, highstrung, depressed and irascible women. Further, the love-shys' mothers had experienced formidable difficulties in the management of their pregnancies and of the childbirth process itself.

Mothers' Personalities

I asked numerous questions about the mothers' personalities. Most of these data will be covered in chapter eight. However, some of the findings need to be discussed here. For example, I asked each man to respond to the statement: "My mother was an extremely tense, high strung person who would often burst into great rages." Note that this question deals directly with the *same traits of personality* which the East Germans found to be related to the giving of birth to feminized boys. Again, tense, high strung, irascible women by virtue of their mental state cause too little testosterone (and related enzymes) to be released within their male fetuses. As indicated earlier, this situation appears to be a clear antecedent of love-shyness in males, but not in females.

Fully 38 percent of the older love-shys and 31 percent of the younger love-shys replied that their mothers had indeed been high strung and extremely tense women who would frequently burst into great rages. In contrast, *only 4 percent* of the self-confident non-shy men saw their mothers as having been this way.

Another representative question is the following: "My mother was always easily angered and very prone to outbursts of temper." Fully 53 percent of the older love-shys and 47 percent of the younger ones responded in the affirmative, compared to just 20 percent of the non-shys. And to the statement: "My mother was always a patient person", 54 percent of the non-shys replied "*true*", compared with only 13 percent of the older love-shys and 19 percent of the younger love-shys.

Two further examples of maternal personality which are appropriate for review here at the following: "When my mother became angry with me during childhood, she would often say and do some very strange and bizarre things." Fully 41 percent of the older love-shys and 36 percent of the younger ones agreed with this statement, compared to only 13 percent of the self-confident non-shys. And in response to the statement: "My mother often threw uncontrollably loud, angry temper tantrums at me", *fully 45 percent* of the older love-shys and 39 percent of the younger love-shys agreed, compared to *zero percent* (nobody) of the non-shy men.

As bizarre as it might sound to some readers, some of the love-shys' mothers would bring up the subject of childbirth-related pain and suffering whenever they were angry and upset about their son's misbehavior or seeming lack of consideration. For some of the love-shys, these maternal rages were frequent, sometimes daily occurrences. Some of the love-shy respondents spoke of their mothers' temper tantrums as constituting a kind of uncontrolled fit that could last for several hours. The following quote from a 35-year old love-shy man should provide the reader with some idea as to the truculent, ego-deflating, persistently belittling, chronic irascibility that many of these women would display.

> "You may find it hard to believe this. I know some of the psychiatrists I've seen have a hard time dealing with it. But from the time I was about four or five until I was about fifteen or sixteen my mother would have these angry fits. Oh, I guess she would have them about every ten to fourteen days or so—whenever she was so angry about something that she just couldn't control herself. Well, one of the things she would do was rip off her underwear and force me to look at the scar from the excruciatingly painful operation she said she had to have when she gave birth to me. I mean she would just rip every damn thing off in a loud and screaming rage and she'd force me to look at her pussy and this scar that she screamed was so horrendously painful. Then she'd flail her arms all over the place and start throwing silverware and coat hangers. And this would go on like for a half-hour or more sometimes. Then she'd grab this really long butcher knife we kept in the silverware drawer. And she'd show it to me, still screaming at the top of her lungs. And she'd hollar that she was going to commit suicide with it. And then she'd run shouting and screaming into the bathroom, and she'd lock herself in there. At that point she'd usually stop screaming. She'd just cry and cry and cry, loudly and then softly. And like I said, that

would sometimes go on for three or four hours before she'd finally go to bed and sleep it off."

And a 40-year old love-shy man had this to offer:

"Listen, for several years while I was growing up I don't think a single day ever went by when my mother wouldn't rant and rave about something. She would holler at the top of her lungs, sometimes for hours, about what kind of goddam sonofabitch and rotten cur I was, and how she wished I was dead or that I'd be hit by a car or something. Then when she would come out of it she would give me all this loving bullshit about how she loved me. And she would try to stroke my head, and I just wanted to get away from her. I couldn't stand her! Even her breath stunk all the time I remember!

I remember one time she got into some kind of argument with her cousin. I remember this well because I remember I was in kindergarten that year. And I can remember the whole flavor behind what happened. Like one day when I came home from kindergarten— they let us go around 12:30 in the afternoon—I walked in and she said there was something she wanted me to do. She said she wanted me to tell this man she was going to dial on the phone how she was going to come back and haunt him when she dies, and all this stuff about how mean and rotten a cur he was and all this. And I remember I was too shy to do it. Well, she accused me of being in collusion with her cousin. And she started screaming and shouting at me and about what a horrible bastard I was if I didn't say these horrible things to the man she dialed. I remember I finally had to do it for her; but I felt horrible and it was very traumatic for me even though I don't remember the guy actually said anything to me."

Now, living throughout one's formative years with a woman manifesting this type of personality could well have inspired the development on a subconscious level of a generalized fear and mistrust of women in general. In essence, maternal tenseness, irascibility, petulance, etc., which the East Germans found to be a cause behind the feminization of male fetuses was quite a widespread feature of the personalities of the mothers of the love-shys who were studied for this book.

Maternal Bashfulness During Pregnancy

Further support for the view that mothers who give birth to chronically love-shy boys are much more nervous and tense than women whose sons do not develop chronic love-shyness can be seen in the pattern of responses to this statement: "My mother probably felt shy or tense or embarrassed about being seen pregnant by people." It should be noted that *none* of the love-shy men studied for this book had been born out of wedlock. There was no rational reason for any of the mothers to have felt nervous or anxious about being seen pregnant. Still, 78 percent of the older love-shys together with 66 percent of the younger love-shys guessed that their mothers had indeed felt shy or tense or embarrassed about being seen while pregnant. Only 11 percent of the non-shy men felt this way.

Mothers' Employment

Tense, petulant women are probably less likely to be employed over very much time than are women who can maintain a genuinely relaxed, flexible, sociable attitude towards people and towards life. With regard to this I asked each man: "Was your mother employed during most of the period during which she was pregnant with you?" And here again, there were pronounced differences among the three groups of men studied.

Of course, twenty to forty years ago it was quite a bit less commonplace than it is today for a woman to remain employed throughout her pregnancy. Many employers used to insist that their pregnant employees quit their jobs either upon becoming pregnant or by the fifth month at the latest. Because of this difference between today and yesteryear I offered each man interviewed three different responses:

1. Yes; she was employed throughout most of the pregnancy.

2. No, she was not employed. But she remained very active socially during this time.

3. No, and she probably remained indoors most of the time.

To be sure, each man interviewed had to guess at the true state of affairs at the time he was still intrautero. Nevertheless, the results I obtained provided confirmation for my earlier findings that mothers of chronically and intractably love-shy men tended to have engaged in quite a bit of social avoidance behavior, especially in regard to an employment situation wherein they might be judged, or wherein the true nature of their personalities might not be so easy to hide over a long period of time.

First, just 10 percent of the mothers of the non-shys had been employed during most of their pregnancy periods. However, *zero percent* (none) of the mothers of the love-shy men had been employed during their pregnancies. There was no difference between the older and the younger love-shys on this issue. *None* of their mothers had been employed during pregnancy.

The most illuminating of the three possible responses was "no, and she probably remained indoors most of the time." *Only 11 percent* of the non-shy men saw fit to select this response, compared to 52 percent of the younger love-shy men and 67 percent of the older love-shy men. In essence, the more severe the love-shyness, the more socially avoidant (and responsibility avoidant) the mothers of these love-shy men had been. As for those indicating "no, she was not employed; but she remained very active socially during this time", the responses were 79 percent for the non-shy men, 48 percent for the younger love-shy men, and 33 percent for the older love-shy men.

Employment Among Mothers of Teenagers

Whereas it had not been considered socially acceptable until recently for conspicuously pregnant women to remain employed, it has long been considered acceptable for mothers of older children to work. Hence, I wanted to find out the extent to which the various groups of mothers had been employed outside the home during the years when the respondents were between 10 and 18 years of age.

The obtained findings revealed that 77 percent of the older love-shys' mothers together with 67 percent of the mothers of the younger love-shys had *never* been employed while their children were growing up—not even during the period when their children were between the ages of 10 and 18. In contrast, this was true for only 19 percent of the mothers of the non-shys.

On the other hand, 54 percent of the non-shys' mothers had been employed *full-time* during this period. This was true for only 20 percent of the younger love-shys' mothers, and for a mere 11 percent of the mothers of the older love-shys.

In America we tend to be quite moralistic about mothers spending enough time with their growing children. And yet various research studies have made it clear that it is the *quality* of the time spent with children that matters, and *not* the quantity. The love-shy men quite obviously had had their mothers around quite a bit more often than the non-shy men did. Yet it would appear that the *same* personality traits which had made it difficult for the mothers to obtain and keep employment had *also* served to reinforce the sons' love-shyness traits and social withdrawal tendencies. First, these maternal traits had probably operated to neutralize the operation of the testosterones and related enzymes while the sons were still intrautero. After birth, these maternal traits had probably served to further exacerbate damage already done. In essence, maternal personality traits probably had an important bearing upon *both the nature and the nurture* of shyness. Thus, these maternal traits had probably affected both the inborn biology of shyness as well as post-partum social learning.

Aggravating the noxious impact of the mothers' personality upon the love-shy was the relatively high degree of social isolation found in their homes and in their kinship networks. This is one of the issues that will be dealt with in the next chapter.

The Issue of Prevention

The ultimate test of the true worth of any book is the extent to which its findings can be used towards preventive efforts. If severe, chronic love-shyness can be prevented from developing in the first place, a tremendous amount of human suffering can be averted. Let us consider some of the ways whereby this might be accomplished.

First, preschool, kindergarten, first, second and third grade boys who are clearly shy, socially withdrawn and avoidant of "rough and tumble" play might be given shots of testosterone from time to time. This is what is currently being done in East Germany, and with a considerable amount of success. Only very small amounts of the hormone need be injected at any one time. However, such hormonal treatment must be accomplished while a child is still young. Once a shy, socially withdrawn boy has gotten as far as the fifth or sixth grade, it may already be too late for hormonal injections to do much good. This is because the self-image normally begins to crystallize by the time a child is 11 or 12 years of age. Thus, by age 12 a boy will normally have developed a negative mental attitude towards both himself and others as a result of the consistently nasty way he has been treated by male peers. His self-image will have become intractably negative, and he will have come to define himself as emotionally incapable of social assertiveness and/or as plainly uninterested in traditionally masculine activities such as "rough and tumble" play. Hence, the earlier such treatment can be started, the better the hope for a cure.

We know that girls who are unpopular with their same-sexed peer group are often quite popular with boys. Unfortunately, the reverse is NOT true. Boys who are unpopular vis-a-vis their same-sexed peers virtually never have an easy time asserting themselves in a friendly way with girls. The all-male peer group provides males with the crucial interpersonal skills and the necessary social self-confidence for rewarding heterosexual interaction. It also provides them with a social network that can prove very useful for making introductions to members of the opposite sex. Therefore, anything which effectively contributes to a boy's capacity for winning the respect and companionship of his male peers will inevitably contribute to his capacity to interact successfully with girls as well. Injections of testosterone early in a passive boy's life might help to insure his later happiness and social effectiveness.[1]

Prevention efforts must also be launched with respect to the *mothers*. Gynecologists, obstetricians and pediatricians all need to be alerted to the seemingly shy, ultra-polite, but actually quite petulant, irascible, truculent (vis-a-vis her son) woman.[2] It is expected that by the turn of the century it may be possible for couples to select the gender of the babies they procreate. Women with the kinds of personality traits specified in this chapter could then be directed towards having *female* offspring only—or perhaps no offspring at all. Since pregnant women who are tense, high strung, etc., can do little or no harm to female fetuses but a great deal of harm to male fetuses, great good might be accomplished by assuring that such women have girl babies only.

It would also make good sense for kindergarten and first grade teachers to make note of chronically passive, socially retiring (isolated) boys who are in their charge. This would permit special clinical services to be made available to these boys and to their families (particularly their mothers). These services might include "Parent-Effectiveness Training" seminars, parents of shy and inhibited children support groups, as well as parent-group therapy, Parents Anonymous groups, and play therapy sessions for the afflicted children themselves.

Of course, in order to provide such services there must be adequate funding of the various social services that can constructively impact upon children. Not only is such funding hard to come by, but those parents whose sons are most in need of help are usually the most reluctant to accept any help or guidance.

Women who are tense, high strung, poison-tongued vis-a-vis their sons, etc., are usually quite conservative and conventional. In essence, they tend to be *highly defensive* about their own shortcomings as these are reflected in the inadequate social behavior of their sons. Generally speaking, the more secure a person is, the more willing she or he will be to admit that she or he does not know all the right answers, or how to put those right answers to work in practical, everyday life situations. Insecure people tend to fear negative evaluations and want to run and hide from any possibility of same. And *this* is the most difficult barrier to be overcome in helping socially isolated, pre-shy little boys. In fact, I would say that it is a substantially more formidable obstacle than any shortfall of economic funding.

During the course of the interviews I conducted for this book, many of the shyest men spontaneously mentioned that their parents had been strongly encouraged by school officials to obtain therapeutic aid. Very often therapeutic help had been offered for the parents and for the child himself. And often this help had been offered free of charge. Moreover, in quite a few instances it had been offered repeatedly (*and repeatedly turned down*) while the boy was still in kindergarten or the first grade.

Therefore, if any campaign to *prevent shyness* is to achieve success, it must first successfully address the problem of the very weak, highly vulnerable egos *of the parents* of the pre-love-shy boys. In spite of all the consciousness raising that has been going on in America over the past two decades, many people still feel that they *own* their children, and that successful parenting skills are instinctual. In their defensiveness, many weak-ego parents will persistently sell themselves a false bill of goods that even chronic, long-term passivity in their sons is merely a "passing stage" that will be "outgrown" in time if just let alone.

To be sure, children *do* outgrow *some* undesirable behavior patterns. But people must be educated as to the difference between traits that are likely to be spontaneously outgrown and those that are not. Surely chronic social isolation, passivity and unpopularity are traits which are not likely to be spontaneously outgrown. Indeed, such traits can only become worse as their manifestation invites bullying, rejection and ignoring from peers; and peers are *crucial* agents in the socialization process.

Another widespread trait among the mothers of very love-shy males is *two-facedness*. Many of the most severely love-shy men complained that their mothers could become totally transformed upon such occasions as the ringing of a telephone or the buzzing of a doorbell. Consider the following remark that was made by a 42-year old love-shy man:

> "There were some scenes you just wouldn't believe. My mother would be screaming and hollaring and wailing at me that she wished I was dead and that I'd get hit by a car and all that. She'd be throwing glassware and books at me and yelling so loud that the neighbors at the other end of the block could hear. Then the doorbell would ring. My mother would open the door, and if it was a friend of hers she'd suddenly become a totally different person. I mean she would start laughing, and she would lovingly invite the friend in and be incredibly nice to her. This happened so many times when I was growing up. And each time I could just puke. I would just seethe inside because some of these friends of my mother would tell me how lucky I was to have such a wonderful mother. All these people would be telling me all the time that my mother was just the nicest, warmest, most generous person they knew, and that I was really lucky. If I could have only told them what a vicious, poison-tongued bitch she always was, I know they'd never have believed me."

In short, you cannot tell a book by its cover. Many of these mothers were viewed by their sons as being extremely status-conscious and oriented towards creating a good impression irrespective of whatever psychoemotional consequences might be involved. Deeply insecure at heart, these women simply could not permit any unpolished side of themselves to be displayed to the public. This may be one reason why (1) they would not accept therapeutic help for their pre-love-shy sons, and (2) they did not, deep down in their hearts, really like, love, or respect their sons very much—even though they would often loudly and angrily protest to the contrary. (These mothers would often remind their sons of how "lucky" they were to have such a mother as themselves!)

In sum, throughout his formative years the chronically love-shy adult male had behaved in ways which with today's knowledge would have made it very easy for him to have been singled out. Simply put, *chronic, pathological love-shyness can be detected in advance.*

However, unless laws can be passed that would assure all children the right to appropriate therapy irrespective of the wishes of weak-egoed, insecure parents, preventive measures might continue to be well nigh impossible to take. Appropriate preventive efforts would certainly entail:

(1) individual and group therapy for the children themselves;

(2) occasional injections of appropriate amounts of testosterone;

(3) twice weekly individual and group therapy sessions for the parents of shy boys, and particularly for the mothers;

(4) *required* attendance by parents at "Parent-Effectiveness Training" seminars operated in accordance with the well-tested and proven principles of Dr. Thomas Gordon. (See bibliography of this volume for Gordon's relevant works. See also the ONE MINUTE MOTHER and ONE MINUTE FATHER works of Dr. Spencer Johnson.)

Notes

1. Injections of *anti-anxiety* drugs with few or no side effects *such as nardil* (see the discussion in chapter 2, page 67), might also prove extremely helpful if these are begun on afflicted boys in early elementary school or even during the pre-school years. See especially Dr. David V. Sheehan's book THE ANXIETY DISEASE. The earlier in life such anti-anxiety drugs are administered, the greater the probability of completely staving off love-shyness and social isolation/unpopularity.

2. Medical researchers should test the hypothesis that the mothers of pathologically shy males have an unusually low blood progesterone level *all the time*, and not merely at or before menstruation. If such an hypothesis is borne out, it would partially explain why the love-shys' mothers had such a difficult time holding a pregnancy and giving birth to healthy children.

Chapter 7

Family Composition

One of the premises upon which this book is based is that it is possible to learn a great deal about the underlying causes of love-shyness by contrasting the backgrounds of men who are severely affected by it with the backgrounds of men who are not affected. For example, if a characteristic is very prevalent in the backgrounds of the self-confident, non-shy men, but very rare in the backgrounds of those who are love-shy, we might reasonably deduce that the absence of that characteristic *may* have some bearing upon the development of love-shyness. Contrariwise, if a characteristic is found to be very commonplace among the love-shys and rare among the non-shys, we might similarly deduce that the characteristic *might* have something to do with the development of love-shyness.

No characteristic or experience could, *by itself*, cause severe love-shyness to develop. However, with a certain number of the wrong characteristics or experiences prevalent in a person's background, severe and intractable love-shyness might be deemed quite likely to develop and to remain dominant over a person's life. Experiences and characteristics add up *not* in a mechanical way, but in a cumulative, synergistic, "chemical" kind of way. In essence, with the right complex of deleterious factors in a person's background, seriously debilitating love-shyness is highly likely to eventuate.

Brothers and Sisters

Each of the 500 men studied was asked to indicate the number of brothers and sisters that he had. In addition, each man was asked to indicate the current ages of each one of his brothers and sisters along with his own current age. Normally this type of questions does not yield particularly interesting findings. And indeed as far as *brothers* were concerned I not surprisingly found that there were no meaningful differences at all between the love-shy men and the non-shy men. In essence,

161

the love-shy men were no less likely than the non-shys to have grown up with a brother around. Moreover, the experience of having an older or younger brother was about equally prevalent in the backgrounds of both the love-shys and the non-shys.

On the other hand, *large differences* were found between the love-shys and the non-shys as far as the experience of having had a *sister* was concerned. Only 14 percent of the self-confident, non-shy men had *not* grown up with a sister around. In contrast, fully 59 percent of the university-aged love-shy men had grown up without having had a sister around. And a full 71 percent (*almost three out of every four) of the older love-shy men had never had a sister.*

On the other hand, fully 51 percent of the self-confident, non-shy males had grown up with two or more sisters, compared to only 6 percent of the younger love-shy men, and *just 3 percent* of the older love-shy men.

An interesting statistical point is of relevance here. American government statistics indicate that approximately one-third of all boys in the United States grow up without a sister. The *non-shy* men studied for this book were, as per the discussion in chapter five, more self-confident and non-shy than the average or typical young man. In essence, as a group they were blessed with an above-average level of self-confidence vis-a-vis the opposite sex. And this may be a reflection of the fact that only 14 percent of them grew up without having a sister around, compared to approximately 34 percent of American men generally, and a full 71 percent of the most severely love-shy older men who were studied for this book. (Again, 59 percent of the younger love-shys did not have a sister.)

Thus we can readily surmise that the experience of having a sister might well have had something important to do with helping to develop masculine self-confidence with women. Indeed, this suggestion becomes all the more potent when it is noted that 51 percent of the very self-confident men had two or more sisters, compared to only 6 percent and 3 percent of the two very love-shy groups.

The Mode of Standardization

There is a well supported (by research evidence) theorem in sociology called the "mode of standardization". Simply put, this theorem stipulates that: the more frequently two different kinds of groups interact with each other (provided that the interaction is not brought about by coercion), the better able to understand and to appreciate each other those two different kinds of people or groups are likely to become. In essence, frequent interaction leads to mutual understanding, liking and loving. Moreover, it also leads to a gradual and ever increasing concordance of attitudes, values, beliefs, hopes, desires, aspirations, and dreams between the two different kinds of people or groups. In short, through frequently interacting, people gradually come to think pretty much alike and also to like and even to love as well as to understand one another.

Years of interviewing very shy men have convinced me that love-shys do not understand women very well at the gut emotional (as opposed to intellectual) level. And what people do not understand they tend to fear. For men with sisters, interacting with females who are in their own age group tends to remove much of the aura of mystery surrounding the female sex. More succinctly, through growing up with sisters around boys are accorded the valuable experience of frequently and directly interacting with female age-mates on a thoroughly informal basis. They are thus permitted to relate to girls as people who are little different from themselves.

Important too is the fact that sisters very often bring their friends home for after school play and for a myriad of recreational activities. Normally adjusted boys similarly invite to their homes their own same-sexed friends. Thus, throughout their formative years youngsters who grow up in families with opposite-sexed siblings are at a clear advantage in that they are accorded the near-daily opportunity to meet and to informally socialize not only with their own opposite-sexed siblings, but also with the close friends of these siblings. During adolescense opposite-sexed siblings can provide an important pool of potential dating partners in the friends whom they invite to the home.

Even when brothers do not date their sisters' friends, as is typically the case when the sister is older rather than younger than the brother, the presence of a sister still provides a growing boy with an unending series of valuable learning experiences. Thus, having a sister allows a boy to perceive girls as real people who can be approached, joked around with, argued with, and whose companionship can be enjoyed. Having a sister provides a man with a head start in being able to *relax* emotionally around women. And the ability to relax and feel comfortable when around women is the first step towards bypassing or overcoming the love-shyness problem.

In her 1976 book entitled DILEMMAS OF MASCULINITY, Mirra Komarovsky cited her own research evidence indicating that *for young men* a history of good relations with *sisters* was a far more important determinant of self-confidence in successful dating and courting of young women than was a history of good relations with brothers or even with mothers.[1] My own data indicated that neither the quality of the brother-sister relationship nor whether the sister was the older or younger sibling, made anywhere nearly as much difference in terms of predicting a man's non-shyness in his informal relationships with women as did the mere fact of his simply having a sister in the first place. Only very few of the men studied for this book had poor or strained relationships with their sisters. And whereas having a younger sister did yield a better payoff for the male than did having an older sister, my own data indicate that even an older sister is far better for a boy than not having any sister at all.

Interactions vis-a-vis Married People

The "mode of standardization" theorem provides a good explanation as to why never married men usually find *married* women considerably easier than never married women to talk with. And, of course, it is no secret that single, never married women typically find married men much easier and more pleasant to talk with than they find never married men to be. Married people are ordinarily used to talking on an intimate basis to people of the opposite sex. After all, they do it with their spouses every day. Thus they do not need to put on any kind of a defensive, sham act. Simply put, married people are less likely than single people to need the protective mask of a role or a script.

Of course, this natural ease which never married people feel when they are in conversation with married people often gives rise to problems. Secretaries who are otherwise quite conventional sometimes find themselves falling in love with their married bosses or job colleagues. Such love relationships often create a great deal of emotional pain and suffering for everyone involved. And yet these same rather conventional women who take such delight in talking with married men (often to the point of getting themselves emotionally entangled) often behave in an annoyingly aloof and disinterested way vis-a-vis the available single, never married males prevalent within their social and work environments. Often the tragedy is that the never married man remains lonely while the never married woman allows herself to become severely hurt over an attached man whom she cannot possibly win. And the never married man remains much more socially inept than he otherwise would if he had the interested involvement of the woman who keeps spurning him in favor of the smooth-talking, non-shy already married man.

Despite extreme and chronic love-shyness, most of the love-shy men interviewed for this book could recall instances wherein they had stumbled upon a conversation with a married woman who had been either in their own age range or younger. And virtually all of these love-shy men were amazed at how easily they could talk with these married women, and at how completely relaxed they had been made to feel by these women's attitude toward them. Many of these men recalled how frustrated and bitter they had felt upon learning that the woman was married or otherwise "taken". In fact, had she not been "taken", it is likely that at least some of these severely love-shy males could have developed a viable and potentially permanent relationship. My point, of course, is that young women who are spontaneous and open, without any pretenses, are much easier for love-shy men to open up with than are single, never married women who feel constrained to play a role. As a result of being unused to interacting with male age-mates on an open, honest, and casual basis, the never married woman in her role playing and mask wearing diffidence erects barriers to free-flowing conversation that are every bit as real and impenetrable as the barriers which the love-shy male erects.

One of the questions to which each of the men in this study responded reflects these problems very poignantly. I asked each man to react to this statement: "It seems that whenever I develop a crush on someone I soon find out that the person is already taken." And 100 percent of the older love-shys fully agreed with this statement together with 86 percent of the younger (university aged) love-shys. In contrast, only 20 percent of the self-confident non-shy men saw fit to agree with this statement.

In having had a good deal of experience at interacting with women (*including sisters*) throughout their lives, the non-shy men seemed to enjoy a relatively easy facility at penetrating the coolness and aloofness barriers that are commonplace among never married women in our culture. Perhaps the non-shys' calm self-confidence and suave, non-threatening bearing assured them of being perceived in much the same way that single women usually perceive married men. Then too, it seems probable that the competitive nature of the non-shys served to render them difficult to discourage.

For the love-shy males, on the other hand, the disinterested airs of single girls cause feelings of fear, anxiety and discouragement. Lacking past experiences with sisters and with other young women, the love-shy take life too seriously. And they are thus unable to roll with the punches and sustain a creative, happy sense of humor about the foibles of human nature—as these foibles affect heterosexual interaction and the various sham acts and pretenses that both genders tend to use on one another.

Implications for Prevention

Unfortunately, it is not possible to assure every boy of growing up in a family which contains a sister. (See the chapter titled "Parenthood Aspirations" for a scientific technique that can allow parents to choose in advance the genders of their future children with up to 85 percent accuracy.) However, there are certain things which parents and elementary school officials *can do* right now to provide sisterless boys (particularly the socially isolated and withdrawn) with a viable alternative to the experience of having a sister.

I would recommend the development of a new children's recreational organization to be called the *"Coed Scouts"*. For many decades such organizations as the Boy Scouts, Girl Scouts, Cub Scouts, Boys Club of America, Brownies, Campfire Girls, YMCA and YWCA, have done big business. But these organizations have all traditionally segregated children according to gender. I believe that this traditional practice is counterproductive in our contemporary quite *coeducational* world. And this is particularly true as far as socially isolated, shy and inhibited young boys are concerned. Satisfactory adjustment in adulthood absolutely requires an ability to get along smoothly and harmoniously with *both* genders. Boys who are shy and withdrawn vis-a-vis their own gender at the elementary school level are almost always afflicted with incipient love-shyness. Thus there can be no question but that such boys would benefit enormously from membership in an organization comprised of equal numbers of girls and boys which entails weekly recreational activities, and which makes it both very easy and very pleasant for the two genders to interact socially.

From the time children reach the age of two, American parents begin taking steps to encourage their children to play in gender-segregated peer groups, and to develop friendships exclusively with individuals of their own gender. Yet research evidence has shown that young children do not *naturally* ("instinctually") gravitate towards gender-segregated peer groups. If left entirely to their own devices a majority of children in fact choose to play in coeducational peer groups.

I believe that the easy availability to all children of a coeducational peer group would represent an extremely useful preventive device for nipping heterosexual love-shyness in the bud. The little boy who will eventually develop into a young man so severely shy with girls that he cannot date or marry *can easily be spotted* in kindergarten and in the first grade. And inasmuch as he *can* be readily spotted, failure to take positive action to stem the tide of his ever worsening love-shyness is both unnecessary, unethical, and immoral. The very shy man is of little use to himself or to his society and community. Failure to take action where it is warrented is tantamount to discarding valuable human resources.

The Only Child

The status of being an "only child" was a great deal more common among the ranks of the love-shy men than it was among the self-confident, non-shy respondents. Only *seven percent* of the non-shy men had grown up as only children. In contrast, 25 percent of the younger (university aged) love-shys and 31 percent of the older love-shy men had grown up as only children.

A note of caution is in order here. The vast majority of research studies in both psychology and in child development that have looked at only children have found them to be *better adjusted* than children with siblings. Indeed, this is especially true for only male children. Boys without any brothers and sisters *normally* enjoy significantly higher levels of self-esteem and social self-confidence than do the large majority of boys with brothers and sisters.

So how come *this* research study revealed a strong relationship between only child status and severe love-shyness? My suspicion is that the experience of growing up an only child serves to increase the chances of extreme shyness *if and only if* incompetent parenting and inhibition genes are involved. It is quite probable that most people who have only children turn out to be at least slightly *above* average in parental competence. In contrast, the data collected for this book strongly suggest that severely love-shy males tend to have had a history of less than adequate parenting.

Thus, for those with parents of normal effectiveness growing up an only child can be an advantage. However, when the mother and the father are less than adequately competent, the only child with the inhibition gene is left with no one around to mitigate the psychoemotional blows that often come to pass. When brothers and/or sisters are around they will usually incur at least some of the parents' wrath and bizarre behavior. And even though many families with more than one child do make a scapegoat out of one specific individual, siblings very often do protect one another to at least some extent from the behavior of hostile, capricious and bizarre parents.

With virtually no exceptions, all of the love-shy men I studied who had grown up as only children recounted a large number of bizarre, erratic and capricious incidents perpetrated by their parents, and particularly by their mothers. Words like "irascible", "abrasive", "truculent", "tense", "high strung", "cantankerous", and "petulent", were typically used by this group to describe their mothers. Even now as adults, virtually none of these only children seemed to like their mothers to any extent.

The love-shys' mothers seemed to have conveyed an extremely frightening and obnoxious image of womanhood—an image that is anything but attractive or alluring. For those who grew up as only children this type of obnoxious behavior had to be dealt with alone and without any help from anyone. Many of the men I interviewed had learned to accept their mother's behavior on an intellectual level. On an emotional level, however, virtually none of these love-shy men had made any headway at all in coming to grips with commonplace events of their formative years.

Kinship Relationships

In traditional societies men and women were seldom left entirely to their own devices in rearing children. If a mother or a father happened to be under great stress or for some other reason could not properly care for their child, a relative such as an aunt or an uncle would take over for a time. In fact, even in the contemporary United States most families seem to be enmeshed in a kinship network which provides a considerable amount of help on occasions when things become a little too tough. Recent studies on child abuse have documented the fact that abusers tend to be far more isolated from relatives, kin, and chosen friends, than nonabusive parents. Men who beat their wives similarly tend to be isolated, as do their victimized wives.

Accordingly, it seemed appropriate to ask both the shy and the non-shy men some questions about the extent to which there might have been other adult relatives around, besides their parents, upon whom they could have depended for emotional support as they were growing up. One of the questions I asked required each respondent to react to the following statement:

> "When I was growing up I had at least 3 or 4 other adult relatives besides my parents to whom I could turn for help and emotional support."

The results were remarkable, and convey a strong suggestion that emotional support networks among relatives and kin serve to enhance children's capacities to cope effectively with stress and to deal competently and self-confidently with the world.

Zero percent of the older love-shy men indicated that the above statement was *true* for them. Only 9 percent of the younger love-shy men indicated that it was true, whereas an impressive 59 percent of the self-confident non-shy men indicated that it was true.

Respondents were given the opportunity to check that this statement was "very untrue" for them, or merely "untrue". The dramatic differences between the three groups of men become accentuated when it is observed that 94 percent of the older love-shys indicated that the statement was "very untrue" for them, compared to 71 percent of the younger love-shy men, and only 13 percent of the self-confident non-shy men.

Each respondent was further asked to indicate just exactly *how many* relatives (other than parents) he had had available for help and emotional support during his formative years as a child and teenager. Fully 53 percent of the non-shy men indicated that they had had three or more relatives to count on. Only 8 percent of the younger love-shy men and *zero percent* of the older love-shy men were able to indicate that while growing up they could count on three or more adult relatives.

In fact, 87 percent of the older love-shy men said that there had been *no* relatives they could have counted upon as a child for help or emotional support. The analogous figures for the love-shy and non-shy university males were 68 percent and 27 percent respectively.

As for *the present time*, fully all 100 percent of the older love-shys and 71 percent of the younger love-shys agreed that *"there is no one I can turn to"*. Zero percent (nobody) of the non-shys agreed with that statement and sentiment.

Quality of Parents' Marriages

There is evidence that the love-shys' parents had somewhat less satisfying marriages than did the parents of the non-shys. However, the issue of divorce versus non-divorce did not differentiate between the three groups of parents. In other words, the love-shys' parents were no more likely than the non-shys' parents to have ever divorced or separated. For example, 20 percent of the non-shys' parents had either divorced or separated. The analogous figure for the older love-shys was 17 percent, and for the younger love-shys it was 23 percent. Looking at divorce alone (excluding separation), only 6 percent of the older love-shys' parents had been divorced. Eight percent of the younger love-shys' parents had divorced. And just 7 percent of the non-shys' parents had been divorced.

However, I asked another question which may constitute a better barometer of marital quality than the issue of divorce/separation itself. I asked each man: "If your parents were not divorced, about how happy would you rate the quality of their marriage?" *Excluding* those men whose parents had actually been divorced, fully 45 percent of the older love-shys and 41 percent of the young love-shys classified their parents' marriages as having been "not too happy" or "unhappy". Among the non-shy men, 31 percent classified their parents' marriages this way.

In another question I asked: "Did your parents get along with each other during your childhood, or was there conflict, fighting, and dis-satisfaction?" And here only 6 percent of the non-shy men indicated that their parents had gotten along with each other *less than moderately well*. In contrast, fully 36 percent of the older love-shy men together with 31 percent of the younger love-shys indicated that their parents had gotten along with each other *less than moderately well*.

I also asked each man: "While you were growing up, about how often did your father praise your mother?" And only 12 percent of the non-shys responded "rarely or never", compared to 30 percent of the young love-shys and 35 percent of the older ones. This question may have some implications in terms of *modeling*. Most sons, including even those who do not get along very well with their fathers, model their own behavior to some extent after that of their fathers. The love-shys' inability to relate to young women in a positive way may be partially attributable to deficits in the ways in which their own fathers had failed to openly model this behavior vis-a-vis their mothers. Of course, as so much evidence presented in this book indicates, most of the love-shys' mothers had been far from charming or attractive. And perhaps their objective qualities and characteristics had done little to inspire praise or admiration from husbands or sons.

To be sure, praise had not flown in a particularly generous fashion in the reverse direction either. I asked each man: "While you were growing up, about how often did your mother praise your father?" And only 6 percent of the *non-shy* men indicated "rarely or hardly ever". In contrast, fully 28 percent of the young love-shys and 33 percent of the older love-shys said "rarely or hardly ever".

In sum, it would appear that the love-shys' parents had had significantly less emotionally satisfying marriages than those of the non-shy men. And this had doubtless been reflected in the ways these parents had openly comported themselves vis-a-vis each other around the house.

However, it also appears that the love-shys' parents had had some aversion to the divorce option. Perhaps there had been an unhealthy, symbiotic dependency between the husbands and the wives in many of these marriages. In other words, frequent turmoil and tension may have been perceived by many of these people as less threatening and less distressing than the idea of divorce or permanent separation. In essence, a tension-filled relationship may have been viewed as preferable to the absence of any close primary relationship at all.

Conclusions

The most commonplace family composition among *both* severely love-shy groups was a pair of parents with an intact marriage, and one or two brothers and *no* sisters. The research data obtained for this book clearly suggest that severe love-shyness is strongly associated with the experience of having grown up in a family without female siblings. "Only child" status was also found to be associated with severe love-shyness. However, it was pointed out that "only children" *with competent parents* are probably at even less risk of developing severe love-shyness than children (of competent parents) who do have siblings.

Finally, severe love-shyness appears to be strongly associated with growing up in a family which does not afford any adult relatives or kin, *other than parents*, upon whom a child can count for emotional support and help. Simply put, the families of the love-shys were much more isolated from relatives and kin, than were the families of the non-shy men. Further, the little kin interaction which the love-shys had experienced throughout their formative years tended to have been much "cooler" and less emotionally satisfying than that which had been experienced by the non-shy men.

Interactions with siblings and with adult relatives and kinfolk can do much to absorb a considerable amount of the stress and turbulence created by emotionally disordered parental behavior. In most cases the love-shys did not have such benefits available to them. On the other hand, most of them did grow up in intact homes. The parents of the love-shys were no more likely than those of the non-shy men to have ever divorced or separated. However, the *emotional quality* of the marriages of the love-shys' parents appears in most cases to have been markedly inferior to that prevalent in the marriages of the non-shys' parents.

Notes

1. Almost two-thirds of the non-virginal men in Komarovsky's study had enjoyed favorable relations with their sisters. This had been true for *only two-fifths* of the sexually inexperienced men whom she studied.

Chapter 8

Parents as a Cause of Love-Shyness

In 1979, sociologists Boyd C. Rollins and Darwin L. Thomas published an important article which reviewed hundreds of research studies pertinent to the relationship between family atmosphere, and passive, socially reticent behavior. I want to underscore that the following statements reflect the quite consistent research results of *hundreds of studies* in the social and behavioral sciences. In fact, the propositions which appear below have become an integral part of what is now considered to be *valid knowledge*. I present these propositions here because they anticipate very nicely and with remarkable accuracy the findings at which I arrived after years of interviewing and studying severely love-shy men. Indeed, most of my own findings of pertinence to maternal and paternal behavior can be subsumed under one or another of the following propositions:

Proposition #1: The greater the amount of warm, emotional supportiveness that is displayed by parents towards their children, the greater the amount of *social competence* that will eventually be developed and displayed by those children.

Proposition #2: The greater the amount of use that parents make of *verbal reasoning* in the disciplining of their children, the greater the amount of social competence that will eventually be developed and displayed by those children.

Proposition #3: The greater the amount and use that parents make of physical coercion in their attempts to influence and control their children, the *LESS social competence* those children will eventually develop and display.

Proposition #4: The greater the amount of warm, emotional supportiveness that is displayed by parents towards their children, the fewer the behavior problems (*of which shyness is one*) that those children will develop and display.

Proposition #5: The greater the incidence of parental coercion (use of force), the greater the behavior problems in children.

Proposition #6: The more parents try to control the behavior of their children, the greater the likelihood that behavior problems will develop.

Proposition #7: The greater the parental coercion, the lower the self-esteem and self-confidence of children.

Proposition #8: The greater the amount of warm, emotional supportiveness that is displayed by parents towards their children, the higher the level of self-esteem and self-confidence that will be developed and displayed by those children.

Proposition #9: The greater the amount of use that parents make of *verbal reasoning* in the disciplining of their children, the greater the amount of self-esteem and self-confidence those children are likely to develop.

Proposition #10: The greater the parental supportiveness, the lower the incidence of schizophrenia in children.

Proposition #11: The greater the parental coercion, the greater the incidence of schizophrenia in children.

Proposition #12: For both boys and girls, the greater the coerciveness of the *opposite sexed parent*, the less adequate will be the child's own-gender sex role orientation. In essence, dominant, coercive mothers tend to breed passive, feminized boys.

Proposition #13: The greater the relative dominance of the father over the mother, the stronger will be the masculine sex role orientation in boys.

Proposition #14: The greater the parental power of the *same-sexed parent*, the greater the social competence of children.

Proposition #15: The greater the coercive control attempts of parents, the greater the social incompetence in children.

Proposition #16: Fathers' emotional supportiveness is strongly associated with a healthy masculine sex role orientation in boys.

It is worth repeating that each of the foregoing sixteen propositions has been well supported by hundreds of well executed research studies.

The research findings pertinent to severely love-shy men which I shall delineate on the remaining pages of this and the following chapter, all corroborate the validity of these propositions. Thus, these propositions are all well worth learning and using in the course of ordinary, day-to-day interaction vis-a-vis all of one's loved ones. To the extent that these propositions are learned and acted upon, to that extent the incidence of severe love-shyness in our society can be *and will be* enormously reduced.

Children are exposed to the large majority of their most influential learning experiences in just two places: (1) the family, and (2) the peer group. Chapter 10 will focus upon the latter. This chapter and the following one will examine the impact which parents have upon the development of severe love-shyness.

Family Atmosphere

The general atmosphere of the family in which a child grows up exerts a cumulative impact upon his view of the world and of himself. Numerous questions regarding family atmosphere were included in the questionnaire. And the findings tended to sharply and consistently differentiate the love-shys from the non-shys.

For example, I asked each man: "Compared to most people, about how happy would you say your family life was during your childhood years?" And fully 89 percent of the non-shys indicated that it had been either "very happy" or "happy". In contrast, this was true for only 31 percent of the younger love-shys and for a mere 19 percent of the older love-shys. In fact, the love-shys differed from the non-shys even more sharply regarding how happy they felt their family lives had been during their *teenaged years*. Fully 82 percent of the non-shys rated their family lives as having been either "very happy" or "happy" during their teenaged years. Only 22 percent of the younger love-shys together with a mere 14 percent of the older love-shys rated their family lives as having been this happy during their teenaged years.

Of course, questions such as these are fundamentally subjective. And some readers may feel that love-shys are "pathological complainers". However, people are governed to a far greater extent by what they subjectively believe to have been the case than by what the objective state of affairs might have been. When the obtained differences to a subjective question are as great as those which obtained here, I think it is reasonable to infer significance for the etiology of love-shyness. If the love-shy are indeed "pathological complainers", we need to concern ourselves with the question of how they got to be that way in the first place. The process of becoming a "pathological complainer" may not be too different from that which is involved in becoming severely love-shy.

Further, there is a *social desirability* element to many of the questions to be dealt with in this chapter. Most people tend to exaggerate the extent of their past family happiness. The tendency of most people to adjudge happiness in a positive direction renders the love-shys' pattern of negative responses all the more impressive and noteworthy.

Extent of Family Emotional Supportiveness

I asked each man: "To what extent did you feel that your parents believed in you and supported you emotionally?" And 67 percent of the non-shy men answered "a great deal", compared to only 32 percent of the younger love-shys and 23 percent of the older ones. Contrariwise, 58 percent of the older love-shy men felt that their parents had provided them with very little if any emotional support. Among the younger love-shys 48 percent felt that they had received very little if any emotional support, compared to a mere 13 percent of the non-shy men.

Meaningful participation by children in dinner table conversation has been found by a good many researchers to correlate highly with active participation throughout adulthood in community and political affairs. Thus, I asked each respondent how frequently he had been able to participate meaningfully in dinner table conversation during his formative years in his parents' home. The obtained differences between the love-shys and the non-shys were quite substantial on this question. For example, 80 percent of the *non-shy* men indicated that their participation in dinner table conversations had been "frequent" or "very frequent", compared to only 36 percent of the younger love-shys and just 23 percent of the older love-shys.

Hence, it cannot be considered surprising that rather substantial differences obtained between the three groups with regard to reactions to this statement: "I always felt free and comfortable about discussing my problems with my parents." In one sense this might be considered a poor item because virtually no child is very likely to "*always*" feel free and comfortable about talking with parents. Nevertheless, 52 percent of the non-shys indicated that the statement was "true" for them. Only 17 percent of the younger love-shys together with just 10 percent of the older love-shys felt the same way. Indeed, 66 percent of the older love-shys and 57 percent of the younger ones felt that the statement was definitely "untrue". Only 19 percent of the non-shys felt that it was "untrue".

The love-shys' parents evidently had not acted particularly interested in what their sons had had to say. I asked each respondent: "As far as you can tell, how interested were your parents and other family members in what you had to say?" Fully 52 percent of the older love-shys together with 45 percent of the younger ones responded that their parents had been either "not too interested" or "not interested", compared to *zero percent* (nobody) of the non-shys. In fact, 74 percent of the non-shy men indicated that their parents had been either "very interested" or "interested". Only 27 percent of the older love-shy men and 34 percent of the younger ones felt that their parents had been "very interested" or "interested" in what they had had to say.

And when I asked: "How frequently did you enjoy informal conversations with your mother about any topic?" only 5 percent of the non-shy men indicated "infrequently". In contrast, 58 percent of the older love-shys together with 46 percent of the younger ones indicated that they had enjoyed such conversations on an "infrequent" basis. The findings when this same question was asked with regard to *fathers* were quite similar. Fully 43 percent of the older love-shys along with 37 percent of the younger ones indicated that they had enjoyed informal conversations with their fathers on an "infrequent" basis. The analogous percent for the non-shy men was *zero* (nobody).

Another question pertinent to parental emotional supportiveness which clearly differentiated the three different groups of respondents was: "When you received a low grade at school on a test or paper, did you feel free and comfortable about discussing the matter with your mother?" Fully 65 percent of the non-shy men indicated the affirmative, compared to only 39 percent of the younger love-shys, and just 32 percent of the older love-shys. In fact, several of the love-shy men spontaneously mentioned that for them to have approached their mothers about a poor performance on a paper at school would really have constituted a case of "double jeopardy". In essence, they could have looked forward to the very antithesis of "emotional supportiveness" from their mothers in this type of situation.

Probably the most "telltale" item in this set was the statement: "My mother sometimes acted as though I didn't exist." Fully 43 percent of the older love-shy men and 35 percent of the younger love-shys indicated "yes" to this statement, compared to *zero percent* of the non-shy men.

I asked the same question with regard to the fathers, and was somewhat surprised to find a somewhat less pathological set of responses than I had found with regard to the mothers. Only 30 percent of the older love-shys felt that their fathers had sometimes acted as though they (the love-shys) did not exist. The analogous percentage for the younger love-shys was 22 percent. Again, none of the non-shys felt that their fathers had ever ignored their existence.

The Komarovsky Study

The 1976 Mirra Komarovsky study titled DILEMMAS OF MAS-CULINITY compared and contrasted the personalities and family backgrounds of virginal and non-virginal Columbia University men. Only a fourth of the undergraduate men in her study were virginal, and she found them to have had significantly lower self-images together with much weaker self-ratings for self-confidence, than had been the case for the sexually experienced men. Moreover, 73 percent of the virginal men fell below the mean for university students on the *sociability* factor; only 29 percent of the non-virgins similarly fell below the mean on sociability. Also, 47 percent of her virginal men fell below average on the *self-acceptance* factor, compared to only 2 percent of the non-virginal men.

Of course, most of Komarovsky's virginal men *were* dating at least occasionally; and a substantial minority of them gave "moral-religious" reasons for not having experienced premarital coitus. Thus as a group Komarovsky's virgins cannot be considered equivalent to the pathologically love-shy men upon whom this book is intended to focus. Nevertheless, Komarovsky's personality profiles for the virginal men are certainly of very much the same sort as the personality profiles for the love-shys of the current study.

With this in mind, it is interesting that Komarovsky found *fathers* to have been more important than mothers in differentiating the virginal men from those who had had sexual experience with a girlfriend. For example, only 42 percent of the virgins had rated their relationships with their fathers as having been favorable. Among the non-virgins, on the other hand, 62 percent rated their relationships with their fathers as having been favorable. In contrast, just under four-fifths of *both* groups rated their relationships with their *mothers* as having been favorable.

> "The virgins reported less satisfactory relationships with their fathers than the non-virgins did . . . . The tests portrayed the virgins as deficient in self-esteem relative to the sexually experienced seniors . . . . It is likely that an unfavorable self-image would drain the son's confidence to take the initiative in sexual advances to women. Thus, we can conclude that unfavorable father-son relationships tended to be associated with virginity by lowering the self-esteem and self-confidence of the son." (Komarovsky, 1976, p. 243.)

Komarovsky's findings are quite interesting inasmuch as my own data seem to lead to a very different conclusion. In most cases, according to my own data, pathologically love-shy men appear to have had *considerably worse* relationships with their mothers than with their fathers. In fact, for many of these men the mother-son relationship had been so extremely bad as well as bizarre that "maternal" behavior may have served as a major factor precipitating severe love-shyness.

One young man seemed to have arrived at quite a bit of insight regarding this matter:

> "I realize now that my mother probably couldn't help doing a lot of the things that she did. But I mean an eight year old kid doesn't really have an intellect yet. And all this stuff from my mother I'm sure had a cumulative impact on me that the intellect I have now just hasn't been able to fend off. I mean, all that stuff affects you more at the gut level. And I think that's what lasts. Your intellect can't fight off all the things that had been programmed into your gut throughout all the years of growing up." (23-year old love-shy man.)

Of course, the love-shys' relationships with their fathers had similarly been far from ideal. However, most of the men had been able to communicate at least a little bit with their fathers. And very few of the father-son relationships seemed to contain the bizarre elements that had been quite prevalent in the mother-son relationships.

Family Democracy

The issue of family democracy is obviously quite closely related to the matter of how open, spontaneous, and unfettered by defensiveness family communication had been. A democratic family environment is one wherein children continually play an active role in the making and revising of all the rules, regulations and policies that impact upon them. It is an environment characterized by high levels of mutual respect and mutual trust. The parents in such families both respect and trust their children because they know that genuine respect inspires respect, that trust inspires trust, and that love breeds love. Such parents intuitively realize that it is always the superordinate figure (i.e., the parent) who must make the first move towards inspiring (*by their actions*) respect, love, trust, etc. And such parents realize the prime importance of open, honest, non-threatening communication that is unfettered by any ambiance of defensiveness or fear.

In looking over the research literature on this subject I realized its relevancy to the love-shyness problem. For example, Robert Lane of Yale University, found that children who had taken an active part in dinner table conversations throughout the years of growing up tended to be far more likely as adults to vote and to take an active part in community affairs. Psychologist Kurt Lewin similarly accumulated strong and consistent evidence indicating that democratically managed families breed young people who are highly self-reliant, responsible, self-disciplined, goal oriented, and socially involved. Shy people have long been known to cringe at the thought of self-disclosure. Unlike non-shys, love-shy people tend to be unable and unwilling to share their deepest thoughts and feelings with others. Keeping to themselves almost all the time, they tend to be uninvolved both socially and politically.

Two of the questionnaire items that were incorporated into this study have a direct bearing upon the family democracy issue. Specifically, I asked each respondent: "While you were growing up, did you have any influence over the making and the revising of family rules and policies that affected you?" The respondents could check any one of four different options: (1) yes, much; (2) yes, some; (3) yes, little; and (4) none.

In sum, fully 82 percent of the older love-shy men together with 69 percent of the younger love-shys had "*little or no*" influence over the way in which their families had been managed. In stark contrast, only 26 percent of the non-shy men similarly indicated that they had had "little or no" influence. Putting it another way, 74 percent of the non-shys had had either "much" or "some" influence over the ways their families had been managed. This had been true for only 18 percent of the older love-shys and for 31 percent of the younger love-shy men.

In fact, 52 percent of the *older* love-shys indicated that they had enjoyed *no* influence at all over the way their families had been run. Only 12 percent of the non-shys similarly indicated "*no*" influence at all in regard to family management policies. Indeed, 36 percent of the non-shys indicated that they had had "*much*" influence in the daily process of family management. Only 4 percent of the older love-shys and 6 percent of the younger love-shys similarly felt that they had had "*much*" influence.

The second question was asked much later on in the interview. This was done to assure overall reliability and validity of the research findings. The second item simply asked each man to react to this statement: "While I was growing up, even though I was a child I usually had a meaningful role in the way our family was run." Fully 73 percent of the non-shy men answered "true" to this statement, compared to only 34 percent of the younger love-shys and 27 percent of the older ones.

Mutual Sensitivity to Needs and Feelings

An increasing number of social scientists are beginning to define "*love*" as *the communication of a compassionate mutual sensitivity to one another's needs and feelings*. In order for a person to reap the benefits of love he or she must first *feel* loved. The data obtained for this book very clearly indicate that the parents (and *particularly the mothers*) of the love-shy (1) did little to make their sons *feel* loved, and (2) had very little if any awareness or insight into the way in which their behavior was impacting upon their sons' psychoemotional development.

> "Ah, she had the radio or the television on all the time. If I came in the room where she was she'd scream at me that she was trying to concentrate. Even during meal times she would have the radio on. I can remember throughout all my school years how my mother and my father would both clobber me if I opened my mouth while we were eating dinner. They wanted to concentrate on what some news commentator was saying. But when I grew older it would be the same old story, even if the program was some stupid contest show or soap opera. Everything was more important than I was. I guess at the time I didn't think of it that way. But as I grew older I began to realize that I was just a sort of distraction to my parents. I was never the main show, or even the cartoon for that matter—ha, ha, ha!" (24-year old love-shy man.)

Most of the love-shys' mothers undoubtedly believed that they truly loved their sons. In fact, many of these mothers frequently *screamed* out that they "loved" their sons. And they sometimes shouted this with great rage! *But they didn't SHOW IT*. In essence, they would say one thing and do something which conveyed a very different message entirely.[1]

Such behaviors as forcing their sons to go to summer camp, and keeping the radio on at the dinner table instead of encouraging their sons to express themselves, illustrate well the crass insensitivity of the love-shys' parents. The emotional needs and feelings of the love-shys had mattered very little if at all. The love-shys' parents had been task oriented and "final results oriented", rather than person-oriented. They had been concerned about shaping and molding a son who would gain status and prestige for them in their local communities. In *that* sense they had cared about their sons. They "cared" that their sons would be propitiously shaped and molded to fit their image of what a good son should be like. But they did not care much about their sons as people with deep feelings, emotions, and needs requiring recognition, respect, and emotional support.

There is an interesting paradox here. On one level many of the love-shys' parents had been quite generous. They gave their sons many material things, and often cried out in exasperated resignation about how "ungrateful" and "spoiled" their sons were. The following interview segment well illustrates this:

> "Oh, my parents were generous alright! The trouble is they were usually generous with the wrong things. Like even when I was a young kid my parents would constantly drag me into the best clothing stores. I was always the best dressed kid in town. They would

constantly buy all these expensive outfits for me. But when I asked them to buy me a toy or a book or a record on the way home, they would complain about how spoiled I was; and they would threaten to beat the shit out of me if I didn't stop agitating them about a toy. They were always very generous about getting me what I didn't particularly want or care about. But when it came to something I really did want the answer was always how spoiled and ungrateful I was, and why I didn't get the hell out and earn the money to buy it myself. The strange thing is—what they were buying me always cost a great deal more money than the things I really did want. And some of the things they bought I seldom even wore." (20-year old love-shy man.)

The preoccupation which many of the love shys' parents had about clothing and appearance is well reflected in the response pattern to this questionnaire item: "Until I graduated from high school, my parents almost always decided what I would wear each day." Fully 33 percent of the older love-shy men *agreed* with this statement, together with 22 percent of the younger love-shys. *None* of the non-shy men agreed with it. In fact, one love-shy man spontaneously volunteered that every morning until the day he graduated from high school his father would come into his bedroom, drag him up, put his socks on for him, and then physically drag him into the bathroom where he (the father) would wash the son's face and remove in a sometimes painful manner any blackheads which had been apparent. And while the father did all this he would angrily rail and berate the son for being irresponsible and uncaring about being late for school.

At one point in the questionnaire, I asked each man to react to the statement: "At Christmas when I was a child my parents almost always gave me too many clothes and not enough toys." And 38 percent of the older love-shy men along with 27 percent of the younger love-shys *agreed*. In contrast, only 12 percent of the self-confident non-shy men agreed with that statement. And in a similar item I asked for reactions to this statement: "My parents tried to wean me from stuffed animals, dolls, and other toys too early in life." Here again there were substantial differences between the love-shys and the non-shys. Fully 27 percent of the older love-shys along with 23 percent of the younger ones *agreed* with this statement. Only 7 percent of the non-shy men agreed.

"Milk" versus "Honey"

In his celebrated 1956 work entitled THE ART OF LOVING, social philosopher Erich Fromm distinguished between two types of "love": (1) *milk*, and (2) *honey*. The "milk" has to do with the provision of food, clothing, shelter, as well as all the material luxeries. "Honey", on the other hand, has to do with conveying to the child a sense of deep personal worth, happiness, vibrancy—a feeling that life itself is intrinsically rich and highly worthwhile.

When people are uncomfortable with life they often develop a grandiose preoccupation with *appearance*, rather than with the *human side* of interpersonal relationships. Highly tense and less-than-happy parents often shower their children with all manner of material goodies—"*milk*", to use Fromm's metaphorical term. When the recipients of all this "milk" do not respond in the expected manner the parents are likely to angrily (and with *hurt* feelings) accuse them of being "ungrateful", "spoiled", "mean", "inconsiderate", etc. Yet in spite of not securing the desired outcomes, these frustrated parents persist in showering their "ungrateful" child with more and more "milk". The vicious cycle repeats and repeats and repeats itself *ad nauseum*: the parents give and the child does not respond favorably. The parents feel hurt and angry and accuse the child of being ungrateful and spoiled. And then the parents go on to commence showering their "ungrateful" child with some other form of expensive "milk".

Of course, we must be clear on what the *true culprit* is here. Moralists have characteristically made the mistake of blaming the excessive supply of "milk". Their advice has always been to stop showering the kid with so much milk because he doesn't appreciate it anyway. "And besides, you're only spoiling him rotten. The more you do for him, the less he appreciates," etc.

The fallacy of the moralist's approach can be readily observed every day in the thousands of children from financially well-off homes who had always received a copious abundance of material goodies and who had never wanted for anything. Most of these children grow up very happy, exuberant, very sociable and socially well-skilled, well adjusted, self-disciplined, and genuinely loving of life *and of the parents as well*. How do such children get this way after having received such an excess abundance of "milk"? Many of such children receive brand new automobiles upon graduating high school, trips to Europe, etc. And yet they turn out charming, love their parents, their parents are delighted with them, and most facets of their lives and of the lives of their parents function quite well.

Simply put, it is NOT a matter of HOW MUCH "MILK" a child gets that makes the difference. A child can receive a surfeit of the material goodies, and still be a real joy both to himself/herself AND to his/her parents. More succinctly, *the thing that makes all the difference in the world is the presence of a significant amount of "honey" to accompany whatever amount of "milk" may be given.* AN EXCESSIVE AMOUNT OF "MILK" CAN

NEVER BY ITSELF "SPOIL" A CHILD OR MAKE HIM/HER SEEM UNGRATEFUL. *But ANY AMOUNT of "milk" given in the absence of a healthy amount of "honey" can and will "spoil" the child.*

As Erich Fromm has convincingly argued, *both* "milk" *and* "honey" are essential human needs. Some minimum amount of "milk" is a *sine qua non* for mere survival. The paradox is that children who receive a very great deal of "milk" from their parents along with very little if any "honey" are scarcely more than "just surviving". As adults they end up "just existing". In the case of the love-shy, they just "hang on" with rather colorless and emotionally hollow lives.

A parent cannot compensate for deficits in the ability to disseminate "honey" by going overboard in the dissemination of "milk". Many of the love-shys' parents had gone "overboard" in disseminating the "milk" of huge wardrobes of clothing, material possessions, the best food, money, etc. Mystified and exasperated by their inability to "reach" their sons, these parents moved toward showering their love-shy sons with a lot of material goodies—as a substitute for the *love* ("honey") which they did not know how to deliver. For these parents to simply have stopped showering their sons with material things would have very likely made matters even worse. The remedy does not lie in the increasing or in the decreasing of the amount of "milk" that is given. The remedy lies in somehow finding ways to teach highly serious, hypertense parents how to deliver "honey" to their children— the *joie de vivre*, the vibrancy, the aliveness, the feeling of self-worth and self-pride, the unshakable feeling that life is beautiful and highly worthwhile despite the inevitable day-to-day problems and minor rejections.

Virtually hundreds of research studies have shown that if a parent is effective and naturally competent at providing the "honey" of life— if the child really enjoys being in the company of his/her parents—the amount of influence the parents wield is very strong indeed. This is because the child has not erected any defensive barriers against the parents. *The most powerful social influence is always that which is least strongly perceived (felt) by those who are being influenced.* When there exists the "honey" of genuine love between parents and children, there is inevitably a continuing flow of open, *unguarded* communication. No one is tense or on the defensive. No one has anything to hide. There is no "lecturing" by parent to child. The child simply and quite automatically internalizes a majority of his parent's values without any awareness at all of the fact that he/she is so doing.

Again, social influence is strongest when it is *least noticed* by the one on the receiving end of the influence. And when the "honey" of spontaneous love suffuses a parent-child relationship it constitutes the most powerful form of fertilizer for strong albeit unfelt influence, and for the child coming to want to *model* his/her behavior after that of the parent.

The upshot of all of this is that people cannot *"own"* a child in the same way that they "own" a material possession. Children are independent souls who are in their parents' charge for a very brief time. The most successful parent-child relationships, like the most successful and happy husband-wife relationships, are those where there is a mutual facilitation of self-actualization, and where both (or all) parties to a relationship are accepted for themselves and *are free to be themselves*. It is only when a person is accepted as he/she is that he/she becomes free to grow and to change.

The love-shys' parents could not accept their sons *as their sons actually were.* The love-shys' parents were always trying to change their sons in some way. And they were quite serious in their efforts in this regard. They could not relax and enjoy their children—a key prerequisite for providing the necessary "honey". They could not *"let go and let God"*, to borrow a useful cliche from meditation experts. Moreover, any seemingly serious message eminating from the radio or television invariably commanded their attention to a far greater extent than their children's presence ever could.

Seriousness

Several of the questions contained on the interview schedule have a strong bearing upon these points. For example, fully 67 percent of the older love-shy men agreed with the statement: "My parents were too serious with me." Among the younger love-shys 54 percent agreed. In contrast, only 19 percent of the non-shy men felt that their parents had been too serious.

In a similar question I asked for reactions to this statement: "My parents would almost constantly lecture to me about the way they wanted me to behave." Here again, 53 percent of the older love-shys together with 46 percent of the younger ones saw fit to agree with the statement. Only 27 percent of the non-shy men felt that their parents tended to constantly lecture them about how to behave.

In being too serious, the parents of the love-shy men never provided a role model for relaxed, informal, friendly interaction. Their children could not really relax and enjoy socializing within the family context. Instead the love-shys learned throughout their formative years vis-a-vis their parents how to erect a defensive wall between themselves and other people.

Inability to forgive and forget can also be seen as reflecting an overly tense, hyperserious attitude towards children and towards child-rearing responsibilities. Such parental attitudes can have a quite negative impact over time upon a child's developing self-image and his/her overall sense of self-worth.

For example, I asked for reactions to this statement: "My parents frequently remind me about and berate me for things they think I did wrong six, seven, or even eight or more years ago." And fully 45 percent of the older love-shy men responded in the *affirmative*. Among the younger love-shys 35 percent indicated that the statement was true for themselves. But among the non-shy men, only 18 percent saw fit to agree.

In a related question I asked: "My parents can't seem to forget things they think I did wrong a very long time ago, and they keep harping away about these things when I am around them and especially when they are angry." Here again, only 12 percent of the non-shy men responded in the affirmative. In contrast, 41 percent of the older love-shy men together with 34 percent of the younger ones indicated that the statement was *true* for themselves.

A hyperserious attitude towards child-rearing combined with crass insensitivity towards a child's feelings can also be observed in issues pertinent to the invasion of privacy. The love-shys' parents were much more likely than the parents of the non-shys to feel that they *owned* their children, and that anything which happened in their child's life was fully and completely *their business*.

As a case in point, I sought reactions to this statement: "My *mother* would sometimes use confidential, personal, or secret information about me to scold or belittle me, or to make fun of me." And fully 42 percent of the older love-shy men together with 33 percent of the younger ones said "yes". In contrast, *zero percent* (nobody) of the non-shy men indicated an affirmative response to this question.

I then asked each man the same question with respect to his *father*. Strong differences continued to exist between the three research groups, although fathers were *less likely* than mothers to have committed this sort of injustice against their sons. More specifically, 27 percent of the older love-shy men together with 20 percent of the younger ones recalled their fathers as having sometimes used confidential, personal information against them. The percent for the non-shy men was again *zero* (nobody).

In another question, 46 percent of the older love-shys and 38 percent of the younger ones indicated that their mothers frequently failed to respect their privacy. Only 5 percent of the non-shy men felt the same way. In fact, 53 percent of the older love-shys and 43 percent of the younger ones agreed that: "My mother was always excessively nosy and inquisitive regarding my personal life." Just 20 percent of the non-shy men agreed that such had been the case as far as their own mothers were concerned.

Another poignant example of parental hyperseriousness can be seen in the following interview quotation:

> "Several times I sort of implied to my mother that I was really interested in girls and that I was really hurting a lot inside because I couldn't get one. Like I told both of my parents on several occasions that I'd really appreciate it if they would help me meet some girls. Anyway, whenever I would even vaguely broach the subject with my mother she would invariably tell me to *finish my education first* (emphasis his). She'd always say to finish my education first. Now I've got seven years of university education and I'm a 36-year old virgin. So what the hell good did all the piss-hole education do me?! I'm still as incapable as I ever was of getting a woman. Besides being too shy, I don't even know how!" (36-year old love-shy man.)

Few of the love-shys had ever discussed their inhibition problems with their parents—at least, not at any length. In many cases the love-shys simply did not have the nerve, particularly in terms of discussing with their parents their shyness problems vis-a-vis the opposite sex. However, in quite a few cases this reluctance to discuss these problems with parents had undoubtedly been brought about by crass insensitivity of parents to the love-shyness problem. Thus, parents would brusquely laugh it off, minimize its importance (particularly in comparison with making same-sexed friends and studying hard in school), swiftly change the subject, or angrily moralize with the son about his "not having the gumption to grab the bull by the horns".

Paternal "Sex Anxiety"

It has been known for quite some time that a condition known as "sex anxiety" in the *father* is related to femininity of attitudes and interests in sons. The "sex anxious" father is simply one who is very uncomfortable about discussing sexual matters. He strongly discourages all sex-related talk within the family, and tends not to be especially demonstrative vis-a-vis his wife, particularly when children are around. Robert Sears was the first social scientist to discover a fairly strong relationship between paternal "sex anxiety" and feminization of interests and behavior patterns in sons. This was in 1957; and since that time scores of other researchers in psychology, in education, and in sociology, have corroborated his findings.

In my own study I simply asked each respondent whether or not his father had been comfortable about discussing sex with him during his teenaged years. Of course, misperceptions can be a problem when a researcher is trying to get young men to respond to a question of this nature. Some fathers could have been remembered as having been "comfortable" about the subject even though they had not been. Nevertheless, there is little reason for suspecting that the non-shys would systematically misperceive their fathers as having been comfortable about sex, while the love-shys would misperceive their fathers as having been uncomfortable about it.

Anyway, 65 percent of the non-shy men viewed their fathers as having been comfortable about discussing sexual matters. In contrast, only 28 percent of the older love-shy men recalled their fathers as having been comfortable about discussing sex. The analogous figure for the university aged love-shy men was 36 percent.

One of Robert Sears' particularly interesting findings had to do with fathers' interactions with their infant children. He found that "sex anxious" fathers picked up their infant sons to fondle and cuddle them significantly less frequently than did the *non*-anxious fathers. Interestingly, anxiety over sex tended not to affect the fathers' behavior vis-a-vis female babies. Girl babies were picked up about equally often by the "sex anxious" fathers as they were by fathers who were not "sex anxious".

Tactile contact with boy babies tended to be avoided by "sex anxious" fathers. And this avoidance of touch by fathers was not compensated for by maternal attention. In general, boy babies were found to be picked up by their mothers significantly less often than girl babies. Sears speculated that most women as well as "sex anxious" fathers tend to feel uncomfortable vis-a-vis the sight of their son's genitalia.

This dearth of tactile contact could be of significance as an antecedent factor in the development of (1) an overly tender self-image, and (2) in the development of severe love-shyness. In his celebrated book titled TOUCHING anthropologist Ashley Montagu marshalled an impressive amount of evidence suggesting that frequent tactile contact throughout the years of infancy and childhood gives rise to an open, trusting sociability, and a relaxed friendliness and openness to others. Montagu's data strongly support this premise for both genders. However, the relationship appears to be especially strong for boys. With data in hand from hundreds of societies around the world, Montagu concluded that boys who had been frequently fondled and touched throughout their formative years made friends far easier and faster than those who had not had this experience.

Discomfort about nudity in the home is doubtless another good index of "sex anxiety". I therefore asked each man: "What was the attitude towards nudity in your home when you were a child?" And I was somewhat surprised to find that even on this relatively controversial issue fully 67 percent of the non-shy men recalled their home atmosphere as having been rather casual and relaxed with regard to nudity. Indeed, this finding might even be considered somewhat amazing in view of the very high prevalence of *sisters* in the homes of the non-shy men. In stark contrast, only 14 percent of the older love-shys recalled their home atmosphere as having been relaxed and reasonably casual with respect to nudity. The analogous figure for the younger love-shy men was 22 percent.

Discomfort about touching, fondling, and about sexual matters generally may be a reflection of underlying shyness and reticence on the part of the father. Of course, all of the love-shys' fathers *had managed* to find a woman! All had had sexual intercourse and all had fathered at least one child. This is far more than any of their love-shy sons had ever been able to do. Nevertheless I asked each respondent to react to the statement: "My father is (or was) a very shy man." And 56 percent of the older love-shys *agreed*, compared to only 26 percent of the non-shy men. The university aged love-shys were "in between" with 48 percent of them agreeing.

As a case in point, I asked each respondent to react to the statement: "My father always seemed to have an easy time spontaneously displaying affection towards my mother even when other people were around." Fully 94 percent of the non-shy men agreed that this had indeed been the case in their own homes. In contrast, only 37 percent of the older love-shys and 49 percent of the younger love-shys viewed this statement as having been correct with respect to the behavior of their own fathers. In other words, the non-shy men were approximately *twice as likely* as the men in the two love-shy groups to recall their fathers spontaneously displaying affection towards their mothers.

In contemporary American society successful heterosexual interaction appears to require a high level of social spontaneity. Men who are emotionally capable of a natural spontaneity vis-a-vis their spouses, lovers, or dating partners, tend to go much farther with women, and they do so much faster. Women feel maximally comfortable with such men, and they want to see more and more of them. In not having had the opportunity to observe such behavior around the house during their formative years, the love-shys lacked a propitious role model upon which they could pattern their own thoughts, behaviors, and subconscious tendencies.

Appearance of the Home

The way parents insist upon keeping their home also reflects upon overall psychoemotional seriousness and upon the ability to relax and to spontaneously enjoy children. In essence, the love-shys' parents tended to have been much more concerned about "appearances" than with genuine, unpretentious, interpersonal interaction.

The following question was contained on all of the questionnaires that were used for this research:

When I was growing up my mother didn't mind if our house or apartment had a casual, "lived in" appearance:

_____False; she always insisted that everything be kept completely neat, straight, and well polished.
_____She insisted that the place be clean, but she was not compulsive about neatness.
_____True; my mother was usually quite relaxed in regard to the appearance of the house or apartment.

Only 5 percent of the non-shy men checked the first option: that their mothers had always fastidiously insisted that everything be kept completely neat and straight, etc. In contrast, fully 47 percent of the older love-shy men together with 36 percent of the younger ones checked this alternative.

On the other hand, the last of the three alternatives was not especially popular among any of the three research groups. Just 16 percent of the younger love-shys and 6 percent of the younger love shys. In essence, most of the non-shy men checked the second alternative.

In a related question I asked the following:

Which of the following comes closest to describing the interior of your house or apartment while you were growing up?

_____Very neat, well-ordered and tidy.
_____Warm, with a casual "lived in" appearance.

And here fully 80 percent of the non-shy men checked the "warm and casual" option, compared to only 37 percent of the older love-shys and 48 percent of the younger ones. Putting it another way, only 20 percent of the non-shys thought their house had usually been kept "very neat, well-ordered and tidy", compared to a full 63 percent of the older love-shy men.

Parental Overprotectiveness

There is evidence suggesting that the love-shys' parents had been more overprotective than the parents of the non-shys. This is especially true as far as moralistic issues are concerned. For example, I asked each man to react to the following: "*Before* I was 17 years old, if I had wanted very badly to see an 'R' rated film, I could usually count on at least one of my parents taking me to see it." Fully 57 percent of the non-shys indicated "true" for this statement, compared to only 23 percent of the young love-shys, and just 16 percent of the older love-shys.

On the other hand, there is evidence that the love-shys' parents were quite *disinclined* to be protective, much less "overprotective", when it came to their sons' unwillingness to fight back against the assaults of school bullies, and when it came to participation in the sorts of "rough and tumble" contact play that boys are "supposed to" relish. Most of the love-shys' parents were, in fact, quite disappointed about their sons' non-masculine behavior patterns. And quite a few of the love-shys could recall numerous instances of having been thrown out of the house and angrily told to go play with the boys. On these occasions the love-shys would almost invariably take long walks or bicycle rides by themselves. And even today most of the love-shys claimed that they find taking long walks and long drives by themselves to be quite conducive to rich fantasy and daydreams. They also find such solitary activities to be a good antidepressant.

Negative Comparison

I asked each respondent "How often did your mother or father compare you unfavorably with your brothers and/or sisters?" And *excluding from consideration all respondents who had been only children*, 47 percent of the older love-shys and 38 percent of the younger ones had experienced such unfavorable comparisons on a "frequent" basis, compared to only 12 percent of the non-shy men.

Such adverse comparisons, particularly when they are made on a frequent basis and in the child's presence, can prove highly embarrassing and can have a very deleterious impact upon a child's developing self-image, self-pride, and sense of self-worth. The fact that the love-shys' parents had been particularly prone towards making such disparaging comparisons can be seen in the pattern of responses to this question: "How often did your mother or father compare you unfavorably in regard to other children of your own age and sex?" Fully 52 percent of the non-shy men indicated that their parents had *never* made such disparaging comparisons. In contrast, only 12 percent of the older love-shys together with 19 percent of the younger ones could similarly say that their parents had *never* made such disparaging comparisons.

In fact, 55 percent of the parents of the older love-shy men were recalled as having made such disparaging comparisons to their sons' faces quite "frequently"; 46 percent of the younger love-shys similarly recalled their parents having done this on a "frequent" basis. On the other hand, only 13 percent of the non-shy men could recall their parents "frequently" comparing them in an unflattering way to other children of their age and sex.

Quite related to the foregoing is the experience of having been criticized, scolded or punished in front of other children or adults. Again, frequent experiences of this sort can have a strongly deleterious impact upon a child's developing self-image and sense of social self-confidence. And they can also have a bearing upon the development of social avoidance habits. It should be recalled that inhibited (melancholic) children find it extremely difficult to forget embarrassing experiences.

I asked each respondent: "How frequently were you criticized, scolded or punished by your parents *in front of* other adults?" And 67 percent of the older love-shys along with 57 percent of the younger ones indicated that this had happened to them "sometimes" or "frequently". In contrast, this experience had happened "sometimes" or "frequently" to only 19 percent of the non-shy men.

The story was very much the same in regard to public scolding and/or punishment taking place in front of other children. I asked each respondent: "How frequently were you criticized, scolded or punished by your parents *in front of* other children?" And despite the fact that few of the love-shys had had any friends while they were growing up, fully 89 percent of the older love-shy men along with 73 percent of the younger love-shys indicated that this had happened to them either "sometimes" or "frequently". The analogous percent for the non-shy men was only 45.

Among those who had checked *"frequently"*, the percents were 49 and 41 for the older and younger love-shy men respectively. Only 5 percent of the non-shy men recalled having been criticized, scolded or punished on a "frequent" basis in front of other children.

The love-shys' parents quite clearly did not model effective or emotionally rewarding interpersonal relationships. They provided no viable model at all for competent and harmonious *conflict resolution skills*. Conflicts arise in all human relationships. And I think the characteristic behavior of the love-shys' parents did much to make the love-shys *fear* conflict and hostility. And in so doing, I think these parents' personalities indirectly inspired socially avoidant behavior. After all, if a person is not involved in any meaningful interpersonal relationships he or she will never need to deal with potentially painful conflicts, hostilities, disagreements, etc. By remaining a social isolate one can assure oneself of *external* harmony (absence of social friction), even though *internal* harmony might as a consequence remain permanently elusive.

The love-shys' fear of potential conflict situations vis-a-vis parents is well reflected in the pattern of reactions to this questionnaire statement: "I always felt free and comfortable about discussing my problems with my parents." Only 19 percent of the non-shy men indicated that this was *untrue*. In contrast, 66 percent of the older love-shys and 57 percent of the younger love-shys indicated that this statement had been *untrue* as far as their formative years in their parents' homes had been concerned.

Forcing the Summer Camp Experience on Children

One of the especially curious findings I uncovered in conducting the interviews for this book was that the love-shys were significantly more likely than the non-shy men to have been to summer camp *at all*— quite irrespective of whether or not they had ever been forced to attend. Only 48 percent of the non-shy men had ever been to a summer camp. In contrast, 83 percent of the older love-shys and 72 percent of the younger ones had been to a summer camp at least once at some time in their lives.

Further, of the non-shys who had ever been to a summer camp, 60 percent indicated that they had *enjoyed* the experience. Of the love-shys who had ever been to a summer camp, *zero percent* of the older ones and just 15 percent of the younger ones indicated that they had enjoyed the experience to any extent at all. On the other hand, *zero percent* of the non-shy men hated the summer camp experience. In contrast, 68 percent of the older love-shys and 57 percent of the younger ones said that they had hated the experience. The remaining men felt indifferent about their experiences with summer camp.

Fully 61 percent of the older love-shy men had been forced by their parents to attend summer camp at least once. Most of these men had been forced to attend during several consecutive summers. Among the younger love-shys 43 percent had been forced to attend summer camp. That figure is substantially lower than the 61 percent figure for the older love-shys. But even it is high by comparison with the 7 percent figure for the self-confident non-shy men. More specifically, *only seven percent* of the non-shys had ever been forced by their parents to attend summer camp. The remaining 41 percent of non-shy men who had been to camp had gone because they had *wanted* to go. (Again, only 48 percent of the non-shys had ever been to camp.)

These findings suggest that the very fact of a child being *forced* to attend summer camp against his/her will is *itself* a good indicator of a pathogenic, *love-shyness generating family*. Hence, this is something about which school guidance counselors and psychiatric social workers ought to be made aware. Indeed, it may be quite prudent to get laws passed at both the state and the federal level barring summer camp administrators from accepting children into their institutions who are there by force rather than by choice.

Summer camp administrators tend to be quite moralistic, and cannot be trusted on their own to accomplish the needed screening of children. In the camp administrator's way of thinking the boy or girl who is sent to camp is very lucky indeed; and he/she ought to be very grateful to his/her parents for their financial sacrifice. Also, most summer camps are profit-making organizations. And this together with various moralistic ideas about how "lucky" these children are, contributes to an ideology that runs rough-shod over the needs and feelings of male children who happen to be passive, inhibited, shy and withdrawn. In essence, camp administrators are *sales people*; and the idea that what they have to offer may be "bad" for some children is *unthinkable* to them. This is as true for those who run YMCA, Boy Scout, and religious camps, as it is for those who manage expensive, private camps. Summer camp administrators have a strong set of vested interests which eventuate in their defending their product in the face of any and all kinds of opposition.

Further, there is evidence that substantial numbers of parents use summer camps as depositories for temporarily getting rid of their children. As a case in point, the following statement yielded a pattern of responses which sharply differentiated the love-shys from the non-shys: "Generally speaking, I think I was less important to my mother than her friends were." Fully 43 percent of the older love-shys together with 36 percent of the younger ones *agreed* with this statement. In contrast, *zero percent* (nobody) of the non-shys chose to agree with the statement.

In essence, it appears that a substantial proportion of the love-shys' parents had failed to display any real sensitivity toward their sons' needs and feelings. And this general insensitivity was eventually reflected in the unusually high popularity of summer camps among the ranks of the love-shys' parents.

Summer Camps as Torture Prisons

Many of the men I interviewed complained bitterly about their experiences of having been "incarcerated" or "imprisoned" in these "torture chambers" known as summer camps. The non-shys had relished and thoroughly enjoyed most of their summer camp experiences because camp provided a copious abundance of opportunities for engaging in the "rough and tumble" baseball/football activities which they had always enjoyed anyway. Thus the non-shys had looked upon camp as a place to hone up their athletic skills, and to meet and compete with many new boys of their own age.

To the love-shy, on the other hand, summer camp had been a place of interminable torture and bullying. It was a place where they had been isolated from *girls*, the one class of human beings in their age group whom they had always *wanted* to be around, to look at, and to longingly stare at.

Actually, the love-shys had many more interests and hobbies throughout their childhoods than the non-shys did. But all of the love-shys' interests and hobbies (except for swimming, which was frequently mentioned) were quiet, solitary ones such as reading, nature study, map collecting, ceramics, listening to music, arts and crafts, taking long walks or bicycle rides, etc. Hence, the summer camp experience failed to "expand" them from the standpoint of interests. In fact, in some ways the camp experience had had a constricting impact. The following comment is illustrative of this:

"I always loved swimming at the beach. When I was a kid I would sometimes spend three or four hours in the ocean without ever coming out. My mother used to scream at me because she thought it might be bad for me to stay in the water so long. Sometimes other kids in the water would talk to me. But I usually swam and rode the waves all by myself. Anyway, one of the things that really surprised me about all the different camps I attended was that I couldn't do much swimming. They give you only one hour of free swimming per day. And by the time you adjust to the cold lake water, the hour is almost up. I took much longer to get my body completely into the water than any of the other kids did. I can't adjust to cold water very fast, and the lake water at camp was much colder than the ocean is. (*Note*: This person grew up in Newport Beach, California.) It sometimes took 45 minutes before I could even get myself into the water; and the other kids would be teasing and splashing me. And that slowed me down all the more, and made me withdraw. It was really bad because they wouldn't let you go in the water without a 'buddy' at the camps I attended. And the kid the counselors assigned me to would be screaming and throwing rocks at me because my inability to adapt to the cold water meant that he couldn't go in either. None of those people would have ever guessed that I was a real 'fish' when I was home and had my freedom at the beach." (20 year old love-shy man.)

Here is another comment that is poignantly revealing as to how thoroughly *out of their element* the love-shys had been at all-male summer camps:

"I remember every day about an hour before lunchtime they made us line up and march in military fashion. I absolutely hated this because I was always getting it from the guys behind me who would be constantly kicking the backs of my ankles. The people who ran this camp must have been absolute animals. I remember the counselors tried to force everyone to shout these horrible chants. I remember one which went:
'You're in the Army now,
you're in the Army now,
you dig a ditch,
you sonofabitch,
you're in the Army now.'

I'd be the only kid who wouldn't cooperate in hollaring these unromantic, horrible, stupid things. And I'd be screamed at and punched by the kids and sometimes even by the counselors . . . . While the kids were hollaring these horrible things and trying to make me keep in step, I'd be in a deep, romantic reverie about walking on a beach or in some beautiful forest somewhere with a beautiful girl who loved me. I would be so deep in my daydreams about being with a girl that I would become totally oblivious to the people who were shouting at me and calling me all sorts of foul names. The fact that I was totally unresponsive to all this abuse got some of the counselors really mad. I remember the only thing that unnerved me was when the kids who were marching in back of me kicked my legs or ankles. But the counselors usually stopped them from doing that. So I was usually able to spend most of this stupid marching time off in my world of romantic daydreams." (36-year old love-shy man.)

Of course, it wasn't just military chanting which turned the love-shys off. *Any* type of repetitive chanting had the same effect on them. Several of the love-shys commented upon how they had gotten into trouble at church or religious meetings that had been forced on them— because they would not partake in the required group chanting. Again, while the chanting was going on they would have their minds off in a world of romantic daydreams. And at the center of all of their daydreams was a beautiful girl friend. As I shall make clear in chapter eleven, a beautiful girlfriend loomed at the center of the love-shys' daydreams *throughout* all the years of elementary school and high school.

Many of the especially salient memories recalled during the interviews by the love-shy men entailed painful scenarios of being forced by counselors to join a baseball playing group out in the bright, glaring sun. Many of the men vividly recalled the extreme discomforts to their eyes of being out in very bright sunshine and being chided and hazed by boys whom they simply did not want to be with. Some of the men felt that the counselors were sincerely trying to do the best thing, and that most of the counselors simply didn't have any awareness of the deleterious impact that their coercive tactics were having.

In the camp craft shop these love-shy men had evidently been enthusiastic artisans. But on the baseball diamond they were listless and unwilling outsiders. Even though they were technically on somebody's team (and *none* of the other boys wanted them to be on *their* team), in reality they were on the baseball diamond only in body and not in spirit. Some of these men, in fact, had kept their hands cuped over their eyes and remained oblivious in the outfield even when a ball passed right by them. Several of the love-shys spontaneously mentioned that they breathed a sigh of relief every time a cloudy day dawned. For even if baseball were to be forced upon them on such a day, they would at least not have to deal with the painfulness of the glaring sun.

Partly because of their noncompetitive nature, the love-shys were like "fish out of water" at camp. Among groups of young boys almost everything is rushed at in a frenzied, competitive way. And boys who do not take an enthusiastic interest in the competition tend to be castigated with an unlimited barrage of highly disparaging, *ad hominem* swear words— like "fuck face", "asshole", "turd brain", "chicken shit", "shitass", "shithead", "fairy queen", "faggot", "cocksucking queer", and scores of others. Parents who go to great trouble to see to it that their children do not see any "R" rated motion pictures ought to be accorded the opportunity of witnessing six or seven year old boys at a *middle-class* summer camp constantly spewing out a never-ending flow of *ad hominem* swear words so venomous that one would be hard pressed to find *any* "R" or "X" rated motion picture that could hold a candle to it!

Enforced participation (and they do not *really* "participate" even when they are forced) in "rough and tumble" contact sports is only part of the picture. Non-shy boys at summer camp tend to become quite ferociously competitive over such matters as the neatness and cleanliness of their cabin. Here again, the love-shys wanted to be *left alone*. To them their cubby hole, trunk and bunk *was theirs*, and it was *their own private business* as to how they kept these things. Most of the love-shys suffered severe physical bullying and cruelty at the hands of their peers during what was supposed to be "clean up time".

Most summer camp counselors are themselves young men who are in no way equipped to deal constructively and appropriately with their love-shy charges. Many of them are working their way through college, and their awareness of the fields of child development and parenting is limited to their recollections of their own parents' behavior. Vis-a-vis children whose temperament and behavior is "mainstream", most young men in camp counselor jobs manage to perform quite well. Withdrawn and inhibited boys, on the other hand, are simply not understood by them. Withdrawn and inhibited boys seldom inspire the best from summer camp counselors. Indeed, even the counselors sometimes end up teasing and hazing such love-shy children.

For example, one love-shy man recounted the following set of experiences surrounding required games of "capture the flag".

> "Every third or fourth night after dinner the counselors used to make us play 'capture the flag' for an hour. I hated this and had absolutely no interest in it. But the thing that makes me shudder even today when I think about it is that the counselors always assigned me to the team that had to take their shirts off. At seven o'clock all the mosquitos came out, and I was absolutely in a torture chamber every time. I went to complain to the camp president about it, and he refused to do anything about it. Nobody would help me. They would come over and take my shirt away so I couldn't put it back on. And for a solid hour I would be flailing my hands all over my body trying to keep the mosquitos away. And the kids would be throwing rocks at me and making fun at me while all of this was going on." (38-year old love-shy man.)

Homesickness

Homesickness is a problem from which many young children suffer when they are sent away from home for the first time. Curiously, however, I do not believe that homesickness had affected any of the love-shy men whom I studied for this book. To be sure, most of the love-shys absolutely hated summer camp. To most of them camp was a real "house of horrors". But despite the interminable bullying and hazing, none of them could recall any deep yearning to be home with their parents. In essence, what the love-shys missed most was *their freedom*, NOT their parents.

Most of the love-shys viewed their parents as callous, insensitive jailors, and not as the benign kinfolk whose warm glow of love they will once again be able to enjoy. Few of the love-shys felt that their parents really cared about or had any awareness at all of their deepest needs and feelings. They saw their parents only as people who *cared* about molding them into a preconceived image of a "normal boy". They did not view their parents as accepting and loving them *as they were*, but only as something which the summer camp experience might help make them into.

The love-shys had always felt quite lonely around their parents. This is not surprising when it is borne in mind that the love-shys had always felt too shy and inhibited about discussing with their parents what had always been throughout their childhoods the most important thing in their lives. In essence, they were too shy about sharing with their parents their daydreams about having a beautiful girlfriend, and about their deep, romantic infatuations with a particular girl at their school. The love-shys' parents virtually never entertained even the slightest inkling about what was *really* salient in their inhibited and withdrawn sons' minds. In this sense, the love-shys and their parents had always been quite total strangers vis-a-vis each other.

And so the love-shys were anxious to "get out" of camp just as a prisoner is anxious to "get out" after he has done his time. The love-shys looked forward to being able once again to take long rides on their bicycles by themselves, to taking long walks, getting back to their music, reading, arts and crafts hobbies, etc. Aside from getting the money, food, clothing, shelter, etc., that they needed, the love-shys tended not to look forward to seeing their parents. They *knew* that the verbally abusive explosions from their parents would soon be recommencing again—within a few days of their arrival home. Indeed, how could the love-shys logically be expected to be "homesick" for their jailors—for those who had been responsible for their incarceration, and ultimately in an indirect way for all the bullying and *ad hominem* hazing that had followed this incarceration? Of course, the parents had sent their sons to camp in hopes that the experience would "make a real man" out of them. Not surprisingly, it didn't work!

Parents and Inheritance

Because of their comparative youth, the issue of inheritance did not come up in any of my interviews with the younger love-shy men. However, it was a major preoccupation for a considerable minority of the older love-shys, and particularly for the 31 percent who had grown up as *only children*. Despite the fact that none of these men had ever enjoyed cordial relations with their mothers and fathers, all felt somewhat guilty and distraught about the fact that their parents had no one to whom to leave their tangible (non-monetary) worldly goods and property.

> "My parents keep reminding me that they have so many nice things, and no one to leave them to. My parents were always very different from me. They always had a lot of friends. And they have this expensive silver service; they have all these expensive dishes, living room set, dining room set, and all kinds of other heirlooms. When I'm around my mother sometimes cries that all this stuff will just have to be auctioned off. You know, like what's the point of leaving stuff like that to a single man who doesn't have any friends, and who lives in a cockroach infested one-room flat! Of course, with all the friends my parents have wined and dined over the years, you'd think they'd have somebody who would be willing to introduce me to some eligible women! You'd think that parents with all those social connections would be able to help their son! I'm their only kid, and yet they won't lift a finger for me. They claim that I'm an embarrassment to them. All they can do is complain and cry that they haven't got anyone to leave their stuff to. All this makes me feel very angry. And yet whenever I think about it I get more depressed than angry because my hands are tied! What can I do about it?!" (39-year old love-shy man who is an "only child".)

> "I think the most painful thing when my mother was dying was that she had no one to leave her heirlooms to. I know she had been praying for grandchildren. Everytime I saw her she would remind me that I had a responsibility to give her grandchildren. And I would have to constantly remind her that I was too shy to get a wife. I mean you have to be able to date in order to be able to get married. And you have to be married in order to have any children. See, my mother thinks I'm a fag, because that's what my dad kept saying before he died. There was nothing I could do to convince her that I was anything but a fag—that there was nothing I wanted more than to have a loving wife and family. I just couldn't make her understand the concept of shyness—that I was as normal as anybody else—just shy . . . . Anyway, what happened was that I inherited 25 percent of what my mother had in the bank. The other 75 percent and all of the heirlooms and house went to my cousin and her family. It was almost funny because my mother never even saw my cousin more than twice a year. I don't think she even liked her very much. I mean she would always criticize my cousin about one damn thing or another. Yet it was my cousin who got all the inheritance, not me." (49-year old love-shy man who had been an "only child".)

> "My parents are really distraught. I hate my parents, and yet I feel really badly about the fact that they are evidently not going to be able to die knowing that their only son is going to be able to lead a

normal life. I guess I wouldn't mind so much if I had chosen to live this way. Like some people choose to be priests. But that's okey because they *choose* to be celebate; they *choose* not to marry or to have children. I never chose to live like this; and yet both I and my parents have to suffer the consequences of a life style which I never chose. I think I'll get the inheritance money. But they've already told me that unless I'm married at the time their will goes through probate, all of their property is going to be given to charity." (41-year old love-shy "only child".)

The "only child" cases seemed to be the most sad and poignant. However, love-shys with brothers and/or sisters had no easy "row to hoe" either with respect to the inheritance issue. Many of the love-shys had become the "black sheep" of their respective families. And this was reflected in the fact that the love-shys visited and/or were visited by their parents a very great deal less often than were their non-shy brothers and sisters. Married siblings, in particular, received a great deal more attention from their aging mothers and fathers than did these love-shy men. And this was true irrespective of whether or not the married siblings had children.

Today an increasing number of journalists and scholarly writers are asserting that the single life represents "a legitimate choice", and that those pursuing this "choice" are no less happy and no more lonely than those who pursue the more traditional choices of marriage and parenthood.[2] The important word here, of course, is *"choice"*. And at the risk of being redundant I must repeat that the love-shy men never *"chose"* their life style. Indeed, their life style is highly antithetical to their desires and to their value systems.

The fact that it is also antithetical to their aging parents' value systems may be entirely beside the point. If an adult child is happy and positive about his *chosen* life style, that child is likely to be perceived by his aging parents as *"a joy to be around"*. On the other hand, if an adult child is quiet and obviously unhappy about the life style with which he is "stuck"—if he is *not* positive and enthusiastic about the life he is leading, then the aging parents are bound to feel uncomfortable, embarrassed, guilty, and not especially proud or happy about having their adult son around.

To be sure, I think that adult sons and daughters who *choose* the single life style incur the wrath and displeasure of their aging mothers and fathers a great deal more frequently than women's liberation and pro-singlehood writers are predisposed to suggest. However, someone who *did not choose* the single life style, but who is living it anyway because of a reason as nebulous and difficult for most people to understand as *love-shyness* (and as seemingly indicative of poor self-discipline and self-control), is far more likely to incur the wrath and displeasure of aging parents than someone who had *chosen* the single life style for reasons he/she is proud and happy to discuss. There is a celebrated cliche in the Bible which states: "By their fruits, so shall ye know them." The negative, unhappy ambiance of the love-shy man represents "fruits" about which aging parents find it very difficult to feel proud.

> "Every time I visit my folks I'm always reminded about how my two younger brothers are married, and about how they have such nice children. My 18-year old kid brother brags right in front of my parents about how he knocked up his wife in the chemistry lab one night when no one was around. Anyway, he *had to* marry her, and he cost my parents and her parents a great deal of money and trouble. But everything is all forgiven with him because he has such a nice baby and I'm the black sheep everybody is ashamed to have for a brother. They wouldn't lift a finger to introduce me to any girl. No, they find it easier to just assume that I'm a fairy—and they just let it go at that. It's in their best financial interests. I mean, my father already told me that unless I get married neither he nor my mother are going to leave me anything. He even showed me his will. And that's what it says." (35-year old love-shy man with two younger married brothers.)

Love-shyness can quite clearly serve to alienate its victims from their siblings. A noteworthy minority of the love-shys had grown up in homes wherein all of the children had suffered frequent harassment at the hands of parents. In many such instances the children had "stuck together" through their respective childhood ordeals. But when they became adults, the love-shys' lack of heterosexual involvements served to gradually alienate them from brothers and sisters with whom they had formerly gotten along satisfactorily. The parents themselves may have had a good deal to do with this. In essence, while drawing up their wills the parents could not "see" leaving as much to progeny who did not appear to have any responsibilities of their own. It made more sense to leave money and property to children who had become parents themselves, and who seemed to be leading some semblance of a "normal" life.

In learning of their aging parents' intentions, it seems likely that many of the love-shys' siblings had encouraged their parents' will-making resolve. After all, it was in accordance with their own vested interests to do so. Why, indeed, should a sibling without any family responsibilities receive as much from the parents' estate as those sons and daughters who had turned out "alright" in spite of everything?! Everybody loves a winner; and it is always easier to be good to people who are ostensibly happy and successful than it is to be good to those whose lives are bogged down by severe psychoemotional problems.

Even when they lived close by, the love-shys' aging parents never or almost never paid their sons any visits. In turn, the love-shys sometimes did visit their aging parents. But the frequency of these visits tended to be far less than the frequency of visitation experienced by the love-shys' married siblings. Moreover, when the love-shys did visit their aging parents the visits were often frought with friction. Often times the love-shys would prod their parents to provide introductions to young women; and that tended to create a great deal of friction. In almost all cases the aging parents tended to feel uncomfortable and quite disappointed about being seen publicly with their love-shy sons.[3]

Showers and Wedding Presents

It appears fairly logical to assume that most of the love-shys' parents would be shy and lonely isolates themselves. But this is evidently not true. In fact, some of the love-shys' parents had quite a few friends. And some of them interacted with their friends quite frequently.

It was in regard to these parental friendships that having a love-shy son tended to create a great deal of embarrassment and strong feelings of deprivation and disappointment. As would be expected, these feelings tended to have been most painful for those parents who had had an *only child* who had turned out love-shy.

Many of the parents had very frequently complained to their love-shy sons that they never had anything to brag about with their friends. Their friends were always boasting about the accomplishments of their sons and daughters. The love-shys' parents, on the other hand, could only hold their tongues on such occasions, and just feel depressed because of their own sons' lack of propitious progress and growth—particularly in the social area of life.

For example, some of the love-shys' parents had spent a considerable amount of money on wedding gifts and shower presents for their friends' children. These parents, of course, expected to be able to revel in the joy of reciprocation when their own love-shy children got married. When this never happened a great deal of bitterness and unhappiness was created in the lives of these aging parents.

> "Every time I see my mother she reminds me of the hundreds of dollars she had spent on Judy's shower and Ted's wedding present and Nancy's wedding present, and so-and-so's shower, and on and on and on. All of this makes me feel even more depressed. I mean, if these people mean so fucking much to my Mom, why the fuck didn't she try to get them to introduce me to some women! When I was growing up she used to spend more fucking time with those fucking people than she ever spent with me. Now that she's old

and retired she still insists on upstaging me so that she can spend time with a new set of friends she now has. Neither she nor her fucking friends would ever do a goddam thing to help me to meet someone who might become a wife for me. So why should I feel guilty because my inability to marry means that my mother will not be able to see me receive all those valuable wedding presents in reciprocation for the wedding and shower presents that she gave! Shit! Let her find me a wife. Then I'll marry and she'll receive her reciprocation!" (50-year old love-shy "only child".)

"Oh, my parents are constantly reminding me about how embarrassed I make them feel. I am the only kid in all my parents' friends' families who has not married. And every time I see them they remind me of that fact. They don't even allow me to come around anymore if there is a chance that any of their friends will be there. I have to phone them first before I come. Otherwise they say they'd be too embarrassed if their friends were there when I showed up. I don't know why! I keep fantasizing that maybe one of their friends might understand my problem and help me meet some women." (42-year old love-shy man.)

In essence, love-shyness very effectively prevents afflicted sons from bringing any real pleasure either to themselves or to their aging parents. Even though most of the love-shys had gotten along quite poorly with their parents throughout childhood and adolescence, presently as adults they did want to make their parents feel proud of them. But they were powerless to do this. The love-shy men tended to become the "black sheep" of their families—people who were viewed as best left forgotten or, at least, not talked about when non-family members are around.

Of course, the love-shys had wanted a lover and marriage partner for many, many years prior to the time when their parents had first begun desiring these things for them. A wife and family was genuinely and truly the goal of each love-shy man who was studied for this book. And in most cases this had been their most cherished goal since the time they had been in the first or second grade of elementary school. If a love-shy man had not very strongly desired a wife and lover, it seems highly improbable that his parents' desire for him to obtain these things would have had any meaningful effect upon him at all. In short, these men wanted to get married *for their own benefit*. The delight and "relief" of their parents would merely have represented an attractive *fringe benefit*, and nothing more.

It is therefore quite clear that love-shyness brings sadness and unhappiness to more people than just the young men who are afflicted with the problem. There is a significant price to be paid whenever any human being is deprived of free choice and self-determination. Simply put, *responsible freedom for all* represents the safest, most happy and productive way of life for any society. And love-shyness is highly antithetical to that goal.

"Get Me a Goose!"

Quite a few of both the younger and the older love-shys had tried to prod their parents into using their social connections to effect appropriate introduction to eligible young women. Many of these efforts on the love-shys' part had been quite forceful. And none had been successful. Many of the love-shys stood in bitter envy of various acquaintances whose parents and kinfolk had allegedly embarked upon *unwanted* matchmaking efforts. They wanted their own parents to do the same thing for them. And in at least a few cases they were quite non-shy about prodding their parents in this regard. I quote the following interview at length because it illustrates quite well the difficult psychodynamics of intractable love-shyness.

"After I had completed three years of graduate school I decided to take off a year. I thought I'd go back to Denver where my parents still lived, and see if I could force them to get me a girl. My father was a successful lawyer, and I knew that he must have had all sorts of connections in the local community. So I thought maybe I could get him to get me a wife. I was just getting more and more depressed all the time. And even though my grades were good and I had successfully completed a Masters degree, I knew that I would be much more effective if I had a wife. A lot of the students in my classes were already married. And I was just desperate. I was willing to just do anything to force my parents into doing something for me to get me a wife.

Well, up to that time I never had the nerve to say anything to my parents about my shyness problems. They thought I was just a slow starter, and like my mother would always keep saying to her friends that I had plenty of time, and I'd get over my bashfulness when the right woman came after me. Well, no woman had ever come after me. And my father kept telling me that I was really lucky. At the dinner table ever since I was a small kid he would tell me 'ahhh, never get married, kid!' He kept saying that even though he had been married to my mother for over 30 years without very much evident fighting or turmoil between them.

Well, I had just turned 25 when I left my graduate school in Seattle. My parents gave me a really cool reception. They couldn't understand why I had turned down my student stipend and would want to return to live with them. Both of them bitched away and bitched away at me to get a job and stop living at home with them. And I kept telling them that I'd leave as soon as they got me a 'goose'. I don't know why. But it was just much easier for me to use the word 'goose' with them. I didn't have the nerve to say 'girl'.

Anyway, they started getting madder than hell at me. Whenever they had company which was quite often, I would tack or scotch tape little announcements to the wallpaper or to the guests' cars which said: 'please get my parents to get me a goose! Mention this to my parents and they'll explain it'.

Then I started doing all kinds of other stuff. Like after my parents went to bed I would take all the cans of food out of the kitchen cabinets, and pile them up one on top of the other, until they went from the floor to the ceiling. And I would leave them balanced like that. My parents thought I was going nuts. And I just kept telling them that I wouldn't stop until they got me a goose. I mean I told them that they hadn't finished their responsibilities with me yet. Even though I was 25, they still had to get me a goose; then they would be finished with their child-rearing responsibilities with me. Like, there are societies all over the world where the parents take upon themselves the responsibility of finding geese for their children. Well, I thought I could force my parents too to get me a goose— I mean 'wife'.

Well, one time my father came home and told me that he might be able to get me a date with one of his secretaries. Actually I kind of liked the girl he had in mind. She was sort of pretty. But I had never met her. I mean, at a business meeting my father took me to he introduced me to her. But he didn't do anything to enable us to sit down and really get to know each other. I mean, I didn't have the nerve to say anything after I said 'hi'. She was busy mixing whiskey sours for all these businessmen. And I didn't have the nerve to go up and try to talk to her—although my father was creating something of a scene trying to force me. Like he just wasn't cool. If he could have only set something up where we would have to talk to each other without me feeling any anxiety, it would have been great.

Anyway, a few days later my father came home and told me that he had told this girl that she should be expecting a telephone call from me. And she had allegedly said 'great' to my father. So for the next several days my father was constantly at me to call. And believe me, I desperately wanted to call this girl because she did seem really nice. But I just couldn't bring myself to get up the nerve. I mean, what could I say? How would I even begin? I just couldn't handle the situation. And my father just became more and more pissed off at me. He kept telling me that I had embarrassed him at work because this girl had been expecting me to call; and I didn't call. I kept telling my father that she was a really nice goose, but that he'd have to work something out that would make it easier for me to get involved in a conversation with her. Anyway, he just got to the point where he just kept telling me to go to hell.

Well, I wouldn't stop with my parents because I had told my classmates back at the U. of Washington that I was taking off a year to find a wife, and that I'd be returning as soon as I had found one. Anyway, I started doing all kinds of crazy things like putting a wet mop on my mother's living room broadloom, and overflowing the toilet bowl. One time when my parents weren't home I took a lot of my mother's stuff down to the pawn shop. I didn't need the money and I wasn't stealing anything because I gave them the pawn tickets and loan money as soon as they got home. I just told them that I wouldn't stop doing these things until they finally fulfilled their responsibilities with me and got me a goose.

Well, my father had me arrested and I spent a night in jail. My father bailed me out the following morning even though he was the one who had me arrested. By this time I was just so frustrated and exasperated about my parents' unwillingness to do anything to help me that I decided to go back to graduate school. I mean even their friends didn't seem to notice all the pleas for help that I had left around in the form of these notes saying that I needed a goose.

Well, I finally went back to graduate school. But I had to go to Oregon instead of back to Washington—because I didn't have the nerve to face the kids and tell them that I hadn't made any progress at all in my quest for a wife." (39-year old love-shy man.)

This case illustrates the fact that some severely love-shy men become quite "passive-aggressive" in their behavioral tendencies vis-a-vis their parents. On the surface these aggressive tendencies appear quite antithetical to shyness. But they are actually loud pleas for help. In the above case this is particularly apparent in this man's having left notes on the windshields of his parents' friends' automobiles.

Grossly immature behavior as well as chronic misbehavior are actually *forms of disordered communication*. The person employs misbehavior as a form of communication when normal modes of communication are constantly ignored or when they simply fail to work. The love-shy male will often use these disordered modes of communication around people he knows well, such as parents, whose presence does not arouse the very low native anxiety-threshold that seems to universally characterize the chronic love-shy.

One problem with the "passive-aggressive" diagnosis is the fear that any genuine helping will actually serve to reinforce or strengthen the "passive-aggressive" tendencies. I believe that this fear is unfounded. Love-shy men use "passive-aggressive" behavior as a *tool*—nothing more. They use it as a tool to get their most basic love needs met. Once these needs are met—through being accorded a wife or lover—there is no longer any need for "passive-aggressive" conduct.

In a later chapter I shall discuss "practice dating", which is the *only* form of therapy which appears to have any constructive effects on love-shys. It is the only form of therapy which extinguishes heterosexual interaction anxieties and gets love-shy men involved in the actual dating and courting of women. Whereas conservative, traditional-minded clinicians perceive "practice-dating therapy" as encouraging passive-aggressive conduct, the available research data suggest that this form of therapy has just the opposite effect upon love-shy males. Love-shy men will *not* benefit from either (1) the "talking cure" of traditional psychotherapy, or (2) from the "good swift kick in the ass" which many people would like to give them.

By the way, in regard to the idea of arranged marriages I included the following statement on each of the questionnaires:

> "I would like to see arranged marriages available as an option in our society so that I could get married without having to suffer the indignity of having to ask women for dates."

Fully 74 percent of the older love-shy men agreed with this statement, along with 56 percent of the younger love-shys. In stark contrast, *zero percent* (nobody) of the non-shy men saw fit to agree.

And in a related question I asked each man to react to this statement: "If I could get married without ever having to go out on dates, I'd jump at the chance." And fully 53 percent of the older love-shys and 37 percent of the younger love-shys agreed. Again, *none* of the 200 non-shy men agreed.

Notes

1. In his books THE ONE MINUTE FATHER and THE ONE MINUTE MOTHER, Dr. Spencer Johnson makes an especially important conceptual distinction between a child's *being loved* and a child's subjectively *feeling loved*. FEELING LOVED is of infinitely greater importance for a child's well-being and future socio-emotional growth than is being loved. Almost all parents passionately assert that they "love" their children. And virtually all manner of abuse can be heaped on a child in the name of "real love", "caring and concern". Many "loved" children simply do not *feel* loved; and as a result they fail to develop in a healthy manner.

2. In point of fact, they may be *less* happy and *more* lonely. In his book THE BROKEN HEART: THE MEDICAL CONSEQUENCES OF LONELINESS, James J. Lynch cites convincing evidence to the effect that the unmarried are a great deal more vulnerable than

the married to all manner of medical and psychiatric problems. His data show that this is particularly true for men.

3. In 1984 a new kind of support group developed which calls itself "*Parents of Gay and Lesbian Children*". This group has proved very beneficial in helping its members with a whole host of problems such as those pertaining to coming to an honest acceptance and compassionate understanding of their sons and daughters, coming to grips with not being able to have grandchildren (where this is applicable), etc. I would suggest that a strong effort should be made to develop a support group called "*Parents of Love-Shy Heterosexuals*". Thus, in addition to a national network of *Shys Anonymous* organizations, a companion network of parents of young men who are victims of severe love-shyness would be most beneficial. Like the parents of homosexuals, the parents of love-shy heterosexuals must similarly (very often) deal with permanent or long-term deprivation of the opportunity to have grandchildren. And the parents of heterosexual love-shys have as much difficulty as those of homosexuals in coming to a compassionate understanding of their children. Further, an effective network of parent support groups might even prove somewhat helpful in getting love-shy sons introduced to eligible women.

Chapter 9

The Family as a Hotbed of Rage and Belittlement

Anger and rage are commonly understood by psychologists as a response to being hurt emotionally, and of being made to feel unimportant. Despite the widely accepted cliche that "actions speak louder than words", people tend to be less courteous to members of their own immediate family than they tend to be with total strangers or chosen friends. Moreover, they tend to be less courteous and respectful vis-a-vis their "flesh and blood" children than they tend to be vis-a-vis their spouses.

In American society we tend to think of the chronically mischievous, hyperactive male child as inspiring the most frequent episodes of anger and rage from his parents. My own suspicion is that the normally sociable, highly active, mischievous lad may be much easier for most parents to understand (and hence to handle), than the fearful, anxiety-prone, socially inhibited boy. The former is much easier than the latter for a parent to understand because the former more nearly approximates the traditional stereotype as to what a "real boy" should be like. People tend to fear and to display hostility toward those things which they do not understand. And there is a great deal about the behavior of a severely shy male child that might well be beyond the average parent's capability for understanding.

In their studies of child abuse many sociologists have been able to show that the *exceptional child* tends to be far more vulnerable to severe physical and psychoemotional abuse than any of his more "normal" siblings. And even though I was not able to interview any of the brothers or sisters of the love-shy men, the impression was quite consistently driven home to me that the love-shys had been treated in a far more psychologically and physically callous way by their parents than the non-shys had ever been. Moreover, the love-shys tended to be in surprisingly consistent agreement that their siblings had been treated better by the parents than they themselves had been. Indeed, fully 81 percent

211

of the older love-shys (who had grown up with siblings) together with 73 percent of the younger love-shys felt that their brothers and sisters had been accorded better treatment than they themselves had been accorded. In contrast, only 5 percent of the non-shy men felt this way.

Temper and Rage

The thing which differentiated the parents of the love-shy from those of the non-shy more sharply than anything else was what might be termed the *rage and irascibility factor*. The love-shys' parents were remembered as being especially fast to display their tempers. For example, 53 percent of the older love-shy men together with 47 percent of the younger ones agreed with the statement: "My mother was always easily angered and very prone to outbursts of temper." Among the non-shy men only 20 percent agreed. Further, 41 percent of the older love-shys along with 36 percent of the younger ones agreed that their *fathers* were always easily angered and very prone to outbursts of temper. Among the non-shys just 21 percent agreed.

One of the statements to which each respondent reacted was: "My mother often threw uncontrollably loud, angry temper tantrums at me." Fully 45 percent of the older love-shy men indicated that this had happened "frequently" or "sometimes", compared to *zero percent* (nobody) of the non-shy men. Among the younger love-shys, 39 percent indicated that it happened "frequently" or "sometimes". On the other side of the ledger, 73 percent of the non-shys indicated that it *never* happened. Only 30 percent of the older love-shys and 39 percent of the younger ones similarly indicated that it had *never* happened.

Of course, almost all parents lose their "cool" with their children from time to time. This is very natural. In fact, it is part of being human. However, parental rages seemed to have left an indelible mark upon the minds of the love-shys whereas the non-shy men seemed to have largely forgotten such incidents.

The memory of parental swearing may similarly have faded from the minds of most of the non-shy respondents. In response to the statement: "When I was a child my *father* would very often swear, hollar and cus at me," 40 percent of the older love-shys and 35 percent of the younger ones indicated "true". Only 14 percent of the non-shy men similarly indicated "true". In response to the statement: "When I was a child my *mother* would very often swear, hollar and cus at me," 48 percent of the older love-shys together with 37 percent of the younger ones indicated "true". Among the non-shys only 6 percent said "true".

When I asked "Has either of your parents ever come after you with a knife?" 16 percent of the older love-shys and 11 percent of the younger ones said "yes". *None* of the non-shy men said "yes". And in response to the statement: "My mother would often scream that she wished I would die or that I was dead," fully 38 percent of the older love-shys and 30 percent of the younger ones indicated that this had happened on several occasions. Only 3 percent of the non-shys indicated that it had *ever* happened to them. As a case in point, one of the young love-shys recounted the following:

> "Oh, every time I go home for a holiday my mother turns really rabid after a few days. She does things like screaming that she can't understand why so many nice kids get killed in automobile accidents and plane crashes while a dirty rotten sonofabitch like me is permitted to live. Ha! Ha! Ha! I mean, she always really says that! Last time I was back there she asked me point blank—why don't I just take my car and crash it into a tree somewhere at 90 miles an hour! She says I'd be doing her and the rest of society a favor, and that I wouldn't have to suffer anymore either . . . . I've never had any suicidal wishes myself. I do feel depressed about the fact that I can't get a girl. But I think my feeling is to a much greater extent one of anger, than of depression. Like I enjoy my studies here at the university. I just get pissed off about the fact that society won't allow me to have a girlfriend just because I'm shy and because I'm not a nervy person." (23-year old love-shy man.)

None of the men in any of the three samples seemed able to recall their *fathers* doing or saying strange or bizarre things. However, some of the fathers were remembered by the love-shys as having been quite punitive and prone to fits of rage. Many of the love-shys recalled their fathers' frequent expressions of disappointment about having an "unmasculine" or "inadequately masculine" boy for a son. And in families where there had been more than one son, the love-shys remembered their fathers as having been a great deal more kindly and friendly in their interactions with the more "masculine" brother. Indeed, this had been true even in several cases where the more "masculine" brother had been an inferior student and had gotten himself into frequent scrapes of one kind or another at school. Thus, misbehavior in the favored or more "masculine" son was more likely to have been overlooked and forgiven by the love-shys' fathers.

Spankings, Beatings, and Physical Abuse

None of the 300 love-shy men interviewed for this book had ever had their bones broken by their parents. None had ever been beaten black and blue, or to the point of being bloodied up. None had ever been thrown into scalding water or placed atop a red hot radiator or stove, etc. In other words, dramatic instances of bizarre forms of *physical* child abuse or neglect are evidently not very common among the ranks of the love-shy.

However, the problem with the available literature on child abuse is that it focuses only on "the tip of the iceberg"—on cases that are maximally dramatic and bizarre. The metaphor of an iceberg is a very useful one in considering the issue of child abuse. Eight-ninths of an iceberg is inconspicuous and unapparent because it lies buried beneath the surface of the sea. In spite of the burgeoning in the reported cases of child abuse today, the vast majority of instances go unreported. Milder forms of abuse, which over the years can have an enormously deleterious cumulative impact upon a child, virtually never reach the attention of public officials.

Males who remain "single, never married" beyond the age of 30, have been found by numerous researchers to have had more stressful childhoods than any other major category of people. As far as love-shy men are concerned, there is no question but that a very uncomfortable family *and* peer group life constituted the major sources of stress. For many of the love-shys interviewed for this book, family stressors never abated. An abusive peer group situation can ordinarily be escaped for long periods— except for instances involving involuntary confinement in a summer camp. In contrast, no child can ever escape his family for very long. A child's dependence upon his parents for food, clothing and shelter obviates his escaping for very long.

The interview data I obtained clearly indicated that *psychoemotional abuse* represented a far more pervasive factor in the family backgrounds of the love-shy men than did physical abuse. Of course, psychoemotional abuse *is child abuse* in every sense of the term. Unlike physical abuse, psychoemotional abuse is almost never detected, much less stopped, by outside officials in the school or local community. Yet such abuse carries an enormous toll; and one manifestation of this toll is quite clearly that of love-shyness.

Despite the fact that psychoemotional abuse was the major theme as far as the family backgrounds of the love-shys were concerned, physical assaults on the love-shys by mothers and fathers had been quite commonplace. Psychologist Hans Eysenck has shown that highly inhibited, sensitive children ordinarily require a far below average amount of discipline because they learn (*when they are CAPABLE of learning*) socially acceptable behavior patterns faster and more thoroughly than extroverts do. And unlike extroverts, once they do learn something, they find it extremely difficult to *unlearn* it, even when it is appropriate for them to do so. Yet the love-shy men who were studied for this book had received a great deal *more* of all forms of "discipline" than the self-confident non-shys. And this had been as true for spankings, beating, and other forms of physical punishment, as it had been for loud, angry, ego-deflating scoldings. And when the love-shys had been beaten, loud shouting and screaming and abusive hollaring on the part of the "disciplining" parent had been invariably an integral part of the scenario.

First, 22 percent of the self-confident, non-shy men claimed that their parents had *never* used corporal punishment. This was true for *zero percent* (nobody) of the non-shys. In both the older and the younger groups, *all* of the love-shy men had received at least some corporal punishment during their formative years.

At the other end of the spectrum, 21 percent of the self-confident non-shys had been spanked or beaten on an average of at least *once or more every ten days* throughout their formative years of childhood. In stark contrast, fully 44 percent of the younger love-shys and 58 percent of the older love-shys had been beaten or spanked on an average of at least once every ten days.

Of course, what constitutes "spanking" or "beating" is very much a question of semantics. The word "spank" is widely used by abusive parents as a euphamism for severe beating and for other forms of psychoemotionally painful abuse. For this reason I asked the respondents about the impliments their parents had used for beating them. And in this regard the parents of the love-shy had been a great deal more indiscriminate in the "weapons" or impliments they chose than the non-shys' parents had been. Better than three-quarters of all groups of parents had relied upon their bare hands most of the time. However, 82 percent of the love-shys' parents (both groups) had relied heavily upon the use of belts; 56 percent of the parents of the non-shys had occasionally used belts, although these were used considerably less frequently by the non-shys' parents than by those of the love-shy.

Nineteen percent of the love-shys' parents (both groups) had occasionally used razor straps; none of the non-shys had mentioned razor straps. On the other hand, 14 percent of the non-shys' parents had occasionally used hairbrushes, compared to 21 percent of the parents of the love-shys (both groups). Straps were mentioned by 62 percent of the love-shys (both groups), compared to just 31 percent of the non-shys. Wooden rulers were used occasionally by 39 percent of the parents of the love-shys (both groups), compared to just 15 percent of the parents of the non-shys.

Sticks or birch rods were mentioned by 38 percent of the love-shys (both groups), compared to just 7 percent of the non-shys. And whereas none of the non-shys claimed to have ever been beaten with heavy wooden paddle boards, these were mentioned by 33 percent of the love-shy men. Dog leashes were similarly mentioned by 19 percent of the love-shys, but by *none* of the non-shys. And 12 percent of the love-shys had been beaten with wooden coat hangers; none of the non-shys had ever been beaten with same.

Perhaps the major difference between the love-shys and the non-shys is that corporal punishment had become an integral part of the normal way of life in *at least half* of the love-shys' homes. This had been true for little more than *one-fifth* of the homes from which the non-shys had come. In essence, the love-shys' parents were a good deal more likely than those of the non-shys to have learned throughout their own formative years to respond immediately to frustration, annoyance and wrongdoing in a *physical* manner. It would thus appear that the love-shys had grown up with parents who had always had an above average amount of difficulty with impulse control.

For this reason, when aroused to anger and rage the love-shys' parents had been much more likely than those of the non-shys to reach for any object or impliment that might have been immediately at hand. In fact, several of the love-shys recounted bizarre stories about all manner of household objects (sometimes even very valuable household objects) being thrown or used to inflict pain. Silverware and dishes were very often employed by the love-shys' parents as flying missiles. However, worthless objects were occasionally thrown as well. If a bag of garbage waiting to be taken out happened to be sitting on the kitchen counter during a temper tantrum, the mother might grab and throw that—quite irrespective of the mess that it made. One of the love-shys' mothers had become so enraged one time when she happened to be sitting on the toilet that she picked up her waste and threw it at her son.

These spontaneous, uncontrolled displays of parental rage constitute another reason why the love-shys were much more likely than the non-shys to be punished with other adults and/or children immediately present upon the scene. Rage often made the love-shys' parents (especially the mothers) lose contact with reality to the point where they would say or scream anything, no matter how bizarre or horrendous it might be. Nevertheless, a significant portion of the love-shys' parents did deliberately wish to inflict as much humiliation upon their sons as they possibly could—with the conscious hope that such humiliation might shock their wayward son "into line". As a case in point, 28 percent of the older love-shys and 23 percent of the younger ones claimed that when they were of elementary school age their buttocks were often bare when they were beaten by their parents. This had been the case for only 2 percent of the non-shys.

Another major difference between the homes of the love-shys and those of the non-shys is that the *mother* tended to be seen by the love-shys as having been the major source of discipline and punishment. In fact, 47 percent of the older love-shys and 38 percent of the younger ones agreed that the mother had done *mostly all* of the punishing in the family. Contrariwise, this had been true for only 6 percent of the non-shy men.

On the basis of these differences, it seems quite possible that the mothers' basic nature and behavioral style may have helped significantly to set the stage for (1) the love-shys' strong fears concerning informal interaction with women, and (2) their basic, underlying nervousness. Again, experimental psychology has clearly taught us that introverts and low anxiety threshold people condition much faster and more deeply than extroverts. Living on a day-to-day basis with an enormously high strung woman certainly could not have done anything positive in terms of promoting a relaxed, easy-going ability to relate in a friendly way with women.

A good example of the nervousness evoked by these mothers can be seen in the following interview segment:

> "Sometimes when my mother was mad, which was most of the time, she would take me by surprise. Like I'd be sitting at the dinner table, and she'd be getting ready to dish out some mashed potatoes from a pot that was sitting on the stove. Well, a lot of times she would take her wooden serving spoon and clobber me over the head with it as she was serving the mashed potatoes. I'd have mashed potatoes all over my head, and there would be mashed potatoes on the floor, and it would be a real mess. A lot of times she would scald me with hot water or with some other hot thing she was serving. It got to the point that every time she passed my seat with something she was serving, I'd duck and wince. And sometimes other people there would laugh at me for doing that . . . . I've been embarrassed several times. I mean sometimes even today as an adult I'd be sitting in a restaurant waiting for my meal. And when the waitress starts putting stuff on my plate I'd duck. I've been asked about that several times, but I don't say anything. Anyway, it never seems to happen when a man is serving me—only if it's a woman." (23-year old love-shy man.)

I asked each respondent to indicate how old he had been the last or most recent time one of his parents had inflicted any physical pun-ishment upon him. And the differences between the three groups of research respondents was quite substantial. The average age for the cessation of corporal punishment for the *non-shy* men was 11.6. For the young love-shy men, on the other hand, the average age had been 15.9. The average age when the *older* love-shys had stopped receiving corporal punishment was 17.2.

When People "Stop Behaving"

Numerous research investigations have revealed that when people are subjected to arbitrary and capricious punishment they typically *stop behaving*. In essence, they don't do anything. Much like the schizophrenic, they stop responding to their environment. Cessation of overt behavior is a commonplace response in situations where (1) "good" behavior is seldom recognized or rewarded in any meaningful way, (2) wherein "bad" behavior meets with arbitrary and capricious punishment incorporating steady doses of hazing, bullying and belittling, and (3) wherein the desired or "good" behavior is beyond the intellectual or psychoemotional capabilities of the individual.

A key finding of this entire research study is that the mothers of the love-shy (and to a lesser extent also the fathers) tended to be unusually capricious in their angry temper tantrums, in their irascible, truculent remarks and psychoemotional hazing, and in their administration of punishment and discipline. The behavioral inertia that is inherent in the love-shyness condition may be construed as a kind of *withholding of behavior*—of *any* behavior. Indeed, the inability of the love-shy to take risks vis-a-vis members of the opposite sex whom they deem attractive may similarly be viewed as a sort of "non-behaving". Moreover, it may represent a kind of "transfer" of non-behaving from the mother to women in general out in the wider social environment.

The family has long been recognized as constituting a kind of microcosm of the rest of society. People who become used to disordered patterns of intrafamily interaction (1) grow to *emotionally* expect similar disordered, arbitrary and capricious patterns of communication outside the family; and they respond within such outside social contexts accordingly. And (2) they may gradually come to develop a brain biochemistry that is different from that of the rest of us, and which is supportive of schizoid, socially withdrawing behavior. Recent research has suggested that long-term involvement in certain types of stressful environmental situations may help to alter the brain's biochemical composition. Presently ongoing research may soon provide us with more definitive answers in this regard.

Corporal Punishment's Negative Consequences

A book could easily be written summarizing all of the research activity that has been conducted pertinent to corporal punishment. Thus my discussion here will necessarily be kept brief and succinct. The main point I wish to make is that in spite of the widespread popularity of corporal punishment in the United States, hundreds of research studies are all in unanimous consensus on the points that (1) corporal punishment *defeats* the purpose of discipline, and (2) it entails a host of very deleterious consequences upon both the child and the parent-child relationship. Readers desiring a good summary of the undesirable consequences of corporal punishment should read my article on the subject in HUMAN BEHAVIOR magazine. (See the bibliography for Gilmartin, 1979.)

The research findings concerning this most important child-rearing topic can be summarized as follows:

(1) Corporal punishment is a self-image/self-esteem lowerer. The more frequent the reliance by the parents upon corporal punishment, the lower a child's self-esteem is likely to be, and the *less positive* his *mental attitude* is likely to become.

(2) Corporal punishment undermines the ability of parents to constructively influence their children. People (*including children*) tend to be most thoroughly influenced in situations wherein they can relax and let down their defensive guard. Corporal punishment creates social distance between parent and child.

(3) Actions speak louder than words. Corporal punishment teaches violence and psychopathic behavior and attitudes. The psychopath doesn't care about the needs and feelings of others because his own needs and feelings had never been shown any genuine concern. Frequently spanked children tend to become either extremely aggressive and bullying towards their peers, or they tend to become extremely passive. Among criminals, the more violent and frequent the criminal behavior, the more frequently and severely that criminal is likely to have beeen beaten by his parents. In general, criminals had received far more corporal punishment than non-criminals.

(4) A history of corporal punishment has been found to be strongly associated with husband-wife violence and with child abuse.

(5) Corporal punishment discourages the development of *internal* self-control. It makes people become overly dependent on *external* forms of control. For this reason, frequency and severity of corporal punishment has been found to be inversely associated with social mobility. In other words, frequently whipped children stand a below average chance of (1) getting a good education, even if they have the native intelligence, and (2) getting and keeping a good, white-collar, middle or upper-middle-class occupational career.

(6) Fear of pain has been found to bear *no relationship* to long-term obedience. Studies have been done with children born with a rare gene that makes them incapable of experiencing pain. Except for their inability to feel pain, these children are quite normal in all respects. In fact, these children have been found to behave themselves just as well, and to grow up just as responsibly, as children of the same ages who are capable of feeling pain. For both (1) the children who *could* feel pain, and (2) for those who could *not* feel pain, whether or not the children were spanked had no relationship to acceptability of behavior. For *both* groups of children the only factor which *did* give rise to good behavior was a harmonious, emotionally satisfying parent-child bond.

Of course, old traditions die hard. And corporal punishment *is* an old tradition in the United States. In the years to come it is certainly to be hoped that our public high schools will (1) educate young people in a sufficiently detailed way as to the adverse consequences of physical punishment, and (2) provide systematic training based upon role playing (psychodrama) of constructive and effective ways of handling interpersonal conflict within the family.

Persistent Belittlement and Ego Deflation

Psychoemotional abuse usually doled out in extreme anger was the major complaint that the love-shys had against their parents. This ego-deflating hollaring and screaming was an *everyday occurrence* in the homes of most of the love-shys. From the time the love-shys were very small children, the hollaring and screaming and shouting of belittling and highly disparaging labels was something with which they had always had to live—until they finally moved out of their parents' homes, usually to attend a university. Some of the love-shys told me that they thought they had immunized themselves against the rantings and ravings of their parents. But given the fact that throughout their formative years they had had to reside within such a highly charged home atmosphere, the absence of a deleterious cumulative effect seems most unlikely.

Consider, for example, the ways in which some of the love-shys respond even today to their parents' rages. Several of the men I interviewed mentioned that they cannot stop themselves from breaking into an uncontrolled spasm of hysterical laughter whenever one of their parents displays a temper tantrum. Others simply escape the situation by locking themselves into their bedrooms until the tantrum subsides. Still others admit that even with their university educations they cannot stop themselves from becoming depressed whenever they have to listen to their parents rant and rave.

And some of them still witness their parents' rages from time to time. According to my interview data even the older love-shys occasionally visit with their aging parents. Of course, these visits are primarily one-sided: the love-shy man visits his parents; the parents seldom or never visit him. The *non-shy* 19–24-year old men were visited by their parents on an average of *five times more frequently* than the love-shy 19–24-year olds were visited. And the older love-shy men were scarcely ever visited at all.

Curiously, some level of partial financial dependence appeared to be a major motive for many of these visits. Some of the love-shys continue even in their 30s and 40s to receive some level of financial support from their parents. The love-shys would visit their parents' home and receive money along with heavy doses of angry, psychoemotional abuse. Some of these love-shys figured that the abuse was simply "the price" they had to pay for the money they were getting. Some of the fathers did not like the way their love-shy sons were dressing, or the sort of employment (many were *under*employed) they were holding. Many of the fathers were still very upset about their adult sons' lack of competitive "masculine" drive. In essence, while the fathers were berating their love-shy sons for holding menial, "dead end" jobs, for dressing shabbily, and for not having any kind of a social life (not "settling down", having a family, etc.), they would simultaneously give them various sums of money.

Throughout their formative years the basic keynote of the psychoemotional abuse the love-shys had received from parents was *persistent belittlement and ego deflation*. As I shall show in the next chapter, this is the same sort of treatment they had been forced to accept throughout their formative years from their *same-sexed peer group*. American society provides no systematic training on the crucially important matter of how to parent. We assume that competent parenting "comes natural", whereas, in point of fact, *it does not*—especially when a parent is charged with the responsibility of raising a difficult or unusual child. And *pre-love-shy boys are unusual children*. (Highly effective approaches to parenting *do* exist; interested readers should consult P.E.T. IN ACTION, and PARENT-EFFECTIVENESS TRAINING, both by Dr. Thomas Gordon. Dr. Spencer Johnson's ONE MINUTE MOTHER and ONE MINUTE FATHER should also be considered "must" reading.)

Most of the love-shys' parents probably did what they thought was best for their sons. I suspect that many of them felt "hurt" by the non-masculine behavior of their sons, and by their sons' intractable and seemingly *deliberate* unwillingness to "straighten up and fly right" as a "*real boy*" should. The more refractory and non-responsive the sons became towards the methods of discipline imposed, the more exasperated, hurt and enraged the parents became. All people like to have control over their lives and over their environments. The love-shys' behavior tended to make their parents feel powerless; and that is a very painful and emotionally disconcerting way for anyone to feel.

Of course, a central part of the problem was that the love-shys' parents could not accept their sons as they were. Certain of the changes the parents had demanded were most probably beyond the native capacities of the love-shy sons. On the other hand, it seems probable that a great deal of constructive change *which might have been feasible* had been unintentionally prevented from happening. Simply put, the parents had, by their actions, defeated their purpose. Their actions had served to prevent *feasible* change.

A child must *feel* unconditionally accepted and loved *as he is* before realistically feasible change can begin to come about.[1] I am using the word "loved" here with a very precise meaning in mind. *Love* can be manifested and displayed only via *communication which reflects a genuine sensitivity to and compassion for the needs and feelings of the loved one.* This is the true operational essence of what "love" is all about.

To be sure, the experiencing of such "true love" would not have proved sufficient to have turned the pre-love-shy boys into highly energetic, "rough and tumble" oriented, "regular" little boys. However, I believe that it most definitely *would* have proved sufficient to prevent sensitive children from becoming love-shy, unhappy and poorly adjusted adults.

Children with the inhibition and low anxiety threshold genes *can* grow up to have a collection of good friends, marriage, career success, and a strongly positive self-image, provided that they are accorded this "*love*" and acceptance when they are in the process of growing up. Again, you cannot get a duck out of a swan's egg. But you can have a mighty healthy, happy, well adjusted *swan* if you accept your swan as a swan, instead of shouting him down all the time in the vain hope that your shouting will somehow inspire him into becoming something else— which he can never do. *Love* as defined above, and unconditional acceptance, are the *fertilizer* for propitious human growth and development. The sooner all people can be taught this message, the sooner our world will become a safer, happier, more productive and harmonious place.

In this regard, *patience* had not been a virtue among the love-shys' parents. Fully 51 percent of the non-shys agreed with the statement: "My *father* was always a patient person." In stark contrast, only 11 percent of the younger love-shys and 3 percent of the older ones saw fit to agree. Regarding the *mothers*, 54 percent of the non-shy men remembered theirs as having been patient. In contrast, only 13 percent of the older love-shys and 19 percent of the younger love-shys recalled their mothers as having been patient people.

Argument Initiation

I asked each respondent to indicate which of his two parents usually started an argument with the other parent. This type of question is, of course, totally dependent upon subjective memory. But it is what a person subjectively thinks and believes that impacts upon him, *NOT* what the objective facts might have been. Thus it is particularly instructive to note that fully 74 percent of the older love-shy men recalled their *mothers* as having "always" or "usually" been the argument initiator vis-a-vis the father. Among the younger love-shys 62 percent recalled their mothers as having normally been the one to start arguments with the father, not vice versa. In contrast, only 33 percent of the non-shy men saw their mothers as having been the usual argument starter vis-a-vis the father. In other words, in the non-shys' families when there was an argument the father was recalled as having been more likely than the mother to have started it.

Parenthetically, I permitted each of the respondents to check an alternative to the mother/father argument question which read: "I never observed my parents arguing." Not very many respondents checked that alternative. Nevertheless, 29 percent of the non-shy men *did* check it, compared to only 5 percent of the older love-shys and 9 percent of the younger love-shys.

Doesn't All of This Contradict the Genetic Perspective?

Given the highly dissonant and often quite tumultuous family backgrounds of the love-shy, it would be easy to conclude that genetic factors are not responsible for very much. Such a conclusion, of course, would be quite false. Throughout this book I have taken the position that severe love-shyness is a byproduct of a synergistic interaction between genetic, karmic, and social learning factors. For example, the mothers and fathers of the typical love-shy man studied for this book had not responded as favorably or as kindly to him as they had vis-a-vis his more normally appearing brothers and sisters. Karmic and genetic (plus congenital) factors determine the social stimulus value of a boy, as per the discussion in chapter four. When a boy's social stimulus value is at marked variance from what family and community norms suggest a boy should be like, that boy will typically *not* be accepted as he is. Indeed, he is far more likely to be disparaged and rejected than would be the case if he were "normal" (as defined by community norms) in terms of social stimulus value.

People with the inhibition and low anxiety threshold genes condition (learn) much faster and more thoroughly than extroverts, ambiverts, and high anxiety threshold people do. And it is especially for this reason that an adverse family background would be expected to do far greater damage to the "thin-skinned", pre-love-shy male than it would to the vast majority of the rest of us who had been born with "thicker skin".

Since the pre-love-shy learn self-related ideas much faster and more deeply and intractably than most people do, they are as a consequence less resiliant than most people. In essence, the shy retain adverse conditioning whereas most of the rest of us can fairly easily shake it off. The adverse conditioning (learning) which the love-shy receive from their families and peer groups serves to strengthen and reinforce the undesirable social stimulus value with which they started out. Thus the vicious cycle is perpetuated, and the love-shy male sinks ever more deeply and hopelessly into the quagmire of an ever worsening social stimulus value.

Thus a human being enters the world with a constellation of *elastic* limits. These elastic limits become progressively less and less elastic and to an increasing extent fully crystallized and etched in cement to the extent that their owner is consistently labeled and to the extent that he internalizes the disparaging label.

Notes

1. In his books THE ONE MINUTE FATHER and THE ONE MINUTE MOTHER, Dr. Spencer Johnson makes an especially important conceptual distinction between a child's *being loved* and a child's subjectively *feeling loved*. FEELING LOVED is of infinitely greater importance for a child's well-being and future socio-emotional growth than is being loved. Almost all parents passionately assert that they "love" their children. And virtually all manner of abuse can be heaped on a child in the name of "real love", "caring and concern". Many "loved" children simply do not *feel* loved; and as a result they fail to develop in a healthy manner.

Chapter 10

Love-Shyness and the All-Male Peer Group

Throughout their lives the love-shys had experienced significantly fewer friendships than had the non-shys; and the few friendships that a minority of them had experienced had been very shallow. In fact, most of the love-shy men I interviewed for this book had been social isolates or "loners" throughout most periods of their lives. For example, I asked each man: "When you were growing up, how many people *close to your own age*, and whom you felt free to contact, did you have readily available to you to help you deal with school and the various other problems and anxieties associated with growing up?" The differences in the pattern of responses between the three groups of men were quite substantial.

Fully 83 percent of the older love-shy men and 65 percent of the younger love-shys indicated that they had had *no one*. In contrast, this had been the case for *zero percent* (nobody) of the self-confident non-shy men studied. In fact, 57 percent of the non-shys indicated that they had had at least three or more close friends throughout their formative years. Only 11 percent of the younger love-shys and *zero percent* of the older love-shys could say that they had had three or more close friends throughout the duration of their formative years. In addition, 73 percent of the older love-shys together with 53 percent of the younger ones agreed with the much more extreme statement: "Throughout most of my life, I never had any friends." *Nobody* among the non-shy men agreed with that statement.

In order to tap the level of satisfaction each respondent felt with his *current* situation I simply asked the following: "In general, do you feel that you have as many friends of the various kinds as you would like?" And 94 percent of the non-shy men indicated "yes", compared to a mere 8 percent of the university love-shys, and *zero percent* of the older love-shy men.

This social distance which the love-shy feel vis-a-vis the human race apparently extends even to relatives and kin. I asked each man:

225

"How many relatives do you see often and consider close friends?" And 84 percent of the older love-shys together with 68 percent of the younger ones said "zero" or "nobody", compared to just 26 percent of the self-confident non-shys. In stark contrast, fully 45 percent of the non-shys saw *"four or more"* relatives often and considered them close friends. This was the case for *zero percent* of both the older and the younger love-shy men.

The basic premise of this chapter is that love-shy men learn very early in life to associate feelings of fear, anxiety and physical pain, with the mere idea of informal interaction amid an all-male peer group. The data which I shall review in this chapter strongly support this basic premise. Moreover, they point to a most pathetic poignancy in the lives of the love-shy.

Most human beings look forward with considerable enthusiasm to opportunities for friendly, informal interaction with peers. In fact, most people learn very early in life to associate friendly socializing with keen pleasure. Being placed in solitary confinement has long been recognized as the most cruel and extreme of all punishments. When all other pleasures have been removed, most people still manage to experience considerable positive feelings from talking with and from sharing ideas with their friends.

Over the years numerous psychologists have focused upon the determinants of happiness. And the one common denominator to emerge from most of these studies is that satisfaction with informal friendships constitutes for most people the single, most important predictor of happiness. The feeling that one is "in the driver's seat" of one's own life has been found by a minority of researchers to surpass "friendships" as a determinant of happiness. But most studies of happiness have clearly demonstrated that *involvement in meaningful roles and relationships with friends and family* constitutes the single, most important determinant of happiness.

Given the fact that most of us associate the idea of friendly peer group interaction with feelings of pleasure, it is doubtless of formidable significance that the love-shy associate the idea of male peers with pain, fear and anxiety. Indeed, the very idea of play within the all-male peer group often conjures up so many strongly displeasureable feelings for the love-shy that they quite commonly take special pains to *avoid* peers. Simply put, the love-shy often *deliberately choose* a life of solitary confinement.

Of course, the love-shys' prison is an internal, self-imposed one. But that observation only scratches the surface. In order for us to truly understand the love-shy we first need to comprehend why they found it necessary to erect their internal prisons (defensive walls) in the first place. This is important, socially valuable knowledge. Armed with this knowledge it may become possible to engineer a kind of elementary school environment which inspires no child into building an insurmountable wall around himself.

The peer group is of enormous importance from the standpoint of ensuring propitious growth and development. This appears to be especially true for males. There is evidence that the same-sexed peer group is of considerably less importance for females than it is for males. For example, women who are unpopular among their same-sexed peers often become highly popular with men. By contrast, males who are unpopular among members of their own sex *virtually never* become popular or even mildly successful with women. The social requirement that males must be the ones to make the first move vis-a-vis the female gender may partially account for this. Males without a network of same-sexed friendships have nothing to support them in their natural strivings to become assertive in a positive, friendly way vis-a-vis potentially eligible female dating partners. Simply put, a reasonable level of success within the all-male peer group constitutes a prime prerequisite for a male's ability to attain even a very mild degree of success in securing female companionship.

The Key Importance for Dating of Friendship Networks

During the past decade sociologists have published numerous research studies which have highlighted the importance of informal friendship networks. One of the key findings to emerge from this work is the fact that most Americans of both sexes initially meet their future marriage partners through their friends. Of course, popular folklore would have us believe that Cupid accomplishes most of his work in such public places as beaches, bars, discoteques, zoos, etc., and that employment situations and dating services also provide fertile soil for the sprouting of incipient romances. The reality of the situation is that women tend to be quite wary of strangers. The reality of the situation is that *informal friendship networks* instigate far more male-female relationships that eventually lead to cohabitation and/or marriage than do all of these impersonal meeting grounds put together.

This represents a social fact of the most profound sort for our understanding of the plight of love-shy men, and for our efforts to understand how they got to be love-shy in the first place. Even the best employment opportunities are obtained some 70 percent of the time through the proper and effective use of informal social networks. Love and work, the two most indispensably crucial ingredients of life, are *both* a direct byproduct of how successful people are in cultivating highly satisfying, quality friendship networks. The more solid our friendship networks are, the more solid will be our satisfactions and rewards in *both* LOVE *and* WORK.

A related fact is that it is actually easier to meet members of the opposite sex through friendship networks than through any other means. It requires a significantly greater amount of courage and self-confidence to initiate a conversation with a total stranger than it does to initiate one with someone to whom one has been introduced by a *mutual friend*. This is true for the vast majority of people, and it is certainly true for those with interpersonal anxiety or shyness problems.

Of course, shyness above and beyond a certain point of severity prevents a person from ever immersing himself into any informal social networks. The real rub is that for those who actually enjoy active membership in informal social networks, *substantially less* social self-confidence and "nerve" is required for meeting potential lovers than is required for people who do not have membership in informal friendship networks.

In other words, more is actually required of the severely isolated, love-shy man, than is required of the moderately self-confident man who has a small network of friends. The former is *forced* to deal with impersonal agencies and meeting places if he ever hopes to obtain a wife. The latter can totally avoid the hard, cold, impersonal world by depending upon his friendship networks.[1]

The Harlow Research

In his work with Rhesus monkeys, University of Wisconsin researcher Harry Harlow found that animals deprived of play amid a peer group while growing up became, upon reaching maturity, totally incapable of reproducing on their own. In fact, this was found to be true even for animals that had *not* been deprived of mother love. Peer group deprived female monkeys refused to permit even very socially successful males to mount them. These sexually disinterested females had to be impregnated by artificial insemination. Upon giving birth they tended to treat their young as though it were feces. They stomped on it, threw it against the cage wall, ignored it, and in some cases actually started eating it. The male monkeys that had been deprived of a peer group while growing up tended to sit in a corner and simply stare at the females. Harlow placed deprived males into enclosures with a large number of normally sexually receptive females. Yet in spite of the favorable gender-ratio and lack of sexual competition, these males refused to make any efforts towards sexual mounting behavior. In fact, in most cases they didn't even make an effort to play with the females. In most cases they simply sat on the sidelines watching and staring.

One thing which particularly struck me about Harlow's findings is that the "watching" and "staring" reaction of the deprived monkeys seems to be very commonplace among love-shy *human* males. In essence, rather than risk making an approach, love-shy human males quite commonly just simply watch and stare and daydream. Moreover, this "staring" behavior seems to persist even in environments offering a favorable gender ratio. There can be six women to every man, and the love-shy male will still "watch and stare and daydream" in lieu of taking positive action.

As Harlow was able to demonstrate in his work with monkeys, play and the multitudinous play-related experiences of childhood constitute a crucial and indispensable preparation for adult roles. And so it is with *human* children. To the extent that a person had been deprived of a childhood incorporating a great deal of happy, carefree play with other children, to that extent he could be expected to come of age inadequately prepared to competently fulfill adult family and employment roles.

The Polish Peasant

W. I. Thomas and Florian Znaniecki, in their book THE POLISH PEASANT IN AMERICA, cite many cases of boys who had been severely mistreated by their parents. Most of these impoverished Polish-American boys responded to such insensitive treatment by developing and maintaining a strong sense of solidarity with their male peers. Those who remained well integrated members of peer networks became effective, well adjusted adults, quite in spite of their past history of abuse at home. The few who lacked a friendship group to turn to in times of severe stress and unfair treatment, tended to become isolated and very poorly functioning adults.

Thomas and Znaniecki's conclusions regarding human children are very similar to those arrived at by Harlow in his work with Rhesus monkeys. In essence, Harlow found that young monkeys could almost always be expected to survive ineffective mothering very well indeed if they had had the benefit of a regular peer group life with fellow young monkeys.

As scores of social scientists have been able to demonstrate, children who do not experience a childhood become very poorly adjusted adults. A person's *social* adjustment as an adult is directly related to his having been actively involved in social play as a child. Child's play is important, especially to the extent that it involves cooperative, friendly interaction with a network of age-mate peers.

At one point in the interviews I asked each respondent in my own study to react to the statement: "I guess I was never really a child." And the pattern of obtained results back up the traditional wisdom about the importance of childhood. More specifically, *zero percent* (nobody) of the self-confident non-shys agreed with this statement. In contrast, fully 71 percent of the older love-shys and 59 percent of the younger ones saw fit to agree with it.

Bullying

A key premise of this book is that love-shy males learn early in life to perceive peer interaction as painful. If this is indeed the case, socially avoidant behavior along with self-imposed social isolation becomes more easily understandable. Again, most people associate informal peer interaction with feelings of pleasure. How and why did the love-shy come to associate such interaction with pain? Let us begin our analysis with a look at the widespread social phenomenon of bullying.

The male peer group among elementary school aged boys can be extremely cruel. The reasons as to why this is the case have been accorded far too little attention by research investigators. There are scores of societies all over the world wherein violence, cruelty and bullying (including psychological hazing) are totally absent phenomena as far as children's peer groups are concerned. In America these painful phenomena are far from absent.

I asked each of my respondents to react to the statement: "When I was a child I was often bullied by other children of my own age." It is important to note that *nobody* among the 200 non-shys indicated that this had been true for them. In stark contrast, fully 94 percent of the older love-shys together with 81 percent of the younger love-shys indicated that it had been true for them. In essence, better than four-fifths of even the younger (university sample) shy men had been frequently bullied while growing up. For the older love-shys almost all had been frequently bullied.

At the risk of redundancy, I would assert that the significance of this finding for understanding the development of love-shyness cannot be too greatly overemphasized. In chapter two I documented how love-shy men differ substantially from non-shys in terms of inborn, biologically and physiologically based temperament. Doubtless the physical and psychoemotional hazing interacted with these "weaker" biologically based inborn temperaments in a synergistic kind of way. The net result of this was undoubtedly to enhance social avoidance tendencies. Because of low inborn anxiety and emotional sensitivity thresholds, the love-shy men studied for this book probably suffered far more psychoemotional pain and scars than a non-shy person would have suffered even if such a non-shy person had been the recipient of the same quantity of bullying and psychoemotional hazing.

A further point is that the *social stimulus value* of running away and not defending oneself "like a man" is doubtless very negative in most American all-male peer groups of elementary and junior high school age. Simply put, if children are going to bully someone, they are far more likely to select a victim whose displeasure and suffering is conspicuous and clearly evident for all to see. It is endemic in the perversion of bullying for the perpetrators to single out those who clearly suffer most, and who are unwilling and unable to defend themselves. This is why the *social stimulus value* concept is so important in understanding bullying and in understanding the evolution of love-shyness and of socially avoidant, self-isolation tendencies.

In a similar question I asked each of my 500 respondents to react to the statement: "When I was a child I never fought back when I was punched." And here again, fully 94 percent of the older love-shy men agreed that this had indeed been the case for them. And among the younger love-shy men 77 percent indicated that it had been the case. In contrast, only 18 percent of the non-shy men indicated that they had never fought back. And several of these men added that it had never been necessary for them to do so because no one had ever punched them in the first place!

Even at the senior high school level the love-shy men studied for this book had received an incredibly large amount of bullying and psychoemotional harassment. For example, 62 percent of the older love-shys together with 48 percent of the younger ones had received quite a bit of bullying even in the 10th, 11th, and 12th grades. This had been true for *none* of the 200 non-shy men whom I interviewed.

Frailness of Body Build

In addition to having a sensitive inborn temperament, body build may have served as another key variable increasing the likelihood that the love-shys would be bullied. Simply put, a frail build represents another element contributing to negative *social stimulus value* here in American culture. Young boys are constantly being programmed by their parents and by the mass media to admire physical strength and daring, and to detest—and even punish—physical weakness and fearfulness.

Because of the biases in American all-male peer group culture which reward the strong and punish the weak, I asked each man to respond to the following: "Comparing yourself to other students of your size, weight, and sex when you were in high school, how physically strong or weak were you?"

Fully 66 percent or almost two-thirds of the older love-shys perceived themselves as having been physically weaker than most of their male contemporaries. Among the younger love-shys the analogous figure was 42 percent. In contrast, only 9 percent of the non-shys felt that they had been physically weaker than the majority of their contemporaries of the same size and weight. Indeed, on the other side of the ledger 55 percent of the non-shys believed that they had been *stronger* than most of their contemporaries. Only 21 percent of the younger love-shys and just 4 percent of the older ones felt that they had been physically stronger than most of their contemporaries. The remaining men indicated that they had been "about equally as strong as most others."

Inauspicious Introductions to the All-Male Peer Group

First impressions can be lasting. Often they set the stage for a person's future orientations toward a particular person or situation. This would certainly appear to be the case as far as the all-male peer group is concerned. The following interview segment can be considered representative:

> "Before I started school I don't remember ever being lonely. I usually had companions, but they were usually girls. I didn't think anything of it actually. There was this one little girl I used to play with all the time when I was three and four years old. In fact, I guess I played with her until we were both about ready to start school. She was the same age as I was, and we enjoyed being together. But our mothers were beginning to get rather nervous that we should be with kids of our own sex. I know my mother was really nervous about my being with this girl all the time. So one day about a week before I was supposed to start kindergarten she takes me to this house a few blocks from where we lived. And I remember there were a lot of boys my age there. I remember they were running

around on the lawn, screaming at each other and knocking each other down. One of the kids had a football, and he threw it at me hard. I was just standing there with my mother, and I practically shit in my pants! She was pushing me to join in, and she was saying things like 'Doesn't that look like fun!' and 'Isn't that fun?' and 'Why don't you run after them and join in?' and 'See, Billy is here! Why don't you join him?'

Well, I was just five years old at the time. And I had never known fear before. But boy! I really felt fear watching these kids! In retrospect, I guess what really bothered me was this idea that what I was watching was supposed to be fun! Jesus! I mean I might just as well have been watching a pack of wild tigers at play! I mean it was like I was watching a totally different species of animal! That's how detached I felt. Even though I was only five I realized right then and there that I was a different breed of animal than these kids I was watching. And I didn't know how to convey to my mother that this stuff they were doing didn't look anything like what I believed to be fun! My mother started to get really angry that I didn't want to join in. And it took several of the other mothers there to convince her not to force me—that I wasn't ready.

And I wasn't holding on to my mother's hand either. Even at that age I wasn't comfortable with my mother. I remember I reacted by backing farther and farther away from both my mother and the kids who were kicking each other and knocking one another down. I just wanted to go off by myself and find my girlfriend to play with.

Actually I was looking forward to starting school because I thought the kids at school would play nicely—you know, games like hide-and-seek, and hopscotch, and other games I played with my girlfriend. When I finally did start school I realized the very opposite was true. And I became more and more envious of the girls with each passing day because I felt I belonged with them. They were doing the things I liked to do while every minute with the boys was like bloody hell." (20-year old love-shy man.)

The foregoing can be considered quite representative of the early peer group experiences of love-shy men. American society expects boys to play with boys, and girls to play with girls. And it expects the two different gender-segregated peer groups to engage in entirely different constellations of play activities. It further expects children to pursue their "gender-appropriate" play activities with gusto and enthusiasm. For boys especially, "rough and tumble" play is expected to be viewed as "fun".

The problem, of course, is rooted in the untenable assumption that children of a particular gender can and should be encouraged to fall into the same mold. Simply put, most parents and educators believe in forcing square pegs into round holes, and in standardizing human personality into two different categories: male and female. I believe that chronic love-shyness along with a lifetime of loneliness and social isolation constitute part of the price that is intrinsic in this traditional and unchallenged way of doing things.

As a case in point, each of the 500 men studied for this research was asked to react to the following statement:

> "When I was six or seven years old, just watching boys partake in "rough and tumble" type play activities scared me to death; I resented any expectation that I try to join in; I wanted just one or two close friends who would play gently and with no chance of anyone getting knocked down or hurt in any way."

Among the older love-shy men, fully 79 percent indicated that the statement had been *true* for themselves. Among the younger love-shy men the analogous figure was 67 percent. On the other hand, *nobody* among the ranks of the self-confident non-shys felt that the statement had ever been in any way true for themselves.

In a related question I asked for reactions to the statement: "When I was a child in elementary school, being knocked down by one of my peers was one of my greatest fears." And here again, fully 87 percent of the older love-shy men indicated "yes, this was true". And among the younger love-shys, 73 percent similarly indicated that the statement had been true for them. In contrast, only 19 percent of the non-shys said that the statement held any truth for themselves.

In sum, the research data I obtained for this book strongly suggest that there is a strong and direct relationship between (1) extent of fear and apprehension upon first coming face-to-face in early childhood with an all-male peer group, and (2) degree or severity of love-shyness in adulthood. Some children take to the all-male peer group *and* the "rough and tumble" almost immediately, as soon as they are introduced to it. For these fortunate souls it is a matter very much like that of introducing a duck to water. The all-male peer group together with the "rough and tumble" is their "natural" mileau. For other youngsters this mileau is foreign and unnatural. Because this latter group of youngsters represents nonconformity from the "mainstream" expected course, there is a tendency to "see" them as being "homosexual" or "sick" or "neurotic" or just plain negative and uncooperative. In most cases such "nonmasculine" boys are none of these things! Homosexuality, for example, has to do with erotic and romantic directionality; it has nothing at all to do with recreational play interests and proclivities. And as for neuroticism, there is mounting evidence that society *creates* neurotics as a result of its insistence that all people of a particular category (e.g., *boys*) must fit into a certain interest and activity mold.

I believe that to the extent that we create *options* for children—to the extent that we afford them *a choice of more than just one type of peer group*, to that extent we are likely to begin observing a sharp dropping off in the incidence of incipient neuroticism, and probably in homosexuality as well.

I think one further point may be in order pertinent to the above case interview segment. Throughout my years of conducting interviews for this book I observed that love-shy men appear to have unusually rich and detailed memories of their early and middle childhood years. In fact, love-shy men are often able to recount in considerable detail incidents that had transpired long before they had even entered kindergarten.

In stark contrast, non-shy men do not appear to have anywhere nearly such rich and detailed memories of early childhood events. Many of the non-shys had difficulty recalling events as recent as their junior high school days, much less events of early childhood. In essence, the unusually sharp and detailed memories of the love-shy may be due in part to their unusually high degree of introspectiveness. But more importantly, such detailed memories may simply reflect their very low inborn anxiety threshold. Again, Eysenck's work has shown that introverts and low anxiety threshold people tend to condition (learn) responses far more deeply, thoroughly, and intractably than more advantaged people. Thus, the fact of not forgetting early childhood memories might simply be a reflection of this tendency on the part of inhibited people to condition deeply and permanently. Indeed, it probably also reflects their inability to "shake off" bad memories.

Masculine Toys

Another manifestation of this "visitor to a strange world" feeling vis-a-vis male peers which I found to have been quite prevalent in the formative years of the love-shy, has to do with toy preferences. Traditional gender-role stereotypes prescribe that little boys ought to be interested in toy guns, pistols, trucks, footballs, baseball bats and gloves, etc. And these same norms prescribe that little boys had better not feel attracted to dolls, figurines, miniature houses, doll house items, miniature animals, etc. However, not all people who happened to have been born of the male sex naturally gravitate in the direction of these normatively prescribed stereotypes. One 19-year old love-shy man had this to say:

"As far back as I can remember, I always found male toys and male activities to be painfully boring. When I was in kindergarten I can remember that the teacher used to prod me all the time to join the boys and play on the floor with the trucks and the orange crates. At that time I used to enjoy making cut-outs with different colored paper. And I enjoyed working with clay quite a lot. But all that was looked upon as being girl's stuff. I hated the thought of getting on all fours with the boys, not only because what they were doing was very boring to me, but also because I felt very uncomfortable about getting dirty."

And a 42-year old love-shy man offered this remark:

"When I was eight or nine I remember my mother used to shoo me out of the house all the time to play with some boys who lived in our neighborhood. I can remember these kids running all over the place with these cap guns and bragging to each other about how expensive and special their own cap gun was. I was just bored stiff by this and by the stupid western movies that these kids enjoyed. I usually just went off on long walks by myself whenever my mother threw me outside. I remember I had to keep the toys I really liked hidden away in an attic crevace because both my parents would swear and cus at me when they saw me admiring my miniature animals. I also had a lot of miniature chests of drawers and miniature silverware and mops. And I liked to play with my model railroad a lot. But I always had to play with these things on the sly, like when my parents weren't home.

I remember one time when I was about nine I really wanted a Charley McCarthy doll (ventriloquist doll) really badly, and I kept nagging my father to buy it for me. There were really a lot of nasty scenes at the dinner table about this because both my parents kept insisting that this was girl stuff, and that I should be interested in guns and baseball, not dolls. But I can't remember one single time throughout my years as a child when I was even the slightest bit attracted to these things. My father took me to five or six professional baseball and football games and I couldn't wait until it was all over. I might as well have been watching a bunch of spiders spin a web, for all the interest it held for me."

I asked each man: "When you were a child between the ages of 5 and 12, did you *prefer* girl-type toys to boy-type toys?" And 83 percent of the older love-shy men said "yes", along with 61 percent of the younger love-shys. *Nobody* among the 200 non-shy men indicated that they had ever preferred "girl-type" toys to "boy-type" toys.

For a follow-up question I asked: "When you were about 12-years old, did you ever play with such items as dolls, miniature furniture, plastic or glass figurines, etc.?" And 88 percent of the older love-shys along with 74 percent of the younger ones indicated "yes". In contrast, *zero percent* of the non-shy men indicated "yes".

These differences could not have been due to the presence of too many girls in the household. Again, 71 percent of the older love-shys and 59 percent of the younger ones had grown up without sisters. Only 14 percent of the non-shy men had grown up without a sister.

Moreover, there is no evidence that the love-shys' parents had wanted a daughter. In fact, all of the love-shy men (both the older ones and the younger ones) believed that their parents had gotten what they wanted in giving birth to a son. And, indeed, some of them had pressed pretty hard in trying to turn their sons into "real boys".

> "When I was about 11 my dad bought me this punching bag which he set up in the basement. And I can remember he used to make me practice using it. It was really horrible because it was just so boring, and the damn thing was making my knuckles become red. I mean he was really stupid because there was no way I could ever fight back against any of those bullies. I don't even believe in fighting. It's stupid!" (20-year old love-shy man.)

The Baseball, Basketball, and Football Syndrome

In American society the mere thought of "boy" conjures up images of "rough and tumble" competition and enthusiasm for the "big three" triumvirate of contact sports—football, basketball, and baseball. So deeply imbedded are these three sports in our concept of masculinity that some young fathers actually go to the trouble of erecting basketball hoops as soon as they learn that their wives are pregnant with male fetuses! People expect the interest and attention of a "healthy" boy of any age to immediately perk up as soon as the very words "baseball" or "football" are mentioned. And people often react with amazement and surprise when these words do not arouse an enthusiastic response. Indeed, miniature and even full-sized footballs and baseballs are often given to boys as Christmas or birthday presents as early in life as age three!

Because of these often uncompromising expectations which pervade our society, I asked each of the 500 men interviewed a collection of questions about his past attitudes *during childhood* towards a variety of sports. For example, I asked: "When you were growing up, how much did you like to play football?" And not surprisingly, *zero percent* of the older love-shys and only 7 percent of the younger love-shys indicated that they had *loved to play it*. In contrast, fully 73 percent or *almost three-quarters* of the non-shy men indicated that they had loved to play football.

On the other hand, *nobody* among the non-shys had ever "disliked" playing football, whereas 89 percent of the younger love-shys and fully 100 percent of the older love-shys had *disliked* the idea of playing it.

Regarding the idea of options, which had seldom been available to the men interviewed, I asked the following:

> "Picture yourself as a high school teenager. Supposing you were given a choice between playing a game of touch football and going bowling. Which would you have chosen?"

Fully 87 percent of the non-shys selected the touch football, compared to *zero percent* (nobody) of the older love-shys, and just 9 percent of the younger love-shys. In essence, 100 percent of the older love-shys and 91 percent of the younger ones selected bowling over touch football. Only 13 percent of the self-confident non-shy men selected bowling over touch football.

In a related question I presented each person interviewed with the following scenario:

> "Supposing you were at an all day picnic as a 15-year old. Suppose one group composed only of boys your own age was going to play games such as football, baseball and basketball all day long. The other group would spend the day learning how to play golf and would be composed of 8 boys and 8 girls. Which group do you think you would have been more likely to have selected?"

Quite interestingly, only 52 percent of the non-shy men selected the group playing baseball, basketball and football, over the coeducational group that was to learn how to play golf. All 100 percent of the older love-shy men along with 98 percent of the younger love-shys similarly selected the coeducational golf-learning option.

These findings suggest that many naturally assertive, "typical" boys could easily find delight in more gentle pursuits such as golf. The fact that golf, like bowling, is a *lifetime sport* that need never be given up represents a powerful argument in its favor. Inasmuch as the sport provides an opportunity for good outdoor exercise, there is no reason why it, along with a good many other non-contact sports, should not be taught to school children—as an option for those wanting nothing to do with baseball, basketball and football.

The "National Pastime"

The so-called "national pastime" fared little better among the love-shys than did football. Only 4 percent of the older love-shys had had any enthusiasm at all for baseball as they were growing up. The younger love-shys had been more open to the sport with 13 percent indicating that they had enjoyed it. Among the self-confident non-shys, on the other hand, fully 86 percent had loved to play baseball.

Thus I asked each man: "At the age of 15, suppose someone had given you a choice between tennis lessons and baseball lessons. Which would you have chosen?" And in spite of the burgeoning popularity and high status of tennis, fully 66 percent of the self-confident non-shys opted for the baseball. In contrast, *zero percent* of the older love-shys and only 5 percent of the younger love-shys opted for the baseball over the tennis.

Part of the love-shys' aversion to baseball may have been due to a higher than average sensitivity to bright sunlight. Fully 64 percent of the older love-shys and 56 percent of the younger ones indicated that bright sunlight made them very uncomfortable. This was true for only 21 percent of the non-shy men. However, it seems likely that the major reasons for the unpopularity of baseball among the love-shys were (1) it is a very non-romantic sport that is always played in gender segregated settings; and (2) it is a "rough and tumble" sport with a high probability of physical injury and pain.

Again, throughout their formative years the love-shys had wanted to play in *coeducational* peer groups. And most of them felt extremely bitter about the fact that American society arranges things in such a way that coeducational play is seldom a permitted option for growing children.

Basketball

Love-shy men tend to view basketball with almost as much trepidation as they view football and baseball. Several of the men I interviewed commented about the flailing hands and arms, and about the inordinate speed. Both of these conditions are intrinsic to the sport of basketball. Of course, the love-shys' big fear was that they could get an eye knocked out or severely injured. In fact, one man specifically commented that he might have become interested in basketball had the sport required all players to wear goggles protecting the eyes along with some other paraphernalia designed to protect the mouth and teeth.

The speed factor was viewed as quite frightening by most of the love-shys because they did not have the coordination to handle it. Some of the love-shys claimed that they could run quite fast as, for example, in a 100 meter dash. But in basketball many maneuvers involving both team mates and opponents must be made while in the process of running. The extremely fast thinking and movement required along with the absence of coeducation in the sport rendered basketball very unattractive to most of the love-shys.

I asked each respondent to indicate whether during his junior and senior years of high school he preferred basketball to volleyball, or vice versa. And fully 95 percent of the older love-shys together with 82 percent of the younger love-shys indicated that they had preferred *volleyball* to basketball. In stark contrast, only 27 percent of the non-shy men had preferred volleyball to basketball during their junior and senior years of high school.

The "Left Out" Syndrome

One love-shy man told me that when his elementary school teachers required him to go outside and play baseball the kids always assigned him to play the position of "left out". Now this individual had *wanted* to play baseball at that time. As I have indicated, the vast majority of the love-shys wanted to have nothing to do with baseball, basketball, football, or any other non-coeducational "rough and tumble" contact sport.

Nevertheless, whether they wanted to be involved in these sports or not, a strong message was made crystal clear to the love-shys time and time again. And that message was: "Get the fuck out of here! We don't want you, shithead! You're not important! You're incompetent!" This message had been pounded home to the love-shys repeatedly throughout their formative years, and irrespective of whether or not a physical education class had been involved. When a physical education class had been involved, the teacher invariably had to force the children to admit the love-shy pupil onto one of the two competing teams.

I asked each respondent to react to this statement: "In physical education classes back in my earlier school days, I was usually the *last person* to be selected for a team when the kids were drawing up sides." Fully 91 percent of the older love-shys together with 70 percent of the younger love-shys indicated that this had indeed been the case. In stark contrast, only 3 percent of the non-shys indicated that they had usually been the last person selected.

After approximately one-third of the data to be collected for this book had been obtained, I added an additional item to the research questionnaire. In essence, I began asking each of my respondents to react to the statement: "In elementary school when the teacher required everyone to play baseball, the kids usually assigned me to play the position of 'left out'." Only 1 percent of the non-shys who had been presented with this statement saw fit to agree with it. In stark contrast, fully 86 percent of the older love-shys together with 62 percent of the younger ones agreed that they had indeed usually been assigned to play the role of "left out".

Now virtually anyone can understand how this sort of experience repeated time and time again throughout the formative, impressionable years could and most probably would operate to drastically lower a child's self-esteem. But what may be less apparent to some readers is that this experience also teaches children to associate peer group (*people*) sociability with negative feelings of displeasure, pain and anxiety. It teaches them to find greater pleasure in solitary pursuits than in sociable ones. Elementary education and physical education protagonists require participation in sports with the ostensible purpose of providing good exercise and cultivating the capacity for friendly sociability. Some educators strongly believe that team sports teach children how to get along with each other. However, the evidence is that shyness-prone boys are *made worse* rather than better off by the types of physical education and "gym" requirements that are imposed upon them.

The old cliche that "one man's meat is another man's poison" is nowhere more true than in the contemporary policy of requiring all boys to play at baseball, basketball and football. Simply put, if we are to prevent love-shyness as well as a host of other psychoemotional disorders, we must insist that educators and parents stop trying to force square pegs into round holes.

It is true that all children need exercise. But it is equally clear that they do not all require *the same type* of exercise. Forcing all boys (just because they are boys) to partake in the same "rough and tumble" exercise is the fastest way of defeating the educator's purpose. Educators want children to grow to love exercise, and to find a great deal of pleasure in it. Yet as a consequence of the experiences forced on children, the more inhibited, sensitive boys learn early in life to despise physical exercise, and to *avoid* it just like any other unpleasant phenomenon. And in avoiding exercise they are *also* avoiding the opportunities for the development of social self-confidence and interpersonal skills—opportunities which are generously accorded boys who *fit* the baseball-basketball-football-loving mold.

Most People Know What Is In Their Best Interests

Most love-shy men seem to know what would have been in their best interests. All children absolutely require a copious abundance of opportunities for socializing with peers. And these opportunities must be looked forward to by *all*. Sociability must be associated with *pleasure* and *not* with anxiety, fear and pain. Sports participation at all ages throughout the formative years must be genuinely FRIENDLY and *NOT* HOSTILE.

Before I review my suggestions for remedying the shyness-generating situations with which all boys in contemporary America are required to contend, let me first present some attitude data. I asked each respondent to react to the following statement:

> "Requiring all boys to play touch football, baseball and basketball in physical education class provides an open invitation to all the bullies and rough necks to gang up on shy and retiring boys who are not interested in and do not desire to play at rough and tumble contact sports."

Only 27 percent of the non-shy men agreed with this statement. And that included many men who very much enjoyed contact sports, but who had long been fully cognizant of the counterproductive consequences which forced involvement in such activities holds for the withdrawn and noncompetitive child. On the other hand, a majority of the non-shy men had taken some pleasure in the overt psychoemotional suffering which these "rough and tumble" sports had caused their more "tender-hearted" classmates. This is reflected in the fact that 80 percent of the non-shy men admitted that when they were school children they had at least occasionally bullied their more withdrawn and inhibited peers.

Whereas only 27 percent of the non-shys agreed with the above statement, fully 95 percent of the older love-shys and 86 percent of the younger love-shys agreed with it. Simply put, most love-shy adults fully realize the deleterious impact that a certain type of required "physical education" activity had had upon them.

In a related question I asked each man to respond to this statement:

> "Ideally, every elementary school and junior high school ought to have its own miniature golf course, bowling alley, and ping pong tables for children of *both* sexes who prefer to play at gentle sports while their more aggressive classmates play at the more aggressive contact sports and games."

Here again, fully 100 percent of the older love-shys and 92 percent of the younger ones agreed with this statement. In contrast, only 43 percent of the non-shy men agreed. And whereas 43 percent is certainly a much lower figure than 92 percent, it nevertheless suggests that as many as half the people in most local communities might be willing to support the above idea.

I then asked each respondent to react to this telltale statement:

> "During my childhood years, I am sure that I would have had many more friends if sports and games a great deal gentler than baseball, basketball and football had been more readily available to me."

Fully 87 percent of the older love-shy men along with 76 percent of the younger love-shys agreed with this statement. In contrast, *zero percent* (nobody) of the self-confident non-shys saw fit to agree with it. And as a check for consistency and reliability, I asked each respondent to react to this very similar item:

> "During my childhood years I am sure that I would have been much happier if sports and games a great deal gentler than baseball, basketball and football had been more readily available to me."

And again there were huge differences in the amount of agreement between the non-shys and the love-shy men. Fully 78 percent of the older love-shys together with 65 percent of the younger love-shys agreed with this statement. On the other hand, *nobody* among the ranks of the non-shy men saw fit to agree with it.

In order to round out the picture, each respondent also reacted to the following statement:

> "My sense of self-confidence and my social skills would both be a great deal better today if sports substantially more gentle than baseball, basketball and football, had been more readily available to me when I was growing up."

Fully 64 percent of the older love-shys together with 52 percent of the younger ones agreed with the statement. *Zero percent* of the non-shy men agreed with it. Of course, no one can be completely sure as to how his development might have proceeded had certain past experiences been different. We are dealing here with a form of speculation. Nevertheless, the differences between the three research groups were so strong and consistent on all of these items that it seems highly probable that a message is being conveyed here which deserves to be taken seriously by parents, educators, and community leaders.[2]

The Solution

We must put a stop to the multitudinous shyness-generating situations to which our male children are exposed every day throughout the entirety of their formative years. I believe that this can be accomplished without imposing any strain upon cramped school budgets, and without inconveniencing boys who truly prefer to select "rough and tumble" forms of play. All children should be expected to take an active part in some sports activities. But all children *must be accorded a choice as to which sports activities they wish to involve themselves in*. The available choices for children of all age levels must be made sufficiently varied to accommodate people of inhibited and melancholic temperament. School districts are already required by law to accommodate the blind, the deaf, and children of all intelligence levels who are slow in learning how to read. Similar accommodations must also be made for children who are exceptional in the extremely important area of *native temperament*.

American education quite fallaciously assumes that making friends "comes natural" to all children, and that relaxed, easy-going sociability is therefore something which need not be taught. For the naturally reserved, making friends and learning "small talk" does not "come natural". Just as slow readers are given a set of learning experiences that is different from that which is accorded the majority of children, a *"different"* set of classroom experiences must similarly be developed for shy and withdrawn, *socially* handicapped children.

Towards this end I believe that a recreation and physical education program that is in harmony with the psychoemotional needs of *ALL* children represents one of the most promising means for the prevention of chronic and intractable love-shyness. Such a program of recreation and physical education *must* incorporate three basic ingredients: (1) children must be permitted a *choice* of activities; options other than "rough and tumble" play *must* be readily available; (2) coeducational sports and games must always be available for those children who want it; and (3) inhibited, melancholic, low anxiety threshold boys must *never* be required to play among a group of children containing bullies or rugged, "rough and tumble" oriented individuals.

This third point is of especial importance. For even if the game were tiddleywinks, if an inhibited boy were assigned to play along side a "rough and tumble" oriented boy, you can *rest assured* that the inhibited boy would very soon be bullied, and would soon learn to withdraw from tiddleywinks! Boys of diametrically opposite native temperaments *must never* be made to play together. Lambs must never be made to play with lion cubs! Just as the mentally retarded are never educated in the same classroom as the intellectually gifted, the highly inhibited must *never* be thrown in with the highly exuberant, aggressive extrovert. This is true *no matter what* sport or game might be involved.[3]

Regarding point #1, I would suggest that the following can and should be made an integral part of the physical education curriculum of every elementary school, junior high school, and senior high school:

(1) *Bowling*: Schools need not construct their own bowling alleys— although such construction might not be a bad idea if it can be afforded. School districts should rent an appropriate number of alleys from commercial establishments. Most bowling establishments are not particularly busy during the mornings

and early afternoons of the five weekdays. Interested children can easily be transported in coeducational groups to the bowling alleys during the various periods of the regular school day.

(2) *Ping Pong (Table Tennis)*: Readers who have ever observed the Chinese play this on television know that there is far more *good exercise* to it than most people realize. All schools can easily obtain an appropriate number of ping pong tables. In essence, these facilities can be made available to children quite cheaply on all school premises.

(3) *Horseshoes*: This can easily and cheaply be made available in every school.

(4) *Miniature Golf*: This is a favorite of most inhibited boys. As with bowling alleys, miniature golf courses can be rented for the various periods of the regular school day. Financially well-off districts can build their own miniature golf courses. Often this can be done at low cost through the creation of summer work projects for young people. The help of art majors at various local colleges can also be sought in this regard.

(5) *Golf*: Like #1 through #4, this is a *life sport*; it is an activity that can be enjoyed throughout the life span. And it is one which can contribute to good physical (as well as mental and social) health throughout the life span. To be sure, few school districts will be able to afford their own golf courses. But such ownership is not necessary. Most schools have immediate access to a plain, grass-covered playground. This can be used to teach interested pupils the basic fundamentals of golf. A significant portion of a golf game can be played on a comparatively small sized playground. Of course, children can also be taken to regular, full-sized courses, after they have mastered the fundamentals.

(6) *Shuffle Board*: This is another gentle, *lifetime sport* that can easily and cheaply be made available on a coeducational basis in all school districts.

(7) *Croquet*: This is a gentle, lifetime sport that has long enjoyed considerable popularity in the United Kingdom. It would be very easy and inexpensive to make it available to all American school children.

(8) *Volleyball*: Most American schools already offer this. However, it needs to become a far more ubiquotous option than it currently is; and it needs to be made freely available on a strictly coeducational basis. Children with an aversion to baseball, basketball and football should always have volleyball available to them as an acceptable physical education option.

Parenthetically, volleyball can also be played in a swimming pool as well as in an indoor gymnasium, or outdoors.

(9) *Swimming*: Swimming is a *lifetime sport* which requires the utilization of virtually all muscle systems. As such, it is a far better body builder than the far more aggressive sports of football, baseball and basketball! Many of our senior high schools already have swimming pools. Elementary schools seldom have them. But indoor swimming pools can be rented for use by school children. For example, children electing swimming as their sport might be required to join up with the YMCA—although this should be transformed into the "YPCA" (Young *People's* Christian Association) thus ending sex-based segregation. Many motels also have indoor swimming pools which might be made available for rent to schools during certain portions of the weekdays. Time spent on Saturday mornings in swimming activities at the "Y" could be subtracted from any given child's required physical education time at school.

(10) *Billiards*: For quite irrational, often mysterious reasons, many people don't like the idea of children engaging in this activity. Yet it provides good exercise, convivial companionship, and it can easily be played coeducationally. In addition, it is a *lifetime sport*, quite unlike the baseball, basketball and football that our society has so mindlessly and cruelly pushed upon all male children.

(11) *Frisbee Throwing*: A sport can easily be developed out of this popular activity. Fine exercise is provided by this activity; yet there is virtually no chance of physical injury and pain. Moreover, children who might be getting too little exercise might be shown how to engage in frisbee throwing (and catching) with their dogs. This is a quite enjoyable activity in which to involve one's canine companions.

(12) *Tennis*: I have found in my own work that many love-shy men are not afraid of the lifetime sport of tennis; although a small number of them commented that they would like to see comfortable eye-protectors devised for the sport. Even in our highly aggressive society, tennis has become a rather high status sport. Given the expressed interest in this sport by many love-shy men, it would appear especially appropriate to build tennis courts for those of our children who are temperamentally averse to "rough and tumble" activities. And tennis can be played "doubles" with two people on each "team". For

example, a boy and a girl can be pitted against another boy and girl.

(13) *Racquetball*: This is another *lifetime sport* which entails some of the same dangers to the eyes as does tennis. However, many love-shy men appear interested in this sport, and protective eyewear can surely be devised for it.

(14) *Horseback Riding*: Curiously, many love-shy men are far less afraid of animals, including horses, than they are of people. School districts should construct small stables for the benefit of interested pupils. I recommend that only the "western saddle" be used. Teaching horseback riding with an "English saddle" is a good way to alienate most children from the sport.

(15) *Tetherball*: This can be quite an aggressive game. Yet shy children like it because no matter how aggressive it becomes, there is virtually no chance of participants suffering any physical injury or pain.

(16) *Hopscotch*: This game provides fine exercise for all young children. And it is high time that we stopped restricting it to girls, or viewing it as a "girls only" activity.

(17) *Bicycle Riding*: Inhibited children often do more of this than extroverted children do. Several of the love-shy men interviewed for this book had gone on 40 and 50 mile bicycle trips all by themselves, as young as age 11 or 12.

(18) *Archery*: This can provide good exercise; and it also entails a competitive element.

(19) *Ballroom and Social Dancing*: This can provide fine exercise, and it is an activity that is intrinsically coeducational. Moreover, it can be incorporated into an interpersonal skills education program. One note of caution, however: most love-shy men dislike any and all forms of rock music. They prefer waltzes, fox trots, tangos, love ballads, big band, jazz, etc.

(20) *Square Dancing*: This entails the same fine advantages as #19. In addition to being a good facilitator for heterosexual interaction, square dancing is also very good exercise. It teaches coordination and the ability to react rapidly to constantly changing cues.

(21) *Jumping Rope*: Perhaps even more than hopscotch, this has traditionally been viewed as a "girl's activity". However, recently it has become a high energy sport that can be made quite demanding from the standpoint of endurance. Contrary to popular opinion, jumping rope can provide outstanding exercise; and can easily be done coeducationally.

(22) *Running*: Many love-shy males engage in quite a bit of this anyway—on their own. It provides good exercise and it can easily be done coeducationally. It can also be enjoyed as a "lead-in" to one of the other activities I have enumerated above. A key benefit of running for the love-shy is that it seems to enhance their rich fantasy life. And it is also a proven antidepressant.

(23) *Darts*: This is one of the most popular of gentle sports. Popular among both males and females on both sides of the Atlantic, involvement in it can easily serve as a catalyst promoting friendly, sociable interaction and conviviality.

(24) *Boccie*: This is an Italian variety of lawn bowling which is played on a small court. For those who insist that children must have *outdoor* exercise, this would represent a fine substitute for regular bowling. A nice, tree-shaded area should be used for constructing the courts.[4]

Some of my critics have charged that the above twenty-four activities do not provide the competition that boys allegedly need to a greater extent than girls. Critics have also insisted that with the exception of volleyball these are not team sports; and that team sports are somehow necessary for teaching boys how to cooperate. The usual contention is that a cooperative spirit is picked up from active participation in baseball, basketball, and football; and that this cooperative and competitive spirit somehow transfers to the business world and to life in general.

I would suggest that competitive drive is essentially a function of native temperament. Boys with an aggressive temperament are highly likely to gravitate naturally towards baseball, basketball and football. And they are similarly quite likely to display this aggressive drive vis-a-vis the business world. Simply put, it is *not* competitive sports that *causes* competitive business drive. Every Sunday afternoon the bars are loaded with rather noncompetitive blue-collar men who have a great love of competitive sports. Instead, *active* participation in competitive sports *AND active* competition in the business world *both reflect* an inborn temperament that is fundamentally aggressive and characterized by a high anxiety threshold.

As for cooperation, girls have long grown up without being required to partake in "rough and tumble" athletics. Yet it seems to me that females display far more of a cooperative spirit vis-a-vis each other than males typically do. Quite clearly, women do not enter adulthood less capable than men of cooperating effectively with others. The notion that participation in "rough and tumble" sports is a necessary condition for inspiring a spirit of cooperation and of friendly competition appears nothing short of ludicrous.

Of course, the available research evidence has documented what is actually a far more important point. When shy and withdrawn boys are *required* to participate in "rough and tumble" activities they withdraw into their private shells all the more completely. By encouraging shy and withdrawn boys to participate, *away from the company of bullies and other aggressive individuals*, in the twenty-four activities I have suggested (in lieu of rugged calesthenics and contact sports), the shy will be accorded the opportunity to (1) *make friends*, and (2) to develop the interpersonal skills and social self-confidence that are crucial to success and happiness throughout life.

In short, requiring love-shys to play football, baseball, basketball, *OR NOTHING*, results in their not being accorded the opportunity to cooperate or to informally associate WITH *ANYONE*. Even those who are "gung ho" for contact sports and rugged calesthenics would have to agree that *SOME* LEARNING IS BETTER THAN NONE AT ALL; and that *SOME* exercise is *far better than none at all*. Except for running, swimming, and frisbee throwing, *all* of the twenty-four activities I delineated require a partner. And if a person is too shy to have friends, it is a good bet that he will go through life without participating in *any* sports activity. In essence, forcing square pegs into round holes always yields counterproductive outcomes.

And baseball, basketball, football, and rugged calesthenics are not even *lifetime sports*. In addition to not providing as much good exercise as swimming and running and several of the other activities delineated above, "rough and tumble" activities cannot even be practiced to any major extent by most people beyond the late 20s.

In sum, options need to be made available to all school children. To be sure, highly active boys must be accorded their opportunities for participating in "rough and tumble" sports. But while they are "doing their thing", the less energetic and more socially withdrawn boys must similarly be accorded the dignity and respect as human beings to "do *their* thing" as well. While the assertive, aggressive boys happily pursue their football, the more withdrawn boys must have the right to run off and pursue their volleyball and bowling and miniature golf and swimming, etc. AND THEY MUST HAVE A RIGHT TO ENJOY THESE ACTIVITIES WITH GIRLS IN A *COEDUCATIONAL* SETTING.

Again, socially withdrawn boys typically feel out of place in gender-segregated contexts. And whenever they are placed in such contexts they immediately fantasize about being with girls anyway. Lacking sisters as many of them do, they desperately need to learn how to interact comfortably with girls and to engage in mutually enjoyable small talk. Hence, it is best that *all* of their required physical education activities be engaged in on a strictly coeducational basis. Such a background of coeducation may accord them the head start they need over their more fortunate male peers—a head start from the standpoint of feeling at home with and comfortable about associating informally with girls.

Physical education enthusiasts typically display a trained incapacity for perceiving their discipline in its proper perspective. To be sure, physical education *is* important. But it can eventuate in positive outcomes for children only to the extent that it (1) operates to enhance social self-confidence, and (2) inspires in children a deep seated need to pursue sports on their own throughout their life spans. To the extent that physical education *blocks* the development of social self-confidence, to that extent it *creates social isolates* who will lack both the nerve and the impetus for pursuing a lifelong program of enjoyable physical activity.

A person *must* have meaningful friends in order to become emotionally "psyched up" for physical activity. Almost all sports including even the gentle ones require at least one partner. In order to have a partner one must first have a friend. And in order to sustain a friendship one must have a certain minimum of social self-confidence; one must feel reasonably good about oneself.

Most of my respondents intuitively realized the truth behind these points. For example, I asked each respondent to react to the statement: "Social skills are more important to happiness as well as to mental and physical health than physical skills and physical fitness are." And 100 percent of both the older and the younger love-shy men agreed. In fact, even among the self-confident non-shy men fully 59 percent registered agreement. As I have indicated, many different researchers have found *friendships* to be the *number one* correlate of personal happiness and mental health. And as a deterioration in mental health is almost always accompanied by a deterioration in physical health, it is clear that the importance of meaningful friendships is far more pervasive than most people realize.

I also asked each of my respondents to react to this statement: "It is more important for a child to be socially well skilled with many friends than it is for him to be physically fit and good at sports." To be sure, in a society such as ours it is virtually impossible to even conceive of a child who is good at sports and who is not at the same time "socially well skilled with many friends." Nevertheless, I thought it might prove interesting to check out the opinions of the respondents relative to this hypothetical situation.

Among the older love-shys fully 100 percent agreed with the statement; and 97 percent of the younger love-shys agreed. The level of agreement among the self-confident non-shys was 79 percent. This quite high level of agreement among the non-shys is particularly interesting given their somewhat lower level of agreement with the earlier statement that social skills are more important to happiness than physical fitness is; only 59 percent of the non-shys agreed with that, compared to 100 percent of the two love-shy groups.

In sum, it is crucial that each child becomes a fully accepted and respected member of a peer group. *Nothing* is more important than that. Boys who are not psychoemotionally suited to "rough and tumble" play *MUST NEVER* be denied a peer group. We must be constantly on guard against overzealous football lovers who would deny meaningful friendships (and the crucial socialization that these provide) to more gentle-hearted boys. By providing children with a choice among a range of attractive sports, we are simultaneously according them a choice among a range of different kinds of peer groups. In this way each child can more easily find and keep friends who have native temperaments similar to his own. And in this way boys who are likely to be best off in *coeducational* peer groups will be able to get their needs appropriately met. In short, a gentle, introspective boy of *any* age should be free to sustain close friendships with members of BOTH sexes. And he should be able to do this with the full support of his elementary school and junior high school educators.

Use of School Letters

For many decades now American society has lavishly rewarded teenagers who perform well at football, baseball and basketball. This lavish praise is well symbolized in the so-called "school letters" that are awarded annually to the high school stars of these sports. It seems to me that a significant component of any program geared to the prevention of intractable shyness is going to have to include *greatly expanding* the range of activities for which competent teenagers are awarded school letters.

For openers I would suggest that every high school throughout the land should award letters for excellence in (1) bowling, (2) volleyball, (3) ping pong, (4) billiards, (5) miniature golf, (6) swimming, (7) shuffle board, (8) tennis, and *all* of the other *gentle* sports that I delineated earlier. Indeed, letters might also be awarded to the high school champions of such nonathletic games as chess and bridge, etc. To be sure, outstanding performance in the contact sports would not be ignored. The idea would be to award one school letter to the most accomplished individual in each activity each year. Indeed, this might also be done for each one of the three senior high school classes: sophomore, junior, and senior.

Recognition in the form of school letters should also be accorded the best pupil in each one of the academic disciplines as well. For example, each year each high school might award three mathematics letters: one to the best sophomore, one to the best junior, and one to the best senior. This would apply to *all* of the acadmic disciplines. This is not to be done merely because cultivation of the intellect is the traditional *"raison d'etre"* of the high school. That would *not* be sufficient reason as there are hundreds of thousands of extremely unhappy and ineffective intellectuals. The *key reason* for these awards is that the greater their number (and the greater the diversity of competencies for which they are awarded), the more young people will be accorded the recognition and respect that they need to grow and flourish emotionally and to come to feel good about themselves. All human beings require recognition and respect; these things must *not* be limited to those who are effective on the football gridiron and basketball court!

Finally, I believe that awards need to be granted for those who go out for dramatics, theatre arts and singing. Most love-shy males are strongly interested in these areas. In fact, most love-shys appear unusually well-versed on subjects pertinent to the arts. Of course, their shyness had long served as a barrier preventing them from being anything more than a passive spectator at theatrical events. And I think this points to the necessity for engineering strong catalysts that would effectively enlist the active participation of the love-shy in artistic and theatrical activities. Dedicated teachers and educational administrators are needed who would gently press the love-shy towards regular and active participation in areas of their interest. Such gentle, "benevolent coercion" might also be effectively employed to involve shys in coeducational programs that might develop in them an above average competency in such areas as trumpet playing, clarinet, piano, solo singing, etc.

The fact that strong but gentle catalysts may be required to motivate the shy is well reflected in the pattern of responses to this questionnaire statement: "After I was 13 or so I usually tried not to sing out loud whenever anyone was around." Only 20 percent of the self-confident non-shy men agreed with this statement, compared to 100 percent of the older love-shys and 83 percent of the younger love-shys.

Football: Should It Be Made Illegal?

One of the most important lessons I learned from the research I conducted for this book is that *bullying costs*. A majority of the love-shys studied for this book had been heavily bullied by their age-mates throughout their formative years. And I have no doubt that this history of almost incessant verbal and physical assault represents a major factor underlying the intractable love-shyness and social isolation from which they suffer today.

It is my belief that football both teaches and encourages bullying behavior vis-a-vis the weak and vis-a-vis children who are disinclined towards physical aggression. Unlike the thousands of hours of violent television programs which male children customarily watch, football is *NOT* a fantasy. FOOTBALL IS REALITY, and children know it. Moreover, young boys are clearly taught from the most tender ages onward that individuals who perform creditably at this violent sport are likely to be handsomely rewarded from the standpoint of money, recognition, popularity, attractive women, and everything else that makes life worthwhile. Simply put, young boys are taught to model their behavior after that of competent football stars.

Exacerbating the situation is the fact that a sizable minority of fathers strongly and sometimes coercively encourage their young sons to take part in "little league football" and to "kill" each other in order to move the football. CBS news magazine "60 MINUTES" ran several segments during recent years in which fathers were shown screaming at their sons *to hit hard*. Indeed, the boys were shouted down quite harshly by their fathers if they were not observed as being sufficiently aggressive and rough. Some of these fathers may have been using their sons to "live out" in a vicarious way their own frustrated fantasies. But whatever psychodynamic may have been involved, this is clearly not a healthy situation.

This overzealous football mentality can easily be seen as *encouraging* young boys to be (1) physically cruel vis-a-vis each other, and (2) as encouraging them not to feel any sense of guilt or remorse in striking out mindlessly and needlessly at one another. People do not talk to one another, or learn anything about one another's needs, feelings and emotions. People who are respected as *"he men"* simply gang up and physically punch out, assault and tackle their imagined opponents. They are not supposed to care *or even think* about human feelings, motives, intellect, etc. They are not supposed to be either intellectually or emotionally oriented; and they are not supposed to be verbal. Mindless physical aggression and nerve are rewarded to a far greater extent than intelligence and benvolent compassion.

In recent years I have aroused quite a bit of controversy at some of my lectures by suggesting that football ought to be made an illegal sport. It is quite interesting that the incidence of violent crime in American society over the years has directly paralleled the burgeoning interest in professional and university football. As televised football has reached more and more young men, violent crime has burgeoned. Moreover, the popularity of football constitutes a far better barometer of this than the phenomenon of fictionalized violence on television. American television has always had a surfeit of violent westerns and crime programs— ever since the days when Americans first began purchasing television sets in large numbers—back in the late 1940s. In contrast, it has only been since the early 1960s that the popularity of televised football has burgeoned.

For those with the "right" native temperament, football enthusiasm is quite contagious. And thousands of male physical education instructors and overzealous fathers have caught it. In their mindless enthusiasm these people have automatically assumed that (1) football is good for all boys, and that (2) if a child had been born a boy it is "only natural" for that boy to want to spend as much time and energy as he can developing football playing skills.

This "football consciousness" has permeated male peer groups at all age levels, as well as the various Cub Scout, Boy Scout, summer camp, and YMCA groups. And it has resulted in the continuing wholesale rejection of the more sensitive, introspective boys who do not wish to pursue this or any similar "rough and tumble" recreational interests. Many sensitive boys are fortunate enough to have supportive parents and relatives who help them to (1) group together with boys *and girls* of similar disposition, and who (2) introduce them to more appropriate recreational and artistic interests.

However, a large number of introspective, introverted boys are less fortunate. Their parents disparage them for being "different". And the teachers at their schools ignore them and thereby deprive them of needed opportunities for earning the recognition and respect that all human beings require for propitious psychoemotional growth and development. Some of these boys are even labeled "queer" or "fag" or "homosexual" or "fairy nice boy" simply because they do not enjoy participating in "rough and tumble" endeavors—as though that had anything at all to do with sexual and romantic directionality—which it *does not*.

There is far too much emphasis upon conformity in contemporary American society. And if we are ever to succeed in preventing intractable, chronic shyness we absolutely *MUST* increase the range of fully respectable alternatives for people. Every person is born with a set of purposes to fulfill; and these purposes are directly related to inborn temperament. There is no rational reason why all male children must be pressed into engaging in "rough and tumble" forms of play. And there is no reason why they must all be pressed into playing in gender segregated peer groups. Further, there is no reason why they should all be constrained to like the same forms of music. It is interesting that record albums containing love ballads (sung by quality male voices) and Broadway show tunes have become very difficult to find in record stores during recent years. As with football, everyone is being shunted towards the "rock" music mold—a mold which simply does not fit all children and young adults. As a result, thousands of children and young people are getting needlessly "left out".

As of January 1983, pressure was beginning to mount for making boxing illegal. For about a century now, children who grew up in impoverished ghetto neighborhoods had often been railroaded and intimidated into involving themselves in boxing competition, just as middle-class children continue to be railroaded and intimidated into taking part in football. The intimidating pressures impacting upon children to participate in football have quite clearly affected a great many more millions of children than pressures to partake in boxing competition. And many hundreds of thousands more have been injured in football than in boxing.

I have no doubt that boxing too should be made illegal. However, football has long had a far more disasterous impact upon our society than boxing has had. Football involves many millions more people. And the insensitive, mindless pressures upon our children to take part in it continue to be far stronger than the pressures to take part in the two-opponent sport of boxing.

Educators often speak of permitting only "touch" football at their schools. However, anyone who has made any observations at schools where intramural football is played fully realizes that "touch" is a grandiose euphamism of the most ludicrous and destructive sort. Boys with the aggressive native temperament appropos to football *invariably* become so keyed up by the excitement of their sport that they *invariably* knock down their opponents quite irrespective of what their gym teachers say about using "touch" only. The football model as consistently conveyed on television *encourages* violence and insensitivity to the feelings and emotions of other male age-mates. And I believe that this violence-prone insensitivity often transfers (for at least some boys) into violence against the community as manifested in acts of vandalism, assault, mindless drinking binges, drunk driving, and other forms of violent crime and uncompassionate disrespect. Football teaches that it is "okey" to use power and coercion to control others.

Because of the billions of dollars that are involved, football is not likely to be rendered illegal soon. It may require the passing of several centuries before our society evolves to the point where compassion will obviate cruelty, bullying and violence. Once that point is reached football will no longer be with us. In the meantime, there is much that we can do to protect our children from the crass, mindless enthusiasm that is endemic in football and in several other contact sports.

The repeated witnessing of violent acts on television has been found by numerous scholars to render young boys significantly more violence prone vis-a-vis their male peers than they otherwise would be. It has also been found to render them significantly less sensitive to and compassionate about the pain and suffering of their fellow human beings. In short, violence in sports (or in crime programs) creates a detached attitude with regard to human feelings and emotions that is very dangerous as well as dehumanizing. And since violence in sports is a reality and *not* a fantasy, it is bound to have a stronger impact than fictionalized programs.

In sum, FOOTBALL BOTH INSPIRES AND ENCOURAGES *BULLYING* and related uncompassionate attitudes, values and behaviors. As such I believe that football and other violent contact sports constitute a serious liability for our culture. And I believe that we will all be better off on the day when such activities disappear from our midst for good.

Current Peer Group Interaction

At the time they were interviewed virtually none of the 300 love-shy men studied for this book were involved with any significant friendships. A small number of them carried on a semi-active letter writing correspondence with "pen pals" located in distant parts of the world. And some of them were occasionally invited by co-workers to attend informal get-togethers. However, none of the love-shys with whom I talked had anyone *of either gender* who they could feel free about spontaneously contacting for informal conversation or for mutual visitation, for going out to a movie or a restaurant, etc. In short, none of these men were integrated into any kind of an informal friendship network.

Most of these men possessed surprisingly good insight into how during their formative years they had learned to associate peer interaction with pain and humiliation. In fact, many of them were too introspective about their pasts. Not having any friends to distract them, many of these men would typically spend a great deal of time each day brooding about the past and the influence that it might have had upon them. Often such brooding would be interrupted only by their listening to their stereos or by their watching television. Most of the private thought and introspection activities of the love-shys (apart from their daydreams about being with a girl) revolved around either (1) their painful pasts and the impact that past experiences might have had upon their ability to secure female companionship, and (2) intellectual topics often pertaining to such matters as music, entertainment, the arts, theatre trivia, psychological subjects, and subjects pertinent to psychic phenomena and the occult.

But there appear to be some other important factors serving to keep most of the love-shys from even wanting male friendships. Most of the love-shys quite frankly indicated that *even if they could get it* they preferred loneliness over the idea of having male friendships. Of course, since they did not want male companionship, there were no feelings of deprivation, yearning, or hurt preoccupation concerning its lack.

Discrepancy Between the Actual Self and the Ideal Self

Simply put, the idea of having a girlfriend was central to both the value systems and the emotional essence of each and every love-shy man studied for this book. In order for a person to appear genuine, to converse spontaneously and in a completely free manner without any sham or pretense, that person's lifestyle must bear at least some degree of congruency with the things that he thinks about all the time, his values, the things that matter to him and are important to him.

In male/male friendships, just as in female/female friendships, people "open up" most freely and frequently about the subjects that are most important to them. And they specifically gravitate towards just those same-sexed friends whose values, interests and preoccupations are essentially the same as their own.

As I have already made clear, romantic male/female interaction occupied as much as 90 percent of the love-shys' daydream content. In essence, heterosexual interaction is enormously important to love-shy men. And for this reason, in order for them to converse on a truly open and spontaneous basis they would necessarily have to find male friends whose interests and values are the same as their own. In essence, they would have to find male friends who are similarly very interested in male/female interaction and who are themselves actually involved in a great deal of informal heterosexual interaction. Of course, the rub is that such a socially successful man would be highly unlikely to be interested in helping or even in interacting with someone who has seldom or never dated. The ideal for the love-shy would be male friends who would somehow take them (the love-shy) by the hands (figuratively speaking) and directly involve them in the sorts of heterosexual-romantic interaction about which they dream.

Hence, in order for love-shy males to begin having meaningful *male* friendships, *they must first solve their love-shyness problems* as far as *heterosexual* interaction is concerned. In order for a love-shy man to have and to keep a male friend, *he must first be actively involved in a romantic love relationship with a woman.*

Some of the interview material I obtained from the love-shys provides some very useful insights in this regard. Please consider the following quotations:

"Well, I've given a lot of thought to the idea of male friendships. I suppose it would be nice. I mean, it might help me. See, if I were going with someone (a girl) it would be just so damned much easier for me to have male friends. I'd have something to talk about with them. But right now, what the hell would I talk about with a male friend? I mean, everything I think about concerns woman! And I haven't got one! If I ever found a male friend who was anything like me, it would make me even more depressed because he wouldn't be able to help me. The guys I would really like to have as friends— I mean the guys who are engaged or going with someone—well, they're not interested in having me as a friend. Like at work, some of those guys think I'm a homo. They don't think I have anything in common with them—which is ridiculous because I bet I do a lot more thinking and dreaming about women than any of them do!" (24-year old love-shy man.)

"This may sound stupid. But I don't feel as though I'm the real me! Like I sometimes feel totally detached from the person I am because the person I am is not able to do the things that are really important to the real me. It's like the person that I am manifesting behaviorally is a total stranger to the real me, the me that includes the things in life that are really important to me. I have no control over the person I'm presenting to the world because my anxieties prevent me from doing the things I would really like to do. If I had any male friends how would I be able to maintain a straight face with them? I mean, what I would want to talk about with them and how I actually behave in real life are two drastically different things. I'd be seen as a hypocrite. The type of male friend I'd like to have would be bored with me because I wouldn't have anything to offer him. I wouldn't even have the nerve to confess my extremely strong desire to have a woman to love." (23-year old love-shy man.)

More succinctly, how can the love-shys be expected to develop *male* friendships when all they ever think about is women and their deprivation of same?! There can be no doubt that all the painful hazing and bullying and forced involvement in baseball, basketball and football which plagued the love-shys in the past continues to have a bearing upon alienating them from the idea of male-to-male interaction in the present. But even if the love-shys could discipline their minds to forget their pasts, they would still have to deal with the problem of having a personality/temperament that is at drastic variance with their most deeply cherished values, interests, and secret goals.

To be sure, the love-shys *could* grit their teeth and *change* their values, interests, goals, etc. But it is seldom realistic to ask a person to do such a thing. To change deeply held values and interests is usually tantamount to *giving up one's whole sense of personal identity* and ego-structure. Values and interests represent the only grip on reality some of the love-shy men have. For them to give these up (very central components of the personal ego) could very easily threaten sanity itself.

Implications for Therapy

After a love-shy man has been successfully helped to the point where he is involved in a stable heterosexual love relationship, I think it makes very good sense for his therapist to help him develop a friendship network. At that point in time the love-shy man will almost always be quite receptive towards the idea of developing male friendships. On the other hand, *before* that time he will usually *not* be receptive. Practice-dating therapy groups (discussed in *section three* of this book) can prove very helpful catalysts in helping the love-shy to develop same-sexed friendship networks and mutual support systems. And their usefulness should be capitalized upon in that regard.

In recent years a controversy has developed among therapists working with the lonely and the love-shy. Many such therapists believe that the almost constant preoccupation love-shy men have with finding someone to love should be discouraged. Karen Rook and Letitia Peplau of the U.C.L.A. Loneliness Clinic have taken a rather crass and arrogant stance in this regard:

> "While lonely individuals are most likely to say that they need 'one special person' or 'a romantic partner', their views do not necessarily represent psychologically sound treatment goals . . . . Having such relationships does not necessarily protect one against feeling lonely, particularly when important social exchanges are not provided through the relationship . . . . We recommend caution in defining relationship formation as *the* goal of intervention with lonely clients . . . . Among the sociocultural factors that we suspect contribute to loneliness are the social stigma associated with being unmarried, and the cultural preoccupation with love relationships. We would call for greater acceptance of lifestyles other than traditional marriage. We urge that the pressure to 'achieve' love relationships be relaxed and that other forms of social relationships, particularly friendships, be given greater status." (Rook and Peplau, 1982, pp. 360–373.)

It has been my experience that the only people *preoccupied* to any extent at all with love relationships are those *without* such relationships. *Felt deprivation gives rise to preoccupation.* And the *only workable way* to stem this preoccupation is to somehow satisfy the unmet need. To be sure, there are certain groups, such as elderly widows, for whom the obtaining of a heterosexual love relationship may indeed be unrealistic. In a society with six times as many widows as widowers, sex ratio considerations alone dictate for some that ways other than heterosexual love and romance be cultivated for assuaging loneliness problems. On the other hand, in the case of the love-shy man there is no logical or necessary reason for a therapist to discourage his/her client from wanting a heterosexual love relationship.

Actually, it would probably not even be feasible for a therapist to do this even if it were indicated. Love-shy men are too intensely preoccupied with their need for a female. It is *only* through releasing this need and preoccupation *through satisfying it* that the love-shy man can begin to appreciate the desirability of building up a network of meaningful, non-romantic friendships. This represents a key reason why the deep-seated emotional need for a love relationship MUST be satisfied *first* before any other worthwhile goals can be worked on.

Secondly, the having and sustaining of male friendships absolutely requires a reasonable degree of harmony between a man's ideal self (deeply held values, interests), and his real or actual self. A real self that is at drastic variance from the ideal or aspired to self *effectively blocks spontaneous, free-flowing communication*. In addition, it makes the love-shy man appear bored and disinterested in what the other members of the all-male friendship network are conversing about. It makes the love-shy man appear excessively self-centered and self-preoccupied.

A person's own cup must be reasonably full before he is going to be in any position to share the content of his cup with other people. Until a love-shy man has made substantial progress towards the attaining of meaningful female companionship, his "cup" is going to be well nigh empty. He is certainly not going to be in a position to freely and unself-consciously *share* anything of his "cup" with *male* friends.

And why should "friendships" have to be of only one sex (one's own sex) anyway! Like many therapists, Rook and Peplau assume that friendship and social support networks must necessarily be comprised of people of just one gender. This represents a very deeply ingrained cultural assumption and bias which (1) is very destructive, and (2) which we need to get away from. This is a key reason why I have stressed throughout this book the desirability of developing a Coed Scouts organization for children—so that those who wish to do so can learn to play and to comfortably interact in strictly coeducational settings from the earliest ages in life onward. Neither children nor adults should have to accept strictly sex-segregated friendship groups. More succinctly, there is no reason why a man (or boy) cannot have a woman (girl) as a lover and/or wife, and other women (girls) as *"just good friends"*.

In general, it is both arrogant and alienating for a therapist to intimate to his/her love-shy client that he/she knows what his/her client needs better than his/her love-shy client himself knows what he needs. It is this very arrogance that led most of the older love-shy men to a firm resolve to never again seek out a clinical psychologist or any other type of professional psychotherapeutic counselor. Simply put, I believe that therapists have a moral obligation to honor their client's presenting problem, felt needs and preoccupation. A person almost always knows (1) what he needs, and (2) what is truly in his best interests, far better than anyone else ever could. The rightful and proper task of a shyness therapist is to help his love-shy client obtain and develop an emotionally satisfying relationship with a woman.

"Society's Goal"

Therapists such as Rook and Peplau speak as though the goal of finding a lover is actually not the love-shy man's goal at all, but merely just *society's goal* which the love-shy man had just mindlessly internalized through the ordinary processes of socialization. In essence, Rook and Peplau are arguing that love-shy men simply mirror and reflect the societal prescription that everyone ought to have an opposite-sexed lover.

The problem with this reasoning is that most of the love-shys had been extremely desirous of an opposite sexed lover ever since they had been small children in kindergarten or the first grade. In other words, these men had wanted the emotionally close and intimate companionship of a girl friend at a time when this desire had been highly antithetical to the mainstream American society's prescription as to what kindergarten and elementary school children *ought to want*. Society tells kindergarten and elementary school children that they "ought to want" to play in strictly sex-segregated peer groups. It also tells them that boys "ought to want" to play at "rough and tumble" sports. In fact, society even goes so far as to prescribe that elementary school boys "ought to" *hate* age-mate girls.

The love-shy men studied for this book had been quite refractory and resistant to these as well as to scores of other societal prescriptions as to how they "ought to" think, feel, behave, and want. The question naturally arises as to why these love-shy men should now as adults all of a sudden become desirous of following society's behavioral prescriptions!

In point of fact, they have *not* all of a sudden become so desirous! The love-shys' strong need for the love of an opposite sexed companion had been very much a part of their essence as human beings since their earliest ages. This intractable urge for a lover had long been their most deeply cherished goal. For love-shy men such a goal is obviously *not* a mere reflection of society's prescription that everyone ought to be mated!

Friendship Networks and Happy Marriages

Finally, the happiest marriages tend to be those in which both the husband and the wife are actively involved in meaningful friendship networks. At least a dozen major research investigations have demonstrated this to be a fact. However, there are at least two ways a therapist can interpret this fact. The *wrong way* would be for the therapist to work first toward the goal of getting the love-shy client to develop a friendship network. The *right way* would be to *first* get the love-shy man into a practice-dating therapy group for as much time as he may need to find and develop an emotionally satisfying heterosexual love relationship. Then, either *concurrent* with practice-dating group therapy (if the client is receptive) or after it has been completed, help the client develop a network of meaningful non-romantic friendships.

Despite all of their seeming dislike for members of their own gender, many of the love-shy men I talked with looked forward with considerable anticipation to what might best be described as *"couples friendships"*. In essence, the love-shys did not want to interact *on their own* with an all-male peer group. But they did aspire to being able to entertain married couples, once they themselves become part of a married couple. They also looked forward to being able to go out *as a married couple* to visit with other married couples.

Many of the love-shy men specifically felt that once they were married they would be able to meet and to interact with a great many interesting male friends—through their wife's efforts. But they wanted to do this exclusively as a couple, *NOT* as a single. None of the love-shys with whom I spoke could see themselves as ever wanting to leave their wives and children at home in order to go out by themselves for purposes of socializing in a sex-segregated peer group. The love-shys tended to view such same-sexed interaction as being quite disparagingly juvenile. They entertained no desire to do it as a married adult; they did not want to do it presently as a single man; and they obviously had not wished to do it even when they had been children and teenagers.

There is a curious paradox here. Many women might view this sort of "home and family oriented" husband as representing an "ideal catch"—almost "too good to be true!" Surely such a man might well be far less prone towards infidelity than the more outgoing type of individual. And yet the severe shyness, inhibition and low anxiety threshold of this sort of man keeps him from being experienced by *any* woman!

People need *both* a network of friends *and* an emotional love-attachment figure in order to be maximally happy and well adjusted. For most males the latter is definitely of far greater importance than the former. For most women the former may be of somewhat greater importance than the latter. Again, there is a great deal of truth to the cliche that *men need women a great deal more than women need men.*

Notes

1. Membership in friendship networks also permits non-shy men to bypass problems created by the initial suspiciousness, fearfulness and hostility that many young women feel and display towards men whom they do not know. The burgeoning rate of violent crime committed by men against women has rendered women (particularly in the cities) more leery, hostile and suspicious of strangers than they have ever been before. Thus, men who can be introduced to women by mutual friends enjoy an especially strong advantage. Again, as severely love-shy men do not belong to any such friendship or kinship group networks, far more is expected and demanded of them than is the case for non-shy or for moderately (but not pathologically) shy men.

2. A very good case can be made for the proposition that love-shy heterosexuals ought not be expected to play *at all* in the company of high energy aggressive extroverts. As of April 1985, the New York City school district opened up the nation's first high school for homosexuals and lesbians. A key *raison d'etre* for doing this was that such children could not learn effectively in regular high schools with all the bullying to which they had been subjected. (High school name is: Harvey Milk High School.) I would suggest that *inhibited, emotionally sensitive boys* (pre-love-shy heterosexuals) are up against essentially the *same problem.* And as such, special *coeducational* education facilities might well be expected to bring the best out of such temperamentally handicapped children. Under conditions of a strong self-esteem a person can far more readily contribute the most both to his own well-being as well as to that of his community.

3. There is some evidence that excessively shy, inhibited boys have an excess of the brain chemical *dopamine* (see Wender & Klein, 1981, p. 220). Unless certain drugs are administered to neutralize some of this dopamine, very shy, withdrawn and fearful behavior is normal.

4. Even though it isn't considered a sport, one of the activities most thoroughly enjoyed by the love-shys as children was swinging on playground swings. Indeed, using the swings tended to be recalled by the love-shys as having been their favorite playground activity. In view of the fact that swinging does represent good exercise, it too could be made available to love-shy elementary and junior high school aged boys while their more aggressive peers play at their "rough and tumble" sports. Further, for those choosing it, swinging can be done on a strictly coeducational basis.

Chapter 11

The Powerful Impact of Preadolescent Infatuations

There is a very cruel and curious paradox in the psychoemotional development of love-shy men which deserves special attention. From the standpoint of *overt behavior* any disinterested person would judge love-shy men to be (1) extremely "late starters", and (2) perhaps not especially interested in women at all. Most people tend to judge others by overtly manifested behavior. Indeed, most of us tend to view overt behavior as constituting a reasonably accurate barometer of a person's wishes, values, attitudes, feelings and aspirations. We tend to view such behavior as a good index as to what is actually going on inside of a person's head. And so it is perfectly understandable that most of us would view as "disinterested" any man in his late 30s or 40s who has seldom or never dated women.

But as I have argued throughout this book, severe and chronic shyness blocks the normal exercising of free choice and self-determination. The love-shy cannot allow their behavior to reflect their deepest wishes, desires, values, etc., because doing so would overcome them with severe feelings of anxiety. In fact, the mere thought of experiencing this anxiety is so painfully forbidding to the intractably love-shy person that he will not allow himself to even fantasize making plans to do the kinds of things he would love to do. To be sure, the love-shy man does spend a tremendous amount of time and energy fantasizing about being with a girl whom he can love. But these fantasies never extend to the practical business of *engineering a viable plan* for actually winning the affections of a girl. The severely love-shy man cannot permit himself to engineer a plan to telephone a girl or start a conversation with one at work or school, or to ask a girl who is attractive to him for a lunch of a coffee date. He cannot calm himself sufficiently to do these things because the fear of the anxiety that would be created from merely thinking about doing them is far too much for him.

The Paradox

The paradox is that love-shy men become romantically interested in the opposite sex significantly earlier in life than do non-shy men. And the more severely love-shy a man is, the earlier in life he is likely to have become deeply interested in the other gender from a romantic/esthetic standpoint. For example, 87 percent of the older love-shy men who were studied for this research indicated that *prior to the age of 13, they had experienced feelings of loneliness for the close, emotionally meaningful companionship of an opposite-sexed age-mate. Similarly, 73 percent of the younger love-shys had experienced such feelings prior to their 13th birthday, whereas none* of the 200 self-confident non-shy men had ever experienced such feelings prior to their 13th birthday.

One of the questionnaire statements to which each man reacted read as follows: "When I was a child of about 10 or 11, there was nothing I used to spend more time daydreaming about than little girls of my age or younger." Here again, *zero percent* of the non-shy men responded in the affirmative. In stark contrast, fully 63 percent of the older love-shys together with 48 percent of the younger ones agreed that the statement had indeed been true for them.

In an effort to get down to specifics, I then asked each man: "What was your grade in school when you first felt a strong, romantic interest in an age-mate of the opposite sex?" The *average* for the 100 older love-shy men was *grade 2.13*. The average for the 200 younger love-shy men was *grade 3.52*. And the *average* for the 200 self-confident non-shy men was *grade 6.43*.

I also checked out the *modes* (the most frequent response) for each of the three groups of men studied. And they were as follows: 34 percent of the older love-shys had first become romantically interested in a girl while in the *first grade*. The mode for the younger love-shys was *grade three*: 29 percent of them checked that. And the mode for the self-confident non-shys was *grade nine*; 38 percent of the non-shy men had not become romantically interested in an opposite-sexed age-mate until they were in the ninth grade.

Some readers may think that even a mean of *grade 6.43* (the mean for the non-shys) is quite young. However, research over the years has clearly demonstrated that most middle-class children of both sexes first become romantically interested in the fourth, fifth or sixth grades. Dr. Carlfred Broderick of University of Southern California, has collected the most extensive amount of data on this subject. However, even in the 1890s most middle-class American boys seemed to have become romantically interested in opposite-sexed classmates by the time they were in the fifth or sixth grades. Writing in the 1902 volume of the

AMERICAN JOURNAL OF PSYCHOLOGY, Sanford Bell cited data (which he had obtained during the 1890s) which jibe very nicely with the far more recent data of Professor Broderick. Parenthetically, nineteenth century novelist Samuel Clemens similarly seemed to have had a keen awareness of prepubescent love. As "Mark Twain" he created the celebrated Tom Sawyer/Becky Thatcher romance.

Many people find this phenomenon difficult to understand because (1) they confuse sex with love, and (2) because they have forgotten their own early romantic interests. And for some reason adult women are a good deal more likely than adult men to forget and to make light of the strong romantic infatuations that they had experienced during their elementary school years. It seems quite probable that erotic sexuality does remain largely latent (at least in the industrialized world) throughout the elementary school age period. But romantic/esthetic needs are not the same as sexual needs. Romantic and esthetic needs seem to manifest themselves very early and very strongly in the lives of some children.

In sum, love-shy men quite typically experience many, many long years of intensely felt deprivation regarding the opposite sex. And this explains why so many of them tend to be so vastly more preoccupied *and obsessed with* thoughts about women, love, romance and sexuality, than the vast majority of men. Felt deprivation tends to give rise to preoccupation and obsession. And this psychological truism is no where better reflected than in the lives of love-shy men.

The usual scenario in a male's development of heterosexual interests goes something like this: Between the sixth and the ninth grades he begins to show strong romantic interests in one or more girls in his classes. He occasionally talks with these girls and attends some parent-supervised parties with them. By the ninth or tenth grade he begins dating. This may be done on a group basis at the outset; but by the middle of his tenth grade year he begins dating on a one-on-one basis. And by the eleventh grade he begins "going steady", although his early "steady" relationships may not remain entirely exclusive over very much time.

To be sure, most American males suffer some inhibitions and twinges of shyness when they first commence becoming romantically interested in a girl. The younger a boy is and the more beautiful the object of his infatuation is, the greater the likelihood that these twinges of shyness may create several weeks of emotionally painful distraction. During these weeks he is likely to be extremely affected by the girl's looks. And he is likely to remain too shy to start a conversation with her or to in any way endeavor to get to know her. It is during this period when the beautiful object of his affections will be the central figure of his daydreams and "wish-fulfillment fantasies.

Research has shown, however, that most American boys suffer these periods of emotionally painful distraction and preoccupation for just three or four weeks. For many of them these painful periods may last for a mere fortnight or less. A teenaged boy of normal emotional health and interpersonal skills may suffer through two or three of these periods between the time of his initial romantic infatuation (in the sixth grade) and the time when he actually marries—say at age 24 or there-about. So that by the time he gets to be 25 years old he will have had to deal with perhaps eight or nine weeks (total) of what a chronically love-shy male experiences at all times from the time he is seven years old until he is a very old man. The self-confident non-shy boy with plenty of male friends and a respected place in his peer group may never experience *any* such periods in his life. The somewhat less fortunate but adequately confident young man may experience a maximum of eight or nine weeks of such "lovelorn" periods.

Simply put, the typical love-shy man commences an intense roman-tic preoccupation with the opposite sex when he is anywhere from kin-dergarten age to the second or third grade. This mental set remains intractably welded to him and intensely affects his waking state from the earliest years of his elementary school career until old age. In con-trast, more normally advantaged males experience these periods of intense preoccupation for only comparatively short periods which seldom last for more than three weeks at a time.

In most cases, once a child has actually initiated a friendship with the object of his dreams, his preoccupations rapidly diminish. And the more accessible the girl remains within his social environment, the less preoccupied he will feel. In essence, to the extent that he feels the sense of personal freedom necessary for talking with her whenever he desires, to that extent there will be no debilitating or distracting romantic preoc-cupation or infatuation.

Social Supports

Most children enjoy a copious variety of social supports. The most important of these eminate from the peer group and the parents. For most children these two systems provide a range of enjoyable distrac-tions. Young children tend to want to keep their romantic infatuations to themselves. But to the extent that they enjoy good relationships with their social support systems, to that extent young children are likely to share their preoccupations and worries. Once these preoccupations have been discussed with peers or parents, solutions are likely to be gener-ated. There is strength in numbers. And whereas prepubescent children occasionally tease each other about romantic interests, "*best* friends" tend to learn about each other's innermost wishes. And they tend to help one another out.

Parents vary in their sophistication and sensitivity regarding heterosexual love matters. One self-confident non-shy respondent recounted this story from his past:

> "I remember I was in the sixth grade, and there was this girl in the other sixth grade class whom I just adored. I didn't have the nerve to say anything to her. But whenever the kids were all out on the playground I used to stare at her whenever I got the chance. I remember two of my friends sort of had infatuations with some of the girls too. So they were understanding, but they weren't much help.

> One day my mother insisted that I tell her why I was so bleery-eyed all the time at the dinner table. She knew I wasn't myself and she guessed that I was in love. And when she said that I had to say 'yes', and I blushed. For the next several days she kept goading me into starting a conversation with her. And my dad kept telling me that my life would be a lot easier once I did. He told me that I was creating a problem for myself. And that it would all be pretty much solved once I talked to the girl, even if she rejected me.

> Well, what eventually happened was that Vince, who was this friend of mine, was having a birthday party. His mom and my mom were always good friends. And my mom got Vince's mom to invite this girl to his party. You know, when I first found out about it I was outraged. Like I was really embarrassed. But I have to admit that that is what solved my problem. I got to meet the girl at the party and we had a long talk. And from that time on I was never really shy anymore around girls. I've felt hesitant for short periods. But except for this time when I was in the sixth grade I never really suffered any really painful shyness." (21-year old non-shy man.)

A key impediment to the effective prevention of love-shyness is that some parents maintain certain rigid ideas about when it is "right" for boys and girls to become interested in each other. Such parents sincerely believe that the sixth grade is just "too damned early"—that such children are just "too young" and that love-shyness at this age is "good for children".

Even though this point of view is understandable, I believe that it is a very socially deleterious perspective which must be countered through concerted educational efforts. Shyness is *NEVER* "good". Shyness obviates free choice and self-determination, and it stands squarely in the way of responsible self-control and self-management. It is one thing for a child to decide out of rational self-interest to avoid exclusive love relationships for a certain portion of his/her life. It is entirely another matter for a child to avoid love relationships as a result of shyness. The first child is *in control* and *in charge* of his/her own life. The second child is *NOT* in command of the ship that is his or her life. And that ship stands a great risk of aimlessly drifting into some rocky shoreline a derelict unless it is stalwartly and decisively directed at its helm. *The child is father to the man*, and children who learn the shyness script do not easily forget it. All too frequently their shyness learnings remain intractably welded in their minds, and they go through life love-shy.

Simply put, SHYNESS IS NEVER HEALTHY—not at *any* age or for *either* gender. Rational self-direction inspired by an internalized set of rational self-controls and a deep-seated feeling of self-worth and self-love is what a happy, productive life is all about. The parents in the above case interview were very wise, sensitive and caring. They exercised their rational ingenuity toward helping their son out of the self-destructive doldrums which deep-seated love-shy infatuations represent for people of *any* age.

Whenever a child (*prepubescent or older*) is in the throes of love-shyness inspired preoccupation, the *best thing* that a caring parent, teacher or peer can do is to tactfully and creatively engineer a way of according that child an opportunity to meet and to enter into relaxed conversation with the object of his infatuations. THE LONGER THE PERIOD OF LOVELORN INFATUATION/LOVE-SHYNESS LASTS, THE GREATER THE PROBABILITY THAT SEVERE LOVE-SHYNESS WILL BECOME A PERMANENT SCRIPT AND LIFE-STYLE FOR THE BOY OR MAN. Moreover, the earlier in life that deep-seated romantic infatuations commence, the more important it is to help the love-shy male interact with the object of his infatuation as a real live fellow human being.

Again, the more severely and intractably love-shy a person is, the *earlier in life* he is likely to have begun suffering deep-seated love-shyness rooted romantic infatuations. In essence, it is *even more important* to help elementary school aged love-shy children than it is to help teenaged love-shy children. Both need to be helped to meet and to interact with the objects of their affections, and to relate to these opposite sexed individuals as fellow human beings. But the research data collected for this book strongly suggest that the *preadolescent* love-shy male is the one who is the prime candidate for a lifetime of chronic love-shyness unless he is helped. He must be stopped from learning the love-shyness script! He is anything but "too young"! Love-shyness is the worst kind of poison for him.

I would suggest that no child should ever have to suffer love-shyness for more than three consecutive weeks at a time. Indeed, *three weeks* might well be considered a good maximum because to the extent that a boy or young man suffers love-shy preoccupation with the *same* girl for more time than that, to that extent he is likely to be headed for a lifetime of trouble and unhappiness. To the extent that highly distracting love-shyness is permitted to fester away in the minds of its victims, to that extent eventual rational self-direction becomes less and less likely.

The American education system needs to teach people how to communicate with each other. People should not be afraid of people! Each child is entitled to have cultivated within him enough self-confidence and pride that the possibility of rejection by a girl does not daunt him from taking constructive action on his own behalf.

The Field of Roses Metaphor

In all of nature the young of virtually no species mature at exactly the same time. Humans are no exception to this. In this regard humans can be compared to a field of roses. Under proper care each rosebud will eventually open up and develop into a beautiful flower. The majority of the rosebuds will commence opening up within a few days of one another. However, some will begin unfolding into beautiful flowers significantly earlier than the rest. And still others will continue on in the rosebud stage long after the rest of the flowers have come into full bloom.

Any horticulturist would agree that prodding the slow buds to open before they are ready will result in serious injury and possibly death. In addition, the resultant flowers will prove much less attractive than those which had been permitted to open and blossom at their own pace. And so it is with the early buds. Any effort that might be made to slow them down and prevent them from blossoming before the rest will result in lifelong damage and possibly even in death.

The paradox here is that love-shy men appear to have been *early bloomers*, and *not* "late" ones as most people are inclined to think. A *genuine* "late bloomer" is a person who truly does not become romantically interested in the opposite sex until he is perhaps long out of high school and into his sophomore or junior year of college. Many perfectly healthy heterosexual men are "late bloomers" of this sort. Love-shy men, however, *are not*! Love-shy men are *early bloomers* who are temperamentally inhibited, and whose well-intentioned but misguided "gardeners" (parents and teachers) tried to force them to stop blooming and to attune themselves to the internal timetables of others instead of to their own internal God-given timetables. Most love-shy men seem to have had parents who either thought love-shyness was "good" or who ignored it and failed to properly read and interpret the lovelorn behavior of their sons.

"Oh, Leave Him Alone; He's Still Got Plenty of Time!"

The early blooming rosebud does *not* have "lots of time" anymore than the late blooming one has "lots of time". Left to fester unattended, love-shyness can quickly and easily become a permanent way of life. Some of the angriest and most bitter comments expressed in the hundreds of interviews I conducted for this book pertained to well-meaning but misguided parents and relatives who had reacted to a respondent's lack of female friends with the statement: "Oh, don't worry! Leave him alone! He's still got plenty of time!"

Simply put, love-shy males at any age do not want to be "left alone". They do not want their love-shyness problems to go ignored and misinterpreted. They want to get out into the flow of life as nature had intended for them. The following interview quotation poignantly reflects the rage which many love-shy men feel towards their parents' noncaring attitudes.

> "I can remember lots of times my mother would have her friends over and someone would bring up the fact that I hadn't started dating yet. I was always delighted whenever this happened because I thought someone might finally do something for me. But my delight always quickly faded to depression because there was always someone there who would say 'oh, leave him alone; he's still got plenty of time'. And my stupid parents would go long with that bullshit reasoning. I didn't want to be left alone, and I would always fervently pray that someone would do something for me that would somehow get me introduced to somebody. But that never happened. Today my parents never invite their friends over when I'm around. But for a really long time all I ever heard was this bullshit that I should be left alone because I've got plenty of time!" (39-year old love-shy man.)

One very important point about time is that it has a way of passing very rapidly. Time must be used. And a key reason why so many of the love-shy men I interviewed were so bitter is that no one had ever cared enough to help them use their time productively. No one had ever helped them use it in a way that might have stood a chance of leading to a satisfactory remedy for their love-shyness problems.

Many people operate on the basis of the untenable assumption that no young man wants his parents to arrange any introductions with girls on his behalf. My own work suggests that most love-shy men are quite nervous and tense about anyone arranging introduction for them because of a fear of not knowing what to say or of how to keep an interesting conversation going. And this nervousness is often miscon-strued as suggesting an antithetical attitude towards arranged introductions.

Most young people do *not* object to tactfully arranged introductions by caring parents, relatives, teachers and friends. And this is especially true with regard to the love-shy. Such introductions serve to expand a person's field of eligibles. An arranged introduction is *NOT* a betrothal! The young person who is introduced to someone still has plenty of free choice as to whom he will select as dating partners and as an eventual marriage partner.

The "Male Lesbian" State of Mind

As I pointed out in chapter five, many of the love-shy men inter-viewed for this book conveyed the impression of being *male lesbians*. A male lesbian is a fully heterosexual man who often wishes that he had been born a female. And yet if he had been born female he would still have felt strongly attracted to women (and *not* to men) romantically, esthetically, sexually, and socially. A male lesbian is a person who from his earliest years onward had never felt any attraction towards members of his own sex—not even for purposes of recreational play. He is a person who had always felt rather strange, detached, and disinterested around age-mates of his own gender, and who had always entertained the fantasy that if he could only win acceptance from an all-girl peer group he could feel "at home" there.

The "male lesbian" state of consciousness *may* be related to inborn temperament, and *may* at least partly explain why the love-shy men tended to have become very romantically attracted to girls from an early point in life.

The Preadolescent Love Experience

Virtually all of the love-shy men I interviewed had very clear and detailed memories of their preadolescent infatuations. And there had been a very great many of these infatuations. Better than two-thirds of the older love-shys and close to half of the younger ones had experienced one intense infatuation after another throughout all of their elementary school years. In short, from the time they had first become interested in a particular little girl, there had scarcely ever been a period of greater than a few months in length during which the love-shys had not been deeply in love (unrequited, of course) with some little girl. These intense love fantasies had consumed a very great deal of the love-shys' time and psychoemotional energy. From the time of their kindergarten or first grade year until the time when they reached their early thirties, most of the love-shys had devoted a great deal of their time to day-dreaming about some specific female with whom they were too shy to even think about making any real contact. Subsequent to the age of 32 or 33, the amount and frequency of these romantic fantasies tended to drop off a bit. But even the love-shys in their 40s still experienced occasional very strong infatuations.

Sixteen percent of the older love-shys and 7 percent of the younger ones had experienced their first very strong romantic infatuations as soon as they started school. Being thrown in with a great many other fellow five-year olds, the love-shys immediately found the girls to be far more fascinating than their own gender. Most of the love-shys had viewed members of their own sex as being quite foreign to them. As one love-shy man expressed it, "I viewed boys as members of another species." And since the teachers tended to discourage efforts on the part of the love-shys to group up with the girls, most of the love-shys became social isolates immediately upon the commencement of their educational careers—in kindergarten.

> "I remember the kindergarten teacher used to get all upset with me because she wanted me to play with the scooters and cars and a lot of other junk that the boys were playing with. I remember I tried doing those things on several occasions. And the praise and encouragement I got from the teacher made me feel really good because I really liked the teacher. But I just didn't enjoy it. In fact, I found it painfully boring. And all the while I would be looking over at the girls and at the things I really wanted to do.
>
> So I guess I just decided very early that I would have to sacrifice my need to please the teacher for my need to feel comfortable and please myself and just be myself. And after about November of my kindergarten year I never played on the floor with the boys again. I worked with craft things. And I became really good at making things out of clay.
>
> I don't remember exactly when I first began to take really strong notice of them. But there were these two twin sisters in my kindergarten class—Rita and Ruth. They were fraternal twins. They looked entirely different. And before Thanksgiving I found myself looking all the time over at Ruth who was the really pretty one. By Christmastime it got to be really intense. When I went to bed at night I

would think so intensely about her before I fell asleep that I would feel really warm and wispy and goosebumpy all over. Parts of my body would go moist, and I would dream that she was sleeping there beside me. You have to understand that I was just five years old at this time. Most of the psychiatrists I've told this to think that I'm putting them on. But I can remember Ruth as clearly as I can remember the things I did at work today. After all these years I've never forgotten her.

By March and April of my kindergarten year my mother was finally beginning to suspect that something was amiss. She thought something was wrong with me because I would come home from school and just sit on the cold front stoop which was made of slate. And I would daydream intensely about Ruth. My mother kept insisting that I tell her what was bothering me. But I didn't have the nerve to say anything. Lots of times she chased me from the slate stoop because she thought I might catch a cold. Whenever that happened I just took a long walk and dreamed about Ruth. Sometimes my mother would scream at me when I came back because I had been away too long. But none of that phased me. I just wished that I could spend forever with Ruth.

Then one day in April of my kindergarten year it all sort of came to a head. My mother was taking me downtown to go shopping. And I was sitting with my mother on the bus. Whenever I went anywhere by bus with my mother she would always give me the window seat and she would sit on the aisle seat. I don't know what the hell happened; but this one time I was sitting in the aisle seat and my mother was sitting in the window seat. All of a sudden Ruth and her sister Rita and their mother got on the bus; and they sat with their backs to the window in that seat that's just at the entrance to the bus across from the driver.

Well, I started to blush, and I smiled uncontrollably. And I just couldn't control myself. I wanted to act like I didn't see them. And I started looking towards my mother—out the window. And she noticed that I was blushing. I mean, tears were coming down my face I was blushing and smiling so intensely! Anyway, my mother insisted that I tell her why I was blushing. And I asked her what she meant. I didn't know what the word blushing meant. Well, it didn't take long for my mother to guess what was happening because I had been okey until those three people, including Ruth, got on the bus.

My mother guessed that I liked one of the little girls who got on. And she kept poking me about it. And I kept my mouth clamped shut more tightly than I ever kept my mouth shut in my life. A few stops before we had to get off my mother got up and went over to

Ruth's mother and started a conversation with her. My mother always had a great deal more nerve than I ever did. I mean she could start conversations with strangers like that. Anyway, she found out from the lady that Rita and Ruth were in my kindergarten class. And when we got off the bus she started teasing me about which one of the two girls I liked—which was ridiculous because Rita wasn't pretty at all.

Anyway, she starts telling me that I shouldn't like either one of them because they were Jewish and we were Catholic. I remember I didn't know what she meant by that. All I know was that when my kindergarten year was over Rita and Ruth moved away. And for a long time I was really depressed because I didn't have the nerve to ask anybody where they moved to." (41-year old love-shy man.)

On the other hand, some of the love-shys came closer to developing genuine relationships with girls during their prepubescent years than they ever did at any later time in their lives. The following interview quotation well illustrates (1) how the love-shys had relied upon passive-aggressive techniques from the earliest time in their lives to issue the attention they wanted from a girl who had attracted their fancy, and (2) how insensitive and non-understanding adults had used whatever tactics they could to discourage and break up prepubescent love relationships.

The second point is of formidable significance from the standpoint of *prevention* because if properly handled these early romantic hetero-sexual interactions could have been used to keep these boys from developing severe love-shyness in the first place. It is far better for a child to have just one extremely close friend than it is for him to have no friends at all. And it is far better for a child to have one opposite-sexed friend than it is for him to have no friends at all.

The following interview presents a case in which the child had at least transcended the point of pure infatuation. In this case the child had actually interacted vis-a-vis his girl friend. And if this interaction had continued over time there can be no question but that some social self-confidence would have been gained. Even if the relationship had eventually died a *natural* death, this social self-confidence would have served this love-shy man well in regard to the practical problem of meeting and initiating meaningful relationships with other females later in life.

"I was only in kindergarten when I first fell in love. There was a girl in my kindergarten class and there was one in my first grade class whom I found myself dreaming about all the time. But throughout all my years of education the love that I remember best of all was the one that I had had when I was in the second grade.

I guess I didn't notice her too much right away. But after a couple of months I began to notice more and more this girl whose name was Phyllis. There were about 30 kids in my second grade class, about half girls and half boys. And whenever anything came up I always wanted to be either in or near the group that contained Phyllis. I started dreaming about her all the time. And nine times out of ten if the teacher called on me and I was off in a world of beautiful daydreams, it was Phyllis that I was dreaming about.

Well, one day when I was fooling around at home I saw my mother looking in some big book she had on the kitchen table. That was when I was introduced to the telephone directory. And I looked up the name 'Springman', which was Phyllis' last name; and I found it there. And it also gave me her address.

Well, I already had a detailed street map of the town where I lived. I don't know why, but maps always fascinated me a very great deal. Even when I was only in the second grade I started to build up a tremendous collection of maps. I had them from every state in the union, and I had detailed street maps from all over. Anyway, I saw that Phyllis lived about a mile and a half away. But I had always loved to take long walks anyway. And I had a dog at that time which my parents always wanted me to walk.

So almost every day I would walk the mile and a half over to Woodside Drive. And I would walk up and down it several times with my dog. And each time I would approach that street my fantasy life would become extremely rich. However, if I saw someone stirring in the window or on the front porch of the house where she lived, I would immediately become overcome by extremely strong anxiety feelings. And I would run like hell in the opposites direction for a few minutes. And then I would return. By the way, all this happened in the spring of 1948. In 1956 when MY FAIR LADY opened I immediately thought of Phyllis the first time I heard the song 'On the Street Where You Live'. And even today whenever I hear that song I always think of the street where she used to live where I would walk up and down with my dog Punch.

Well, about this time like when I would be staring at her in class she would begin smiling at me. I would start to blush. And I think the teacher became somewhat disturbed about this. Like the kindergarten and first grade teachers that I had had, this teacher was sort of peturbed about the fact that I never wanted to play with the boys. Anyway, after a few weeks I stopped blushing when our eyes met. I would smile at her and she would smile at me. But we still hadn't arrived at the point where we were actually saying anything to each other. But she knew I liked her. And I was very happy about the fact that she seemed to like the fact that I liked her. In fact, I don't think I've ever been so happy in my life—even though I was still too shy to start a conversation with her.

Well, one day when I was walking down her street with my wire-haired fox terrier her mom came outside and called me by name. At first I was extremely nervous and started to walk the other way. But she seemed very friendly, and she called me by name. She told me not to be afraid, and that she wanted me to come in and have some cream soda and cookies. Well, I felt extremely shy. But something made me turn around and start walking her way towards the house. Her mom seemed extremely nice, and when I walked in the kitchen Phyllis was there and she smiled and said 'hi'. And I finally became involved in my first real conversation with a girl!

That was in March of my second grade year. And from that point on we became very close friends. Every day as soon as school was over I would walk down to her house, and we would play together until dinner time. And then I would go home. My mother found out about my friendship with Phyllis. And she was glad I finally had somebody to play with even if it was a girl. One day my mother asked me to invite Phyllis home for lunch, and I did. And I remember we had lamb chops. And my mother seemed delighted with her. I was very happy. You have to understand, we didn't always agree about everything. I mean there were things I wanted to do that she didn't want to do. But it didn't matter. For about three months we were inseparable.

By the way, wouldn't it be great if even by the time you got to be of college age all you had to do was walk up and down a girl's street a few hundred times with your dog and you'd get invited in by her mother?! That's one reason why I'd like to see arranged marriages become available in the United States—at least for shy people.

I remember I became eight years old pretty close to the end of the school year. And my mom threw a birthday party for me. Actually this was quite unusual because she only threw two parties for me while I was growing up: one in the second grade and one in the fifth. This particular party was a really special time for me because it was one of the very few times while I was growing up that I was really happy. My mom invited a lot of kids, some of whom had been teasing me quite a lot about spending all of my time with Phyllis. But I didn't care. I was glad to have them at my party. And strangely enough, I felt kind of pleased about things even though they were teasing me. Even though I had just turned only eight, I sort of suspected that some of the kids who were teasing me might have been jealous of me.

Shortly after that time my school let out for the summer. And my parents forced me to go away to summer camp. I always hated camp, but my dad always insisted that I go because he thought it might make me turn magically into his idea of a real boy. As you can see, that never happened. But what did happen was that when I arrived home at the end of the summer I didn't have the nerve anymore to go visit Phyllis. I had been looking forward to seeing her all summer long. But when I arrived home for some reason I somehow lost my nerve. Nevertheless, one day around Labor Day I did say that I was going to take a walk down there with my dog. And my mother told me she did not want me to go. She told me that she had this outing planned that would involve a lot of boys my age and their parents. And she insisted that I get ready to go on that. She was still after me to become a real boy.

I guess the real clincher, though, was the school. Both Phyllis and I continued attending the same school throughout our third, fourth, fifth and sixth grades. But the school made sure that we were assigned to different teachers for all four years. I mean there were two third grades, two fourth grades, two fifth grades, and two sixth grades. And I don't think it could have been pure chance by the wildest stretch of the imagination that we were kept separate for all four of those years. And you know even to this day I still feel very angry about that. Like if we had been together again in the third grade it would have been very easy for me to continue seeing her. Even if we had been separated for the third grade and put back together again in the fourth grade it would have been easy for me to start seeing her again. But the way they worked it, I just lost all the confidence that I had built up the preceding spring. One day when I was in the third grade I heard through the grapevine that both Phyllis and her mother were wondering why I didn't come around anymore. When I heard about that I felt really depressed. But I just didn't know what to do because by that time I had lost my nerve. And I was afraid that if I did try to see her again I wouldn't be able to think of enough things to say to her. And silence has always made me extremely nervous." (43-year old love-shy man.)

This case interview poignantly illustrates how parents and other well-meaning adults often do far more harm than good in their dealings with love-shy and pre-love-shy boys. It also illustrates how trying to force a small child into becoming something which he is not can almost always be counted upon to give rise to very disappointing results. If the friendship-love relationship in this case had been encouraged or at least not discouraged, this 43-year old man might well have grown in the ways that nature had intended for him to grow. And today at 43 he would not be a severely love-shy, single, never married virgin.

This particular case study was interesting in still another way. As I have stated, virtually all of the love-shy men whom I interviewed could remember with great clarity each of the many love infatuations that they had experienced throughout their elementary school years. However, this particular man had saved photographs of his Phyllis kissing him at his eight-year old birthday party. While I was interviewing him he brought out several copies of two different photographs. And he suggested that it might dress up this research report in an appropriately incisive manner if I printed them. They appear on the next page. One shows him being kissed by Phyllis while some of his male peers look on. The second one depicts him standing with Phyllis and her girl friend.

Beautiful, Driving Obsessions

There is a long standing tradition in American society to belittle and disparage preadolescent infatuations. The term "puppy love" exemplifies the tendency on the part of many adults to make light of the early

manifestation of heterosexual love and romance. Yet all of the research evidence currently available strongly suggests that even very young children *feel* the emotions of romantic infatuations every bit as strongly as adults do. To be sure, not all prepubescent children experience these strong love feelings for a person of the opposite sex. But those who fall in love at seven or eight seem to experience the emotions of love every bit as strongly as do those who fall in love at eighteen or at twenty-eight or at thirty-eight.

What the ultimate causes of the preadolescent love phenomenon are is anybody's guess at this juncture in time.[1] Some social scientists are beginning to suspect that the need for heterosexual love and romance has a genetic basis, and that it is conceptually distinct and entirely different from the biologically rooted need for sexual expression. Some think that the need for love and romance is more closely related to the need for esthetic satisfaction than it is to the need for sexual pleasure.

(See Vernon Grant's book titled FALLING IN LOVE.) Suffice it to say that the need for romantic love manifests itself in many young children long before there is any capability of *sexual* performance.

Some social scientists have speculated that prepubescent love interest may be a reflection of a dearth of love in the family of orientation vis-a-vis the mother and father. A vulnerability to unrequited romantic infatuations *at any age* may quite possibly reflect deficits in family love. But normal romantic boy-girl interests at the elementary school level do not appear to reflect any shortfall of family love.

In fact, unusually early heterosexual romantic interests do not appear to be very closely related to a dearth of love in the family of orientation. Professor Broderick's research showed that 57 percent of all children with unusually early heterosexual-romantic interests enjoyed happy, loving relationships with their mothers and fathers. The analogous figure for children who did not manifest such unusually early boy-girl romantic interests was 83 percent. Thus in America there is only a mild association between early romantic interests and poor relationships with mothers and fathers.

But this statistical association is obviously far too weak to explain the phenomenon of very early boy-girl romantic attachments because *a majority* of the children who did become romantically interested very early in life (57 percent) *also* enjoyed happy, healthy relationships with their families. Further, there are several hundred societies in the preindustrial world wherein it is most unusual for a child *not* to become interested in the opposite sex by the age of six or seven.

As I documented in chapter one, people perform better (often *much* better) than they ordinarily do when they are involved in a love relationship that is mutual and reciprocal. This is known to be especially true for males of all ages. Only unrequited love, which is the basis of "infatuation", is taxing on people's time and psychoemotional energies. Only unreciprocated love seems to yield destructive, self-defeating results. And only unrequited love appears to cause the development of intense obsessions that keep a child, teenager or adult from attending to constructive, action-oriented behavior.

The love-shy seven year old needs to be dealt with in exactly the same manner as the love-shy seventeen year old and the love-shy twenty-seven year old. All need to be helped to stop excessive daydreaming and to *commence living!* All need to be helped to reach out to the member of the opposite sex in whom they are interested. The fact that a majority of a love-shy child's classmates may not as yet have reached the point of having heterosexual romantic interests is actually quite immaterial. People must be helped in their effors to climb each step of life *as they themselves reach each step.* Preconceived timetables that everyone is "supposed to fit" need to be discarded; such timetables invariably lead to destructive consequences.

> "I remember when I was about nine my dad made me join the Cub Scouts. It wasn't too bad; but I can remember dreaming all the time about girls being there instead of boys. I mean I took part in most of the activities, but I did so without saying much to anybody. Like, the kids used to refer to me as the 'man of few words'. I never really made any friends in the Cub Scouts even though I was with them for three years—all the way through the fourth, fifth and sixth grades.
>
> Maybe I can explain a little better what I mean. Like when I was about eleven we went on this overnight hike up around the Delaware Water Gap. And I enjoyed getting out into nature. But I didn't want to talk to anybody. All the guys found me unsociable, and the three fathers who led us on this trip I don't think liked me too much either. Like, I'd be off in a world of deep fantasy as I was walking along. And I just didn't want to be interrupted from what I was daydreaming about because it was always much more beautiful than the stupid, boring things the other 11 and 12-year old boys were talking about—and the stupid, ridiculous songs they were singing—Jesus!
>
> Well, at that time I was really in love with the 8-year old sister of one of the boys in my Cub Scout den. And I remember as I was walking along I would be dreaming that she was right there with me and that she and I were talking. And there would be other pretty girls in my classes who I would be daydreaming about. I mean, I'd see all of them there with me in my mind's eye. But most of the time I would be daydreaming just about my favorite girl—Jenny. She was my den mate's sister I just told you about. And even though I was just eleven, I can remember getting moist and goosebumpy all over as I dreamed she was there inside my sleeping bag with me.
>
> Anyway, when I was twelve I finally got out of the scouts, even though my parents didn't want me to. I just didn't see any point in staying in because I wasn't getting introduced to any girls. I mean, if my den group had been coeducational, there's no way in the world anyone could have ever gotten me to drop out. I just didn't want to participate in anything anymore where girls weren't present." (22-year old love-shy university student.)

Nearly all of the love-shys spoke of having resented the American custom of segregating the sexes. Virtually all social organizations for elementary and junior high school aged young people are gender-segregated. And these include the Cub Scouts, Boy Scouts, Boys Club of America, Campfire Girls, Brownies, Girl Scouts, YWCA, YMCA, etc.

Even at the senior high school level virtually all extracurricular activities continue to be gender-segregated.

The love-shy men I studied had known what they needed better than any of their parents or teachers. They *knew* that they needed a copious abundance of opportunities for relaxed, informal heterosexual interaction. Such opportunities had been denied them by a system that they preceived as being totally unjust and insensitive to their needs—and totally uncaring about their strong (albeit secret) desires for the companionship of an opposite sexed friend.

This represents a key reason why the love-shy tended to withdraw from social activities organized for children and young people. They saw no need for further informal contact with age-mates of their own gender. Like the young man quoted at length above, *what is the point of going on a hike with a bunch of age-mates of your own gender if all you do the entire time is daydream about being with and talking with a GIRL!?*

All of this flies in the face of a quite stubborn bias which continues to prevail in our society. Many people strongly believe that it is *"natural"* for boys in the eight-to-thirteen-year age range to want to spent their time exclusively with same-sexed age-mates. It is also widely believed that senior high school boys "naturally" prefer to spend the majority of their free time engaging in "rough and tumble" athletics with age-mates of their own gender. To be sure, most American boys develop these *typical* preference patterns—most probably because (1) they have been socialized (programmed; hypnotized) to do so, and because (2) these preferences are in consonance with their native temperaments anyway. However, *not all prepubescent boys fit these "typical boyish" preference patterns.* AND IT IS ALWAYS COUNTERPRODUCTIVE TO TRY TO FORCE SQUARE PEGS INTO ROUND HOLES.

The love-shy might well have been "premature" by conventional American standards in their overwhelmingly strong heterosexual companionship interests and fantasies. But in blocking any form of realization of these fantasies many of these seemingly precocious boys may have learned to associate feelings of "naughtiness", anxiety, and "disobedience" with the thought of being with a girl. In other words, the feeling that their desires for close, female companionship were somehow "not right" for them at their age, may have transferred to a more general anxiety pertinent to heterosexual interaction that remained with them long after they had arrived at an age when heterosexual interaction *is* considered appropriate by society. Simply put, unless a child is involved in a clearly dangerous type of activity, it is always best to both permit and encourage him to grow and develop in his own way.

An organization called the "Coed Scouts" could clearly become a godsend for boys with this sort of temperament and seemingly precocious need for emotionally intimate heterosexual interaction. If such an organization could be made a socially acceptable alternative for children of both sexes who want it, units could be established which cross-cut school districts so that in the unlikely event that not enough boys from one district wish to join, there would always be a sufficient number of pre-love-shy boys from surrounding districts to fill the gap. Coed Scouting groups would provide for such activities as hiking, swimming, arts and crafts, music, visits to museums and live stage shows, etc. Indeed, the only activities that would be ruled out would be the rough contact sports such as basketball, football, baseball, softball, etc.

A Preadolescent's Preference for a Sister

The love-shys' tendencies to have spent countless hours daydreaming and fantasizing about being involved in mutually gratifying interaction with a female companion sometimes extended even to the idea of prompting parents to procreate a baby sister. The following interview quotation is both interesting and poignant:

"Well, as I told you I was an only child. And I can remember when I was about eight I kept prodding my mother to get me a baby sister. I don't know; I guess I must have kept pestering her about it for five or six months or more. Anyway, one day my dad told me that she couldn't have anymore children, but that they were thinking about adopting one. My dad wanted another son, and he couldn't understand why I kept asking all the time for a baby sister. I guess he thought that if you're a boy you should want a brother. Well, I knew I definitely didn't want any damned brother. I wanted a baby sister.

Well, one day my father came home with some papers about an adoption. Up to that point my mother hadn't said anything. But she suddenly became quite upset. And she and my father argued until late into the night about adopting. Anyway, my dad came into my room the next morning and told me that my mother definitely did not want to adopt a child, and that I would be better off anyway because they would have that much more to give to me.

For a long time after that I was really disappointed. But after awhile I began to feel relieved. If my dad had gotten his way and adopted another boy I would have really been in trouble. I don't know what I would have ever done with a brother around! I hate boys!" (35-year old love-shy man.)

The Principle of the Superordinate Goal

There is a well established principle in the social sciences which states that whenever the cooperation of two people is enlisted towards the completion of some task that is of equivalent importance to both (*and which cannot be successfully completed except through the close cooperative enterprise of the two people*), those two people will come to like each other, they will become friends, and their values, attitudes, goals, etc., will tend to become increasingly similar. This is known as the *principle of the superordinate goal*. And it would seem to me to be particularly applicable to the problem of dispelling bashfulness and social distance between an elementary school boy and girl who may have a romantic interest in each other. Of course, it would be equally applicable to the problem of helping older love-shys as well. The principle has been found to work quite irrespective of the ages or genders of the people involved.

In elementary schools it is usually quite easy for a teacher to engineer social experiences entailing superordinate goals. For example, a teacher can enlist the cooperation of a boy, and the girl in whom he is interested, in the completion of some sort of project for the classroom or for the school. They could be asked to do something that would require them to spend quite a bit of time studying and researching together in a cooperative way. The teacher can make such assignments in a nonchalant way which suggests to the particular boy and girl that there had been no special reason for grouping them together. A teacher can do much to provide the sort of warm mutual introductions that stave off blushing and other manifestations (internal and external) of painful embarrassment.

Love in the Middle Childhood Years

Even though it is somewhat unusual for children to fall in love with opposite sexed age-mates as early as kindergarten or the first grade, by the fourth, fifth and sixth grades such strong romantic attachments are quite commonplace throughout middle-class suburban and small town America. Love-shy boys differ in their romantic attachments from boys of normal psychoemotional adjustment in essentially *seven* ways: (1) they become deeply romantically interested in girls at least three or four years earlier, usually by kindergarten, the first or second grades; (2) they rarely transcend the point of unrequited infatuation. Thus, they never actually socialize in any way with the object of their affections.

(3) They are usually social isolates, whereas boys of normal psycho-emotional health sustain many male friendships. In fact, Broderick found that fourth and fifth grade boys with girl friends had significantly more *male* friendships than did boys of the same age without any girl friends. And (4) the need to daydream about and the yearning to be near the object of their infatuation represents a dominating, driving force in the love-shys' lives; they care about very little else. Male peers, parents, schoolwork, etc., simply do not matter to them. All that matters is the love object.

The fifth (5) major point of difference is that love-shy boys both prefer and need a coeducational environment for *all* of their activities. Love-shy boys don't like their own gender much, whereas non-love-shy prepubescent boys enjoy "boyish" all-male activities quite in spite of their romantic interests in girls which, again, are *reciprocated*. And (6) the love-shy preadolescent boy tends to be strongly infatuated with just one girl at a time, whereas his more "normal" male peers tend to develop romantic interests in a lot of different girls. Lastly (7) the love-shy occasionally become deeply infatuated with television and movie actresses of their own age or younger, whereas the "normal" boy confines his romantic interests strictly to accessible girls.

The following interview quotation is illustrative of typical behavior in a fifth grade love-shy boy. Again, it is quite normal for fifth grade boys to develop and maintain strong romantic love interests. However, the love-shy boy daydreams while the adjusted, happy boy interacts. In this sense the two different lifetime scripts (love-shy and "normal") begin to manifest themselves at about the fifth grade year. The adult social behavior of a love-shy man is little different from the behavioral style of the love-shy fifth grader.

"I didn't really do much after school until I got to be in the fifth grade. Up until that time I just sort of hung around. But that year they cleared a bunch of vacant lots about a half-mile from where I lived. And they created a park where kids could play at all kinds of stuff. I rode my bike there one day and I saw this really pretty girl. I didn't know her name, but I knew she was one grade behind me in school. All I can tell you is that love just all of a sudden hit me and I was overwhelmed. For the next two years I don't think I ever missed a single day at that park. I would take my bike there every single day after school. Most days she never came. In fact, I guess she only showed up there about once every two weeks or so. But that was enough to force me to go there every single day. I mean, if something held me up from getting to the park it was like I would be just overwhelmed. My spirit would just be jumping out of my insides! Strange and really strong feelings would penetrate throughout my whole body. And I just couldn't stand still. I just had to get there even though I knew she might not show up.

Actually I never talked to her. All I ever did was look her way as long as she was anywhere near me. If she would look in my direction I would just feel overwhelmed as though hot lead had just passed throughout my entire bloodstream. And I would look away from her for a second. And then I would just run two or three laps around the park, or I might get on one of the swings and swing myself real hard. I think the other kids must have thought that I was crazy because sometimes I would just run and run whenever she would look at me. And as I would run or swing myself I would be dreaming about being in bed with her, or at the beach in the sun together, or just sitting quietly watching television together. This was long before I knew anything at all about sex.

After awhile I guess she must have begun to suspect that I really liked her. But she never tried to start a conversation with me or anything. I never had the nerve to say anything to my mother or father about it. In fact, I never had the nerve to say anything to my folks about any of the girls I ever fell in love with. I just quietly suffered by myself all through my life." (35-year old love-shy man.)

Self-Disclosure Inhibitions

One of the particularly difficult problems in helping the love-shy prepubescent child is that of getting him to "open up" about his problems, hopes, needs, wants, aspirations and desires. Young children who are shy are almost always afflicted with an inability to self-disclose. And very often they will not disclose what they *really* want and need, or what is *really* bothering them unless and until they are accorded plenty of warm, non-threatening encouragement and time. They must be able to trust the person to whom they self-disclose, and they must feel free about contacting the teacher, parent, counselor or therapist, at any time in the future, be it by telephone, letter, or in person.

Many school districts retain just one or two clinical psychologists. And these very few persons are expected to successfully trouble-shoot all of the emotionally disturbed youngsters who surface throughout a district that services several thousand pupils. Obviously this cannot be accomplished with any degree of effectiveness without the input of a great deal more resources for the hiring and retaining of trained people.

A 37-year old love-shy man shared this poignant story with me about how he had been too shy to tell a school psychologist what he *really* wanted to tell her during his one visit with her.

"I remember I was in the third grade, and one day I was sent in to see the school psychologist because I was regarded as different than the other kids. They seemed to think that I needed help. Anyway, there were ten different elementary schools in our district, and this psychologist only came by our school about once every two weeks or so.

Well, I was given the entire school day with this psychologist. I was only about eight years old at the time, and it was really interesting. I mean she gave me all these tests. Most of the tests were spoken, so I didn't have to write anything. And she seemed to be a very nice person.

Well, at one point she asked me to make a list of the three things I most wanted in all the world. I vividly remember this because she also said that I was definitely going to receive my number one wish. I was just a little kid, and I didn't know how she could be so goddam certain. But I remember her calmly saying that I'd better choose my number one wish with care because I was going to receive it— whatever it was. She said that she had helped all of the kids she had seen get the thing that they had listed as number one.

Well, I remember this more vividly than most other things in my childhood because the only thing I could think of was a girl friend. I knew I wanted a girl friend more strongly than anything else in the world. But I just didn't have the nerve to tell her that! There was this girl in the other third grade class. Actually, she had been in my second grade classroom the year before. But now we had different third grade teachers. And what I really wanted was any-thing that might enable me to spend all my free time with her and make her my best friend.

Well, I remember I was stone silent for what must have been five minutes. It seemed like ages. And she was really confused about it. I mean I had done a lot of talking up to that point. And I took all her oral intelligence tests without any problems like this developing. She was really confused.

Well, what finally happened was that I said I'd tell her my second and third wishes first, and that I'd have to come back to wish number one. Well, I covered wishes number two and three rather fast. And then I began stalling again. This time instead of not saying anything I started elaborating on as many details as I could think of about my second and third wish. The funny thing is I couldn't tell you now what my second and third wishes were, even if my life depended on it. All I can remember is that I did a lot of talking about my second and third wish so that I would not have to talk about my first wish. I was really nervous and I wanted to bide myself some time. But I really couldn't think very easily because I was talking about something entirely different from what I was trying to think about.

Well, finally I just couldn't think of anything else to say. I couldn't stall her anymore, and I had to get to the first wish. Well, dammit, I just didn't have the nerve to tell her. So I finally told her that I wanted a dog! Actually I did want a dog, but that wasn't what I really and truly wanted more than anything else in the world. I wanted a girl friend. And I remember that for the rest of the school year I went through mental turmoil inside because I didn't have the nerve to tell her what I really wanted.

You know what? Well, I don't think two weeks went by before my father came home one night with a standard poodle puppy! I know neither of my parents had especially wanted a dog. I think this school psychologist must have talked to them. Anyway, this psychologist's prophecy was fulfilled at my expense! I was delighted to have the dog, but I would have exchanged it in an instant for what I *really* wanted. I didn't get my *real* number one. To this day I keep wondering what would have happened if I had told her what my *real* number one desire was!"

To this 37-year old man this incident had long taken on a kind of occult, mystical significance. However, even if the psychologist had been unable to get him the specific girl friend whom he so dearly craved, she should have at least been made aware of what had truly been on his mind. She should have been made aware of what his strongest desire *actually* was. For without this information there was really no chance of her ever truly helping him in a whole host of other ways—including the ways which had been of pertinence to the reasons for his having been sent by his third grade teacher to see a school psychologist in the first place.

In cases similar to this one the child needs to be accorded regular access to a trained psychologist. Moreover, the child needs to be shown various alternative ways for getting his information across, if he is too shy to say it all out loud. In the above instance the child had become able to explain his true feelings and wishes upon actually receiving the dog. In fact, to listen to him today he may have even been ready on the very next day of school—*if the psychologist had been there* the next day ready to listen to him.

In sum, troubled youngsters need to have regular access to friendly, nonthreatening clinical staff. In addition to this regular access, they also need to be supplied with alternative means for relaying important information to therapeutic staff. Again, letter writing is an important alternative means of contact. Another might be in-depth hypnosis. Generally speaking, most children are far more hypnotizable than adults. And this is a fact that should be constructively capitalized upon.

Not having the nerve to talk about strong heterosexual love needs and desires is a condition that often persists among love-shy males well into adolescence, and sometimes even into adulthood. It is a problem which can and often does prove quite costly to parents who may be operating under the illusion that conventional psychiatric treatment will work to turn a love-shy son into someone who behaves in a "normal" and socially desirable fashion. The self-disclosure reticence that prevails among the love-shy often wrecks havoc upon parents and relatives *in addition to* the victims themselves. The following case interview well illustrates this point.

"I remember back in 1953 I was a sophomore in high school. And I wasn't doing very well. My parents were always being called in because I wasn't performing up to what was thought to be my intelligence and ability. And I was always acting up. Like, the kids would constantly bully and tease me all the time. And the way I dealt with that was to play the clown. In fact, I think I was even better than Jerry Lewis. Jerry Lewis was my role model at that time. And I was even more 'far out' in real life than he was on stage.

Anyway, the real reason I wasn't doing well academically was that I just couldn't stop myself from daydreaming all the time about this girl who I was in love with. She didn't even know I existed. But from the moment I got up in the morning until I went to bed at night all I could do was dream about all kinds of beautiful stories involving me and her. I would be in class. But I just couldn't keep my mind on anything the teacher would be saying. And when I tried to read a textbook I would hold the book open and look at it with my physical eyes. But my real eyes were off with my beloved girl whom I desperately wished I could have. Sometimes I would have the book open to the same page for an hour or more. Sometimes I would even get headaches because my physical eyes would get tired looking at the print while I personally was not actually reading the print.

Anyway, the principal convinced my father to take me to this psychiatrist. I remember she charged my father $20 per visit. That was a lot of money in those days. And I knew my father wasn't rich. Like, he didn't make all that much money. And I began to feel worse and worse about it because I began to recognize that psychiatry was really bullshit. Like when I first went to see this doctor I thought she was going to do something to me. But after I completed the initial battery of tests, all there ever was was talk. And during most of the sessions there were these prolonged silences. Sometimes we would just sit there and stare at each other for twenty whole minutes or more before anybody said anything. And it was still $20 a meeting.

The thing that really upset me the most about all of this was that I really wanted to tell her about my daydreams. I mean I really wanted to tell her about how I longed to have a real live girlfriend whom I could love, and how all I ever thought about was this girl. Well, I went to see this woman every week for almost two whole years. And in all that time I never really had the nerve to tell her what I was really like—like what was really going on in my mind all the time. Of course, she would keep telling me that I would talk when I became ready. Well, after two years I still didn't have the nerve. And when the principal told my father that all of this didn't seem to be doing any good, he finally let me stop seeing this psychiatrist. Of course, since then I've had fifteen years of psychotherapy with several different psychiatrists who *did* know about my need for a girlfriend. So I guess it probably wouldn't have done any good anyway if my first psychiatrist had known about it." (46-year old love-shy man.)

Media Inspired Love Infatuations

Psychiatrists have occasionally suggested that it is "safe" for a socially incompetent person to fall in love with a television or movie star because there is virtually no chance of his ever being rejected by her. The probability of a movie star ever entering upon the accessible social networks of a love-shy person is virtually nil. In fact, even a highly self-confident young man might accurately be seen as highly unlikely to ever meet up with a film actress to the point at which he might be able to actually converse with her.

Only a comparatively small minority of the love-shys' major infatuations had involved television or motion picture actresses. Nevertheless, almost all of the love-shy men I studied for this book had experienced at least two romantic infatuations with media starlets before they got to be of college age. In other words, most of the romantic infatuations that the love-shys had suffered had involved accessible women. But a sizable minority of their deepest infatuations had involved media starlets.

Several of the strongest and most intense infatuations mentioned by those interviewed had involved preadolescent girls. For example, one man told me that as a 14-year old eighth grader he had fallen in love with Brigette Fossey, the 7-year old starlet of the French movie FORBIDDEN GAMES. In fact, he had been so "turned on" by her and by the content of the movie itself that he sat through it 44 times!

One of the most interesting comments made by any respondent concerned the family drama I REMEMBER MAMA, which ran on CBS Television every Friday night from 1949 until 1955.

> "Well, I guess there was only one television actress that I ever really fell in love with; and that was Robin Morgan. She played Dagmar on a program called I REMEMBER MAMA, which I used to watch all the time when I was a kid. Actually, I never really watched that much television compared to the amount that the other kids seemed to watch. But this was a program that I wouldn't miss for anything. And I remember it was on at a time which sometimes got me into trouble. Like, I was in junior high school for a lot of the time that it was on the air. And the school periodically threw parties. And the parties were always held on Friday nights. I can remember there were several times when I wanted to attend some social function at my school. But it was held on a Friday night. And I just couldn't go because if I did I would have missed Robin.
>
> I remember some of the teachers used to accuse me of being anti-social. Actually this happened quite a bit because I remember I didn't have the nerve to tell them the real reason why I couldn't come. I remember they'd angrily come up to me and insist that I tell them what was so important that I couldn't come to the party. And I'd say something like 'I don't know'. My parents often got pissed off at me too. But I never had the nerve to tell them anything. They never would have understood.
>
> Like if they only had held the parties on Saturday nights or even on Sunday nights I know I would have gone to them. But I know I would have suffered immeasurably if I ever missed one of the I REMEMBER MAMA programs. Like even if they had had video tape machines then as they do today I could have had the program copied while I attended the parties. I even suggested to some of the teachers that if they started the functions at 8:45 instead of at 7:30 I'd be able to come. See, I REMEMBER MAMA was on only from 8 to 8:30; and I could have gone anywhere after that." (44-year old love-shy man.)

The foregoing well illustrates another way in which romantic infatuations can have a deleterious impact upon propitious socioemotional growth—particularly when such infatuations concern inaccessible media figures. Of course, during their pre-teen and teenaged years love-shy children manifest many rather grandiose hints that their lives are headed for serious trouble. Yet in spite of the middle-class home backgrounds from which they come, their parents somehow ignore the often not-too-subtle clues and messages which are repeatedly displayed. In some cases this may be due to the parents themselves being shy and unsure of themselves.

And as is obvious in the above case, the school is seldom of much help either. This particular school was at least sophisticated enough to run social functions for its students. But staff had simply not been available to the boy (now a 44-year old man) that was sensitive enough to pick up on what was *actually* going on in his life. Without an awareness of what was happening in his life there was no viable way of (1) helping him towards a viable solution to his love-shyness problems by getting him introduced to some *accessible* girls, and (2) of assuring his attendance at the Friday night social functions.

The Biochemistry of Falling in Love

The past few years have yielded a great deal of new knowledge about what lies at the basis of the beautiful and glorious feelings we all feel when we fall in love. Talk show host Phil Donahue nicely summarizes much of this material in his 1985 volume THE HUMAN ANIMAL (see especially chapter six of that work).

The available data indicate that romantic love feelings commence in the region of the lower brain that is known as the hypothalamus. The hypothalamus is composed of a dense cluster of nerves which controls hundreds of bodily functions and impacts in a large host of ways the entire nervous system. Whenever a person subjectively perceives another human being as romantically appealing a portion of the hypothalamus transmits a message by way of various chemicals to the pituitary gland. And in turn the pituatary releases a host of its own hormones which rapidly suffuse the entire bloodstream. The sex glands respond to these hormones by rapidly releasing into the bloodstream their own hormones which have the effect, *even among preadolescent children*, of creating a more rapid heartbeat and a feeling of lightness in the head. Simultaneously the nerve pathways in and around the hypothalamus produce chemicals that induce—provided that these chemicals continued to be produced over a long period of time—what people refer to as "falling in love".

What current research especially needs to focus upon is the question of whether love-shys have a hyperactive hypothalamus that commences to respond and react with "love chemicals" significantly earlier in life for them than for most human beings—and whether these hypo-thalamus responses are stronger and more persistant over the first three decades of life for the love-shys than for non-shy people. As I have already documented in chapter two, many components of the lower brain stem are much more hyperactivein introverts than in ambiverts and extyroverts. The neurons of the locus coeruleus and of other parts of the ascending reticular formation of the brain appears to be much more hyperactive among inhibited people than among the uninhibited. Thus, there is little reason to suspect that the "love nucleus" component of the hypothalammus (itself a part of the lower brain) might not also be hyperactive for highly inhibited, very shy men.

If this is so it would provide a key portion of the explanation as to why so many of the love-shy fall so deeply in love as early in life as age 5—much earlier in life than most people experience powerful feelings of romantic love. It would also partially explain why love-shy men tend to fall in love so easily and so often right from the earliest years of elementary school through the years of middle adulthood. Simply put, for severely love-shy men the "love nucleus" portion of the hypothal-amus may *"awaken to full operation"* seven or eight or nine years pre-maturely, long before adolescence is arrived at with its normal surge of sex hormones. The prepubescent child who does not have any aware-ness of sex or of erotic feelings (as these do not usually occur prior to adolescence) interprets the powerful feelings he does feel as being those of overhwelming romantic love.

Among the first signs of "falling in love" is a giddy high similar to what might be obtained as a result of an amphetamine boost. This "high" is a sign that the brain has entered a distinct neurochemical state. This occurs as a result of the hypothalamus releasing a chemical sub-stance (probably phenylethylamine) that is very much like an amphet-amine and which, like any "upper", makes the heart beat faster and confers energy. This biochemically-based "high" is experienced by any-one "in love" quite irrespective of their chronological age. The problem for the love-shy *of any age* is that they are emotionally incapable of harnessing the energy that is a byproduct of their biochemically-based "high". In essence, they are incapable of following through, flirting, and winning the attention of the loved person. If they did follow through and were rejected, the biochemical "high" would quickly and fairly easily come to a halt. In not being able to make the approach to the love object the biochemical "high" remains endemic in the love-shy child's brain for an indefinite, usually quite lengthy period of time. And the elemen-tary school boy (or man as the case might be) becomes *"hooked"* on his own brain biochemicals. In short, for the love-shy male who cannot approach the girl, love swiftly becomes an overwhelming strong addiction that is probably every bit as strong and demanding as a drug addict's addiction to amphetamine might be. (The ability to share many experiences with the love object would operate to remove the "rosy colored smokescreen" of infatuation, thus preventing this addiction.)

Of course, any "high" has to end. The evidence suggests that males who are able to start conversations with girls in whom they become interested are highly unlikely to experience any painful "crashes". At least their susceptibility to such "crashes" will remain very low until early adulthood. And even then they will be susceptible only if a boy-girl love relationship of many months duration breaks up against their wishes. In contrast, love-shy males are susceptible to such "crashes" from the age of five simply because their inability to start a conversation with and to get to know their "love-object" causes a long-term preoccupation and fantasy world to develop that can and does often last for many months. As the cases reported in this chapter suggest, all a 5 or 7 or 9 year old boy need do is look at his love-object in a school hallway or on a playground, and his hypothalamus will cause the release of a shot of blood amphetamines that are as potent (and distracting) as a shot out of hell! Despite the tendency of naive parents to use the disparaging expression "puppy love", the biochemical basis of love is really no different for the eight year old than it is for the adult.

A key consideration for anyone who gets hooked on drugs is that of *withdrawal*. Whether a person gets hooked on pills or on natural drugs that the brain produces, the "crash" of withdrawal can be highly distracting and debilitating for a person of any age. But of especial interest here is the finding that people who "crash" after having been deeply in love tend to have an unusually strong craving for chocolate. Very noteworthy is the fact that chocolate is high into phenylethylamine—the very substance that is released by the brain into the bloodstream as a concomitant of falling in love. When the love-feelings cease the body craves chocolate because it has developed a tolerance to the phenylethylamines which it is no longer getting—because the brain has stopped secreting them.

As I shall document in chapter fifteen of this book, from early childhood the love-shy men studied for this book had always had a significantly above average craving for chocolate and other sweets; and they tended to consume significantly more of these items than did the non-shy men. This consumption of chocolate and sweets tends to aggravate the love-shys' problems in a whole host of ways as we shall see. For now, suffice it to say that this craving for sweets may be due in part to constantly being in the throes of hopeless and terminated, unrequited love experiences.

Finally, Jack Panksepp, a chemist at Bowling Green State University, has obtained evidence indicating that the brain also produces chemicals called *opioids* (which are quite similar to the highly addicting opiates) when a person falls deeply in love.

Chapter Postscript

One of my fondest wishes is to see American parents institutionalize a new tradition which loosens up on children as far as early dating, informal heterosexual interaction, and even sexual expression are concerned. Children *of any age* should not be discouraged from having a "best friend" of the opposite sex. I believe it is always wrong to discourage expressions of love and romance—feelings which are all too scarce in our world. And to discourage children *of any age* from having a close, "best friend" of the opposite sex is tantamount to discouraging *monogamy* and monogamous proclivities; and this too is not an adaptable or prudently compassionate course of action to take in our high-divorce, rapidly changing world. Males and females do need each other in loyal, monogamous unions; and this is true for people of all ages—not just for married adults.

And despite the often oppressive conservatism in contemporary homophobic America, parental attitudes towards early dating and towards relaxed, spontaneous, unaffected heterosexual interaction, can actually be seen from any logical standpoint as actually promoting homosexual interests and behavior. To be sure, for children and young teenagers in contemporary America, it is actually easier to be a person of homosexual interests (because privacy is much easier to come by) than it is to be a person of heterosexual interests—although this should not be interpreted as contradicting my earlier research-based assertion that true homosexuality and true heterosexuality are both inborn and that you cannot change a heterosexual child into a homosexual one or vice versa. (However, experience *may* move a bisexual person more in one direction than towards the other.)

Finally, the most powerful cause of unwanted pregnancy among American teenagers today is failure of many of them to accept their monogamous, loving premarital coitus as morally right for themselves. In other words, conservative parents and religious leaders fan the flames of the unwanted teen pregnancy problem as a result of the norms which they intimidate young people into internalizing. Contraceptive use makes premarital sex deliberate and premeditated, and thus such judicious precautionary measures will usually not be carefully and consistently taken by young people who are not *truly comfortable* with their monogamous, loving, contraceptively protected premarital sexual love-making. Scores of recent studies strongly support my position in regard to this. The interested reader should consult my upcoming volume titled PREMARITAL BIRTH CONTROL.

NOTES

1. Ibid., pp. 294–297. In essence, it would appear that love-shy males are most probably (from very early childhood onward) significantly above average on the brain amphetamines which cause people to fall in love. This surfeit of "love amphetamines" is probably operative for the love-shy from the preschool years onward. In contrast, for most people who are not afflicted with severe shyness these "love amphetamines" probably do not begin to become operative until shortly before the onset of pubescence. Of some significance is the probable fact that there is *no minimum age* with respect to when the *love* hormones might begin working upon a person's brain. In contrast, there *is* a minimum age for the operation of the *sex* hormones: they cannot commence influencing a person prior to the onset of pubescence.

Chapter 12

Beauty and the Love-Shy

In his book entitled FALLING IN LOVE, Vernon Grant cites evidence that in the first phase of romantic attraction visual and auditory factors (appearance and voice) are vital. He argues that this phase is "of crucial importance", since if it fails, further opportunities for informal interaction which would have revealed other facets of personality, interests, etc., *will not be sought*. A newly met person of the opposite sex might offer considerable potential as someone who is highly desirable with compatible values. However, in disregarding opportunities for further contact, a potential dating partner would never be able to find this out. Thus it would appear that physically unattractive individuals are at a considerable disadvantage in the dating and marriage marketplaces.

Chronically love-shy men have an unusually strong penchant for physical beauty. To be sure, virtually everyone loves beauty. However, one of the most significant findings of the study upon which this book is based is that beauty is quite a bit more important to the love-shy than it is to the non-shy. My findings further suggest that the love-shys' very strong need for beauty constitutes one of the several major reasons for their remaining shy and without the regular companionship of a woman. This attribute of the love-shy is so important and so little recognized that I decided that a separate chapter of this book should be devoted to the subject.

This need for beauty which the love-shy feel is very strong as well as highly generalized. And it extends to such things as dogs, automobiles, music, natural scenery, as well as to women. And it clearly suggests a major reason as to why most love-shy men could never be really well satisfied—particularly since their own level of physical attractiveness tends to be at least somewhat below average.

One of the older love-shys was telling me about his very strong love for dogs. He lived in a small apartment with three dogs: a Golden Retriever, a Standard Poodle, and an Afgan Hound. I was mentioning to him about how dog ownership commonly provides many single people with outstanding opportunities for easily meeting and talking with attractive humans of the opposite sex. Yet a memorable feature of my interview with him was how he "absolutely despised" all "ugly" dog breeds such as the toys, and those with turned-in snouts, such as the Boston Terrier, Boxer, Bulldog, etc., those with large heads, such as the Chow Chow, those with asymmetrical appearances such as the Basset Hound and Dachshund, etc. In short, even amid the world of dogdom, this avid but chronically love-shy dog lover could only bring himself to like or appreciate the *beautiful* breeds. To quote him: "It just boggles my mind how anyone could possibly want to own a Bulldog or a Boston Terrier; those things are uglier than puke! I love dogs, but they've got to be beautiful! I'd sooner own a cat than even look at any of those ugly breeds."

Fortunately for this chronically love-shy man, it is usually possible for people to *choose* their breed of dog, their type of automobile, their brand of music, etc. If a person has the appropriate purchasing power, he is free to make any and all of these decisions irrespective of how shy he might be. On the other hand, neither money or education nor anything else of a tangible nature can ever be used to "purchase" the love and companionship of a beautiful woman.

The Need for Beauty

As I have indicated, the love-shy men studied for this research very seldom or never dated. They were all far too shy to assert themselves with women, and particularly with women whom they found attractive. However, they desperately wanted to date and to spend all of their time with just one opposite sexed partner whom they could love. Being deprived of the very thing which they had always wanted more strongly than anything else, they tended to fantasize and daydream to a far above average extent. Daydreaming has long been recognized as constituting a vicarious form of wish-fulfillment. And in being unrestricted in terms of what they envision for themselves, frequent daydreamers tend to be quite unrealistic in terms of what they expect pertinent to feminine pulchritude.

I asked each respondent: "Compared to other teenagers at the time you were a teenager, were fantasies and daydreams *more* OR *less* important to you?" And *zero percent* (nobody) of the non-shys indicated that daydreams and fantasies were *more* important, compared to fully 87 percent of the older love-shys and 61 percent of the younger love-shys. In contrast, 32 percent of the non-shys thought that daydreams and fantasies had been *less important* to themselves than to most others of their age. Only 2 percent of the younger love-shys and *zero percent* of the older love-shys thought that daydreams had been less important to themselves than to most other young people. The remaining respondents checked "daydreams were neither more nor less important to me than to most others of my age and sex."

The fantasies enjoyed by these men typically entailed being warmly loved by very feminine, nurturant, non-assertive but liberal-minded women with long hair, beautiful faces, and very little or no make-up. They tended to fantasize women with a rather delicate, ethereal beauty, and with a gentleness and vulnerability that is not realistically likely to be found in today's world.

But curiously, most of the younger love-shy men seemed to maintain a sense of optimism that they could or would somehow one day magically be able to win such a specimen without taking any positive steps on their own initiative. Their fantasies and daydreams revolved almost exclusively around the imagery of already having such a beautiful woman. Virtually none of the shy men ever spent any time visualizing themselves taking positive steps to introduce themselves or to otherwise allow themselves to become acquainted with available and accessible women. Clinical psychologists often recommend that shy people engage in mental rehersals in their mind's eye. The 300 love-shy men studied for this book engaged in a great deal of daydreaming; but almost none of this was directed towards the actual solving of their love-shyness problems vis-a-vis real, live, accessible women.

A key theme of this chapter is to suggest that "real, live, accessible women" are not beautiful enough to meet the unrealistically stringent demands and needs of the love-shy. Simply put, the love-shy will not fantasize a female face that is not sufficiently beautiful to constitute a *wish fulfillment*.

As a case in point, I asked each man to respond to this statement: "I would much rather not date at all than date someone whose face is insufficiently attractive to please my esthetic and romantic sensibilities." Fully 98 percent of the older love-shy men agreed with this statement compared to only 49 percent of the non-shy men. Among the younger love-shys, 74 percent agreed.

Of course, 49 percent is itself a rather high figure. But as we shall shortly see, the non-shys were themselves well above average in physical attractiveness, whereas the love-shys were at least somewhat below average. People of great physical attractiveness tend to become involved with lovers who possess approximately similar levels of attractiveness, whereas those of lower levels of attractiveness will, everything else being equal, gravitate towards lovers with lover levels of physical attractiveness. The love-shy men realized this natural principle intuitively and often intellectually; *but they could not accept it emotionally*. And this may be a key reason behind their love-shyness and their avoidance of women who *might* otherwise have been realistically accessible to them.

A further illustration of this uncompromisingly romantic attitude of the love-shy can be seen in the pattern of response to this statement: "I would not want to date anyone to whom I could not visualize (fantasize) myself as being married." Fully 64 percent of the older love-shys together with 46 percent of the younger ones *agreed*. In contrast, only 4 percent of the self-confident non-shy men saw fit to agree. Again, most love-shy men would like to somehow magically bypass what many of them perceive as the cruel indignity of dating, and just somehow wake up one morning married to the esthetically lovely, beautiful girl of their dreams.

An even better example of the dramatically different ways the shy and the non-shy think can be seen in the pattern of results for this question:

> Assuming that you were able to get along with both *equally well*, which of the following two girls would you rather marry?
> A. girl whose face is (to you) extremely beautiful, but with whom you have a very mediocre sex life;
> B. A girl whose face (as you see it) is on the plain side, but with whom you enjoy a consistently terrific sex life.

Zero percent (nobody) of the self-confident, non-shy men selected the girl with the beautiful face, whereas 49 percent of the younger love-shys together with 73 percent of the older love shy men selected the girl with the beautiful face over the one providing the consistently terrific sex life.

Hence, the need for a girl with a beautiful face tends to be far greater among love-shy men than it is among non-shy men. In fact, for most love-shys it is probably accurate to assert that the need for a girl with an esthetically pleasing, beautiful appearance dominates over all other needs. More succinctly, most love-shy men are prone to subordinate the desirability and importance of other feminine attributes (including those related to personality) to those which pertain to physical (and especially *facial*) beauty. Again, love-shy men seem to need women with long hair, beautiful oval faces, little make-up, and youthful appearances. And indeed, the need for a *young* girl poses additional problems for the severely love-shy *older* men in their late 30s and 40s.

A good illustration of the sometimes quite uncompromisingly rigid tastes in feminine beauty that are so prevalent among the love-shy can be seen in the following quote from a 23-year old love-shy man:

"One thing that really pisses me off about some of the women on this campus is when they cut their hair. There are a lot of women around who are really pretty. I can recall a few who I used to even daydream about a lot. And then one day they appear in class with their hair all cut short and they expect all their girlfriends and everyone else to lavish praise on them for their new hair style. I get so mad at these times I could just throw up! I mean somebody ought to tell these women the God's honest truth—that their new hair style makes them look worse than shit! Then maybe they'd grow their hair back and look pretty and romantic the way they should. I think it's really a rotten sin when a formerly pretty girl wrecks her appearance by having her hair cut. I've seen a lot of girls around here go from actually being very attractive to being totally ugly—and all because they had their hair cut. I especially despise the so-called duck tail cut on a girl. Whoever invented such a hair style for a woman ought to be shot! It totally robs a girl of her femininity and it really looks worse than shit as far as I am concerned!"

One 21-year old love-shy man expressed his feelings this way:

"I'd love to have a really wonderful sex life with someone. But look at it this way. You can only have sex just so much. I always dreamed of having a girl I could really enjoy looking across the dinner table at. Let's face it: a person spends a much, much larger portion of his life eating than he does having sex or doing just about anything else. I keep thinking how wonderful it would be to be able to have a really pretty face to look at all the time, and to know that she'll always be with you no matter what. I know that if I could get a girl with a really pretty face and long hair to love me, I'd easily remain loyal to her forever."

Another extremely shy 45-year old virgin wistfully recounted this story:

"It may seem strange for me to say this. But I really wish I could be made not to care about pretty faces and physical attractiveness in women. If somebody could just hypnotize away my need for a girl with a pretty face I would really jump at the chance. I've had several bad memories that still haunt me with guilt. Let me tell you about one thing that happened to me back in November of 1964. I was 26-years old at the time, and I had finally gotten up enough nerve to meet girls through a computer dating firm. They would send me names, addresses and phone numbers. I didn't have enough nerve to use a phone; so I would write to them and arrange meetings that way.

Well, they paired me up with this girl who I think really liked me. I remember she was living alone in New York, and she was from

Kearney, Nebraska. I took her to the show at the Radio City Music Hall, and then we went to a Howard Johnson's restaurant where we had sandwiches and a long conversation. I remember her apartment building was down near Canal Street somewhere, and I remember taking her back there on the subway. She didn't seem to want to leave me, and she asked me at least three or four times when I'd be seeing her again. She asked me to come into her apartment, and that she was going to make hot chocolate. I told her that I'd call her again soon; but I knew I never would because she just didn't have a pretty enough face. Her hair was long enough for me, and she was thin enough. But her face just wasn't pretty enough.

I hadn't begun to think much about that incident until a few years ago. I mean I can count on the fingers of just one hand the number of girls in my whole life who invited me in or said they wanted to see me again. It's not that she was ugly. Actually, she wasn't bad looking. It's just that I've always had this dream that haunts me night and day. I've always dreamed about having a girl with a really beautiful, romantic face. If that girl had only had the right looking face, I'm sure I would be married to her today. I mean the only reason why I could not call her again was that her face just didn't fit the face in my dreams. If she had been exactly the same as she was, but with a really pretty face, I know I would not have been too shy to call her again. I know I could have easily called her an unlimited number of times. It's just that I couldn't see myself marrying someone who did not have a really romantic looking, pretty face."

Clearly the foregoing case is very sad; but it is also very typical of the past experiences of many of the older love-shy men. More succinctly, this quote demonstrates that the very powerful psychoemotional need for a lover with a pretty face constitutes *one of the several major reasons* why these men are remaining (against their wishes) "single, never married", and without female companionship well into their late thirties and forties.

A further point alluded to in the foregoing quotation is that the love-shy tend to feel more comfortable and they tend to converse more fluently when they are in the company of a less-than-beautiful girl than when they are with the type of girl who is so attractive that marriage to her is immediately visualized and envisioned. In essence, the closer a girl comes toward meeting a love-shy man's tastes and predilections in the physical (*especially facial*) attractiveness department, the more shy and inhibited he is likely to be in his efforts to converse with her.

As a final example of this highly romantic, beauty-oriented attitude of the love-shy, I asked each man to react to the following: "I would never want to experience premarital sex with anyone to whom I could not envision (fantasize) myself as possibly being married at some future time." I offered *three* alternative answers, one of which was "true because I would never want to have premarital sex at all." But this third alternative was very unpopular among all three groups of men. Only 6 percent of the older love-shys selected it, along with 11 percent of the younger love-shys, and *zero percent* of the self-confident non-shys.

Hence, the love-shy do not appear to be particularly averse to premarital sex or to premarital cohabitation. Thus, with this fact in mind it is illuminating to note that *fully 94 percent* of the older love-shys agreed with the statement compared to only 19 percent of the non-shys. The younger love-shys were in-between with 68 percent agreeing. On the other hand, *none* of the older love-shys said "false", whereas 21 percent of the younger love-shys and 81 percent of the non-shys indicated "false".

In other words, non-shy people tend to be emotionally capable of socially interacting with all kinds of women, even up to and including the point of full sexual intimacy. The more severely and chronically love-shy a man is, the more averse he is likely to be to even the mere thought of having sex with someone who does not please his esthetic and romantic sensibilities. Indeed, the most extremely shy men do not even wish to go out on informal dates with women who do not meet their esthetic and romantic expectations.

Again, these findings do not reflect any moral conservatism among love-shy men as far as the premarital sex issue is concerned. Love-shy men *do want* premarital sex, and they fantasize having it a very great deal. But they only want to have it with the esthetically beautiful girl of their dreams. The more non-shy a young man is, the less discriminating he is likely to be in this regard. And this is why very self-confident men are likely to experience premarital sex with a wide variety of different women, including many whom they would never even dream of marrying.

In sum, love-shy men tend to be much more demanding and more unrealistic in their requirements pertinent to the physical attractiveness factor than non-shy men. They tend to be uninterested in the idea of even casually dating a girl unless they are able to visualize themselves married to her. And in order for them to visualize a girl as a marriage partner, she must possess the usual "long hair, pretty face, trim figure, etc." syndrome.

And so the love-shy would rather not date at all than date someone who does not incorporate these characteristics. Most love-shy men would not allow themselves to even dream of having sexual intercourse with anyone who did not possess them. The only physical characteristic upon which the love-shy might be construed as being somewhat *less* demanding than the non-shy is that of *breasts*. Most of the love-shys in both groups indicated that they were turned off by large breasted women.

They tended to prefer women with small-to-medium sized breasts, comparatively thin legs, and thighs, and trim figure. This finding did not surprise me inasmuch as psychologists have known since the late 1960s that introverts tend to prefer small-breasted women, whereas extroverts tend to prefer those with large breasts. In fact, there appears to be a rather strong statistical relationship between how extroverted (outgoing) a man is, and how large he wants the breasts of his female partner to be.

Whereas extroverts tend to be governed first and foremost by the *attractiveness of personality* factor, breast size is typically the first specifically physical factor they notice in a woman. In the case of the love-shy the face is invariably the first and foremost physical feature of a woman to receive focused attention. It must be pretty (no make-up), and it must have long (straight or tousled) hair, with no complex or fancy hair styles. When the love-shy do look beyond the face, the second item likely to capture their attention is the legs/thighs (which they like thin), followed by the rear end, which they like small and well-rounded. Very unlike the extroverts, breasts are not noticed by them at all, unless the breasts are viewed as being too large.

Of course, as the man in one of the above interview excerpts pointed out, people spend a great deal more time eating than they do having sex. As most love-shys see it, if a man cannot enjoy being able to gaze romantically across a candle-lit dinner table at a young, beautiful face with long hair, there is really no point at all in getting married or even in bothering to date. This is the quite rigid, uncompromising nutshell essence of the way most severely love-shy men think and feel.

In essence, the love-shy (for whatever reasons) expect too much! Indeed, even if they were attractive men themselves, their expectations might still be considered by any reasonable person as being "too much"! Of course, in most cases the love-shy are *not* attractive—a fact which renders their situation vis-a-vis the opposite sex even more impossible for them. Let us now examine why.

The Love-Shys' Own Esthetic Attributes

Sad though it may indeed be, most areas of social life proceed on the basis of an equality of exchange. Unless a man has something special to offer such as fame, an unusually high income, artistic talent, outstanding interpersonal skills, sense of humor, etc., he is likely to have to settle for a woman of an attractiveness level similar to his own. Of course, an unattractive man can choose not to marry, and to find satisfactions in other areas of life. He can also endeavor to *compensate* for his plain appearance by becoming unusually effective at interpersonal skills, sense of humor, etc. As we have seen, love-shy men cannot bring themselves to *"choose"* not to marry. And the mere thought or upgrading their social finesse arouses in them far too much painful anxiety.

I asked each of the 500 respondents several different questions about their looks. Perhaps the most basic and representative of these simply asked each man to rate his own physical attractiveness along a ten-point scale, with *"0"* representing the ugly end and *"10"* representing the extremely handsome or beautiful end. The average or mean score for the 200 self-confident non-shy men was 7.36, whereas for the 300 love-shy men (older and younger ones combined) it was 5.17.

I was frankly somewhat surprised that the mean score for the non-shy men was as low as 7.36. But, of course, this figure as an average score suggests that most of the non-shy men do not have delusions of grandeur about their purely physical qualities. In essence, the non-shy men had been able to develop healthy self-images and strong interpersonal skills quite in spite of their less than perfect looks. The love-shy had not been able to do this. Indeed, the average to somewhat below average looks of the love-shy merely served to aggravate and to depress even further their low self-confidence relative to the mere thought of asserting themselves in a friendly manner vis-a-vis attractive women.

Some of the other questions I asked pertinent to physical attractiveness yielded considerably greater differences between the non-shys and the love-shys. For example, I asked each man: "During your teen-aged years how did you tend to rate your overall physical attractiveness?" Fully 65 percent of the older love-shys along with 61 percent of the younger ones rated their teenaged physical attractiveness as having been "below average". In contrast, not one single man among the 200 self-confident non-shys similarly rated his attractiveness as a teenager that poorly. Indeed, 53 percent of the non-shys rated their attractiveness as a teenager as having been "above average". Only 5 percent of the younger love-shys and *zero percent* of the older ones rated themselves similarly.

Inasmuch as attractiveness during the teenaged years may be important for helping young people get off on the right foot in terms of social self-confidence and positive self-esteem, I deemed it important to ask a quite related question in another part of the questionnaire. Occasionally, questions dealing with similar matters yield disparate results. However, this certainly did not happen regarding this matter of self-assessed past physical attractiveness.

I asked each man to react to the statement: "When I was between the ages of 12 and 16, I think I was a good deal less attractive than most others of my age and sex." For reasons I am not sure of, the wording to this question yielded lower self-evaluations than did the wording to the earlier question. Nevertheless, the self-confident non-shys still rated themselves as having been considerably more attractive than did the two love-shy groups. More specifically, 25 percent of the non-shys agreed that they were indeed less attractive than most other young people at ages 12 through 16; but 68 percent of the younger love-shys and a whopping 74 percent of the older love-shys similarly thought that they had been less attractive than most other young people.

Of course, many people improve substantially in physical attractiveness as they mature and grow out of adolescence. But for individuals who start out with already weak egos and very low inborn anxiety thresholds, inferior physical attractiveness levels during the teenage years may leave an indelible mark upon the personality, even when objective physical attractiveness improves substantially as young adulthood is entered. More succinctly, attractiveness level as a teenager may represent one of the key factors which get people used to looking at themselves in a certain way. If a person starts out feeling considerably less attractive than most others, that negative self-feeling may have considerably greater "staying power" than it would have had if it had originated later in life as opposed to during the highly formative years of adolescence.

Again, these points must be taken into serious consideration if we are to deal with love-shyness in a constructive, effective fashion. If (1) a person considers himself to be a good deal less attractive than most others of his age and gender, and if (2) *that same person* has a much stronger need for a physically attractive love partner than most others have, then quite clearly that person is asking for (and indeed *requiring*) far more of a potential partner than he can give in return.

To be sure, less-than-attractive men *can* successfully win beautiful women as life-long lovers; indeed, this happens all the time. But these less-than-attractive men almost invariably have a great deal to offer in terms of warmth, interpersonal skills, charm, and positive self-esteem— the very attributes which the love-shy so severely lack. Money, high status career, and education, can also serve as compensators. But as I shall document in a later chapter, career, money, *and especially an extensive education* usually fail quite miserably to attract women. It is only when these attributes *combine* with strong social self-confidence, sense of humor, positive self-image, etc., that they can and often do occasionally work to enable a less-than-attractive man to compensate for his less-than-handsome looks.

Moreover (and this is the shocker from the standpoint of the love-shy), if a man *lacks* a good education, high status career and financial wherewithall, he may still be able to win the girl of his dreams if he has the strong social self-confidence, interpersonal finesse, positive self-esteem, and sense of humor. And this is so even for a man whose looks are less than ideal!

Beauty and the Older Love-Shys

The strong need for a beautiful marriage partner creates a near-impossible situation for the *older* love-shy men. The process of aging does not appear to cause the love-shys to lose much of their strong and uncompromising need for a woman of etherial beauty and youth. Some of the older love-shys justify their need for a youthful woman by what they consider to be their God-given human right to procreate children of their own. However, I suspect that even if children were not an issue these men would still absolutely require youth and beauty in a marriage partner.

Because the older love-shys themselves have so little to offer from the standpoint of personality, charm, and handsome looks, the older they become the poorer their chances are likely to be of ever getting what they want. And on a semiconscious level many of them realize this. The following interview segment illustrates the despair which many of the older love-shys don't even allow themselves *to feel*—a despair from which they try to emotionally disassociate themselves.

> "When I was in college it was impossible enough for me to attract any women whose looks appealed to me. Now—Jesus Christ!—look at me! I'm worse off now than I had ever dreamed I'd be back then. My hair is rapidly disappearing. I mean I'm balding and I can't do anything about it. The little hair I do have is turning grey. And even though the doctors tell me I'm not overweight, I have this big pot belly. Jesus Christ! What can I do? I'd still do anything to get myself a really beautiful girl. My feelings on that haven't changed one whit over the past 25 years. But I guess I stand about as much chance of marrying a pretty woman as a damned cockroach does! That's why I have all these video tapes here. See—I can at least watch these and get some of my needs taken care of. It helps me to forget the way things actually are." (49-year old love-shy man.)

A particularly interesting "adaptation" to this state of affairs made by 14 percent of the older love-shys was that of membership in foreign correspondence clubs. One man volunteered that he was carrying on an active correspondence with three different Mexican girls, all 20 to 25 years younger than he. None of these girls could even write in English. He had to translate each of their letters from Spanish to English. Yet he maintained a fantasy that the whole endeavor was worthwhile because their photographs appeared satisfactorily "pretty" to him. This man had never actually traveled to Mexico to meet any of the women with whom he was corresponding. Even so, all three of the girls had hinted quite broadly in their letters at their interest in marriage, particularly to an American.

Mexico was not the only country to which some of the love-shys were corresponding. Such countries as Taiwan, Japan, Hong Kong, Philippines, India, Pakistan, and Sri Lanka, were also on the list. The fantasy of all of the men engaged in this type of correspondence was that it might somehow be easier to impress an attractive foreign girl who may be strongly desirous of gaining permanent entry into the United States. Several of the men implied that the *only* way they felt they had any chance at all of "getting" a truly attractive woman might be through one of these foreign correspondence clubs.

> "Well, the way I look at it they've got something I want—pretty faces (he holds four photographs up to my face). And I've got something they all want. They all want to become American citizens. I mean with American girls I haven't got any chips to bargain with—especially any American girl who is really pretty and young enough. Like I said, I couldn't marry anyone who wasn't pretty and young. I have to be turned on with my eyes of else I couldn't make a move. I don't know! I've got a fine education. But university degrees are like used toilet paper to American women. You just can't impress an American woman. I wish I could, but I can't. So I'm hoping I can get something going with one of these foreign girls." (48-year old love-shy man.)

What will ultimately develop as far as these correspondence "romances" are concerned is anybody's guess. Suffice it to say that none of the men carrying on these letter-writing campaigns had ever actually met any of the girls. Despite that fact, several of them were spending a large number of hours every week engaged in this type of correspondence. The process of writing to a stranger is evidently a very time consuming and difficult one.

Clothing

I asked each man to react to the statement: "Clothes don't seem to look as well on me as they do on most others of my age and sex." And 64 percent of the older love-shys along with 53 percent of the younger love-shys *agreed*. In contrast, *none* of the 200 non-shy men saw fit to agree. Indeed, 77 percent of the non-shys insisted that the statement was definitely "false" as far as they personally were concerned, whereas just 4 percent of the older love-shys and 7 percent of the younger ones said that it was "false". The remaining men indicated "uncertain".

As part of any viable campaign to prevent or cure love-shyness, clothing needs to be taken into account as an important consideration. The old cliche that "clothes make the man" may represent somewhat of an oversimplification. But those ignoring the inherent wisdom behind this cliche stand to miss out on one of the easiest and least anxiety-provoking steps toward the amelioration of love-shyness. Clothing is something that is within the capacity of virtually all people to control as they wish. This is surely as true for love-shy people as it is for those who are self-confident and socially successsful.

Despite the quite substantial importance of good grooming in our society, I was frequently appalled by the dull, drab colors, old-fashioned styles, and wrinkled garments which many of the love-shy men wore. Simply put, the non-shy men interviewed for this book both dressed and groomed themselves *very noticeably better* than the love-shy men did. And the non-shys tended to smell quite a bit better than many of the love-shys did. (See the chapter on "medical symptoms and the love-shy" for a discussion of the hyperprespiration problem.)

To put it succinctly, most love-shy men need a great deal of gentle but authoritative guidance, instruction, and unobtrusive supervision pertinent to the ways of good grooming, clothing purchase, color matching, hair styling, etc. A person may be somewhat limited in terms of what he can do with the face and body with which he had been born. But there are very few limits on any person in the area of grooming, clothing, etc.

Cloning as a Future Option

While it is quite true that love-shy people need to be helped towards the most propitious maximization of what they've got, I think it is *equally true* that research needs to be stepped up on ways of assuring maximum physical attractiveness to everyone right at the outset of life. In recent years numerous social scientists have been able to convincingly demonstrate that physical attractiveness *does count* in terms of a person's overall life chances. Indeed, it counts *heavily*, and it counts almost as much for males as it does for females.

It has been found, for example, that highly qualified but homely men are less likely to be hired for various business jobs than only moderately well qualified but very handsome men. In a University of Michigan study a large number of men were divided up into three different groups based upon adjudged level of handsomeness. There was the most handsome one-third, the middle one-third, and the least attractive one-third. Fake resumes were constructed for the least handsome one-third in order to make them appear to be by far the best qualified job candidates. Resumes for the *most* attractive one-third were tailored to make each candidate appear adequately qualified but far from outstanding. In addition, the least attractive one-third of men were given an intensive training seminar in how to groom and to interview successfully for the particular jobs which they were after. The most handsome men were given no such training.

In spite of all of this, almost three-fifths of the men hired were from the most attractive (handsome) one-third. (If pure chance had been operating, only 34 percent of the most handsome one-third would have been hired.) Only 11 percent of the men hired were from the unusually well qualified but *least* handsome one-third of men. (Again, if pure chance had been operating, at least 33 or 34 percent of the *least handsome* men would have been hired.)

In short, even on the employment scene wherein males are typically evaluating males, *looks matter.* And the higher and more prestigious the position, the more they matter. Every business and industry is concerned with good public relations. And as any American who watches network television news reports knows, handsome faces draw handsome crowds and *win* at the ratings game!

Over the years many fascinating studies on the influence of physical attractiveness have been conducted by elementary educators. For example, teachers tend to evaluate their more attractive pupils more highly than they tend to evaluate the less attractive but equally intelligent ones. Moreover, this positive bias favoring the attractive students has been found to apply just as strongly when women teachers evaluate girl students and when male teachers evaluate boy students, as it does when teacher-pupil evaluations are cross-sexed in nature.

Many studies have shown that handsome/pretty faces are customarily seen by people of all ages (and levels of attractiveness) and by people of both genders as being more (1) honest, and (2) intelligent. Honesty and intelligence are highly valued characteristics in our society. And positive biases regarding these matters can significantly affect life chances. Undoubtedly the "self-fulfilling prophecy" comes into play here. In essence, *when we come to define certain things or ideas as real, those things or ideas tend to become real in their consequences.* If a moderately intelligent but unusually handsome person is treated as being exceptionally bright, he is likely to very soon become exceptionally bright—because of the way he is treated by everyone.

Studies of dating and courtship have similarly underscored the supreme advantage of being esthetically attractive/handsome. Young people of both sexes often give lip service to the proposition that *personality* is the most important factor determining whether or not they will want to date a person for a second time. However, actions speak louder than words! And several studies involving computer dances on university campuses have documented the fact that for *both women and men*, perceived level of physical attractiveness of the date is the *number one* determinant as to whether additional dates with the same partner will be sought or desired. If a date is seen as "pretty" or "cute", etc., then even serious shortcomings of personality as well as partner incompatibility are often overlooked. The physical beauty/handsomeness sets up a kind of "rosy colored smokescreen" so that such deficits are not even noticed or reflected upon. Simply put, an attractive person enjoys positive social stimulus value. And as such he/she is the one who is most likely to be enthusiastically sought out as a dating partner.

There are no easy answers to the physical attractiveness problem. It seems clear that the only way this issue could be fairly resolved would be to work out a way whereby *everyone* can be born with the same very high quality level of physical (especially facial) attractiveness.

Whenever I bring this issue up with my students, I invariably receive the rejoinder that each and everyone of us has his or her own tastes in beauty; and that what pleases one person may not please another. However, in recent years a great deal of evidence has been marshalled which indicates a remarkable amount of agreement among Americans and western Europeans as to what is beautiful and what is not. In fact, studies have shown that people of all ages and of both genders tend to employ pretty much the same criteria in judging physical and facial beauty. Moreover, people of all ages and of both genders tend to agree almost completely in terms of how they would rank order a large number of photographs in terms of facial beauty/handsomeness.

The *cloning of human beings* may constitute the only truly fair and ultimate answer to the physical attractiveness problem, and to the unfairness of the fact that we are not all born alike in terms of level of beauty/ handsomeness. One 23-year old love-shy man expressed it this way:

> "If the cloning of human beings could be made socially acceptable, every boy no matter how shy he is, could be guaranteed a really beautiful girl with long hair and a pretty face to make love to. Nobody would ever have to be left out because everyone would have the same high quality looks. Each man would also be extremely good-looking, no matter how shy he is. In fact, I don't think that a really shy guy could stay shy for too many years—because he'd see that

he's just as good-looking as the really aggressive guys, and the girls would be coming up to him. I think that fact alone would ultimately give him a real boost in self-confidence. I mean, the girls would be just as likely to approach him as they would an assertive guy. Everyone would be able to have sex with somebody as nice as the girls in their daydreams."

Because some readers may be somewhat uncertain as to what *cloning* is, I want to define and explain it briefly and succinctly. Simply put, cloning is a procedure that would permit the full and complete duplication of the body of a specific human being. It is a process that would be tantamount to "xeroxing" a particular person's body.

For example, suppose that a couple wanted to have a boy by clonal reproduction. And suppose that they wished for their son to look exactly the same as the father when he grows up. In this case the husband would go to his doctor and have several cells removed from his arm or, perhaps, from the inside of his cheek. These cells would be examined under a microscope, and a particularly healthy-looking one would be picked out. The doctor would then remove the selected cell's nucleus, and then place that nucleus into one of the wife's egg cells. Of course, the nucleus of the wife's egg cell would first have to be removed, after which the nucleus from the husband's cell would be placed in its stead.

Finally, the physician would implant this doctored cell into the wife's uterus wherein nature would be allowed to take its course. Thus no sexual intercourse would be involved in reproduction by cloning. In cloning, the ovum cell is *"fooled into thinking"* that fertilization has taken place. Hence, it proceeds to divide and to subdivide until a totally new human being is formed whose body is a carbon copy in every detail of the person from whom the original nucleus had been taken.

Curiously there is some controversy as to whether or not it is now possible to clone a human being. In 1978, David Rorvik published a book entitled IN HIS IMAGE: THE CLONING OF A MAN, in which an alleged case of human cloning was detailed. Most scientists insist that this was a fictionalized account. However, inasmuch as most Americans oppose the idea of cloning, the case investigated by Rorvik had allegedly been completed in full secrecy. Both the family of the cloned man and the scientists who allegedly accomplished the cloning process wanted their privacy to be fully assured.

I asked each man studied to provide me with his reaction to this statement:

"When cloning of humans becomes readily available it will be just about the most wonderful scientific advance in all of history because from that point onward no girl would ever have to be born non-beautiful and no boy would ever have to be born non-handsome or without an appropriately assertive temperament; and there would still be hundreds of thousands of bodies to choose from, so people would not all be born alike."

Fully 46 percent of the older love-shys together with 34 percent of the younger love-shys agreed with this statement, compared to *only one percent* of the self-confident non-shys. On the other hand, 70 percent of the non-shys indicated *strong* disagreement with the statement. Only 32 percent of the younger love-shys together with 18 percent of the older love-shys similarly indicated *strong* disagreement.

Most of the objections to cloning centered around either (1) religious values, or (2) fear that cloning would result in the standardization of human beings. However, I sensed a third (3) factor which may be of equal importance. Cloning is not in consonance with the vested interests of already attractive persons. Under conditions of near-universal cloning, an already attractive man would have less basis for experiencing a feeling of superiority and victory for having won the love and affection of a beautiful woman. This is because *all men* would be winning equally attractive women. And this would be due to the fact that all women would be of the same very high level of physical attractiveness. And, lest we forget, all men would similarly be of the same very high level of physical attractiveness.

As for the fear that cloning would make everyone look the same, it needs to be stressed that there is a *virtually infinite number of possibilities* for high levels of physical beauty or handsomeness. Just as all people now have unique looks (and we can easily tell people apart except for the occasional pair of identical twins), all people can rate a high "10" on the beauty/handsomeness scale and still have looks which are entirely unique. Again, there is an infinite range of possibilities for beautiful faces. Mother nature could never run out of possibilities in regard to this matter.

Of course, during the first two or three centuries after the cloning of humans first becomes available, the range of facial and physical styles would necessarily have to be a good deal less than infinite. But people would still be able to tell each other apart very easily. For example, when a woman wished to have a baby, she and her husband would go to a special store—something like a wallpaper store. In a wallpaper store customers are shown books loaded with hundreds of wallpaper samples. The young couple desirous of a child would similarly be shown books loaded with tens of thousands of photographs of available bodies. If a couple wished to have a daughter, they would be shown the girl books; if they wished to have a boy, they would be shown the boy books.

Each of the 100,000 or more photographs for each gender would be cued to a particular laboratory located somewhere in the United States or western Europe. If a couple decided that they wanted to have *Girl #96,125*, they would be directed to that particular lab wherein hundreds of cheek cells from that particular very attractive woman are waiting. Simply put, the nucleus from one of those cells would be inserted into the wife's denucleated ovum, and she would have a baby daughter who would grow up to look exactly like the body of the woman that they had picked out in the book loaded with photos.

During the first century of so of this procedure, the ovum would develop inside the wife's body, and pregnancy would progress just as now. The only difference is that the wife would be rendered pregnant through the cloning process instead of via sexual intercourse. Two or three centuries from now, on the other hand, it will doubtless become feasible for a baby to grow to term in a factory uterus—outside the wife's body. Inasmuch as factory conditions can be standardized, the chances for a perfectly healthy baby would be greater than they ever could be if the baby were to be carried inside the mother as now. Inasmuch as humans will be able to have babies without going through a pregnancy, women will be able to preserve their youthful beauty for significantly longer periods of time. And they will also be able to fully avoid the pain and suffering that has always been integral to the pregnancy and childbirth process.

At the present time most people seem to have strong objections to research activity that would lead us toward being able to efficiently clone human beings. Of course, people have always tended to fear that which they do not understand. Most people fear that cloning would remove the uniqueness and individuality which today represents each person. However, if a human being is *not* his or her body, if a human being is fundamentally *spirit* and *NOT* body, then cloning would quite clearly *not* remove the individuality and uniqueness which are so important to each one of us.

For example, suppose that in a given year 200,000 Chevrolets *of the same model* were to be produced and sold to the public. Each of the 200,000 owners still considers himself or herself to be a unique person with highly individualistic tastes, talents, predilections, and ways of doing things. And, in fact, each purchaser *is* a unique individual.

The soul can be seen as being directly analogous to the automobile purchaser, whereas the human body can be seen as analogous to the automobile. The purchaser is free to keep and to drive his or her "vehicle" in any way that he or she chooses. There will always be a uniqueness about that because the purchaser (i.e., "*soul*") is unique.

How much better for all of us life would be if (metaphorically speaking) the *only* available vehicles were Rolls Royce vehicles and Mercedes vehicles, and the situation continued to prevail that everyone on the earth plane had to have a vehicle (physical body)! Why would anyone want to be stuck with a Toyota body or a Chevy body when he or she could just as easily own a Rolls Royce body or a Mercedes body?! To be sure, if the karmic lessons that a soul had yet to learn could *only* be learned through ownership of a Toyota body or a Chevy body, then that soul would be "out of luck" as far as incarnating onto this particular earth is concerned. That soul would have to be born on some other less highly evolved "earth" in some other solar system.

The analogy isn't perfect because, unlike models of Rolls Royces or Mercedes, there is a virtually infinite number of possibilities for the perfect human body. There is an infinite number of possibilities for beautiful faces and for beautiful bodies, just as there is an infinite number of possibilities for ugly bodies and for bodies with low native intelligence, and shy, inhibited inborn temperaments.

The reader should think for a few minutes about how much better the quality of life would be for each one of us if *everyone* could be born with such attributes as a beautiful face, gorgeous physique or figure, high native intelligence, a pleasantly outgoing but not-too-aggressive (bullying-prone) temperament, etc. With such an optimal combination of traits everyone would be at a propitious advantage from the standpoint of developing a healthy self-image, social self-confidence, and enjoying a high level of happiness and productivity throughout life.

And most importantly, everyone would be able to date, court, make love with, and marry someone whose appearance thoroughly pleases even the most demanding esthetic tastes and predilections. Everyone's body would be beautiful, and yet everyone's body would appear totally unique. Love-shyness would be a thing of the past, as would such conditions as chronic illness, short longevity, and physical aggressiveness (bullying). Simply put, I would assert that there is no area of research that is of more enormous importance from the standpoint of promoting and improving man's ultimate chances for supreme health, happiness, productivity and evolution, than research into the cloning of human beings.

Of course, most of the foregoing is based upon the assumption that the soul (eternal sense of consciousness and of self) enters the body at birth and not at conception. To an increasing extent contemporary scientists are veering towards the viewpoint that conception merely triggers off an electromagnetic energy force field which commences to gradually shape and build a body (shell) which will ultimately be inhabited by a person if it (the fetal body) is seen through to term. In essence, conception causes the creation of (1) the physical body, and (2) the etheric (electromagnetic force field) body. *At birth* the soul joins with the physical and etheric bodies to create a new person. Again, if the only available bodies are "10s", then all of the awaiting souls *must* choose such high quality bodies.

Hypnosis

Inasmuch as unrealistic expectations regarding feminine pulchritude constitute one of the main stumbling blocks impeding the love-shy from getting what they sorely want and need, hypnosis may hold some possibilities as a means toward bringing these unrealistic expectations into line. The major problem inherent in pursuing this tactic is that love-shy men tend to be unusually difficult to hypnotize. The love-shy tend to maintain a very robust, rigid set of defenses. In order for hypnosis to work, the person receiving the treatment must have the emotional capacity to place these defenses in abeyance.

Most love-shy men would gladly submit to hypnosis, especially if they felt that it would remedy their inhibition problems vis-a-vis women. Thus, from an *intellectual* standpoint the love-shy tend to believe in hypnosis; and they tend to be quite enthusiastic about its potentials as a therapeutic modality. However, from an *emotional* standpoint they tend to be *non*-acceptant of it. Love-shy men tend to have very little control over the emotional side of themselves. Unfortunately a person cannot ordinarily be hypnotized unless and until he is capable of accepting hypnosis on *both* the emotional and the intellectual levels. In fact, accepting hypnosis on an emotional level is actually of far greater importance from the standpoint of ultimate success than is the idea of accepting it on a purely intellectual level.

Because of its controversial nature, very few professional therapists have undertaken to learn hypnosis. Hence, there are far fewer people truly competent at administering hypnosis than are actually needed by society. Aggravating the problem is the fact that only about one professional hypnotherapist in twenty is capable of hypnotizing virtually anybody to the point of a deep trance. And a deep trance is what would be required in order for viable and effective help to be delivered to the love-shy.

A solution might be for such professional groups as the American Medical Association and the American Psychological Association to renounce their biases against educating as many new clinicians as possible into effective hypnotherapeutic techniques. If more people in the helping professions endeavored to learn hypnosis, there would eventually be a higher ratio of available practitioners who could hypnotize truly difficult but intellectually willing subjects—such as the love-shy. In addition to lowering the love-shys' requirements in terms of feminine beauty, hypnotherapeutic techniques might also help towards enabling the love-shy to calmly handle their anxiety fears. Indeed, hypnosis might even hold some possibilities (for at least *some* love-shys) from the standpoint of preventing interpersonal anxiety attacks and "people-phobia" altogether.

Accentuating the Positive

As getting the love-shy to cut back on their wants may be unrealistically difficult, a more potentially productive course of action might be to teach them ways of upgrading their own attractiveness and desirability vis-a-vis the opposite sex. The love-shy can certainly be taught (1) good grooming and dress habits; (2) exercise and diet; and (3) interpersonal skills together with a positive mental attitude. People who *appear* neat, well-dressed, and happy, are invariably perceived by others as being a good deal more attractive, "cute", handsome, etc., than they *actually* are. On the other hand, people who usually appear "down in the dumps", unkempt and dischevaled are likely to be perceived as being *less* attractive (handsome) than they *really* are.

Of course, simply "knowing" these truths could never prove sufficient to upgrade a very low self-image, or to transform a negative mental attitude into a positive one. Because the intellectual part of man is much weaker than the emotional part, any cognitive awareness of truth must be backed up by active participation in appropriate social-emotional support groups. Alcoholics, drug addicts, child abusers, gamblers, overeaters, homosexuals, etc., all have their support groups. Support groups operate in such a way that intellectual insights can be capitalized on by all members. Support groups provide that needed element of warmth, friendship, and caring, that is indispensable to propitious growth and change.

Love-shys do not have any support groups. And in this regard I would suggest the development of an organization that might be called *Shys Anonymous*. Patterned after the Alcoholics Anonymous model, Shys Anonymous would be composed of shy persons of both genders and of all ages. Through a host of organizational activities significant help together with positive motivation would be provided for its membership. The services of professional counselors could also be retained on occasion for purposes of facilitating group interaction, psychodrama, therapeutic role playing, etc.

Shys Anonymous would provide important reinforcement for positive behavior and dress patterns. Its membership would display genuine caring and concern for each other—something which most love-shys never experience throughout their formative years, from either parents or peers. Just as homosexual organizations provide true and meaningful friendships for their members, Shys Anonymous would provide an important source of caring friends to the heterosexual love-shy.

The concept of "Shys Anonymous", like that of the "Coed Scouts", is a very important one. And I shall have a good deal more to say about it in the therapy and prevention chapters (Part Three) of this book.

Summary

Whereas love-shy men tend to be somewhat less good-looking than most non-shys, they tend to be significantly more demanding than most non-shy men in terms of wanting and needing a very beautiful girl. Whereas most non-shys enjoy meeting and dating women of all types, the love-shy only want to meet and date women to whom they can visualize themselves married. And the crux of the matter is that most love-shys cannot visualize themselves married to anyone who does not have long hair, a pretty face, and a youthful trim figure.

If a terrible accident were to suddenly blind the love-shy, they might actually stand a substantially improved chance of ultimately getting married. In essence, normal eyesight may actually constitute a liability for many of the love-shys because it obviates their getting close to women who could easily become potential mates. Love-shy men tend to be inordinately governed by the need for esthetic beauty in a mate.

> "Well, a number of people have told me that my expectations are unrealistic. I used to live in the dorm, and the guys there used to tell me that there were a lot of girls around who would probably go out with me if I only asked them. They used to tell me that the girls I was really interested in were all too far above me, and that I should try to start conversations with girls who were more plain in appearance.
>
> Well, anyway, I'd be willing to do it if I could visualize myself getting turned on by one of these plainer girls. I've always wanted to get married. But it just isn't worth it if looking at the girl's face and body doesn't make you want to make love to her. With a plain girl it would be just like going through the motions, sort of like a machine. I wouldn't be able to really feel anything at all. And I don't see why the pretty girls should be considered above me. I have a 3.5 average;

that's better than any of the guys who are dating pretty girls manage to do." (20-year old love-shy man.)

Up until now this strong penchant that the love-shy have for physical beauty has been given virtually no research attention. A key purpose of this chapter is to convince the reader that the physical attractiveness needs of the love-shy constitute a very major reason as to why they have remained chronically love-shy and without any major drive towards asserting themselves in a friendly way with women. If the love-shy could be helped to emotionally accept women of a wider range of physical attractiveness characteristics, their problems might stand a good chance of being healed.

Chapter 13

The Sexual Lives of the Love-Shy

The major purpose of this chapter is to contrast the sexual lives of the love-shy men with the sexual lives of the self-confident non-shys. Things are seldom what they seem. And I decided that it would be a mistake to assume that love-shy males are completely inactive from a sexual standpoint. To be sure, they *are* quite totally inactive from the standpoint of both heterosexual and homosexual love-making. As a matter of fact, 62 percent of the younger love-shy men and 36 percent of the older love-shys had never been out on so much as *one single date* with a girl in their entire lives. And none of the remaining men (not even the ones with membership in commercial dating services) had ever averaged more than four dates per year.

Hence, all of the love-shys studied for this book were *quite virginal*! And none had ever had any homosexual inclinations or leanings. However, there are sexual outlets other than those which involve *people* of *either* gender.

Masturbation

On a self-administered questionnaire which was privately filled out by each man, I asked: "Generally speaking, about how many times *per week* do you ordinarily masturbate these days?" And 85 percent of the older love-shys indicated that they currently average two or more ejaculations per week via masturbation. The average for these 35 to 50-year old virginal men was 4.18 ejaculations per week experienced through the various modes of sexual self-stimulation.

In spite of their considerably more youthful age, only 67 percent of the younger (university age) love-shys indicated that they usually averaged two or more ejaculations per week via masturbation. The average for this 19 to 24-year old group was 3.19 ejaculations per week via masturbation.

In stark contrast, *none* (zero percent) of the self-confident non-shys averaged two or more ejaculations per week via masturbation. In fact,

58 percent of the non-shys told me that they *never* masturbated at all. Only 3 percent of the younger love-shys and zero percent of the older love-shys similarly indicated that they never masturbate. Parenthetically, the average number of ejaculations averaged per week *via masturbation* by the non-shy men studied for this book was only 0.35.

Of course, the self-confident non-shys as a group were quite sexually active with women. I therefore asked each of the non-shy men how often *per week* he had sexual intercourse. And the average for the 200 non-shy men was 3.5 copulations per week.

Now this may seem like a lot; but the really interesting and socially significant comparison among these three groups of men is that which pertains to average *total* weekly outlet. In essence, what happens when average number of weekly ejaculations via masturbation is *added* to average number of weekly ejaculations via sexual intercourse, for each one of the three samples of men?

Simply put, the older love-shys come up with a *higher overall average* than do the 200 highly self-confident non-shy 19–24-year old men. In particular, the average for the non-shy group was just 3.85 ejaculations weekly, whereas the older love-shy men averaged a whopping 4.18 ejaculations per week! Of course, none of the love-shys' ejaculations involved actually being with anyone on an objective level. But on a purely subjective level all of these love-shy men had been deeply involved in romantic fantasies incorporating being wrapped up in the bodies of highly attractive women.

At 3.19 ejaculations per week, the younger love-shys were evidently the least sexually active of the three groups. And yet even this 3.19 figure can be considered somewhat high by comparison with what usually prevails for the typical, sexually active college or university student. For example, college and university men engaged in premarital cohabitation are known to average with their lovers only 2.5 copulations per week. And allowing for additional masturbatory activity, it seems improbable that their total weekly average would be a very great deal higher than the 3.19 (ejaculations per week) figure belonging to the younger love-shy virgins.

Love-Shyness and Sexual Desire.

Of course, the key point to be recognized here is that love-shy men are very far from being "disinterested in sex" or in any way incapable of having erections. In fact, at least one researcher believes that he has uncovered physiologically-based evidence indicating that love-shy men may have *somewhat stronger sex drives* than self-confident non-shy men.

That researcher is Hans J. Eysenck of the University of London. And his evidence points to generally stronger and more urgent sexual drives among men whose native temperament places them in the first (melancholic) quadrant of the Eysenck Cross of Inborn Temperament (see *figure one* on page 41), than among men whose temperaments are less nervous and less introverted.

Specifically, the *high versus low anxiety threshold* ("emotionality") dimension has been found by Eysenck to be fairly strongly related to sexual drive, whereas the introversion-extroversion dimension has been found to be generally unrelated to sexual drive. In other words, extroverts and introverts do not differ from one another in terms of strength and urgency of sexual drive. However, people with low anxiety thresholds (high on "emotionality") do tend to have substantially stronger sexual urges than those with high anxiety thresholds (low on "emotionality").

What this means is that BOTH very shy people (*emotional introverts*) AND very aggressive, extroverted, nervous and unstable people tend to have stronger than average sexual urges. The latter group of men can usually be predicted to release these urges in sexual promiscuity and in very frequent sexual activity with their wives and lovers. Very love-shy men, on the other hand, can be expected to display their strong sexual urges in an unusually high rate and frequency of solitary masturbatory activity.

And this is exactly what I found to be the case for most of the love-shy men interviewed for this book. As a group the love-shys tended to average a greater number of orgasms per week than the highly self-confident non-shy men, including even those who were premaritally cohabitating with a lover. The love-shys manifested their highly charged sexual drives in frequent masturbation, whereas the non-shys manifested their more normal or "moderate" sexual drives via regular sexual intercourse at the rate of about 3.5 copulations per week. (Again, the older love-shys averaged 4.18 orgasms per week, *all* through solitary masturbation.)

The problem for the love-shys is that frequent masturbation does not provide for a very satisfying sexual or emotional life. Of course, it is *not* the masturbation itself which causes the unhappiness and emotional turmoil. The problem emerges from the fact that men who masturbate a very great deal usually do so because their fears and anxieties prevent them from making contacts with women and from cultivating emotionally meaningful relationships with them. None of the love-shys seemed to feel any guilt about their masturbatory activities. And none seemed to be influenced by any of the ancient myths surrounding masturbation. But all felt severely frustrated by the fact that they were not living up to their true and loving potential. In essence, being without a woman made them all unhappy and dissatisfied.[1]

By the way, masturbation among university aged young people has been found by a number of psychologists to relate to emotional adjustment and mental health very differently for females than for males. For example, young men who masturbate three or more times per week tend to be unhappy, nonsociable, shy, and rather poorly adjusted. Among college age females, on the other hand, such behavior has been found to reflect very fine mental health, non-shyness, assertiveness, high levels of sociability, social spontaneity, self-confidence, happiness, and androgeny of attitudes and values.

Felt Deprivation Creates Preoccupation

When a person is deprived over a very long period of time of something which he dearly wants, that person is highly likely to become preoccupied and even obsessed with the thing of which he has been deprived. This is a long-standing tenet of the science of psychology. And I believe that it may explain, at least in part, the unusually high frequency of masturbation among the love-shys. Love-shy men tend to be extremely interested in sex. They have books on the subject and copies of PLAYBOY and PENTHOUSE magazines strewn all over their apartments. And many of them have color photographs of attractive women (both nude and clothed) hanging all over their walls. In spite of their high rate of premarital sexual intercourse, I did not observe anywhere nearly as much of this sort of thing in the living quarters of the non-shy men.

In essence, sexual preoccupation can be seen as being reflected in frequency of masturbatory activity. And it is certainly very often reflected in the frequent need to read about sex or to gaze upon the pictures of attractive women. In contrast, those whose sexual appetites are fairly well satisfied tend to have little need to read about the subject or to admire the photographs of inaccessible women.

Degree of Satisfaction with Sex Life

I asked each of the 500 respondents to rank the overall extent of his satisfaction with sexual life on a scale ranging from "0" to "10". I indicated that a ranking of "10" would represent a very high level of satisfaction with one's sexual life, whereas a ranking of "0" would represent extreme dissatisfaction. The *average* ranking for the 100 older love-shy men was only 0.85; and for the 200 younger love-shys it was a mere 1.57. In stark contrast, the average for the 200 self-confident non-shy men was 8.61. Hence, in spite of the love-shys' very high rate of mastubatory orgasms, their general level of satisfaction with their sex lives was vastly lower than that of the non-shy men. Again, the older love-shys were averaging more orgasms per week than the non-shys. Evidently the very fact of frequent involvement in love-making *with a woman* tends to be far more closely related to sexual satisfaction than the number of orgasms or ejaculations experienced on a per week basis.

In a related question I asked each man to rank how satisfied he felt with his sex life along the following seven-point scale:

1. makes me very happy;
2. makes me moderately happy;
3. makes me slightly happy;
4. neutral;
5. makes me slightly unhappy;
6. makes me moderately unhappy;
7. makes me very unhappy.

Here again, the differences between the love-shy men and the non-shy men were quite substantial. The average ranking for the self-confident non-shys was 1.36. In stark contrast, the average ranking for the older love-shy men was 6.71; and for the younger love-shy men it was 6.07.

I also asked each man to rank himself on the *same seven-point continuum* with regard to his feelings of satisfaction pertinent to "being in love and being loved". Not surprisingly the differences between the love-shys and the non-shys remained just as great as they had been in regard to the "sex life" issue. More specifically, the non-shy men averaged 1.71 on "being in love and being loved", whereas the younger and older love-shy men averaged rankings of 6.29 and 6.97, respectively.

Sexual Values and Attitudes

As I have indicated, all of the love-shy men studied for this book were virgins. All were quite totally lacking in experience from the standpoint of any and all forms of sexual expression other than masturbation and related sexual self-stimulation activities. Yet strangely enough the *attitudes* and *values* of the love-shy men pertinent to sexual matters were surprisingly normal and "modern". In fact, they were quite typical of those held by unmarried American males generally. Further, the love-shys' sexual attitudes and values might even be regarded by some readers as being demonstrably on the "liberal" side. And this represents further testimony for the fact that *behavior does not always reflect attitudes*—especially as far as love-shy males are concerned. Let's look at a few examples of this.

I asked all respondents to react to the following statement:

> "Monogamous, loving, contraceptively protected premarital sexual intercourse should be considered fully socially acceptable for all people 18 years of age and older."

Fully 86 percent of the non-shy men together with 91 percent of the older love-shys agreed with this statement. The younger love-shy men were the most conservative of the three groups with only 79 percent agreeing.

In fact, only 6 percent of the older love-shys and 11 percent of the younger ones would *never* personally want to have premarital sex under any circumstances. The analogous percent for the non-shy men was *zero* (nobody). Yet in spite of this seeming liberality and sexual tolerance, *zero percent* of the 300 love-shy (older and younger) men approved of casual or promiscuous premarital sexual activity. Thus none of the love-shys looked at all favorably upon "one night stands", sex with call girls, pick-ups, prostitutes, or sex with someone after less than two months' acquaintance and steady friendship. In contrast, 73 percent of the self-confident non-shys could accept some casual or "promiscuous" premarital sex—especially that which might involve pick-ups, "one night stands", and sex with a dating partner after having known her for less than two months.

Questions pertinent to premarital cohabitation tended to meet with a positive response by all three groups of men. Approximately 85 percent of all three samples approved the idea of monogamous premarital cohabitation as an integral part of courtship; and most of these men would eventually like to engage in it themselves. In fact, 38 percent of the non-shy men *were* premaritally cohabiting at the time they were interviewed for this book; and 53 percent of the non-shys had already premaritally cohabited with a girl at some point in their lives.

However, the attitudes of the love-shy men towards premarital cohabitation were substantially more romantic than those of the non-shy men. Most of the non-shys indicated that they would be enthusiastic about cohabiting with *any* willing girl. On the other hand, the love-shy men of both groups would only wish to premaritally cohabit with someone with whom they were already deeply in love and who was sufficiently physically attractive (e.g., "long hair and pretty face") to turn them on visually.

In another interesting attitude item I asked each respondent to react to this statement: "A teenager should normally be free to entertain his best friend of the opposite sex in his bedroom at home without parental supervision." Fully 71 percent of the non-shy men together with 84 percent of the older love-shys agreed with this statement. The extent of agreement among the younger love-shy men was 69 percent.

On the other hand, this controversial statement gave rise to almost no differences among the three groups of men who were studied for this book:

> "Teenagers should have a thorough knowledge of contraception and should be free to freely and guiltlessly obtain it through medical sources without parental knowledge if and when they decide to engage in premarital sexual intercourse."

Only 6 percent of both the non-shys and the younger love-shys *disagreed*. Disagreement among the older love-shy men was limited to only 4 percent.

Moral Liberality versus Conservatism

In an effort to assess the extent to which the respondents were "absolutists" or "relativists" as far as their views of "morality" were concerned, I decided to gauge each man's opinions regarding this "relativistic" definition of morality: "Any behavior is moral and *non*-sinful except that which impinges upon the happiness and well-being of our fellow human beings." The *older* love-shy men were the most accepting of this position with 77 percent of them endorsing it. The self-confident non-shy men were second in line with 69 percent endorsing it. The younger love-shys were the most conservative group: just 63 percent indicated agreement with the statement.

Another statement of considerable interest to which each man reacted was the following:

> "Some have spoken of our changing views regarding sexual behavior as being indicative of *moral deterioration*, while others have spoken of this as being indicative of *moral change*. Still others have referred to it as *moral evolution*. Please check the position which most closely approximates your own point of view:

Moral deterioration;
Moral change;
Moral evolution."

On this statement the *younger* love-shys fell somewhat "out of line": 28 percent of them checked "moral deterioration", compared to only 6 percent of the non-shys and 10 percent of the older love-shys. For the "moral change" option there was virtually no difference among the three groups: it was checked by 36 percent of the younger love-shys, by 37 percent of the non-shys, and by 38 percent of the older love-shys. "Moral evolution", on the other hand, was checked by 57 percent of the non-shys, by 52 percent of the older love-shys, and by 36 percent of the younger love-shys.

I also asked for reactions to this political statement: "Some bathing suit optional beaches should be made available for people who enjoy being nude outdoors." Again, the similarities among these three groups of "single, never married" men turned out to be far more striking than the differences: 87 percent of the non-shys together with 89 percent of the older love-shys indicated *agreement*. Agreement was similarly indicated by 85 percent of the younger love-shy men.

To be sure, if any of the foregoing statements were to be read to a group of middle-class parents residing in the suburbs, the level of expressed liberality ("permissiveness") would doubtless be substantially lower than that which obtained for these three groups of "single, never married" men. However, this book is geared towards the goal of understanding the problems of severely love-shy single men. And this can only be accomplished by comparing such chronic love-shy singles with singles who are *not* love-shy. Obviously, there would be nothing to be gained by comparing them with middle-class parents who reside in the suburbs!

Hence, a key conclusion to be drawn from these data is that there are very few *if any* significant differences between non-shy single men and love-shy single men as far as attitudes toward human sexuality are concerned. Simply put, conservative or prudish sexual attitudes/values appear to have no bearing at all on why or how the love-shy got to be the way they are. Severe love-shyness cannot be explained by sexual values.

By the way, one of my colleagues recently suggested that the love-shys might have been better off if social forces had led them to embrace conservative sexual values. Love-shy men don't get any coital sex anyway. And if they were conservative they could join up with a conservative religious group which might help them meet a girl. As of the late 1970s and early 1980s, fundamentalistic religious groups were doing much better than the more moderate to liberal "mainstream" churches in attracting and holding young people, and particularly attractive young women.

Unfortunately, love-shy men tend to be quite disinclined towards joining anything! They are particularly disinclined towards the idea of joining (or even remaining near, for more than a few minutes) any group with any semblance of zealous militancy, or any group that endeavors to standardize personalities, appearances, and value systems through moralistic and/or militaristic intimidation. Love-shy people tend to associate any kind of zealousness and/or militancy with *bullying*. And the love-shy sustain a deep loathing for any and all kinds of bullies, including those who might be operating in the service of what fundamentalists might construe to be Jesus Christ.

On the other hand, it appears that most love-shy men *might* be amenable—if they were both literally and figuratively *taken by the hand*—to joining moderate to liberal "mainstream" churches such as Presbyterian, Episcopalian, Congregational, Disciples of Christ, Reformed Judaism, Christian Science, Spiritualism, Religious Mind Science, etc. This is a complex and important issue which I shall deal with more fully in a later chapter.

Unusual Sexual Directionality

In a study of this nature I realized that it would not be possible to obtain absolutely certain, completely valid data on the most intimate aspects of the men's sexual lives. Throughout the many months of data collecting which this book required, I was constantly gratified by the extent of willing and often gracious cooperation that I received. And I did not want to press my luck too far with this group of highly sensitive, love-shy men. I knew that this was to be a study of love-shyness, not of sexuality. And I did not want to risk the sort of problems that might have surfaced had I asked many in-depth questions pertinent to sexual history. My only major concern was to make certain that each man studied was heterosexually oriented as opposed to homosexually oriented, and that each of the love-shys was a virgin. And I am quite satisfied that I succeeded well in this regard.

However, it is known that prolonged deprivation of female companionship often gives rise to unusual erotic penchants, even among heterosexually oriented men. Among the 300 love-shys interviewed for this book only three *openly and conspicuously* revealed any unusual fetishes. Some of the other love-shys may similarly have had unusual fetishes without wanting to discuss or reveal what they were. Each of the men choosing to discuss unusual erotic penchants belonged to the ranks of the older love-shys.

For example, a 36-year old love-shy man became amazingly open with me about the fact that he often took his golden retriever to bed with him. When I first began my interview with this man he was quite reticent and somewhat tentative in many of his answers. But as the interview wore on he began to open up in a way that suggested the possibility that years might have passed since anyone had ever shown any personal interest in his life or in his interests and opinions.

The reader should understand that this man *did not prefer* his golden retriever to his fantasy of ultimately having a beautiful human girl friend with whom to go to bed. In fact, he insisted that holding his golden retriever in all sorts of intimate sexual embraces made it easier for him to fantasize being with a girl. On one level his behavior had an almost comical touch to it. He called his dog by the name of "Sextimus", and related to it while I was there as though it were a human being. He fed the dog expensive cuts of meat and other human foods. And when he took his "Sextimus" to bed he had a regular ritual in which he would systematically wash its snoot and paws so that it would be "in sanitary shape" for "making love".

During much of the time this interview was being conducted this man and his retriever were lounging upon a large, king-sized bed. He was only partially clad, and at several points he unhesitatingly kissed his "darling little Sextimus" right on the mouth! The more excited his thought processes became in response to various interview questions, the more ostentatiously tactile he became with his dog. It was as though the dog had become a combination emotional support and security blanket to him, and he just couldn't let go of it.

The second man was a 38-year old commercial artist who kept a large and beautiful collection of expensive barbie dolls on conspicuous display throughout his apartment. In addition, he had a large collection of doll clothing that most surely would have been the envy of any prepubescent little girl.

> "Whenever I feel really lonely I get one of my prettiest dolls and I take her to bed with me. Like sometimes I'll take off all of my clothes and I'll have three or even four dolls there with me, and before I know it my tuutuu (sic) will get really hard. I especially like the silky little dresses that some of my dolls wear. They feel so sexy to the touch. I only wish (he starts blushing) that one of my dollies could just magically turn into a real live girl!"

This man may have occasionally gone beyond the using of barbie dolls as catalysts for masturbation. His bedroom contained two human-sized female mannequins, both of which were fully clad in brightly colored dresses. At one point he intimated that he had paid in excess of one thousand dollars for one of these two oversized dolls. Both of them were obviously among his most cherished possessions.

The third man did not reveal his unusual erotic penchants during the course of the interview. Three weeks after being interviewed for this research this 39-year old man mailed to me (the researcher) a lengthy letter in which he described his strong coprophiliac interests. Too shy to discuss the matter face-to-face with anyone, he nonetheless indicated that he was strongly desirous of someone from the scientific community learning about his case.

Specifically, from the time this man had been a child he had always had a strong sexual fascination with his bowel movements, especially when they "come out real long and soft". And on those occasions when he had a bowel movement of the "right" feeling and texture—an event which he claimed happened only about once every couple of months—he would become "uncontrollably aroused" from a sexual standpoint. Using vegetable oil "to enhance the effect", he would roll the bowel movement around in his hands, sometimes for several hours; and he would enjoy several ejaculations while in the process of doing this. He would save his "nicer poopoos" in plastic bags, sometimes for several days. And at several points during this time span he would pick his bowel movement out of the plastic bag and begin getting sexually recharged again. During the course of this behavior he would fantasize being with a "really beautiful young girl" who had "long hair and a pretty face" and who "also liked long, soft, beautiful oozie-goozies".

This man worked as a high school biology teacher, and had earned an M.S. in his discipline. In spite of his unusual behavior and fantasy life, he appeared to be in sufficiently adequate contact with reality to be able to competently handle his job. Thus, he had regularly maintained his coprophiliac interests, fantasies and behaviors throughout his life, and had been having orgasms inspired by the holding of beautiful "oozie-goozies" since his earliest teen years. His unhappiness issued from his being totally without female companionship as well as from certain obvious inconveniences which his sexual penchant had created for him. Thus, he had always been afraid to go to the toilet at work or at school for fear that he might "take an unusually beautiful oozie-goozie" while he was away from home, and thus suffer "severe sexual trauma" because he might not be able to "pick it up and fondle it."

Fending Off Unwanted Overtures

As extremely passive people, some of the love-shy men had had difficulties in fending off homosexual strangers who had wanted to become involved in sexmaking activity. None of the respondents had ever been to bed with a homosexual. But several had experienced difficulties on busses or subways or in other public places. Typically an óverly aggressive homosexual would (1) misperceive the love-shy man as being a homosexual, and (2) that overly aggressive homosexual would persistently move his hand onto the love-shy man's crotch area. Rather than becoming sexually excited by this, the love-shys would characteristically become extremely nervous and upset. They would perceive the overly aggressive homosexual as "just another aggressive, extrovert bully", and they would change seats or make some concerted effort to just get away from him.

In at least one situation recounted by a 20-year old love-shy man, getting away was not so easy to accomplish.

"Well, this happened during the week between the end of the spring quarter and the beginning of the summer quarter. I didn't want to go home because I figured it just wouldn't be worth it for only one week. So I stayed in the dormitory. Anyway, one night I left the student union building after having some refreshments, and I started walking back to my dorm room. All of a sudden this guy comes up to me and starts acting really friendly. He said he had just come down here from Eugene, Oregon, and was lonely and wanted to meet some people. There was something about him I didn't like; but I couldn't put my finger on anything except his very hoarse, raspy voice. I had often been lonely myself; so I didn't want to seem unfriendly. Anyway, he invited himself into my dorm room, and everything was okay for the first fifteen minutes or so. But then he asks me to remove one of my shoes. I thought that was a strange request, but I did it for him. And he held the shoe up really close to his eyes. I thought he was straining to read something in it. Anyway, next he asks me to take my socks off; and then I knew something was fishy! All of a sudden he rushes down and takes my socks off. He holds them up to his nose real hard. And I was shocked. I didn't know what to say or do. Then he grabs my foot and holds that real hard up to his nose and puts it in his mouth! I start screaming; but I was really worried because I knew there weren't many people around who could hear me. This guy starts grabbing me and trying to force me on to my bed. I don't know how I did it, but I managed to grab for the door knob, and I managed to get it open. By that time the guy had ejaculated, and you could see all this stuff staining right through his pants. He had so much nerve! Believe me, that wasn't the end of him. He tried to get into my room on three more occasions before I finally saw the last of him. I mean he would stand outside my door sometimes for an hour at a time asking me to let him smell my feet. I couldn't even leave my room to take a leak because he'd be standing out there trying to get at my feet!"

Being Misperceived as Homosexual

Fully 97 percent of the older love-shy men and 58 percent of the younger ones claimed that they were often mistakingly perceived by people as being homosexual. For many of the older love-shys this misconstrual was an almost daily occurrence. People who saw them regularly would begin to notice that they are never with anybody. As a result of never being seen in the company of a woman, acquaintances in their apartment building or dormitory would begin to suspect homosexuality; and some of these people would occasionally become quite overt in the manifestation of their suspicions.

University students who never date and are never seen in the company of women are often publicly labeled "fag". And there are evidently many people of both sexes who automatically assume that any man remaining unmarried and without the companionship of a woman past the age of 30, must be homosexual.

Many of the love-shys interviewed for this book could remember receiving a steady barrage of ego-castigating name-calling from the time they were young children in the earliest years of elementary school. Many young children use such disparaging names as "fag" and "queer" and "fairy" and "faggot" without even knowing what the literal denotations and meanings of such words are. And many of the love-shys could vividly remember hearing these words shouted at them when they were merely eight or nine years old.

Of course, nonconforming children of the male sex receive all sorts of verbal hazing and name calling. However, even when the love-shys grew old enough to learn the true meaning of some of these disparaging labels, they never thought seriously for any length of time that they might actually be a homosexual. To most of the love-shys, being labeled a "homosexual" was nothing more than just one more reflection of the fact that no one truly understood them or appreciated them, or were even willing to try. Furthermore, some of the love-shys perceived these false labels as merely reflecting the gross stupidity that they saw as being characteristic of all bullies.

Many sociologists believe that a consistent exposure over a long period of time to a particular disparaging label—such as "homo" or "fag" or "fairy"—will result in the internalization of that label, and the consequent transformation of the labeled person's self-image. According to this theory a teenager who is frequently labeled a "fag" by many different people on a daily basis should in time actually become a "fag"; and he should begin behaving like a "fag" with all of a normal fag's sexual predilections and fantasies. This quite popular *labeling theory* obviously did not prove valid for any of the 300 heterosexual love-shys who were studied for this book. And the fact that all of the disparaging homosexual labeling had failed to have any effect (in terms of creating a desire to experiment with homosexual behavior) provides a strong argument in support of the proposition that true homosexuality is *inborn*.[2]

Most of the love-shys simply ignored the majority of the name-calling to which they had been subjected during their formative years. As children physical bullying had bothered them a great deal more than verbal hazing. But presently as adults most of the love-shys were very much bothered by the quiet whisperings and intimations behind their backs that they are homosexually inclined. To the love-shy men these whisperings and negative glances represented proof that they had no real control over the way they were "playing themselves" on the great "stage" of life. It represented proof that they were not *commanding their performance* in accordance with their wishes, values and desires—that they were not now and never had been truly in the *driver's seat* of their own lives and destinies.

And in this way the love-shys felt themselves to be worse off than most homosexuals. In manifesting a homosexual ambiance, most homosexuals are only being true to themselves. To be sure, in American society there is a heavy price to be paid for being a homosexual. But a true homosexual can at least pay the price (if he *must* pay it) with the knowledge in mind that he is at least playing his "true self" in the "drama of life". In stark contrast to the homosexual, the heterosexual love-shy man (especially after he passes the age of 30) is often required to *pay the price* for being something that he is not. In short, he often has to pay some of the price of being a homosexual (1) even though he knows he is *not* a homosexual, and (2) without being able to enjoy any of the rewards and emotional securities that come with being (and accepting oneself as) a homosexual.

Being Misperceived By Homosexuals

Just as love-shy men are often misperceived as homosexuals by heterosexual men, a great many of them are also misperceived as homosexual by homosexual men. Many of the love-shys spoke of having been frequently importuned or befriended by homosexual men. This must evidently happen quite a bit on university campuses because the younger love-shys seemed to have the greatest number of stories to share. And most of the situations that had happened to the older love-shys had similarly occurred during their days as university students.

None of the situations the love-shys shared with me had been traumatic or seriously anxiety-provoking. There are evidently very few overly aggressive homosexuals. In fact, most of the homosexuals discussed in the interviews had simply wanted to make a friend. And in approaching a lonely, love-shy heterosexual, the homosexuals had doubtless believed that they were approaching someone who belonged to their element. Of course, some of these homosexual men may not have been specifically after sex as their major goal. Some of them may simply have noticed areas of conspicuously similar interests (e.g., music, the arts, etc.) between themselves and the love-shy heterosexual men they approached in an effort to befriend.

> "Yes, there was this one guy I really felt sorry for. This happened three years ago when I was a freshman. I was really innocent then. I didn't know anything. Like now I would certainly know that this guy was a homosexual. But at the time this occurred, the very idea 'homosexual' had never even crossed my mind.
>
> Well, this guy always ate alone in the dorm dining hall. And I always ate alone too. One day he came up to me and asked to join me. And I was only too happy to ask him to sit down with me. He seemed like a nice guy; and we had a lot of interests in common. Like, he went to the movies a lot, and we both liked the same kinds of music. Anyway, after chatting with him several times in the dining hall, he invited me to go out to dinner with him. He was a senior; and even though he obviously wasn't popular, I was still flattered. So I went.
>
> Well, about half way through the meal he brings up his sexual preference. I was really dumbfounded because, like I told you, I had never heard very much about homosexuals, and I certainly had never met one before. I mean, he wasn't pushy or anything. Like I said, he was really a nice guy. I really felt sorry for him because he obviously was lonely just like I was. I remember he was really surprised and sort of incredulous when I told him that I didn't know what he meant when he said he was a homosexual. He was really surprised that I wasn't a homosexual because he said that I showed all the signs. But like I told him about how I had always dreamed about being with a girl, ever since I was a first grade kid in elementary school. I mean, being with a girl was my constant preoccupation. And I remember feeling guilty because I was dreaming about being with a girl even as I was eating dinner with him! I shared my feelings with him about how I was always dreaming about certain girls on

campus whom I admired, and about how extremely shy I was. And I remember how he said that he was bored and could not relate to that.

Well, he said he was shy too. And he realized after all I had told him about myself that I really couldn't be a homosexual. Anyway, I offered to be his friend, but that I'd never be able to do anything sexual with him. Actually, I was somewhat surprised when he rather coldly turned me down. He told me that in view of my overwhelmingly strong interest in girls that it would really be better if we didn't see each other again. He asked me to keep our conversation strictly confidential. I remember that because he seemed rather concerned about it. Anyway, I agreed because I did feel sympathy for his position. And I didn't have any friends anyway I could go jabbering to. I saw him a lot in the dining hall after that. But we never again chatted. And he never even responded when I said 'hi' to him in the hallways." (22-year old love-shy man.)

However, not all of the love-shys abstained from friendships with homosexuals. In fact, the relatively few love-shys who had any meaningful friendships at all quite typically claimed that their best friend was a homosexual, or that they had enjoyed meaningful but quite non-romantic friendships with homosexuals in the past. In these cases there had never been any sexual interaction with the homosexual friend inasmuch as the latter had been fully capable of respecting the love-shy man's heterosexual tastes. However, in most cases these friendships gradually tapered off and died out without any ado. The following is typical of this pattern:

"For about three years my only real friend was a homosexual. Don't laugh, but I didn't even know he was homosexual until about two years into our friendship. We would always be going to movies and shows together, and when he moved away we corresponded regularly for about a year. I've visited his home a lot of times; and I always enjoyed listening to records with him. We both like Broadway show music; and both of us have large collections of really good show albums, many of which have been out of print for years.

Anyway, he finally confessed his homosexual instincts one night when we were in the apartment of this friend of his listening to out-of-print show albums. He kissed the guy on the lips several times with me right there watching. And after we left he discussed the situation. I told him there was no way I could practice any homosexual behavior. I told him that I didn't consider it sinful or wrong or anything like that—but that I was just emotionally turned off by it. Anyway, he said he had realized what my feelings were ever since he had first met me, but that he'd really like it if we could still be friends. As for myself, I liked him and I couldn't see any point in not seeing him anymore just because of his sexual preferences. I mean, he was the only friend I had, and his companionship was kind of important to me. I remember he could play the piano by ear, and I really envied him for that. I sometimes used to spend hours just watching him play the piano. But I'd always be dreaming that I was the one who was playing, and that there was a really beautiful girl there with me.

Anyway, after a while I started going more and more into my shell. I knew I wasn't being my real self. I never actually broke up with Kevin. I just stopped answering his letters—not because he's a homosexual. That part didn't bother me. If I had had a girl friend I was close to I would have done my damnedest to sustain my friendship with him because I really liked him and we shared a lot of interests. But I wasn't being my real self without a girl friend. And I knew I didn't want to be friends with anybody of my own sex until after I had found a girlfriend I could be close to. Heterosexual or homosexual, it didn't matter. I just didn't want to be around guys, *period*, until I could get myself a girl of my own." (24-year old love-shy man.)

On Envying Homosexuals

Even though none of the love-shys had any homosexual inclinations, almost half of them indicated that from time to time they felt quite envious of homosexual men and women. To be sure, they did not envy them for their sexual life styles and predilections; indeed, the mere thought of engaging in or even observing any homosexual activity revolted the 300 love-shy men with whom I spoke. What the love-shys did envy about homosexuals is that *homosexuals have a place to go.* And they are a recognized social category and a political force, whereas heterosexual love-shys are not.

There are innumerable "gay" social organizations, support groups, "gay" bars, "gay" baths, "gay" newspapers and magazines, and indeed even "gay" apartment complexes and "gay" clothing stores! In addition to all of these resources, the homosexual community incorporates numerous legal and psychotherapeutic organizations where free or quite inexpensive help can be obtained, and through which *meaningful companionship with like minds* can be experienced and enjoyed. Indeed, many of the larger cities today even provide "gay" churches headed by "gay" clergymen.

"Well, it may be hard for you to understand this, but a lot of the time I really envy the homosexuals. Sometimes I really wish that I were psychologically capable of being one because at least they have someplace to go. Do you know what I mean? They know who they are, and they can always find a sympathetic ear if they need one. There are places for them to go and organizations for them to belong to. There's nothing for the shy person who is not a homosexual. Myself, I'd even try being a homosexual. But even the thought of going to bed with a guy disgusts me. I don't think it's immoral or anything. It's just something that revolts me and there's no way I could bring myself to do it. But guys who can do it are sure as hell a lot better off than shy heterosexuals like me." (24-year old love-shy man.)

This feeling is quite commonplace among the ranks of severely love-shy men. Because the love-shy male lacks any social support systems, even the world of the homosexual often looks better than his own. In order to be happy and stable, all human beings require regular and active involvement in meaningful roles and relationships. Of course, not all homosexuals take an active part in the amenities that are available to them. There are love-shy homosexuals as well as love-shy heterosexuals, and the prevalence of such love-shyness may be no different amid the homosexual community than it is among heterosexuals.

Another reason why heterosexual love-shy men often envy homosexuals is that the latter are permitted to play the *passive role* in interpersonal relationships and in the game of seeking out a stable love mate. In short, the passive homosexual can still find love and love relationships quite in spite of his passivity. Much like a woman in the heterosexual community, the passive homosexual can simply go to a "gay" bar or a "gay" bath, or to some homosexual support group, and simply wait to be approached by potential lovers. He does not need to make the first (assertive) move himself. He is not constrained to take the initiative as a prerequisite for being accorded the right to have someone to love. Indeed, just like a woman in the heterosexual community, the passive homosexual man can place himself in a "gay" bar, and he can keep rejecting and rejecting and rejecting potential lovers until a potential lover comes along who strikes his fancy.[3]

In sum, heterosexual love-shy men are not recognized as representing any kind of a social category or political force with important needs worth attending to. There may indeed be far, far more heterosexual love-shy males in America than there are homosexuals. Yet because heterosexual love-shys appear to be an *invisible* group (because they create no conspicuous social embarrassments), their needs and their very existence normally goes totally ignored.

NOTES

1. The very high incidence of frequent masturbation among the love-shys quite clearly suggests that even very severe love-shyness is *not* associated with any fundamental inability to have an erection. In essence, love-shyness does not appear to be related to impotence.

2. The verbal abuse had doubtless acted essentially as a *self-esteem lowerer* rather than as a homosexual identity creator.

3. And, of course, an obvious reason why shy heterosexual men envy homosexuals is that for the latter there is a *congruence* between attitudes and wishes on the one hand, and behavior on the other. The homosexual has *chosen* not to marry and/or associate on an intimate basis with women. The shy heterosexual man has *not* chosen this sort of lifestyle and in fact hates it. Thus, the reasonably well adjusted homosexual enjoys free choice—something about which the shy heterosexual man can only dream.

Chapter 14

Love-Shyness and the Criminal Mind

At first glance love-shyness and criminality would appear to be poles apart. But as is so often the case, things are seldom what they seem! Stanford Univeristy professor Philip Zimbardo became an expert on life behind prison walls long before he launched his well-known investigation into the shyness problems of univeristy students. And one of the particularly intriguing conclusicns of his work was that many criminals are very shy.

Zimbardo sees shyness together with low social self-confidence and serious deficits in interpersonal skills as driving many people towards (and sometimes over) the brink of committing criminal acts. Crimes of violence both within and outside of the family, as well as rape, robbery, and political/religious extremism, are believed by an increasing number of criminologists to be due at least in part to a fundamental reticence about friendly, honest, open, sociable interaction. In fact, from the age of about eleven onward delinquent boys have been found by many researchers to have a very hard time making friends. And compared to non-delinquent boys, those running the criminal course tend to not even like very much the very few friends they do have.

Most severely love-shy men have similarly grown up to truly feel that no one really gives a damn about them. And, of course, if a person genuinely feels that nobody cares about his human needs and feelings, it is but a short step for that person to renounce any thought about caring for the needs and feelings of the other human beings in his environment. "Since nobody has ever cared about me, why the hell should I give a damn about anybody?" This is the nutshell essence of the psychopathic way of thinking. It is a very dangerous way of thinking, and it often gives rise to serious criminal conduct.

Intrigued with Dr. Zimbardo's thoughts on this matter, I decided to include some applicable questions on my own shyness questionnaire. The purpose of this chapter is to summarize my own findings on the possible relationship between love-shyness and the potential for criminality and/or violence.

Violent Fantasies

I asked each repondent: "Have you had fantasies during the past month in which you saw yourself as being very violent with some person or group?" Quite in spite of the fact that the love-shys were much more pacifistic and anti-war in their ideological belief systems than were the non-shys, it is most intriguing to note that fully 71 percent of the older love-shys and 66 percent of the younger ones answered "*yes*" to this question! And it becomes all the more intriguing when it is observed that only 12 percent of the self-confident non-shy men similarly answered "yes".

Moreover, with most of the love-shys these violent fantasies do not appear to be a recent thing. I asked each man to respond to this statement: "When I was a child between the ages of 10 and 15, I often had fantasies about taking violent revenge against some person or group." And fully 89 percent of the older love-shy men along with 66 percent of the younger love-shys agreed that this had been true for them. In contrast, only 47 percent of the non-shys similarly indicated that it had been true for them.

Violent fantasies appear to have been much more common among both the love-shys and the non-shys during childhood than now. Nevertheless, the interview data clearly suggested that such violent fantasies had been a much more commonplace, everyday occurrence for the love-shys. The non-shys tended to have violent fantasies in response to stimulating crime and western movies, television programs, and contact sports (while involved in the role of either participant or observer). On the other hand, the love-shys never watched contact sports either on television or in person at stadiums. In addition, they tended to avoid crime and western programs because they found them "too unromantic". Unlike the non-shys, their violent fantasies tended to crop up on a near-daily basis in response to bullying from peers and punitive interaction from parents in the home.

One 22-year old love-shy man shared the following with me as an example of a frequent, quite violent fantasy:

> "When I was 14-years old my parents forced me to go to camp for eight weeks. And there was this kid there who kept throwing rocks at me. Whenever he saw me he immediately stooped down to pick up a rock to throw. Every day this kid just made my life more and

more miserable. I tried to get the counselors to put a stop to it. But their disciplinary action against this kid met with only limited success. Anyway, I got to the point where I was planning strategies to bludgeon him to death while he slept. I kept dreaming about how I would sneak into his cabin at 3 in the morning while he was asleep. I'd have a really big rock—but not so big that I couldn't get a good grip on it. And I'd just hit him over the head as hard as I could as many times as I could. And then I'd sneak away. I kept thinking these things over and over, until just a few days before the eight weeks ended I actually had found the rock that I would use. And I kept it in my bed with me."

Several of the love-shys had frequent fantasies about how they would set fire to their parents' homes. These fantasies were all very much like the foregoing. The person saw himself sneaking into the garage at 3 o'clock in the morning and grabbing a container of gasoline which he would dump all over the living room and stairwells. These fire-setting fantasies were particularly commonplace among those love-shys who had received a great deal of corporal punishment at the hands of their parents.

As indicated in chapter ten, most of the love-shys had suffered a tremendous amount of bullying at the hands of their peers as they were growing up. And this is doubtless a key reason why they developed social avoidance tendencies and learned to find social isolation less painful than the physical and psychological abuse they had to sustain whenever they were around age mates.

Bullying

In view of this history of having been severely and frequently bullied, I decided that it might prove interesting to ask each respondent about the extent to which *he* had taken part in the bullying of others during the time when *he* had been an elementary school child. And I think it is instructive to note that fully 100 percent of *both* the older love-shys *and* the younger love-shys claimed that they had *never* taken any part in the bullying of anyone. In stark contrast, only 20 percent of the non-shy men claimed that they had *never* bullied anyone when they were in elementary school.

In essence, these findings would appear to suggest two things: (1) the love-shys had been very violent in some of their fantasies, with most of this fantasy violence directed towards their persecutors. But in terms of *actual behavior*, the love-shys had been far less violent and less cruel as children than the non-shys. Secondly (2), these findings would appear to suggest that "healthy" boyish development in American society quite commonly gives rise to quite a bit of cruelty and capricious violence against others. And, of course, this arbitrary and capricious bullying causes suffering which often leaves lifelong emotional scars.

Of course, having been the victim of so much violence and bullying throughout the formative years would be bound to have some impact upon one's thought processes. People who commit particularly bizarre, irrational crimes of violence are frequently those who had been quiet youngsters who never fought back and who always seemed to do what their teachers told them without overtly complaining. Criminologists have speculated that for some "Casper Milktoast" type personalities the pressures gradually build up over the years. And for some people with this type of personality the bubble eventually bursts and a particularly heinous, violent and bizarre crime ensues. Unfortunately, the problem for scientists is that they cannot as yet predict with any accuracy just exactly *which* "Casper Milktoasts" *will* at some later time explode and become dangerously violent. Most "Casper Milktoasts" *never* become violent. They simply seethe away inside and gradually develop a host of psychoemotional and physical ailments in lieu of eventually exploding with violence towards others.

Similarity to Child Abusers

The similarities between the backgrounds of the love-shy and those of certain violence-prone types are quite striking and deserve some comment. For example, consider what is known about men who severely batter and abuse their wives and/or children. Virtually all of the scores of research studies on family violence that were completed in the ten years from 1972 to 1982, point to the following five major antecedent factors differentiating violent husbands from non-violent ones: (1) social isolation; (2) poor interpersonal/communicational finesse; (3) stress; (4) low self-esteem along with strong feelings of personal insecurity; and (5) an extensive history of having been the *victim* of violence, especially vis-a-vis parents.

Now, in looking over the full range of data obtained for this research, it immediately becomes clear that love-shy men differ most strongly from the non-shy on just these five variables. First, most love-shy men traveled through life as isolates without any meaningful friendships or relationships with relatives and kin. Secondly, the love-shys tended to be conspicuously lacking in interpersonal/communicational finesse. Thirdly, lacking the emotional satisfactions which most people enjoy (*and which love-shy men dearly want to have*), they are under quite a bit of stress and emotional turmoil. And as will be documented in chapter fifteen, this turmoil is reflected in a wide range of medical and emotional symptoms. The love-shy obviously possess far lower self-esteem than the non-shy. And finally, the love-shy had received far more abuse at the hands of *both* parents and peers than had the non-shy.

Of course, we must be careful about drawing unwarrented conclusions from this. For example, studies have shown that violent husbands tend to date and to marry rather early in life. In essence, unlike the love-shy (who *had wanted* to marry quite early in life), violence-prone men tend not to be without female companionship for periods of any significant length. They may not be as relaxed, flexible and sociable vis-a-vis women as are most healthy men. But they quite clearly are not as disadvantaged in these areas as are the love-shy.

In sum, the love-shy entertain many more violent fantasies than do the non-shy. But as yet no conclusions of any predictive value can be drawn as to whether any particular love-shy man will become violent at some later time in his life. For the love-shy the story seems to be one of *dreaming and not doing*. And this would appear to apply as much to violence as it does to manifesting the more constructive emotions such as loving and asserting oneself vis-a-vis persons of the opposite sex.

Psychopathy

In addition to their fantasies about violently acting out, another attribute which love-shy men seem to share in common with incarcerated criminals is that of psychopathy. As indicated before, psychopathy rests upon a deep-seated feeling that no one really gives a damn about what is likely to happen to one. And, of course, if a man genuinely believes that no one really cares about *his* needs and feelings, it is only one small step for him to arrive at the conviction that there is similarly little or no need for him to "give a damn" about the needs and feelings of others.

In this regard I asked each of my respondents to react to the statement: "No one is going to care much about what happens to you when you come right down to it." And only 7 percent of the self-confident non-shys felt impelled to agree. In stark contrast, fully 73 percent of the older love-shys together with 49 percent of the younger love-shys agreed with this statement.

Of course, many of the love-shys were quite alienated from relatives, kin and family. And I think that may constitute a major reason for their widespread tendency to agree with the above statement. In essence, the love-shys were not only isolated from the standpoint of being without chosen friendships, but they also felt very little confidence in any of their blood relatives as help sources. To reiterate an earlier finding, *zero percent* of the older love-shys and only 9 percent of the younger ones had had the benefit during their formative years of three or four adult relatives other than parents to whom they could have turned for help and emotional support. In stark contrast, fully 59 percent of the self-confident non-shys had had the benefit of the help and emotional support of three or more blood relatives other than parents. In a related question, 87 percent of the older love-shys could not name a single blood relative (apart from parents with whom very few of them had enjoyed good relationships) upon whom they could count for help and emotional support. This was also the case for 68 percent of the younger love-shys. But among the self-confident non-shys, only 27 percent were incapable of naming any names.

Of course, the presence of certain psychopathic attitudes is not likely to eventuate in serious criminal or violent conduct unless a host of other factors are also present in a person's life. Most (but certainly far from all) criminal activity requires at least some ability to meet and to informally socialize with other procriminalistic types. The love-shys' "people-phobia" had evidently served well to insulate them from any opportunity to informally associate with those who might have made criminal activity seem like an appropriate or propitious course of action. Simply put, just as love-shyness had served well to insulate its victims from desirable "growth facilitating" experiences, it had also served equally well to insulate them from any opportunity to engage in the large majority of different forms of criminal deviance.

Most of the love-shys I studied read quite a bit; and all of them gave evidence of being rather sedentary, "low energy", "stay-at-home" type people. Hence, it is possible that like most people who read quite a bit, the love-shys had developed a life philosophy that militated against psychopathic wrongdoing. Intellectual and spiritual awareness can both do much to counter psychopathic tendencies.

Shoplifting

When it comes to nonviolent crimes which can be committed without the benefit and cooperation of any accomplices, shoplifting would appear to fit the bill very nicely. Yet I was somewhat surprised to find that the love-shys had been *less* involved than the non-shys in this sort of activity. For generations now it has been argued that kleptomania is a reflection of a search for love; and that the love-less often steal *things* as a substitute for the lack in their lives of *real love*. Of course, it requires some amount of "real nerve" in order to engage in shoplifting. And this might explain the fact that the love-shys were less likely than the non-shys to have engaged in it. Another factor of some importance might be the fact that most shoplifting among teenagers is done as part of a group—in an effort to "prove" masculinity, courage and daring—rather than as an effort to own things as "love substitutes".

In any case, 19 percent of the non-shys claimed that they had "sometimes" or "frequently" engaged in shoplifting. In contrast, *zero percent* (nobody) among either the older or the younger love-shys had "sometimes" or "frequently" engaged in shoplifting. On the other side of the ledger, 71 percent of the older love-shys had *never* engaged in shoplifting. In contrast, only 36 percent of the self-confident non-shy men claimed to have *never* engaged in shoplifting. Among the younger love-shys, 59 percent claimed to have never engaged in shoplifting.

Marijuana Use

Most young people who experiment at parties with marijuana never got into any legal difficulties as a result. Nevertheless, frequent or regular use of marijuana is believed by many social scientists to reflect a sort of crime-prone psychopathy.

I asked each of my respondents to indicate the approximate number of times during the past two months that he had used marijuana. And 88 percent of the older love-shys together with 71 percent of the younger love-shys indicated that they had not used it at all. By contrast, only 34 percent of the self-confident non-shys were non-users. Indeed, on the other side of the ledger fully 58 percent of the non-shy men had used marijuana *five or more times* within the two months prior to the interview. *None* of the older love-shys had used it that often, and only 14 percent of the younger love-shys had used it five or more times within the two month period immediately prior to the interview.

Of course, marijuana smoking is a *highly social* brand of noncon-formity. Everything else being equal, it would not ordinarily be expected that relatively isolated, lonely people would become involved in much marijuana use. Friendship networks are normally needed in order for people to know where to go in order to safely purchase marijuana. In addition, direct involvement in friendship groups is usually needed as a catalyst for providing the impetus and social facilitation necessary to the promotion of marijuana experimentation. Love-shy people tend to have very few if any informal friendships. As such they appear to lack the kinds of opportunities and social supports that serve to promote experimentation with drugs.

Several studies published during the late 1970s showed that among university students there is a high positive correlation between sexual involvement and experimentation with marijuana. Students who were involved in premarital sexual relationships were, in essence, found to be far more likely than those not so involved to have tried marijuana. The main reason why these two types of activity tend to be found together among young people is that both seem to be associated with a spirit of adventure, with high sociability, and with a willingness to take risks. Love-shy men, as this book quite clearly documents, tend to be bogged down by inertia. As a group they tend to be anything but adventurous. Indeed, they are extremely fearful and reticent about taking risks, even when the risks are in their best interests and are very mild in nature. And in spite of the love-shys' intellectual desires to be sociable, it is clear that they are anything but sociable. Hence, their comparative absence from the drug scene can be considered quite understandable and expected.

Alcohol Use

Hans Eysenck found that virtually all of the alcoholics he studied were high on inborn introversion and high on inborn emotionality (low anxiety threshold). In short, he found that alcoholics tend to possess essentially the same type of inborn temperament as do the love-shy. For this reason I was quite surprised to find that the love-shy men who were studied for this book were significantly *less likely* than the self-confident non-shys to be heavily into alcohol use. For example, I asked each man interviewed to provide me with an estimate of the number of drinks containing beer, wine or liquor, he usually consumes during a typical week. The average for the older love-shys turned out to be 4.83. In contrast, the self-confident non-shys estimated that they took 9.21 drinks during the course of a typical week. The younger (univeristy age) love-shys were in between with an average of 8.43 drinks per week.

Looking at the data another way, 79 percent of the non-shy men imbibed four or more alcoholic drinks per week, whereas among the older love-shys only 33 percent imbibed that many. The analogous figure for the younger love-shys was 50 percent.

I further asked each man to respond to the statement: "I never or very rarely become intoxicated from too much drinking." And only 21 percent of the self-confident non-shys indicated that this was true for themselves, compared to fully 72 percent of the older love-shys and 43 percent of the younger love-shys.

Of course, these findings do not assure that over the long haul the love-shys might not be more vulnerable to alcoholism or to undisciplined drinking binges than the non-shys. Nevertheless, there is a strong suggestion here that as of the time the data were collected the love-shys were engaged in a good deal less undisciplined drinking behavior than the non-shys.

I would suggest that a key reason behind these findings is that for most people drinking is a *sociable* sort of behavior. Inasmuch as the love-shy were "people-phobic" and certainly not very sociable, their lower average intake of alcoholic beverages can probably best be explained in exactly the same way that their lower level of marijuana use was explained. In essence, the love-shys simply do not have any friends with whom to drink. And since there is no one around to facilitate them in social, convivial, recreational drinking, the drinking in which the love-shys do partake is probably quite likely to be done strictly on their own. And this is exactly what I found to be the case.

For example, I asked: "Do you ever drink alcoholic beverages *alone*?" And 32 percent of the older love-shys answered *"yes, frequently"*, *compared to zero percent* of the self-confident non-shys. The younger love-shys were in between with 14 percent admitting that they *"frequently"* drink all by themselves. In fact, when those respondents who said "yes, they *occasionally* drink alone" were added to those who said "yes, they *frequently* drink alone", the differences between the love-shys and the non-shys remained rather substantial: 13 percent of the non-shys frequently or occasionally drank alone, compared to 44 percent of the two groups of love-shy men.

Another interesting difference of less serious significance was the fact that a majority of the love-shy men had never developed a taste for beer. Only 4 percent of the love-shys ever drank beer at all, whereas beer was the major alcoholic staple among the ranks of the non-shys. Both the older and the younger love-shy men tended to prefer mixed coctails, brandy or bourbon with ginger ale, and various wines. Further, the love-shy men in stark contrast to the non-shys almost never drank in bars.

Of course, beer drinking has long been integral to masculine culture here in the United States. The love-shys (1) had long rejected traditional masculine culture with all of its football and beer drinking, and (2) they were in most cases lonely isolates of poor social self-confidence. Especially because of the second factor, they could not be expected to have developed a taste for beer. Of course, this is not to intimate that men who choose beer are necessarily better off from the standpoint of health and safety implications than men who choose other forms of alcoholic beverages. Beer drinking men from college age onward often overdo things to the point of endangering both themselves and others. However, there are some obvious negative signs of a very different nature in the drinking patterns of the love-shy men.

For a very long time research on alcoholic beverage consumption has shown that people who drink alone in their homes or apartments tend to be substantially more likely to eventually become alcoholic than those who do not drink alone. The fact that the love-shy men had many more severe frustrations and anxieties in their lives (and the fact that their lives were obviously a great deal less happy and satisfying) than did the non-shys, would appear to render them especially vulnerable to eventual alcoholism. Again, Hans Eysenck found that virtually all of the alcoholics he studied were both highly introverted and very low on inborn anxiety threshold. These same characteristics apply on an equally universal basis to severely love-shy men.

On the other hand, the reader should remain mindful of the fact that as of the time the data were obtained only 7 percent of the self-confident non-shy men were averaging "one or no alcoholic drinks per week". Among the love-shy men, on the other hand, 44 percent of the older ones and 36 percent of the younger ones were averaging "one or no drinks per week".

In the future it would be both interesting and useful if some researcher would follow up a large number of love-shy men, and see just how many of them eventually do become alcoholics. For the moment, at least, the question of whether or not love-shyness leads to problem drinking patterns will have to remain unanswered.

The fact that love-shy men (1) are not peer group oriented, and (2) the fact that they never had any need to overtly manifest or "prove" their masculinity in the company of others, may have served well to keep them free from the dangers and pitfalls of problem drinking.

Finally, it has often been said that melancholic men (inhibited men with low native anxiety thresholds) tend to be prone towards *using* alcohol as a solvent for their psychoemotional inhibitions. The idea, of course, is that through "getting stoned" many very inhibited people finally become capable of doing or saying things in the company of others which they would really like to do or say—but which they do not have the nerve to do or say in the sober state.

The data which I collected from the love-shy men who were interviewed for this book has strongly convinced me that *all melancholic men are not alike*. Simply put, it would appear that the defense system of love-shy melancholics is far too strong and rigidly intractable to permit *using* alcohol as a tool for dissolving inhibitions. Just as most of the love-shy men would be too fearful and nervous to permit a hypnotist to hypnotize away their inhibitions, for the *same reason* they would be too fearful and nervous to permit alcohol to dissolve away any of their inhibitions. In essence, love-shy men would appear to be a special type of melancholic. Whereas the typical alcoholic usually finds a sense of relief in using alcohol as an inhibition solvent, the love-shy melancholic seems to tremendously fear *losing control*. And this great fear of loss of control may well be what keeps most love-shys from ever becoming involved in problem drinking or in alcoholism. Most of them drink on occasion (and alone) only because they "enjoy the taste" of their favorite coctails or wine. Most love-shy men seem to dislike the "feeling" which the imbibing of more than two or three drinks creates. In essence, when love-shy men drink they drink for the taste and not for the feeling. Non-shys, on the other hand, drink for "friendly sociability", and they often look forward to "that light-headed feeling".

Staring and Following

In surveying the full range of findings that were uncovered by this study, there appears to be only one area wherein some of the love-shys seem to have gotten themselves into a sort of trouble that entails legal implications. This area pertains to compulsive staring and following behavior. As a case in point I asked each man to respond to this statement:

"There have been times when I have stared for long periods at a girl whom I have found very attractive; but as soon as she would look in my direction I would immediately look away."

Fully 97 percent of the older love-shy men together with 71 percent of the younger love-shys indicated that this had been "true" for them. In stark contrast, only 11 percent of the self-confident non-shy men indicated that this statement was true for themselves.

Of course, the more important question is that of whether or not this behavior had ever led to any negative confrontations or disciplinary action. And here, fully 42 percent of the older love-shys together with 31 percent of the younger love-shys did admit that they had at one time or another gotten into trouble because of their inability to stop themselves from staring at a girl or girls whom they had found very attractive. Moreover, only 9 percent of the self-confident non-shys had ever gotten into any trouble due to this sort of behavior.

At this point the reader may be somewhat confused because it obviously requires some amount of "nerve" or non-shyness in order to engage in this sort of compulsive behavior. Of course, most non-shy men never had any need to engage in this sort of compulsive behavior;

they could *interact and communicate* face-to-face with the women of their choosing.

While the love-shys were engaging in this staring behavior, as well as during periods between episodes, they would fantasize and daydream very deeply and long about the particular girl with whom they were uncontrollably infatuated and towards whom they had felt impelled to stare. Their fantasies made her out to be a sort of "saint"—someone who would somehow *understand* them and their love-shyness problems. (Many of the love-shys had remained incredibly "innocent" in this regard until their early 30s, when some of them started to become quite cynical.) Many of the love-shys had fantasized about how this girl of their dreams would really like to meet them, and about how this "angel" of a girl would one day find a way to assume the assertive role in opening up a friendship with them.

Contributing to the compulsive quality of this staring behavior and greatly enhancing the strength of the compulsion to stare, was the fact that these love-shy men would often spend many hours of each day, sometimes over a two or three month period of time, daydreaming about the girl in whom they held the infatuation. Of course, the problem was that any time the girl actually looked as though she might be ready to make an actual move towards the love-shy man doing the staring, that love-shy man would instantly become overwhelmed with fright. And he would either very quickly walk or run away, or he would turn his head in a different direction. Much of this staring behavior had occurred in university libraries. And frequently the love-shy man would respond to a girl's gesture by immediately looking back down at his book—the very second the girl began to look his way.

Needless to say, this sort of behavior had been very unnerving and upsetting to most of the women who had been victimized by it. Most people tend to fear that which they do not understand. And most of the victimized women found this staring (then looking or running away) behavior to be exceedingly strange. And they did not know how to respond to it.

American society does not provide its young women with the type of behavioral repertoire that is required for correctly interpreting and responding to this sort of extremely love-shy male behavior. Consequently, some of the stared at women in time became quite worried and even frightened. And they often went to the police or to the Dean of Women, or to some other authority figure (e.g., campus security) to try to get something done about it.

Occasionally these romantic compulsions of love-shy men can become extremely frightening and even traumatic to some women. Of course, the women selected are almost always quite attractive—with the usual "long hair and pretty face" that is strongly preferred by most love-shy men. Attractive women normally have a good sized network of informal friendships. In addition, they are usually above average in assertiveness compared to the majority of women. This represents an interesting paradox because while the love-shy male usually fantasizes that by some magic stroke the girl will become friendly and loving towards him, he almost always dreams his ideal love-object to be a very beautiful but shy and inhibited, quite socially unpopular person—just like himself. Of course, in reality feminine beauty and low social self-confidence would appear to be well nigh mutually exclusive categories. Very rare indeed is the beautiful girl who is not also very sociable and very socially self-confident.

Because they have a good sized network of close friends, most of these stared at women have a good many people towards whom they can turn when they are faced with anxiety-provoking incidents, such as that of almost constantly being stared at by some seemingly "weird" young man who is a total stranger to them. Of course, the women selected for this unwanted attention usually have no way of knowing that the young man who is doing the staring is about as "harmless as they come". A woman's lack of knowledge of a young man and her total lack of understanding about his behavior will almost always render her subject to serious emotional trauma when and if, in addition to staring, he *also begins following her.*

I asked each respondent to react to the statement: "There have been times when I have followed a girl whom I have found attractive all over campus or town; but I have looked away whenever she looked in my direction, and I have not said anything to her because of my extreme shyness." *Zero percent* (nobody) of the self-confident non-shys indicated "yes" to this statement. On the other hand, 44 percent of the older love-shys along with 35 percent of the younger love-shys indicated that the statement was "true" for themselves. Moreover, fully 19 percent (almost one-fifth) of the older love-shys together with 13 percent of the younger love-shys agreed that they had "gotten into trouble" at one time or another as a result of an uncontrollable urge to follow a girl all over campus or all over town without ever saying anything to her.

The trouble that ensued was variable, but always extremely painful to the love-shy man who, again, had fantasized his love-object to be a kind of goddess and saint who would somehow "understand" him. One young man who had grown up in a small community in Alabama, had been made to spend a night in jail as a penalty for his persistence in following a girl around. He had received several warnings to stop following her; but he couldn't bring himself to stop. Several other love-shys had suffered bruises and welts as a result of having been accosted by male friends or brothers of the attractive girl whom they had been staring at and/or following. However, the most commonplace sort of "trouble" seemed to be that of (1) disciplinary action at their university, or (2) being terminated from their employment for "sexually harassing women".

One 36-year old love-shy man told the following story about how he had been suspended from college and sent home by the disciplinary dean when he was a sophomore at his undergraduate university.

"I grew up here in Los Angeles. But I wanted to attend the University of Montana because I wanted to see what life was like outside this city. I didn't get along very well with my folks. And I had heard that the people up in Montana were supposed to be much friendlier than those here in L.A. I mean, I really thought that if the people were really friendlier as everybody was saying, then I should be able to get some girl to come after me. You know what I mean? Like I figured that sooner or later some girl up there would make friends with me, and everything would be okey from that time onward. I could get married if I could get the right, friendly girl to make friends with me.

Well, my father was a successful accountant, and he had enough money to pay the out-of-state tuition up there in Montana. And I was really looking forward to moving up there because, like, I went to high school in Canoga Park. And Valley girls are just all shit! I mean, they're just not romantic. I wanted to get a girl as fast as I could who would be really romantic and beautiful.

When I got up there I was really bitterly disappointed. I mean the countryside was nice enough. I used to enjoy taking long drives all over. But everybody ignored me. And even though my father was paying for a double room for me in the dormitory, by March of my freshman year I ended up having the room all to myself. And in my sophomore year my roommate moved out by Columbus Day weekend, and they didn't assign me anyone else. So I had my double room all to myself all during my sophomore year. And I used to dream a lot about how nice it would be if I could get a girl in there with me. I had the place all to myself, and it would have been so beautiful.

Anyway, it took until my sophomore year until I spotted someone who I really liked. This girl was a freshman, and she had the most beautiful long, dark hair you ever saw. She had a really beautiful face with a kind of ethereal look to it, like she had come from some other world. And she had blue eyes and narrow, thin legs. I mean she was really perfect! But I had never dated anyone in my life, and I knew that I couldn't just go up to her and say anything.

So pretty soon I began making mental notes of the times of day and places around campus where I saw her. I spotted her a lot in the library; and I couldn't take my eyes off of her. I couldn't concentrate on a thing. I'd sometimes have my book turned to the same page for hours on end whenever she was there. And by Thanksgiving I was following her all over the campus. Several times she looked like she was going to approach me. And I got so frightened I had to go to the bathroom. I mean, I was just shaking all over. I knew I wanted her more badly than life itself. But I would shake all over whenever she would turn around and look my way.

Anyway, one day this big, tough-looking adult accosted me as I was peering through a first floor window at her where she was attending a math class. The guy showed me a police badge. And I was really shocked. I mean this guy looked like an overgrown, overaged football player. He wasn't wearing a uniform or anything. Anyway, he asked for my student 'ID', and took down all the information on it. And he said I'd soon be hearing from the dean.

Well, I got called into the dean's office the next morning. In fact, he made me cut my English class in order to come because he said it was extremely important. Anyway, after I got there he started asking me all these questions I was just too shy to answer. And then he said he was going to send me to the university psychiatrist; and that if I was caught anywhere near this girl again I would be suspended.

Well, my insides felt like they were being torn out. I mean I realized that there wasn't any way I could really ignore this girl. I had been spending 24 hours a day dreaming about her, and she was a part of me. There was no way I could just forget she existed. I mean, just one look at her made my day; although it also made my heart beat extremely hard, and it made me feel almost out of breath just to look at her.

I went to the shrink because I had to. And he was just as bad as the shrinks my father had sent me to back home. In fact, I'd say he was even worse because he was extremely condescending towards me. And he said he couldn't do anything about getting me introduced to any girls. I mean if he wouldn't make any effort to introduce me to any girls, I figured he was worthless to me. I mean, what good is any psychiatrist unless they give you what you need? I needed a girl I could love. And whenever I asked him to introduce me to some girls all he ever did was ask me what my feelings were about his refusal to do so! Isn't that the stupidest goddam thing you ever heard?! Psychiatrists are all for the shits! I never met a one I really liked because they don't want to give you the kind of help you really need!

Anyway, to make a long story short, I was accosted again by this plainclothesman about a week before Christmas vacation was scheduled to begin. There was no way I could make like this girl didn't exist on the same campus with me. And the dean suspended me for it. I lost a whole year of work because of this incident. It was really the most painful time of my life because no one would give me the help I really needed. When I got home my parents were more hateful of me than ever. My father sent me to this expensive shrink in Santa Monica. And it was the same old shit. This time the psychiatrist was a nice guy. But just like all the others he wouldn't do anything to really help me except for one thing. He did put me into a group therapy situation where there were some girls. But most of them were too old for me. And the one girl there of my age was just too damned hostile."

This case is not dissimilar from many others uncovered by this research. In fact, it can be considered quite representative in a good many ways of the plight of the love-shy. Of course, this is notwithstanding the fact that as a result of their own plight and internal turmoil the love-shy occasionally (albeit unintentionally) cause others considerable turmoil and suffering, as in the case of the girl in the above interview who had been followed and stared at interminably. As I have indicated, people tend to most strongly fear those things, situations *or people* which they do not understand. Thus, it would appear that some education at both the high school and the college/university level might be in order in terms of rendering young women aware of the motivational psychology of love-shy men. Young women need to be advised that love-shy men are not in any way dangerous, despite the fact that love-shy following and staring behavior appears to be inordinately "weird".

Sadly, the man in the above case interview is now 36 years of age. Yet he is presently just as virginal and just as inexperienced with women as he had been during his University of Montana days. The psychotherapeutic treatment that had been foisted on him over the years did virtually nothing to effect any kind of a solution to his problem of chronic, intractable love-shyness vis-a-vis women. Thousands of dollars had been spent on psychotherapy for him. But the psychotherapeutic technologies employed in dealing with him had all proved totally refractory to his needs. This is an issue of the most profound importance. And it along with a viable, workable remedy will be introduced and detailed in part three of this book.

Another behavior which got some of the love-shy men into trouble was that of writing love-letters to a girl with whom they had become infatuated. For example, a love-shy man might use various means to find out a girl's name. A few of the men spoke about how they had sneaked up to a girl's books and papers in the library while she was away from her study table or on a break in the bathroom. After receiving the love letters these shy men had written, the women often became very nervous and upset. Often they would respond by going to the police or the dean or to some other legal source about the matter. This outcome served to further disillusion many of the love-shy men about women. Indeed, this type of (to them) hostile response caused many of the love-shy men to become all the more lethargic about doing anything constructive to remedy their love-shyness situation.

One love-shy man had been fired, and another had been called on the carpet at work, because of love letters which they had surreptitiously sneaked onto the desks or lockers of young women employees in whom they had been infatuated. In both cases the young woman had responded by taking these innocent love letters to the boss. Both women had evidently been quite nervous about the letters because they had had no acquaintanceship with the young man at all. They didn't even know who he was. Again, the very hostile, punishing response on the part of these women had proved quite traumatic to the love-shy men. It made them more fearful of women than ever, and it served to disillusion them all the more strongly about their chances of ever being able to secure meaningful female companionship.

Six of the men interviewed had initially gotten into trouble for following women as early as their high school years. Again, this suggests that the grosser symptoms of love-shyness often manifest themselves early enough and conspicuously enough for appropriate interventive methods to be pursued. Therapeutic interventive methods are not pursued because the tools in the traditional psychiatric armentarium are simply not suited to the task at hand.

Psychologists and psychiatrists continue to quite wrongly assume that their methods only "seem" ineffective, and that "in time" the love-shy man will improve—"when he is ready"—if he continues seeing a therapist year after year. Because of legal difficulties and many highly anxiety-provoking, traumatic incidents precipitated by women who had been the victims of this staring and following behavior, most love-shy men do eventually cease their following and their staring activity—although it is far from easy for them to do so. But even though the love-shy man no longer creates problems for his community as a result of his following and staring behavior, he continues to pose a profoundly unhappy problem to himself. And his community simply ignores him and passes him off as "some kind of weirdo".

By the way, none of the foregoing is intended to imply that staring and following behavior automatically ceases after it has been punished. Of the men studied who had gotten into trouble for their staring or following behavior, 62 percent had gotten in trouble a second time as a result of staring at or following a *different* girl. And 38 percent had gotten into trouble yet a third time. Usually anywhere from four months to a year will pass between infatuations that are so strong that they precipitate following or staring behavior. The needs of many of the love-shy men appear to be so strong that they outweight both rational caution as well as fears and anxieties pertinent to hostile confrontations vis-a-vis the girl at whom they had been staring or following.

Because it is easier to hide as well as to deny, the recidivism rate for staring behavior is much higher than it is for following behavior. Some of the older love-shy respondents admitted that even now they occasionally find themselves repeatedly staring at a certain girl whom they find attractive. One university man brought a movie camera on campus and hid himself behind windows, shrubs and doorways where he filmed the object of his intense infatuation as she walked by presumably unaware of what was happening. Doing this kept this love-shy man from making a fearful nuisance of himself and getting himself into additional serious difficulties. Even among those love-shys who are now in their 40s, the urge to stare occasionally overwhelms them, and they give in to it quite in spite of the risks.

The Hinkley Case

It is difficult not to notice the similarity between the psychology of the love-shy men studied for this research, and that of John Hinkley, the then 25-year old man who tried to assinate President Reagan. Hinkley had been obsessed with fantasies about youthful movie star Jodie Foster. And these fantasies eventually led him to the bizarre conclusion that he could somehow favorably impress the object of his infatuation with an act that would immediately gain him worldwide and infamous notoriety.

In addition, there is considerable evidence that John Hinkley might have been a love-shy young man, as per the criteria for love-shyness which I delineated at the outset of chapter five. For example, Hinkley had never dated at all while he was in high school. In fact, according to his parents (interviewed on ABC News Magazine "20/20"), Hinkley had long wanted to have a girl friend; but he had never made any effort to actually interact socially with girls, or to date. According to Hinkley's parents, their son had been a social isolate from the eighth grade onward.

I think it should be stressed that none of the love-shys studied for this book had ever had the interest and fascination with guns that Hinkley had. Indeed, there seemed to be no interest in guns and firearms at all among any of the 300 love-shy men whom I interviewed. In contrast, a good-sized minority of the self-confident non-shys did have some degree of interest in such activities as riflery and hunting.

On the other hand, the obsessions and compulsions which the love-shy men steadfastly maintained for women who struck their esthetic fancy could be roughly compared to those of John Hinkley. Hinkley had been so thoroughly obsessed with thoughts of Jodie Foster that he could scarcely concentrate on anything else. And so it was with the love-shy men who could not bring themselves to stop their compulsive staring at or following the objects of their infatuation.

There was another interesting similarity worth mentioning. Hinkley's fantasy that shooting President Reagan would somehow cause Jodie Foster to like him could be compared to the equally improbable (albeit vastly less dangerous) fantasy that the women who were followed or stared at would somehow be charmed enough to magically endeavor to initiate a romantic friendship without causing any anxiety feelings (to the love-shy man) while in the process.

And so (1) obsessions and (2) compulsions with respect to beautiful women combined with (3) a psychoemotional inability to relate in any meaningful way to *available* women, all seem to present a series of common denominators between the Hinkley case and the cases of many of the love-shy men who were studied for this book.

Difficulties Concentrating

The obsessions of the love-shy burn and waste away a tremendous amount of psychic energy that could be used for constructive purposes if the love-shy could be successfully helped towards the attaining of their goal of an attractive women who would love them.

Obsessive and compulsive thoughts, most of which pertain to their deprivation of female companionship and love, do much to prevent love-shys from concentrating their energies upon constructive activities and endeavors. For example I asked each respondent: "Do you have trouble concentrating while reading or studying?" And 84 percent of the older love-shys along with 62 percent of the younger ones said "yes". In contrast, only 6 percent of the self-confident non-shys admitted to having serious difficulties with concentration while reading or studying.

Occasionally some of the love-shys suffered from obsessive thoughts even at times when they were engaged in recreational activities. For example, one man comments:

> "Sometimes like when I'm at a movie I won't be able to concentrate because I'll have these thoughts that I just can't allow myself to forget. Sometimes these thoughts aren't even really important,

although other times I'll want to remember them for some reason. So I always carry paper and pen with me no matter where I go. Like when I'm watching a movie I'll be able to concentrate on things better if I simply write down my thought—even if it's an unimportant thought. And so I write it down. And then the movie will remind me of some other idea. And again I won't be able to concentrate and enjoy the film until I write it down. I have over 3,000 note cards with these ideas on them. I keep them in a disorganized mess, and I never look at them. But I just couldn't throw them out because at one time or another I just couldn't concentrate on something until I wrote down an idea on one of the cards." (50-year old love-shy man.)

As a final illustration of some of the problems created by obsessive thoughts, consider the following interview excerpt:

"Sometimes something will happen that will make me forget what I was thinking of. I really hate more than anything to forget what I was thinking of. And sometimes I'm in mental turmoil for a long time whenever this happens, unless I can make the thought come back to me. Like if I forget a thought while I'm listening to a lecture or watching a movie, I just won't be able to concentrate for the rest of the presentation. I get so upset that I almost cry when this happens. That's why I become so upset if somebody knocks on my door, and the knocking causes me to forget what I was thinking. That can really ruin my whole evening—unless I get lucky and I can remember what it was I had been thinking of. (24-year old love-shy man.)

Chapter 15

Medical Symptoms and Love-Shyness

One of the most fascinating parts of my research on love-shyness dealt with the issue of medical symptomology. Few areas in the study of shyness are frought with more myths than this one. The typical psychologist often takes for granted the idea that psychosomatic symptoms arc a consequence of shyness; and that once shyness symptoms are cured all of the various medical problems from which a shy person suffers will just naturally go away.

In contrast, the data revealed by my research strongly suggest that *certain* medical symptoms may have a major bearing upon the creation and the maintenance of severe and pathological degrees of shyness. Of course, no one factor or set of factors will ever prove sufficient to cause severe love-shyness in males. Severe love-shyness is caused and maintained by many factors operating in synergistic interaction with one another. Medical factors now appear to be an important part of this synergy of causative factors. And it is the purpose of this chapter to pinpoint just exactly which medical factors may be important in cases of incipient as well as chronic love-shyness. Additionally, this chapter will provide the reader with further clues as to how to spot the pathologically love-shy man of the future while he is still in the earliest years of his elementary school career.

All respondents were asked some fifty different questions about their health and about various kinds of symptoms that are often thought of as "psychosomatic" in nature. I had originally hypothesized that love-shy men would be far more likely than non-shy men to have suffered from virtually any and all of the symptoms asked about. However, it turned out that such was not the case.

Headaches

For example, 23 percent of the older love-shy men indicated that they suffered from frequent headaches. The exact same figure of 23 percent also obtained for the younger love-shys. And among the self-confident non-shy men 21 percent said that they suffered from frequent headaches. Quite clearly the difference between 21 percent and 23 percent is insignificant; and indeed this difference could easily have occurred by chance. Simply put, love-shys are no more likely than non-shys to suffer from headaches. And by the way, headaches are probably the "number one" psychosomatic symptom prevalent in America today!

Backaches and Back Trouble

Backaches and back trouble cost American business and industry more money each year than any other type of medical problem except for alcoholism and headaches. The cost of this problem in lost wages and in absenteeism is staggering. And yet among the three groups of men studied for this book, back trouble was not very commonplace at all. Only 5 percent of the older love-shys together with 3 percent of the younger love-shys indicated that they had ever had any problems with their back. In contrast, 8 percent of the self-confident non-shys had occasionally experienced one problem or another with their backs.

Hence, it would appear that back trouble may represent one medical problem to which love-shy men are *less* vulnerable than self-confident non-shy men. I would speculate that the major reason for this lower level of vulnerability probably has something to do with the love-shys' long-standing disenchantment with participation in any type of "rough and tumble" sports. In avoiding typically "masculine" activities the love-shys were, in essence, protecting themselves against possible back injuries.

Bedwetting

Lately there has been a good deal of discussion about parents mishandling the enuresis (bedwetting) problem in young children, and creating pathological degrees of self-consciousness and low self-esteem in the process. Especially since little boys are a good deal more vulnerable than little girls to the enuresis problem, I decided to ask each of the respondents whether or not he had wet his bed at any time *after his fourth birthday*.

Again, the findings were somewhat surprising. Fully 55 percent of the highly self-confident non-shys admitted that they *had* wet their beds subsequent to reaching the age of four. The analogous figures for the two love-shy groups were 54 percent for the younger love-shys and 49 percent for the older love-shys. In essence, if these data are true it appears that love-shy males may have actually been slightly *less* likely to have wet their beds during early childhood than self-confident non-shy males!

Weight Problems

On weight problems there was similarly very little difference among the three different groups of men studied. Four percent of the self-confident non-shy men complained of being overweight, compared to 5 percent of the younger love-shy men. Among the older love-shys the figure was a bit higher—8 percent. Nevertheless, the message remains quite clear that even among pathologically love-shy men in their late 30s and 40s, less than one out of every twelve suffers from any kind of a weight problem. More succinctly, weight problems in men do not appear to be either a cause or an effect of severe love-shyness.

Constipation and Diarrhea

Among all three samples fewer than one percent of the men complained about either constipation or diarrhea. Nervousness has often been said to wreck havoc upon the digestive track, and to cause diarrhea in the very shy. However, the love-shy men of both groups engaged in so much social avoidance behavior that it is not really possible to accurately test this viewpoint with the data at hand. Suffice it to say that neither constipation nor diarrhea appear to differentiate love-shy men from non-shy men—at least not as far as the data collected for this book are concerned.

Problems of the Nose

One of the few medical symptom areas that did serve to sharply differentiate the love-shys from the non-shys had to do with problems of the nose. Indeed, if one were to predict among a large group of elementary school boys just exactly who is likely to go on to a life of chronic and painful love-shyness, there does not appear to be any better or more readily observable *medical* predictor than that of difficulties involving the nose.

Numerous questions pertinent to nasal difficulties were asked of all respondents. What follows is a summary of the rather thought-provoking results which the reader should find quite easy to review and to understand.

1. "My nasal passages are often severely blocked even when I do not have a cold."
   Percent saying *"true"*:
   > *Zero percent* of the non-shy men;
   > 53 percent of the younger love-shy men;
   > 66 percent of the older love-shy men.

2. "I have always had greater difficulty than most people in breathing through the nose."
   Percent saying *"true"*:
   > 11 percent of the non-shy men;
   > 45 percent of the younger love-shy men;
   > 56 percent of the older love-shy men.

3. "I often find it easier to breath through the mouth than through the nose."
   Percent saying *"true"*:
   > 26 percent of the non-shy men;
   > 58 percent of the younger love-shy men;
   > 67 percent of the older love-shy men.

4. "I use more than twice as much kleenex as most people even when I don't have a cold."
   Percent saying *"true"*:
   > 3 percent of the non-shy men;
   > 37 percent of the younger love-shy men;
   > 45 percent of the older love-shy men.

5. Item on list of 25 medical symptoms: "difficulty breathing through the nose".
   Respondents were asked to check those symptoms on the list of 25 which they had.
   Percent checking "difficulty breathing through the nose":
   > 10 percent of the non-shy men;
   > 42 percent of the younger love-shy men;
   > 56 percent of the older love-shy men.

None of these questions pertained to colds or to other infections of the upper respiratory track. I shall focus a bit later on the issue of headcolds. At the present juncture we need to focus on the fact that love-shy males, *from very early in childhood onward*, seem to be a great deal more likely than most people to suffer difficulty in breathing through the nose.

For centuries the great philosophers have made passing comments about the relationship of *nasal breathing* to a sense of personal freedom. And in eastern religion and in Spiritualism it has been taught for better than 4,000 years that a blocking of the *left* nostril issues forth a blocking of the ability to love and to express feelings emotionally; whereas a blocking of the right nostril creates a blocking in the effective flow of the intellect and of the verbal expression of ideas.

Of course, even if a person wishes to discount the viewpoints of the ancients, there are certain empirically based facts which cannot be ignored. For example, virtually all severely love-shy men agree that they suffer from a lack of a sense of personal freedom. Indeed, most of the love-shy men interviewed for this book claimed that they had never felt anywhere nearly as free as most of their contemporaries seemed to be. And these men made it clear that this lack of a sense of personal freedom was not due to any *external* constraints of any kind. Pathologically love-shy men often use the word "inertia" to describe their inability to take the kind of positive, constructive action on their own behalf which they know they should take, and which they usually know (from an intellectual standpoint) how to effect.

The well-known British psychiatrist Robert Laing, has similarly noted how men who seem to be caught in chronic ruts (often in spite of strong intellectual assets), quite typically complain of an inability to breathe freely through the nose—and how as a result of not being able to breathe freely they do not feel free.

If we accept the view that the human body is a kind of energy force field that is dependent for healthy functioning on a steady flow of incoming energies from external sources, then it seems quite clear that a chronic blocking of the nasal passages may have a bearing on a blocking of energies that are crucial to (1) feeling free, and (2) to effective social interaction with other people.

Recent research at the University of Bucharest in Romania, has documented the fact that man's body is suffused by an energy field that is often called an aura. Dr. Florin Dumitresko has taken color motion pictures of this aura using Kirlian photography apparatus. And he has found that when no acupuncture points show up in a person's Kirlian photographs, that person is healthy. However, when dots show up on a person's Kirlian photographs, those dots point directly to the section of the body with incipient or already present illness or pathology. In short, behind the Iron Curtain Kirlian photography is already being used quite successfully for diagnostic purposes.

And thus far these studies have supported the beliefs of the ancients that important sources of energy, quite apart from air, are fed into the body with oxygen *via the nose*; and that when breathing must take place through the mouth and not through the nose, the Kirlian aura (human energy field) loses its healthy luster and weakens. Of course, important energies also enter the body through the acupuncture points themselves. But nasal breathing now appears to be crucial for the receipt of energies which are necessary for healthy functioning. These energies are very important for enabling a person to feel free and in control of his life. If you block a person's nasal breathing, very quickly he will begin to feel bogged down in a kind of inexplicable, vague inertia.

Implications for Shyness Prevention

Until quite recently most health professionals have rather curtly and summarily dismissed nasal breathing problems as being purely psychosomatic—except, of course, instances that clearly involved head-colds. The very high degree of specialization within the medical profession is undoubtedly a major reason for this. Most physicians know little about the nose and quite often have as little awareness of debilitating *inborn* nasal conditions as the man on the street.

Today more and more physicians are becoming aware of the fact that a significant minority of people are born with a condition known as "deviated septum and polyps". Males are a good deal more vulnerable to this problem than females, and it is also more common among people of Irish and British ancestry than it is among other groups.

The *septum* is the cartilage which separates the two nostrils. Very often, even when the exterior of the nose is quite normal, this cartilage renders one side of the nose much smaller than the other. Consequently, the mucous which collects within the nose is not afforded proper drainage. In essence, the mucous is prevented from being blown out.

Nasal polyps quite frequently accompany the deviated septum. However, unlike the deviated septum, people are seldom born with nasal polyps already in place. Instead they are born with a vulnerability for such polyps to develop. People with allergies are believed to be highly susceptible to nasal polyps; and children with allergic problems will commonly begin developing polyps well before they complete their elementary school education.

When the deviated septum and polyps coexist in a person's nose, nasal breathing ranges from very difficult to well nigh impossible. The polyps and deviated septum prevent the flow of mucous out of the body, and very often obviate the flow of air through the nose even when no mucous is present. Further, when the victim of this problem does catch a cold, he is likely to suffer from it a great deal longer and more severely than another person who catches the same headcold germ but does not have a deviated septum or nasal polyps. This is because the polyps provide germs with a much larger array of places to hide and to be protected than what would ordinarily be available in the normal upper respiratory track.

The symptoms described to me by most of the respondents with nasal breathing difficulties sounded very much like "deviated septum and polyps". Very few of the men studied had ever been to a nasal specialist. In every case those who had been to see a specialist indicated that "deviated septum and polyps" had indeed been what they were suffering from. Those who had visited nonspecialists tended to have been summarily dismissed as having a psychosomatic symptom; and if the doctor gave them anything at all for the problem it was merely a prescription for a nasal spray.

Hence, my first recommendation to any love-shy person with chronic nasal breathing problems is to seek out a nasal specialist. These specialists are called rhinologists and are nowadays listed under that designation in the Yellow Pages of all major urban telephone directories.

Elementary school teachers can place themselves in the front line of attack relative to problems that can become chronic and intractable, and cause lives to become unhappy and nonproductive. The parents of all children with nasal breathing problems should be strongly urged by elementary educators to take their children to a rhinologist for a complete diagnosis. This is all the more important if teachers observe a child with chronic nasal breathing problems who is also chronically shy and who is an isolate or does not make friends as easily and readily as most children.

If surgery is recommended by the physician, it should be performed. Nasal polyps can quite commonly be removed under a local anesthetic right in a doctor's office. However, when a deviated septum is present a general anesthetic must be used. And the child (or adult) will be required to remain in the hospital for just one overnight period. Thus the procedure is considered minor surgery; it can be quickly and easily performed. However, its impact on a child's life may be anything but minor. Such a surgical procedure might remove from a child one of the more important factors that contribute to the development of severe and intractable love-shyness and behavioral inertia.

A further issue that may be of especial relevance to the love-shyness problem is that nasal breathing difficulties may impede the free flow of necessary oxygen to the brain, especially during sleep. A key characteristic of love-shy men is that they suffer considerable difficulty in thinking quickly and clearly under stress. A person who usually breathes quite freely through the nose may be getting significantly greater amounts of oxygen and other life energies than the person who is usually bogged down by nasal stuffiness. The more oxygen a brain receives, the more efficiently it can operate and the faster it can think. For example, joggers and runners frequently report that their thought processes tend to be in peak form immediately after a work-out session. Such flooding of the brain with oxygen not only helps to cure depression, but it may also help the brain to function more efficiently.

Hence, the inability of many a love-shy man to "think on his feet" when he is under stress and anxiety may be due *at least in part* to the blocking off of the free flow of oxygen and other energies that pass through the nose. Mouth breathers may be taking in significantly fewer of these energies (and oxygen) than nose breathers. This is another good reason why a love-shy man should waste no time in getting his nose checked out by a reputable rhinologist, especially if he has long suffered from nasal breathing problems.

Conversations with many of the love-shy men in their apartments convinced me that the deviated septum with polyps can aggravate self-consciousness. Many of these men use a veritable mountain of kleenex each day. In fact, many of the love-shys had used kleenex on the floor all over their living quarters. The necessity of using so very much kleenex is bound to render a person a bit apprehensive about interacting much with others. It is especially likely to render him nervous about inviting others to his living quarters.

Finally, the presence of a deviated septum with polyps often causes a large piece of "snot" to pop out of a person's nose quite by surprise when he is not ready with a kleenex. For example, a person will blow his nose in a kleenex several times without much of anything coming out. Then two minutes later he might press one finger against a side of his nose to force some air through, and a large piece of solid mucous pops out. Several of my love-shy respondents commented about this matter, and indicated that they often worried about it accidentally happening publicly. Of course, such large pieces of mucous often spontaneously leave the nose by way of the alimentary canal (rear of the nose); and several love-shys claimed that on numerous occasions they almost choked when this spontaneously happened to them upon lying down in their beds.[1]

Hyperactive salivary glands constitute another condition which causes many love-shys to use an excessive amount of kleenex. This problem will be dealt with later in this chapter under "hypoglycemia".

Allergies

Fully 66 percent of the older love-shys and 43 percent of the younger love-shys had been diagnosed at some time in their lives as having one or more allergies. The same had been true for *zero percent* (nobody) of the self-confident non-shy men. Inasmuch as allergies are widely believed by rhinologists to contribute to the development of nasal polyps, the much more widespread prevalence of diagnosed allergies among the two love-shy samples than among the non-shy sample cannot be viewed as surprising.

Of course, shyness with its psychoemotional consequences of being "left out" socially may serve to somewhat lower a person's resistance to allergies. This is one reason why many people seem to undergo a spontaneous remission of all their allergies as they grow into adulthood and become socially self-confident. On the other hand, there are many people for whom allergies remain chronic—especially those with lower levels of interpersonal competence. And people afflicted with such chronic allergies are often likely to develop the nasal polyps problem.

The polyps develop in the upper respiratory track as a way of preventing pollins from getting into the interior of the body. Thus the nasal polyps serve as a kind of "protective" shield or barrier. But in so doing, they block and often totally obviate a person's nasal breathing. And the person comes to experience the dearth of personal freedom referred to earlier. Of course, respiration can always proceed through the mouth; but necessary energies may be useless to a person unless they enter the body through the nose. This may be one reason why people with headcolds often feel "drained of energy".[2]

Dry Mouth

Not surprisingly, the problem of dry mouth was about four times more prevalent among the love-shys than among the non-shys. And whereas nervousness can cause dry mouth, it would appear that its most usual cause is simply that of not being able to breathe through the nose. In essence, air coming in and out of the body through the mouth will inevitably serve to dry out the mouth's tissues.

Many of the love-shy men were very self-conscious about halitosis (bad breath); and this problem seemed to be similarly related to dry mouth as well as to hypoglycemia—a problem which will be dealt with later in this chapter.

The Common Cold

People with chronic nasal breathing problems have long been known to suffer a good deal more than most people from the common cold. Therefore, it cannot be considered surprising that the two severely love-shy samples suffered substantially more from the common cold than the self-confident non-shy men did. Shyness and particularly the problem of being without a love-partner is widely believed by physicians in the United States to bring on the common cold. This is because the stress of being without love and companionship can lower the resistance of the various bodily defense systems. In their articles on the common cold many doctors cite the lyrics which Frank Loesser wrote for the GUYS AND DOLLS song titled "Adelade's Lament" back in 1950:

> The average unmarried female, basically insecure,
> due to some long frustration may react with psychosomatic symptoms
> difficult to endure, affecting the upper respiratory track.
> In other words just from waiting around for that plain little band of gold,
> a person can develop a cold.
> You can spray her wherever you figure the streptococci lurk.
> You can give her a shot for whatever she's got, but it just won't work.
> If she's tired of getting the fish eye from the hotel clerk,
> a person can develop a cold.
> The female remaining single just in the legal sense
> shows a neurotic tendency, see note . . . note . . . note;
> chronic, organic syndrome, toxic or hypertense
> involving the eye, the ear and the nose and throat.
> In other words just from wondering whether the wedding is on or off,
> a person can develop a cough.
> You can feed her all day with the Vitamin A and the Bromo fizz;
> but the medicine never gets anywhere near where the trouble is.
> If she's getting a kind of a name for herself and the name ain't his,
> a person can develop a cough.
> And furthermore just from stalling and stalling and stalling the wedding trip,
> a person can develop la grippe.

When they get on the train for Niagara and she can hear church
bells chime.
The compartment is air conditioned and the mood sublime.
Then they get off at Saratoga for the fourteenth time,
a person can develop la grippe, la grippe, la post nasal drip,
with the wheezes and the sneezes and a sinus that's really a pip.
From a lack of community property and a feeling she's getting too
old,
a person can develop a death of a cold!

Of course, an important question that needs to be raised is that of
why love-shy people are so much more likely to choose headcold symptoms and nasal breathing symptoms rather than headaches, backaches,
stomach aches, overweight problems, cramps, constipation, diarrhea,
fevers, accident proneness, etc. As yet no one has been able to come
up with a satisfactory answer to this question. Moreover, it seems very
likely on the basis of the facts already presented here that at least some
of the headcolds from which love-shy people suffer are due in part to
the presence of a deviated septum and/or nasal polyps. Colds which
last for an inordinate amount of time are particularly likely to be sustained and aggravated by the deviated septum and polyps problem.
And this point is well supported by the research data of the medical
specialty of rhinology.

The following represents a summary of the questions asked pertinent to the common cold. The fact that the older love-shys suffer from
considerably greater problems pertinent to the common cold than the
younger love-shys do, suggests that there may be a direct relationship
between severity of love-shyness on the one hand, and the common
cold on the other.

1. "It is not unusual for me to catch a cold that lasts three or four
   weeks or even longer."
   Percent saying "*true*":
   > 19 percent of the non-shy men;
   > 44 percent of the younger love-shy men;
   > 63 percent of the older love-shy men.

2. "I suffer from a good many more colds than most people do."
   Percent saying "*true*":
   > 6 percent of the non-shy men;
   > 25 percent of the younger love-shy men;
   > 48 percent of the older love-shy men.

3. "I find that I suffer far more severely from colds than most
   people do."
   Percent saying "*true*":

                5 percent of the non-shy men;
                23 percent of the younger love-shy men;
                42 percent of the older love-shy men.

4. "Lots of times my colds have been so severe that I think I might have passed as much water through my nose as through my bladder."
Percent saying *"true"*:
        3 percent of the non-shy men;
        22 percent of the younger love-shy men;
        35 percent of the older love-shy men.

5. "My colds are worse than most other people's colds."
Percent saying "true":
        12 percent of the non-shy men;
        31 percent of the younger love-shy men;
        54 percent of the older love-shy men.

6. Item on list of 25 medical symptoms: "runny nose". Respondents were asked to check those symptoms on the list of 25 which they have.
Percent checking "runny nose":
        6 percent of the non-shy men;
        44 percent of the younger love-shy men;
        63 percent of the older love-shy men.

Two medical facts pertinent to the common cold are that (1) men tend to catch fewer of them than women do, and (2) as a person becomes older he or she is likely to catch fewer and fewer colds. In spite of these basic facts, it is particularly noteworthy that the *older* love-shy men tended to catch a considerably greater number of colds than the younger love-shys did; and they suffered a good deal more severely (and longer) from them. Hence, these findings tend to support the viewpoint that as love-shyness increases in severity and intractability (and thus prevents a person from exercising free choice and self-determination over his life), headcolds are likely to become an increasingly prevalent part of an individual's life.

Regarding the first point, women may be more vulnerable than men to headcolds at least partly because of the unique distribution of hormones in their bloodstream. As the data reviewed in chapter six of this book suggest, severely love-shy men (while they were still in the intrauterine environment) may have failed to receive a sufficient exposure to masculinizing hormones. In this sense love-shy men may be more similar to women in certain biochemical respects than they are to members of their own gender. If this is indeed the case, it may partly explain the unusually high vulnerability to headcolds which most love-shy men seem to have.

Another interesting point suggested by the foregoing findings is that *severity* of cold suffering appears to be a somewhat better barometer of love-shyness than *frequency* of colds. In other words, even though the love-shy do tend to suffer from more frequent colds than the non-shy, it is the (1) severity of suffering, and (2) the length of time the average cold lasts, that makes the most difference.[3]

Reactive Hypoglycemia

Hypoglycemia means *low blood sugar*. It is caused by the Isles of Langerhans in the pancreas sucreting more insulin after a meal or snack than the body requires. No reliable data are available as to the true prevalence of reactive hypoglycemia in the United States. However, most estimates vary from 25 percent to 45 percent of the population. In essence, probably somewhere around one-third of all Americans suffer from it to some extent; and about 10 percent of the population suffers from it quite severely. It is a problem which quite frequently remains undiagnosed; and it is one about which a considerable portion of physicians are biased and incapable of professional objectivity.

Reactive hypoglycemia *may* (and I underscore the word "*may*") be important in arriving at an accurate understanding of the genesis of severe love-shyness. This is because many of the symptoms about which love-shy people most often complain tend to be quite commonplace among reactive hypoglycemics. In short, love-shy people *and* reactive hypoglycemics tend to share a number of common symptoms. To be sure, not all hypoglycemics are love-shy. However, there is evidence suggesting that most males with reactive hypoglycemia tend to be socially inhibited.

First among the symptoms common to both love-shyness and hypoglycemia is chronic fatigue and low physical energy. *Inertia*, that feeling of somehow being powerless to remove the invisible chains that bind one to the ambiance of a boring life, represents a key manifestation of chronic fatigue. And a full 47 percent of the older love-shys complained of this, compared to only 11 percent of the self-confident non-shys. The analogous figure for the younger love-shys was 30 percent.

Reactive hypoglycemics are most likely to feel uncomfortably tired (1) upon waking up in the morning, and (2) shortly after eating a meal or a snack. People who feel especially tired even though they've slept well for a good seven or more hours are particularly likely to be afflicted with hypoglycemia. The hypoglycemic's blood sugar is especially likely to be quite low after the extended fast represented by a full night's sleep. On the other hand, the fatigue that ensues for the hypoglycemic shortly after eating is due to the fact that the ingested sugars and starches (which turn to sugar) quite rapidly cause a lowering of the blood sugar by causing the Isles of Langerhans to release too much insulin. It is for this reason that teachers, parents and therapists should pay particularly close attention to this finding:

I asked each respondent to react to this statement: "I often feel sleepy after eating breakfast and I return to bed when it is feasible for me to do so." *Zero percent* of the self-confident non-shys indicated that this statement was true for themselves. However, 21 percent of the younger love-shys and 25 percent of the older love-shys responded to the statement in the affirmative.

Breakfast here in the United States is the most hypoglycemic meal of the day inasmuch as it is made up almost exclusively of sugars and starches: cereals, pancakes, toast with jam, etc. In fact, pancakes are undoubtedly the worst of all foods for people with reactive hypoglycemia because of the syrup—which is pure liquid glucose, and is hence very rapidly absorbed into the bloodstream.

A related statement to which all of the respondents reacted was the following: "During my high school years I was usually so tired after my last class that I was anxious to get home so that I could take a nap." And again, *zero percent* of the self-confident non-shys agreed, compared to 22 percent of the younger love-shys and 31 percent of the older love-shys. In short, almost one-third of the most pathologically love-shy men of this study suffered from a major symptom of reactive hypoglycemia. Of course, this does not prove that each of these men actually had hypoglycemia. I am not a physician and could not legally conduct a test of any respondent's blood sugar. However, recent medical studies on high school teenagers have shown that young people who experience extreme tiredness by the end of the school day (1) usually *do* have reactive hypoglycemia, and (2) eat and drink significantly more than the usual amount of high sugar content foods, such as soda pop, candy, pasta, cakes and pastries, etc.

And indeed this is what I also found with respect to questions pertaining to both past and present eating behavior. For example, I asked each respondent to estimate the number of cans of soda pop he drank *per week* when he was approximately fifteen year old. Of course, memory does fade with time. But there is little reason to believe that it would fade differently for the love-shys than for the non-shys. Thus it may be significant that the older love-shy men had recalled drinking an average of 5.41 cans of soda pop per week at the age of fifteen. The figure for the younger love-shys was 4.85 cans, and that for the self-confident non-shys was just 3.36 cans.

Many of the love-shys had long maintained a strong penchant for sweet drinks involving milk and chocolate or malt. The older love-shy men recalled averaging 6.57 such drinks per week during their teen years, compared to only 4.43 such drinks for the younger love-shys and 2.27 for the self-confident non-shy men.

Regarding candy bars, the older love-shys estimated that they had eaten an average of 4.87 candy bars per person per week during their teenaged years. In contrast, the self-confident non-shys had eaten an average of only 2.21 candy bars per person per week. The younger love-shy men were in between with an average figure of 3.73 candy bars.

And regarding current behavior, much of this same "sugar addict" behavior seems to be repeating itself. For example, most of the men in both love-shy groups presently use two teaspoonfuls of sugar for every cup of coffee or tea which they drink. On the other hand, the non-shy men usually use just one teaspoonful.

The chronic fatigue and lethargy feelings that are symptomatic of reactive hypoglycemia can and often do serve to strengthen and reinforce love-shyness. One way they can do this is through enabling the afflicted individual to feel perfectly justified in avoiding extracurricular and other social activities so that he can go home and rest. The fatigue that accompanies reactive hypoglycemia provides a constantly ready excuse for social avoidance. And as such it represents one of the many ways whereby normal social-emotional growth and development can be stunted.

Of course, as a *very real* medical condition, reactive hypoglycemia and its numerous symptoms are anything but figments of a weak-willed person's imagination. The symptoms are quite real and in extreme cases can even be life-threatening. It is therefore highly desirable for parents, teachers, and young people to become aware of the symptoms of reactive hypoglycemia so that a proper diagnosis can be made when such symptoms appear. With the right diet young people with reactive hypoglycemia can regain huge amounts of energy which they never suspected they had latent within them. (This is especially true if a physician checks them over for the full array of food allergies. See chapter 16.) Inasmuch as severe shyness is usually indicative of a kind of behavioral inertia along with low energy, the correct medical treatment together with a non-hypoglycemic diet could scarcely help but alleviate at least a few of the most stubborn and intractable symptoms of severe shyness.

To be sure, a chronic, low energy level is not always related in any way to hypoglycemia. Sometimes it is a function of biochemically based depression. Sometimes it is merely a psychosomatic byproduct of a boring lifestyle. This is why a correct medical diagnosis is of the utmost importance. However, my own research has led me to believe that reactive hypoglycemia is a fairly widespread concomitant of severe love-shyness. In fact, there are sound reasons for speculating that as many as two-thirds of all young men who are too shy to date and to socialize with women (in spite of genuine heterosexuality) are victims of reactive hypoglycemia.

One of the questions I asked of each man interviewed was: "Compared to people of your own age and sex, how much *energy* do you see yourself as having?" It should be noted that this question is loaded with what social scientists call "*social desirability valence*". How many young people in today's high energy society could easily admit to themselves and to others that they possess a dearth of energy? Probably not many! Thus, for this reason the obtained results for this question may very likely represent an *underestimation* of the true state of affairs.

With this point in mind, 55 percent of the older love-shy men together with 44 percent of the younger love-shy men viewed themselves as having *less energy* than most people. This was true for only 13 percent of the self-confident non-shys. In short, the love-shys were approximately four times more likely than the non-shys to perceive themselves as suffering from a dearth of energy compared to the majority of people in their respective environments.

Frequent or chronic lethargy (low energy level) is, of course, the main symptom of reactive hypoglycemia. And it is well reflected in the often unpleasant task which each person has to face each and every day—namely, getting up out of bed in the morning. And in this regard I asked each man to react to the statement: "Even when I've slept for a good seven hours, I still seem to have much greater difficulty than most people in getting up out of bed in the morning." And 62 percent of the older love-shys along with 50 percent of the younger love-shys agreed. In contrast, only 17 percent of the non-shy men saw fit to agree with that statement.

I also asked each man to give me an estimate as to the number of minutes it *usually* takes from the time he wakes up in the morning until the time he actually gets up out of bed. The averages for *weekday mornings* were: 16.3 minutes for the older love-shys; 12.9 minutes for the younger love-shys; and 7.71 minutes for the non-shys. The averages for *weekend mornings* were: 38.6 minutes for the older love-shys; 28.5 minutes for the younger love-shys; and 22.2 minutes for the self-confident non-shy men.

Getting up out of bed in the morning had long been an exceptionally unpleasant chore for a good many of the love-shys. In fact, some of the love-shys even went so far as to speculate that below the college level their educational careers might have been at least somewhat more successful if early morning hours had not been required. And the data back them up on this point. The love-shy men were much more likely than the non-shys to have been *better students* at the university level than they had been at the high school level. And several of the love-shys speculated that a key reason was that at college they could either avoid early morning classes altogether, or if they were unfortunate enough to have an 8:00 AM class they could go back to bed after it was over—a tact which had simply not proved feasible below the college level. Simply put, love-shy boys might well benefit from a different type of school hours: 11 AM to 5:30 PM was suggested by several of my love-shy respondents as being far more suitable for themselves than the current 8:30 AM to 3:00 PM. In essence, the number of school hours would remain the same; the virtue of the later schedule is that it would permit more children to arrive at school well rested and in a better position to learn.[4]

Other Hypoglycemic Symptoms

Whereas frequent or chronic tiredness represents the dominant symptom of reactive hypoglycemia, there are some other symptoms I wish to mention, particularly since they too were found to be considerably more prevalent among the ranks of the love-shys than among the ranks of the non-shys.

For example, hypoglycemic young men often suffer from severe leg cramps, especially upon waking up in the morning. In fact, such severe cramps often quite rudely and painfully awaken hypoglycemics in the middle of the night and cause the victim to instantly rise and sit hard upon the calf of the leg. Among the respondents studied for this book, such severe leg cramps were three times more commonplace among the love-shys than they were among the non-shys.

Acid stomach is another fairly frequent side effect of hypoglycemia, and 33 percent of the older love-shys (and 24 percent of the younger love-shys) suffered from this, compared to just 12 percent of the non-shy men. Ulcers, on the other hand, were not commonplace among any of the samples studied. None of the older love-shys had them, whereas only 6 percent of the self-confident non-shys and 4 percent of the younger love-shys indicated any problem with ulcers. (Fewer than 5 percent of all three samples indicated stomach aches to be a frequent problem.)

Halitosis

One of the most widespread concomitants of hypoglycemia is halitosis or "bad breath". Of course, this is a problem that a person can very easily have without being cognizant of the fact! Be that as it may, 44 percent of the older love-shys and 37 percent of the younger ones believed that they had this problem "quite a bit of the time", compared to only 3 percent of the non-shy men. Bad breath can create a good deal of self-consciousness and can significantly aggravate shyness feelings by encouraging more and more avoidance behaviors. And, by the way, this is also true with respect to an extreme fear of catching headcold germs—a quite commonplace fear among the love-shys. Clearly, there is a vicious circle here; the more a person avoids social interaction, the more inhibited and fearful he becomes, and the less socially competent he is likely to become relative to his contemporaries.

It is important to note that halitosis or "bad breath" also relates quite closely to the problems of deviated septum and nasal polyps, which were discussed earlier. The necessity of breathing through the mouth almost all the time serves to dry out the mouth quite rapidly. And to the extent that a person's mouth is dry it is also far more likely than otherwise to exude a foul odor. In short, two medical problems which appear to be quite commonplace among love-shy men are also known to contribute to a high probability of bad breath: (1) reactive hypoglycemia, and (2) deviated septum with nasal polyps. Halitosis is a strong catalyst reinforcing love-shyness, social inertia, and social inactivity. Correct medical diagnosis and treatment (along with regular use of non-hypoglycemic breath mints) can effectively remove these medical conditions as a cause.

The problem of finding proper breath mints is not an easy or simple one. Most men with reactive hypoglycemia have to use prescription products here because most over-the-counter products will cause (1) excessive feelings of fatigue, and/or (2) a foul after-taste, and/or (3) excessive salivation.

Hyperactive Salivary Glands

Hyperactive salivary glands have also been found to relate to the broader medical condition of reactive hypoglycemia. This problem can also be exacerbated by certain food allergies. People who are allergic to milk very often secrete too much very thick and foul-tasting saliva. Of course, sometimes the problem is caused by enlarged salivary glands.

However, hypoglycemia can and does cause people to produce too much saliva—a problem which caused so many of the love-shys I interviewed to use an inordinate amount of kleenex. As an antidote, most love-shy men seem to drink unusually large amounts of water. On the job or at school they remain close to the water cooler because water is just about the only thing they have been able to find which keeps their mouths feeling moist and pleasant without producing any adverse side effects—apart from a fairly frequent need to urinate. Again, most healthy people can simply poke a "life saver" or a piece of hard candy into their mouths as a means of feeling more comfortable. Most love-shy people cannot seem to be able to do this without feeling severe fatigue, an uncomfortable feeling in their stomach, or a very bitterly unpleasant after-taste. Unfortunately, sugar-free breath pills seem to cause the same unpleasant effects for them.

A good illustration of the problems which many love-shys have in dealing with hypersalivation can be seen in the reactions I obtained for the following statement: "I am often psychologically incapable of swallowing my own saliva". Only 5 percent of the self-confident non-shys agreed with this statement, compared to 26 percent of the older love-shys and 18 percent of the younger love-shys.

The problem of hypersalivation seems to be, at least in part, sex-linked. For example, females (of all ages) are very rarely observed to expectorate in public. And whereas this may to some extent be due to the greater concern that many females feel about etiquette, it seems likely that basic biochemical differences between the two sexes may also have a good deal to do with the matter. The fact that females almost never have the amount of phlegm to expectorate in the morning upon arising which men have, may also reflect this possibility.

In regard to this matter, I asked each man to react to the statement: "I feel that I have to spit much more frequently than most people." And 65 percent of the older love-shys together with 53 percent of the younger ones said "yes". In contrast, only 38 percent of the non-shys indicated that they felt they had to "spit" more often than most people. By the way, in psychoanalysis frequent spitting has long been viewed as a reflection of *anger*. And there is, of course, a possibility that the greater *anger* (at themselves and others) of the love-shys may be partially responsible for this symptomology. On the other hand, I think it is highly unlikely that such anger could be the *only* cause.

Finally, in regard to the issue of milk allergies, I asked each man to react to the statement: "Milk seems to cause very heavy, bitter-tasting saliva to form in my mouth." And 33 percent of the older love-shys together with 27 percent of the younger love-shys *agreed*. In contrast, only 13 percent of the non-shy men agreed.

Hyperprespiration

A further problem which many medical specialists believe to be a concomitant of reactive hypoglycemia is copious overprespiration. Most of the body's sweat glands are of the *merocrine* type and thus do not produce an odor. Only the *apocrine* sweat glands produce a foul odor, and these are the ones that are located under each arm pit.

Given the high prevalence of the other hypoglycemic symptoms among the love-shys who were studied for this book, it is not surprising that 73 percent of the older love-shys and 66 percent of the younger love-shys agreed with this statement: "My underarm prespiration seeems to be far heavier than most people's and is much more difficult to control." In stark contrast, *only 15 percent* of the self-confident non-shy men saw fit to agree with this statement.

Like halitosis, the odors created by overactive apocrine sweat glands can easily serve to enhance self-consciousness and exacerbate love-shyness. Moreover, these problems are not particularly easy for love-shy people to discuss. Normally, the love-shy will avoid discussion of such problems, even when face to face with a physician or a psychiatrist. And, of course, this self-disclosure reticence renders it all the more difficult for helping professionals to provide appropriate aid. One cannot remedy a problem unless it is placed squarely on the table for all concerned to see and to understand.

Surgery is one available means for curing the hyperprespiration problem—although this solution should not be accorded too much emphasis as it may not be warrented except in the most extreme cases. However, some of the apocrine (under arm) sweat glands can be surgically removed. Many such operations have been performed; and it does seem to be a procedure which alleviates the "body odor" problem to some extent. Of course, hypoglycemic love-shys should attend *first* to their reactive hypoglycemia problem. If a licensed physician provides a positive diagnosis of reactive hypoglycemia, appropriately treating that problem will automatically reduce (and possibly even cure) all of the side symptoms which I have been discussing, such as hyperprespiration, halitosis, leg cramps, acid stomach, fatigue, etc. If hyperprespiration *continues* to be a problem after the hypoglycemia has been treated and the diet has been reformed, *then and only then* the chronic body odor problem might be effectively alleviated through having some of the underarm sweat glands excised.

Exacerbating the problem of chronic body odor is the love-shy man's great allergic sensitivity to the various over-the-counter deodorants. Each man studied was asked to respond to this statement: "Conventional deodorants cause painful blisters to form under my arm pits." And fully 31 percent of the older love-shys along with 25 percent of the younger ones responded in the affirmative, compared to *zero percent* (none) of the non-shy men. It is because of such allergic reactions that many dermatologists do recommend surgery for the excising of some of the underarm apocrine sweat glands. But in the meantime there are prescription deodorants and special soaps which may serve to substantially alleviate the problem.

Depression

A final symptom which many physicians have found to be a typical concomitant of hypoglycemia is depression. In contrast to the other symptoms discussed in this section, this one is often psychological in nature—although in extreme and chronic cases it may have a biochemical basis, as per the discussion in chapter two. Depression would seem to be quite logically related to chronic love-shyness, especially in view of the love-shy man's tendency to avoid social activity vis-a-vis the other sex which he so strongly craves.

In any case, 72 percent of the older love-shys and 51 percent of the younger ones checked "frequent feelings of depression" on the medical symptom checklist. In contrast, *none* of the 200 self-confident non-shy men saw fit to check "frequent feelings of depression".

To be sure, the effective treatment of reactive hypoglycemia might not relieve all or even most of the depression from which love-shy men are prone to suffer. On the other hand, "nipping hypoglycemia in the bud" among young children could well prevent such symptoms as chronic depression from developing in the first place. Depressed feelings cannot be so easily remedied among older people. Love-shy middle-aged and young adult males have grown so used to socially avoidant behavior and have developed so many bad habits that some form of behavior therapy (such as practice-dating) is likely to be necessary for successfully helping them. However, purely medical (as opposed to psychological) treatment can serve as a very helpful and perhaps even absolutely necessary catalyst for facilitating the effective functioning of the more psychoemotionally-based therapies.

Furthermore, we must keep a constantly watchful eye for effective ways of preventing severe love-shyness from developing in the first place. The need for accurate medical diagnosis and treatment of the various symptoms discussed in this chapter cannot be overemphasized. Remove the problem while the child is young and the problem is likely to be gone forever, provided that parents and teachers become dedicated to *lovingly* ensuring that the child sticks to a good diet. They must make sure that hypoglycemic children understand both emotionally and intellectually the reasons behind that good diet, so that each child has the benefit of a well-developed set of *internal* controls and does not need to depend upon coercive external controls. Indeed, the parents must also maintain a warm, nurturing environment so that the child is not afraid to go out, make friends of *both* sexes, and take social risks.[5]

Throat Clearing and Coughing

One of the characteristics that I have long noticed among socially inactive men is that they tend to clear their throats and/or cough significantly more often than anybody else. You can enter any university library during any month or season of the year, and find that the most persistent bookworms quite commonly approach the point of creating a public nuisance with their frequent and often loud coughing and/or throat clearing. (Maybe this is a latent way of crying out for loving heterosexual attention!)

The sheer fact of sustaining a dedicated, serious attitude towards academic study by itself is not sufficient to create this coughing/throat clearing syndrome. There are many young men who are quite serious about their academic work and who very seldom find it necessary to clear their throats or cough. Of course, such young men are usually the ones who are emotionally capable of maintaining a reasonably well balanced life. They may study for five or six hours per day; but they *also* have their lover around them five or six hours per day as well. Moreover, quite often their lover will be found studying in the library at the same table with them.

In essence, heterosexually active young men very seldom cough, and this seems to be true irrespective of how much time they devote to serious study. Years ago it had been believed that the dedicated student had to lead somewhat of a monastic existence. Today we know that this simply is not so, and that an active premarital sex life (provided that it is monogamous and contraceptively protected) is more likely than not to facilitate the successful attainment of both academic and vocational goals.

Of course, coughing and frequent throat clearing in many cases may be closely related to the type of nasal problems discussed earlier. But as these behaviors are often engaged in quite frequently and loudly in public places (such as university libraries), they may represent an exasperated cry for help—unconsciously made. These are very shy men we are talking about here—the very last type of persons we would expect to be making loud, ugly noises in public places. And yet they do it all the time, possibly with the unconscious fantasy in mind that someone (perhaps an attractive, youthful, maternal figure) will come to their rescue and tend to their most deeply felt but long ignored social-emotional needs.

Heterosexually inactive young women seldom have such strong needs, and so they seldom cough the way love-shy men do. This is because they are usually able to find the emotional intimacy that they need through their same-sexed female friends. In American society heterosexual men are very seldom if ever able to satisfy their most deeply felt emotional needs through same-sexed male friends. Only a female will do for this purpose. And this is a key reason why sociologists and psychologists have long recognized the fact that men of all ages need women a great deal more than women need men.

All of the men studied were asked to respond to the statement: "I have a tendency to want to clear my throat a good deal more often than most people." And not surprisingly, 60 percent of the older love-shy men and 47 percent of the younger love-shys said "*yes*", compared to only 19 percent of the self-confident non-shy men. Moreover, in response to the statement: "It seems that I feel the urge to cough a good deal more often than most people", only 6 percent of the self-confident non-shy men agreed, compared to 40 percent of the older love-shys and 32 percent of the younger love-shys.

Gas

Love-shy men do not appear to be anymore prone to gas problems than the non-shy. In fact, not one member of either the love-shy or the non-shy samples indicated either "chronic gas" or "frequent need to fart" as representing any kind of a noteworthy problem.

Eyeglasses

I believe that America has long passed the time when very many boys are bullied or hazed because they wear eyeglasses. In this regard I believe that we have "grown up" and matured at least a little bit as a culture. My father who grew up attending Catholic schools in Jersey City, New Jersey, during the second and third decades of this century, has often commented upon how eyeglass wearers had been routeinly singled out for both verbal hazing and physical bullying. In working class neighborhoods some of this still goes on. But in middle-class school districts it has become relatively uncommon.

Be that as it may, the wearing of eyeglasses continues to remain a component of the love-shy stereotype. Many people continue to associate the image of the eyeglasses-wearing schoolboy with the notion of social ineptitude, withdrawal, and excessive studiousness. Of course, many people look good in glasses. Nevertheless it may indeed be that the wearing of eyeglasses gives a young boy a head start towards the quagmire of intractable, chronic love-shyness.

At the time the data for this research were obtained only 27 percent of the non-shy men regularly wore corrective lenses, compared to 59 percent of the younger love-shys and 78 percent of the older love-shys. Also of interest is the fact that better than one-third of the non-shys who wore glasses wore contact lenses. In contrast, not one love-shy man in either group wore contact lenses. Of course, this fact may reflect the unusually low sensitivity threshold of love-shy men. It requires some degree of eyeball insensitivity for a person to be able to tolerate contact lenses.

Of course, not every person wearing eyeglasses had commenced wearing them during childhood. In fact, it is widely believed today that the many tensions and stresses that are associated with prolonged and intense study *create* myopia and sometimes astigmatism as well. Since love-shy men often endeavor to become highly competent at an academic subject in an effort to compensate for their social-emotional immaturity (lack of dates with women, unpopularity, etc.), their need to remain highly successful at college often creates considerably greater stress for them than it does for well-balanced, psychologically well-adjusted young men. Love-shy men have considerably more to lose if they do not perform well at school. The self-confident have their friends; love-shys are frequently friendless.

In this regard I asked each respondent who wore corrective lenses whether he began wearing them (for the first time in his life) *before or after* his 16th birthday. My hypothesis was that the love-shy would be much more likely than the non-shy to have commenced wearing eyeglasses *after* the 16th birthday because they had had a much stronger need that the non-shy to pursue scholarly goals with a dedicated seriousness.

The hypothesis was borne out. Among the non-shy men who wore corrective lenses, only 9 percent had commenced wearing them *after* their 16th birthday. In stark contrast, 35 percent of the younger love-shys who wore glasses and 41 percent of the older love-shys who wore glasses had commenced wearing them *subsequent to* their 16th birthdays. More succinctly, the love-shy eyeglass-wearers were about four times as likely as the non-shy wearers to have begun wearing the corrective lenses *after* the 16th birthday.

In sum, love-shy men often endeavor to develop intellectually as a means of compensating for serious shortcomings in their social-emotional lives. In so doing they often strain themselves quite formidably. And a byproduct of this emotional strain is even greater love-shyness, social inadequacy, myopia or astigmatism, and (often) a less attractive facial appearance. This is especially so given the widespread tendency among the love-shy to wear eyeglasses with rather dark and heavy plastic frames. Non-shy men very seldom wear such heavy frames. Thus, the love-shy obviously need guidance in selecting eyeglass frames which serve to maximally upgrade facial appearance.

Shortness of Stature

I checked the height of each of the 500 men interviewed for this book. And there were no significant differences at all between the love-shys and the non-shys in this regard. Simply put, love-shy men do not appear to be anymore likely than non-shy men to be excessively or noticeably short.

Of course, inequalities in this regard during early adolescence or childhood can leave emotional scars. But even here, the love-shy men were no more likely than the non-shys to have been unusually short during childhood.

I asked each man whether he had reached adolescence (1) earlier, (2) later, or (3) at approximately the same time as other boys in his class at school. And even here there were few differences among the three samples. For example, 11 percent of the non-shys claimed that they had arrived at adolescence later in life than their male classmates. This had similarly been true for 14 percent of the older love-shys and for 17 percent of the younger ones. On the other hand, 31 percent of the non-shys claimed that they had become pubescent earlier than most other male children. The analogous figure for the younger love-shys was 12 percent, and for the older love-shys it was 13 percent. Hence, a clear majority of all three samples (58 percent of the non-shys, 71 percent of the younger love-shys and 73 percent of the older love-shys) felt that they had arrived at adolescence "at approximately the same time as most others of their sex".

Of course, as I made clear in the chapter titled "Beauty and the Love-Shy", the love-shy men had been far less likely than the non-shys to have been in any way satisfied or happy with their level of attractiveness during their teenaged years. Suffice it to say, though, that the *source* of the love-shys' dissatisfaction seldom had anything to do with being excessively short of stature.

Acne

At the time the data for this research were obtained, none of the 500 men appeared to have any noteworthy skin problems. However, it is well-known that a history of teenage acne often leaves mild to serious emotional scars. And it is for this reason that I deemed it appropriate to ask each man a question about acne problems that might have been suffered during adolescence.

Not surprisingly, 63 percent of the older love-shys and 53 percent of the younger love-shys had had "moderate to severe" cases of teenage acne. In contrast, this had been true for only 26 percent of the self-confident non-shy men. Inasmuch as love-shy people are more sensitive and more easily hurt than the non-shy, selective memory may have been operating here. Thus, in view of the positive mental attitude that prevailed among them, the non-shys may have been more likely than the love-shys to have forgotten their former problems with acne—and with a good many other things as well.

Irrespective of whether or not this had indeed been the case, it seems apparent that acne might well have contributed at least slightly to the social withdrawal habits and the self-consciousness tendencies of the love-shys. Acne is a quite noxious condition for teenagers. And in this regard it is heartening to note that between 1979 and 1983 enormous advances were made in the effective treatment of even the very worst cases of acne. Any teenager with such skin problems must be accorded ready access to the services of a competent dermatologist.

During adolescence as throughout life males do differ among each other in terms of the relative amount of the hormone androgen in their blood streams. Androgen is the hormone that is responsible for acne. The more excessive the amount of androgen in the bloodstream, the more severe the acne problem is likely to be.

From before they are born until late childhood, love-shy boys appear to suffer from a dearth of testosterones in their bloodstreams. On the other hand, they do not appear to suffer from any shortfall of most blood androgens—the *other* male hormone. In fact, throughout their teenage years most love-shys may well suffer from an *excess* of certain blood androgens. Of course, it may be that the love-shys' body physiology is less equipped than that of the non-shy to handle the on-rush of *both* androgens and testosterones that occurs with the onset of adolescence. In essence, the physiology of non-shy males during childhood may better prepare their bodies for smoothly and harmoniously absorbing the onrush of male hormones that occurs with the inception of pubescence. An inability in a person's body to smoothly handle such an onrush may help to cause such symptoms as severe acne.

The fact that androgens are closely associated with acne problems ties in with one of Hans Eysenck's (University of London) most fascinating findings. Eysenck found that very shy people tend to have significantly stronger sex drives than non-shy people. He found that the stronger and more persistent a man's anxiety feelings tended to be, the stronger would be his sex drive and the more frequently he would feel the need to masturbate. As I have already documented, love-shy men tend to masturbate far more frequently than do the non-shy. In fact, my own work showed that when one adds up the total number of ejaculations men experienced per month from all sources (e.g., masturbation, sexual intercourse, heavy petting, etc.), age for age the love-shy experience quite a few more orgasms than do self-confident, socially active men.

This is an important point because it documents a side of the love-shy man about which very few people are aware. The more deprived a man feels of the things he most desperately wants, the more severely preoccupied he is likely to become with respect to the source and substance of his felt deprivation. Hence, the typical love-shy man devotes much more time than the non-shy man to masturbating and to daydreaming about copulating with a beautiful girl of his choice.

So a very cruel paradox here is that severe teenage acne serves to (1) exacerbate teenage unpopularity, particularly vis-a-vis the opposite sex, and to (2) increase self-consciousness and the self-defeating habit of social avoidance. But that very teenage acne is caused by the very same thing (i.e., excessive blood androgen) that *also* causes an unusually heightened sexual interest—an interest which is effectively blocked from fulfillment by the acne and related shyness and social self-consciousness.

Parenthetically, an amusing side point is that just as high blood androgen tends to be related to "horniness" in boys, it is *also* related to "horniness" in girls. More succinctly, the "horniest" high school girls can easily be spotted because they are the ones with the most conspicuous cases of acne! Of course, females have relatively less blood androgen than males do. And this is why the most severe cases of teenage acne are always suffered by males and not by females.

As a final point, the fact that the love-shys had consumed significantly more sugary items during their teenage years than the non-shys had may also have served to exacerbate their skin problems.

Insomnia

The love-shys were somewhat more vulnerable to insomnia than the non-shys. *Zero percent* of the non-shy men indicated that they "often had difficulty falling asleep." On the other hand, 19 percent of the older love-shys and 16 percent of the younger love-shys "often" experienced difficulty in falling asleep.

Stuttering

Only 5 percent of the older love-shys and 4 percent of the younger ones appeared to have any problems with stuttering at the time the interviews were conducted. However, only 44 percent of the older love-shys and 47 percent of the younger love-shys indicated that stuttering had *never* been a problem for them. In contrast, 97 percent of the self-confident non-shys indicated that stuttering had never been a problem for them. In addition, none of the non-shys seemed to have any speech problems at the time the interviews were conducted.

Buck Teeth

Fully 26 percent of the older love-shys and 19 percent of the younger ones indicated that they had had problems with buck teeth. In contrast, only 6 percent of the non-shy men mentioned this as a problem.

Hypochondria

The love-shy men appeared to be considerably more vulnerable than the non-shys to a fear of germs. This was no doubt related to the fact that when they do catch headcold germs they do seem to suffer a good deal longer and more severely than most people. In any case, 16 percent of the older love-shys and 10 percent of the younger love-shys indicated that they do not like to handle door knobs. This was true for *zero percent* of the non-shy men.

In another question I asked for reactions to this statement: "After touching the floor (like after completing push-ups) I always want to go to a sink and wash my hands." Fully 46 percent of the older love-shy men together with 31 percent of the younger love-shy men agreed. *None* of the non-shy men saw fit to endorse the statement.

In another question I asked for reactions to the following: "I would not eat a banana until after I first cut out any and all black or gray spots." Fully 65 percent of the older love-shys together with 52 percent of the younger love-shys agreed. Among the non-shy men the level of agreement was 33 percent.

And 31 percent of the older love-shys along with 25 percent of the younger love-shys checked that they were sometimes fascinated by their bowel movements. This was true for just 4 percent of the non-shy men.

Finally, 68 percent of the older love-shys and 52 percent of the younger ones indicated that they always wash their hands immediately after taking the garbage out. This was true for only 35 percent of the non-shy men.

Psychotherapy

Finally, I asked each man whether or not he had ever in his life sought help from a psychiatrist or clinical psychologist—for any reason. And not surprisingly, fully 100 percent of the older love-shys responded in the affirmative, along with 37 percent of the younger love-shys, and only 3 percent of the self-confident non-shy men. However, the experiences that the love-shys had had vis-a-vis psychotherapists had been far from satisfactory. In fact, *all* of the love-shys interviewed for this book who had had psychotherapy at some point in their lives had major complaints to voice about their experiences. *None* of them had found therapy to be at all helpful from the standpoint of reducing their shyness and severe inhibition vis-a-vis women. Yet in spite of their stinging and often angrily voiced complaints, 24 percent of the older love-shys and 27 percent of the younger love-shys were actually seeing a therapist at the time they were interviewed for this book.

Chapter Postscript

Los Angeles area physician Dr. Steven Rosenblatt is now quite successfully using a form of needleless acupuncture to totally cure pre-pubescent children of allergy problems. Through realigning the electromagnetic energy force field of certain portions of the surface skin where it is found to be out of proper alignment (i.e., a malaligned "aura"), allergies can be entirely done away with.

As per my comments in the first four chapters of this book, an aura with various electromagnetic deficiencies has been found to be related to and to cause all manner of physical and psychoemotional problems. Per chance, intractable forms of shyness may be among these problems. This chapter has, of course, demonstrated a clear relationship between difficult allergy problems and shyness. It is obvious that much serious research is sorely needed on acupuncture and on the relationship between the body's aura and the full variety of physical and psychoemotional problems.

NOTES

1. Frequent nose picking as well as frequent scratching of the interior of the nose, appeared to be quite conspicuous problems of both groups of love-shys. The problem of severe nasal itches may be related to allergies. On the other hand, the more problematical symptom of a frequent need to pick one's nose is doubtless caused to a major extent by nasal polyps and deviated septum. In short, any obstruction which renders it difficult to pass mucous will have the effect of frequently creating a supply of dried-up phlegm in the nose. And, of course, this is what causes a person to feel a need to pick his nose.

Needless to say, nose picking behavior entails a very negative *social stimulus value* here in American society. Hence, the frequent need to pick one's nose is bound to have an exacerbating impact upon feelings of self-consciousness and of severe love-shyness.

2. But there is another way in which allergies can exacerbate other health problems. People with allergies often suffer from attacks of *itchy nose*. And as will shortly become apparent, the love-shys were found to be extremely susceptible to this problem. Scratching an itchy nose with one's fingers represents a major way by which infectious headcold germs are "caught".

3. In recent years the University of London has produced some fascinating research findings on the relationship between the sun's light rays and the seasonality of headcold suffering. Headcolds are caused by many variables which synergistically interact with one another. The variable of the sun's light rays has been largely ignored up to now in spite of the demonstrable seasonality of headcold suffering. It is clear that much more research needs to be done in this area.

4. In his recent work entitled STRESS FREE LIVING, Dr. Clay Sherman comments on an experiment that had been conducted in an elite boarding school for high school students. There were two groups in this experiment: (1) a group that was given a heavy daily dosage of malted milks, pastries, soda pop, candies, and other high sugar foods; and (2) a group that was kept low on such foods. At the end of the academic year during which the study was done, the first (high sugar) group was found to be significantly lower than the second group on such factors as: proportion of students holding high student offices in government, demonstrated interpersonal skills, demonstrated ability to get along well with and enjoy the company of other students, grade-point average, ability to concentrate well, quality of relations with adult authority figures, and athletic ability. At the beginning of the experiment both groups were equal in terms of the type of students that composed them. Thus, we have one more strong piece of evidence here that high sugar diets may represent a major variable (interacting in synergy with the other variables delineated in this book) giving rise to intractable love-shyness. Aggravating the situation is the fact that many depressed young people will eat sugary items in order to assuage feelings of depression and/or worthlessness and shyness. In this way such young people become progressively worse rather than better. The sugary remedy *worsens* the disease.

5. Of course, children and teenagers often eat a lot of sugary foods as a *substitute* for the *love*, caring and concern that they are not getting from parents, peers, and opposite-sexed age-mates. Thus, it is quite possible that love-shy males own a much stronger need for such things as sugary pastry, sweet cereals, candy bars, malted milks, soda pop, etc., than do those young people who feel well loved, liked, etc., and who are excited about all the interesting and enjoyable *social* activities which they have to pursue each day.

With this in mind, it should be patently obvious than it may not normally be very easy to "unhook" sugar addicts from their sugary food needs. Quite clearly, parents will *not* be able to successfully rely upon coercive tactics in their efforts to motivate their love-shy sons to change their snack food diets.

Another point of interest is that shy people tend to use an above average quantity of *salt* on certain of their foods. An addiction to salt is often a reflection of overworked, overstressed adrenal glands. As anxiety-prone people tend to be highly overstressed, their adrenal glands might well be overworked. And this would give rise to a craving for salt.

Chapter 16

Love-Shyness and the Innate Sensitivities Issue

Love-shys seem to be far more "sensitive" than most people. So what else is new?! It almost goes without saying that shy people are "sensitive". They are more sensitive than most people to rejection. Compared to most people, their feelings are more easily hurt. Real or imagined insults throw them off balance to a far greater extent than what is typical for most people. But what is not well-known is the fact that love-shys also suffer from a large host of sensitivities that are not ostensibly related to "people phobia" or to interpersonal interaction considerations. It is about these *"other"* sensitivities that this chapter will be concerned.

I believe that the study of sensitivities may offer us some important clues as to the causes of severe love-shyness. The research data obtained for this book dealt with only some of the potentially important sensitivity-related questions and issues. For example, are love-shy men more likely than most people to have *food allergies*? And if so, to which foods and/or chemical additives are they allergic? As per the data reviewed in chapter fifteen, we know that love-shy men had always been (throughout their lives) more vulnerable than most people to a host of allergies. Inasmuch as they are more sensitive than most people to a wide variety of pollins, dust, animal dander, etc., it is not at all improbable that many love-shys *may* have a variety of food allergies which may be exacerbating their problems and rendering their situation all the more chronic. It is certainly to be hoped that medical researchers will in the very near future check out a sample of love-shys for the full range of food allergies. In order to successfully help the love-shy, this sort of information and knowledge must be deemed quite indispensable.

The issues of native temperament which were dealt with quite thoroughly in part one of this book, suggest a strong biological base for love-shyness—a base which causes social learning to progress propitiously for some and more or less problematically for others. The issue

393

of sensitivities suggests another biological base for understanding love-shyness. This is so because not all sensitivities could have been learned. Indeed, this is why the study of sensitivities is so thought-provoking and challenging—challenging particularly of preconceived biases.

In essence, there are no easy or "pat" answers to the problem of accurately understanding the etiology of severe love-shyness. As for myself, I do not pretend to a full understanding of all the data to be reviewed in this chapter. This is why I want to present my findings in some detail—so that interested people from all walks of life can begin asking all of the right questions pertinent to the etiology of severe and chronic love-shyness.

Bodily Itches

Bodily itches surely represent one of the most interesting of sensitivities. It is readily apparent that some people have a well above average number of itches. Indeed, some people appear to be almost always scratching themselves somewhere, whereas others almost never seem to feel the need to scratch. Could such differences between people be attributable to inborn biological factors? Unfortunately medical science has yet to furnish us with an answer to this question Suffice it to say that love-shyness appears to be fairly closely related to frequency of bodily itches.

For example, I asked each respondent: "Compared to most people, to what extent are you bothered by itches in many different parts of your body?" And 30 percent of the older love-shys along with 23 percent of the younger love-shys said *"very frequently"*, compared to *zero percent* of the self-confident non-shy men. In contrast, 41 percent of the non-shys said that they were *never* bothered by bodily itches. Only 19 percent of the younger love-shys and 11 percent of the older ones similarly indicated that they were *never* bothered by bodily itches.

Of course, it should be noted how a greater proportion of the older love-shys than of the younger ones had been frequently bothered by itches. Inasmuch as it is a fair assumption that as a group the older love-shys were more severely shy vis-a-vis women than the younger ones, the message appears clear: the more severe the love-shyness, the greater the amount of bodily sensitivities. The older love-shys had made it through to ages 35 to 50 in the "single, never married" category, *not* out of personal choice but because of shyness. Therefore, if sensitivities are related to love-shyness, we would logically expect such sensitivities to be more conspicuously manifest among the ranks of the older love-shys than among the ranks of the younger ones.

I also asked each respondent: "Compared to most people, how often do you find it necessary to scratch yourself in various parts of your body?" Here 30 percent of the non-shy men indicated "*never*", compared to just 13 percent of the younger love-shys and 7 percent of the older love-shys. At the opposite extreme, 34 percent of the older love-shys indicated that they had to scratch themselves "*very often*", compared to 25 percent of the younger love-shys and *zero percent* (nobody) of the non-shys. In fact, even more dramatic were the responses to this statement: "Lots of times I have so many itches all over my body that I scarcely know where to scratch first." Here 36 percent of the older love-shys and 27 percent of the younger love-shys agreed. But not one single non-shy man saw fit to agree with the statement.

Climate

In his extensive work at New York University, Dr. Alexander Thomas has been able to document the fact that people are born with different degrees of sensitivity to heat, to cold, to pain, to light, and to several other forms of bodily discomfort. Expressed scientifically, people are born with different discomfort thresholds.

Some of these thresholds are sex-linked. For example, women have a lower threshold for cold than men do, whereas men have a lower threshold than women for heat and humidity. In studying young babies, Dr. Thomas found that as he decreased the heat in a room the girl babies began crying sooner than the boy babies. On the other hand, as he raised the heat of the room, the boy babies commenced protesting earlier than did the girl babies.

Dr. Thomas and other scientists have found that these differences among people and between sexes tend to remain surprisingly stable throughout life. For example, men will typically derive less enjoyment than their wives out of vacationing in such hot, humid resort areas as Miami Beach, Bermuda, Honolulu, the Bahamas, Tahiti, etc. On the other hand, wives will usually display impatience sooner than husbands with such cooler vacation spots as Ireland, Scotland, Norway, the Alps, the Canadian Rockies, the Oregon and Alaska coastlines, etc.

But what is even more interesting is the fact that the differences which have been found between the two sexes are considerably less than the differences among members of either of the two sexes. For example, some women can tolerate cold far better than the vast majority of men, whereas many men can tolerate heat and humidity far better than the vast majority of women. It is useful to know that differences in the ability to tolerate heat and cold are at least in part sex-related.

However, differences in tolerance levels *among people in general* are far greater than the average differences between the two gender groups.

The love-shy men studied for this book gave evidence of being a good deal less tolerant of *both hot and cold* weather than the non-shys. But as expected (given their previously documented tendency towards hyperprespiration), the love-shys also gave evidence of being bothered to a considerably greater extent by heat and humidity than by cold. (Curiously, this turned out to be one of the few ways the love-shy men seemed more similar to "typical" members of their own gender, than to "typical" members of the female gender.)

Each respondent was asked to react to this statement: "It would be wonderful if I could live in a breezy climate where it never gets colder than 40 degrees Farenheit, or hotter than 60 degrees Farenheit." And according to the results, only 14 percent of the self-confident non-shy men agreed, compared to 58 percent of the older love-shy men and 42 percent of the younger love-shy men. Many of the non-shy men specifically added that they took great pleasure in the changing of the seasons. And many of the men whom I interviewed in California claimed that this was something they especially strongly missed about the east and midwest.

The love-shys, on the other hand, tended to take little pleasure in the changing of the seasons. They tended to prefer weather that was *constantly comfortable*. For most of the love-shys, October seemed to be the favorite month of the year. By and large, the love-shys tended to prefer constant spring and fall, with no summer and no winter.

For some of the love-shys, even October entailed a noticeable deficit: they did not like the diminishing length of the days. Some of the love-shys interviewed in normally comfortable, coastal California complained that they wished there could be a place in the United States where the day length would be constantly the same. These men wanted it to become dark at 8:30 or 9PM throughout the year. A few men interviewed in California felt that their state should be on *Mountain Time,* and not Pacific Time. Similarly, several of those interviewed in New York felt that New York and New England ought to be in the Atlantic Time Zone along with Nova Scotia, New Brunswick, and Prince Edward Island.

Some writers have suggested that one of the reasons for the surfeit of homosexuals in San Francisco, Santa Monica, and other coastal areas of California, is that there is only about a 10 degree Farenheit difference between average January temperatures, and average July temperatures. To be sure, a cosmopolitan, tolerant, urban atmosphere doubtless has even more to do with the plentitude of homosexuals in such places. But the possibility that a moderate and relatively unchanging climate (without too much sunshine) may also have something to do with it should not be discounted.

To be sure, there are many significant differences between homosexuals and heterosexual love-shys. But as I have documented, there are also some very interesting similarities. And one of these similarities is the penchant so commonplace among both homosexuals and heterosexual love-shys for a constantly comfortable, moderate, unchanging weather picture.

Bright Sunlight

Of the various sensitivities, few may be of greater significance than sensitivity to bright sunshine in accounting for the tendency among some children to withdraw from certain types of outdoor activity. And, of course, in American society this type of sensitivity would logically be expected to eventuate in more social harm to a boy child than to a girl child.

Each of the 500 respondents was asked to react to the following statement: "When I was a child I could not enjoy playing in bright sunlight; I could enjoy myself much easier in the shade or in cloudy weather." The obtained results indicated a level of agreement almost three times as great among the love-shys as among the non-shys. More specifically, only 21 percent of the non-shy men agreed with the statement. In stark contrast, fully 51 percent of the younger love-shys and 60 percent of the older love-shys agreed with the statement.

Again, peer group interaction must be made pleasurable and rewarding if a child is to develop any motivation at all for pursuing such activity. If a child perceives outdoor play as unrewarding and possibly even painful, he will endeavor to avoid such activities to an ever increasing extent. In American society girls are perfectly free to avoid playing in bright sunlight *without* incurring the hostile wrath of their peers. In fact, there is little reason to expect that the peer group life of a girl would be adversely affected at all by her unwillingness to take part in play activity within the context of bright sunshine. She will always be able to find plenty of friendly and sympathetic peers who, like herself, prefer to play indoors or outside the context of bright sunshine.

American methods of socializing boys tend to be quite rigid and cruel in this regard. Boys are not only strongly discouraged from playing within the framework of a coeducational peer group, but they are also quite often the victims of a dearth of play options. Their peers, and often their parents and teachers as well, commonly expect them to play at baseball and football. And no alternative sports, such as ping pong, bowling, indoor volleyball, etc., are made available as an option.

Wool

One of the more widespread sensitivities is that of wool. Many people cannot wear it or use it because it feels like painful pin or needle pricks when it touches the skin. Very sensitive people cannot even wear a woolen sports jacket because the noxious effect of the wool penetrates right through the shirt that they are wearing, and sometimes through the undershirt (if they are wearing one) as well.

Only 7 percent of the self-confident non-shy men indicated that they could not wear wool. In contrast, 40 percent of the younger love-shys and 54 percent of the older love-shy men indicated that they could not wear woolen items because of the often severe feelings of discomfort (especially itchiness) that such clothing items create.

Of course, a key question to be raised is that of why love-shy men are far more likely than non-shy men to find wool uncomfortable, and why they are more likely than the non-shy to find weather warmer than 60F and cooler than 40F uncomfortable and disconcerting? Are all such differences *really learned* in every case? Or do such differences between the love-shy and the non-shy reflect some basic, genetically rooted, biologically based (inborn) differences? All differences which undermine flexibility and adaptability are bound to render life more problematical and less enjoyable for the love-shy than for the non-shy. By itself, sensitivity to wool is a very minor thing. But it *may* (and I underscore the word *"may"*) relate to some broader based, genetic characteristics that differentiate love-shys from non-shys right from the very beginning.

Physical Pain

This is another area wherein sensitive males are at a far greater disadvantage than sensitive females. Several questions were asked of each of the 500 men studied. The first of these concerned the following scenario: "Picture yourself on a camping trip with a good many people of all ages. The area in which you are camping has some mosquitos and gnats. Compared to the other members of your party, to what extent do you think you would be bothered by the mosquitos and gnats?"

Nobody among the 200 self-confident non-shys thought that they would probably be bothered *more than* most of the other people. In contrast, fully 66 percent of the older love-shys and 45 percent of the younger love-shys thought that they would be bothered by the mosquitos and gnats to a greater extent than the other people. Several of the love-shys told me that they had an unusually strong sensitivity to mosquitos, and that whenever there are any mosquitos they "always" come after them first. Some of the love-shys attributed this to the fact that their blood is somehow "sweeter" and "different" from the blood of most people. Others thought that their problems with mosquitos might be due to their very light skin.

In a further question I simply asked each man whether he considered himself to be more or less sensitive than the majority of people to physical pain. Only 7 percent of the non-shy men considered themselves to be more sensitive to pain than most people, compared to 39 percent of the younger love-shys and 57 percent of the older love-shys. On the other side of the ledger, 24 percent of the non-shy men considered themselves to be "a great deal less sensitive to pain than most people". Not one single man in *either* of the two love-shy groups considered himself to be a great deal below average in physical pain sensitivity.

In numerous cases great sensitivity to physical pain stimuli had caused some of the love-shy men a considerable amount of embarrassment. One of the younger love-shys told me about an incident that had taken place at Glacier National Park. This man had been part of a tour group of the outback that had been composed of people of both sexes and of all ages. And for quite a while during the course of a hike through a woodland area he found himself swatting his hands so incessantly and dramatically that he could not even hold on to his camera. There had been two elderly women in the group; and even they had not reacted to the mosquitos with anywhere nearly the extreme flailing and swatting movements that this love-shy man had displayed. He felt quite embarrassed by his behavior, and by the fact that he had been less able to deal with the mosquitos than anyone else in his tour group, including the old ladies.

Several stories of this nature suggest the possibility that *allergic reactions* to insects may affect the love-shy to a considerably greater extent than they affect the non-shy. Further, such sensitivities may quite possibly be attributable to inborn, genetically rooted factors. Hopefully medical research will soon shed some light on this matter. Suffice it to say that such strong and conspicuous sensitivities in *male* children are highly likely to attract bullies. Inordinate degrees of sensitivity to or fear of physical pain can have an extremely negative affect upon a male's ability to get along successfully with his same-sexed peer group. Such fears can render a male child highly vulnerable to persistent bullying, and to the social avoidance patterns discussed earlier.

Fear of Pain in Medical Settings

In view of the quite substantial number of often chronic medical problems from which the love-shy suffer, I found it especially interesting that the love-shy tended to visit medical doctors a good deal *less often* than the non-shys. To be sure, there are many psychoneurotic people who visit medical doctors a great deal more often than the majority of the population. But all people with psycho-emotional problems are NOT alike! And it appears that one of the major identifying characteristics of love-shy men is that of *under-visitation* with doctors at medical facilities.

One of the questions I asked of each man was: "I would avoid having a strongly recommended (but not absolutely required) surgical procedure performed on me because of fear of pain, discomfort, and being put to sleep." And 45 percent of the older love-shys along with 32 percent of the younger love-shys indicated "yes, that is true". In contrast, *nobody* (not one single person) among the non-shy men indicated that the statement was true for themselves.

In essence, almost one out of every two of the most severely love-shy men tend to fear potential pain so enormously that they would sacrifice their health and their physical well-being just in order to avoid entering a hospital for strongly recommended work.

Of course, there may be some additional fears which account for this aversion to doctors and to medical facilities. For example, during the interviews some of the men shared with me their negative fantasies and worries about how they would be extremely nervous and shy about screaming and hollaring in pain with other people around. One of the most commonplace worries was that of being seen nude by the nursing staff. Urinating and defecating constituted another anxiety. As one man said to me:

> "I wouldn't have the nerve to go to the bathroom. I mean they make you use these bedpan things when you are confined to your bed. I'd never have the nerve to do that with the nurses and other people there! I think I'd just go insane because of the horrible lack of privacy!" (24-year old love-shy man.)

And some of the men recounted embarrassing scenes from their childhood days. Often these scenes related to an inability to "take" an injection without crying out in pain, whereas other children (including girls) who were getting inoculations at the same time had remained silent and nonresponsive to any pain. The love-shys tended to remember their embarrassed feelings all too well. Indeed, remembered negative feelings from a very long time ago often haunted the love-shys to the point of distracting them from their involvement in productive pursuits such as work or study.

One 37-year old love-shy man told me about how he could remember jumping on tables and chairs in doctors' offices in order to avoid being given necessary inoculations. In fact, several of the love-shys recalled having to be held down by parents and medical staff in order to receive required injections. In some cases this behavior had occurred as late as age 14 or 15.

Several of the love-shys confessed that they break out in a cold sweat whenever they enter a physician's office for any reason. In essence, love-shy men tend to be inordinately nervous, and this often shows up even to the point wherein the medical staff comments upon it. Interestingly, a good predictive barometer that might be used to predict chronic love-shyness early in life is the knee-jerk response. One physician with whom I spoke commented that whenever he gives the knee-jerk test to a particularly shy or fearful male, the leg of that male will typically overreact, sometimes to an inordinate degree. Thus the tendency for the love-shy to quite automatically overreact in a hypernervous fashion seems to extend to all manner of things, including even the mild hitting of the knee with a rubber hammer.

In sum, love-shy males tend to have an extremely strong fear of pain and of anxiety. And these fears tend to keep them away from health care delivery systems for sometimes inordinate lengths of time. Despite their myriad medical symptoms, most of the love-shy obtain medical examinations only when these are absolutely required for employment or for some other education or career-related reason.

I found that this tendency to avoid medical services did not extend quite so strongly to the avoidance of dentists. Most of the love-shys had learned to relax to a sufficient extent upon the administration of novacaine. Unfortunately, medical doctors seldom deal in local anesthetics. And it is this fear of loss of control brought about by the potential administration of a general anesthetic (and being placed on a breathing machine) that the love-shy especially strongly fear. And they also fear the severe pain and nausea that often accrues from being brought out of anesthesia.

Curiously, none of the love-shys studied for this book had ever had a major surgical procedure performed on them. In essence, their worries were all rooted in what they had heard from others. Worries and fears rooted in personal experiences tended to be confined to the pains they recalled suffering as children upon being given required inoculations.

As I suggested in the preceding chapter, a good many of the love-shys may need a deviated septum and polypectomy procedure performed upon their noses and nasal cavities. Several of the older love-shys mentioned that such a procedure had been recommended to them, but that they had turned it down out of fear of pain and anxiety. Thus it is fair to assume that at least a few of the love-shys are permitting quite uncomfortable and socially debilitating medical conditions to remain uncorrected simply out of a fear of pain and of anxiety.

Miscellaneous Sensitivities

Each of the 500 respondents was asked about several other miscellaneous sensitivities. Obviously, there was no way for me to cover the gamut as far as this issue is concerned. Suffice it to say that every question I raised vis-a-vis each respondent revealed the love-shys to be substantially more sensitive than the non-shys.

For example, I asked each man to react to this statement: "It doesn't bother me much when a pair of rubbers are rubbed against each other (causing a squeek), or when chalk on a blackboard squeeks." Fully 60 percent of the self-confident non-shys replied "yes, it does *not* bother them". In contrast, only 16 percent of the older love-shy men and 36 percent of the younger love-shys could say that such squeeking sounds do *not* bother them.

Of course, this might seem like a "very little thing". But among elementary school and junior high school aged boys this sort of sensitivity is exactly the type of stimulus that invites bullying. In essence, the love-shys tended to have received more and more of the very things they hated and feared the most strongly. Usually such squeeking sounds caused the love-shys to experience painful chills up and down their spines. Non-shy people are significantly less likely to experience this painful sensation, although 40 percent of the non-shys studied for this book *had* experienced it. Thus, even socially self-confident people have *some* sensitivities. Of course, in *not overreacting* to such painful stimuli, the non-shys had not been forced to listen to as many such disconcerting squeeks as the love-shys had been forced to listen to.

Quite related to the foregoing was the following statement: "I can't handle a certain type of expensive, glossy paper (some expensive Christmas cards and department store boxes are made of it) because it causes chills to run up and down my spine." This question may have been somewhat vague for some respondents. Nevertheless, fully 26 percent of the older love-shys and 15 percent of the younger love-shys responded in the affirmative. In contrast, *nobody* among the 200 non-shys interviewed indicated that they could not handle a certain kind of paper.

Of considerably greater significance to the life of a typical male child was the following statement: "Most people seem to be able to enter cold water (such as a fresh water lake or ocean) a very great deal faster than I can." As I indicated in chapter six, many of the love-shys had enjoyed swimming a very great deal when they were children. Yet in spite of their enjoyment, they took much longer than most children to get used to (or "adapt to") cold water. And this had gotten quite a few of them into painful difficulties vis-a-vis their male peers.

In any event, fully 95 percent of the older love-shys and 69 percent of the younger love-shys *agreed* with the statement. In contrast, only 6 percent of the self-confident non-shy men agreed that they required much longer than most people to enter cold water. Obviously, these differences are quite substantial; and they may well relate to basic differences in body chemistry between the love-shys and the non-shys.

In another question I asked for reactions to this statement: "I can't stand it when one of my fingernails becomes even the slightest bit rough." And 57 percent of the older love-shys together with 40 percent of the younger love-shys agreed. In contrast, only 2 percent of the non-shy men agreed.

Another statement that was reacted to quite differently by the three samples of men was: "My eyelashes often seem to cause me itches and other discomforts." Fully 31 percent of the older love-shys together with 22 percent of the younger love-shys agreed. In contrast, *zero percent* of the non-shy men agreed. A related statement to which I elicited reactions was: "The corners of my eyes frequently itch." Here again, 56 percent of the older love-shys and 42 percent of the younger love-shys agreed. *Zero percent* of the non-shy men agreed.

And of relevance to encounter group therapy was the following statement: "Sitting on the floor or on the ground is very uncomfortable for me." Fully 73 percent of the older love-shys along with 51 percent of the younger love-shys agreed. In contrast, only 27 percent of the non-shy men agreed. In fact, several of the love-shys claimed that sitting on the ground for more than ten or fifteen minutes invariably caused their legs and arms to begin hurting. Of course, several others also claimed that sitting on the floor was "unsanitary" because it necessitates placing hands on that which people walk upon. This issue will be dealt with more fully in section three of this book.

Annoyance at Petty Stimuli

Love-shy men show considerable evidence of being unusually irked and annoyed by minor stimuli. In addition, it appears that certain stimuli such as minor discomforts (e.g., a rough fingernail) can distract them to a far greater extent than such stimuli can distract most people.

In some cases this tendency to be easily annoyed may be nothing more than a byproduct of chronic isolation from people. Thus the tendency to become easily annoyed may more often be a *consequence* of love-shyness rather than a cause. On the other hand, extreme manifestations of hypersensitivity may to some extent be rooted in inborn, genetically based considerations. In short, love-shy people may have a lower inborn threshold with respect to the experiencing of certain kinds of stimuli. And if this is so, these same hypersensitivities may also be partly responsible for the heightened self-consciousness which love-shy men commonly feel when they are around people in purely social situations wherein there is no script.

Consider the issue of the rough fingernail. Of course, women might be somewhat more likely than men to agree that a rough fingernail is disconcerting or distracting. But I suspect that a woman's concern here might more usually be attributable to concern for personal appearance than concern about bodily discomfort. The fact that the non-shys were less than one-twentieth as likely as the love-shys to be bothered by a rough fingernail may reflect (at least in part) a greater ability on their part to "*lose themselves*" in the many activities in which they are involved. The ability to become "lost" in what one is doing has long been recognized as an index of mental health, happiness and adjustment.

In lacking such adjustment the love-shy are often unable to "lose themselves" even when they are involved in activities which they enjoy. Thus this inability to become lost in what they are doing might well render them much more likely than the majority of people to notice and to be distracted by a rough fingernail, bodily itches, etc. In essence, the very active tend to be so thoroughly involved with life that such minor stimuli would not even be noticed or recognized in most cases as a bodily discomfort.

Like rough fingernails and bodily itches, grains of sand in one's shoes may well be more readily ignored by highly active people. But then again the speed with which a person is likely to notice a grain of sand in his shoes may itself be partly a function of an inborn, genetically based discomfort threshold. In this regard I asked each man: "To what extent could you walk around with a small grain of sand in one of your shoes and not be aware of it?" And 98 percent of the older love-shys together with 81 percent of the younger love-shys indicated that it would be *"quite likely"* that they would be aware of such a grain of sand. Only 41 percent of the self-confident non-shys felt likewise. Of course, 41 percent is a much higher figure than the 2 percent of the non-shys who would be aware of a rough fingernail. However, what is really impressive here is the *significantly greater sensitivity* of the love-shy men.

By the way, fully 33 percent of the non-shy men indicated that they would probably not be aware at all of such a grain of sand in their shoes. In contrast, *zero percent* of the older love-shys and just 4 percent of the younger love-shys indicated that they would probably not be aware of a grain of sand in their shoes.

The love-shys' unusually high level of sensitivity can similarly be observed in the pattern of responses to this question: "If you felt a grain of sand in your shoe, how likely would you be to stop within 30 seconds, take your shoe off and dump it out?" And 100 percent of the older love-shys along with 77 percent of the younger love-shys indicated that they would be "quite likely to stop and dump it out". In contrast, this was true for only 38 percent of the non-shy men.

Loud, sudden noises also bother the love-shy a good deal more than they bother the non-shy. Hence, the love-shy tend to be substantially more sensitive than the non-shy to the antics of extroverted boys. For example, I asked for reactions to this statement: "I hate it when extroverted, joyriding youths bellow crazy remarks out of their car windows at passing pedestrians." And 97 percent of the older love-shys along with 81 percent of the younger love-shys replied in the affirmative. In contrast, only 18 percent of the non-shy men saw fit to agree.

And as I have already pointed out, most love-shys absolutely despise any type of rock music. It is worth underscoring the point that they hate such music for esthetic reasons, and not for moral ones. As several love-shys pointed out in the interviews, "it violates my esthetic sensibilities". And more than one love-shy man asserted that "rock music is no more comfortable to listen to than the incessant roar of a jackhammer digging up a city street."

Eye Color and Hair Strand Width

Is eye color related to love-shyness? Probably not. But for whatever it may be worth, I did find an interesting difference here. Fully 38 percent of the older love-shys and 36 percent of the younger love-shys had *blue eyes*. In contrast, only 21 percent of the self-confident non-shys had *blue eyes*. Of course, blue eyes are caused by a recessive gene. And it could be that inhibition might be mildly related to the presence of that gene.

Finally, I asked for reactions to this statement: "The width of each of the strands of hair on my head appears to be a great deal narrower (thinner) than most people's hair." And 46 percent of the older love-shys together with 39 percent of the younger love-shys *agreed*. In contrast, only 7 percent of the self-confident non-shy men agreed. Down through the ages many philosophers have believed hair strand width to be related to inhibition, social withdrawal tendencies, and psycho-emotional sensitivity. These data would certainly appear to back up such philosophical speculations.

Some Concluding Observations

Wender and Klein (1981) cite an unpublished paper by Seymour Kety and Dennis Kinney, in which evidence was presented linking extreme shyness (and schizoid personality) with high wheat and rye consumption. Very shy men tend to eat a great deal of breakfast cereal. In fact, some of them appear to eat far more of high-wheat cereals than what could be considered typical of Americans generally. And they also tend to have a strong preference for citrus fruits over other types of fruits—another food predilection that has been found to be strongly associated with extreme introversion.

Psychiatrists Kety and Kinney conducted two studies involving wheat consumption. Each of the two studies contained an experimental group and a control group. Schizoid personalities in the experimental groups had sharply reduced their intake of high-wheat cereals whereas the schizoids in the control groups continued eating the high-wheat diet to which they had grown accustomed. In both experiments the experimental subjects (low wheat diet) gradually became progressively more sociable and less schizoid in their behavior than the controls (high wheat diet).

If these findings continue to hold up over time, then it may be that extremely shy people in many cases have a food allergy—to wheat—which interacts with genetic susceptibility in such a way as to produce deviant degrees of behavioral inhibition, timidity, shyness, and low initiative.

Finally, there is a possibility that severely love-shy people inherit a genetic susceptibility to invasion (early in life) by a schizoid-inducing virus. Over twenty studies during the past four decades have shown a consistent 5 to 15 percent increase in pre-schizoid births during the winter and spring months as compared to the other months of the year. This phenomenon has been reported for a large array of both northern hemisphere and southern hemisphere countries—although the effect tends to be most marked in geographical areas wherein seasonal variations are decidedly pronounced. In view of the fact that the love-shy males studied for this book tended to be especially likely to have been born in the spring (see chapter 4), this is a potentially noteworthy finding the nature of which deserves careful investigation.

According to Wender and Klein (1981), researchers have hypothesized that this increase in pre-schizoid births during late winter and spring may be associated with a greater than average susceptibility (among those with an initially weak constitution) to infectious diseases during that time of the year, and to a greater prevalence of viruses at that time. It needs to be stressed that we are still in the kindergarten of awareness as to what is actually going on here. And it is clear that an enormous amount of new research on the biological/physiological/genetic basis of severe shyness is sorely needed.

Chapter 17

Some Psychological Characteristics of the Love-Shy

In looking over the wide range of information I collected for this book I discovered many items upon which there were enormous differences between the love-shys and the non-shys. A large portion of these items concerned matters of pertinence to style of thinking, personal introspection, and psychoemotional make-up. The primary purpose of this chapter is to fill out the picture on what love-shy men are really like as human beings "deep down inside".

Being Friendly Requires Nerve

Most Americans regard open friendliness as the "natural" state of affairs. Indeed, seemingly unfriendly people are often viewed with suspicion, and they are typically seen as being hostile. At best they are avoided, and they are commonly labeled as "weird" or worse. This is particularly true as far as males are concerned. Unfriendly women are merely likely to be viewed as diffident and perhaps rightfully suspicious vis-a-vis people whom they dont' know. In contrast, unfriendly or seemingly "weird" men tend to be viewed in a hostile fashion. And as a consequence they are ignored or shunned.

Important too is the very widespread tendency to equate behavior with attitude. Simply put, if a person behaves in an unfriendly manner, we tend to view his *attitude* as being unfriendly—even when it is anything but unfriendly. People cannot react and respond to that which they cannot see. Similarly, if a young man is never observed interacting informally with women and if he is always seen alone, the natural tendency is to perceive him as being a homosexual, or perhaps as a "closet queen". And this is true irrespective of how thoroughly heterosexual in predilections that person might indeed be.

Of course, very few people are telepathic. And even those who are may be turned off by the sensing of a strong feeling of negativity and doleful sourness in a love-shy man's aura. The point that needs to be stressed, however, is that for the love-shy attitudes and overt behaviors seldom coincide. The love-shy person cannot command his performance in the direction of his wishes because he is not in the "driver's seat" of his own life. A love-shy man may sustain very liberal, humanitarian attitudes towards others. But due to the fact that he constantly avoids informal social interaction he is likely to be perceived by others as being anything but humanitarian, and anything but "warm and caring".

Again, most Americans judge others *by what they can see*. Attitudes and values cannot be directly observed. And in fact they remain entirely hidden unless and until the person holding them opens up and shares them with others. And even then he may not be believed if his *observable behavior* continues on in a highly asocial, socially avoidant fashion—or in a fashion that appears to contradict the substance of what he says. Consider the cliched expression: "Your actions speak so loudly I cannot hear a word you are saying!"

Let's look at a few examples of these social avoidance tendencies. I asked each respondent to react to this statement: "It requires a tremendous amount of nerve to be friendly with people." And *zero percent* (nobody) of the non-shys said that they agreed. In contrast, fully 52 percent of the younger love-shys and 76 percent of the older love-shys indicated that they agreed with that statement.

Focusing attention upon the opposite sex I asked for reactions to this statement: "It requires a tremendous amount of nerve to be friendly with the opposite sex." And here again, *zero percent* of the non-shy men agreed. In contrast, fully 100 percent of the older love-shy men together with 77 percent of the younger love-shys agreed.

Even more illustrative of the love-shys' behavioral and psychoemotional thought style was the pattern of responses to this statement: "I would sooner avoid someone I know on the street than risk accidentally saying 'hello' to a stranger." *Zero percent* of the non-shy men endorsed this statement. In contrast, fully 87 percent of the older love-shys along with 68 percent of the younger love-shys indicated that the statement was true for themselves.

Extreme Self-Consciousness

A well nigh universal behavior trait of the love-shy is *extreme self-consciousness* when in or near the company of an eligible woman. In essence, the love-shy are intensely preoccupied with the self and cannot "let go and let God". Intense self-preoccupation is, of course, the same phenomenon as extreme *tenseness*. Love-shys are quite unable to relax when in the company of (or anywhere near) a potentially eligible female. And this inability to relax not only ushers in painful anxiety spells, but it also makes clear-headed thinking and communicating virtually impossible.

The minds of virtually all human beings function best and most efficiently when they are relaxed and comfortable. Tension creates a phenomenon known as *"tunnel vision"*. Afflicted by tunnel vision (the *natural* outcome of feeling tense, worried, and intensely self-conscious), ideas for topics of conversation simply cannot and do not come to mind. Effective small talk absolutely requires a relaxed, comfortable feeling of mind.

As a case in point, taking an examination under conditions of a very worried, tense state of mind makes it extremely difficult for a person to do his/her best. The right answers just do not seem to come to mind. The student might have indeed learned the material very thoroughly; but the worry and the tensed-up feeling *blocks and constricts* the "pipe-lines" of truth and knowledge that serve as a conduit for the required facts from the brain's storehouse or memory banks into the conscious mind. This is the essence of "tunnel vision". In contrast, when the person is relaxed and confident and positive in mental attitude, the right answers all manage to quite easily pass into conscious awareness.

And so it is in situations wherein there is no purpose apart from pure, unadulterated sociability. When the fear of the likelihood of anxiety (anticipatory anxiety) causes the person to tense up and to become extremely preoccupied with his own self instead of with the person with whom he is talking, he finds that his mind goes completely blank— which contributes to an even worstening of the anxiety–and relevant ideas just don't come to mind. Immediately upon leaving the anxiety-provoking social encounter, on the other hand, hundreds of very good ideas suddenly flood the mind—because the anxiety and tenseness stimulus has been removed. But it is then too late!

Telephones

If love-shy men are made nervous by the mere thought of purely sociable, friendly interaction on a face-to-face basis with others, the idea of using a telephone does not operate to make them feel anymore comfortable. For example, 100 percent of the older love-shys agreed with the statement: "Telephones have always made me nervous." The analogous figure for the younger love-shys was 76 percent. In contrast, just

11 percent of the non-shys agreed with the statement. (A figure as high as 11 percent might well be considered surprisingly high for the non-shys, given their tendency not to fear face-to-face interaction.)

And the love-shys had evidently learned to adapt to their fear of telephones. Many of them dealt with their telephone aversion by writing letters when they had to communicate with someone. For example, 41 percent of the older love-shys and 30 percent of the younger love-shys indicated that if given a choice they would invariably choose to write someone a letter in lieu of calling them on the telephone. *None* of the non-shys indicated that they would resort to letter-writing in lieu of making a telephone call.

By the way, only 3 percent of the older love-shys kept telephones in their private apartments. The analogous figure for the younger love-shys was 23 percent. In contrast, *all* of the non-shy men kept a private telephone in their place of abode.

Assertion Phobia

Besides being "people-phobes", the love-shy appear to possess strong phobias regarding even the simplest forms of social assertiveness. For example, consider this statement: "Lots of times when I am eating among a group of people I do without salt because I haven't got the nerve to ask someone to pass me the salt shaker." *Zero percent* of the non-shy men indicated "yes" to this statement. Yet fully 37 percent of the younger love-shys and 58 percent of the older love-shys would sooner do without salt than ask someone to pass it.

This question regarding "the passing of the saltshaker" illustrates as poignantly as anything the sheer *social invisibility* of the love-shy. A person can only become visible and noticed to the extent that he takes some social risks and asserts himself. The love-shy had learned to sustain a self-imposed camouflage; the net result of this is that whenever they are amidst a group of interacting persons they are "invisible"—they are there in body but not in spirit. And this is reflected in the virtually universal tendency among the love-shy to enter into a world of day-dreams whenever they are amongst a group of interacting people—unless one of the people whom they are with makes the first move towards starting a conversation. Then and only then does the love-shy person "open up".

Asking for directions represents another example of this fear of self-assertion. I asked each respondent to react to this statement: "I would have to drive many miles out of my way before I would ever be able to get up enough nerve to ask someone for directions." Fully 46 percent of the older love-shys together with 34 percent of the younger love-shys indicated that this was true for themselves. In contrast, *none* of the non-shys revealed any inhibitions at all about asking people for directions.

A Life-Threatening Scenario

Suppose that your physician together with several of his/her esteemed specialist colleagues got together and told you that you had only six months to live. Suppose that they further advised you that for at least the first five of these six months your activities need not be impeded in any way. In other words, you will be able to do virtually anything that you wish to do for the first five of your remaining six months of life.

This scenario has become a favorite of motivational psychologists who travel around the United States and Canada trying to inspire people towards using their valuable time more productively, happily and effectively. Accordingly, I presented it to all 500 of the men who were interviewed for this book. I wanted to get their reactions as I was particularly curious as to whether or not the love-shys would respond to it noticeably different than the non-shys.

The differences I obtained turned out to be quite remarkable. For example, not one man among the 100 older love-shys believed that his life style would change very much at all—especially from the standpoint of his relationships vis-a-vis other people. In essence, for the typical love-shy man, the fear of experiencing anxiety in social situations is more forbidding than the fear of death itself.

A few of the love-shys told me that they would take everything out of their bank accounts and use much of their remaining time traveling. And a few of them would use this as an opportunity to cheat their credit card companies. Some of them spoke about quitting their jobs and spending endless hours listening to their stereos, watching television, or going to the movies. However, *none of them* (and this is the important point) seriously thought that the six-month time limit would in any way have the effect of making it any easier for them to approach a woman, or for them to risk rejection in purely sociable, social situations. The following might be considered typical of the responses I received from the older love-shy men:

> "Well, I'd certainly quit this stupid-ass job; I know that much! Then I guess I'd take everything out of my bank account and I'd use the whole time just traveling all over the place. I'd probably also get all

the cash I could from these so-called credit card loans. Like if I only had five months I might as well get all I can. They're not going to be able to take any action against me if I'm going to be dead! . . . . I know what I'd really like to do. I'd really like to just get myself a really fabulous woman and just do nothing but have constant sex for six months. But I know I'd never be able to even ask a girl out, much less have sex. Even with only six months to live, I know I'd just flip out of my gorge just to even think about approaching a pretty woman. I just couldn't take the anxiety. The fact that I had only six months to live wouldn't make a damn bit of difference because I'd still have to deal with the anxiety. And I know that I'd never be able to deal with the anxiety. Like I told you, I can't even *think* about starting a conversation with some woman who is attractive to me. It blows my mind too much. So I'd just use the remaining time traveling. That's a whole lot better than nothing." (44-year old love-shy man.)

By the way, the responses of the younger love-shys were little different from those of the older ones. On the other hand, the non-shy men tended to phrase their responses strictly in terms of their personal involvements with friends, lovers, relatives, and other loved ones. Many of the non-shys would also travel. But all would do so with a lover and/ or with close friends and family.

Items Clearly Earmarking the Love-Shy

Many of the statements which I presented to all respondents sharply differentiated the love-shy from the non-shy. In essence, these are statements which were reacted to very differently by the love-shy men than by the non-shy men. For the interest and convenience of the reader a representative sampling of these statements is provided below. Underneath each statement the percent of each group of men saying "*true*" is indicated.

1. "When I like someone I am able to let them know it without difficulty."
    82 percent of the non-shy men.
    6 percent of the younger love-shy men.
    Zero percent of the older love-shy men.

2. "I find it very difficult to display emotion and feeling."
    19 percent of the non-shy men.
    66 percent of the younger love-shy men.
    93 percent of the older love-shy men.

3. "When I would like to be friendly with someone, I often feel that I know what to say but I just haven't got the nerve to say it."
   Zero percent of the non-shy men.
   79 percent of the younger love-shy men.
   100 percent of the older love-shy men.

4. "I often feel that I don't know what to say in certain types of informal social situations."
   6 percent of the non-shy men.
   93 percent of the younger love-shy men.
   100 percent of the older love-shy men.

5. "I find it easy to relax with other people."
   100 percent of the non-shy men.
   14 percent of the younger love-shy men.
   7 percent of the older love-shy men.

6. "I sometimes take the responsibility for introducing people to each other."
   88 percent of the non-shy men.
   23 percent of the younger love-shy men.
   Zero percent of the older love-shy men.

7. "Being introduced to people makes me very tense and nervous."
   Zero percent of the non-shy men.
   82 percent of the younger love-shy men.
   100 percent of the older love-shy men.

8. "I would avoid walking up and joining a large group of people."
   Zero percent of the non-shy men.
   79 percent of the younger love-shy men.
   100 percent of the older love-shy men.

9. "After I was about 13 or so I usually tried not to sing out loud whenever anyone was around."
   20 percent of the non-shy men.
   83 percent of the younger love-shy men.
   100 percent of the older love-shy men.

10. "I often feel on edge when I am with a group of people."
    Zero percent of the non-shy men.
    75 percent of the younger love-shy men.
    86 percent of the older love-shy men.

11. "I tend to withdraw from people."

Zero percent of the non-shy men.
84 percent of the younger love-shy men.
96 percent of the older love-shy men.

12. "I find it easy to start conversations with people at parties and informal social gatherings."
    93 percent of the non-shy men.
    Zero percent of the younger love-shy men.
    Zero percent of the older love-shy men.

13. "I find it easy to start conversations with people *of the opposite sex* in informal social situations."
    100 percent of the non-shy men.
    Zero percent of the younger love-shy men.
    Zero percent of the older love-shy men.

14. "I am seldom at ease in a large group of people."
    Zero percent of the non-shy men.
    67 percent of the younger love-shy men.
    92 percent of the older love-shy men.

15. "I feel relaxed even in unfamiliar social situations."
    54 percent of the non-shy men.
    Zero percent of the younger love-shy men.
    Zero percent of the older love-shy men.

16. "I often feel tense or nervous in casual get-togethers in which both sexes are present."
    Zero percent of the non-shy men.
    94 percent of the younger love-shy men.
    100 percent of the older love-shy men.

17. "If the chance comes to meet new people, I often take it."
    96 percent of the non-shy men.
    21 percent of the younger love-shy men.
    11 percent of the older love-shy men.

18. "I don't mind talking to people at parties or social gatherings *provided that they* make the first move in opening conversations with me."
    Zero percent of the non-shy men.
    89 percent of the younger love-shy men.
    100 percent of the older love-shy men.

Sense of Humor

Sense of humor is one of the most important ingredients of what American women deem to be a winning personality in a man. Hundreds of research studies on dating and courtship have shown this to be true. In fact, several studies pertaining to success in marriage have similarly shown *"sense of humor"* to be a factor of formidable predictive value. Certainly it is no laughing matter! A successful marriage requires mutual compassion; and compassion requires communication. A relaxed sense of humor constitutes a major element of communication skills.

It is precisely with respect to sense of humor that one can easily appreciate how "the rich get richer while the poor get poorer." The love-shy had gone through so much unhappiness and negativity throughout their formative years that it soured their personalities and removed what little sense of humor they might once have had. Indeed, the love-shys' pasts probably developed in them a trained incapacity for even developing much of a sense of humor. Their past experiences had made them extremely self-centered, self-conscious, and self-preoccupied. And it is very difficult for such a personality to relax and to be naturally spontaneous enough to "roll with the punches" and to display any humor.

This can be seen quite clearly and poignantly in the pattern of responses to this question: "Compared to most people, about how often would you say you laugh?" Fully 100 percent of the non-shy men checked either "often" or "very often", compared to just 22 percent of the younger love-shys and a mere 6 percent of the older love-shy men. On the other hand, fully 63 percent of the older love-shy men together with 45 percent of the younger ones indicated that they seldom laugh. *Nobody* among the non-shys indicated that he seldom laughs.

In a related question I simply asked: "In general, do you find it easy to laugh?" And fully 100 percent of the non-shy men said "yes", compared to only 20 percent of the older love-shys along with 34 percent of the younger love-shys. Several of the love-shy respondents told me that as young children they had been able to laugh quite easily, but that they had somehow lost the ability over the years. Indeed, one 39-year old love-shy man told me that it has probably been approximately twenty years since the last time he had laughed. Other love-shys made similar albeit less extreme comments.

The ability to spontaneously laugh is important not only from the standpoint of being looked upon favorably by others, but also from the standpoint of sheer physical (medical) health and longevity. Several studies have shown that laughing aids digestion, circulation, blood pressure, and many of the metabolic processes that pertain to the generation of life-preserving enzymes and enzyme activity. The fact that the ability to spontaneously laugh has a strong bearing upon mental health surely goes without saying.

Fully 100 percent of the non-shy men agreed that they "get a lot of fun out of life". This too, it would seem, has a strong bearing upon the sense of humor a person is likely to be perceived by other people as having. Only 23 percent of the older love-shys and 35 percent of the younger love-shys could similarly concur with the statement that they get "a lot of fun out of life". And in a related question I asked:

> "Some people seem to be good at being happy; they enjoy life regardless of what is going on, get the most out of everything. Others are the opposite; they never are as happy as they might be. Where do you fall?"

Fully 95 percent of the non-shy men indicated that they were "very good at being happy". This was true for only 4 percent of the older love-shy men and 11 percent of the younger love-shys. In contrast, 96 percent of the older love-shys rated themselves as being "fair" or "poor" at being happy, compared to *zero percent* of the non-shy men; 70 percent of the younger love-shys rated themselves as being "fair" to "poor" at being happy. The remainder of them checked "pretty good at being happy".

The love-shy men tended to attend motion pictures quite a bit more frequently than the non-shy men. Yet fully 100 percent of the older love-shys and 73 percent of the younger ones indicated that they usually try to avoid motion pictures that are classified as "light comedies". This was the case for *zero percent* of the non-shy men. As I shall show in a later chapter, most of the love-shys wanted to be *emotionally engrossed* while attending a motion picture. In contrast, the non-shys tended to be primarily interested in merely being entertained. Again, the non-shys could laugh easily at many different things; the love-shys, on the other hand, tended to find light comedies extremely boring and lacking in substance.

Quite related to the natural and spontaneous ability to laugh (or cry), is the ability to display emotion generally. It is not at all unusual for American men to develop a trained incapacity for displaying emotion. And the pathologically love-shy appear to have been especially vulnerable in this regard. For example, 93 percent of the older love-shy men along with 66 percent of the younger love-shys agreed that they found it very difficult to display emotion or feeling. Even among the non-shy men the analogous figure was a surprisingly high 19 percent—almost a fifth of those interviewed. Nevertheless, it seems quite apparent that an inability to be spontaneously real in one's interactions with others is a very central aspect of the love-shyness problem.

Control Over the Good and Bad

Love-shy men do not feel as though they enjoy any significant degree of control over the impressions other people have of them. I asked each man: "How much control do you think you have over the *good* things that happen to you in life?" And 100 percent of the non-shys thought that they enjoyed a good deal of control over what happened to them. In contrast, only 40 percent of the younger love-shys and just 27 percent of the older love-shys thought that they had any significant amount of control at all over the good things that happen to them in life.

The story remained much the same when I asked: "How much control do you think you have over the *bad* things that happen to you in life?" Only 6 percent of the older love-shys together with 25 percent of the younger love-shys thought that they had any control at all. In contrast, 73 percent of the non-shys thought that they had a substantial amount of control over the bad things that happen to them in life.

Of course, this 73 percent figure is a good deal lower than the 100 percent figure that applied to control over the *good* things that happen in life. This would seem to reflect the fact that even non-shy, happy, well-adjusted people typically feel that they enjoy less control over the bad which might happen than over the good.

Loneliness

The relationship between loneliness and love-shyness is more complex than most people imagine. I tested each of my respondents for loneliness through the use of a 20-item scale that had been developed at U.C.L.A. during the mid 1970s, by Dr. Letitia Anne Peplau. The scale together with the instructions for responding to it follows:

For each of the following twenty statements please use the following legend:

"1" = I *never* feel this way.
"2" = I *rarely* feel this way.
"3" = I *sometimes* feel this way.
"4" = I *often* feel this way.

Please *circle* whatever number is closest to the truth for you for each of the twenty statements:

1. I am unhappy doing so many things alone. 1 2 3 4
2. I have nobody to talk to. 1 2 3 4
3. I cannot tolerate being so alone. 1 2 3 4
4. I lack companionship. 1 2 3 4
5. I feel as if nobody really understands me. 1 2 3 4
6. I find myself waiting for people to call or write. 1 2 3 4
7. There is no one I can turn to. 1 2 3 4
8. I am no longer close to anyone. 1 2 3 4
9. My interests and ideas are not shared by those around me. 1 2 3 4
10. I feel left out. 1 2 3 4
11. I feel completely alone. 1 2 3 4
12. I am unable to reach out and communicate with those around me. 1 2 3 4
13. My social relationships are superficial. 1 2 3 4
14. I feel starved for company. 1 2 3 4
15. No one really knows me well. 1 2 3 4
16. I feel isolated from others. 1 2 3 4
17. I am unhappy being so withdrawn. 1 2 3 4
18. It is difficult for me to make friends. 1 2 3 4
19. I feel shut out and excluded by others. 1 2 3 4
20. People are around me but not with me. 1 2 3 4

The mean (average) loneliness score for the 200 non-shy men was 27.4. The mean score for the 200 younger love-shy men was 60.9; and the mean score for the 100 older love-shy men was 73.2.

In essence, it would appear that the love-shy suffer from a great many more feelings of loneliness than do the non-shy. However, a problem with this interpretation is that 97 percent of the older love-shys together with 74 percent of the younger ones *also claimed* (when I directly questioned them about it) that they *never* experienced any feelings of loneliness *for people of their own sex*. Simply put, the large majority of love-shy men do not seem to care about the fact that they do not have any real friendships with people of their own gender. Indeed, quite a few of the respondents specifically indicated that they did not even want any friendships with people of their own sex.

Thus it would appear that the twenty statements on *Peplau's Loneliness Scale* were all interpreted by a majority of the love-shy males in strictly cross-sexed terms. It should be noted, of course, that the scale items are all *gender-neutral*. In other words, none of the twenty statements have any bearing at all upon loneliness for the opposite sex as opposed to loneliness for one's own sex. Similarly, none of the items require an interpretation of loneliness for one's own sex as opposed to loneliness for the opposite sex. Yet the love-shy men interviewed for this study all seemed to think strictly in terms of their long-term deprivation of cross-sexed companionship.

For example, item #4 tended to be interpreted: "I lack opposite sexed companionship". Item #18 tended to be interpreted as: "It is difficult for me to make friends with the opposite sex". And so on for each of the other eighteen statements. In stark contrast, the non-shy men did not tend to think in these cross-sexed terms at all. Only the love-shy tended to interpret the scale exclusively in cross-sexed terms.

I asked each man to respond to this statement: "It wouldn't bother me at all if I had no friends of my own sex. Just so long as I had friends of the opposite sex I'd be alright." Fully 86 percent of the older love-shys and 61 percent of the younger ones agreed with this statement. In contrast, only 12 percent of the self-confident non-shy men agreed with it.

> "What the hell would I want a male friend for! All they ever talk about is baseball, basketball and football! I can't stand their interests or their crass, coarse manners. Whenever I even hear guys talk with each other I want to get away from them as fast as possible because it's too depressing. I want a girl! That's the only thing I've ever felt lonely for. I've never felt lonely for a male friend in my entire life!" (20-year old love-shy man.)

Despite the differences which obtained between the love-shys and the non-shys on the *Peplau Loneliness Scale*, I got the distinct impression from my many interviews that love-shy males in general tend to have *a much weaker need for people* than (probably) the vast majority of the population of human beings. To be sure, the love-shys are far from content with their lot. But at the same time their needs for people tend to be restricted to their deeply felt need for just one (usually beautiful) opposite sexed person with whom they can love and live.

Another impression I got (and I may be wrong about this one) is that the younger love-shys seem to suffer from a good many more bouts of really painful loneliness than the older love-shys do. The older love-shys seem to have adapted to their lot in life. And even though they are far from content with that lot or willing to accept it as their "just desserts", they do not appear to become bogged down by as many lengthy periods of debilitating depression as do the younger love-shys.

> "Oh, twenty years ago there were sometimes weeks at a time when I couldn't even study or concentrate on any of my work. I would flunk courses I didn't have to flunk. Sometimes at 3 o'clock in the morning I'd just be overwhelmed with an uncontrollable urge to just get up and take a really long walk. That used to happen a lot

of times. Every time I became infatuated with some girl at work or school I'd get this uncontrollable urge to take five-mile walks at any time of night, no matter how late. I'd be just so damned depressed. But I'd be even more depressed if I just laid there. I just had to get up and run and run and run. And when I'd get back I'd be sapped of every ounce of energy, and still I'd be depressed—but I guess not as depressed as I would have been if I didn't run. I mean, I'd some-times get these really beautiful fantasies when I'd take long walks. I'd see myself really making it with a beautiful girl.

It's been a really long time since I was that badly off. I guess I started to calm down when I was about 32 or 33. Right now I guess I feel more angry than depressed. Like I'm angry at society for depriving me of a chance for a wife and family simply because I'm shy. I mean that really pisses me off. And that's how I feel—pissed off, not depressed or even lonely so much." (47-year old love-shy man.)

The foregoing feelings seemed to be quite typical of many of the older love-shy men. These feelings may merely be a reflection of changes in blood-androgens and blood-testosterones that gradually accrue as a person becomes older. Hence, blood hormone changes could affect cer-tain emotional feelings (e.g., restlessness and depression) without caus-ing any changes in basic beliefs concerning deprivation, being a long-term victim of unjust treatment, etc.

In sum, I would say that love-shyness is far from being in any way synonymous with loneliness. Love-shy males tend to think of "loneli-ness" strictly in terms of their long-term deprivation of meaningful, loving *female* companionship. From this it can be concluded that mem-bership in any kind of support group or friendship group that is strictly (or even primarily) male in membership composition is something that would drive most love-shy men to distraction. Therapists need to keep this point in mind. An all-male group almost invariably meets with strong feelings of resistance, boredom, disinterest, and even hostility, as far as love-shy men are concerned. They drop out of and avoid such groups because they do not perceive such group involvements as speak-ing in any way to their deeply felt needs and vested interests.

Simply put, an all-male group will not in any way correct feelings of loneliness among love-shy men. It will not correct such feelings because involvement with male peers is not seen by love-shy men as being therapeutic. To the love-shy, *females* are the only human beings worth knowing or informally associating with. There is an old cliche that it is possible for a person to be quite "lonely" out in a crowd. Love-shy males characteristically *feel* quite "lonely" when they are in or around groups of men. Never having developed the ability to truly "let their hair down" and relax while in the company of men, they feel that only female companionship can accord them what they *really* need.

Loneliness and Experimental Social Psychology

Experimental work in the field of social psychology has led to a better understanding of the dynamics of loneliness. Much of this work has had a direct bearing upon the problem of love-shyness. And it is worth looking at in this regard.

A set of experiments by Schachter (1959) demonstrated that, given the opportunity, people confronting a stress-inducing experience will usually tend to seek out the informal social support of other people— even strangers if necessary. Experimental subjects who thought they were going to experience a series of painful electric shocks, and subjects who anticipated experiencing only very mild electrical stimuli were given a choice between (1) waiting alone, and (2) waiting with other subjects for a brief period while final preparations were made for the experiment. In essence, Schachter found that the greater the anticipated pain, the greater the tendency was for subjects to choose to wait amid the companionship of other people. He interpreted this pattern as reflecting heightened needs for reassurance, distraction, information, and social comparison, among subjects experiencing greater stress.

Sarnoff and Zimbardo (1961) largely replicated Schachter's results; but they also demonstrated the fact that people do not always seek social affiliation or emotional support in the face of severe stress or anticipated pain. These researchers distinguished between *fear* of an inherently dangerous, painful external object, and *anxiety*, the latter of which is negative emotional arousal *that has no clear source* or which stems from *objectively harmless objects or social situations*.

In addition to replicating Schachter's fear arousal conditions (anticipation of electric shock), their study also included an anxiety arousal condition in which male college students were led to anticipate having to suck on a variety of nipples, baby bottles and pacifiers—as in a contrived, embarrassing situation of the type which used to be televised as "entertainment" on such television shows as CANDID CAMERA and PEOPLE ARE FUNNY.

As expected, there was far greater variation among the experimental subjects in emotional arousal in the *anxiety* condition than there had been in the *fear* condition. More importantly, high levels of emotional arousal in the *anxiety* condition led to a marked preference among the subjects for *waiting alone* rather than with other subjects. *Almost all* subjects in the *fear* condition chose to wait for their anticipated ordeal amid the companionship of other people.

Sarnoff and Zimbardo suggest that if people are emotionally aroused for reasons that are largely idiosyncratic to their own unique personality or (possibly) not socially acceptable, they will tend to fear many kinds of informal social contact. And even potentially beneficial emotional support will only serve to increase their anxiety.

Because the *anxious* person tends to be aware of the element of *inappropriateness* in his feelings, he is loath to communicate his anxieties to other people. To avoid being ridiculed or censured, he conceals anxiety aroused by stimuli which he guesses do not have a similar effect upon others and which, he feels, ought not to upset him. Thus when *anxiety* is aroused a person should tend to *seek isolation from others*. On the other hand, when *fear* is aroused and he is unable to flee from the threatening object, he welcomes the opportunity to affiliate with other people.

The love-shy man (deep down) is clearly embarrassed about his inability to "connect" with any woman. Since women do not constitute an objectively dangerous sort of stimuli, the painful inability to approach and to initiate conversations with them represents an *anxiety*, NOT a *fear*. In American society it is considered socially unacceptable for men (far more than is the case for women) to harbor anxieties. Indeed, it is considered even more socially unacceptable for men to permit their lives to be virtually *governed* by their anxieties.

The lives of the love-shy are, in point of fact, quite governed by their anxieties. And I believe that this represents a formidable reason as to why virtually none of the 300 severely love-shy men studied for this book had any strong desires to informally affiliate with members of his own gender. Many of the love-shy men specifically told me that *once they managed to get themselves a girl* they would definitely want to have some male friends. But as long as they were without their heart's desire—because of these socially unacceptable *anxieties* which they were allowing to control their lives—they felt very uncomfortable whenever they were amid the informal companionship of fellow males whom they might have otherwise very much enjoyed having as friends.

This represents another reason why I believe that love-shy males of *all* ages (including prepubescents) must *first* be therapeutically helped to informally affiliate with women/girls. I believe that this *must* be done BEFORE they will be in any way amenable to therapy aimed at the cultivation of same-sexed friendships. As long as (1) love-shy males desperately crave female companionship, and (2) as long as they are governed by these *socially unacceptable anxieties* which cause them to avoid opportunities for friendly, sociable self-assertion vis-a-vis women, they can be expected to go to considerable lengths to avoid sociable interaction with fellow males.

Another experimental study with clear implications for our understanding of love-shy males was conducted by Freedman and Doob (1968) at Stanford University. Using a clever experimental maneuver, they made some of their subjects feel *"different"* from those around them, whereas other experimental subjects were made to feel "pretty much like others of their own age and sex." Hence, subjects who were told (after taking a battery of personality tests) that they were very unlike others of their age and sex *tended to elect working alone* on a contrived experimental task. This was especially true if none of the other experimental subjects in the room knew that they (the deviant subjects) were actually "deviant". More succinctly, most of the experimental subjects run by Freedman and Doob chose to work in a group with other people. The only subjects who chose *not* to work in a group with other people were either (1) those who had been made to feel "deviant" as a result of being shown fake personality test results that made them appear to be highly "deviant", and (2) those whose real or actual personality test profiles indicated that they were indeed (in reality) quite different from others of their age and sex.

Love-shy men are, of course, quite demonstrably "deviant". How, indeed, could a *totally virginal*, heterosexual man in his thirties or forties be anything but "deviant"! Most of the 300 love-shy men studied for this book were even more "deviant" than that, inasmuch as most of them had never even kissed (or been kissed) by a girl or woman! Many of them had never even dated. In this sense, severely love-shy men must be considered quite directly analogous to Freedman and Doob's "unknown deviant" laboratory condition. Thus, you cannot spot a 40-year old male virgin on the street just by looking at him. You cannot spot a severely love-shy 19-year old male who has never been kissed, just by looking over a group of 19-year old individuals.

These "deviant" (involuntarily nonconformist) men tend to be quite embarrassed about their *non-behavior*, about the fact that their "non-behavior" is at drastic variance with their value systems, and about the way their interpersonal anxiety vis-a-vis women has dominated and ruled over their lives. Thus, we might reasonably guess that most of them don't especially care to be "found out" or "exposed"—as could quite easily happen within the context of any all-male peer group.

And, of course, many love-shy men further feel that the all-male peer group will misperceive them as "homosexuals". After all, how can 19–50 year old men who are totally without any form of heterosexual experience (and who are not priests) be anything but homosexual! That is the way popular lay-reasoning works. Most people are not even aware of the fact that about 40 percent of all homosexual men marry; about 35 percent of them have children. And about 80 percent of them pass through a period of quite rampant *heterosexual* promiscuity before they finally come to terms with and accept their true homosexual identity. Again, homosexuality is a totally different "animal" from heterosexual love-shyness. Doubtless, there are some *homosexual* love-shys. But they are most assuredly in the minority, just as *heterosexual* love-shys represent a small minority (1.5 percent) of all *heterosexual* men.

In sum, people who feel "different" from others of their age and sex are highly unlikely to want to affiliate with friendship groups composed of same-sexed peers. Their desire to hide their deviancy until it is rectified will make them prefer aloneness to being in the company of others who might become hostile and disapproving. Of course, aloneness is not the same as true loneliness. Again, many of the love-shys studied for this book did not appear to suffer very frequently from true loneliness. Most of them preferred to be alone; and most of them tended to seek out solitude from those of their own gender. Unlike a truly lonely person, being "alone" did not usually make the love-shys feel depressed. When they did feel depressed (or angry) it was because they lacked an intimate female companion, NOT because they did not have any friends.

Moreover, there appears to be some indication that even the depression that is caused by being without an opposite sexed intimate tends to dissipate somewhat with advancing age. The older love-shys *appeared* to be demonstrably less depressed than the younger love-shys— despite the fact that their loneliness scores were higher than those of the younger love-shys. The older love-shys seemed to react to their plight primarily with feelings of anger, cynicism and fatalism. They appeared to be pretty well resigned to their plight, but nevertheless were very angry about it. The younger men appeared to be less cynical and less angry, but more prone to frequent bouts of painful depression–again, related exclusively to being without a girl friend, *never* to being without male friends.

Because *anxiety* does not entail any objectively dangerous stimuli, and because it is not warrented from a purely rational standpoint (society stipulates that men are "supposed to be" more *rational* than women), love-shy men are basically "cowards" who cannot and will not help themselves by "taking the bull by the horns". They have "allowed" their emotions to overrule their rational intellects. Their anxiety state with respect to informal heterosexual involvement further makes them want to be alone in order to avoid the disapprobation of their own gender.

Envy of Female Privilege

The many conversations I had with the love-shy revealed a deep-seated attitude of envy towards female privilege. In most cases this envious attitude focused primarily upon the right of the female to be passive in male/female relationships, and to exercise *control* over her life destiny simply by saying "no" to each male (and amorous advance) until the *"right"* male (and amorous advance) came along. In essence, merely by *playing the odds*, women could usually end up getting what they wanted simply by exercising *negative control* vis-a-vis somebody else's (*a male's*) assertive risk-taking. In not being able to work this way themselves, the love-shy men perceived themselves as second class citizens—as "surplus refuge" whose feelings and needs society simply didn't care much about.

And there were many other areas of life where envy of the female sex was evident. One young man told me about how his parents would not allow him to use a multi-colored umbrella he had purchased—because "only females have a right to use pretty umbrellas." A few people mentioned hitchhiking, and the fact that a girl is usually picked up within two or three minutes, whereas a male will frequently have to wait for three or four hours. Another love-shy man who liked to sing recounted this story:

> "When I got to high school one of the first things I did was to sign up for the chorus class. For some reason I was never shy about getting up to sing so long as I could do it before a large audience as part of a structured program, and not before some small group of people like a bunch of guys at somebody's house. Anyway, when I joined the class I was shocked out of my bloody wits. The teacher told me that I was a base, and he assigned me to sing base. I soon found out what base actually was—that it was the shit ugliest part of music—the garbage dump of the chorus. Well, I just didn't cooperate. I insisted on singing the beautiful notes that the composer wrote. They allowed the girls to sing the notes that the composer wrote. They call that soprano. But they give the boys the shit to sing just because they have the misfortune to be male.
>
> Anyway, all the guys around me kept bullying me and punching me as I would be standing there singing the soprano part—which is the only decent and pretty part of a song. And they would be punching me, trying to get me to sing the shitty base along with them. Anyway, before the first concert the teacher threw me out of the class for refusal to cooperate. I mean this is just another illustration of how girls are treated as prima donnas while boys are always

left to do the ugly dirt. It was just as well anyway because I didn't even like the kind of material we were required to sing. I like to sing the love ballads of Jerome Kern, Richard Rodgers, Cole Porter, and the like. All they had us sing was religious and patriotic garbage. I hate religious and patriotic music.!" (21-year old love-shy man.)

In essence, love-shy males often insist upon singing their own song and marching to their own drummer—quite in spite of their introverted tendencies. The above young man had been told that the base part contributes a countermelody that typically enables an audience to enjoy a choral piece better than they otherwise might. However, his feelings had been dominated by two major questions:

1. Why should *men* be discriminated against? Why should all men have to sing the ugly part simply because they are male, while all girls get to sing the pretty part just because they happen to be female? That is arbitrary and capricious discrimination against the male sex.
2. Singing base or even listening to it being sung removes all the joy from the activity of singing. The fact that the audience may enjoy it is quite beside the point. *I* have to enjoy what *I* am doing or else *I* won't have anything to do with it.

Another major area wherein females were often bitterly envied had to do with the draft and the military. This subject will be dealt with in a later chapter. At this juncture suffice it to say that the love-shy feel that *they are human beings too,* just as females are; and that males have emotions and feelings just as females do. Hence, the love-shy deeply resent the United States military treating males, but not females, as "dispensable pawns", and forcing them to suffer severe physical pain and injury, and exposure to enormously anxiety-provoking situations. They also resent the way military organizations endeavor to standardize male personalities, and the way they put males, but not females, through a host of degradation ceremonies—such as hair cutting.

Again, there is the quite frequently recurring theme in the love-shys' conversations that males, unlike females, are *"dispensable" and "surplus"*—*that they count for much less as human beings than females do; and that their feelings and emotional needs count for nothing.* I think these feelings are largely due to the deep-seated introspective tendencies that are endemic in highly inhibited, love-shy people. And they are undoubtedly also due to the heavy amount of bullying and mistreatment the love-shys had been forced to endure throughout all their years of growing up.

"I've been around, and I've never seen any girl bullied the way boys are bullied. Why shouldn't I be envious when all through life I've seen males required to take all kinds of abuse just because they are males. Girls are treated in a far more humane way by everybody. Parents don't beat girls the way they do boys. At school it's always the boys who are getting it from the teachers. And the worst cruelty of all is what you have to take from people who should be your buddies." (19-year old love-shy man.)

Some of my colleagues have suggested that love-shy males may have some latent transsexual tendencies. But none of the love-shys with whom I talked had any desire at all to have their genitalia removed so that they could become women. Of course, many of the love-shys did wish that they had been born female in the first place. But they did not wish to become women during their *current* lifetime. Indeed, if by some stroke of magic the love-shys were suddenly transformed into women, they would *all* remain highly attracted sexually (and in every other way) *to the female sex.* This is why I suggested in chapter five that severely love-shy men are *"male lesbians"* at heart. They are "closet heterosexual" males who, even if they were women, would still want the love and the sexual attention of another *woman*, and NOT of a man.

Chapter Postscript:

On the Johnny Carson "Tonight Show" of Thursday, December 6, 1984, Dr. Joyce Brothers appeared and presented a fascinating finding of relevance to this book. People with different native temperaments tend to prefer different types of *fruit*. Asked to pick a fruit from a plentiful supply of different types, shy-inhibited people (who tend not to communicate much at all in purely social situations but who nonetheless tend to be highly dependable, loyal and potentially highly monogamous) tend to gravitate primarily or exclusively towards *oranges, grapefruit*, and/or *pineapples*. In essence, a strong predilection towards citrus fruits over other types of fruits may reflect, from an early age in life onward, intractable shyness and behavioral inhibition. (It would not *cause* these things; in essence, a preference for citrus over other types of fruits may *reflect* these traits of temperament. Unfortunately, no questions dealing with fruit preferences were included in the research study upon which this book is based.)

In Appendix III of this book the reader will find a table which summarizes the mean *Eysenck Personality Questionnaire* (EPQ) scores for the non-shy and for the love-shy samples. (A more detailed table can be found in Gilmartin, 1987—JOURNAL OF PERSONALITY article.)

Chapter 18

Parenthood Aspirations

The vast majority of the love-shy men expressed a desire to eventually have children of their own. Few of the older love-shys were optimistic about ever being able to achieve that desire. Nevertheless, 86 percent of the older love-shys and 100 percent of the younger love-shys *did want* to procreate children of their own—if the fates would allow them to do so. Expressed somewhat differently, *none* of the younger men interviewed for this book wished to go through life childless. There were no differences in this regard between the self-confident non-shy men and the younger love-shy men.

On the other hand, there were *big differences* between the love-shys and the non-shys when it came to the matter of gender preferences. I asked each man how many children of each sex he would eventually like to procreate, if his wishes could come true. And whereas 86 percent of the older love-shys would indeed like to have children, only 17 percent of them would like to have sons. Fully 69 percent of the older love-shys would want *daughters only* if they had children. Again, 14 percent of the older love-shys preferred not to have any children at all, even if they somehow could manage to eventually get married.

The story was much the same for the younger love-shy men. Even though *all* of the younger love-shys would eventually like to have children, only 28 percent expressed any desire at all for sons. In essence, 72 percent would want their future wives to somehow procreate *daughters only* for them.

Of course, the self-confident non-shy men had a quite different set of predilections. As a 200-person group, the non-shy men wished to procreate 145 sons for every 100 daughters. Most of them wanted to procreate children of *both* sexes. But if they could have their way they would procreate almost three boys for every two girls.

The non-shy men also wanted larger families. Compared to the love-shy men, the non-shys seemed to be considerably less mindful of the social desirability of "zero population growth" and of the perils of the population explosion. In essence, the non-shy men registered a preference for an average of 2.63 children each. The younger love-shy men wanted 2.28 children each—a figure which would also contribute to uncontrolled population growth. Only the older love-shys wanted fewer than two children per family. Excluding the fourteen older love-shys who did not want to have any children at all, the remaining 86 older love-shy men wanted to have an average of 1.8 children per family.

Expressed in more detailed terms, 50 percent of the non-shys wanted *three or more* children, compared to only 22 percent of the young love-shys, and just 5 percent of the older love-shys. None of the non-shy men wanted to have only one child. However, 7 percent of the younger love-shy men together with 22 percent of the older love-shys would be perfectly content with just one child. Those hoping to have two children included 50 percent of the non-shys, 71 percent of the younger love-shys, and 59 percent of the older love-shys.

Thus, it would appear that love-shy men tend to be quite normal in their desires to have children. Indeed, they might even be viewed as being a bit more socially responsible than the non-shys, inasmuch as they tended to desire somewhat smaller families than the latter. Quite clearly, love-shy men aspire to the goal of being able to enjoy a normal family life. The one thing which sharply distinguishes them from the non-shys is their overwhelming preference for daughters rather than sons. The large majority of the non-shy men wanted to eventually have both daughters and sons, with "two sons and one daughter" being the most commonplace preference pattern among them. In contrast, almost three-quarters of the love-shy men wanted daughters only. And some of them were quite adamant about this preference.

> "Well, I'll tell you. If the fates dictated that I had to have a son, I would definitely prefer not to have any children at all. Of course, if I really had my druthers I'd have two little girls. In fact, I even know what I would call them—Sarah and Jenny. That's what I really would like. But if I had to have a boy I would much rather not have any kids at all. Like I told you before, I just don't like boys. A boy is a horrible thing to be in this country. Boys are subjected to all kinds of indignity, and they're not accorded the respect that women are. They have to suffer a lot more than women. And in childhood they are either chastized and bullied all the time, or they are forced to take part in a lot of rough, boring games where people are likely to suffer a lot of pain and injury. There's no pleasure in that. But I think that having my little Sarah and Jenny would be just terrific— especially if I could get a beautiful wife to go along with the bargain!" (35-year old love-shy man.)

> "I would really love to be able to have children. But I gotta tell you. I don't know what I would do if my wife gave birth to a son. I've always hated baseball, basketball and football. I don't like any of the things that boys are supposed to like. I just wouldn't be able to be any kind of a companion to a boy, unless he were like me. And Jesus Christ! In this lousy world we're living in I hope to God I wouldn't have a boy like me. I know I just wouldn't want to do that

to anyone. I would never want anyone to have to suffer the kind of life I had to suffer when I was growing up. I know I'd much rather not have any children at all than have to deal with that. I would want my kids to be happy. And with me as their father, I don't see how that could come about unless they were girls." (24-year old love-shy man.)

"Well, I don't like boys. In fact, I hate boys. I know because I was a boy myself. And a boy is a terrible thing to be in this world. Sometimes I think that the world would be a better place if everyone could somehow be a girl—if from now on no boys would ever be born again to anyone, and people had children by being artificially inseminated with only female sperm. There wouldn't be anymore war or bullying or cruelty. And there would be no more danger of a nuclear holocaust, and no more crime. The world would be a much safer place to live. And you could still make love. Everyone would be a lesbian, so there would still be a lot of sex. And the sex would be a lot better because there wouldn't be anymore violence and cruelty and rape." (22-year old love-shy man.)

"Ahhhh, boys are dirty and aggressive. And I don't know how I'd handle one. I guess I'd have to leave the boy up to my wife, and I'd take care of the little girl. Have you ever noticed the fingers of little boys? Yuck! They're disgustingly filthy and sticky. The paws of my goddam dog are cleaner and more sanitary. Little girls can be kept clean. They are manageable, and you can sort of show them off. I mean you can dress them and take them out to different places and be proud of them." (37-year old love-shy man.)

"Well, I like the theatre. In fact, everything that I really enjoy doing seems to be considered sort of feminine by people. I wouldn't have anything in common with a boy. I wouldn't know how to relate to one. I know I could relate very easily to a little girl. If I had daughters I know they would both grow up happy and well-adjusted. They would both be really wanted kids, and they would both be well taken care of. I don't know what I'd even name a son if I had one. I've got the names of my daughters all picked out already. I decided several years ago that I'd call them Lisa and Becky. What would I call a boy?! Attila and Hitler are the only things I can think of—or maybe Fletcher, after my airedale—or maybe Stinky and Smelly! Ha Ha Ha!" (39-year old love-shy man.)

Even among the minority of love-shy men who *did* want to have a boy (17 percent of the older love-shys and 28 percent of the younger ones), there was quite a bit of evident uneasiness about the prospect. Incidentally, *all* of the love-shys wanting a boy had registered a preference for "one boy and one girl". And all of them seemed to be motivated by the desire for the opportunity to experience the idyllic old-fashioned, traditional type of family life with children of both sexes present in the home. In fact, consistent with this preference pattern several of these love-shy men indicated that they wanted the boy to be born first in that "the boy should always be older than the girl".

> "I think I'd really like to have one boy and one girl. Yeah, I've done a lot of thinking about it, and that's what I want—only I want the boy to be born first. I think brothers and sisters get along better if the boy is the older one. And maybe they can introduce each other to boyfriends and girlfriends as they get older . . . . The only thing— I think I'd try to get my wife to assume primary responsibility for rearing my son. Like, you know, after all I've been through I wouldn't want to screw him up. Like I wouldn't want to take any chances, you know? I'd see if I could get my wife to let me have primary responsibility for the girl, and I'd let my wife deal with the boy all the time. Like I know I'd really like to have a son. But I'd sort of like to raise him from a distance—oh, I don't know how to express this—I don't know. I mean, I'd like to encourage my son and watch him grow. But I'd want to be sort of out of the picture—you know what I mean? The girl, if I had one, —well, I know I'd want to really spend a lot of time with my daughter. I mean I'd really want to be with her almost all the time. I'd want to take her places and do a lot of fun things with her. I don't know how I'll be able to do that without my son feeling sort of left out. But I'd get my wife to give my son a lot of love, and I'd encourage him to go out and play with his friends." (23-year old love-shy man.)

> "You know, I haven't given it much thought. But I think it would be sort of interesting to raise a son. It would be a neat experiment— I mean with a guy like me as the father! I wouldn't be able to take him to any baseball games because I hate that stuff. But I'd take him to all the Broadway shows and movies, and I'd encourage him to study music. Like if he became really good at the trumpet or the saxophone, or even the piano, he could join a jazz band at his school and gain popularity that way. I don't know. I don't think there would be somebody like me born two generations in a row! I just know that my son would be a whole lot better off than I was! I just know it!" (38-year old love-shy man.)

Fear of Discipline

Fears and anxieties pertinent to the taking of disciplinary action represent another very important reason for the love-shys' very strong predilections for female offspring. Girls are usually viewed as being easier than boys to discipline. They are widely viewed in American society as being the better behaved of the two genders. And they are viewed as being more responsive to discipline—especially to the gentler, milder forms of discipline. Of course, the self-fulfilling prophecy undoubtedly plays a role here. What people expect is ordinarily what they get!

Of course, a key common denominator among love-shy men is that they want to do everything "gently". They want to have a "gentle" life. Coping effectively with people or situations that "make waves" is much more difficult for love-shy people than for non-shy self-confident people. Further, the love-shys had no satisfactory past role models for effective parenting. They knew they wanted to reject the model posed by their own parents. But apart from ideas which they could get from reading books, they had no substitute role model with which to replace that which they had rejected.

There can be no question that the love-shys' own sour memories of parent-child interaction served to dampen their enthusiasm for (1) handling parent-child discipline problems that are bound to develop in every family from time to time, and (2) for procreating *male* offspring. The love-shy's own parents had not provided a benign or competent role model for managing tasks pertinent to social influence. Generally speaking, the most powerful social influence tends to be that which is least strongly perceived by the person (child) who is to be influenced. People (including children) tend to be easiest to influence when they are in a situation that they truly enjoy—a situation wherein they can let down their defensive guard. The reason why the peer group is such an effective source of influence for most children is that vis-a-vis its members a child usually feels free to "let down his/her hair" or defensive guard. The love-shys' parents tended to rely primarily upon coercive, belittling, ego-deflating disciplinary tactics. And unfortunately, most of the love-shys' homes had not been emotionally relaxing or enjoyable places in which to spend time.

> "To be perfectly frank about it, I know I'd never be able to discipline a boy. I'd have to leave everything up to my wife as far as discipline goes. I just wouldn't ever be able to deal with it. Just the mere thought of disciplining a boy child in any manner at all fills me with painful anxiety feelings. I don't know; I just don't feel that way about a little girl. I think I'd be able to deal with a little girl really well. I mean, I really feel confident about being a good parent to a little girl. I don't have any fears about that at all." (41-year old love-shy man.)

> "What would you do if your son got real bratty? I couldn't handle that. I wouldn't even want to handle that. I mean I realize that girls sometimes do bad things too. But somehow I just don't feel nervous about dealing with that. I've had a really hard life up to now. And if I were able to have kids I'd want to create a nice, tension-free

environment. Having a boy is like asking for trouble. I think I'd go to a doctor and see if I could get him to make sure that my wife and I only had girl children. Like if it were a boy it could be aborted; or it could be given up for adoption. I read where you can make $20,000 by giving up a child for adoption. If my wife were willing, that's what I'd want to do with a boy child." (47-year old love-shy man.)

Recycled Fathers

By the way, the only other group of American males, apart from the love-shy that has been found to have a strong preference for pro-creating female offspring, is that of recycled fathers. A *"recycled father"* is a man who had already raised one family. Now that he is in his 40s or 50s and newly remarried to a second wife who is likely to be as much as two or more decades his junior, he decides to procreate a second crop of children. He is especially likely to want to do this because his young wife has never procreated children of her own.

Men who become fathers in their 40s or 50s seldom want to have anything more to do with little league baseball and football, etc. In that regard their feelings tend to be very similar to those of love-shy males of all ages. Thus, they want to procreate female children because it is easier and more relaxing to raise a girl—and because far fewer things can go wrong in raising a girl than in raising a boy.

Selecting the Gender of One's Future Children

For the benefit of love-shy readers, there are three different approaches which can be used for selecting the gender of one's future child. To be sure, many people object to the idea of allowing husbands and wives to exercise control over this area. However, my own research has convinced me that a good 85 percent of all American husbands and wives either (1) do not wish to exercise such control, or (2) they are insufficiently motivated for going to the trouble of doing so. Hence, there is little reason for moralists to become alarmed here. With only 10 or 15 percent of married couples exercising control over the selection of their children's genders, it is doubtful whether society's sex ratio would be affected to any significant extent. Remember, most people want more sons than daughters. The love-shy represent the *very opposite* of this predilection, thus giving society some much needed female children. Everything else being equal, it is quite reasonable to expect that having children of the desired sex would increase the probability of high quality, competent parenting. And that would benefit everyone, child as well as parent.

The most widely used technique today for choosing one's baby's sex is simply *amniocentesis combined with abortion*. This method has been available only since the mid-1970s. And it involves having an appropriately qualified physician test the amniotic fluid surrounding the growing fetus. This is a procedure which can be accomplished quite early in pregnancy. And besides enabling the prospective parents to learn of the presence of certain genetic abnormalities, it also permits the ascertaining of whether the fetus is a male or a female.

Most (but certainly far from all) physicians consider it unethical to abort a healthy *female* fetus simply because the parents wish to have a boy. However, it is comparatively easy to get a physician to abort a *male* fetus because the parents desire a female child. Again, the widespread desire that most people have for procreating boy babies renders most physicians rather squeamish about aborting female fetuses for gender selection purposes—unless the pregnant mother already has three or four daughters and wishes for her final child to be a son. Inasmuch as a very strong need for female children is far more unusual than a very strong preference for male children, the love-shy should encounter comparatively little difficulty in locating physicians willing to abort their wives' male fetuses—provided that their wives are also uncomfortable about the idea of procreating a male child.

Unfortunately, one out of every twenty-three men manufactures only one kind of sperm. A man who is biologically capable of synthesizing *only* androsperms (male sperm) would have to resort to some form of artificial insemination *via a donor* if he and his wife were strongly intent upon having a female child. Of course, most men can simply "try again", and hope that with the second try the fetus will be female.

Pre-Selecting Prior to Conception a Baby's Sex

There is an easy-to-learn technique which can increase up to *about 60 percent* the probability of having female offspring. This technique has been developed and thoroughly researched by Dr. Elizabeth Whelan of the Harvard University Medical School. And it involves the timing of sexual intercourse relative to the moment of ovulation. Interested readers will find a readable and quite fascinating account of this procedure contained in a paperback book entitled BOY OR GIRL? By Dr. Whelan.

In view of the large amount of ongoing research pertinent to the issue of pre-selecting a baby's sex, it now seems likely that by the year 1995 a foolproof, 100 percent effective means will be available to anyone who wishes to employ it. In all probability this method will entail taking a pill which will kill off all of the androsperms (boy sperms)—assuming that one wishes to procreate a female child. However, at the moment prospective parents desirous of having a female child can only increase the odds in their favor from the original 50-50 provided us by mother nature, to 60-40. (Those interested in having a *male* child can increase *their* odds to 68-32 by following Dr. Whelan's directions.)

In order to preselect a baby's sex it is necessary for the wife to keep detailed records of her menstrual cycles over a period of some six to eight months. Towards this purpose a fertility kit should be purchased from a drug store. This will contain a special, detailed thermometer and a spool of tes-tape. The main objective is for the wife to be able to predict with a high level of accuracy the time when during any given cycle she will ovulate. And she will be able to achieve a high level of predictive accuracy through (1) regular use of the thermometer each morning immediately upon awakening, (2) testing cervical mucous for the dates upon which it is most elastic, slippery and clear, and (3) use of the tes-tape, which is a special kind of litmus paper that is capable of responding color-wise to chemical changes in the cervix.

Simply put, couples desirous of a *girl baby* should be sure to copulate within about a day and a half *prior to* the moment of anticipated ovulation. And during the crucial copulation sexual intercourse should be preceded by an acid douche consisting of two tablespoons of white vinegar to a quart of water. The wife should try to inhibit herself from experiencing orgasm during the crucial (girl baby-making) copulation.

Finally, those wishing to have a girl need not abstain from sexual intercourse during the first half of the cycle. In fact, a low sperm count slightly increases the probability of female offspring. So frequent intercourse prior to the crucial copulation one day prior to ovulation will prove beneficial. But it should not be any more frequent than once every two days. Daily intercourse would render the sperm count too low for fertilization to be likely.

The Eugen Jonas Method

The third approach for selecting the gender of one's future child is an astrological one devised by Czechoslovakian physician Dr. Eugen Jonas. Using this approach on some 35,000 female patients over a 30 year period, Jonas claims a 90 percent success rate for it. No one knows exactly how or why it works. And as author of this book I would recommend caution in its use. The Whalen technique *may* be more reliable. However, for those who might be interested in trying out the astrological approach, here is a very brief, capsule summary as to how to do it:

1. Have a trained astrologer draw up a natal horoscope *for the wife*. The chart should be accurate *to the nearest minute*.
2. Ascertain the number of degrees and minutes separating the wife's natal Sun from her natal Moon. This should be done by moving *counterclockwise* from the position of the Sun to the position of the Moon.
3. Get a detailed ephemeris (from a bookstore or library) for the current month and year. Then find the day during the wife's current menstrual cycle during which the Sun and the Moon will be the *same number of degrees apart from each other* as they had been at the moment she was born. Using an ephemeris for the current month, this will be very easy to calculate.
4. The day *during each menstrual cycle* when the Sun and Moon are the same number of degrees apart from each other as they had been at the moment of the wife's birth is the *wife's most fertile day for that cycle*. Pregnancy would be most likely to occur on that day.[1]
5. Using your ephemeris, notice what sign the Moon is in during that day. If the Moon is in (1) Taurus, (2) Cancer, (3) Virgo, (4) Scorpio, (5) Capricorn, or (6) Pisces, your wife will conceive a *girl* if you can get her pregnant on that day. If the Moon is in any of the other six signs, *don't have intercourse* because if you do and your wife becomes pregnant, she will have a boy. (*Note*: The Moon changes signs every 2.4 days; so one-third of the time you will have to calculate just exactly where, in terms of sign, the Moon is during the portion of the day when you are having sexual intercourse.)

Shyness and Contracepting

As I have shown, love-shy men tend to *prefer* smaller families than non-shy men. However, if the love-shy were to actually become actively involved in regular sexual intercourse, they might actually end up fathering *more* rather than fewer children than the non-shy men! For example, I asked each man: "Would you be too shy to ask the clerk in a drug store for a package of condoms or vaginal foam?" And fully 97 percent of the older love-shy men together with 87 percent of the younger ones said "*yes*", they *would* be too shy! Only 6 percent of the non-shy men indicated that they were "too shy" to purchase a package of condoms.

Lee Rainwater, a sociologist at Washington University in St. Louis, has extensively studied the fertility behavior of working-class midwesterners. And one of his strongest and most consistent findings has been that men with inhibitions pertinent to self-disclosure and to sexuality tend to have much larger families than more sociable, socially self-confident men. He points out that many husbands remain quite shy vis-a-vis their wives, even after several years of marriage. These husbands never discuss with their wives their own most deeply held feelings; and they do little to make their wives feel comfortable about discussing intimate needs and feelings.

Use of any form of contraception or birth control necessarily entails some discussion between husband and wife. Because inhibited men feel very uncomfortable about such discussions, contraceptive responsibility is left entirely up to the wife. And since the wives who are married to such men are themselves quite often ill at ease on matters pertinent to sexuality, they too are usually not especially prone towards the taking of any contraceptive precautions. Thus, even in the area of family planning, the love-shy may be disinclined towards taking over the "driver's seat" of their own lives.

NOTES

1. Technically, in order to successfully practice astrological birth control you must abstain from sexual intercourse on the date of the wife's natal sun-moon alignment, as well as on the three days preceeding that date. The best day for having sex if you wish to maximize your chances for pregnancy is the date immediately before (one day prior to) the date of the wife's natal sun-moon alignment. The sex of the baby to be conceived will be determined by the moon's position on the date of the wife's natal sun-moon alignment during her *current* menstrual cycle. Thus, if the moon is in an even numbered sign when she conceives, the baby will be a girl; otherwise it will be a boy.

Readers wishing to explore this fascinating subject further are urged to read ASTROL-OGICAL BIRTH CONTROL by Shiela Ostrander and Lynn Schroeder (Prentice-Hall, 1972). Because this book has become quite scarce, interested readers are urged to make use of the interlibrary loan programs which are available in most local and college/university libraries. With a copy of the book in hand, you can photocopy those pages which you might wish to use as a reference.

Chapter 19

Career, Money, Education, and the Love-Shy

Most psychologists today agree that there are essentially two avenues to happiness, effectiveness, and constructive productivity as a human being. In his book THE ART OF LOVING, Erich Fromm called these *creative work* and *creative love*. All people need to become involved in networks of roles and social relationships in both love and work that are meaningful and important to them. To the extent that a person loses or is deprived of the ability to travel with reasonable harmony along either the "love avenue" or the "work avenue", he is likely to be headed for trouble. Both love and work appear to be quite necessary, especially for men.

The purpose of this chapter is to review the data that were obtained on matters pertinent to career, money and education. The 200 younger love-shys and the 200 non-shys were all college and university students. As all 400 of these men were between the ages of 19 and 24 at the time the interviews were conducted, I did not pay much attention to their social class backgrounds. Of course, time will determine what each of these men actually does with the education that he gets. There was no way of determining at the time of the interviews just how successful the 19 to 24 year olds would eventually become.

However, it can be said that all of the non-shys and younger love-shys came from middle-class to upper-middle-class homes. Most of them had grown up in suburban areas of the major metropolitan areas of New York and Los Angeles. And over 90 percent of them had resided throughout most of their formative years in single family houses.

The demographic characteristics of the 100 older love-shy men were in several important respects quite amazing and noteworthy. Unfortunately, at this time there is no way whereby the *representativeness* of these 100 older love-shys can be accurately ascertained. Nevertheless, the following characteristics of these men stand out and are worth noting:

Level of Attained Education

Fully 93 percent of the older love-shys had completed an undergraduate B.A. or B.S. degree. Only 24 of these 93 men had completed their degrees in practical, career-related disciplines such as business, engineering, and computer programming. The remainder had majored in liberal arts, social science and humanities discipline. Majors in philosophy, art, psychology, sociology, education, history, geography, theatre arts, creative writing, and English and American literature, were the most prevalent in the backgrounds of *both* the older and the younger love-shy men.

At the time they were interviewed, only 31 percent of the younger love-shys were majoring in fields related to business, engineering, or computer programming. Fully 62 percent of them were majoring in liberal arts, social science, humanities and education related disciplines; and 7 percent of them were still "undecided" as to a major. In contrast, only 23 percent of the non-shy men were majoring in liberal arts, social science and humanities disciplines; and only 3 percent were in the "undecided" category. The remaining 74 percent were all majoring in career-related disciplines of a traditionally masculine nature, such as business, engineering, architecture, computer programming, etc.

Regarding education beyond the undergraduate level, 42 percent of the older love-shy men had completed at least one graduate degree. Five of the older love-shys had completed an M.B.A. (masters degree in business administration), whereas another 6 percent had completed a masters degree in an engineering discipline. The remaining 31 men had completed their masters degrees in liberal arts, social science or humanities disciplines. In addition, there were three Ph.D.s in the sample; and all three of these men had earned their advanced educations in liberal arts disciplines.

Unemployment and Underemployment

Fully 16 percent of the older love-shys were unemployed at the time they were interviewed. And another 9 percent were employed on only a part-time basis because they were unable to find a full-time job. These statistics are quite noteworthy because as of the year 1982, only 3.6 percent of white, college educated men were unemployed. In essence, the love-shy appear to be extremely prone towards unemployment, prolonged underemployment, and/or part-time employment.

Annual Incomes

The average annual income for the older love-shys was only $14,782 (data obtained 1979–1981). Given the fact that 93 percent of these love-shys had completed an undergraduate degree and 42 percent of them had completed at least one graduate degree, it clearly follows that these men represent a significantly *underrewarded* and ignored segment of the American population.

The average annual income of the 24 older love-shys who had completed at least one degree in business, computer science or engineering, was $21,163. Of course, this figure is still well below what would normally be expected for a group of university-educated 35 to 50 year old men. But it is also quite clearly superior to what the majority of the older love-shys were achieving from a financial standpoint. This represents a major reason why severely love-shy men probably need to exercise better care than most people in the managing of their educational preparation. For severely love-shy men it would appear that *amount* of education is of substantially less importance than *substantive content* of education. For example, the average annual income for the 31 older love-shys with *graduate degrees* in the liberal arts, social sciences and humanities, was only $16,912–a figure still substantially lower than the $21,163 which love-shys with a B.S. degree in business or engineering were getting.

Places of Abode

All of the 100 older love-shy men were residing in small rented apartments at the time the interviews were conducted. In fact, many of them were living in one-room bachelor apartments. And even though I as the author of this study was the only judge, I would say that only 27 percent of these men were living amidst what could reasonably be considered "pleasant surroundings". For the most part the apartment buildings were located in less-than-attractive neighborhoods. Most of the buildings were quite old. And the living quarters themselves tended to be quite cramped and cluttered.

Childhood Socioeconomic Status

Judging by questions pertinent to (1) occupation of the father, (2) neighborhood of residence while growing up, and (3) type of housing while growing up, it seems quite reasonable to conclude that the older love-shys had become *downwardly mobile*. Fully 92 percent of the older love-shys had grown up in private, single-family houses which were located in attractive suburban neighborhoods. And virtually all of their fathers had held middle to upper-middle-class occupations.

Thus, it would appear that the outstanding educational backgrounds of the older love-shy men were not sufficient to compensate for deficits in social self-confidence and in interpersonal finesse. Sociologists typically use the term *"status inconsistent"* to describe the general life style of people whose educations far surpass their incomes and occupational prestige levels. "Status inconsistents" are seldom happy, content, or productive. And the life situations of the older love-shy men well illustrate this point.

Implications of Money for Love-Shyness

Money has always been a great aphrodisiac. With some exceptions men who have a comfortable amount of it are much more likely than the financially less comfortable to feel good about themselves. They are also more likely to feel in control of things. They are more likely to feel as though they are in the "driver's seat" of their own lives.

And so there is evidence of another vicious cycle operating here. Love-shyness appears to be a cause (in conjunction with a non-technical education) of low income and of career instability. Indeed, it appears quite evident that low income and career instability both serve to aggravate and to exacerbate love-shyness problems. Both render the love-shy less and less self-confident about even the mere thought of making the first move vis-a-vis a woman.

It has often been said that *"a man's career is his penis"*. Because of differential gender role socialization, a man's very sense of personal identity is likely to be wrapped up in what he does for a living, to a considerably greater extent than what is the case for most women. Further, having only enough money to "get by" is itself hardly conducive to a free attitude towards spending, "letting go" and having fun. Worry and concern over "having enough" can render even a non-shy person considerably less self-confident in the company of women than he ordinarily would be.

Sociological research data have demonstrated again and again that the chances for a successful "pursuit of happiness" vary a great deal as a function of *income*. In a 1977 national survey that asked people how happy they were, 46 percent of them with family incomes over $20,000 said that they were "very happy". The proportion of "very happy" people dropped to 33 percent for the $10,000 to $19,999 income range, and to 29 percent among people whose annual incomes were below $10,000.

Thus, even when it is considered by itself apart from other variables, income wields a formidable impact upon happiness, contentment, and overall self-esteem. With only enough money to "get by", the alternative courses of action available to people become severely restricted. Especially for men with love-shyness problems, self-confidence vis-a-vis the opposite sex is bound to be adversely impacted upon to at least some extent. After all, it is the man who is supposed to (in our society) do the paying, the wining and dining, *and the impressing*. Not having the funds is likely to make it all the more difficult, especially for older love-shy men, to begin taking constructive action.

Shyness in the Job Search

Love-shyness does not exist in a vacuum. Men who are severely love-shy are quite likely to be unusually shy in other important areas of life as well. Many of the (1) skills, and (2) states of mind, that are requisite to success in winning meaningful female companionship are *also* requisites for success in the world of employment. For example, let's consider the attitude of the love-shy towards the risk-taking enterprise of searching out a good job opportunity in the first place.

I asked each man: "How shy would you be about telephoning an executive about an *advertised* job opening? Assume that the executive's name is given in the job ad." *None* of the non-shy men indicated any shyness at all here. In contrast, fully 63 percent of the older love-shys and 52 percent of the younger ones indicated that they would be shy about making the telephone call. It should be noted, of course, that *all* of the older love-shys had been out in the workaday world for at least ten or more years. Thus, the 63 percent figure must be considered quite shockingly high.

One 36-year old M.B.A. holder from California State University at Fullerton, worked as a $15,000 per year clerk in an insurance firm. He had held this position for almost four years despite his conspicuous overqualification for it. The following represents a quote from one of my interviews with him:

> "When I first got out of school I made really good money for awhile.
> But the tensions on the job were just getting to be too much for me.
> They were asking me to do a lot of things I just didn't have the

nerve to do. And I think some of the guys who worked in my department thought I was snubbing them. Anyway, I heard that they had gone to the boss and they succeeded in getting me fired. I guess I wasn't too friendly. But I just haven't got the gaul to be friendly. I mean it takes a tremendous amount of nerve to be friendly with people. You know—I'd see the guys in the restroom. And what else could I say to them but 'hi'?

Anyway, I managed to get two other good jobs since then. One of them I got through an employment agency. Fortunately I didn't have to pay anything for the job because I only lasted three months on it. I mean they were asking me to do all sorts of things that just made me too nervous. Like I was always being asked to call people up on the telephone. And one time they even asked me to invite a customer out for lunch. I had to refuse because I just haven't got the nerve to do something like that. They never taught us anything like that in my graduate school of business. You might not believe it, but I was always a good student!

After I lost this job five years ago I just began to feel that the job search just wasn't worth it. I mean it just made me too damned nervous. I would come home each day a nervous wreck, and I couldn't sleep each night worrying about what I would say to this employer or that employer the next day. The people I was supposed to hit it off with were all just too outgoing for me, and I knew that no matter what my resume said or how good my grades at school were, they just didn't like me.

So one day this employment agency referred me to this insurance job. They told me that if I performed well I'd eventually make a good salary. But the raises so far only amount to about $500 a year before taxes. So I don't like the money too much. But at least I don't have to worry about anxiety-provoking situations all the time. I guess I am in a bit of a rut. But I just haven't got the nerve to look for something else—at least not now. Anyway, what would I tell my supervisor if I had to cut out in the middle of the day for some job interview somewhere? I just wouldn't have the nerve to tell my supervisor that I was on the lookout for a better job opportunity."

Regarding this last point, several of the older love-shys talked about how they had just walked out of certain jobs without giving their employer any notice, because they "just didn't have the nerve to tell their employer that they wanted to quit." Two men advised me that at 5 o'clock on the last day they wanted to work for an employer they dropped a letter in the mailbox advising the employer that they were quitting and that they would not be back. Hence, it should be easy for the reader to appreciate why many of these men were not well-liked at their former places of employment!

The Unadvertised Job

It is an established fact that only 25 to 30 percent of the best jobs and career opportunities are advertised. The large majority of the most desirable positions (some 70 percent or so) are obtained through informal social networks. People can very effectively tap into these informal friendship networks (1) by contacting their own and their parents' friends and relatives, and (2) by contacting executives in the fields of their choice, and asking these executives for a few minutes of their time. These meetings are technically called *"advice calls"* as opposed to "employment interviews" because the job seeker is neither responding to a job ad nor asking for a job. In essence, he is merely asking for advice and for personal names of appropriate executives with whom it might prove productive to talk. Simply put, the key purpose of an "advice call" is to try to plug into an influential executive's social network.

Such personal meetings are usually solicited by telephone. And the task of obtaining the interviews and going through them effectively requires some degree of poise, "nerve", and relaxed, natural friendliness. Most love-shy men are seriously lacking in these attributes. And as such they are deprived of the route to most of the best employment opportunities. For example, I asked each man:

> "How shy would you feel about telephoning a major executive of a company and asking him about the possibility of any job openings developing in his department in the near future? Please assume that you are not responding to a job ad; you simply want to discuss possible opportunities with this major executive. How shy would you be about doing this?"

Fully 100 percent of the older love-shy men indicated that they would be too shy to do this. Among the younger love-shys 79 percent thought that they would be too shy to try it. In contrast, only 12 percent of the non-shys thought that they would be "more than moderately shy" about making such a telephone call. And parenthetically, all of even this 12 percent indicated that they would go ahead and do it anyway quite irrespective of their nervousness about the matter.

As a final example, I asked each man: "How shy would you feel about walking in unannounced on an executive in order to discuss with him possible job opportunities that have not been advertised?" Several of the love-shy men insisted that this shouldn't even be tried—that it was "discourteous" and simply "not done". Of course, research shows that it *is* done a very great deal by the most successful job seekers.

The results indicated that fully 100 percent of the older love-shys together with 82 percent of the younger ones felt that there was no way they could ever possibly do such a thing. In contrast, only 27 percent of the self-confident non-shys indicated that they would be shy about the matter. In addition, only 5 percent of the non-shy men indicated that they would definitely rule out doing it.

Nowadays all major American cities have a number of so-called "executive search services". These organizations are not employment agencies because they do not place people or solicit job openings from area companies. In fact, it would be illegal for them to do so in that a license is required for operating an employment agency. Executive search services do not have this license. They earn their money by acting as a consultant to the man or woman who is in search of a better career opportunity. Their fees are high, ranging from a low of $1,500 to a high of $3,000.

Four of the older love-shy men had done business with such firms. The following interview excerpt amply demonstrates the severe and costly problems that love-shyness creates.

> "As you know, I have a Masters degree in European history. And there just isn't any way of getting a job with that type of background. I had always wanted to teach in a junior college or in a high school somewhere. But nobody wants history teachers anymore. I had been driving a cab for over two years and I was really tired of it because here in Los Angeles it's so damned dangerous, and you have to work six nights a week in order to even get by financially.
>
> So I saw this ad in the LOS ANGELES TIMES about how a $20,000 a year job could be guaranteed to educated but underemployed people. I went to the address indicated and was subjected to this really well polished sales spiel. I remember the offices there were incredibly plush, and the people were so friendly. Anyway, they were so convincing that I invested $1,800 of my hard-earned dollars on the spot. Since my shift at the cab company is from 4 PM to 1 AM, I thought I could easily do whatever they wanted me to and still earn the money I needed to get by.
>
> Well, I want to tell you I was really very deeply disappointed by what happened. I think that was the blackest time of my entire life because they were asking me to do all kinds of stuff I just didn't have the nerve to do. I tried to get my money back. I mean I contacted the Better Business Bureau, the Legal Aid Bureau, some of the consumer protection and consumer fraud groups, and a whole bunch of other places. But all I could get was their sympathy. They couldn't do anything for me because of the fine print in the contract I had signed.
>
> This executive search place had all kinds of testimonial letters from people boasting of the terrific jobs they had been able to get with the help of this company's service. But they make you go out on

these advice calls. You have to contact a lot of people all the time, cold. Like I always thought of commission selling as the cruelest, most horrible job in the world outside of wartime combat itself. Well, this stuff they were asking me to do was just as impossible for me as a commission selling type of job would be. The only people they will ever really help are those with no anxiety feelings. You know, like insensitive people who have no qualms about approaching strangers cold. I mean if anybody is *that* nervy, why don't they just take some selling job and save themselves $1,800! I don't know! This whole damn world is just a cruddy, cruel place!" (46-year old love-shy man.)

Shyness On the Job

Just as severe shyness effectively obviates an effective job search, it also greatly interferes with certain facets of on-the-job performance. For example, I asked each respondent the following question: "You feel that you have been performing well in your occupation; but it has been over a year since you received your last raise. How shy would you feel about approaching the supervisor and discussing the matter with him?" Fully 94 percent of the non-shy men replied that they would *not* feel shy at all about doing this. In contrast, only 17 percent of the younger love-shy men and *zero percent* of the older love-shys felt that they could approach the supervisor about the matter without feeling painfully shy about doing so. In addition, 86 percent of the older love-shys together with 68 percent of the younger love-shys felt that they would be "very shy" to "extremely shy" about approaching the supervisor and asking about the possibility of a raise. None of the non-shy men felt this shy about the idea of asking for a raise.

Further, in response to a question about whether or not they would *actually* indeed ask for a raise if a situation similar to the above happened to them, 89 percent of the non-shy men said that they "definitely would", compared to only 33 percent of the younger love-shys and just 19 percent of the older love-shys.

The following scenario also revealed quite substantial differences between the love-shys and the non-shys: "A colleague who has been goofing off a good deal gets a raise and a promotion while your efforts on behalf of the company have apparently gone unnoticed. How shy would you feel about discussing your feelings with your supervisor?" Fully 100 percent of the non-shys said that they would be "quite confident and self-assured" about doing this. Only 41 percent of the younger love-shys and 24 percent of the older ones similarly felt any degree of self-confidence at all about discussing the matter with the supervisor.

Shyness in employment situations seems to entail many other problems as well. For example, love-shy men are often too shy to attend to certain tasks that are a part of many jobs. Many of them are too shy to use the telephone. And virtually all of them are too shy to use the telephone if the task has anything at all to do with selling, with collecting, or with the filing of any complaints. Many forms of informal face-to-face socializing that are required by many jobs are similarly beyond the ken of most severely love-shy men. And, of course, several of the love-shys interviewed for this book had gotten themselves into serious trouble at work because of their inability to stop staring at certain attractive women. Indeed, some of the men had been fired for such staring (unintentional harassment of women).

Further examples need not be given. Clearly, love-shy men possess too much "thin skin" and hypersensitivity for effective success-striving and competitiveness in today's business world. Indeed, the foregoing discussion should provide incisive support for the view that a university education in intellectual skills and technical knowledge only will often lead to a life of career failure and underachievement—particularly as far as the love-shy are concerned.

Employment Attitudes

Some of the questionnaire items employed for this research are of particular relevance to the issue of employment success and effectiveness. For illustrative purposes, I shall present nine of these items together with the obtained percentage results. There is no need for any commentary here. The following data provide a poignant and forceful argument to the effect that love-shyness and employment ineffectiveness are both caused by some of the same deficits of personality. Thus, if you either cure or prevent love-shyness, you necessarily at the same time cure or prevent many forms of employment ineffectiveness and underachievement.

1. "I am a competitive person by nature." Percent who agree:
     Non-shy men: 100 percent.
     Younger love-shy men: 55 percent.
     Older love-shy men: 32 percent.

2. "I don't work any harder than I have to." Percent who agreed:
     Non-shy men: 19 percent. Younger love-shy men: 55 percent.
     Older love-shy men: 48 percent.

3. "I seldom work to full capacity." Percent who agree:

Non-shy men: 13 percent.
Younger love-shy men: 44 percent.
Older love-shy men: 55 percent.

4. "I'm just not the goal-setting type." Percent who agree:
   Non-shy men: 5 percent.
   Younger love-shy men: 29 percent.
   Older love-shy men: 33 percent.

5. "I get discouraged easily." Percent who agree:
   Non-shy men: *Zero* percent.
   Younger love-shy men: 79 percent.
   Older love-shy men: 100 percent.

6. "I can persist in spite of pain or discomfort." Percent who agree:
   Non-shy men: 100 percent.
   Younger love-shy men: 57 percent.
   Older love-shy men: 40 percent.

7. "I seldom if ever let myself down." Percent who agree:
   Non-shy men: 72 percent.
   Younger love-shy men: 27 percent.
   Older love-shy men: 4 percent.

8. "I enjoy making decisions." Percent who agree.
   Non-shy men: 88 percent.
   Younger love-shy men: 50 percent.
   Older love-shy men: 38 percent.

9. "I don't impose much structure on my activities." Percent who agree:
   Non-shy men: 21 percent.
   Younger love-shy men: 43 percent.
   Older love-shy men: 38 percent.

Some Positive Recommendations

The experience of interviewing hundreds of people has convinced me that there are certain steps which the love-shy can take that will minimize the difficulties they are likely to encounter in the employment sector of life. The recommendations that I shall make here are applicable primarily to young people who are still in school. Parents, teachers and advisors of love-shy men will be able to be of especial service to their charges if they reflect carefully upon the following points.

First, love-shy boys and young men need clearly established, *realistic career goals*. And the earlier in life they are able to commit themselves to these goals, the better off they are likely to be. It is not enough that the love-shy be able to visualize themselves in the mind's eye attaining these goals, although that is important. What is *most important* is that these goals, once attained, permit the successful pursual of a career path which is life-long and which permits *stability*.

Among the older love-shys who were interviewed for this book, few had given any serious thought to what kind of work they would engage in as adults. And the younger love-shys were scarcely any better off in this regard. Most of both groups of love-shy men had labored under the false and misleading notion that if they merely completed a university degree in something, they would be alright. Indeed, the saddest cases of all entailed men who had assumed that if they successfully completed an M.S., M.A., or a Ph.D., they would just naturally be alright.

As I have documented throughout this book, the love-shy tend to follow the law of least resistance in almost everything they do. And this is doubtless a key reason why they experience so many stumbling blocks in arriving at some semblance of success and happiness. Career-wise, the first mistake most of them make is in their choice of an *academic major*. Here the love-shy veer toward those fields which are (1) most interesting to them, and (2) which are easiest for them to accumulate an impressive grade-point average.

A cardinal rule which all love-shy men should memorize before they even set foot in a college or university is this: THE CHOICE OF A MAJOR IS OF INFINITELY GREATER IMPORTANCE THAN GRADE-POINT AVERAGE. To put it bluntly, A STRAIGHT "C" AVERAGE IN THE *RIGHT DISCIPLINE* WILL BE OF VASTLY GREATER VALUE TO THE LOVE-SHY THAN A STRAIGHT "A" AVERAGE IN THE *WRONG* DISCIPLINE. Good grades can be helpful. But the *courses* in which such grades are earned is a matter of far greater importance than the good grades themselves. Completion of a major in a technical field with only a "C" average will very likely get a love-shy man a much better career opportunity than will an "A" average in a non-technical discipline that is not clearly related to the job market.

Some areas of employment require much greater social self-confidence than others do. Generally speaking, *the greater the amount of technical knowledge that is required for entrance into a career field, the less social self-confidence and interpersonal finesse that field is likely to require.* Contrariwise, the smaller the amount of technical training and knowledge a field requires, the *MORE* that field is likely to demand in terms of interpersonal finesse and social self confidence.

Of course, there are certain ascetic moralists passing themselves off as "therapists" who argue that the love-shy would benefit enormously from entrance into employment situations that require assertiveness and interpersonal self-confidence for financial survival. My own observations have convinced me that such psychoemotionally harrowing employment situations (e.g., commission sales) cause the love-shy to withdraw even more deeply into their shells. And they cause ever worsening feelings of discouragement, personal worthlessness, and financial failure.

During their undergraduate years most love-shy men drift into academic majors that usually come under the headings of *liberal arts, social sciences,* and *humanities.* These majors include such fields as theatre arts, psychology, sociology, English and American literature, music, philosophy, history, anthropology, education, geography, and political science. Often the love-shy will be attracted to these disciplines because they seem to offer something in terms of self-knowledge.[1] Thus, they provide what some in the helping professions call *bibliotherapy*—self-insight derived from the reading and studying of books. Some love-shy men become so delighted by their expanding self-awareness that they actually go on to earn masters and doctorate degrees in these disciplines. And in so doing, they often render themselves unemployable. This is true because it is *far, far more difficult* for a person *with a graduate degree* in one of these disciplines to obtain a job in some mainstream area of business, than it is for a person with merely a bachelors degree in one of them to get a job.

Intellectual self-enlightenment or "insight" is now recognized by most psychologists as being quite useless from the standpoint of curing love-shyness. Insight is an *intellectual* attribute, and as such it does not even begin to deal with a person's fears about experiencing interpersonal anxiety. The love-shy are victims of a kind of *people-phobia.* And like any phobia, the *emotional* (NOT the intellectual) components of the person must be effectively reached and affected if therapeutic advances are to be made. Given the fact that there appears to be a strong biological-physiological base behind the overstrong anxiety-prone feelings of the love-shy, it seems likely that for any therapy to work it would have to deal with these inborn biologically based components of shyness *as well as* those facets of shyness that are rooted in faulty learning.

It can be asserted with considerably certainty that love-shy men who major in technical fields and who develop salable, technical skills, adjust to their adult lives a great deal better than do love-shys who major in the liberal arts, social science, education and humanities disciplines.

Therefore, the love-shy college student who feels that he must take some of these *"self-knowledge"* courses should either (1) attend college a fifth year so that he can complete his *technical* degree and still take the "self-knowledge" courses that he so desperately wishes to take, or (2) complete his *technical* degree first and then take the "self-knowledge" courses (while he is working) in the evening division of some nearby college or university.

A socially self-confident person need not be anywhere nearly so careful. Such a person can emerge from his university training with a "C" average and a degree in English or psychology or geography, etc., and end up making $30,000 or more in his second full year of employment—for example, in some sales capacity. Approximately 85 percent of all Americans with annual incomes in excess of $60,000 derive those incomes from commission sales work. And most of these jobs require no specialized or technical training of any sort. Indeed, many of these jobs realistically permit incomes in the $30,000 range within the first year on the job. Second and subsequent years can easily net the conscientious, competitive worker $60,000 or more.

There is no shortage of sales career opportunities. But these jobs all require individuals who are (1) naturally sociable, (2) relaxed, (3) socially self-confident, (4) high on interpersonal finesse, (5) high on positive mental attitude, and (6) unusually insensitive to interpersonal anxiety. This last point is the most crucial. Successful sales people all have unusually high anxiety thresholds; social kinds of stimuli simply do not unruffle them. In stark contrast, love-shy males suffer from a severe and chronic people-phobia. Temperamentally they are 180 degrees different from what is required for success in a career involving commission sales work.

There is an important reason for my citing commission sales work in this chapter. Most love-shy men without some form of technical training eventually end up working in commission sales for various quite brief periods of time. And inevitably the experiences they encountr during these periods prove quite traumatic and emotionally harrowing for them. It is not simply a matter of extreme polar opposites attracting— although I think that may have at least something to do with the fact that love-shys without technical skills almost always manage to get roped in on at least one or two selling jobs. There are two key factors which I think are of prime importance: (1) commission sales jobs are plentiful, and sales managers will commonly "try out" two-thirds or more of all people who walk through the door asking for a job. University graduates and others with white-collar backgrounds will almost never be turned away. Thus, in sales work those who are taken on are allowed by the manager to "recruit" and to "screen" themselves. Only about two out of every 100 eventually "make the grade". The other 98 voluntarily quit after varying lengths of time.

The second (2) key factor is that love-shy men do not possess the charm, polish and finesse necessary for talking themselves into white-collar career positions that do not require a technical degree. There are plenty of such jobs "out there". But such positions ordinarily require the applicant to be "hooked in" to a social network, and to have friends and/or relatives who are willing to speak on his behalf. As the data in this book have made painfully clear, love-shys have few or no friend-ships, and their kinship networks similarly tend to be very weak, non-existent, or very unhelpful.

To be sure, young men are occasionally recruited for good, entry level career opportunities through newspaper job ads. However, in such cases the employment interviewer will almost always opt for the charm-ing, handsome, well-groomed young man who appears naturally friendly, relaxed, sociable and spontaneous. The love-shy young man simply cannot compete—not even if his university grade-point average had been far superior to that of the sociable charmers who are accorded the better opportunities. The net upshot of all of this is that LOVE-SHY MEN NEED A SALABLE TECHNICAL SKILL WHICH WILL EFFECTIVELY PERMIT THEM TO COMPENSATE FOR DEFICITS IN THEIR PERSON-ALITY AND LOOKS.

On Selling an Employment Interviewer

People who emerge from college with liberal arts degrees have occasionally been known to obtain business-related career opportunities outside the fields of sales and marketing. But this is actually very rare. In order to obtain such a career opportunity a person would ordinarily have to *sell* an employment interviewer on the prudence and desirability of creating a new position just for him—and hiring him for that position *without* advertising it. Accomplishing something like this typically requires a charming, highly sociable personality with a good sized friendship network. It also requires an above average physical appearance together with an ability to articulate one's ideas vis-a-vis the interviewer in a relaxed yet incisively convincing, winning way.

In contrast, the person with an academic background in such prac-tical fields as accounting, finance, engineering, etc., virtually never finds himself in the highly uncomfortable position of having to sell an employer on the idea of creating a new position just for him. The employer has placed an ad for someone with a background in engineering, accounting, etc. And all the job interviewee needs to do is to convince the interviewer that he would be a more suitable candidate for the job than his competitors. If he fails to win the position, little is lost. A trained accountant, engineer, etc., can travel to any metropolitan area of his choosing and find a copious abundance of employment advertisements for applicable positions. A person without technical training cannot do this.

In short, a person without technical training must depend upon the power and charm of his personality to win and to keep employment opportunities. The love-shy tend to lack both the power and the charm factors as well as the physical attractiveness assets that would be instrumental in motivating an employment interviewer to think twice about them. More importantly, the severely love-shy individual is normally so emotionally incapable of even trying to sell an employer that he ends up making no attempts at all.

In the nutshell, this is why severly love-shy, college educated men without technical training almost always end up underemployed. They end up in lower level clerical positions and as cab drivers, door-to-door canvassers, etc. Such unstable and disappointing employment situations serve to lower the love-shys' self-images to an ever worse degree. Such positions similarly serve to further reduce the love-shys' chances of ever meeting an appropriate woman for dating, courtship, and marriage.

The Importance of Being in Demand

Rugged individualists often delight in reminding us of a statement which the playwright George Bernard Shaw once made. In effect, "the people who get on in this world are those who are constantly on the lookout for new opportunities; and when they cannot find them they create their own opportunities." No evidence has ever been presented suggesting that love-shy men are any less intelligent than the rest of us. Indeed, many love-shys have no shortage of creative ideas. The problem is that they do not have the nerve to do and say the things which their God-given native intelligence tells them to do and say.

This is why it is of the utmost importance for love-shy men to take whatever steps may be necessary while they are young to give themselves the virtue of being *in demand* from a career standpoint. Inasmuch as their love-shyness obviates their being "in demand" socially and heterosexually, creative, meaningful and enjoyable work represents one area wherein it is within the realm of feasibility for them to find some sense of positive enthusiasm for their lives—and also some semblance of a social life. Involvement in meaningful, well-paid work can do much to bolster a person's overall self-esteem. And it can further serve to increase even a severely love-shy man's romantic chances.

Because of their thin-skinned, low anxiety threshold attributes, it is simply not realistic to expect severely love-shy men to "create their own opportunities" when the going (employment-wise) gets tough. And this is why in counseling severely love-shy men I always make it a point to emphasize as strongly as I can the desirability—*indeed the necessity*— of their choosing and completing a college major which will place their services *in demand* as far as the labor market is concerned. Since love-shys are not emotionally capable of "hustling", they must be prepared to carry what they have to offer (technical knowledge) *in their minds*. And that technical knowledge must be of a sort which society deems to be in demand, and which will continue to be in demand for the foreseeable future.

In this regard, love-shys owe it to themselves to *get the objective facts* regarding job trends in the areas of specialized career endeavor that they are considering. University professors are *the last place* to go to in order to acquire this information. Professors have a personal vested interest in selling their discipline to naive but reasonably intelligent undergraduates. This is one reason why we have so many highly educated cab drivers and welfare recipients today. Colleges and universities are essentially *sales organizations* in the same sense as Bristol Myers, General Mills, General Motors, Colgate-Palmolive, Encyclopaedia Britannica, and Coors Beer, etc., are sales organizations. Moreover, each individual university department represents a separate sales organization with strong vested interests in assuring plenty of students (both graduate and undergraduate) for its teaching staff.

This is why young people need to obtain their information on career trends from as many *objective* sources as possible. City libraries and personnel agencies can provide many helpful hints in this regard. So can frequent surveys of the employment advertisements that appear in the major daily newspaper of the metropolitan area in which one hopes to reside. Except for sales and marketing, *the greater the number of job ads that appear for a particular occupational or career category, the safer that occupational or career category will prove for the love-shy individual*.

Alleged "Frills" in Education

There has been a great deal of discussion in recent years about the alleged "frills" in education. Many well-meaning conservatives want education to "get back to the basics" of the "three Rs". They angrily clamor against the use of school resources and public funding for such "frivolous" activities as interpersonal skills training, sex and family life education, parenting education, music, and even recreation.

I think we might all stand to benefit a great deal by giving careful thought and consideration to some comments recently made by well-known American industrialist and mulit-millionaire M. R. Kopmeyer. As Kopmeyer pointed out, all we need to do is have a good look around at the hundreds of educated derelicts and chronically unemployed and underemployed individuals. An assessment of their situation should incisively convince anyone that education of the intellect *by itself* is quite insufficient to provide young people with all the ingredients they will require to be successful and happy in today's world. Positive mental attitude, social self-confidence and strong interpersonal finesse rank *at the head of the list of what is actually required*. And the sort of education recommended by conservative "back to basics" protagonists does not even begin to speak to these highly crucial human attributes. (Remember the study cited in chapter one: better than 90 percent of all employment terminations in middle-class white-collar employment are caused by *interpersonal shortcomings*, NOT by unsatisfactory technical competence/ performance.)

A person can possess an outstanding graduate education and a very high grade-point average. *And he can still fail*. On the other hand, in today's society there are thousands of enormously successful individuals who never got beyond high school. Indeed, there are many high school graduates who had been quite bored with school, and who managed to move straight upward to $50,000 and $60,000 per year careers (particularly in sales) without taking any additional formal education above and beyond their high school training.[2]

Very often that which is touted as "frills" lies at the very core of what is *truly* important, whereas that which is deemed to be of central importance is *really* of quite secondary importance and can be picked up at any time of life. For example, it is well known that technical, academic, intellectual skills can be effectively learned *at any time in life*. Yet is it *also* well known that deficits in the self-image, psychoemotional life, mental attitude, social self-confidence, etc., cannot be remedied anywhere nearly as easily after a child has grown beyond the ages of approximately 12 or 13. In short, giving people what they need in terms of social self-confidence, positive mental attitude and psychoemotional health, seems to entail a *time limit*—not a rigid time limit, but a time limit nonetheless. In stark contrast, the learning of intellectual skills such as reading, writing and arithmetic, knows *no time limit*. Unlike the emotions, the intellect can be educated with equal effectiveness at any point in life. Indeed, for some people (e.g., the hyperactive), education can actually be accomplished far more easily in the late teens and twenties than it can during middle and late childhood. And, of course, some normally bright individuals ought not attend college until they get to be 25 or more years of age.

Higher Education as a Mode of Compensation

Many love-shy men seem to *use* higher education as a mode of compensation for deficits in their social self-confidence. Some of these men accept as valid the proposition that they must defer the gratification with which a love mate would supply them, in order to successfully attain some educational goal. And as the years go by such love-shy men become progressively less and less mature by comparison with their age mates in terms of the ability to relax and to enjoy the friendly companionship of fellow human beings. Thus, they become less and less competent at the art of acquiring a wife.

American universities are filled with graduate students who are years ahead of their age-mates in intellectual maturity, but who remain sadly in the kindergarten of awareness as far as social and psychoemotional maturity is concerned. As Spiritualist clergyman Paul Mastorakos recently expressed it, these people possess enormous intellectual knowledge, but they lack the rudiments of plain, ordinary "horse sense".

One 35-year old love-shy man with a Ph.D. in adolescent psychology (of all fields!) recently expressed his feelings this way:

> "One of the main reasons why I worked so hard on my doctorate for all those years is that I thought I'd finally be able to get an attractive girl to be really impressed with me. But after I finally had the degree in hand I found out that it impressed nobody. In fact, I became more shy than I had ever been. And the very few women I have managed to talk to seemed to react as though the Ph.D. were actually a liability rather than an asset. A lot of women seem to become frightened of me as soon as they find out I've got a Ph.D. I think realization of the fact that education doesn't help is one of the most bitter pills I've ever had to swallow!"

For many highly inhibited young men higher education may actually help to create a *trained incapacity* for truly "being oneself", and for being able to (as Spiritualists often say) "let go and let God". Further, higher education is often perceived by severely love-shy men as a means by which status, recognition, and worthwhileness as a human being can be acquired. Indeed, a good half-dozen of the men who were interviewed for this study spoke of how they had fantasized women being impressed with their Ph.D.s and M.A.s. Some of these men had actually fantasized women asserting themselves in actually trying to commence a romantic relationship. Thus, a good-sized minority of severely love-shy men had evidently believed that women think so highly of advanced degrees that socially assertive, friendly behavior on the part of the man would no longer be required.

As suggested by the above interview excerpt, once these men had actually obtained their advanced degrees they were bitterly disappointed. Not only were the women they encountered quite unimpressed with the idea of getting to know a man simply because he had achieved an M.A. or a Ph.D., but employers were even more unimpressed. Thus, after spending ten or more years at full-time study in a university, these men were not only incapable of winning the admiration and affection (or even the interest) of a woman, but they were *also* (in most cases) unable to obtain respectable full-time employment.

In sum, social skills vis-a-vis the opposite sex do not exist in isolation. Such skills *transfer* to the world of employment and business. And they provide an important basis for career success and for lifelong productivity. A history of happy childhood play that in adolescence and young adulthood leads to an easy social effectiveness with women, *also* leads unmistakably to competence and effectiveness in the highly competitive world of contemporary employment in business and industry.

Putting First Things First

Which is more important—that a 17-year old young man successfully master his high school trigonometry course, or that he develop the ability to comfortably interact on an informal basis with the 15–17 year old women in attendance at his high school? Most American parents, teachers and community leaders would be swift to assert the overriding importance of the former. Popular wisdom is unfortunately sometimes *extremely wrong*. And following it can sometimes cause a young person to go from bad to worse. Those who proffer such folk advice usually have the young person's best interests genuinely at heart. But the action and advice that they offer quite frequently cause the afflicted young man to become *increasingly incapable* of concentrating upon conceptually difficult material.

To be sure, not all 17-year olds having difficulty with mathematics are love-shy. But for those who are—i.e., for those who are never or almost never seen interacting with opposite-sexed age mates, it is my suggestion that any permanent improvement in study and concentration habits will have to await improvement in the interpersonal skills/informal heterosexual interaction sector of life. Simply put, help the young man to surmount the love-shyness barriers *first*. And once that is accomplished you will very likely experience the pleasure of witnessing that young man *soar* in his academic abilities and accomplishments. You will also have the pleasure of seeing him mature (from a psychoemotional standpoint) almost overnight.

Love-shyness will seldom keep a person of normal intelligence from attending and passing most *liberal arts* university/college courses. In contrast, the ability to take and successfully pass the sort of university courses which *pay off* in today's highly technical job market normally requires a reasonably serene, trouble-free state of mind. Such a state of mind is an impossibility for someone who has long been constantly deprived of that which he has wanted most strongly, and who can perceive little or no real hope for the future as far as finding the ability to obtain his secret desire (a girlfriend) is concerned.

In sum, for young men of high school and college age who are lonely and shy a *priority emphasis* needs to be placed by educators upon developing interpersonal skills and social self-confidence—as per the discussions to follow in chapters 22, 23, and 24. Afflicted young men should be encouraged to place academic mastery in temporary abeyance until such time as a normal social life has become feasible for them.

Moving During the Formative Years

Even though it is a minor point, the data I obtained for this book suggest that the love-shys had attended a greater number of schools than the non-shys had. For example, between the ages of 5 and 18, fully 54 percent of the self-confident non-shy men had not moved at all. In contrast, only 38 percent of the younger love-shys and 35 percent of the older love-shys had made no moves between the ages of 5 and 18.

On the other side of the ledger, 34 percent of the older love-shys and 31 percent of the younger ones had made *three or more moves* between the time they were 5, and the time they had reached their 18th birthday. Only 12 percent of the non-shy men claimed to have moved three or more times between their 5th and 18th birthdays.

For naturally outgoing children from loving families, geographic moves during childhood and adolescence are not very likely to adversely impact upon psychoemotional or social self-confidence development. On the other hand, boys with a strong inhibition gene (the unusually inhibited and introverted) may quite possibly be adversely impacted upon by childhood geographic moves. This is likely to be especially true in cases where quality parenting skills are wanting, and where there is a dearth of warm and meaningful intrafamily communication involving the children. Again, good communication lies at the very heart and soul of love. Genuine compassion requires communication. And in our highly competitive society, boys with the inhibition gene require much more of this from significant ego supports such as parents, than do more biologically advantaged children.

NOTES

1. Another factor strongly attracting many love-shy men to the liberal arts is the opportunity to sit in classrooms populated mainly by young women. Several of my love-shy respondents advised me that they had found it "painfully depressing" and highly distracting to sit in a classroom composed exclusively or even primarily of fellow male students. Some of the love-shy men had dropped out of such technical, career-related majors as accounting, engineering, computer programming, etc., just in order to be able to take classes which might (they hoped) permit them to interact with women students. After graduating college all of these men had regretted such decisions. But equally sad is the fact that sitting in a lot of "liberal arts" classrooms proved quite insufficient to get the love-shy men actually interacting with any female students. Thus, the love-shy men would merely look and stare at the girls in their classes; they would not (because of severe shyness) actually interact with any of them. (As I have tried to clearly demonstrate in this chapter, introverted, inhibited college and university males belong in technical, career-related majors because they do not have the "chutz-pah" that is absolutely required for seeking *or holding* a job as a liberal arts graduate.)

Chapter 20

Politics, Religion, and the Love-Shy

The best one-word description for the love-shys' politics would be *"alienated"*. As far as the love-shys were concerned, the existing political structure "couldn't care less" about them, and wouldn't be the least bit interested in helping them out in any way. Thus, the love-shys' attitude seemed to be: "Why should I give a damn?! As far as my life and well-being are concerned things will obviously remain the same no matter who gets into office! Nobody gives a damn about the plight of love-shy men!"

And on the basis of these feelings, it cannot be considered surprising that only 18 percent of the older love-shys and 23 percent of the younger ones had bothered to vote in the most recent general election. In contrast, fully 62 percent of the non-shy men had voted in the most recent general election.

And yet most of the love-shys seemed to identify with quite liberal social and political viewpoints. During the past several years liberal politicians have become increasingly exasperated by the fact that truly liberal people are not particularly likely to either register or to vote. The older love-shy men represent as good an illustration of this point as one might be likely to find. For example, 96 percent of the older love-shys had favored George McGovern in the 1972 election. Yet only 15 percent of them had bothered to even register for the vote that year. (Those who had registered, however, *did* vote.)

I asked each man a good many questions pertinent to social and political issues. Suffice it to say that the two love-shy groups came out significantly more liberal than the non-shy group, quite in spite of the youthful ages of the latter. Perhaps the non-shys saw themselves as having a vested interest in preserving the "status quo" inasmuch as the traditional ways of doing things had led them to become so happy and socially (and romantically) successful. Never having gotten very much out of the currently prevailing "system", it cannot be considered surprising that the love-shy men tended to be rather disenchanted with it.

In spite of their quite evident liberality, I found the love-shys to be rather strangely disinterested in the idea of identifying themselves with the Democratic Party. To be specific, fully 83 percent of the older love-shys and 64 percent of the younger love-shys identified themselves as being either "independents" or as just plain "uncommitted". In stark contrast, the non-shys were much more likely to identify themselves as being either Republicans or Democrats. Only 32 percent of the non-shy men saw themselves as being either "independent" or as "politically uncommitted"—quite despite their youthful ages.

Religion

Just as the love-shys had become quite alienated from politics, they had similarly become alienated from conventional religious participation— probably for much the same reasons: Conventional religious structures had never done anything to help them become involved with meaningful female companionship. Indeed, most of the love-shys tended to view conventional religious organizations as being rather sour on the idea of informal heterosexual interaction among unmarrieds—even though such interaction is a prerequisite in our society for marriage and parenthood.

However, the religious factor is not a simple one. For example, only 4 percent of the older love-shys and *zero percent* of the younger ones considered themselves to be nonreligious, agnostic, or athiest. In contrast, fully 36 percent of the non-shy men regarded themselves as being nonreligious, agnostic or athiest; and this included several who occasionally attended conventional, organized church services! In essence, most love-shys appear to be religious. But their approach to religion is deeply personal and private. They view religiousness as a personal state of mind and prefer not to attend organized church services.

Many of the love-shys had become alienated from religion by the militant overzealousness of fundamentalist Christians, some Roman Catholics, and other similar "born again" groups. This is not surprising given the strong tendency among the love-shy to feel uncomfortable around groups of people wherein there is any type of social pressure to conform either behaviorally or attitudinally. Love-shy men appear to have an unusually strong need to think for themselves, and to remove themselves from any situation wherein there is social pressure to conform to a certain thought style or behavioral mold. This explains their strong aversion to anything military in nature, to anything involving contact sports and athletics; and it seems to explain their aversion to organized religion as well. The love-shy are not joiners; they have an inordinate fear of having their sense of identity swallowed up by any formal organization.

Several of the love-shys had been alienated from organized religion by the disinterest and/or inability among the clergy to help them with their shyness problems. For example, some of the love-shys had written to clergymen of various mainstream denominations including Catholicism. And in their letters they had requested help in meeting potential female companions. The following interview segment can be considered typical of what usually happened in these cases:

"Well, I got the names and addresses of some Presbyterian ministers out of the Yellow Pages, and I wrote to them. One of the ministers was really nice, and he invited me to join his church, which I did. To be perfectly honest, I really didn't find anything wrong with any of the church services. They were quite nice. There wasn't any hell-fire and brimstone crap, and nobody tried to force any straight-laced religious dogma down my throat. The problem was that practically everybody who came to the church services every Sunday morning was either very old or very young. I mean it was basically a family service. There were a lot of children, and I used to enjoy listening to the children sing. It was really nice because the singing was never confined to the usual depressing hymn stuff. But I mean it was all family.

After the service there was usually a social hour. And there were almost no young women in their early 20s, which is what I was looking for. Like I said, they were all families along with a good number of elderly ladies as well. Now how the hell was that going to benefit me?! I liked the church because there didn't seem to be any fanatics associated with it. But after three or four months of attending the services I finally quit because I realized there was no way I was ever going to meet anybody there." (37-year old love-shy man.)

In several cases the ministers had responded to the love-shys' letters by inviting the love-shy man to join a weekly church therapy and prayer group. But again, the composition of these groups invariably lacked the presence of any young, never married women. These clergyman therapists and group facilitators had evidently been no less competent than the usual psychotherapists that are found in private practice. Indeed, they were perceived by most of the love-shy men as being warm, sincere, and well-intentioned. But with only married women, divorced people, alcoholics, elderly people, etc., attending the meetings, the love-shys tended to see little point in continued participation.

Paradoxically, the stricter, more fundamentalistic demoninations often do attract a large contingency of impressionable, insecure young women. But again, love-shy men inwardly rebel at the thought control and strong social pressures which prevail among the various funda-mentalistic "born again" sects.

> "I strongly disagree with their belief that the Bible is the word of God and that it should be interpreted literally. But I went to a few of their meetings because I noticed that there were a lot of attractive girls my age there. I contacted the pastor by writing him a letter. I thought he might be able to get me introduced to someone. All that happened was that he interviewed me and invited me to come to a social event. When I arrived there I certainly wasn't disappointed by the attractiveness of the girls who were there. But the minister didn't actually do anything for me. I mean he came up to me and said he was delighted that I came. Then he introduced me to a guy, of all things. This guy he introduced me to was more interested in getting me to accept Jesus into my life than in getting me introduced to any of the women. I always believed in Christ anyway; but I just didn't like their attitude. I mean, it was as though only this guy really knew Christ and I didn't really know Him, and I wouldn't be saved unless I saw things their way. Actually, I didn't even have the nerve to tell the guy my real reason for being there. I thought the pastor might have told him; but I guess he didn't.
>
> There was also a lot of loud singing in unison—sort of like what fraternity men do at their beer brauls. I just didn't like the way my problem was totally ignored. And I especially didn't like the way I was forced to take part in these stupid group chants. I guess maybe it's just as well—because even if I had met a girl there I never would have been able to practice that kind of religion with her. I would have insisted that she come with me over to a more staid and sensible denomination. I know I would never be able to live with a woman who insisted on being a member of any of those crazy "born again" groups." (23-year old love-shy man.)

The love-shy seem to require a sort of "big brother" who will take them under their wing, and who will see to it that meaningful hetero-sexual interaction does take place and that it is actively and continuously facilitated. When such an unusually benign, highly altruistic "big brother" is not provided, the love-shy often become anxiety-ridden and/or lose interest. For example, consider the following:

> "Well, I grew up Catholic. And at various times I've written letters to the priests asking them if they could help me with my problem. My parents have also contacted their bishop about my problem. And the thing is, nothing has ever come of all this. At home the bishop invited me to come to a young people's party. And the two different Catholic churches I contacted near the university campuses where I went to school—the same thing happened. They invited me to attend a young people's party. Well, I went to three of these. The

only reason why I was able to go is because they had a layperson accompany me. There were no priests at all at any of these affairs, even though they were all held on church property. A layman took me inside all three different times. But once I was inside, everything was left entirely up to me. There were enough girls there. But I felt so anxiety-ridden that I escaped all three times after less than a half-hour of walking around the dance floor. I knew how to dance, but I just didn't have the nerve to approach anyone. And the church had not assigned anyone to get a girl for me. If they had assigned me to a girl, even if I didn't like her I would have stayed. But I would have to be assigned and put together with someone. There is no way I would ever have the nerve to do that for myself." (47-year old love-shy man.)

It would thus appear that the leaders of organized religion do have a viable potential for effectively helping the love-shy. However, as yet this viable potential has not even begun to be realized. Love-shy men enormously fear social ambiguity. They cannot "survive" within the context of an unstructured party situation. They must be engaged in highly structured social activities that entail and in fact *require* direct face-to-face cooperation with eligible females. It is not sufficient for a clergyman to merely introduce a love-shy man to an eligible female. The love-shy man must be tactfully aided towards the end of becoming enmeshed in a conversation with the woman to whom he has been introduced. Those ministers who would be most helpful in this regard are going to be those who can get a love-shy man introduced to a fairly steady stream of new, eligible women, and who can directly foster the development of good, solid conversations with each.

Love-shy men cannot be left alone in unstructured party situations. They must be closely supervised and kept occupied with people. If this is not done they will escape either physically and/or in fantasy. Dependency is a prerequisite for any kind of socialization or therapeutic experience. Dependency is a temporary albeit indispensable stage through which all severely love-shy men must pass. Thus, clergymen and other therapeutic counselors need not feel uncomfortable about this need of the love-shy "to be taken by the hand". Once a love-shy man has gained a sufficient minimum amount of social self-confidence plus a suitable female companion, he will no longer display any need for being directly dependent upon someone for help.

Amenability to Religious Participation

Love-shy men appear to be quite disinclined towards joining *anything*. Most of them appear to be *particularly* disinclined towards joining (or even remaining near, for more than a few minutes) any group with any semblance of zealous militancy, or any group which endeavors to standardize personalities and value systems through moralistic and/or militaristic intimidation and brainwashing. Love-shy men tend to associate any kind of zealousness and/or militancy with *bullying*. And the love-shy sustain a deep loathing for any and all kinds of bullies, including those who might be operating in the service of what fundamentalists might construe to be Jesus Christ.

Some of the love-shy men I interviewed were quite aware of the match-making that goes on in many strict, conservative Christian churches. For example, devout young men of the Latter-Day Saint faith are expected by their church to devote two years to missionary work. But after their education and those two years of religious service have been completed, such young men are expected to begin thinking seriously about getting married. And those LDS men who remain into their late 20s without partners are quite commonly helped by church officials to obtain same.

However, very few of the love-shys I talked to had ever been tempted to join up with any strictly conservative religious organizations. Most of them felt that they could not compromise their integrity. And some of them disagreed so strongly with fundamentalist Christian viewpoints that there was no way they could seriously entertain the idea of even temporarily affiliating with any such organizations. To quote from one man:

> "I'll be damned if I'm going to become a bloody hypocrite about this thing. It wouldn't work out anyway because I know I could never live comfortably with someone whose views I disagreed with so strongly. How would we raise our children? I mean, how would we communicate about the things in life that are really important?! I've never been an athiest. And I wouldn't mind attending church again if the girl I married wanted to go. But it would have to be a moderate denomination with a minister who is either moderate or liberal. As far as I'm concerned, I feel just as uncomfortable around 'born again' Christians as I do when I'm around athiests. There's got to be a happy medium. And I'm not going to become a hypocrite just to marry someone I could never see eye to eye with!" (22-year old love-shy man.)

On the other hand, it appears that most love-shy men *might be amenable—if they were (figuratively speaking) taken by the hand*—to joining moderate-to-liberal mainstream churches such as Presbyterian, Episcopalian, Congregational, Disciples of Christ, Christian Science, Spiritualism, Religious Mind Science, etc. However, in order to keep a love-shy man in the congregation, a minister or pastor is going to have to successfully accomplish three goals: (1) he must offer religious services and informal social get-togethers (with well-structured activities) that are attended by a large number of young, "single-never-married", attractive women; and (2) he is going to have to engineer a system for making introductions between the love-shy man and eligible girls. And thirdly (3) he is going to have to make sure that the love-shy man is comfortable after he makes each introduction, so that the love-shy man actually remains behind and talks with the girl. Clergyman readers who might be interested in helping the love-shy should carefully study Chapter 22 of this book which deals with *"practice-dating therapy"*. That material should serve as a source for potentially fruitful ideas. Actually there is no legal or practical reason as to why religious leaders could not become perfectly good practice-dating therapists!

A Rejoinder to Ponder

Certain people never get tired of suggesting that a love-shy teenager or young adult might benefit from joining the Latter-Day Saint Church (Mormons). The LDS Church requires of its young men a great deal of assertive proselytizing activity. Usually two young men are sent out to work together on such endeavors. And this along with the prescribed missionary work (allegedly) has a tremendous impact upon building self-confidence, ego strength, and positive self-discipline.

Now this viewpoint makes just about as much sense as a similar one which states that "going away to a university for four years will tremendously boost a love-shy boy's self-esteem and social self-confidence." In point of fact, the university experience *does* boost a shy person's *intellectual* self-image. But it does nothing by itself to remedy interpersonal self-confidence deficits vis-a-vis the opposite sex, or social fearfulness and inhibition.

A key finding of my research on love-shyness is that love-shy men are often quite self-confident in social situations *where there is a script*, where there is a *specific role* to play. On the other hand, in social situations that are *purely informal*, where there is no purpose apart from pure, unadulterated sociability, the situation is *far too ambiguous* for the love-shy man to function: and thus he *"freezes"*, or he escapes and runs away (either physically or, if he cannot do that, then *in fantasy*).

The proselytizing and missionary roles in the LDS Church are both impersonal and highly structured, as is the role of university student in the classroom. Learning how to self-confidently get up and deliver a speech before an audience can confer a substantial amount of self-confidence upon a love-shy man. But unfortunately it WILL NOT be the *sort* of self-confidence that will enable him to initiate friendly conversations with people or get himself a girlfriend/lover/wife. Simply put, self-confidence in well-structured, impersonal, unambiguous situations where there is a definite script (role) to play WILL NOT CARRY OVER AND CREATE SELF-CONFIDENCE IN UNSTRUCTURED SOCIAL SITUATIONS INVOLVING YOUNG WOMEN WHEREIN THERE IS NO PURPOSE APART FROM PURE, UNADULTERATED SOCIABILITY AND FRIENDLINESS!

Of course, as a final note it must be added that LDS missionary work is all done on a strictly sex-segregated basis. It goes without saying that a sex-segregated environment is the very last thing that a love-shy man needs!

Spiritualism

Throughout the past twenty years I have been deeply interested and involved in the study of psychic and occult phenomena. For this reason I decided to throw in a small number of questionnaire items of pertinence to spiritualism and psi phenomena. In some respects the results I obtained were quite surprising. At the very least they provide some interesting clarification regarding the *ways* in which some of the love-shy men are religious.

As I indicated earlier, to most love-shys religion is a very deeply personal and private matter. The following research findings provide some suggestions as to the way love-shy men think from a religious standpoint. And they highlight some of the ways whereby their "personal" religious thought may differ from that of the majority of people who are involved in conventional, mainstream religious participation.

First, 100 percent of the older love-shys together with 87 percent of the younger ones believe in "life after life". Surprisingly, only 50 percent of the non-shy men expressed a belief in the concept of "life after life". Further, only 6 percent of the non-shy men indicated any belief in reincarnation. In contrast, fully 38 percent of the older love-shys and 31 percent of the younger love-shys indicated a belief in reincarnation.

I asked each respondent to react to this statement: "Mind and brain are two different things; brain is just a temporary channel for the mind, and the two can exist completely apart from one another." The differences between the three respondent groups were quite substantial with regard to this issue. Only 35 percent of the non-shy men saw fit to agree with the statement. In stark contrast, fully 85 percent of the older love-shys and 73 percent of the younger love-shys registered agreement.

Related to the foregoing was the question: "Cases are frequently reported involving communication with and visitations from the discarnate spirits of deceased persons. Do you believe that some of these reports might be authentic and valid?" Fully 64 percent of the non-shy men indicated "*no*", compared to just 37 percent of the older love-shys and 46 percent of the younger love-shys.

The subject of out-of-the-body experiences has become increasingly popular of late. A person having an out-of-body experience genuinely believes that his/her sense of consciousness and sense of self have left the physical body. Out-of-body experiences are believed by many people to support the view that the real self or "soul" is something that is separate and apart from the physical vehicle. Fully 75 percent of the older love-shy men registered a belief in the concept of out-of-the-body experiences. The younger love-shys were second most believing with 63 percent endorsing the concept. On the other hand, only 43 percent of the non-shy men indicated a belief in out-of-the-body experiences.

As for a basic belief in the reality of extra-sensory perception, the non-shy men were much more open-minded. Fully 79 percent of the non-shys accepted the reality of "ESP" as an established fact. The analogous figures for the two love-shy groups were 97 percent for the older ones and 89 percent for the younger ones.

Lastly, I asked each man whether he accepted a basic principle of Spiritualism which holds that God exists within and throughout all of nature, including the minds of all human beings. Fully 93 percent of the older love-shys together with 87 percent of the younger ones indicated basic agreement with this viewpoint. I suspect that few of these agreeing respondents had much awareness of the implications of this principle. Be that as it may, just 42 percent of the non-shy men endorsed it as being valid.

In sum, the love-shys appear to be quite a bit more "open" than the non-shys to an "other worldly" type of orientation and world view. To some extent this may be a byproduct of the fact that *this world* has not provided the love-shys with the range of rich satisfactions and experiences with which it has provided the non-shys. Long term deprivations have forced the love-shys to look in unusual directions for the possibility of satisfactions. And in hitting upon the psychic and occult, many of them felt privileged—as though they were in possession of a secret knowledge and awareness which the majority of people are "too dense" to be able to share. In essence, the non-shy men were experiencing a sufficiently rich life right in the here and now; and many of them did not feel any special need for a higher spiritual world, or for personal immortality.

By the way, I am not making these statements in order to disparage a belief in Spiritualism or in psychic and occult subjects. Years of intense study have convinced me personally of the fundamental validity of many occult ideas. I am merely suggesting that people who feel driven from an early point in life to study Spiritualism and the occult have very often had to deal with a range of hardships and privations. Compared to others of their age and gender, they have not had as smooth or as easy a time in coping with life. In a 1975 monograph on the psychological correlates of a belief in psychic phenomena (by Notre Dame University priest and sociologist Andrew Greeley), a very similar conclusion was reached.

On the other hand, a number of anthropologists have suggested that Spiritualism is the *only* form of religious belief to have prevailed throughout 80 percent or more of all human societies down through history; and that the conventional American approach to religion is *actually* the unusual one. Thus, conventional Christianity as practiced by most Americans appears to be a good deal more concerned with *social control* than with satisfying man's truly spiritual needs. In essence, to many Americans religion operates primarily as a policeman and martinet, rather than as an agent offering true peace of mind, serenity, and a life purpose. This is why the term "God fearing" is used so much more often than the term "God loving".

In any event, the love-shy do not like to be *"controlled"* or in any way bullied or harassed. This may be a key reason why the ideas of Spiritualism appeal to a good many of them so much more than does conventional, organized religious participation. Spiritualism provides for the satisfaction of spiritual needs *without "controlling"*.

Chapter 21

Movies, Music, and the Love-Shy

Many people believe that it is possible to learn a great deal about a person from an analysis of his/her cultural tastes and interests. I shall confine my attention in this chapter to music and to motion pictures as the love-shy (especially the older ones) tended to have a great deal to say about both. Films and music appear to be very important in the lives of most love-shy men. Presumably this is because these media provide rich food for fantasy, along with a good deal of vicarious gratification.

First it is important to point out a curious paradox uncovered by my data. I had originally hypothesized that love-shyness would go hand in hand with the passive activity of seeing a great many motion pictures, and with the deriving of vicarious gratification from same. And indeed I *did* find that the *older* love-shys tended to spend a substantially greater amount of time in motion picture theatres than the self-confident non-shys. However, what surprised me was that the *younger* love-shys tended to see significantly *fewer* motion pictures than either the older love-shys or the non-shys. In fact, the younger love-shys tended to be involved in a serious dearth of activities—*period*! And this lack of involvement tended to apply almost as much to such passive pursuits as film viewing as it did to active ones.

I asked each respondent how many motion pictures he had gone to the theatre to see during the four week period immediately preceding the interview. I stressed the fact with each respondent that I was only interested in motion pictures that he had seen in a theatre. I wanted to make certain that the respondent would not include anything that he might have seen on television.

In the four week period prior to being interviewed, the older love-shy men had seen an average of 4.77 different films. The analogous figure for the younger love-shys was only 1.64 films. Curiously, the self-confident non-shy men had averaged 2.28 films in the four weeks prior to being interviewed.

On the other hand, my interview data did strongly suggest that when the love-shy see a motion picture they really like they tend to pull out the stops. And this applies almost as much to the younger love-shys as it does to the older ones. Thus, love-shy men tend to go back to a theatre to view favorite pictures over and over and over again. Indeed, several of them boasted that they had sat through a film as many as five times in one sitting! A few of the love-shy men had seen certain films so very many times that one wonders how they could have possibly kept from becoming bored. Of course, as per the discussion in the chapter titled "Love-Shyness and the Criminal Mind", love-shy men appear to be especially susceptible to very deep and unrelenting obsessions.

Basically, love-shy men are especially prone to become obsessed with anything which they consider to be romantic and esthetically pleasing. They love motion pictures which incorporate well-structured, romantic love stories that tug at the heartstrings and which "grab a person" emotionally. Simply put, they love to be emotionally engrossed through the vicarious experiencing of love and romance, especially when the romance involves a girl whom they consider to be naturally beautiful.

Many of the love-shys spoke of remaining transfixed in their movie chairs from 2 o'clock in the afternoon until midnight, just watching over and over again a film and/or female movie star of their obsessions and romantic preoccupations. For example, one 39-year old love-shy man had seen the 1973 film JEREMY 86 times, at least in part because he was so overwhelmed by the appearance of the star, Glynnis O'Connor. Another 43 year old love-shy man had seen JEREMY 42 times, and then found a way to obtain a 16mm print of it through the underground. Even though he was earning a gross of only $9,000 per year at the time, he paid $1,000 cash for the JEREMY print. This, again, is ample testimony as to the powerful motivation provided by deep-seated obsessions with beautiful women and/or romantic stories.

The film stars most often named by the love-shys as sources of deep-seated romantic obsessions and infatuations included the following: Glynnis O'Connor (JEREMY), Goldie Hawn (BUTTERFLIES ARE FREE), Kathrine Ross (THE GRADUATE), Julie Biggs (NOBODY WAVED GOODBYE), Brigitte Fossey (FORBIDDEN GAMES), Janet Margolin (DAVID AND LISA), Kay Lenz (BREEZY), Yvette Mimieux (TIME MACHINE and JOY IN THE MORNING), Catherine Deneuve (UMBRELLAS OF CHERBOURG), Mary Badham (TO KILL A MOCKINGBIRD and THIS PROPERTY IS CONDEMNED), Carol Lynley (BLUE DENIM), Hope Lange (PEYTON PLACE), Sondra Locke (THE HEART IS A LONELY HUNTER), Isabelle Huppert (THE LACEMAKER), Anice Alvina (FRIENDS and PAUL AND MICHELE), Olivia Hussey (ROMEO AND JULIET), Mary Steenburgen (TIME AFTER TIME and MELVIN

AND HOWARD), Barbara Hershey (LAST SUMMER), Tuesday Weld (PRETTY POISON), and (quite interestingly) Jodie Foster (TOM SAWYER and THE LITTLE GIRL WHO LIVED DOWN THE LANE). Parenthetically, none of the love-shys mentioned TAXI DRIVER!

Of course, the love-shys' need to become deeply lost in the vicarious experiencing of romantic emotion must be considered perfectly understandable in view of both their backgrounds and their problems. The love-shys had been quite totally lacking in the opportunity to experience emotion directly in their own lives. Virtually all of them seemed to suffer from what psychiatrists like to call "affect hunter". Indeed, by the love-shys' own admission, people often comment to them that they (the love-shys) seem to be incapable of expressing emotion because they are almost never observed laughing or displaying their feelings.

Many of the love-shys had commenced their obsessions with certain motion pictures while they were still quite young. One man saw the French language film FORBIDDEN GAMES fifteen times when he was only in the eighth grade. Eight of my respondents had seen DAVID AND LISA in excess of a dozen times while they were still in high school. However, many of their comments made it quite clear to me that a naturally beautiful female star is seldom sufficient to please a love-shy man, much less bring him back for a second viewing. For example, virtually all of the love-shys enthusiastically agreed that Bo Derek was one of the most beautiful women they had ever seen. Yet none of the love-shys who had seen the film "10" had liked it. Most of the love-shys had found it to be dreadfully boring because it contained an unstructured, highly confusing story with no love or romance. Simply put, it did not engross the emotions. It did not touch the heartstrings.

On the other hand, "10" was one of the comparatively few films which a small number of the self-confident non-shys had seen multiple times. The non-shys had loved it whereas the love-shys hated it—despite the fact that both groups agreed with the premise that Bo Derek is an extremely beautiful woman.

A further example can be seen in the fact that BUTTERFLIES ARE FREE was one of the love-shys' top favorite films of all time. Many love-shys had seen this film multiple times, and at least one man had seen it 24 times! Yet BUTTERFLIES ARE FREE was the *only* Goldie Hawn film to be seen more than once by any love-shy man. In essence, her other films failed to deeply involve the emotions. Through the eyes of the love-shy, BUTTERFLIES ARE FREE was the only one that was not a mere "shallow comedy".

In this sense, the romantic and emotionally engrossing character of a film's script may have more to do with the likelihood of a love-shy man developing a romantic infatuation with a film star than the issue of which actress plays the romantic role. One love-shy man had seen the original stage play of BUTTERFLIES ARE FREE with Blythe Danner in Ms. Hawn's role. And he claimed to have enjoyed Ms. Danner a good deal better than Ms. Hawn. Even at Broadway's steep ticket prices, he went back to see the stage version of BUTTERFLIES ARE FREE a total of six times!

There is nothing to be gained by discussing in detail all of the films which deeply fascinated each love-shy man who was interviewed for this study. However, I think it is appropriate to describe some of the films which precipitated deep and lasting obsessions in a significant fraction of the love-shy men who witnessed them. Again, I believe that it is possible to learn a good deal about the love-shy by studying films that deeply and thoroughly obsessed them over a substantial period of time. Further, a probing of the quality and flavor of these films can help to foster an understanding and an appreciation of the sort of male-female love relationships to which the love-shy aspire and which they tend to view as idyllic. Such a probing will also serve to highlight the sort of feminine pulchritude and vulnerable, nurturant attitude which enthralls the imagination of severely love-shy men.

I asked each man interviewed to name every motion picture he could think of which he had seen *"a minimum of at least five times."* Fully 87 percent of the older love-shys together with 69 percent of the younger love-shys named at least one such motion picture, as did 55 percent of the self-confident non-shy men. Most of the older love-shy men named at least seven such films, whereas the younger love-shys tended to name just two or three. The non-shy men tended to name just one or two films each; and the number of times they had seen each of the films they mentioned had seldom exceeded five or six.

Altogether, the 300 love-shy men named 63 motion pictures, whereas the non-shy men named only 20. The two lists which I have presented below represent a rank ordering of all the films mentioned as having been seen within a theatre five or more times. The figure in parentheses is the year the film was initially released. After year of initial release I have indicated the greatest number of times the motion picture had been viewed in a theatre *by any one love-shy man*. Most of the first twenty films had been mentioned by at least six love-shy men. Films with the *same number of times* indicated after year of release, were rank ordered according to the number of respondents who mentioned them. For example, five love-shy men had seen THE PARENT TRAP (#14) fifteen times whereas only three had seen FRIENDS (#15) fifteen times. Hence, THE PARENT TRAP is ranked higher than FRIENDS.

Finally, I placed a line underneath the first seven films on both lists. Many analysts believe that a scrutinization of just the first seven films on each list can teach us more about key personality differences between the love-shy and the non-shy, than a more thorough coverage can. Others find it easier to make useful comparisons when the lists are kept comprehensive.

The foregoing two lists suggest several key differences between the love-shy and the non-shy. First, the love-shy men named many more serious artistic works than did the non-shy men. This would tend to support the view that feminine beauty and esthetics are substantially more important to the love-shy than they are to the non-shy. Many of the films on the love-shys' list were "shoestring budget" films; indeed,

Figure Five

LIST OF ALL FILMS WHICH RECEIVED MENTION BY THE LOVE-SHY MEN AS HAVING BEEN SEEN INSIDE A THEATRE AT LEAST FIVE OR MORE TIMES

1. Jeremy (1973) 86 times.
2. David and Lisa (1962) 46 times.
3. Forbidden Games (1952) 44 times.
4. The Umbrellas of Cherbourg (1965) 37 times.
5. The Graduate (1967) 29 times.
6. Butterflies Are Free (1972) 24 times.
7. Marty (1955) 19 times.
8. Fiddler on the Roof (1971) 18 times.
9. Romeo and Juliet (1968) 17 times.
10. Nobody Waved Goodbye (1965) 17 times.
11. Peyton Place (1957) 17 times.
12. The Exorcist (1973) 17 times.
13. Show Boat (1950) 16 times.
14. The Parent Trap (1961) 15 times.
15. Friends (1971) 15 times.
16. West Side Story (1961) 14 times.
17. Brigadoon (1954) 14 times.
18. The Dark at the Top of the Stairs (1960) 14 times.
19. The Harrad Experiment (1973) 13 times.
20. A Little Romance (1979) 13 times.
21. Our Time (1974) 12 times.
22. Carousel (1956) 12 times.
23. Ice Castles (1979) 12 times.
24. Love Story (1971) 12 times.
25. The Lacemaker (1977) 12 times.
26. Kramer versus Kramer (1979) 11 times.
27. Bus Stop (1955) 11 times.
28. Goodbye Columbus (1969) 11 times.
29. Breezy (1973) 11 times.
30. The Ressurection (1980) 11 times.
31. From the Terrace (1960) 10 times.
32. The Music Man (1962) 10 times.
33. Joy in the Morning (1965) 9 times.
34. Time After Time (1979) 9 times.
35. Billy Jack (1972) 9 times.
36. Alfie (1967) 9 times.
37. Oklahoma! (1955) 9 times.
38. Parrish (1961) 8 times.
39. All the President's Men (1976) 8 times.
40. My Fair Lady (1964) 8 times.
41. The Time Machine (1961) 7 times.
42. The Sound of Music (1965) 7 times.
43. Blue Denim (1959) 7 times.
44. South Pacific (1959) 7 times.
45. Paul and Michele (1978) 6 times.
46. Inherit the Wind (1961) 6 times.
47. Le Bonheur (1965) 6 times.
48. Where the Lillies Bloom (1974) 6 times.
49. Fraternity Row (1977) 6 times.
50. Three Little Words (1950) 5 times.
51. Mary Poppins (1965) 5 times.
52. Family Life (1973) 5 times.
53. Straw Dogs (1971) 5 times.
54. The Effect of Gamma Rays on Man-in-the-Moon Marigolds (1972) 5 times.
55. Paper Moon (1973) 5 times.
56. The Heart Is a Lonely Hunter (1967) 5 times.
57. The Student Prince (1954) 5 times.
58. Dangerous When Wet (1954) 5 times.
59. The Trial of Billy Jack (1974) 5 times.
60. Three in the Attic (1968) 5 times.
61. S*W*A*K (Sealed with a Kiss) (1973) 5 times.
62. Rose Marie (1954) 5 times.
63. Till the Clouds Roll By (1945) 5 times.

Figure Six
LIST OF ALL FILMS WHICH RECEIVED MENTION BY THE SELF-CONFIDENT NON-SHYS AS HAVING BEEN SEEN INSIDE A THEATRE AT LEAST FIVE OR MORE TIMES

1. Animal House (1978) 8 times.
2. M*A*S*H (1970) 7 times.
3. Star Wars (1977) 7 times.
4. Star Trek (1979) 6 times.
5. "10" (1979) 6 times.
6. Smokey and the Bandit (1977) 6 times.
7. Raiders of the Lost Ark (1981) 6 times.
8. Superman I (1979) 5 times.
9. Rocky (1976) 5 times.
10. 2001: A Space Odyssey (1967) 5 times.
11. Halloween (1978) 5 times.
12. The Empire Strikes Back (1980) 5 times.
13. One Flew Over the Coocoo's Nest (1975) 5 times.
14. Gone With the Wind (1939) 5 times.
15. Grease (1978) 5 times.
16. Death Wish (1974) 5 times.
17. The Godfather I (1971) 5 times.
18. Blazing Saddles (1974) 5 times.
19. Superman II (1981) 5 times.
20. True Grit (1969) 5 times.

four of the top ten had been filmed in black and white. And three of the top ten were foreign: #3 and #4 were French, and #10 was Canadian. (Altogether 6 of the 63 films were French.)

The 63 films on the love-shys' list can be classified primarily into two categories: (1) "heavy", emotionally engrossing love stories, and (2) escapist musicals with a strong romantic flavor. In fact, even the science fiction items on the love-shys' list (#34 and #41) were preeminently love stories. Hence, this would appear to provide further testimony as to what the love-shys both want and actually most strongly need to have in their personal lives. It points up the thing of which they feel most severely deprived.

To be sure, a small number of items on their list appear somewhat "out of place": particularly #12, #30, #39, and #46. However, even these films were tightly knit and emotionally engrossing compared to their counterparts on the non-shys' list. Of course, many of the love-shys sustain a strong interest in subjects pertaining to the occult and to Spiritualism; and most of them are politically and religiously liberal. However, films on spiritual or political themes will evidently not appeal to the love-shy unless they are (1) emotionally gripping, and (2) intellectually accurate and credible.

A key feature of the non-shys' movie list is that all twenty of the films on it were enormously popular and made many millions of dollars.

And except for items #13 and 14, the material on the list can be sorted into essentially three categories: (1) escapist space fantasies, (2) raucous, slapstick comedy, and (3) blood, guts and gore. Moreover, none of the top seven films on the list contained any of the emotionally engrossing, romantic components which are of such enormous importance to the love-shy. Only 25 percent of the films on the non-shys' list could be said to contain reasonably strong, emotionally engrossing ingredients: #8, #9, #13, #14, and #17.

Since completing my research I have had the opportunity to show the non-shys' movie list to several severely love-shy older men. And whereas most of these people admitted that they did enjoy ONE FLEW OVER THE COOCOO'S NEST, the SUPERMAN series, and to a moderate extent GONE WITH THE WIND, the majority of the non-shys' favorite films had been painfully (and sometimes irritatingly) boring to the love-shy.

I have already commented on the film "10" (#5 on the non-shys' list) which had starred Bo Derek. But far more irritating through the eyes of the love-shy were M*A*S*H and 2001: A SPACE ODYSSEY. Many of the love-shys to whom I talked were extremely amazed that these films could have done as well as they did inasmuch as both were "emotionally vacuous". To the love-shy, "2001" represented two hours of veritable nothingness apart from the lovely Johann Straus waltzes. (Some of the love-shys had gone to see this film only because Keir Dullea, the star of their enormously enjoyed DAVID AND LISA, was in it.) And M*A*S*H was viewed as being even more irritating because it was composed of two hours of plotless, ambiguous, unrelated skits that simply failed to "hang together", which were filmed in a military context (which love-shy men hate), and which were totally devoid of any semblance of romantic love and of feminine nurturance. The other space films listed by the non-shy men contained most of these same unappreciated attributes, although they were much less intensely disliked than "2001" and M*A*S*H.

The Love-Shys' Prime Film Experiences

For as far back as many of them could remember, motion pictures and the theatre had provided the love-shys with their only strongly positive emotional experiences. In contrast to the non-shys who were *living life*, the love-shy men had learned early in life to depend for their delights upon the vicarious experiencing of emotion. Most of them had begun getting "hooked" on films sometime between the ages of 10 and

14. The following statement from a 42-year old love-shy man provides some idea as to how this happened.

"Until I was about ten I was really bored with most of the stuff my parents took me to. On Saturday afternoons my parents occasionally made me go with the other kids to see these horrible westerns and war movies. I was just so bored; and I hated being with the roudy kids I was forced to go with. And most of the stuff my mother took me to was drama. And I guess I was really too young to understand it.

But when I was about ten I remember we were visiting Florida. This was back in 1950, and my parents took me to see the film SHOW BOAT. Well, I guess that's what really did it for me because I was enthralled. When I got home I went to see the film at least a dozen times, I was just so overwhelmed by the music and the romance. My parents just couldn't understand what fascinated me so much. But they let me go. Movies were cheap in those days, and it was a chance for me to get out of the house.

Well, after SHOW BOAT I began going to the movies more and more. I don't know. I guess it's a lot like Skinner's pigeons pecking away for nourishment. If you provide a highly rewarding experience every now and then, the pigeon will peck away forever. Well, most of the kids my age wanted to see crummy westerns and war movies; and I realized that I probably liked musicals best. So I started seeing a lot of them. And a lot of them like BRIGADOON and CAROUSEL and THREE LITTLE WORDS and OKLAHOMA! really turned me on because they had a lot of beautiful music and love and romance. But sometimes I was disappointed, like with SINGING IN THE RAIN. I didn't like that one because it had no plot, and I couldn't understand it.

But I guess the real clincher came when I was in the eighth grade. I read in the newspaper one day that there was a movie playing about a love relationship between a 6-year old girl and an 8-year old boy. My sense of excitement was immediately aroused because when I was 6 and 8 years old I was really in love with a girl in my class at school. But just like now, I didn't have the nerve to do anything about it.

Well, the name of the film was FORBIDDEN GAMES. And I didn't know it before I went into the theatre, but it was in the French language with subtitles. I had never seen any foreign language films before. And when I saw the subtitles I thought—Boy! I really threw my money away! But wow, was I wrong! I had entered the theatre at one in the afternoon; and I was so overwhelmed by the experience that I didn't leave the theatre until 11:30 that night. I didn't even think about food or anything. I just sat spellbound through it for five straight showings.

Well, when I got home my parents both threw a fit. I remember they beat the hell out of me for staying out so late and not calling them. But I didn't care. I was just so in love with Brigitte Fossey, the six-year old girl in the film, that I just had to go back to the theatre as quickly as I possibly could. I was really hooked!

Anyway, during the next four months FORBIDDEN GAMES played at four different theatres in my area. And I went back to see it every chance I got, and I just stayed to see it at least three times each time I went. The theatre managers just couldn't understand me. And when I told some of the teachers at school about it, they were even more mystified! But I was really hooked, and deeply in love!"

FORBIDDEN GAMES dealt with a love relationship between a 6-year old girl and an 8-year old boy. The story chronicled what happened to the girl after both of her parents had been killed in the June 1940, Paris bombing. Thus, the little girl started wandering around and was eventually taken in by a poor farm family whose eight-year old son immediately fell in love with her. As children, some of the love-shys had had fantasies that their own parents might someday pick some little orphan girl off the street for them! So there was a great deal in this film to which the love-shys could relate. (Several of the love-shys had wanted their parents to get them a sister.)

The boy in the film had the unusual hobby of stealing crosses from cemetaries, and using these crosses in his family's barn for the burial of dead mice and cockroaches. By the middle of the film the strong love interest between the young boy and girl had succeeded in distracting their respective preoccupations away from death and towards each other.

DAVID AND LISA (film #2 on the love-shys' list) hooked many of the older love-shy men to films when they were attending college. Still others became fixated to this charming story of an intense love relationship between two teenagers resident in a home for emotionally disturbed adolescents when they themselves were only in high school. Two of the love-shys had first seen the film when they were only in the seventh grade, and several others had become hooked on it in the eighth and ninth grades. As had been the case for FORBIDDEN GAMES, many of these men had spent entire days in the theatre viewing this film over and over and over again.

In discussing why they liked DAVID AND LISA so much, several of the love-shys suggested that the film conveyed a powerful message which very few contemporary psychiatrists seem to have learned. The usual "wisdom" among practicing psychiatrists is that a person must lose his neurosis and become emotionally healthy *BEFORE* he can be considered entitled to the loving companionship of a woman. Expressed another way, a person must love himself before he can really love others.

The essential theme behind DAVID AND LISA, however, was to show how love itself (including all the compassionate communication of caring and concern that this entails) can serve as a powerful therapeutic (*causative*) force in giving rise to the *loss* of neurotic thought/behavior patterns, and to the movement towards emotional health, happiness *and* self-love.

Expressed in more scientific terms, *love* (when it is mutual and reciprocal) is a powerful *independent variable* (cause) giving rise to the *dependent variable* of emotional health and effectiveness. Thus, a key reason behind the feelings of exasperation which most love-shy men had felt regarding the psychiatrists who had treated them, was the implied assumption that "only after you get well can you have a girl; you're not entitled to one now". More succinctly, conventional psychiatry may be putting the cart *before* the horse! Heterosexual love appears to be the most enormously powerful of all therapeutic forces.

Especially intriguing is the fact that several of the love-shy men had fantasized for many years about having a girl all to themselves just like Janet Margolin, the girl who had portrayed Lisa in the film. Thus, even though Lisa was a victim of adolescent schizophrenia, many of the love-shy men would have liked nothing better than to have had her as a girl friend and wife! One reason why this fantasy may be noteworthy is that love-shy men are commonly viewed as being pathologically passive and dependent themselves. Yet the fantasies recounted to me about DAVID AND LISA suggest that many love-shy men would just love to have a really beautiful girl who nurtures their positive emotions, but who is totally dependent upon them for support and protection. Of course, as a schizophrenic Lisa was totally dependent. There was no way that she could have been expected to care for herself.

However, there was one motion picture that surpassed even FORBIDDEN GAMES and DAVID AND LISA in terms of leaving an indelible impact upon the love-shy and in terms of keeping many of them well furnished with intense memories that will last a lifetime. This film was JEREMY, a 1973 budget film about an intense love relationship between two New York City high schoolers. One man who had been living on food stamps because his graduate school education rendered him "overqualified" for every job for which he applied, spent $1,000 to illegally obtain a 16mm print of the film through the underground. Another man had seen the film 86 times—which is more times than any love-shy man studied for this book had seen any other film. Altogether, seventeen of the love-shys had seen the film 20 or more times; and most of the other love-shy respondents who had managed to see it at all had been sufficiently "fired up" by the experience to return to the theatre for multiple viewings.

The boy in the film was depicted as being quite shy. But in spite of this he found a way to win the affection of his sweetheart through becoming an expert cellist. Despite the fact that the lovers in this film were high school students, the romance depicted was an intense and "heavy" one. There were two catalysts which quite effectively served to "hook" the love-shy on to this film: (1) the fact that the hero himself was depicted as being love-shy; and (2) the physical appearance of the heroine. The first of these factors made it exceedingly easy for the love-shy to immediately identify will all aspects of this film. And despite the fact that the starring actress was an unknown, her beauty served to effectively haunt the love-shy men to a far greater extent than did Olivia Hussey in ROMEO AND JULIET, or Ali McGraw in LOVE STORY and GOODBYE COLUMBUS.

Jeremy's girl was portrayed by Glynnis O'Connor. And those interested in learning about what type of girl love-shy men would be especially desirous of winning would be well advised to study Ms. O'Connor's appearance and portrayal in this film. It was mentioned by no fewer than 25 of the love-shy men as representing the quintessence of perfection in feminine pulchritude and loving nurturance. Indeed, one man wistfully lamented that he would give up virtually anything and everything if he could somehow be supplied with an 18-year old clone of Ms. O'Connor!

Teenage love (including *very young* teenage love) was a major theme among the films seen by the love-shys five or more times. In addition to JEREMY and DAVID AND LISA, other films in this category which received many mentions included NOBODY WAVED GOODBYE, FRIENDS, PAUL AND MICHELE, A LITTLE ROMANCE, PEYTON PLACE (original 1957 version), BLUE DENIM, ROMEO AND JULIET, ICE CASTLES, OUR TIME, and WEST SIDE STORY. And, of course, many other films on the love-shys' list dealt with love relationships among the college aged. And FORBIDDEN GAMES dealt with love among prepubescent children, as did S*W*A*K. While it was too late for their being included on the love-shys' list, 1982 (after all the data for this book had been obtained) ushered in four new films of this genre which will doubtless enthrall thousands of contemporary love-shys: L'ADOLESCENT, VALLEY GIRL, PARADISE, and GREGORY's GIRL. And in 1983 there was the Australian film LONELY HEARTS, and the American film JOHNNY BELINDA.

May-December romances constitute another theme which, for understandable reasons, enthralls many older love-shy men. The 1973 film BREEZY, with the late Bill Holden in the part of the older man, excited many of those interviewed. And the then 19-year old Kay Lenz,

Mr. Holden's love interest in that picture, received many votes from the love-shys as "the perfect woman". Ms. Lenz's role in BREEZY depicted her as being wildly assertive, nurturant, and yet flamboyantly unconventional and nonconforming. These too are traits which are very rare in attractive young women; such traits seem to excite quite well the romantic fantasies of the love-shy.

Another May-December romance worth mentioning here is contained in the Frank Loesser musical THE MOST HAPPY FELLA (1956). As this was a live stage show and not a motion picture, it is not contained on the love-shys' list. However, it is noteworthy that a 44-year old love-shy man interviewed for this book claimed to have seen the show six times *while he was still in high school*! Thus, it is almost as though precognition had been operating here in that we have a person who had been deeply enthralled by a May-December romance (involving a very love-shy man) while he was still in high school!

THE MOST HAPPY FELLA was a serious work about a 60-year old, single-never-married grape farmer who became infatuated with a restaurant waitress during one of his trips to San Francisco. He is too shy to start a conversation with her, so he leaves her a love note along with an expensive piece of jewelry. The two correspond by mail over a period of several months. And at one point he sends her a photograph of his handsome young foreman, claiming that the picture is of himself. Lonely and in need of a loving man, the young girl travels to the old man's farm. And on the day of her arrival the lovelorn old man becomes so nervous and anxiety-ridden that he has a near-fatal accident in his truck as he heads for the railroad station to pick her up. Despite this, she comes to the farm, copulates with the handsome foreman, thinking that he is Tony, the 60-year old hero; and she swiftly becomes pregnant. By the end of the show the old man wins over and marries the young sweetheart, and accepts her baby as his own.

This is the sort of story that inspires immediate identification in many love-shy men. And that is why they had wanted repeated exposures—although all two hours and fifteen minutes of THE MOST HAPPY FELLA was commercially recorded; and it remains available in record stores to those interested. Parenthetically, the then 52-year old author-composer of THE MOST HAPPY FELLA, in 1956 married the 20-year old girl (Jo Sullivan) who played the heroine in THE MOST HAPPY FELLA!

Because it was filmed in black and white it is seldom seen anymore. But the 1955 film MARTY remains one of the most "applicable to the love-shy" of any motion picture ever made. It depicts a 34-year old love-shy butcher who is anything but handsome, and who would very much like to have a wife. By the conclusion of this exceptionally engrossing film by Paddy Chayefsky, he succeeded in getting one. However, the love-shy butcher (Marty, played by Ernest Borgnine) had had the advantage of being well integrated into (1) a caring Italian kinship network, and (2) an informal network of same-sexed peers. These are advantages which love-shy men *in the real world* tend not to have. As I have indicated, such informal networks are exceedingly important in terms of helping people get introduced to eligible opposite sexed individuals. Nevertheless, MARTY was sufficiently enthralling to enough of the love-shy respondents to warrent place #7 on their list of all-time favorite films.

Numerous musicals were included on the love-shys' list of most frequently viewed films. And many of the older love-shys interviewed in the New York and Los Angeles areas had enjoyed seeing a good many musicals performed live on stage. Richard Rodgers, Jerome Kern, Cole Porter, Frank Loesser, Jule Styne, Arthur Schwartz, George Gershwin, Jerry Herman, Steven Sondheim, and Harold Rome, appeared to be the composers most admired by the love-shy men. But Lerner and Loewe's BRIGADOON was the musical most often mentioned as being evocative of a never-ending supply of rich fantasy.

In fact, BRIGADOON was often mentioned in connection with two H. G. Wells movies, THE TIME MACHINE (1961) and TIME AFTER TIME (1979), both of which were often mentioned among the films seen five or more times. Of course, the love-shys were far less likely than the non-shys to prefer science fiction related entertainment. Yet both THE TIME MACHINE and TIME AFTER TIME *are* science fiction. The crucial element that they have in common (and what distinguishes them from STAR WARS, 2001: A SPACE ODYSSEY, STAR TREK, etc.) is that both are *deeply romantic*. Moreover, both along with the musical BRIGADOON, ask the same poignant question which seems to thoroughly fascinate the love-shy. In essence, "Would you be willing to sacrifice *forever* everything you have in this world for the permanent, unconditional love and devotion of the heavenly beautiful girl of your dreams?" Parenthetically, LOST HORIZON asks this same question, although none of the respondents cited that work.

In the case of BRIGADOON, hero Tommy Albright stumbles upon an enchanted village amidst the mist and mountains of Scotland. The village becomes incarnate (materializes) for only one day every one hundred years. And, of course, during his day there he meets and falls in love with an enormously nurturant, exquisitely beautiful girl with the much preferred (among the love-shy) features of long, dark hair and pulchritudinous, oval face. In very short order Tommy has to decide whether to give up his home, family, friends and career back in America, for the eternal love and devotion of this beautiful girl. And, indeed, after briefly visiting the crass vulgarity of an airport bar he ends up choosing the beautiful girl and remaining forever behind in BRIGADOON—much to the amazed dismay of his traveling companion Jeff Douglas.

In the case of H. G. Wells' THE TIME MACHINE, the hero travels forward thousands of years in his brilliant invention. And he meets a girl of heavenly, ethereal beauty, called Weena—played by Yvette Mimieux in the 1961 film, and by Mary Steenburgen in the 1979 version. And as in BRIGADOON, the hero opts to sacrifice everything for his beloved.

Music

The love-shys in both age groups tended to prefer vocal love ballads, Broadway show music, brassy jazz music, easy listening, film soundtracks, and light classical works. A few of them mentioned having a strong liking for country and western. On the other hand, rock music of any kind tended to be strongly disliked by the love-shys. Their objections to it, however, were based on *esthetic*, and not on moral grounds. Simply put, love-shy men prefer anything with rich and beautiful melody; and they dislike anything which is noisy, loud, dissonant, or unmelodic. For most of the love-shys, *melody* appears to be the most important element in music. And in this regard many of their contemporaries would doubtless consider them to be "old fashioned". Thus, musical beat and lyrics matter a good deal *less* to the love-shy than does melody. Love-shy men prefer singers who by virtue of their talents can best bring out the melody. They prefer such artists as Steve Lawrence, Frank Sinatra, Robert Goulet, Sammy Davis, Jr., Gordon MacRae, Nat King Cole, Mario Lanza, Al Martino, Vic Damone, etc. Curiously, the love-shy mentioned very few female singers, although some of those that were mentioned include Barbra Streisand, Karen Carpenter, Julie Andrews, Barbara Cook, and Ethel Merman.

In contrast, the non-shy men were heavily into "rock". In fact, most of the non-shys studied for this book seldom listened to anything other than what might be described as "hard rock". Several of them did mention that they also enjoyed country and western, rhythm and blues, and jazz. And a few voiced the cliched viewpoint that they "like all kinds of music". Upon scrutinizing the contents of their record collections, however, it became obvious that "rock" is pretty much the only sort of music for which they ever spend any money.

Nevertheless, there was one point of similarity between the musical tastes of the non-shy and the love-shy. Both groups tended to dislike classical music—although the love-shy indicated a liking for some of the "lighter" classical forms, such as certain of the more melodic works of Chopin, Tchaikovsky, Straus, Gregg, Borodin, Shubert, Offenbach, etc. Thus, as seen by the love-shy, both "rock" and the "heavier" forms of classical music share an interesting common denominator: both suffer from a dearth or near total absence of melodic beauty.

The love-shy perceive much of what is defined as classical music as being as "choppy" and dissonant as some of the worst "rock". Stravinsky's "Rite of Spring" illustrates a piece that is as dissonant and devoid of melodic beauty as anything that can be found in "rock". And many of Beethoven's symphonies are also quite choppy and lacking in melodic flow. All in all, most of the older love-shys would probably rate such composers as Rodgers, Kern, Loesser, Gershwin, Porter, Styne, Youmans, Straus, Schwartz, Romberg, Herbert, Loewe, Lane, etc., as having made more distinguished contributions to music than most of the so-called "classical" composers.

Implications

Musical tastes might seem to be a "personal thing". However, most people aspire towards being able to *share* the music they enjoy with other people. And the love-shy are no exception to this. The problem is that those in charge of running musical events and of financing record albums tend to think primarily in terms of the five "currently mainstream" musical tastes: (1) rock; (2) country and western; (3) classical; (4) rhythm and blues; and (5) gospel and religious. Very few love-shy men sustain an interest in *any* of these areas. Record stores have come to be of little help. Back in the 1950s and 1960s, most record stores offered music for a wide range of different tastes. Today rock music dominates the space in most record stores; and what little is left over tends to be given over to country and western, and to classical.

This problem of imbalance (and of trying to force everyone into the same mold) is well reflected in the fact that such outstanding singers as Steve Lawrence, Tony Bennett, Al Martino, Robert Goulet, and even Frank Sinatra, find it very difficult to obtain the financial backing that is required for making albums. Choral groups such as Ray Charles Singers, Percy Faith Singers, etc., are not making albums at all anymore. And jazz music is similarly becoming increasingly difficult to find. Even Broadway show music has pretty well died off as a musical category inasmuch as rock music has taken over the dominant role in the Broadway theatre. Today new show albums are both created and sold almost exclusively by mail order through such organizations as those headed by Ben Bagley and Bruce Yeko. Aside from certain specialty record stores found only in London, New York and Los Angeles, such material simply isn't handled commercially anymore.

The love-shy tend to be as "different" from the mainstream in their musical tastes as they are in a whole host of other ways. If the love-shy are to be helped, I would suggest that groups need to be formed in all major cities and on all university campuses, which *respect* their tastes and interests, and which provide for the playing and enjoying of the types of music which they enjoy. Properly organized and managed, such groups could serve as a powerful catalyst for facilitating the initial meeting and the informal heterosexual interaction of love-shy people. Some of these groups might specialize in jazz; others might specialize in traditional Broadway of the 1920s through 1960s; and still others might specialize in the more quiet varieties of easy listening and light classical music. Many love-shys strongly prefer the *"intimate piano bar"* type of scenario (involving a skilled pianist and possibly a singer or two) wherein traditional show music is played.

Through the creation of such organizations, love-shy people could be encouraged to form groups and to both share and enhance their musical interests and knowledge within the sphere of the particular musical catagories to which they can best relate. Of course, love-shys are not "joiners". And this is why various kinds of catalysts are needed to facilitate their getting out of their apartments and involved in things. This is the main concern of *Part Three* of this book: *"Therapy and Prevention"*.

Part Three

THERAPY AND PREVENTION

Anyone who truly believes that shyness is caused *exclusively* by learning will *NEVER* succeed at engineering a successful mode of therapy for the problem. A *balanced* perspective is a MUST.

Chapter 22

Practice-Dating Therapy

So far in this book we have examined the causes and the consequences of severe and chronic love-shyness. Those who have read up to this point will surely agree that love-shyness can be an extremely debilitating and excruciatingly painful condition that entails formidable repercussions for the victim's ultimate stability, success and happiness in life. Fortunately, however, the situation is far from hopeless. Just within the past fifteen years a tremendous amount has been learned about ways of successfully treating and preventing love-shyness. And it is the purpose of this and the following chapter to examine the best and most promising of what has been learned up to now.

At this time we already know a very great deal about ways of effectively preventing severe love-shyness from ever developing in the first place. But because there is quite a bit of resistance to the engineering of various modes of prevention, it appears likely that severe love-shyness will retain its current prevalence for quite some time into the future. This is why it is of the utmost importance for love-shyness victims to enjoy easy access to modes of therapeutic treatment that are as efficient, effective, and non-anxiety-provoking as possible. And of the approaches that have heretofore become available, make no mistake about it— "practice-dating therapy" is the approach most applicable to the needs and psychoemotional characteristics of severely love-shy men.

Behavior Therapy Approaches

Practice-dating is a form of *behavior therapy*. All forms of behavior therapy are oriented towards the goal of successfully *extinguishing* inappropriate anxieties and fears. Traditionally, this had entailed bringing the person face-to-face with the thing that he most strongly feared. There is obviously no way of successfully forcing an extremely nervous and inhibited man to approach and start a conversation with a girl who interests him. Yet conventional "shyness clinics" often assign this sort of thing as a "required homework exercise".

The vast majority of severely love-shy men will not cooperate in any exercise that arouses too much painful anxiety, or even the fear of experiencing painful anxiety. And by the way, this includes guided imaging. The vast majority of severely love-shy men find it far too anxiety-provoking to even *visualize* themselves making a friendly overture vis-a-vis a girl. Inasmuch as it requires very little to painfully arouse the very low native anxiety threshold of a love-shy man, the task of engineering workable therapeutic programs has *not* been an easy one.

Nevertheless, my work with love-shy males has convinced me that almost all of them *will cooperate* when someone else takes the responsibility of arranging introductions on their behalf. This is especially true if these arranged introductions are followed by a program of structured activities in which the love-shy man will not feel emotionally threatened in any way. In short, severely love-shy men will not cooperate with any type of therapeutic program that requires them to make the first move with a woman (in reality and/or in mental imagery), and which affords no structured system that would incorporate cushions against unexpected events causing anxiety attacks.

Despite this, it might surprise some readers to learn that even severely love-shy males would in most cases willingly and even enthusiastically participate in a program that requires going out on therapist-arranged dates. Thus, I asked each love-shy man the following question: "Would you participate in a form of therapy that in addition to involving many coeducational group discussions also *required* you to go out on dates that were prearranged for you by the therapy team?"

The results for this question were heartening, and need to be carefully reflected upon by all those who aspire to engineer therapeutic programs that would help the severely love-shy. Specifically, 92 percent of the older love-shy men indicated "*yes*" to this question, and *all* of the remaining 8 percent said "*maybe*". The younger love-shys were slightly less enthusiastic. Yet even among the younger love-shys fully 83 percent said "*yes*"—they *would* participate in such a program—and another 12 percent indicated "maybe". Only 5 percent said "no", they would not be willing to participate in such a program.

Further verification of the love-shys' psychoemotional ability and willingness to accept therapy involving arranged meetings with the opposite sex can be seen in the pattern of responses to the question: "Would you enroll in a computer dating service?" Fully 87 percent of the older love-shys and 65 percent of the younger ones indicated "*yes*". In stark contrast, it is interesting to note that only 18 percent of the self-confident non-shys said "yes". Presumably this is because the non-shys experience little or no difficulty in meeting all the women they could possibly deal with.

Several forms of practice-dating psychotherapy have been developed. All of these require the client to date and to informally interact with preselected opposite sexed age-mates. Thus, matches are arranged by a therapeutic staff. And it is the responsibility of each client (1) to go out on dates with the assigned individual, and (2) to attend weekly or twice-weekly 90-minute group sessions during which each young man and woman is accorded an opportunity to discuss anxieties, problems, difficulties, apprehensions, etc., and to participate in some structured exercises in psychodrama and role playing.

Practice-dating is based upon the *extinction model* of behavior therapy. In practice-dating the irrational interpersonal anxieties associated with informal heterosexual interaction are "extinguished". This is accomplished through repeatedly exposing the love-shy man to the basic fear-producing stimuli—i.e., the opposite sex. This exposure is effected through engaging the love-shy client in a well-structured program of enjoyable and non-anxiety-provoking dating and conversational activities.

Practice-dating *does not* require its clients to jump into the deep end of the swimming pool before mastering the basic rudiments of successful functioning at the shallow end. Thus, practice-dating clients are not expected to initiate conversations with women whom they don't know—until they have progressed to the point at which they have become personally ready to do this.

Practice-dating as a systematic mode of behavior therapy was developed at the University of Oregon during the early 1970s, by psychologists Hal Arkowitz and Andrew Christensen. Since that time, Dr. Arkowitz (now at the University of Arizona, Tucson) has taken the lead in publishing the greatest number of scholarly papers on this mode of therapy. However, numerous scholars and clinicians have become involved with it. Moreover, some credit for its development must also go to Dr. Joseph Melnick of Indiana University, who in 1973 published the first scholarly paper on practice-dating while Arkowitz and Christensen were still engrossed in the engineering of their seminal work in this area.

The "Practice-Dating" Model

At this juncture I should like to present a composite sketch of the best and most essential features of practice-dating therapy. Much of the ongoing work pertinent to practice-dating remains exploratory in nature. Nevertheless, the heretofore published research results suggest that upwards of 95 percent of the most severely love-shy males can be sufficiently cured by this approach to permit normal participation in dating, courtship and marriage. Simply put, practice-dating therapy is the *only remedy* heretofore devised for dealing with love-shyness that *really works* even on the most difficult and intractable cases.

Practice-dating is obviously not going to prove appropriate for dealing with all growth-stifling forms of shyness. But for shyness vis-a-vis the opposite sex *it really works!* And, of course, it is difficult to imagine a young man cured of his love-shyness who does not enormously benefit from the standpoint of social self-confidence gains in all other areas of his life. Once a young man is accorded the emotional freedom to love a woman, he is bound to gradually begin opening up in a wide variety of other types of social situations.

Practice-dating therapy is conducted in groups composed of six men and six women. An exactly even gender ratio is absolutely mandatory in this form of therapy. In addition, the women clients must all be of the same age or younger than the male clients. Because love-shyness has always been a far more painful problem for men than for women, a significantly greater number of men than women usually sign up for it. And similarly, the women clients tend to drop out of therapy a good deal sooner than the men, either because a cure is effected for them sooner or because some of them lose interest or become disenchanted—something which virtually never happens for the men.

This means that *waiting lists* must be used for the male clients. I have found that time means something very different to the love-shy than it does to most people. For example, a year represents a long time to most Americans. To the love-shy it means next to nothing. If love-shyness entails no other virtue, it at least teaches patience—perhaps *too much patience!* At any rate, each male desirous of practice-dating must wait for an opening. On large university campuses the wait required seldom need be more than a month or two. Large state university campuses will sometimes have as many as three 12-person groups operating simultaneously. This means that 18 men and 18 women can often be helped at any given point in time.

The most effective practice-dating programs incorporate two 90-minute group therapy sessions each week. Each of a group's twelve members is expected to attend these. Each meeting is led by one and sometimes two clinical psychologists. And occasionally one or two graduate students of clinical psychology will also be in attendance to help as facilitators. The therapy is conducted in an office that is large enough to comfortable accommodate the twelve clients and the therapeutic staff. Folding chairs are typically used; these are placed in a circle so that everybody is facing each other. Tables are not employed as these impede full vision. Each member of the group must be able to see the full body of every other member; and the seating is always boy-girl-boy-girl-boy-girl, etc., throughout the full circle. *Chairs are always used* in this form of therapy. There is no sitting on the floor or sitting on pillows or cushions, as commonly obtains in nonprofessionally operated encounter groups.

Before a client is accepted he or she must agree to the ground rules. This agreement should be effected both formally and informally. Even when the therapy is being provided free of charge as on university campuses, each group member should be expected to sign a written contract, thus committing himself/herself to all necessary rules and policies. At the same time, the therapeutic staff must approach their clients with a confident, positive mental attitude. Their attitude should be that this is an approach which *will work successfully* for all who follow the rules.

The number of weeks during which each practice-dating group will meet will vary quite considerably. Normally shy university students of both sexes typically reach the point where they can date on their own after only about ten or twelve weeks of therapy. Of course, severely love-shy men are *not* "normally shy", and they will require a good deal longer—probably from a low of six months to a maximum of two years. In this regard, there is no time limit. Each person can feel free to remain with the program for as long as he or she may require. For a man the usual criterion indicating a satisfactory "cure" is the ability to comfortably initiate contacts with women who are not associated in any way with the practice-dating clinic.

Prior to initially joining his or her group, each client needs to be given a brief orientation regarding behavior therapy techniques, and this should include how and why they work. Toward the conclusion of each 90-minute therapeutic session the chief facilitator assigns each of the twelve group members to a person of the opposite sex. During the early weeks of therapy this person selected by the therapist will be a fellow client from within the group.

The instructions require each of the twelve members to go out on a date with his or her preselected partner some time before the next scheduled group meeting. Assuming that meetings are held for 90-minutes each Monday and Thursday afternoon, the "date" would have to be experienced by each member prior to the Thursday or Monday afternoon meeting. Each date is required to last for a minimum of two hours. And it can involve any activity of the couple's choosing except going to the movies, watching television, studying together, or anything that might discourage or obviate informal conversation.

It is made clear to each participant during the very first group meeting that silent periods can and probably will develop from time to time during each assigned date. Participants are counseled about the fact that silent periods are normal, and that they are nothing to worry about. During later therapeutic meetings a variety of techniques of relaxation and of meditation are taught. Love-shy people tend to be quite tense, and this makes it quite difficult for them to get in touch with themselves and to truly be themselves. Indeed, tenseness also makes it unusually difficult for a person to think of things to talk about. Tenseness invariably blocks the creative flow of ideas.

Each assigned date requires a specific time and place for getting together. This part must be arranged by the clients. And, in fact, it is usually arranged by the love-shy male. However, this is a task that is usually quite easy for most love-shys to handle because the therapist had specifically directed the two specific people to contact one another by telephone for the two-hour date. Thus, the girl is *expecting* the young man to call; and she would normally feel constrained to phone him if he failed to make the contact within a reasonable time. Furthermore, she had already met the young man at the therapy meeting. Inasmuch as he knows whom he is calling and since he knows that she is expecting his call *because it had been assigned*, he can follow the prescribed instructions without feeling any noteworthy apprehensions. He can negotiate a time and place for the meeting without feeling threatened in any way because he, the girl to whom he has been assigned, and all other practice-dating clients had agreed to the same set of ground rules.

At the next 90-minute therapy meeting on Thursday or Monday afternoon each of the twelve members will discuss his/her experiences on his/her "practice-date". Participants are encouraged to be frank during these sessions so that everyone is able to gain an awareness of his/her strengths and of areas wherein improvements are warrented. Much of the time during each therapy meeting is devoted to interpersonal skills training, grooming, posture and poise, speech patterns, etc. Psychodrama and role playing also figure quite prominently in the therapeutic exercises that are commonly used.

Again towards the end of the 90-minute period the therapist will pair up each of the twelve clients—this time to a different member of the opposite sex. And prior to the following Monday's (or Thursday's) meeting each participant will again be expected to get together with his/her assigned date for a two-hour outing.

The same procedure is followed for each meeting. Again, many practice-dating clinics provide for only weekly meetings. Twice-weekly meetings are definitely preferable as these provide for a more intensive immersion of each client in the various facets of the treatment process. However, for most clients progress tends to be remarkably rapid even when the group meetings and assigned practice dates are limited to once per week.

During the early weeks of involvement in the program, dating is limited to the women in the group. Thus, each love-shy man will be accorded the opportunity to get to know the six women of his group quite well. And since women tend to require fewer weeks/months of this therapy than the men do, the average love-shy man will probably be assigned to as many as nine or ten different women who become members of his group. In other words, as one female client drops out, another is immediately added. Again, this is necessary in order to keep the gender ratio even and to assure effective therapeutic progress for all.

If more than one practice-dating group is being operated simultaneously—and this is very often the case on larger university campuses—each male and female client will be given a list of all men and women currently involved in practice-dating therapy. These lists will include just the name of the person and his/her telephone number. It is quite commonplace for love-shy male clients to begin phoning women on this list several weeks prior to the time when this is actually prescribed and required by the therapist. Thus, the experience of going out on assigned dates with each of the six female members of his group will have so effectively worked to extinguish many of his anxieties that he soon becomes able to contact women whom he does not know but whom he knows to be involved in practice-dating groups other than his own— or who had been involved in practice-dating therapy at some time in the past. Graduates and/or dropouts from practice-dating therapy are noted on the list so that the men can distinguish between the names of women who are currently involved in the therapy, and the names of those who are no longer involved in the program.

Along about the sixth week of the practice-dating regimen, the therapist specifically assigns each male client the homework exercise of phoning a female member of another practice-dating group for a date. Usually by this time this therapeutic exercise arouses little anxiety. He has already dated each of the six girls in his own group approximately twice; and he knows that the girls in the other groups are going to be as psychologically open to his call as the girls in his own group. Every six or seven weeks dances are held for members of all the practice-dating groups; and attendance by all is required at these. The comparatively few severely love-shy men who after six weeks of treatment remain emotionally incapable of calling a girl member of a practice-dating group other than their own are now accorded the opportunity of formally meeting *all* of the female clients. Particularly inhibited men are accorded special attention at these dances by the therapeutic staff. And this attention operates to diminish shyness-related anxieties to the point wherein even the most severely love-shy male client gradually becomes emotionally capable of approaching any female practice-dating participant, irrespective of whatever therapy group to which she might belong.

And so the heterosexual interaction anxieties of each participant become progressively lessened with each new dating experience. Assigned dates with the six members of a person's own group serve to "get the ball rolling". Subsequent assigned dates with members of other practice-dating groups serve to further facilitate this process. At the outset each of these dates is assigned by the therapist. The participants must arrange by telephone for time and place; but the therapist makes clear to each male just exactly whom he is supposed to call. However, as the weeks pass more and more males become emotionally capable of calling non-assigned women on their own. At first the non-assigned women called are fellow members of the various practice-dating groups. The calling and arranging of meetings with non-assigned women is strongly encouraged and rewarded after the fifth week of therapy— provided that the date with the assigned woman is also experienced some time prior to the next group meeting. During the first five weeks members are asked to confine their dates to the partners who had been specifically assigned to them. And effective screening constitutes a major reason for this policy.

Screening

Few non-shy men will be comfortable with the various exercises engaged in by the practice-dating therapy groups. Nevertheless, a non-shy male will occasionally slip into a group quite irrespective of all the careful screening that is done involving paper-and-pencil personality tests, shyness tests, one-on-one interviews vis-a-vis psychologists, etc. Because of the relative shortage of women clients relative to men clients, it is important that inappropriate male clients be weeded out of the program as early in their involvement with it as possible. This is because (1) their presence in the group is at the expense of far more needy men who remain on the waiting list, and (2) because their presence exacerbates the anxieties of women participants who may not be emotionally ready for confident and assertive male behavior. In fact, if too many inappropriate males were to slip into practice-dating programs it would serve to arouse the suspicions and defensiveness of the women participants—thus making it all the more difficult for the genuinely love-shy males to do the required homework exercises and make the required telephone calls.

One way of dealing with this problem is to prohibit any non-assigned dates during the first five weeks of involvement in the program. However, the most prudent approach is to subject all male applicants to a screening process that is sufficiently thoroughgoing that comparatively non-shy males can be detected and weeded out beforehand. Borderline or mildly shy males can and should be assigned to a "shyness clinic" or to an "assertiveness training" program similar to the one operated by Zimbardo and his associates at Stanford University. Zimbardo-styled "shyness clinic" programs will frighten away all severely and chronically love-shy men. But for the *borderline shy* they appear to accomplish a substantial amount of good. One man's meat is another person's poison!

Indeed, it might even be suggested to males *graduating* from practice-dating programs that they might benefit from attendance at a shyness clinic or assertiveness training group. In essence, they might be told: "Now you have the female companionship that you've always wanted plus the emotional freedom necessary to enjoy this companionship and, if necessary, to seek out additional female companionship. However, there may still be other areas of your life where you are still too shy and inhibited: e.g., employment seeking, starting conversations with strangers, being friendly and open with people, filing necessary complaints about bad service, giving public talks, making cold telephone calls in sales work, making friendly and sincere comments of praise vis-a-vis clients before you get down to business with them, giving compliments, etc. Participation in a shyness clinic or an assertiveness training group can help you grow in the directions of your choosing in all of these areas."

Dealing with the Love and Beauty Problem

As I have clearly documented earlier in this book, the issue of female pulchritude often represents one of the toughest stumbling blocks in helping love-shy men. Since the days of ancient Egypt, Greece and Rome, we have known that beauty (especially facial beauty) is the prime stimulus inspiring a man to become romantically infatuated with a woman. Indeed, beauty often triggers a love-shy man's infatuation long before he has ever met or interacted in any way with the women possessing that beauty. And to be sure, the rules and policies of practice-dating therapy cannot change this quirk of human character. But these rules and policies *can curb* this penchant and preoccupation with beauty, *at least* to the extent that it is not allowed to interfere with the promotion of the kinds of psychoemotional growth that practice-dating is designed to facilitate.

And so the therapist makes clear at the outset that clients are not expected to fall in love with or to develop any type of lasting romantic commitments to their practice-dating partners. Of course if a romantic interest develops anyway, *then fine*! However, the purpose of practice-dating as a therapeutic modality is to enable love-shy, socially inactive men and women to get to really know and appreciate the opposite sex as living, thinking, feeling human beings just like themselves. Practice-dating is further intended to remove false and destructive illusions about the other sex—illusions which promote separateness, mutual suspicion and non-interaction. The belief that only conspicuously attractive women are worth getting to know and appreciate is one of the most destructive and self-limiting of these illusions.

In short, whereas extinction of destructive shyness-related anxieties is the main function of practice-dating, other functions are also of crucial importance. Severely love-shy men typically live deep in a world of fantasy. And this fantasy is highlighted by a mental set incorporating highly pulchritudinous female faces. It is the indispensable job of practice-dating therapy to catalyze the love-shys into moving out of their fantasy worlds into the world of actual social interaction with real, live women.

One of the first things love-shy men learn in practice-dating is that women who at the outset appeared to be of only average looks often turn out to be incredibly charming and worth knowing on a long-term basis. Indeed, love-shys often begin to fall in love with some of the practice-dating partners whom they see often. It is not necessary that a man like each of his practice-dating partners equally well. Such would obviously be unrealistic. However, he must learn to deal with all of his assigned partners as potential friends. And he must learn to go beneath the superficial surface of overt personality and get to know and truly appreciate at least a few of his practice-dating partners.

Thus, we are dealing here with prime therapeutic goals. Therapy is deemed to be far from complete with any man who persists in interacting with all of his assigned dates with a detached attitude because none of them befit his mental set incorporating a beautiful face, long hair, thin legs and thighs, etc. Emotionally detached attitudes are picked up intuitively by the practice-dating partners; and these are among the matters that are dealt with during the twice-weekly group therapy sessions.

Of course, it may surprise some readers to learn that not all of the women electing to receive practice-dating therapy are of only average attractiveness. In fact, some of them are surprisingly attractive. And some of them even have the "long hair and pretty face" which love-shy men typically crave. I think the *average* attractiveness level of love-shy *males* receiving practice-dating therapy tends to be a slight bit below the average male attractiveness on any given university campus. But this does *not* appear to be the case for women clients of practice-dating therapy. The attractiveness level of the women clients tends to be quite on a par with the general female attractiveness level of the campus upon which they are taking courses.

Self-consciousness problems pertaining to level of personal attractiveness are dealt with during the group meetings. For example, there are frequent discussions about various techniques of upgrading grooming patterns, making clothing purchases more wisely, etc. But more importantly, the positive mental attitudes and enhanced self-confidence which the therapeutic regimen promotes also serve to significantly enhance the ostensible physical attractiveness levels of all practice-dating participants. Thus, *it is true* that people of both sexes look better when they feel positive about themselves, and when they are fired with enthusiasm about life. Practice-dating serves to accomplish these goals.

Of crucial importance is the fact that people tend to learn some very important things about themselves only to the extent that they interact regularly and informally with other people—particularly with those of the opposite sex. This is why love-shy men quite commonly experience an almost religious awakening when they come to find genuine delight in being with an opposite-sexed companion who (from an objective standpoint) is not highly attractive. Love-shy men often begin to perceive exquisite physical beauty in the many subtle aspects of someone who at first meeting had not appeared conspicuously attractive. Once this begins to happen, the love-shy man is freed to begin noticing and relishing all sorts of richness in the *personalities* of the women whom he is dating. This is important because it is on the basis of these attributes of personality that most emotionally mature, well-adjusted people eventually make their final selections of a marriage partner.

The Alcoholics Anonymous Model of Mutual Caring and Concern

One of the key therapeutic goals is to make the therapeutic group a cohesive unit and, indeed, a kind of quasi-kin group that will provide emotional supports for its fellow members when they are in need. The development of close same-sexed friendships among each of the six same-sexed members is strongly encouraged. Same-sexed members of a group are encouraged to see each other outside of the group, and to help each other with various problems that might crop up. For example, when a member fails to show up for a meeting a fellow male member is asked to go check up on the missing person, and to help him deal with any problems that might have arisen. Difficulties or avoidance of the assigned homework exercises involving dating or the arranging of assigned dates is also dealt with through the promotion of interested involvement by fellow members of the client's own gender, and often of the opposite gender as well.

On some campuses the graduates of practice-dating remain so enthusiastic about what the program had done for them that they agree to interact as friends with neophytes (new practice-dating clients) of their own gender. The development of close, emotionally meaningful friendships with these experienced former clients is strongly encouraged. Alcoholics Anonymous has long encouraged such friendships among its experienced and inexperienced members. And this has long been a prime factor accounting for the huge success of "AA" in keeping its members "on the wagon".

Again, love-shy people (especially males), similar to many other kinds of deviants in society, tend to have had a long history of very little or no kin-group support or meaningful kin-group interaction. People with such a history tend to benefit in important ways from becoming members of *quasi*-kin groups that are appropos to their needs and interests. Such quasi-kin groups currently include Alcoholics Anonymous, Gamblers Anonymous, Parents Anonymous/Mothers Anonymous (both for child abusers), Gray Panthers, Gay Liberation Front (for homosexuals), Mothers of Terminally Ill Children, Families of Cancer Victims, etc. At various points in this book I have suggested the development of a Shys Anonymous/Love-Shys Anonymous that would serve the needs of afflicted heterosexually oriented persons of all ages, and that would also provide for the development of a much needed political power base. The membership of the 12-person practice-dating therapy groups can serve many of these same functions.

Visualization and Mental Rehearsal

A basic precept of behavior therapy is that the physiological and neurological mechanisms of the human body cannot tell the difference between (1) actual behavioral experience, and (2) the *same* experience vividly imagined and visualized. Visualization exercises have a long and distinguished history as a viable therapeutic modality. In fact, their use goes back as far as the days of ancient Egypt. And during the middle ages of western civilization they were an integral and often feared (misunderstood) part of the practices of the religion of witchcraft. Today visualization exercises are as likely to be championed by hard-headed, pragmatic business leaders as they are by witches and warlocks. Indeed, visualization and mental rehearsal have become an accepted part of the *routeine preparation* of such widely diverse groups as star athletes, gymnists, golfing pros, tennis stars, professional football players, renouned piano and trumpet players, actors and actresses, star salespeople, business and sales managers, and American astronauts.

The question as to why visualization and mental rehearsal work so effectively is beyond the scope of this book. However, some clues are provided in chapter 23. Doubtless visualization is closely tied to certain metaphysical and occult processes such a psychokenesis (PK), meditation, thought becoming form, etc. Suffice it to say here that visualization and mental rehearsal are rapidly becoming an integral component of practice-dating therapy—which is itself a form of behavior therapy.

Normally the visualization exercises are assigned as homework, although occasionally an individual group member or two will be helped through a visualization exercise during a group session. It must be stressed that performing these homework exercises requires considerable self-discipline—more self-discipline, in fact, than many practice-dating clients are capable of. This represents a key reason as to why severely love-shy men absolutely require a support group; and fellow practice-dating clients of both sexes constitute an outstanding basis for a support group.

As visualization exercises tend to be most effective when they are practiced in the early morning upon arising and just before going to bed at night, it is just at these times that fellow clients of practice-dating groups are asked to pair up with each other and to catalyze each other's efforts towards the actual *doing* of the visualization and meditational exercises.

In essence, clients are asked to work in twos. One member induces the other into a light meditative trance. Once that member has been made to feel deeply relaxed, a scenario involving friendly, assertive heterosexual interaction is introduced. It is introduced by being read from a 5 by 8 card very quietly to the recipient in the trance. Usually the scenario will involve approaching or talking to a girl with whom the entranced subject has long wanted to make social contact. As these sessions usually last twenty minutes to a half-hour a piece, only one person can be the recipient of the help per session. Thus, if client "A" is the recipient during a morning meditational session, then during the evening session the roles will be reversed and client "A" will help client "B" by reading a visualization scenario and inducing in client "B" a light meditational trance. Eventually, of course, it is hoped that each practice-dating client will feel impelled to do these visualization and mental rehearsal exercises on his/her own. But severely shy people are characterized by a high degree of behavioral inertia as well as an attitudinal pessimism and cynicism that commonly obviates taking any action at all.

Approaching these feelings of discouragement and their consequent behavioral inertia with a moralistic air—as many American psychotherapists do—is invariably counterproductive. It is perfectly
understandable as to why severely shy men are bogged down by inertia.
And the support groups precipitated by well-run practice-dating therapy
groups provide for an outstanding remedy.

In sum, a person tends to become what he/she thinks about. Support groups composed of both sexes are needed to almost constantly
monitor the thoughts, self-talk, and the visualizations of severely love-
shy people. Visualization exercises entailing friendly, assertive behavior
vis-a-vis opposite sexed eligibles is known to substantially facilitate
improvements caused by the practice-dating therapy itself. More specifically, practice-dating therapy and visualization/mental rehearsal exercises operate in synergistic interaction with each other to catalyze the
most rapid psychoemotional and social growth in love-shy men.

The "Second Plateau"

A therapist friend of mine once asked a love-shy client: "What the
hell would you do with a girl after you actually got her home with you?!"
This is the nutshell essence of what the "second plateau" of love-shyness
is all about.

There are basically two different plateaus of difficulty in dealing
with heterosexual love-shyness. And practice-dating must effectively
remedy both of these in order to prove successful for people in any
lasting way. The first of these plateaus has to do with initiating a relationship with a woman and getting it launched. As I have shown, the
very thought of doing this arouses a tremendous amount of anxiety in
the love-shy and usually works to keep the majority of love-shy males
from ever getting anywhere near the second plateau.

The second plateau has to do with *being oneself*, and with being
able *to relax* and *to communicate on a feeling level* vis-a-vis the person with
whom one hopes to develop a lasting relationship. Most love-shy men
find that they devote the first four or five dates with a person to superficial small talk. This small talk represents a kind of "prepared script".
As a form of self-disclosure it is limited to such topics as what they are
majoring in, what they are doing or wish to do for a living, where their
family lives, what the father does or did for a living, television shows
and movies, trivia, the weather, and other similar forms of what for lack
of a better word might be termed "bullshit"—or "bullpoopoo" if you
prefer!

Several love-shys told me that their first few dates with a girl are
very reminiscent of their first two or three visits with a new psychiatrist!
Thus, they find themselves bored with the very words that are pouring

out of their mouths because they have been over these same words ("prepared script") so many hundreds of times with so many hundreds of different people. Most human beings sooner or later become very tired of reiterating the same material about who they are, what their interests and hobbies are, what their parents are like, etc., that very little of the true self is permitted to show when this type of "bullpoopoo" is discussed.

The jist of this is that many people lose their nerve again after they have run out of all of these superficial conversational topics. Love-shy men will typically stop seeing a woman they really care about (1) because there are now too many uncomfortable silences due to the fact that they cannot think of anything more to talk about; (2) because they haven't got the nerve to kiss the girl goodnight or to commence any other form of physical love-making; and (3) because the girl as a result of her own shyness (and feelings of insecurity vis-a-vis the love-shy man) is of no help in overcoming these barriers.

Practice-dating therapy is charged with the responsibility of getting each of its clients past this barrier posed by the "second plateau". The experience of dating and informally interacting with a variety of assigned women helps out considerably in this regard. In essence, a large amount of experience with practice-dating serves to foster an increased ability to relax in the company of women, to be oneself, and to perceive women of different levels of attractiveness as being non-anxiety-provoking, non-threatening human beings just like themselves. To the extent that people are not tense or in the throes of anxiety, to that extent new and creative thoughts and ideas start to easily flow from the mind.

Of course, the practice-dating itself is not enough to ready a person for competently and successfully getting past the hurdle represented by the "second plateau". This is why a variety of exercises are incorporated into each of the group meetings. Love-shy men tend to be extremely defensive and fearful of exposing their vulnerabilities. Lacking the interpersonal skills, they also lack the finesse and social spontaneity necessary for smoothly moving towards such physical displays of affection as kissing, necking, petting, etc.

Make no mistake about it! Such physical displays are *normatively prescribed* in our culture after a certain number of dates have transpired with the same woman. And a woman will very seldom feel comfortable about accepting additional dates with a man who does not respond to these normative prescriptions. Indeed, she is quite likely to begin *wrongly* perceiving such a shy and inhibited man as being a "latent homosexual". As she cannot understand him, "latent homosexual" seems to be a logical enough label to apply to him—even though it is a quite false label.

In American society we tend to be so preoccupied with the far more typical male behavior of "moving too fast" with a woman, that we tend to neglect the fact that men who "move too slowly" with a woman (for other than overtly stated religious reasons) *also violate norms*. And these normative violations are often a good deal more difficult for a woman to deal with than the "moving too fast" type of violation. Most young women have received a good deal of socialization from both peers and parents about ways of successfully dealing with the excessively "fast mover". Never having received any socialization about ways of dealing with the excessively "slow mover", the typical woman tends to become confused, worried and upset. Again, people tend to most strongly fear those things (behaviors and *behavioral omissions*) which they have never been prepared to understand.

When the relationship is right, love-shy men tend to have as much if not more "desire" than non-shys. It must be emphasized that the entire life history of most love-shy men is one of emotional blockage from doing many of the things they would really like to do. Thus, the inhibition gene is an extremely cruel and constantly vigilant taskmaster. This is one reason why Zimbardo has likened shyness to a *prison* that is every bit as real and in some ways even more restricting than a real prison would be. In America we learn from early childhood to judge attitudes, values, intentions and desires, *by behavior*. With love-shy men you cannot do this because their *behavioral omissions* very often do not accurately reflect what they truly want, value and desire. Thus, the mental prison created by the inhibition gene prohibits love-shys from manifesting behavior that is *congruent* with their feelings, attitudes and desires.

When a Practice-Dating Participant Fails to Show Up

There will be times when a practice-dating participant fails to show up for a required group meeting. Most of the time the reasons for this are legitimate. But because the degree of commitment to practice-dating is almost always stronger for males than for females, absentees are more likely than not to involve female participants.

An absent female means that one of the six male members will have to go without a practice-date for the coming half-week or week, unless one of the remaining five women participants is willing to experience two practice dates. Thus, the therapist can (1) either arrange it so that one of the women (perhaps a different one each time) is assigned to *two* practice dates, or (2) a rotational system can be used. If a rotational system is employed, then each of the six male participants in a group takes his turn at *not* having a practice-date prior to the next group meeting.

There is, of course, no fully satisfactory or "smooth" method for handling no-shows. If the absent member did not phone in prior to his/

her intended absence, it is very important that the therapist and/or two or three of the group members phone that absent member as soon as possible after the missed meeting. The purpose of the call is (1) to ascertain whether or not the absent member wishes to remain a part of a practice-dating group, and (2) to encourage further participation if the absent member is inadequately committed to further involvement. If the absent member cannot be brought back into the group, it is important that they be replaced as rapidly as possible so that the sex ratio can be kept even at six males and six females.

As I have indicated, it will always be easy to replace male members. And in order to keep matters fair and orderly, waiting lists should be used for this. Efforts need to be kept constantly ongoing for purposes of recruiting female participants. Indeed, waiting lists can also be used for interested women. And these can include (1) any young woman who wishes to enhance her interpersonal skills and social self-confidence vis-a-vis the male sex, and (2) already self-confident young women who wish to do some "community service" and help out. For example, sorority girls could be offered an opportunity to earn "brownie points" for community service, by committing themselves for a period of time to a practice-dating therapy group.

Thus, the level and severity of love-shyness among potential female participants need not be anywhere nearly as "desperate" or "painful" as it needs to be for participating males. In other words, only those males *really* in need of it should be assigned to a practice-dating group. Less needy males can be referred to a "shyness clinic". And appropriate screening needs to be done towards this end.

Participants who phone in an intended absence will usually be much more deeply and sincerely committed to the practice-dating program. For this reason, it should be a policy of all practice-dating groups that absences be phoned in *in advance* whenever this is feasible.

In most instances, those phoning in an anticipated absence can still be assigned a practice-date for that half-week (or one week) period. And, of course, this should be done. As practice-dating groups (if they are worth their salt) are basically *support* groups and *friendship groups* in addition to being therapy groups, some of the regularly attending members can fill in the absent member on the basic essence of what he/she had missed—and of any special instructions pertinent to this week's (or half-week's) practice-date.

In cases wherein the level of commitment to practice-dating is sufficiently strong, absentees (other than those who had phoned in their *intended* absence) can still be assigned a practice-date for the applicable half-week or one-week period. If the therapist maintains a reasonably accurate handle on each participant's level of commitment (and the friendship bonds within a practice-dating group have become strong), a practice-date can be assigned over the telephone to a female participant who had not shown up for a group meeting.

"Going Outside"

University-based practice-dating therapy programs should make copious use of local area high schools. Most men prefer women who are a few years their junior. And this is especially true for love-shy men, most of whom possess an above-average need to have a woman partner who will "look up" to them and see them as being "someone special". Through advertising and promoting practice-dating programs in local area high schools, the gender ratio problem as well as problems created by absenteeism can both be greatly minimized.

In due course all high schools will have their own practice-dating therapy programs. But until they do it is best to upgrade to the maximum the one practice-dating program that might exist in any given community. This "going outside" to the high schools would be geared almost exclusively towards the recruitment of *female* participants. A minimum age of 18 might be insisted upon for *male* participation. However, in return for their cooperation in making a practice-dating program a success, love-shy males in the selected high schools could be guaranteed priority status for receiving practice-dating therapy as soon as they turn 18 or graduate from high school. Such a promise should go over well with love-shy high school males (1) because such males tend to *live in the future* anyway, and (2) because very few love-shy high school males would wish to "practice-date" with women who are older than they.

Again, love-shy males are extremely romantic; and it is simply not seen as "romantic" for a male to date a woman who is older than he. Further, the love-shy male needs a feeling of power, influence, superior knowledge, etc., over his dating partner and potential lover. And one way of securing this self-confidence boosting feeling is through dating a girl who is younger by at least a few years. In this respect local high school girls could be extremely good for love-shy university-age males. Further, the girls would be "safe"! Remember: love-shy males are extremely fearful of assuming any kind of assertive role vis-a-vis the female sex in informal social situations.

Waiting Lists

There are two methods for developing waiting lists for love-shy males desirous of practice-dating therapy: (1) the "first come, first served" method, and (2) the "severity of the problem" or "severity of need" method. The latter would include such considerations as *how many years* the individual has suffered from his chronic love-shyness, whether or not he has *ever* dated or interacted informally with girls, etc.

If college and university practice-dating therapists engage in an active program of recruitment of high school aged girls and non-college attending girls into the program, lengthy waiting lists for needy love-shy males should not be a problem. However, when waiting lists do develop I personally recommend the "severity of need" method be given priority over the "first come, first served" method. A combination of both methods can and inevitably will be used. But sensible screening methods along with just plain human compassion would dictate that those most in need (1) stand to benefit the most, and (2) will pose the most interesting and stimulating challenges for the therapeutic staff. In short, the most prudent screening policies will assure that those most in need will receive the most prompt and thoroughgoing therapeutic attention.

Practice-Dating Therapy for High Schoolers

Practice-dating therapy needs to become easily accessible to people of *all* ages. However, the category of persons for whom this mode of therapy would ultimately do the most good is that of love-shy high school students. This is because the nipping of problems in the bud serves to *prevent* many long years of needless suffering. Further, there is evidence that the younger a client is, the easier it is to get a therapeutic approach to work for him/her. Simply put, therapy works faster and easier for younger clients.

As I stressed earlier in this book, love-shyness even among five and six-year old children *is destructive* and needs to be remedied. Shyness blocks free choice, self-determination, and the taking of personal responsibility for one's actions and inactions. This is a very dangerous state of affairs in a society such as ours that *assumes* the operation in the lives of all citizens of self-determination and personal responsibility. Social norms may stand in the way of developing practice-dating programs for elementary school aged and junior high school aged youngsters. Nevertheless, the wise, prudent and sensitive parent or teacher will see to it that seven-year old Johnny develops the sense of personal freedom *to talk* to six-year old Suzie instead of daydreaming about her all day long. And they will work towards the engineering of social festivities that will get Johnny and Suzie working together on projects. In essence, they will get Johnny and Suzie interacting through means which are subtle, tactful, non-threatening, fully natural, and non-embarrassing. It if is indeed best for Johnny to avoid emotionally intimate interaction with a girl until he is much older, then he should be furnished with information which *might* lead him to decide on a rational, voluntary basis to avoid such interaction. But such would have to be *his* decision. Neither he nor anyone should *ever* have to avoid heterosexual interaction because of the genetically induced (inhibition gene) mental prison of love-shyness!

In our society the high school represents the youngest level at which the instituting of practice-dating therapy programs would be normatively practicable. And such instituting *should be done*! Love-shy high schoolers must never be dealt with via the immoral, laissez-faire attitude: "Oh, leave them alone; they've got plenty of time". Love-shyness problems *do not* take care of themselves with the passing of time. Left alone love-shyness problems can and do become increasingly worse, NOT better! And furthermore, even though it may not be feasible to offer practice-dating therapy *below* the high school level, I believe that informal heterosexual interaction programs *for boys without sisters* can quite easily be justified and supported, even at the elementary school level.

What *justice* is there in 90 percent of a high school class attending dances and proms when Johnny cannot go because he is afflicted with the inhibition gene and its consequent love-shyness prison syndrome?! It is *wrong* to assume that behavior (or behavioral inaction or omission) always reflects personal preference—e.g., that the reason why Johnny isn't going to dances is because he really doesn't want to go, or because he is really a "latent homosexual", or because he "isn't ready yet".

In American the modal (most commonplace) age for the commencement of dating is 15. This is the case for young people of *both* genders and for middle-class suburbanites and small town residents. The term *"modal"* means that more boys and girls commence dating at 15 than at any other age that is either older or younger than 15. Young people need to feel as though they are a part of the mainstream of things. They also need to feel as though they have some control over their own lives. To be sure, mindless conformity to the dictates of *either* parents *or* peers doesn't make any sense. But allowing a situation to persist wherein the love-shyness syndrome *dominates* the lives of certain young people *makes even less sense*. In order for a young person to make rational decisions and to act in accordance with these decisions, he/she *cannot stay shy*!

Again, practice-dating therapy can be expected to work both faster and easier for high school aged teenagers than for university aged young people. Strong practice-dating programs at the high school level represent strong *preventive medicine* that will ultimately benefit not only the treated love-shy individuals but the wider society as well. Success in the employment sector and everywhere else depends to a greater extent upon social self-confidence and interpersonal finesse than it does upon technical knowledge or formal education. Rare indeed is the high school boy who would rationally choose to remain at home while 90 percent of his fellow classmates are in attendance at parties with "dates" of the opposite sex. Socially inactive love-shys tend to manifest scores of symptoms each and every day, thus letting both parents and teachers know who they are. It is time that we heeded these symptoms and accorded our young people a behavior-oriented remedy that *really* works. Practice-dating therapy fills the bill!

The Termination of Therapy

There is only one major criterion for determining when a formerly love-shy man no longer requires further participation in practice-dating therapy. Simply put, when a man *on his own* contacts a woman who has never had anything whatever to do with practice-dating, the need for this form of therapy is on the verge of being over. Thus, if a man feels secure about contacting new women in the outside world towards whom he feels attracted, the practice-dating experience has successfully accomplished its essential job.

Most love-shys seem to reach this point within approximately six to twelve months of the time when they initially commence therapy. Thus they begin telephoning women whom they meet in their university classes, places of business, etc. In fact, many of them begin to initiate relationships on their own by starting conversations with women on an in-person basis. The fact that some of these initial attempts lead to rejection or to one or another type of "turn down" is no longer emotionally unnerving to them. They have become able to assert themselves in a relaxed, friendly way vis-a-vis women they do not know because their six to twelve (or more) months of practice-dating therapy had served to successfully *extinguish* their fears about experiencing anxiety and because it had served to drastically raise their social self-confidence level. The minor anxieties which they do experience from time to time no longer impede them in any significant way.

An increasing number of practice-dating therapists today also want to make sure that their clients have mastered "the second plateau" before they totally leave therapy. Hence, once a man becomes capable of asking for dates on his own he may discontinue the "practice-dating" aspect of this therapy. But he will continue attending the practice-dating group therapy meetings until he has come to feel confident about (1) exposing his true feelings vis-a-vis his girlfriend after he has reached the seventh or eighth date with her and the usual "bullshit" superficialities can no longer be discussed or rehashed; and (2) kissing his girlfriend and getting started with the physical/sexual manifestations of loving and romantic feelings.

In some cases practice-dating therapists will operate separate groups for those who have successfully completed the basic therapy. Groups which are operated for those who have completed the basic therapy are usually kept fairly small, seldom exceeding five or six members. The ideal is for each group to be composed of three men and three women. Thus, important exercises in psychodrama and role playing can be easily facilitated. Video-tape machines are often used as an adjunct to these exercises. Such technology permits the client to become more mindful of his style of conversation and of informal heterosexual interaction. And like psychodrama itself, it permits him to more rapidly (and accurately) become cognizant of the way he impacts upon other people.

Psychodrama and Role Playing

Much of each 90-minute period in practice-dating group therapy is devoted to exercises in psychodrama. In psychodrama the therapist presents the group of clients with a scenario which entails informal heterosexual interaction, and which might well be expected to arouse anxiety in a love-shy person. One man and one woman will usually be singled out for each exercise in psychodrama. The girl might be asked to play the person in whom the love-shy man has a strong romantic interest. A scene is described by the therapist, and the two people are asked to improvise a "play" over about a ten minute period of time.

In psychodrama each participant is given the opportunity to improvise a role within the safety of the therapy office. And occasionally the scenario described by the therapist at the outset of an exercise will require a "role reversal", in which case a man might be asked to play a girl, and the girl will be asked to play a love-shy man. During each exercise the video-tape machine will commonly record everything that is going on so that the participants can review it all afterward, and so that the other members of the therapy support group can more easily make constructive suggestions so that the next "performance" in a similar situation can be better, more successful, rewarding, etc.

Psychodrama has been found to represent an extremely powerful therapeutic device. Through its use people get to experience what it feels like to exist "in the shoes" of another human being. And as per the old proverb: "You never really understand a man (or woman) until you get to walk a mile in his/her moccasins." In essence, the procedure teaches compassion and understanding of others, as well as self-knowledge.

There is a process in successful interpersonal relationships which sociologists call *"role taking"*. Role taking *is not* the same thing as "role playing". Role playing simply involves playing a role—taking on the vested interests and "soul" of a particular character. Fine actors do that all the time; it is an integral part of their work. However, in *role taking* a person tries to "feel for" the other person (e.g., dating partner) with whom he/she is interacting, and whom he/she is hoping to influence in some way (e.g., accept an invitation for a second date, accept an invitation to "go farther" sexually, etc.). In "role taking" a person tries to anticipate the thoughts and feelings of his/her partner all the while the informal interaction is proceeding.

Generally speaking, the better a person becomes at "role taking", the easier it becomes for him/her to move the relationship in the direction of his/her choosing. The other person comes to *want to* "go along". They feel safe and secure with the person who is good at "role taking", because they have come to trust him/her to respect their feelings, needs and wishes.

The role playing exercises that are endemic to psychodrama quite effectively teach the participants both "role taking" and "role playing". When the exercises are carried out in a supportive, noncompetitive setting (as in practice-dating therapy), they enable the person to come to grips with whatever he/she may be doing wrong, and to plan for a more effective "performance" in the future. Thus, the exercises gradually serve to enormously upgrade social self-confidence and social finesse vis-a-vis the opposite sex.

No Time Limit

One of the most important virtues of practice-dating therapy is that there are no time limits to it. If a client appears to be suffering from a particularly intractable case of love-shyness, he is made to feel free about remaining with the program for as long as he chooses, and for as long as he needs it. Regardless of whether a person remains in therapy for a brief period of time or for a long period of time, the *principle of extinction* remains the dynamic whereby destructive inhibitions and anxiety fears are gradually relinquished. A small minority of men (especially older love-shys) have to "practice-date" scores of women before they become disinhibited enough to loosen up and contact women on their own. Everybody has his/her own internal "clock" or "timetable", and it is viewed as counterproductive to "give up" on a person simply because he/she is taking a long time to display meaningful growth or progress.

Of course, the therapeutic regimen is not entirely permissive. All participants must go out on all assigned practice dates; and all must attend the many group meetings and participate in the various exercises which take place at these meetings. In addition, there are various home-work exercises. But on the other hand, failure of a client to cooperate in these matters is far less of a problem with practice-dating therapy than it is with "shyness clinic" therapy and "assertiveness training" therapy. Again, in practice-dating, clients are never asked to do anything that is beyond their psychoemotional ability to handle, as a prerequisite for remaining in therapy.

Further, practice-dating therapy trains its participants to be respon-sible to some extent for each other. As in Alcoholics Anonymous, people who have progressed quite a bit are encouraged to make friends with and to look in on less experienced and still somewhat frightened practice-dating participants. The idea is to make the newer participants feel as though their new group really does "give a damn" about their welfare. Again, practice-dating provides for the development of quasi-kinship groups—just as "AA" is a quasi-kinship group. Participants are made to feel that their fellows truly care about them and about their progress and growth.[1]

Thus, the most severely love-shy men sometimes have to experi-ence several complete turnovers of women participants in their particular practice-dating group. Nevertheless, the method works. Better than 90 percent of even the most intractably love-shy males manage to eventually improve to the point at which they can effectively compete for women on their own. In essence, therapy that works is invariably *a form of socialization*. And a prerequisite for any kind of socialization *IS depend-ency*. The purpose of socialization is to enable a person to function ade-quately on his or her own—to provide him/her with the "bootstraps" (including the social self-confidence) by which he/she *can* "pull himself/herself up".

Psychologically speaking, love-shy men are *very late* in fulfilling certain very crucial *developmental tasks*. Psychoemotionally their growth will remain stunted unless and until they do manage to fulfill these. Our society had failed to facilitate the love-shy (provide the requisite socialization) in the fulfilling of these "developmental tasks" when they (the love-shys) were in the "normal" and "expected" age bracket for their fulfilling—ages 13 through 16 throughout most of America.

In essence, practice-dating is charged with doing for these men *at a very late time* what society (including parents and teachers) had failed to do for them at the *appropriate* times. Again, it cannot be too strongly stressed that *dependency is a prerequisite for socialization, which is a prereq-uisite for any kind of mature and productive INDEPENDENCE and self-sufficiency*. At the normal ages for the commencement of dating and informal heterosexual interaction the love-shys were ignored because they lacked the charm, attractiveness and poise of the majority of their fellow junior high schoolers. Practice-dating is simply a matter of accomplishing the "dirty work" which our highly competitive society had chosen to leave undone.

Exceptionally Stubborn Cases

The *only* men who cannot be cured by the practice-dating experience are those who cannot or will not do the assigned exercises. All told, this comes to less than five percent of those who commence practice-dating, and less than ten percent of all men actually in need of it. (This extra five percent accounts for the group that simply cannot be benevolently coaxed into a practice-dating group.)

However, there are certain men—about 15 percent of those who enter practice-dating—who never seem to reach the point where they become emotionally capable of approaching women for dates strictly on their own. *All* of this 15 percent eventually gets "cured", and occasionally their needs are taken care of within a good deal less than a year's time. Thus, some of their love-shyness problems are remedied even before those of some of the men who will eventually become capable of asking for dates strictly on their own.

Of course, what happens is that these men eventually find themselves in the midst of a mutual love relationship with one of their practice-dating partners. Just as it frequently happens outside of therapy in the "real world", love-shy men sometimes find themselves "in love with" (*infatuated*) a girl who either doesn't care for them or who may not be aware of the fact that the man has a crush upon them. Such problems are dealt with during the therapy sessions. And when the group sessions prove inadequate for that task, one-on-one therapy is provided for the love-shy man.

But if a man remains in practice-dating therapy long enough, sooner or later he will find himself with a girl with whom a mutual love relationship is genuinely feasible. This seldom happens vis-a-vis any of the six girls in the *initial* therapy group. When it does happen it involves either a girl from a different practice-dating group, or it involves someone to whom the love-shy man had been assigned after one or two complete turnovers of women in his own group. Typically when this happens it will happen within six months to a year of the time when practice-dating therapy had first been commenced. Men with even the most severely stubborn cases of love-shyness will invariably find that it happens to them within a maximum of 18-months of full-fledged involvement in the assigned practice-dating exercises.

When a close, *genuinely mutual* love relationship does develop out of a set of assigned dating experiences, the man is given the option of either (1) remaining in therapy until the normal therapeutic goal of complete self-sufficiency in soliciting dates has been achieved, or (2) of dropping out and pursuing a strictly monogamous courtship relationship with his chosen love-mate. If he chooses the second option (and about 75 percent of love-shy men do), he is given the freedom to return for either one-on-one or group treatment at any time in the future the felt need might arise.

This represents a controversial point among traditional psychotherapists of even the behavior therapy persuasion. The reason, of course, is that those men have not arrived at the ostensible therapeutic goal of full self-sufficiency. They remain as yet emotionally incapable of assuming the assertive role vis-a-vis women they do not know, and of constructively dealing with anxiety feelings accruing from the inevitable rejection that is part and parcel of "the dating game" in American society.

It comes as a surprise to most traditional psychotherapists that a large proportion of successfully married American men had never in their lives asked a stranger for a date. As I documented earlier in this book, many men are introduced to their future wives by members of their extended kinship and/or friendship networks. Simply put, it is *not* merely love-shyness-related anxieties vis-a-vis the female sex which keep some severely shy men from ever marrying. Of perhaps equal importance is the fact that the chronically love-shy male HAS NEVER HAD THE EXPERIENCE OF BEING AN INTEGRAL PART OF ANY SOCIAL NETWORK, kinship related, friendship related, or otherwise. As with Alcoholics Anonymous, Parents Anonymous, etc., the practice-dating therapy group represents an important substitute for the kin family network and friendship networks which love-shy people lack. If *EVERY* man *HAD TO* introduce himself to women he did not know, it is highly likely that the marriage rate in American society would be a very great deal *lower* than it actually is. Thus, therapists may be expecting more out of love-shy men than what is commonly expected of men generally here in the United States.

And so I would suggest that it is both unreasonable and counterproductive to expect *all* love-shy men to approach strange women as a hard, fast prerequisite for their being able to marry. The experiencing of marriage and family life is so crucial to socioemotional growth and maturation that to deny a man the opportunity to participate in these institutions simply because he cannot assert himself with strangers is positively immoral. In fact, psychoemotional inhibition in regard to the idea of approaching strange women may even have its positive albeit quite latent functions. For example, such inhibition may operate to assure sexual fidelity throughout the duration of a marriage. In *that* sense, love-shy men may actually make better-than-average husbands—*if* they can simply be accorded the sort of catalyst they require for becoming involved with a suitable female partner. Practice-dating therapy appears to be the best such catalyst yet to come along.

So if a man falls in love with and marries one of his assigned practice-dates, the mission of practice-dating therapy as far as that man is concerned must be considered to have been successfully accomplished. And if a severely love-shy man is patient and remains actively involved in practice-dating long enough, it is *virtually inevitable* that he will eventually be assigned to someone with whom he will be able to progress towards marriage. It should please most traditional-minded therapists to learn that the large majority of love-shy men in therapy eventually manage as a direct result of the practice-dating experiences to have their heterosexual interaction anxieties fully extinguished. But for the 15 or so percent of severely love-shy men who do not respond to this anxiety-extinguishing process, it is nice to know that they *will* inevitably meet and marry someone through their practice-dating participation *if they simply "hang on" long enough*.

Conclusions and Recommendations

Given its very high degree of documented effectiveness, it is very apparent that practice-dating as a therapeutic modality for love-shys needs to become far more widely available than it is at present. For example, no practice-dating programs have as yet become available outside the context of large university environments. Up to now the work that has been done on practice-dating therapy has focused entirely upon college and university students as clients.

I think it is high time that practice-dating be made available to older love-shy clients. At this juncture in time this could be accomplished in three ways:

(1) State university practice-dating clinics could be expanded in such a way as to service severely love-shy adults from the surrounding community. This is one of many ways through which universities could to some extent give back to the local communities which support them. Advertisements could be placed on a frequent basis in local newspapers; posters could be affixed throughout the community. And the interest of local television and radio news and talk show people could easily be captured. Brief, 15-second ads could also be prepared for

local television networks. In short, it would require little time to build a large adult clientele. The only two problems would be (a) the necessity of waiting lists for prospective male clientele due to the dearth of interested women, and (b) securing the interest of a sufficient number of women who are still young enough to comfortably procreate children; i.e., ages 20 to 30.

(2) Individual therapists in private practice could easily become involved in the delivery of practice-dating therapy services. Most clinical psychologists and psychiatrists in private practice already devote a substantial portion of their time to the administration of group therapy sessions. Through advertising and through the obtaining of free publicity via television and radio news and talk shows, private practitioners could end up providing far greater and more lasting help to people than their traditional "talking cure" group therapy sessions ever could provide.

(3) Public health clinics, health maintenance organizations, group medical practices, etc., have become widely available throughout virtually all parts of the United States. Practice-dating can be and should be one of the regular services which these various types of health clinics offer to the public.

Of course, readers should not be left with the impression that practice-dating is as yet widely available even on university campuses. In fact, I think it can be considered highly tragic that this therapeutic modality is presently available on only a comparatively few campuses. Conventional shyness clinics patterned after the Zimbardo model and assertiveness training therapy are both far more widely available. There are essentially two key reasons for the dearth in the availability of practice-dating:

(1) Most clinical workers in the helping professions possess the basic human trait of *laziness*. Let's face it. It is much easier for a clinician to conduct a form of therapy that merely involves conversation in his/her private office than it is for him/her to deal with such matters as waiting lists, advertising and publicity, assigning men and women to each other for meetings that are to take place outside the context of the therapy office, etc. Personally I do not believe that practice-dating needs to represent anymore laborious a task for a competent therapist than any of the more conventional therapies. It is certainly no more taxing than the operation of a shyness clinic (Zimbardo model). However, the initiating of a practice-dating program does require some guts and some sense of adventure on the

part of the therapist. A therapist has got to have a *non-shy*, innovative spirit in order for him/her to be willing to pursue practice-dating to the point of actually engineering and administering a program in it. (I think there is reason to believe that most therapists are themselves a bit on the shy side.)

(2) There is little need for a practitioner to take risks when he/she can maintain a lucrative practice and get along well with his/her colleagues by following traditional therapeutic modalities. Simply put, most therapists in private practice do not wish to be conspicuous or in any way noticeable for being "different" or innovative. Practice-dating is as yet somewhat of a non-conformist approach to therapy. And professional organizations composed of psychiatrists, clinical psychologists and psychiatric social workers, all tend to be very much on the conservative side. Therapists involved in the administration of practice-dating clinics may fear the possibility of not receiving their fair share of referrals of new clients. The traditional folk wisdom in all psychotherapeutic fields is that dependency of the client upon the therapist must be discouraged at all costs. Practice-dating is often misperceived as fostering dependency and as discouraging self-sufficiency. Thus, most psychotherapists like to *"adjust"* to and work within the "status quo".

More succinctly, traditionally oriented psychotherapists (who are usually the ones with the power and influence) believe in stressing *adjustment* both for themselves as well as for their clients. In recent years the entire field of psychiatry has been soundly criticized for this. To be sure, adjustment of a person to his/her social environment is healthy up to a point. On the other hand, *adjusting* to various forms of social pressure, oppression and injustice *is not healthy*. In the Soviet Union political dissidents are often thrown into insane asylums under the pretext that they are "mentally ill" because they disagree with "the system" in some ways. Until quite recently American psychiatry dealt with homosexuals as "sick" individuals simply because they are different. Even today, young women who do not wish to stay home for thirty years and take care of the needs of a husband and a large brood of children are sometimes seen as being "sick"—particularly by fundamentalistically oriented religionists.

The conventional therapist believes that love-shy men need to "adjust" to the currently prevailing norms which prescribe the assertive role for men vis-a-vis women, and which prescribe that all young men must be able to handle ambiguity (practice-dating is a highly structured sort of program). The conventional therapist similarly believes that any matchmaking activity done by a therapist on behalf of a shy person is merely a "cop out". (The coloquial term "cop out" has become for most psychotherapists a kind of "pat" rejoinder for *any* idea of which they disapprove. Utter the words "cop out" and it automatically becomes unnecessary to use the *thinking faculty* for coming up with a *real* argument of rejoinder.)

The practice-dating therapist, like most other *behavior therapists*, believes that people learn *by doing*, and that the longer the love-shy remain uninvolved in social activities, the more socially incompetent they are likely to become—and the more poorly they are likely to think of themselves.

The behavior therapist believes in extinguishing destructive anxiety reactions (like love-shyness) by gradually and continually exposing the client to the anxiety-provoking social stimulus (i.e., *women*), and by assuring that these exposures are systematically controlled in such a way that (1)*none of them* are too threatening or anxiety-provoking for a particular love-shy client, and (2) that each one provides for the experiencing of strong feelings of pleasure and accomplishment. Most importantly, a behavior therapist believes that a person cannot lift himself up by his own bootstraps if he has no bootstraps to begin with. Behavior therapy (practice-dating) provides the bootstraps. Thus, it is *a form of socialization process* which, upon completion, assures that the client will be able to get all of his essential needs met—that he will be able to competently accomplish goals for himself (like securing a wife) that he could not do before the therapy had begun.

Traditional therapists typically believe (by action if not by intellectual conviction) in forcing square pegs into round holes, and in catalyzing people into "adjusting" their personalities *to the way things are*. Hence, most of them are socially and politically conservative; e.g., "society's alright; it's the patient who must change". Most traditional therapists are "wedded" (intractably committed) to one or another "talking cure" perspective. And if a client does not respond positively, then there must be something wrong with the client: e.g., "too many defenses", "he's not ready yet", "he *enjoys* resisting treatment", etc. The idea that there might be something wrong with the perspective itself—or that a certain perspective simply *does not "fit"* a particular client—is something that never seriously enters the mind of the conventional psychotherapist. Indeed, it is against their *vested interests* for such an idea to enter their minds. Simply put, the operating assumption of most traditional psychotherapists is that the perspective they are using *fits everyone*. In the nutshell, THIS IS WHY CONVENTIONAL THERAPEUTIC MODALITIES HAVE INVARIABLY FAILED QUITE MISERABLY IN THE TREATMENT OF SEVERELY LOVE-SHY MEN who had been born with the inhibition and low anxiety threshold genes.

Practice-Dating and the University Campus

If your university campus does not offer practice-dating therapy, I suggest that you frame some well-written letters to your student newspaper about it. Contact the student body president, the local community newspaper, local television and radio stations, religious leaders of moderate denominations—as many different kinds of people as you can. Indicate to them that practice-dating therapy is greatly needed. Give them a copy of this book. Make it clear that practice-dating provides for by far the highest "cure rate" of all therapeutic approaches in dealing with severely love-shy men. And indicate your sincere belief that love-shy men have as much right as anybody to enjoy the good life, to be able to enjoy dating, courting, to be able to marry and to enjoy active involvement in a rewarding social life.

At the present time there is a shortage of academic positions for psychologists. However, if enough pressure was brought to bear, advertisements could be placed in the CHRONICLE OF HIGHER EDUCATION, and in certain employment periodicals of the American Psychological Association, the American Medical Association, and the American Psychiatric Association, for academic/clinical and/or counseling psychologists and psychiatrists *with a special competence in the administration of practice-dating therapy.*

In short, it should now be possible to insist that all university campuses have someone readily available at all times who has a professional competence in the specialized area of practice-dating therapy. Remember the old saying that "the customer is always right". Colleges and universities are literally begging for customers, even to the point of having to advertise on television and in all other media. A sales organization must please its customers if it is to stay in business and to flourish.

The readily availability of practice-dating therapy could be a formidable boon to any college or university. If such a program were well advertised, love-shys from all over would want to go there and matriculate on a full-time basis. Love-shy people are customers; and as *consumers* of higher education they need to make clear to the sales organizations delivering educational services just exactly what their needs and requirements are.

For several very good reasons it is perfectly legitimate and reasonable to expect that all campuses with 2,500 or more students have a practice-dating therapist readily at hand. For example, we know that the love-shy are underachievers who cannot concentrate on their work anywhere nearly as well as they could if they had the sense of personal freedom necessary to enjoy female companionship, dating and courtship, and to lead a well-balanced, diversified life. Hence, even hard nosed academics can be convinced on the basis of available empirical research data that academic goals can be more readily and effectively achieved by students who possess a sense of personal freedom about the governance of their personal lives, and who are able to initiate and to sustain meaningful heterosexual love relationships.

If there is a shortage of already trained therapists in the specialized field of practice-dating, then the large scale appearance of a surfeit of employment ads requiring practice-dating therapists will assure that a plethora of graduate programs in psychology, psychiatry and social work focusing on practice-dating will commence to sprout up so that the demand can be fulfilled. Indeed, *it can be guaranteed that this will happen*! When the pay and the various other rewards are right, the employment needs and requirements of an organization tend to be met quite rapidly.

Some Militancy Needs to be Displayed

If in seeking therapeutic help for your love-shyness you end up in a so-called "shyness clinic" where you are told that for your homework exercise you have to go out and "start a conversation with a stranger", *WALK OUT*! Remember that *you* are the customer! And it is up to the deliverer of a service to correctly ascertain customer wants and to satisfy them. As I have already stressed, "shyness clinic" therapy is totally worthless from the standpoint of successfully remedying chronic and severe love-shyness problems. And the same is true for the various "assertiveness training" programs and encounter groups that are operated, and in which the love-shy often get "roped in".

We know today that practice-dating is the therapeutic direction which offers the greatest hope for the severely love-shy. Hence, practice-dating therapy is the therapeutic modality which must be insisted upon. And corollatively, we must insist upon the development of graduate programs in psychology that work to create practitioners who are properly educated to competently fulfill this demand.

Needless to say, this same militancy is required to an even greater extent vis-a-vis traditional psychotherapeutic practitioners who insist upon using one or another of the "talking cures". Psychoanalysis, client-centered therapy, rational-emotive therapy, etc., will simply not work for severely love-shy men. Similarly, the various forms of conventional group therapy are also a waste of time and often do more harm than good inasmuch as they commonly arouse a tremendous amount of hostility and backbiting among the component members.

Love-shy men would do well to find others with problems similar to their own. There is safety in numbers as well as political power and clout. Heterosexual love-shys remain pretty much the only minority group without a political power base. To be sure, a love-shy man in almost all cases would be far too shy and inhibited to take strong political action on his own. But in the company of other love-shys it is likely that a considerable fraction of love-shys could fight for their rights quite vociferously and with a steadfast attitude. This is especially true for that 30 percent of love-shy males whose shyness does not extend to public speaking or to a range of *impersonal* type social interactions.

Thus, when one is fighting for one's rights there *is* a purpose apart from pure, unadulterated sociability. Therefore, when love-shys are joined together with many others of like mind, there is no reason why a significant minority of them should feel shy or inhibited. Of course, inertia can be a problem inasmuch as a long history of no success at all in the social realm of life can and usually does lead to a feeling of weariness and a concomitant disinclination to take any action at all.

This is why the locating of other men with love-shyness problems can serve as a powerful catalyst to effective political action. For example, on a university campus a group of only five or six love-shy men could attract considerable notice to themselves by peacefully marching and carrying placards in and around the administration building and/or student counseling center and departments of psychology and of journalism/media studies. These placards could back up articles and "letters to the editor" published in the university newspapers. And they could contain such slogans as: PRACTICE-DATING THERAPY *NOW*; MALE LESBIANS UNITE! LOVE-SHY PRIDE; SHY PRIDE; CLOSET HETEROSEXUALS UNITE! HETEROSEXUAL LOVE-SHYS UNITE! LOVE-SHYS NEED LOVE TOO; LOVE-SHYS UNITE; PASSIVE COWARDICE IS A VIRTUE; PASSIVE COWARDS DON'T MAKE WAR! etc.

To be sure, I am not recommending that love-shys become obstreperous rabel-rousers. It is highly unlikely that any of them would have the psychoemotional capacity to do this anyway. What I am recommending is that they take steps to become more politically aware and less politically inconspicuous. If homosexuals can march around insisting upon their rights and chanting "Gay Pride", then it is clear that heterosexual love-shys might be able to make some real progress on their own behalf by similarly banding together with others who share their problem and handicap.

Homosexuals have made some formidable progress over the past fifteen years. And much of this progress can be directly attributable to their vociferously bringing the unfairness of their plight to public attention (*including* the solicitation of *media* attention). Even in large cities, homosexual men used to be discriminated against to a far greater extent than they are today. Yet if the heterosexual love-shy man stops to ponder the issue for a moment he will realize that he has been discriminated against and ignored in a whole host of ways to a far greater extent than homosexual men have ever been discriminated against or ignored. Homosexual men have places to go. They have a whole host of publications which advise them of gathering places, counseling services, bars, support groups, medical services, gay baths, recreational events, political groups, etc. In short, there are organizations designed to help homosexuals establish a social network of meaningful friendships.

As I have stressed throughout this book, heterosexual love-shy men *lack* any social networks. They are isolates who had always been ignored and made surplus garbage (dispensable pawns) by society. They are probably the only major category of people in American society that *lacks* any organized group or publication to look after and defend their rights and needs.

And so marching about with placards would (1) make it far easier for other *closet heterosexuals* and *male lesbians* (heterosexual love-shy men) to come out of the closet and meet and plan strategies with others of like mind and experience. In short, it would help love-shys to get together and make friends with people of their own temperament. It would enable them to establish themselves in meaningful social networks and make their *existence* (along with their basic human needs) known to society through the mass media of radio, television, and newspapers. In fact, I can guarantee that the television cameras would soon be around if a fair sized bunch of heterosexual love-shys marched together carrying placards with statements similar to those designated above. Television news reporters are always on the alert for what appears to be unusual and intrinsically interesting.

Secondly (2), such peaceful marching about would have the effect of alerting university administrators to the needs of their campus and local communities. Sooner or later they would have to take some action by way of bringing in trained and competent practice-dating therapists, and perhaps nude jacuzzi and sexual surrogate therapists as well. At the very least, authority figures would be made aware of the *existence* of a group of highly deprived people whose needs have been totally ignored for far too long.

And finally (3), the public attention that such marching would attract would render it increasingly easy to develop local chapters of a soon-to-be nationwide (support group) organization called *Shys Anonymous* or (*Love-Shys Anonymous*). Indeed, *Coed Scout*ing organizations for children and teenagers might similarly be launched in this way.

NOTES

1. Indeed, since practice-dating groups are really *support groups* (along the "AA" model), men and women who have been fully graduated from regular participation in practice-dating are *also* encouraged to look in on and help anxious neophytes who might occasionally be too nervous to show up for meetings or assigned dates.

Chapter 23

Some Therapeutic Adjuncts

There are several therapeutic modalities which can and most probably should be used as concomitants to practice-dating therapy. The purpose of this chapter is two-fold: (1) to discuss the therapeutic adjuncts that are likely to accomplish the greatest good for love-shy men and women; and (2) to delineate the most important rejoinders to those who would assert that practice-dating is not a suitable therapeutic modality for the love-shy.

The Nude Jacuzzi Experience

A jacuzzi bath is a circular bath tub approximately two feet deep, which is large enough to accommodate some six or eight people. It is characterized by warm, vigorously swirling waters which constantly move, and which remain quite comfortably warm but not hot. In recent years it has become a very helpful psychotherapeutic device. And it has become recognized as a sure-fire socio-sexual "ice breaker" and as a highly effective social relaxant. A high quality jacuzzi bath will easily permit eight people of both sexes to climb in and enjoy the quite unique, disinhibiting sensations. Indeed, an invitation to jacuzzi bathing has been found by numerous therapists to almost always make it very easy for even comparatively shy people to shed their clothes quite rapidly amid mixed company.

Jacuzzi bathing typically provides an intrinsically very sensual experience for all who participate. Physiologically, the warm swirling water tends to raise blood pressure and to give rise to an unmistakable "high" feeling. Thus, besides turning everybody on, jacuzzi bathing is intrinsically disinhibiting. It makes it unusually easy for most if not all participants to let down whatever psychoemotional defenses they might have brought with them.

After just a few minutes in a bath with a collection of nude friends of both sexes even the most reserved participant is likely to giggle and laugh and almost totally lose any feelings of reserve that he or she might have had upon initially arriving on the scene. Herein lies the basic psychotherapeutic thrust of the nude jacuzzi experience. And herein lies the reason why an increasing number of therapists interested in treating shyness are finding the jacuzzi to be of enormous value in dealing with inhibited teenagers and young adults. During the past few years some very promising work with coeducational nude psychotherapy has been done utilizing jacuzzi baths. Therapists report that the warm, swirling water greatly facilitates therapeutic social interaction, and that even the most intractably shy man becomes remarkably disinhibited by the middle of the third jacuzzi bath session, at the latest.

Better than half of the love-shy men I interviewed indicated that they *would be willing* to experience coeducational nude jacuzzi therapy as part of an optional set of exercises engaged in during the twice-weekly practice-dating group therapy meetings. Up to now very few practice-dating therapists have had the guts to incorporate nude jacuzzi therapy into their armamentarium of therapeutic skills. This is doubtless because up to now virtually all practice-dating therapy has been conducted in college and university environments wherein conservative boards of regents and administrators have had to be contended with. However, the success of nude jacuzzi therapy at places like Escalan (Big Sur, California), has convinced me that it would represent an extremely powerful *and extremely beneficial* therapeutic adjunct. To be sure, it would be counterproductive to require participation in nude jacuzzi therapy as a prerequisite for continued participation in practice-dating therapy. However, nude jacuzzi group therapy *should* be made available to all practice-dating clients. All should be gently and tactfully encouraged to take part by experienced practice-daters of both genders. (It is, of course, surprisingly easy to be nude when everyone of both sexes in your immediate social environment is also nude.)

Unwritten university policies (and most of the feared policies *are* unwritten and *not* official) can be circumvented by holding biweekly jacuzzi sessions at off-campus locations. Non-university psychologists would have to be retained for leading the nude group jacuzzi sessions. Thus, at the outset it might be best if the regular, university-affiliated practice-dating therapist was not the person to actually conduct these. Participants would undoubtedly have to pay some fee for the nude jacuzzi therapy service. But I am convinced that the experience and the consequent therapeutic gains would be well worth the asking price.

Nude jacuzzi therapy is especially helpful in getting the severely love-shy person over what was earlier described as the "second plateau" of shyness. It represents an additional highly valuable catalyst for facilitating the dropping of a rigid set of defenses and the baring of the expression of true feelings. In short, nude jacuzzi therapy can greatly facilitate the love-shy towards the ultimate goal of truly being themselves.

Parenthetically, among men and women who have commenced sexual activity with each other, the jacuzzi experience provides a kind of "built in" form of birth control. Research at the Claremont Colleges in California has shown that when the testicles are kept submerged under hot water for five minutes or more (and a nude jacuzzi session usually lasts for at least 50 minutes), the sperm in a man's scrotum are all killed off and he becomes quite infertile for a period of several hours. It has been speculated that this may be one reason why middle-class people have always had smaller families than poor people. Middle-class people have always been more likely than the poor to bathe prior to making love.

Therapy Employing Sexual Surrogates

Any truly comprehensive program calculated to guarantee a complete cure for intractable, chronic and severe love-shyness *MUST* incorporate a program facet that entails use of sexual surrogates. At the outset I want to stress that sex surrogate therapy is *only a facet or component* of what I believe would comprise a thoroughly effective program for the curing of *all* of even the most stubbornly love-shy men. Sexual surrogate therapy would never work *by itself* to relieve a person of intractable love-shyness. Indeed, it might render a severely love-shy man emotionally capable of satisfying himself with prostitutes but as emotionally incapable as he ever was of developing an intimate relationship with an eligible, potential marriage partner.

But just as sexual surrogate therapy is not being recommended here as a sole therapeutic modality for the extremely shy, it *is* being strongly and enthusiastically recommended as a necessary and perhaps *indispensable adjunct* to practice-dating therapy. The United States is still very far from being a sex positive society. Even today there are so many people who are quite uncomfortable about most topics and issues of a sexual nature. And this is why the sexual surrogate component to the love-shys' therapeutic package that is being recommended by this book necessitates some very strong defensive efforts.

Briefly, a sexual surrogate is a young woman who has been trained in techniques of helping men to overcome various sexual problems such as premature ejaculation, impotence, and inability to please a woman. Today hundreds of sexual surrogates are employed in various sex therapy clinics throughout the United States. About 60 percent of the clientele served by these women are married; the other 40 percent are single and divorced. In the majority of instances sexual surrogates work directly under the supervision of a certified clinical psychologist or psychiatrist. However, in recent years a small number of sexual surrogates have themselves completed the Ph.D. and licensing training that is necessary to running their own operation.

Up to now the rate of success eminating from the work of sexual surrogates has been extremely high. In fact, some studies show that the surrogates have provided very valuable help to virtually every man whom they have seen. The first American clinic to employ sexual surrogates was operated by the famous Masters and Johnson sex research team in St. Louis, Missouri. And they too have reported remarkable success rates over the years.

However, what is of especial importance from the standpoint of this book is the fact that sexual surrogates working under the auspices of licensed clinical psychologists have been enormously successful in helping *male virgins* in the 28 to 40-year old age group. Indeed, one of the major categories of people up to now to have sought therapy from sexual surrogates has been the chronically love-shy, single-never-married, male virgin in the 28 to 40-year old age range.

Moreover, there is a valuable side benefit which seems to accrue from sexual surrogate therapy with the severely love-shy. Thus, this form of therapy seems to have the effect of substantially weakening the love-shys' need for a woman with the classical "long hair and youthful, pretty face" syndrome. As I have documented, the love-shys' needs and requirements relative to feminine beauty tend to be both rigid and highly unrealistic. Further, these demands constitute a major reason as to why love-shy men have no interest in approaching or talking to or in initiating relationships with most women. Insofar as sexual surrogate therapy has the effect of sharply reducing the strength of these unrealistic needs, it is thus removing a major impediment to informal heterosexual inter-action for the love-shy.

Of course, anxieties pertinent to *having sex* are not synonymous with heterosexual (social) interaction anxieties. None of the 300 love-shy men studied for this book had ever had sex with anyone other than themselves (masturbation). And love-shy men must learn how to self-disclose vis-a-vis a woman in a comfortable, serene way. They must learn how to relax and to enjoy emotional sharing with another human being.

But what appears to happen in therapy involving sexual surrogates is that THE EXTINCTION OF ANXIETIES PERTAINING TO HAVING SEX *TRANSFERS* INTO THE SIMULTANEOUS EXTINCTION OF HETEROSEXUAL-SOCIAL INTERACTION ANXIETIES! In other words, general interpersonal anxieties regarding informal interaction vis-a-vis attractive members of the opposite sex appear to be almost fully extinguished by and through the process of extinguishing sexual anxieties. And this applies as much to virginal men who have never made love to a woman in their lives, as it does to married men who had been suffering sexual difficulties prior to treatment.

These new and provocative findings raise a question that is of enormous importance for the proper therapeutic treatment of the virginal love-shy. In particular, *a man's sexual anxieties and fears may to a greater or lesser extent lie at the very heart of his anxieties pertinent to informal socializing vis-a-vis women*. And if this is indeed the case (and the available evidence is pointing in that direction), then any therapy for the love-shy which stands a good chance for *lasting* success is going to have to come to grips with the *sexual* anxieties problem. In short, the capacity of the love-shy for (1) developing interpersonal self-confidence and finesse for successful heterosexual interaction, and (2) for overcoming heterosexual interaction anxieties which obviate meaningful socializing with women, may rest in large part upon their ability to overcome their specifically *sexual* anxieties vis-a-vis the female sex.

In view of the foregoing, I would recommend that therapy incorporating use of sexual surrogates be made available to *all* love-shy men 18-years of age and older. All major university campuses and all major urban clinics should have sexual surrogate programs readily available to all men who present evidence that they have suffered from chronic and severe love-shyness. These programs need to receive the same level of federal and state funding as do other medical and mental health programs for, as I have clearly documented, chronic love-shyness has a profound impact upon all levels of emotional *and physical* health.

Right now therapy involving the use of sexual surrogates sells for $75 to $100 per 90-minute session; and programs claiming success at curing the chronically love-shy seem to require about 30 sessions of work over some 30 weeks time. This price structure is obviously far beyond the means of most afflicted young men. And so steps need to be taken to incorporate it under the regular, normal health insurance programs that presently embrace all the medical/psychiatric health needs and requirements of most university students. Inasmuch as only 1.5 percent of all university males suffer from severely intractable love-shyness, it appears evident that sexual surrogate therapeutic programs would not be widely used by the general run of young men. Under conditions of careful psychiatric screening, men with little need for the program can easily be kept out of it.

Programs claiming success with the chronically love-shy ordinarily run for a full 30 weeks. In most cases the men involved in these programs had never been nude with a woman in their lives. And they had never seen a nude woman apart from what they might have observed in "skin flicks" or "nudie" magazines. None of them had ever looked at the genitals of a real, live woman; and none felt at all comfortable about either their own potential nudity or that of a possible female partner.

The first several weeks of the typical program does not entail any nudity. Instead the surrogate works with the love-shy man on what have come to be known as "sensate focus" exercises. Sensate focus is a sort of relaxing meditation. The client closes his eyes, relaxes, and concentrates very deeply upon the feelings of touch that he is experiencing from the touching and massaging activities of the surrogate. The first several weeks may focus primarily on hand-holding and hand caressing. After the client begins to feel reasonably "at home" with that, they move on to the caressing of other parts of the body. Usually it takes until the fourth or fifth week before the surrogate successfully moves the client on to the point wherein both he and she can remove their clothes (bathing trunks).

At the outset a jacuzzi bath may be used as a catalyst to facilitate helping the very shy young man come to grips with the fact of being nude in the same room with a nude woman. Of course, all the while this is going on the young man is learning something about conversational skills with a woman. And he is also learning about various physical pleasuring skills. He is learning how to translate his highly sensitive attitudes towards women *into action* of a type that will benefit both himself and a future female love partner whom he will later be emotionally equipped to pick out.

With each advancing session the sensate focus exercises continue. The young man gradually learns how to relax as the surrogate commences pleasuring each increasingly intimate part of his body. And simultaneously he learns (*by doing*) how to effectively pleasure the increasingly intimate parts of a woman's body. Exercises leading up to and involving actual sexual intercourse may not necessarily commence until the twentieth session or later. After that time the young man may go through the various stages of foreplay and copulate with his surrogate two or even three times during the course of the 90-minute therapy period.

These exercises are a necessary and, in fact, indispensable part of the program and of its ultimate therapeutic success. Moralists have criticized (not unexpectedly!) all therapeutic programs involving sexual surrogates as constituting a thinly-veiled form of prostitution. Of course, moralists by their very nature have always been uncomfortable with all non-marital manifestations of sexuality anyway. Thus, they can be accurately deemed part of the love-shyness problem in American society,

NOT of its solution! Moralists need to be advised of the fact that in order for a love-shy man to attain that ultimate goal of a lasting marriage (which they themselves so enthusiastically exalt), they must allow that love-shy man to experience whatever therapeutic regime the best empirical research points to as being best at painlessly and successfully conquering the love-shyness problem.

Moreover, prostitutes as they currently exist in America today could not be led to accomplish the types of exercises that sexual surrogates do every day at the direction of licensed clinical psychologists and psychiatrists. Most prostitutes have an underlying hostility and dislike for the male gender. And even though some prostitutes have developed reputations for being remarkably effective "talking therapists" of real compassion and understanding, these are the exception rather than the rule. Further, the amount of time a prostitute normally alots each client is far too limited for a severely love-shy man to achieve any lasting benefits. The prostitute is normally oriented towards sexual intercourse only—or towards whatever sexual maneuver will successfully bring a male client to climax as efficiently and rapidly as possible. Simply put, all that has been learned over the past two decades about the profound therapeutic impact of sensate focus exercises would likely be lost on the prostitute. Her business does not allow her to very patiently pursue the slow, systematic course *with the same love-shy man* over a 30-week course of time. And, by the way, none of the 300 love-shy men studied for this research had ever so much as even considered going to see a prostitute. Generally speaking, love-shy men view prostitutes with a sense of fear; they fear being "taken" financially, and they fear sexual embarrassment.

One potential problem with severely love-shy men is that they might be especially vulnerable to "falling in love" with the sexual surrogate. Needing love so badly, it is not difficult to understand why the love-shy might be particularly vulnerable towards developing a deep-seated infatuation with anyone of the female gender who shows them genuine compassion and sincere, personal interest.

Suffice it to say that comfortable ways have been developed for keeping the love-shy man from falling in love with the surrogate. In fact, along about the 15th week of treatment he is strongly encouraged to begin dating. Of course, young men in practice-dating therapy would already be dating anyway. For them sexual surrogate therapy would merely be an important adjunct to the basic practice-dating program. And that is essentially what I am recommending.

However, those receiving sexual surrogate therapy who are *not* simultaneously involved in a practice-dating program would be strongly urged to enroll in a reputable dating service or marriage bureau, and to permit themselves to meet women through that. This would be especially true for men who remain too shy to socially assert themselves vis-a-vis women even after 15 weeks of sexual surrogate therapy. Of course, in most cases after the standard thirty weeks of sexual surrogate therapy even the most severely love-shy men are going to be dating and informally socializing with women. And they will be doing this in a way that is far more comfortable and emotionally rewarding for them than anything they had ever up to that point in their lives experienced.

In sum, I am not claiming here that therapy incorporating sexual surrogates is any kind of a panacea. In fact, I personally believe that this form of therapy needs to be employed as a simultaneous *adjunct* to other forms of therapy, and particularly (under *ideal* circumstances) to practice-dating therapy. However, sexual surrogate therapy with its accent on sensate focus exercises and on learning how to feel at home with the physical expressions of love, can and will make a powerful contribution to the ultimate "cure" of any love-shy man. Such therapy can do wonders in getting a person past the barriers and stumbling blocks posed by the *"second plateau"* of love-shyness. Programs which do not involve use of sexual surrogates stand less chance of ultimate and lasting success than those which do. And, of course, that is the ultimate acid test.

Finally, we must not permit moralists to limit the use of sexual surrogate therapy to the ranks of older men. I believe that the kind of severe love-shyness from which the 35 to 50-year old male virgins of this study suffered could have been prevented from reaching such enormous proportions had these men been placed in sexual surrogate therapy programs when they had been 18 or 19 or 20 years old. Indeed, had these men received practice-dating therapy on top of sexual surrogate therapy, it is highly unlikely that any of them would still be love-shy today.

Use of Audio-Cassette Programs

Practice-dating therapy programs often incorporate use of certain audio-cassette programs. Such recorded programs are often used in more conventional "shyness clinic" work as well. In practice-dating their use can and often does function on a subliminal level as an effective catalyst speeding and facilitating the remission of destructive symptoms.

Certain programs have been found to be especially helpful in this regard. The object of the most effective programs is to inspire the listener into programming his/her subconscious mind with more positive, life-enhancing self-images. Thus, the love-shy male is shown the powerful impact that *mind* can have over "matter", and how a person tends to become what he/she thinks about most of the time. Used by themselves these cassette programs provide little more than an intellectually stimulating experience. However, when they are used in conjunction with a therapeutic regimen with which the love-shy client can live and cooperate (e.g., practice-dating therapy in combination with sexual surrogate therapy), the impact can be very positive and beneficial at a meaningful, gut level. In other words, the client may actually begin to apply the various cassette messages to his life, and particularly to his emotional preparations for and actual interactions with his assigned practice-dates.

For those not familiar with the therapeutic use of audio-cassette programs, this much must be delineated here: (1) The programs are *not* listened to during the valuable group meeting time. Each client has his/her own copies of the cassette programs, and he/she listens to them as part of a program of regular homework exercises. Secondly (2), the cassettes are to be listened to *repeatedly*, NOT just once or twice. This is the only way the subconscious mind can begin to be affected and appropriately influenced by the messages. For example, a client may be asked to listen to a particular cassette once daily for ten days, and then three times per week for the ensuing thirty weeks.

It is not the purpose of this book to list all of the best material that is currently available. Nevertheless, it has been my experience that the following cassette programs constitute a highly worthwhile investment for any practice-dating therapy program:

1. THE PSYCHOLOGY OF WINNING, by Denis Waitley.
2. THE STRANGEST SECRET, by Earl Nightengale.
3. LEAD THE FIELD, by Earl Nightengale.
4. KOP's KEYS TO SUCCESS AND HAPPINESS, by M. R. Kopmeyer.
5. FOCUS, by Mike McCaffrey.
6. WINNING FROM WITHIN, by Shad Helmstetter.
7. REV. IKE (Frederick Eickerenkotter). Includes some 16 individual cassettes which can be purchased singly.
8. THE NEUROPSYCHOLOGY OF ACHIEVEMENT, by Steven DeVore.
9. THE PSYCHOLOGY OF ACHIEVEMENT, by Brian Tracy.

Bibliotherapy

Therapists can also require their clients to read certain books. And some of the group meetings that are integral to a practice-dating program can be given over to discussions of the personal meaning and practical applicability of insights contained in these books to the love-shyness problem. Love-shy people often respond well to anything which contains empirical documentation. In general, they tend to spend a good deal more time with books than do the non-shy—although most of the most appropriate books have become available in condensed form on audio-cassettes.

Of course, therapists need to be quite sparing and need to exercise considerably care regarding the books and articles they might incorporate into their practice-dating therapy programs. Textbooks and scholarly monographs need to be avoided as clients will seldom cooperate in reading this type of material anyway. In fact, this is one reason why audio-cassette programs will usually make a considerably more prudent investment—particularly since they can be comfortably listened to over and over again. Nevertheless, there have been some short, incisively written books that have proved useful. And these include such items as:

1. IN THE MIND's EYE, by Arnold Lazarus.
2. THE MAGIC OF BELIEVING, by Claude Bristol.
3. THINK AND GROW RICH, by Napolean Hill.
4. GETTING WELL AGAIN, by O. Carl & Stephanie Simonton.
5. THE BODY ELECTRIC, by Thelma Moss.
6. THE ANXIETY DISEASE, by David V. Sheehan.

Meditation

To an increasing extent practice-dating programs are incorporating an emphasis upon the teaching and practicing of various techniques of meditation. This is done not merely because love-shy people find it very difficult to relax when they are in informal, unstructured social situations. To be sure, the development of an ability to relax *does* represent a most desirable "side effect" of competency at meditation. But this is only one of the many benefits to which regular periods of meditation can be expected to lead.

In recent years we have learned that regular meditators are far less likely than non-meditators to come down with a host of serious diseases including heart disease, high blood pressure, and cancer. We have also learned that regular meditators tend to get along with other people considerably more harmoniously than do non-meditators. Virtually all of the evidence indicates that meditators tend to be happier in their personal lives and more productive in everything that they do, than non-meditators. And they tend to be substantially more likely than non-meditators to function on a goal-oriented basis.

One of the most thought-provoking studies on this subject was recently published by a group of Canadian scientists. It was found, for example, that meditation drastically reduced the recidivism rate among a large group of researched former prisoners. Two groups had been studied; and each of these was composed of criminals of the same types and of the same approximate sentence lengths. One group was accorded systematic training in various techniques of meditation, whereas the other group was given no such training. All members of each of the two groups were accorded regular group therapy throughout each of their respective stays in prison. Similarly, all members of both groups were accorded access to a variety of programs that had been designed to facilitate adjustment in the law-abiding community upon release from prison.

Simply put, no program ever attempted by the prison system of British Columbia had ever even come close to the success rate of the meditation program. Meditators were less than one-fifth as likely to recidivate as non-meditators. Thus, after a year-long follow-up the men who had been taught meditation while in prison managed to adjust far more successfully to life in the outside community. (The year-long follow-up commenced from the date of each man's release from prison.)

There are many different forms of meditation. In practice-dating therapy we need concern ourselves with only two: (1) meditation for one-ness with the God-mind or "universal cosmic intelligence"; and (2) systematic visualizations. There are hundreds of techniques that can be subsumed under the first type. Practice-dating therapists teach six or seven of these and encourage their clients to use whatever one makes them feel the most comfortable.

Meditation requires some disciplined effort along with a high level of commitment. People need to set aside two 20-minute periods each day, and they must have the dedication to use these for actual meditation. Love-shy people find this more difficult to do than most people. And this is why therapists encourage love-shys to get together in a support group with some of their fellow therapy-mates (of either sex) outside of therapy, and meditate together at pre-designated times.

Few love-shys actually succeed at reaching the "brilliant white light" during their first year or so of following a disciplined program of meditation. Nevertheless, real progress *is* made—and this includes the fact that regular meditation appears to catalyze success at the regular assigned dating exercises. Hence, regular meditation appears to speed up therapy; and this is especially so when it is practiced together with other fellow love-shys.

Systematic visualization is a much easier form of meditation. And it can be engaged in during the regular therapy meetings as well as at almost any other time. A person can do it while walking or (to some extent) even while driving his/her car. It simply involves *"seeing"* in the mind's eye what one wishes to come to pass. In addition, it involves *feeling* and *genuinely believing* that what one is visualizing is very much in the actual process of coming to pass. And that nothing can stop this progress towards the attainment of just and honorable goals.[1]

Systematic visualization can also involve the seeing of a brilliant green or white light penetrating and suffusing (and thus *healing*) the physical body of an ill individual. This approach is less applicable to practice-dating, although it has occasionally been used with beneficial results. The visualization of "the light" in this form of meditation is voluntarily directed by the awake ego. In the first form of meditation one *arrives* (without any help from the personal ego) at the "brilliant white light" after months and sometimes years of practice and dedicated effort.

One point about meditation that is of considerable importance is that visualized goals tend to take on an especially formidable power (for the good) when the visualization is simultaneously engaged in by several people (friends or therapy-mates) while they are either together in a group context or in their respective places of residence. If the later procedure is used, a specific time should be agreed upon and set aside by all group members. For example, it might be agreed that every night from 10:00 until 10:10 the entire group will stop whatever they are doing and intensely visualize a particular desired outcome for a predesignated group member. Or they might simultaneously visualize the person they are trying to help being suffused by a pale of powerful white light. Of course, the member selected would change from time to time so that each member would get his/her turn on many different occasions. This procedure can be followed even if one of the group members happens to be spending a few nights in another time zone. For example, if a member of a group which regularly meets in San Bruno, California, has to spend a few nights in New York, he/she would do the exercise from 1:00 AM to 1:10 AM—the equivalent of 10:00 PM to 10:10 PM Pacific Time.

Down through history systematic visualization has been practiced with often amazing results by witches and warlocks in their eleven-person covens. Today these methods are being disseminated by sales trainers and by university graduate schools of business administration. They are being taught to men in middle-management, often at considerable financial cost to employers. And their successful mastery has been found in many business-related research studies to clearly differentiate between people who "make it big" in their business careers, and those who manage to perform only adequately.

Recently these techniques have been taken over by certain quite successful oncologists (cancer specialists). The work of Dr. O. Carl Simonton and his wife Stephanie, at the Fort Worth Cancer Counseling Center, is rooted in training patients in the dedicated and persistent practicing of these techniques. Dr. David Bresler of the U.C.L.A. Pain Clinic, has also encouraged his patients to use these techniques—and with quite substantial success.

Systematic visualization is simply an issue of "mind over matter". It is a form of psychokinesis ("PK"), sometimes called "telekinesis". All matter including the human body is simply a form of energy that is vibrating at comparatively low rates. The concerted effort of, for example, eleven people all simultaneously focusing on the same goal, appears to do much to cause that goal to come to pass.

Of course, hard-nosed academics do not like to become involved in this subject. Many of them fear the ostracism of their colleagues. And others are just plain *"prejudiced"* against the thought of entertaining hypotheses pertinent to this and related subjects. A key indication that it *is* worth looking into, however, can be seen in the fact that so many highly successful business people swear by it. Amidst a group wherein success is measured almost entirely by monetary profit, it seems highly unlikely that systematic visualization would be dealt with at all if it did not have an impressive history of bringing about positive, measurable results. *Thought is a powerful energy form.*

Systematic visualization exercises which can be incorporated into practice-dating therapy include the following:

(1) For ten minutes at an agreed upon time each night each of the twelve members of a practice-dating group intensely visualizes in his/her mind's eye a particular fellow member happily and successfully "making it" with a member of the opposite sex. This visualization must be strongly felt *and believed* as well as seen and heard in the mind's eye and ear. The recipient of the exercise for a particular evening must simultaneously be involved in the visualization as well—on his or her own behalf.

(2) For ten minutes each night each group member sees in his/her mind's eye a powerful pale of red light suffusing the entire body, and especially the brain, of a preselected group member. Red is the color of energy in occult studies. And love-shy people are often melancholic or highly discouraged people who are

bogged down in the throes of psychoemotional inertia. Red light is therefore appropriate. After the red light is used for a while, the group may also use a powerful pale of green light to bring peace and freedom from anxiety, and then a powerful pale of white light.

(3) Each of the twelve members of a therapy group will be encouraged to systematically visualize on his/her own behalf at several different times each day. Each member will be asked to both see and feel himself/herself to be exactly the person he/she wishes to become—particularly in reference to happy and successful man-woman interaction. Thus, the self-image gradually comes to be reprogrammed. People tend to move towards becoming that which they intensely see, feel, hear, and believe in their mind's eye and ear.

As a final point, both regular meditation and systematic visualization must be seen as *therapeutic adjuncts ONLY*. It is important to stress this point because love-shys tend to be substantially less competent than most people at any and all forms of meditation. Through the use of the right audio-cassettes and/or books most love-shys can be easily convinced *on an intellectual level* of the worth of these approaches. However, these methods work best only when the user has fully incorporated his/her belief into his/her emotional gut essence. Simply put, the user must arrive at the point at which he fully and intensely believes with all his heart and soul that which he is directing himself to "see" in his mind's eye.

The practice-dating client cannot justifiably be criticized for failing to do these exercises properly. As long as he or she does them *at all*—this is all a therapist can reasonably ask. Accepting ideas and visions on an emotional level as well as on an intellectual level IS NOT a purely voluntary process. If it were purely voluntary, no other therapeutic exercise would be required to accomplish the desired end—not even practice-dating.

Thus, the various meditational techniques can be considered useful therapeutic adjuncts which can serve to catalyze therapeutic gains. A comprehensive therapeutic program for love-shys will use them. But program leaders will fully realize that such techniques cannot be placed at the nucleus or core of therapeutic emphasis. The indispensable *core* of a practice-dating therapy program is the *twice-weekly practice dates* which are regularly assigned by the therapeutic staff. *Nothing* can substitute for these. Everything else, especially the meditation exercises, should be considered mere aids which may to a greater or lesser extent operate to catalyze improvements.

Why Not Simply Use Commercial Dating Services?

At this point many readers may be wondering why commercial dating services could not be used as a form of self-administered practice-dating therapy. Today all major metropolitan areas are well supplied with dating services and, in the case of New York, with more traditional marriage bureaus as well. However, the owner-managers of these organizations do not have an easy "row to hoe". They are not to be envied!

There are three major reasons why commercial dating services cannot be counted upon to help in the remedying of male love-shyness. These reasons can be classified under the following headings: (1) gender ratio; (2) commercial vested interests; and (3) the psychoemotional handicaps endemic in love-shyness prevent most of its victims from taking proper advantage of dating services even when they do join. A sizable proportion of the clientele of most dating services *is already composed* of love-shy men. And as indicated in chapter five, the cooperation of 22 percent of the older love-shys studied for this book together with 12 percent of the younger ones, was obtained through the help of a New York area dating service.

The Gender Ratio Problem

The management of dating services do not like to talk about this issue. And in point of fact the problem of imbalanced gender ratios is not really their fault anyway. Imbalanced gender ratios and the inability to do anything about it (other than develop better and more expensive advertisements) constitutes the *number one* reason why so many dating services go bankrupt and fold. It is also the main reason why dating services usually require a man to be at least 21 years of age (and sometimes 24) before they will accept his enrollment. Thus, dating services can be of no help to love-shy high school and undergraduate college and university males because most such people are below the minimum age required for joining.

For the age-group of 21 to 25-year olds, there are typically anywhere from *five to twenty times* as many male members as there are female members. And this is true even in a society that is often alleged to have many more marriage-oriented women than marriage oriented men! Further, this highly problematical gender-ratio situation is aggravated by the fact that ninety percent or more of love-shy men want their "love-mate" to be at least two or three years *younger* than themselves. Indeed, older love-shy men often want their women to be *twenty* or more years *younger* than themselves. And they want women who are both

(a) physically attractive with the "long hair and pretty face", and (b) both willing and desirous of "mothering" or "nursing" them out of their love-shyness-based inhibitions.

Unlike some contemporary psychologists, I believe that it *is* normal and healthy for a man to prefer the "nurturing, maternal type" of woman. I believe that it is unnecessary as well as undesirable for a therapist to try to dissuade a man from these predilections. Nevertheless, the facts are plain. Whereas there are plenty of attractive, warm, nurturing, motherly women "out there", this type definitely *does not* do business with commercial dating services—especially as far as the 18 to 30 age group is concerned. Indeed, such women are "taken up" fast (during their late teens and early twenties) by the non-shy as such women are very much "in demand"; and the demand far exceeds the supply.

Most commercial dating services will accept women as young as 18. But very few women this young ever enroll. Even so, most love-shy men even in their 40s want to date attractive, "single-never-married" women in their late teens and twenties. And many such older men cite as justification for their preference the fact that they would still like to have one or two children, and birth complications are much more likely to accrue to women over 30. Sad though it might be, most love-shy men past the age of 35 will probably never be able to become fathers even if they do eventually manage to obtain a woman. Of course, this may ultimately result in less human suffering if it helps to cause the inhibition and low anxiety threshold genes to die out.

Imbalanced gender ratios create other serious problems as well. And via adverse "word of mouth" advertising among female friendship groups the imbalance is preserved or made even worse because women become motivated against joining. For example, each month the typical dating service sends out the names, addresses and telephone numbers of the recommended "matches". Typically an 18 to 24-year old women will receive between 30 and 50 names for each month during which she remains a member. The typical 21 to 24-year old man will receive *only one or two*. Occasionally if he is lucky he may be given three; but never more than that.

The net result of this is that the home telephones of 18 to 24-year old women ring endlessly. The women and their roommates or families are virtually "driven up the walls" by this situation. And in short order they become irritated, angry and psychologically alienated from the whole business. Often they end up having their names removed from the list, or they advise each male caller that "they are already engaged", or some other "bullshit" lie.

Meanwhile most of the male members become angry and upset. They had spent their good money on a dating service; and the one or two women whose names they received this month do not even want to meet them. Quite understandably many men become quite angry, and they call the dating service office and accuse the staff of sending them an outdated list. Some of the women assert to their male callers that they had "dropped out" of the dating service six months earlier. "Bullshit", *yes*! But sometimes the inexperienced and severely love-shy man is not entirely certain about that. In any case, highly reticent love-shy men are ill-prepared to deal with this sort of situation over the phone. And many of them do not call the women whose names they receive at all. Instead they write letters to the women—most of which go unanswered. And when the letters are answered, they too are likely to say something like "I am going with someone now", or "I am already engaged", or even "I am already married"!

Another problem accruing from the gender-ratio imbalance is the surfeit of divorced women who do business with dating service firms. Given their "starry-eyed" romantic attitudes, most love-shy men do not want to date a divorced woman. They figure that if she divorced one man she can just as easily divorce again. Such women are seen by the love-shy as "expecting far too much". But a more important issue, I believe, is the love-shys' very strong need for a nurturing love-mate who will stick by them "through thick and thin", and who will never reject them. Many love-shys view the prospect of remaining single all their lives as less terrible than the thought of marrying and then being victimized by divorce.

In short, love-shy men want someone who will fall in love with them and give them unconditional acceptance. Love-shy men fear argumentation and friction. They are highly romantic and in need of the sort of young women who would never even have a chance to think about joining a dating service. Again, the type of girl the typical love-shy man wants is quite likely to have already been won by somebody by the time she gets to be 19 or 20.

In sum, for men in the 35 to 44 year age range the gender ratio in most commercial dating firms is about 50:50. And for men who are 45 years of age or older there are actually more women than men in the typical dating service membership. On the other hand, for men in the 25 to 29 year age range there are usually about ten men for every one woman; and in the 30 to 34 year old age range there are about three times as many male members as there are female members. Thus, at least as far as younger age men are concerned we have here another indication that men seem to want and need woman a great deal more than women want or need men. Despite what demographers say about there currently being a shortage of men in the younger, marriage-oriented ages, this is certainly *not* reflected in the membership rolls of commercial dating services! IF ANY WOMAN UNDER THE AGE OF 35 IS *REALLY* SERIOUS ABOUT WANTING A HUSBAND, SHE HAS MERELY TO COMMISSION THE SERVICES OF A COMMERCIAL DATING ESTABLISHMENT AND SHE WILL BE INUNDATED WITH MORE MEN THAN SHE CAN HANDLE!

Commercial Vested Interests

At the outset I must say that I have no opposition or hostility to business. Business has often been thoughtlessly maligned by naive pseudo-intellectuals who would not be enjoying one-fourth of their current surfeit of luxuries if it were not for business and the free enterprise system. However, all businesses must show a profit in order to stay afloat. And in the case of dating services, the showing of an adequate financial return is often very difficult indeed. Of course, making their services better, servicing the needs of clients better, and advertising better, all represent viable ways of improving things. Unfortunately, dating services have not as yet been able to figure out how to successfully engineer the attainment of these desirable goals. A dating service proprietor may launch his/her business with a highly conscientious, deeply caring attitude. Yet almost always this attitude will be shot through to shreds by the everyday trials of running the business and keeping it afloat.

I have interviewed the proprietors of six different dating services located on the east and west coasts. And these proprietors seem to agree that as many as 30 percent (almost one-third) of their male clients are "pathologically shy" or severely love-shy. Most of these proprietors would like to spend some time personally counseling their love-shy male clients. But none of them are equipped from the standpoint of either education or time to be able to do this. All would like to hire a professional counseling staff. But none has the resources to hire *so much as one* university trained clinical psychologist, psychiatric social worker, or counselor. The hard financial realities of managing a business obviate providing any one client with very much time or attention.

Related to this is the problem of *vested interests*. Every business and, indeed, all human beings have these. And a person would have to be a veritable "Jesus Christ" not to take these interests into account in the conducting of his/her affairs. In the case of dating service owners, care is taken to keep prospective members "in the dark" about such problems as gender ratio imbalance, shortages of single, never married women, women members prematurely discontinuing their memberships, the difficulty of actually getting a date, etc. If dating service owners were frank about these matters, most of them would no longer even have a business! Further, if owners either hired a counseling staff or endeavored to conduct such counseling themselves, they would be taking much needed time away from the mechanics of running their businesses. Moreover, even if they did provide some counseling to the love-shy, the realities of the dating service business make it very unlikely that *real help* could be accorded. In essence, the severely love-shy male would be no closer to the attainment of his goal even if his dating service did endeavor to provide him with some counseling.

Finally, dating service proprietors seem to be exasperated by the behavior (more accurately the *non-behavior*) of the chronic love-shy. The reasons why will become clear in the next section.

Barriers Posed by the Love-Shys' Psychoemotional Handicaps

Sooner or later many of even the most extremely love-shy men sign up with one or more dating services. Some readers may have difficulty understanding this inasmuch as "dates" obtained through such organizations are essentially blind dates—and blind dates should, everything else being equal, prove very anxiety-provoking for the love-shy.

The gist of the matter is that dating services provide an excuse for calling a woman. Again, love-shy men, like all people with inborn inhibition, hve a very difficult time handling socially ambiguous situations. In order for a man to telephone someone whom he sees at work every day (and whom he believes he would like to get to know from a romantic standpoint), necessitates providing an explanation. Immediately upon picking up the receiver the woman will ask "who is this?" and "why are you calling?" The second question (indeed, the very thought of it) arouses great anxiety in love-shy men. What, indeed, can they say? How can they admit that they have a romantic interest in the person? And how can they defend this personal interest?

The dating service bypasses this highly anxiety-provoking step. The love-shy man merely has to respond: "I received your name and telephone number from the ABC Dating Service, and I guess you received mine as well." I believe it is because the dating service *bypasses* this ambiguity-laden and highly anxiety-provoking step that it attracts so many love-shy men. Again, as many as 30 percent of the male clients of dating services are severely love-shy.

Sooner or later almost all urban and suburban men who are not hooked into cohesive kinship networks and/or friendship networks will enroll in some sort of dating service. And, of course, *one* reason why women are much less likely than young men to enroll is that a much

higher percent of women *are* hooked into kinship and friendship networks. Women's friendship groups do not require the competitive success that is normally called for in male friendship groups.

A key problem for many love-shy dating service customers is that
they do not have the nerve to make the telephone calls. Some of them
cope with this problem by introducing themselves *by letter* to the women
to whom their dating service had assigned them. And occasionally they
do succeed in getting a date this way. But more often than not their
letter (often a very lengthy one) goes unanswered. Thus, the love-shy
man's confession of severe shyness turns most women off. This is especially likely to be the case for any woman who is already inundated with
telephone calls from men who are not shy—or at least not too shy to
make a telephone call.

A related problem for the love-shy is that most dating services
provide their women clients with the option of listing *only* their name
and telephone number. In essence, the information which the love-shy
man receives by mail very often does not include an address. And when
the address is missing he obviously cannot mail a letter to the girl. Some
dating services permit a woman to give out *only* her telephone number;
in these cases neither the name or the address is provided to male
"matches". This "social ambiguity" scares the hell out of severely love-
shy men; and they are forced to wait for a "match" which includes a
name as well as a street address.

Exacerbating the situation is the fact that very few love-shy men
keep a telephone in their private apartments. In fact, this is one trait of
the love-shy which exasperates most dating service managers. Of course,
love-shy men are not always too shy about using their work phone to
register complaints about not receiving a street address. Inasmuch as
dating service managers and telephone clerks are untrained from the
standpoint of understanding love-shyness, they are seldom in a position
to be of any help. Their attitude is usually: "If you can't call her, there's
nothing we can do." There is nothing in the dating service contract
which stipulates that street addresses must be given out. Of course,
some love-shys write a letter anyway, and mail it to the dating service
for forwarding. Assuming that the dating service does forward these
letters, it is fair to say that such forwarded mail is virtually never answered
by the women receiving it.

Dating services cannot and do not provide the special type of coeducational group therapy that invariably accompanies and is integral to
practice-dating therapy programs. As such, dating services cannot begin
to deal with the sort of love-shyness problems which develop as the so-
called "second plateau" of a man-woman relationship is approached by
a client. Few love-shy clients ever ask an assigned "match" for a second

date; and this is true even when they like her. Love-shy men tend to be extremely awkward at the end of a date. They do not know how to smoothly conclude it, or how to deal with the expectation that they ought to kiss the girl. Most love-shy men have never kissed a woman in their lives. On rare occasion a love-shy man will succeed in getting three or four dates in a row from the same girl. But his severe inhibition and inability to "be himself"—to cope with the ambiguity of what to talk about once all the superficialities have been covered—is enough to keep him from either telephoning or even writing the girl for additional meetings. Again, this tends to be true even when he very much likes the girl and would attempt to continue seeing her if he had the sense of personal freedom to be able to do so.

There is an interesting paradox here that was commented upon by two of the dating service owners I interviewed. Love-shy men are often *extremely* talkative when they are on a first date with someone whom they think they like. Indeed, they are sometimes talkative to the extent of appearing to dominate the interaction. However, their "conversation" might more aptly be described as "lecturing"; the woman usually ends up saying very little. Often times the woman may at first enjoy the fact that she is dating a very talkative and seemingly intelligent man. She may even have trouble "seeing" him as shy because of the way he always seems to have a never-ending series of things to say, and because of the way he *appears* to dominate the conversation.

But by the time the fourth date has concluded he is likely to be "scared shitless" about contacting the same woman for an additional meeting. This severe diffidence is obviously not due to any unwillingness or disinclination towards making a permanent commitment. A permanent commitment is what love-shy men want more than anything else. The problem is that they are emotionally incapable of dealing with the "second plateau". And the dating service staff are business entrepreneurs; they have no way of helping the shys over this most disconcerting "hump". (Of course, it would doubtless eventually become *very good for business* if these entrepreneurs did endeavor to figure out an effective way to help!)

A Corroborating Study

Up to now surprisingly few research studies have been conducted on commercial dating firms. However, what little work has been done tends to support the conclusions which I have delineated in this chapter. Probably the best study heretofore to become available was published in 1972, by K. M. Wallace. Wallace both established and maintained an introduction service for research purposes only. He kept his club going for ten years and over that period of time attracted some 6,033 members.

Wallace was able to compare and contrast his membership with the general population on several important dimensions. To be specific, he found quite significant differences between his club members and a comparison group of nonmembers on the *sociability* and *inhibition* factors. The club members were more likely to be quiet, nonaggressive, and shy, and therefore unable to compete effectively in the dating and mating game of our society. On the other hand, Wallace also found that his club members were better educated than the analogous group of nonmembers that had been drawn from the general population. Not surprisingly, his club had attracted many more male members than female members. And indeed, the sociability, shyness and education differences between the club members and the comparison group of nonmembers were much greater for the males than for the females.

Attractiveness and Education

It came as somewhat of a surprise to me that most of the love-shy men with dating service experience had *not* been displeased with the physical attractiveness level of the "matches" to whom they had been assigned. While there are obviously many formidable barriers which operate to impede dating services from helping severely love-shy men, it is heartening to learn that a dearth of feminine pulchritude does not appear to be one of these barriers.

Secondly, all of the dating service proprietors with whom I spoke agreed that their male clients had well above average educations. In addition, the education level completed by the typical love-shy male client appears to be even higher than that which had been completed by the average male client who is not conspicuously love-shy. Similarly, all of these proprietors agreed with my own conclusion that love-shy men tend to be underachievers (status inconsistents) when it comes to annual income and job prestige level. Thus, in contrast to the majority of male dating service clients, love-shy clients typically have income and job prestige levels that are substantially inferior to their own levels of completed education.

All in all these data suggest that women are not likely to be particularly impressed by a man's academic degrees or by his advanced academic and intellectual attainments. (In fact, there is evidence that the wives of highly educated husbands tend to have poorer self-images than the wives of men with more moderate educations.) Younger love-shy readers, in particular, need to pay heed to this point. A major motivation among love-shy men for obtaining an advanced education is that women will be favorably impressed. The hard, cold reality of the matter is that women tend to feel most at home with men who are relaxed and natural, with a good sense of humor, and who can communicate on a spontaneous *"feeling"* level.

Love-shy men are commonly perceived by their dating service "matches" as being quite tense and nervous. They are also seen as being too serious, and as "all head and no heart". Thus, the years of academic study put in by many love-shy men may well serve to aggravate these women-alienating tendencies by developing a trained incapacity for spontaneous, natural, humorous, relaxed socializing. Inasmuch as love-shy men experience virtually no social life at all at the universities they attend, their behavioral and thought tendencies tend to become geared almost exclusively towards the serious, towards that which is very "deep" and abstract, and towards personal problem areas, most of which they are too shy to discuss.

Perhaps some love-shys pursue an extensive amount of higher education as a way of finding some sense of personal identity and of securing a range of personal self-satisfactions which most people secure through informal social interaction with friends and family. Most people establish a firm sense of personal identity through informal friendly interaction. Those who lack informal friendships may seek their sense of personal self-worth through achievements in higher education.

The American system of education is in many ways destructively one-sided and ridiculously imbalanced in its emphasis. It develops man's intellect yet totally ignores the fact that psychoemotional and spiritual growth are also needed for internal harmony and for the ability to compete *and to USE* attained intellectual awareness in the service of both self and society. Thus, people absolutely require a certain level of social self-confidence and of interpersonal finesse. It has often been said that highly educated people lack ordinary "horse sense". I think that what they *really* lack is *psychoemotional integration*. Practice-dating therapy can do much to remedy this lack of psychoemotional integration in a substantial proportion of poorly balanced male students—*namely the love-shy*.

Leaving the matter of remedying these deficits to commercial dating services is obviously not going to work. As per the material reviewed in this and the preceding chapter, practice-dating therapy quite clearly appears to be the best and only truly sensible remedy for severe love-shyness. The time has arrived for taking action geared toward developing viable practice-dating programs throughout the United States, and making these available to people of all ages who are in need.

Self-Image Psychology as a Therapeutic Adjunct

This book has stressed the *biological* basis of love-shyness. And most contemporary writers continue to assume that self-image psychology is incompatible with a biologically based point of view. But rather than being mutually exclusive, I believe that these two positions complement each other and provide for a better balanced and more accurate understanding of love-shyness than could be arrived at from adherence to either position alone. The purpose of this section is to delineate the key principles of self-image psychology, and to show how they effectively complement the biological viewpoint that I have so strongly stressed throughout this book.

Maxwell Maltz, one of the great leaders of contemporary psychology, has labeled the self-image *"psychology's single most important discovery this century"*. Of course, the self-image has always been with us. But it has taken until comparatively recently for modern man to become mindful of its enormous importance for shaping and determining the quality of all aspects of our lives.

The Key Principles

Let us imagine two levels of thinking: the *judge* and the *robot*. The "judge" represents the *conscious* level of the mind. It is responsible for collecting information from the environment, putting it into the mind's memory bank, and making rational decisions. In contrast, the "robot" represents the *subconscious* level of thinking. And among its major responsibilities are (1) the storage of information in the so-called *memory bank* of the mind, and (2) goal-seeking. Indeed, in certain highly significant respects the subconscious mind *is* the memory bank, and it operates very much like a computer.

Now, like a computer the subconscious mind or "robot" *cannot tell the difference between what is right or wrong, good or bad, false or true information.* Like a computer it is fundamentally *without any intelligence* of its own. Like a computer it cannot think for itself. It must depend totally upon what is programmed into it.

The information storage and goal-seeking functions of the subconscious mind can be compared to a robot auto-pilot. And as we know, auto-pilots are devices which can be programmed to seek a target. The torpedo and the ballistic missile are good examples of this. Both are guided by highly sophisticated electronic systems that seek a target unerringly through the use of feedback. The human brain and mind operate in very much the same way.

Thus, the *judge* part of the human mind cannot make a decision without first clearing that decision with the *robot*. The "robot" checks its memory bank (which contains all the true *and false* information that up to that time had been programmed into it), and it then relays that information back to the "judge" for action. Of course, it would logically seem natural that a person's "judge" would control his "robot" in a kind of master-slave relationship. But unfortunately, *JUST THE REVERSE IS TRUE! The subconscious "robot" controls the conscious "judge" level of thinking!* Action frequently takes place without consultation with the "judge". But no action can ever take place without reference to the computer "robot" (including all the substantive content of the *memory* of that computer).

Every moment of every day we program our "robot" self-image to work either for us or against us. Since like a computer it is only a mechanism having no "judging" function, it strives to meet the objectives and goals that we set before it, whether positive or negative, true or false, right or wrong. Its most basic function is to follow instructions based upon previous inputs, just like a computer reading its tape and responding automatically.

Contemporary behavioral scientists are pretty much in agreement that a person's "robot" subconscious is not capable of distinguishing between actual experience and that which is vividly imagined as a result of strongly felt fears and anxieties. Thus, a person's subconscious "robot computer" stores emotional fantasies as though they were his/her own reality. Many of a person's everyday decisions and behaviors are based upon information that has been stored in the subconscious "robot computer" as truth. Much of this information is merely a figment of a person's imagination that is shaded and colored by his or her current environment. In sum, to a greater or lesser extent *we are all slaves to our subconscious computer robots*. And according to this viewpoint, few people have more fully and totally succumbed to this slavery than the chronically and intractably love-shy.

One of the especially noteworthy properties of self-image psychology is that it underscores the enormous power and flexibility of the human mind. As a case in point, there are certain Pacific Ocean societies wherein at certain times during the year *everyone* walks barefoot across approximately fifty feet of red hot coals. These coals hover between 800 and 1,200 degrees Farenheit on ceremonial occasions. And yet tribesmen ranging from very young children to the elderly walk barefoot across the hot coals without (1) experiencing any pain whatsoever, and (2) without any tissue damage of any sort accruing to the heels or soles of the feet.

The "fire walkers" have been extensively studied by anthropologists, journalists, media people, physical scientists, etc. And there can be no question about the fact that these people actually do go through their ceremony without experiencing any pain or tissue damage. How is this accomplished? How could such a phenomenon be "humanly possible"? The answer seems to be that everyone in these "fire walker" societies is presented with a consistent set of messages virtually from the time of birth. Children of these societies are never presented with any contradictory set of messages. In essence, there is never *any* reason for *any* of these people to doubt their capacity to walk barefoot over the hot coals during the designated ceremonial occasions. These peoples had always been conditioned ("*programmed*", if you prefer) to believe that the Gods would uphold them from any pain or harm as long as they followed certain long-standing customs according to tradition.

To the self-image psychologist *socialization is programming*; and it is also a highly potent form of *hypnosis*, especially when the messages programmed are clear and consistent—in essence, when each elder or teacher programs (hypnotizes) the *same* message. Quite similar to Spiritualists, many self-image psychologists believe that each and every human being contains an element of God. They believe that if the individual is programmed (hypnotized) into trusting the God within, the accomplishments that can be effected stagger the imagination.

Of course, some amazing things have been accomplished in our own society using plain, ordinary hypnosis. For example, any person who is amenable to deep hypnosis can be rendered fully refractory to pain as well as to tissue damage. Some people are capable of hypnotizing themselves in the dentist's chair, and of not feeling any pain at all—even though the dentist had administered no anesthetic. Others can program themselves into having an out-of-the-body experience while the dentist is working, and thus avoid pain in that way.

A person can be placed into a very deep trance (*if* he is amenable), and he can be told that an ice cube is going to be placed into the palm of his left hand—when in fact a red hot half-dollar piece is placed into the palm of his hand. Upon receiving the red hot half-dollar (after it had been taken from atop a red hot grill on a stove), the person will characteristically enfold his fingers around it as though it were a real ice cube.

After such an experiment has been completed it is observed that no tissue damage of any kind had been done to the person's hand. Contrariwise, if the hypnotized person is handed an ice cube and told that he is receiving a red hot half-dollar piece, *then real pain* plus a severe burn blister will immediately happen.

Celebrated psychic Jack Schwartz is able to force a long dagger right through his arm, and then remove it, without causing himself any pain or tissue damage of any kind. Indeed, he does this all the time at his shows in Europe. And, of course, Watergate conspirator Gordon Liddy developed some notoriety for his ability to hold his hand over an open flame—without experiencing any pain or suffering tissue damage.

Hundreds of other fascinating examples could be cited. The message of all of this material is that *under propitious circumstances* the body can be made the servant of the mind. The body is nothing more than a very dense form of energy which can be, *under the right circumstances*, shielded from harm by the much higher form of energy represented by the mind. For example, in the case of the "fire walkers" the bioplasmic body (which suffuses the physical body) creates a temporary shield on the heels and soles of the feet which serves to obviate both pain and tissue damage—temporarily, as per the serenely held belief system of the person. The same thing happens to the palm of the hand of the hypnotized person who receives the red hot half-dollar piece.

Spiritualists delight in citing certain of Christ's statements which can be found in the Matthew, Mark, Luke, and John sections of the New Testament; e.g., "According to your faith, so be it unto you"; "As a man thinks in his heart, so is he"; "All things are possible to him that believeth"; and "Greater things than these shall ye do". Thus, a serene but deeply held conviction that what one envisions will come to pass, will almost always cause it to indeed happen. The problem for severely love-shy men is that they find it very difficult to be serene and comfortable about their beliefs and convictions. They can accept all of this material on an intellectual level, but they are incapable of dealing with it on a gut-emotional level—*where it counts*. And as any hypnotist will agree, severely love-shy people are among the most *non*-hypnotizable parts of the human population. They are simply too tense to simply "let go and let God".

Blending Self-Image Psychology with the Biological Perspective

Self-image psychologists strongly stress the idea that WE *choose* what goes into the robot computer of our subconscious minds. In essence, WE choose to do the original programming. We choose to permit the governing and goal-seeking information to get into our subconscious minds in the first place.

As author of this book it is my position that this is *only partly true*. Much of the most potent and influential programming of our "robot subconscious computers" goes on while we are still very young and impressionable. Thus, a young child is in no position *to personally choose* the information about himself and his environment which will manage to get recorded on the "computer tape" of his subconscious "robot computer" mind. His parents, significant adults, and childhood bullies are the ones who do this sort of choosing, never the small child himself. Small children are quite emotionally dependent (and this is rooted in biological dependency) upon parents, and this sort of near-total emotional dependency is a prerequisite for the most thoroughgoing socialization. Thus, emotional dependency constitutes the optimal set of circumstances for the programming of minds (*deep hypnosis*) which is what the *socialization* process is all about. Young children are maximally suggestible; and this suggestibility provides the most perfect fertilizer for the hypnotizing and programming of minds and of mental sets (which can swiftly become quite intractably rigid.)

When the messages of parents and of childhood bullies are consistent, they will inevitably cause the programming and hypnotizing of impressionable minds, no matter how ridiculously false these messages might be. In essence, the socially inhibited child (with genetically rooted inhibition and low anxiety threshold) often receives a one-sided set of self-labels. And without his even being aware of it, these self-labels are easily programmed into the robot computer tape of his subconscious mind.

Secondly, the social stimulus value of a young boy has a very strong influence upon the nature and tenor of the messages that are likely to be fed to him over time. It is certain that boys who because of inborn inhibition and low anxiety threshold do not like "rough and tumble" play are likely to be accorded a steady stream of stingingly disparaging messages about themselves. And many of these are bound to get programmed into the subconscious (computer tape) mind. An adult can use his rational intellect to censor out mostly all disparaging messages. An impressionable child is unfortunatly not in a position to be able to do this. In addition, there is likely to be a consistency in the messages an impressionable child receives which far surpasses any consistency in the messages an adult receives from different people in his or her life.

Theoretically it is perfectly possible for a male with high inborn inhibition and low native anxiety threshold to develop a fully healthy self-image—*and* to be totally *un*afflicted with shyness. Unfortunately, within the context of contemporary American society it is extremely unlikely that such an eventuality could come to pass. A *girl* with such inborn elastic limitations might well develop a strongly self-confident disposition. And a boy born among the Zuni or Hopi Indian tribes might similarly do so. But a *boy* born within the mainstream of American society is highly unlikely to do so.

Native, inborn attributes all have their social stimulus values. And these social stimulus values interact with the pre-existing biases of people; and they thus call forth social reactions—including disparaging or positive labeling. These labels create strong *visualizations* which get indelibly programmed into the robot computer of the subconscious mind. Thus what starts out as an *elastic* inborn limit swiftly becomes crystallized and "etched in cement".

Of course, of equal importance in explaining the rigid, intractable behavior (or *non*-behavior) of the love-shy is the low native anxiety threshold itself. Moralists and self-image psychologists commonly insist that a love-shy person "could take the bull by the horns" *if he wanted to*, and as a rational adult discard all the trash (false beliefs) from the computer tape of his subconscious mind. Thus, he "could" engage in a rational *house cleaning* operation. Given that the love-shy person "could" do this, why doesn't he?

The problem is that the emotional part of man's mind is far stronger than the rational, intellectual part. And this is a fact that has long been supported by physiological psychologists. The emotions serve as the *cement* which keep both false and true ideas intractably welded to the computer tape of the subconscious mind. Further, the emotional bond between a young child and his parents (the precondition of emotional dependency), not only facilitates socialization, but it also causes all of the values and ideas (both false and true) which parents impart to become *indelibly imprinted* in the child's computer memory bank (subconscious mind). Thus, the emotions serve as a kind of *cement* which effectively keep certain ideas in an individual's mind for life.

Unfortunately, those with very low native anxiety thresholds have far more of this *cement glue* than do those with the advantage of higher native anxiety thresholds. From a purely intellectual standpoint (the "rational judge" part of the mind), the love-shy man is as capable as anybody else of separating what is true from what is false. He is also just as capable as anyone of determining which ideas need to be discarded from the computer tape that is stored in his subconscious mind.

As a poignant illustration of how powerful this "cement" can get, more than one love-shy man told me that he feared the experiencing of anxiety worse than he feared death itself. Many of the love-shys described anxiety feelings as being of the most overwhelmingly excruciating nature—as something which must be avoided even more scrupulously than death itself. Moralists, rational-emotive psychologists, and self-image psychologists, often see anxiety as something which is quite ephemoral. But to those with low native anxiety thresholds, anxiety is as overwhelmingly and stingingly real as anything of a tangible nature ever could be.

Just as inborn attributes all have their good or bad social stimulus value and call forth social reactions that are in conformance with those values, a person's inborn anxiety threshold *itself* places a highly effective albeit elastic limit upon any rational housecleaning he might consciously (intellectually) want to do of the content of the robot computer of his subconscious mind. If the false information (together with all the "cement" represented by the very low native anxiety threshold) could be removed from the subconscious computer tape, the love-shy person's problems would clearly be solved. Unfortunately, this "housecleaning" appears to be feasible only for shys with reasonably high native anxiety thresholds.

Finally, a person's general level of self-esteem is always a byproduct of how closely the following two factors agree:

(1) the person's behaviors and behavioral omissions;
(2) how the person thinks *and feels* deep down in his "gut" about his behaviors and behavioral omissions.

When these two factors are in reasonable harmony the person will have a healthy level of self-esteem. To the extent that there are marked discrepancies between these two factors, then to that extent the person will be bogged down by an unsatisfactory general level of self-esteem.

Among love-shy men the discrepancies between these two factors are very formidable indeed. And these discrepancies are in large measure responsible for the crystallization of what might otherwise have remained the *elastic limits* of inhibition and low anxiety threshold. Thus, inborn limits which had started out flexible lose their flexibility; and they become reified into the behavioral manifestations of intractable, life-long love-shyness. The steady stream of grossly disparaging labeling from parents, peers and teachers has a great deal to do with the ultimate reification (hardening) of these elastic limits.

In sum, in recent years self-image psychology has had a great deal to say about the problem of shyness and about how to remedy it. Many of the ideas eminating from this perspective are quite sound. And they deserve serious consideration by anyone interested in the love-shyness problem. But there are some pitfalls in this perspective as well, four of which are of especial importance: (1) self-image psychologists operate under the assumption that practically everything is learned; they ignore research evidence which pertains to inborn, biologically based human differences, particularly as these relate to personality. Second (2), they often assume that a person is responsible for everything that gets into his/her "robot computer" subconscious mind. Thirdly (3), self-image psychologists typically *quite wrongly* assume that the content of the subconscious robot computer mind is amenable to the workings of the rational intellect. And fourthly (4), self-image psychology enthusiasts tend to be ultra-rightist social-political thinkers. Blindly and with childlike innocence they enthusiastically give assent to the creed: "If it is to be it is up to me!"

Self-Image Therapy

Therapy based upon self-image psychology involves the systematic teaching of two key activities: (1) visualization, and (2) affirmation-making. At the outset I must stress that what I am about to recommend should never be applied to the love-shy *by itself* as the exclusive mode of therapy. When used along with nothing else, visualization and affirmation-making invariably fail to help the severely love-shy. On the other hand, when these techniques are *combined* into a comprehensive practice-dating therapy package, they will most probably work to facilitate therapeutic progress.

Affirmation-Making and Self-Talk

We all talk to ourselves almost endlessly each and every moment of each and every day. In fact, it is very difficult not to talk to ourselves. This is one reason why meditation is so difficult for most adults to learn. Meditation is difficult because it requires stilling and quieting the conscious mind to the point where self-talk stops. It requires bypassing the personal ego to the point where the subconscious mind can be reached.

All words contain both a denotation as well as a connotation. In addition, words almost invariably conjure up images *along with emotional feelings*. Reality is in very large measure subjective and socially constructed. Each one of us constructs his/her own reality by and through his/her regular patterns of self-talk and affective visualizations.

More importantly, there is a remarkably powerful telekinetic power to the mind and to the thought (energy) patterns which it broadcasts. Thought tends to create form, and we tend to become that which we think about most of the time. A key common denominator universally present among the pathologically love-shy is *negative self-talk*. To be sure, the love-shy did not originate the various negative, self-disparaging messages they continually give themselves. Such negative ideas originated from people outside the self. Nevertheless, these negative ideas and thought patterns constantly create negative self-talk. As the love-shy do not have friends to *distract* negative thinking patterns, the negative self-talk tends to be much more constantly ongoing for the love-shy than it is for other types of so-called "negative thinkers".

Hence, an important component of therapy for the love-shy is a *reversal* of these negative self-talk tendencies. Again, this is *NOT* as central a component of therapy as the practice-dating exercises. Indeed, practice-dating can accomplish a very great deal just from the standpoint of *distracting* a love-shy man from his negative thinking habits. With practice-dating he will not have so much time on his hands!

Nevertheless, if we do indeed tend to become what we think about, it is clear that negative self-talk must be replaced by positive self-talk. *"Faith"* is a double-edged sword that can benefit or severely hurt a person. If Christ's statement "according to your faith, so be it unto you" is true, then the love-shy must be conditioned to replace negative faith with positive faith. Rare indeed is the love-shy person who can accomplish this sort of goal on his own. This is why support groups are so important. This is why I have stressed the desirability of developing Shys Anonymous groups, practice-dating therapy groups, coed scouting groups, etc. In order to muster the necessary self-discipline and ego strength for accomplishing necessary exercises, a love-shy person needs to be enmeshed in meaningful social support/friendship groups (coeducational in nature) which he sees and interacts with regularly.

The first step in mastering positive self-talk is that of learning and using positive self-affirmations. The most enormously successful business people have been intensively studied by empirical researchers. And one of the things which better than 90 percent of them have in common is the frequent use of positive self-affirmation and positive self-talk.

Affirmations need not be objectively correct, and they must *always* be stated in the *present tense*. There is no time or space at the higher vibrational levels of energy. The following statements illustrate positive self-affirmations which self-image therapists might prescribe for the severely love-shy:

1. I am already very successful with women.
2. Attractive women compete for my companionship.
3. I am a happy-go-lucky person with a genuine and much appreciated sense of humor.
4. I am deeply and sincerely loved by a woman who matters greatly to me.
5. Women respond in a positive, friendly manner to all of my friendly overtures.
6. Women enjoy being in my company.

7. I am an excellent conversationalist with women.
8. I am always able to assert myself in a friendly, courteous way whenever I am around women.
9. I am always relaxed and completely able to enjoy myself whenever I am in the company of women.

Each word of statements such as the foregoing contains an *affective* element. This is commonly referred to as the *connotation*. And with each repetition of a statement, the feeling tone of that statement gradually reprograms the self-image. All of this takes time to happen. The love-shy need to be facilitated in their efforts to do the homework assignments. They need to be helped towards the development of ego strength/self-discipline. Audio-cassette programs of the sort I recommended earlier can be of considerable help as far as the positive affirmations are concerned. But above all the love-shy require good therapists and a network of meaningful friends (support groups).

For love-shy clients who are familiar with the positive mind science movement and who have already made some progress towards meditating regularly, some affirmations can be prefaced and concluded with the following standard words and phrases which I have italicized below. This approach is best pursued immediately upon concluding one's period of meditation:

"Through the power of the universal God-mind within me, I affirm that I am already popular and well-liked by women. *And for this realization I give thanks. And so it is."*

It is further important that the love-shy be conditioned to stop their thought processes in their tracks whenever they catch themselves engaged in negative self-talk. Self-talk, whether it is positive or negative, operates to program the robot computer of the (subconscious mind) self-image. Again, the self-image is the mechanism laden in the subconscious memory bank which governs all aspects of our lives. When the self-image is positive it leads to positive outcomes. When the self-image is negative, failure inevitably dominates the person's life.

Because it is quite difficult for love-shy men to get into the habit of controlling their thoughts in a positive direction, cassette programs have been devised which can be repeatedly played during a person's free moments. It is just when a person is relatively free of responsibility and in a state of reverie that self-talk normally wields its deepest impact upon the shaping of the subconscious robot self-image. In self-image therapy the shy client is asked to keep a positive self-talk cassette playing during as many such times as possible, especially during the first several months of therapy.

For readers who are interested, the best such cassette program is titled WINNING FROM WITHIN: THE COMPLETE AUDIOCASSETTE ENCYCLOPEDIA OF WINNING SELF-TALK, by Shad Helmstetter. It can be obtained through the Nightengale-Conant Corporation, at 7300 North Lehigh Avenue, Chicago, IL 60648. Three highly recommended six-cassette programs of a more *instructional* nature are THE PSYCHOLOGY OF WINNING, by Denis Waitley, THE NEUROPSYCHOLOGY OF ACHIEVEMENT, by Steven DeVore, and THE PSYCHOLOGY OF ACHIEVEMENT, by Brian Tracy. (See the bibliography at the end of this book for more information.)

Visualization

Seeing things in one's mind's eye is the second major component of self-image psychotherapy. In visualization the love-shy client is asked to engage in mental rehearsals of informal social interactions with women. Thus, the love-shy client will "see" himself actively engaged in a pleasant conversation with an attractive women. He both *sees* and *feels* himself to be relaxed and comfortable during the encounter. And he sees himself handling the situation successfully and in a way that is perceived by the women involved as winningly charming.

There are many biases in the scientific community against the idea of visualization having any real effect for the good. However, the research data which have heretofore become available overwhelmingly support the efficacy of its use. For example, a study was conducted on a large number of high school boys of relatively equal athletic ability. The boys were sorted into three separate groups; and all three groups contained boys of essentially the same characteristics and abilities. As a case in point, the members of each of the three groups were able to throw basketball free throws with an accuracy rate of 23 percent.

The boys in the first group were asked to go to the gymnasium every morning between 10 and 11 o'clock, and do nothing but practice basketball free throws. They spent an hour at this every morning for a month, after which time they were tested. And their accuracy rate had shot up to 46 percent.

The boys in the second group were advised not to go near the gym. Instead they were told to go to a special room every afternoon between 2 and 3 o'clock, and to spend that hour (each school day for an entire month) doing nothing but visualizing themselves throwing basketball free throws, and "making" each one with 100 percent accuracy. At the end of the month this group was similarly tested. And their accuracy rate had shot up to 44 percent—almost as high as the accuracy rate of the boys who had actually been practicing basketball free throws for the month.

However, there was a third group which managed to achieve even more remarkable results. The boys in the third group engaged in *both* types of practice activity. They practiced actually throwing free throws each morning between 10 and 11. And then in the afternoon they also spent the period between 2 and 3 o'clock visualizing themselves throwing free throws and "making" each and every one they threw. At the end of the month this third group tested out at 66 percent accuracy at throwing basketball free throws.

Simply put, active participation in a regular set of programmed visualizations (in which the person actually "sees" himself and "feels" himself actually involved in the successful pursuit of an activity) can work wonders towards the end of bringing a love-shy man up to an average to above average level of social effectiveness. When such visualizations are regularly practiced along with active real-life social participation (*as in practice-dating therapy*), the beneficial effects are commonly multiplied.

Today visualization exercises are regularly practiced by virtually all major sports and entertainment stars. Readers who have any doubts about the validity of this assertion need only check it out. For example, golf professionals will often spend several hours before an important event just standing in their living rooms with their eyes closed, and visualizing their successful completion of the moves they expect to execute and which they expect to win. In their mind's eye and ear they can both see and hear the crowds with all the relevant smells, atmosphere, environmental ambiance, etc. They both see and feel the entire experience before it actually occurs.

Tennis and basketball stars have similarly discussed their successful utilization of these methods. Professional piano players and trumpet players have used them with formidable success. Successful sales people and other business professionals similarly use them all the time. And lately a burgeoning number of therapists have integrated visualization exercises into their therapeutic programs with great success. Interested readers are well advised to ponder the contents of a book titled IN THE MIND's EYE, by Dr. Arnold Lazarus. Lazarus is an eminent clinician who has employed these techniques on his patients with a very noteworthy degree of success. In fact, similar techniques are now being used for the treatment of disorders of the physical body. (See especially Dr. O. Carl Simonton's book GETTING WELL AGAIN, and THE MIRACLE OF METAPHYSICAL HEALING, by Evelyn Monahan.)

These visualizations must be felt and believed by the person on a deep down gut level. Visualization works best when it is accompanied by the positive self-talk and positive affirmation exercises which I have already discussed. As is true with a great many other things in life, these exercises are a great deal easier to discuss than to actually practice. The exercises themselves are certainly not difficult to do. The problem for the severely love-shy is simply that of a deep down cynical attitude of fatalism that "the whole thing is just a bloody waste of time." This attitude of negative expectancy is a logical outgrowth of many, many years of inner pain, suffering and social deprivation. These deep down cynical attitudes render it difficult for a person to force himself to sit down and take the necessary time to do the exercises. Typically, the love-shy man has been so programmed that "deep down" he feels and inwardly "knows" that it "just ain't gonna work".

These feelings which appear to be almost universally endemic among older love-shy men can be successfully reversed only through active involvement in some sort of social support network. This is a key reason why practice-dating therapy groups are so indispensable to the successful treatment of the love-shy. Many contemporary psychotherapists view the insights of self-image psychology as "tremendously good news". But what good is "good news" if a client lacks the catalysts necessary for him/her to make proper use of it?! Again, these catalysts are the social support groups and, in particular, active involvement in practice-dating therapy. Without these catalysts, self-image psychology becomes nothing more to the love-shy than a bunch of interesting intellectual insights.

The Self-Fulfilling Prophecy

The self-fulfilling prophecy has a strong bearing upon self-image psychology. *When we come to define AND VISUALIZE IN OUR MIND's EYE certain things or ideas as real, those things or ideas tend to become real in their consequences.* What we "see" in our mind's eye is what we get. When we come to accept a label that has been consistently placed upon us, we begin to clearly visualize ourselves as fitting that label, regardless of whether it is a good or a bad label. This visualization is basically tantamount to programming the "stupid robot computer" of our subconscious minds—the robot computer which contains all the memory bank and whose substantive content totally governs how we function in the "driver's seat" of our lives. To repeat, our robot computer subconscious minds are gradually programmed by us each and every minute of every day by the content and strength of the *visualizations* and *self-talk* we have, and by the belief we maintain in the veracity of those visualizations and self-talk.

The "driver's seat" concept makes a good metaphor. The way people can and will "drive" or govern their lives is entirely a function of the substantive content of the computer tape of their robot subconsciouses. Throughout their formative years love-shy males are typically labeled "shy", "unpopular", "incompetent", "withdrawn", "chicken shit", "uncooperative", "inhibited", "unsociable", etc. Each of these words incorporates an image or mental picture. And this picture is permitted upon its every thought to become indelibly imprinted upon the computer tape of the subconscious mind.

Some Rejoinders for Traditional Psychotherapists

There are certain criticisms that come up in response to any discussion of practice-dating therapy. In fact, these same criticisms are typically voiced in regard to *any* behavior-oriented style of psychotherapy. And I believe that each is deserving of some attention in this book.

The Symptom Displacement/Symptom Need Argument

There are many psychotherapists practicing in America today who continue to seriously believe that neurotic people *need* their symptoms. The fear, of course, is that if a symptom is "taken away" from a person, he/she will develop a new and perhaps even worse symptom than the one he/she had had originally.

The symptom displacement hypothesis has been extensively studied both by behavior therapists as well as by hypnotherapists. And no support of any kind has ever been found for it. Indeed, seldom does more than one patient out of every two hundred develop a new symptom after the old one has been taken away. And almost never does a person develop a symptom that is worse than the original one had been.

In short, *people do not "need" their symptoms.* People develop love-shyness symptoms as a consequence of a *bad fit* between (1) inborn temperament, and (2) societal expectations as to what is "proper" and expected behavior for their gender. The mysterious unconscious psycho-dynamics with which orthodox psychoanalysts waste their time have absolutely nothing whatsoever to do with it. The research that has been done clearly indicates that people are *enormously relieved* to be rid of their symptoms. The orthodox psychoanalyst wants to give assent to the rights of the "unconscious" over the rights of the rational "conscious" mind. The behavior therapist and the practice-dating therapist, in stark contrast, want people to govern their lives with the rational, conscious parts of their minds. In essence, they want all people to enjoy free choice and self-determination.

Insight

Many practicing psychotherapists believe that *insight*, gradually acquired, into the underlying sources of one's undesired symptoms will progressively cause those symptoms to slowly dissipate and fade away.

Of course, few social scientists would argue that insight is of no value. In fact, intellectual insight is both interesting and deeply fascinating. It can be counted as one of the major reasons why so many love-shy men had majored in the behavioral and social sciences while they were in college.

The problem with insight as a therapeutic tool is that it affects only the rational cognition. It impacts only the intellectual part of man. It does virtually nothing about neutralizing or extinguishing anxiety feelings (or the fear of anxiety attacks), or about breaking the bond between severely painful anxiety feelings and a harmless social stimulus, e.g., an attractive girl or woman. In short, intellectual awareness will not even so much as touch the anxiety problem. In order to extinguish anxiety the emotional part of man's mind must be reached and thoroughly impacted upon. And, of course, it is the purpose of all the basic practice-dating exercises to do just that.

To be sure, practice-dating clients do derive a great deal of intellectual insight about themselves (and the sources of their love-shyness) from fully participating in the various required exercises. However, this insight comes about as an indirect byproduct of participating in the therapy. It is far from being the major therapeutic goal. Love-shy people definitely do not require a great deal of insight in order to get over their symptoms. What they do require is that their heterosexual interaction anxieties be extinguished. Once this severely debilitating anxiety is erased, a person becomes free to develop the social self-confidence and interpersonal finesse that he requires.

Encouraging Dependency and Low Self-Sufficiency

A major fear surrounding practice-dating therapy is that practice-dating will operate to encourage an unhealthy dependency. Because this is the most commonplace and also the most destructive criticism (if it is taken seriously), I have commented upon it at various points throughout this book.

To summarize, better than 85 percent of all practice-dating clients go on to find lovers and marriage partners for themselves. In short, they do not *depend* on practice-dating therapy to find them a spouse—although they are free to do so if they wish.

But more important is the fact that *dependency is a prerequisite for any kind of true socialization*. Love-shy men are quite clearly victims of inadequate socialization. And the *only cure* for inadequate socialization *is socialization*—which necessitates a therapeutic relationship of at least temporary dependency. In order for a person to grow, he/she must go through periods of temporary dependency. In fact, the most mentally healthy, happy people tend to be at least partially emotionally dependent upon certain ego supports (e.g., lovers, spouses, parents, best friends, etc.) throughout their lives.

My many years of studying love-shy men have convinced me that a lack of involvement with social support (friendship) groups lies very close to the heart of the love-shys' problem. In point of fact, very few Americans manage to find their marriage partners strictly on their own without the helpful support of friendship networks in which they are involved. In this respect I think it is quite clear that traditional psycho-therapists tend to expect much more (i.e., the unreasonable) from the love-shy, than plain, ordinary non-shy people characteristically deliver. Again, most healthy people do sustain some dependency upon friend-ship support groups. Why shouldn't the love-shy? For the love-shy a good practice-dating therapy group is nothing more than a good social support group very much like "AA" is for alcoholics, and like Parents Anonymous is for child abusers.

In short, I believe that most traditional psychotherapists sustain an irrational fear of dependency. Because they do not understand what moderate, healthy dependency upon ego supports is all about, they tend to fear it. We all tend to fear that which we do not understand. Dependency is a healthy thing unless it is abused.

Love-shy men are indeed well above average on dependency needs, and well below average on some (but not all) forms of self-sufficiency. In terms of having gotten used to living, managing, and traveling on their own, most love-shys probably possess an *above average* degree of self-sufficiency. They are below average only in terms of their need for help in the heterosexual interaction aspect of their lives.

Thus, the "right" level of dependency may vary from person to person, from woman to woman and from man to man. Rigid require-ments and expectations in this area may do more to stifle propitious psychoemotional growth than to promote it.

The Love-Shys' Need for Structure, and their Fear of Social Ambiguity

Many orthodox therapists believe in assuming an *"or else"* attitude with severely love-shy men. In other words, "either do the homework exercises and confront socially ambiguous situations *or else* get the hell out of therapy!" Such therapists believe that "giving in" to the love-shys' fears only serves to reinforce the fears and to slow down their eventual extinction.

Fortunately, the available research has indicated that "giving in" to fears about having anxiety attacks *does not* cause the love-shy person to take too long in getting rid of his symptoms. In fact, the reverse is true! The easier the transition can be made between (1) being love-shy and (2) being non-shy, the better the client will cooperate with the therapeutic regimen, and the sooner he will show very marked improvements. Forcing a person to confront those things he is not yet ready to confront only forces "departure from the field". In other words, the person "escapes" therapy because it is too frightening for him. Such "therapy" clearly cannot be construed as therapeutic!

Practice-dating is a highly structured therapeutic system. It is a therapeutic approach which removes most of the social ambiguities which love-shy people fear. And this is why moralistic psychotherapists oppose it. However, the acid test is that practice-dating therapy *works* for the love-shy, whereas the approaches promoted by moralistic psychotherapists *fail miserably*.

The "Responsibility" Argument

Client-centered psychotherapists are especially likely to raise this issue. Personally I am not at all opposed to the philosophy of client-centered therapy. Client-centered therapy (along with participatory democracy) represents a great way to rear healthy, happy, responsible children. For the most effective handling of everyday problems of decision-making, the client-centered approach cannot be beat.

However, severe love-shyness is *NOT* an "everyday problem of decision-making"! If a man has clearly demonstrated year after year after painful year that he is *not* capable of solving his own problem, then a behavior-oriented approach to therapy (such as practice-dating) must be sought. The client-centered approach in such cases would represent nothing more than an immoral and exasperating waste of time.

Client-centered therapists believe that for client-owned problems an approach called "active listening and reflection" yields the best results. The therapist serves as a sounding board, giving no advice. Using the pronoun "you" ("you-messages"), he simply reflects back to the client the client's message. For example, the client says: "I'm feeling goddam pissed off today"; the therapist reflects back: "You're feeling very upset about something today".

Usually after an hour or so of client-centered therapy, the client has arrived at some sort of decision or resolution about his problem. He thanks the therapist for the "help", not realizing that the therapist didn't suggest *anything*. For people with ordinary, everyday problems, the client-centered approach *does* teach responsibility and autonomous self-sufficiency. It teaches each person that he/she does have a tremendous amount of wisdom within, if he/she would only take the time to reflect.

Of course, love-shy men are, if anything, far too introspective. They are always reflecting about something! But the most important issue is that love-shy men simply haven't got the nerve to *follow through* on their own decisions once they have come to those decisions. The love-shy know precisely what they want and how to get it. What they lack is the *nerve* (freedom from anxiety) to *use* their knowledge and to take rational charge of their own lives. Client-centered therapy can be of no help with this. In contrast, practice-dating therapy can work wonders.

The "It's Too Mechanistic" Argument

Like other forms of behavior therapy, practice-dating has been accused of being "too mechanistic". This criticism is especially likely to be voiced by (1) client-centered therapists, (2) gestalt therapists; and (3) humanistic therapists.

Having read through this and the preceding chapter, I doubt whether many readers would agree with the premise that practice-dating therapy is "mechanistic". To be sure, the theory explaining how anxiety is extinguished (i.e., gradually exposing the person in controlled doses to the anxiety-provoking stimulus) is "mechanistic". But the delivery of practice-dating therapy entails *and indeed necessitates* a deep and sincere sensitivity to the uniqueness of each client. In fact, a key reason why this form of therapy is as successful as it is, is that it is *more* sensitive to idiosyncratic human foibles and weaknesses than most forms of therapy are. Again, the acid test is that the approach *works*. Not only does *it work*, but practice-dating appears to yield *lasting* cures.

In sum, MEANINGFUL FEMALE COMPANIONSHIP VERY EFFECTIVELY BRINGS LOVE-SHY MEN OUT OF THEIR SHELLS. *Female companionship* constitutes a VERY POWERFUL THERAPEUTIC *CAUSE*; it is *NOT* merely a therapeutic EFFECT! Simply put, frequent and active heterosexual involvement is the very best psychotherapy for love-shy men. Many therapists convey the impression to their love-shy clients that having a lover is a natural byproduct of having an emotionally healthy personality. This may be true. But it is *at least equally true* that having a lover *is itself an important cause* for the development of an emotionally healthy, happy personality. As I documented in chapter one, love has been found to galvanize the spirit of even very healthy people, and to cause them to become more effective and successful in *all* areas of their lives. The powerful therapeutic impact of being enmeshed in a mutual heterosexual love relationship appears to be as strong *or stronger* for the love-shy as it is for the socially successful non-shy.

NOTES

1. Such visualization exercises facilitate the *extinction* of anxiety reactions; the subconscious "robot computer" mind cannot distinguish between what is real and what is *vividly imagined*.

Postscript to Chapter 23

During the 1983–1985 period, psychiatrists and neurologists together with pharmacologists managed to develop certain drugs which may offer some hope for those suffering from social phobias including love-shyness. These drugs are reputed to effectively prevent a person with a social phobia from experiencing anxiety when he/she is involved in a social encounter.

A genuinely effective drug that would obviate feelings of anxiety might prove useful in two contexts: (1) as a *preventive* measure in dealing with withdrawn *prepubescent* youngsters and with young adolescents who are just beginning to want to date and to develop cross-sex friendships; and (2) as an *accompanyment* to the modes of therapy discussed in this and the preceding chapter—especially practice-dating therapy. As a *sole* method of therapy I believe that even highly effective drugs will prove highly unsatisfactory.

Thus, even if a severely love-shy man could be *guaranteed* that he would not experience any anxiety when in the company of a woman, he would still be forced to deal with the *inertia* problem. He would still be forced to get up out of his comfortable chair and risk potentially embarrassing situations. The fear of the unpredictable, of not knowing what to say or how to handle various types of situations, etc., would still operate to keep a love-shy man from entering social contexts on his own wherein there might be some possibility of meeting up with eligible women.

In essence, arranged "matches" through practice-dating therapy together with a coeducational support group composed of fellow shys still represent by far the best hope for solving the problem of severe love-shyness. Using one of these new drugs while on a "practice date" might well facilitate therapeutic change in the direction of the love-shy man's wishes and desires. The same might also be said for hypnosis—i.e., for that small minority of love-shys who might be amenable to being placed into a deep trance and given a series of post-hypnotic suggestions (that would help to instigate social action and obviate the experience of anxiety). But drugs by themselves—no matter how good they are—can never conquer social inertia or program a love-shy's mind (like a robot) so that embarrassing or awkward scenes cannot happen.

Chapter 24

Some Recommendations Concerning Prevention

The purpose of this chapter is to suggest certain steps that can be taken now that would effectively serve to prevent severe love-shyness from ever developing in the first place. To the extent that love-shyness can be prevented, to that same extent therapeutic measures will become increasingly unnecessary. Unfortunately, we are living in the type of world wherein it can be expected that severe love-shyness will continue to be with us for quite some time into the future. Most people are inclined to be at least somewhat hostile towards the idea of instituting the sort of plans which would effectively reduce the incidence and prevalence of severe love-shyness. Indeed, most preventive schemes tend to be viewed as "radical", and as being just too "far out" to be feasible within the context of our sort of conservative, rugged individualistic, democracy. Nevertheless, to the extent that intelligent, compassionate citizens take steps to institute some of the preventive measures which I shall suggest, to that extent severe love-shyness will become a great deal less widespread than it is today. No one person can effectively provide the society with the sorts of changes that are needed. However, each one of us can do a great deal of good for human happiness by instituting new and creative plans for those children and young people over whom we have personal responsibility.

Research on Gene Splicing

The most potent hope for abolishing severe love-shyness altogether lies in genetic research. We all need to support research on gene splicing with all the money, enthusiasm and moral support that we can muster. I believe that the greatest hope for mankind today lies in the advances which can and will be made over the next 100 years in the field of genetic research.

Of course, the big problem here is that most Americans tend to be quite frightened of genetic research. Again, people tend to fear most strongly (and behave in a most hostile manner toward) those things which they do not understand. I would strongly suggest that scholars working on genetic research need to adamently sustain their convictions and press forward with their work quite irrespective of the tenor of public opinion. A great deal can be done without large financial grants, simply by taking full advantage of university resources and facilities. Further, there are many private agencies and individuals who are enthusiastically willing to support even the most controversial of genetic research. And such generosity needs to be fully capitalized upon.

As I indicated in the chapter titled "Beauty and the Love-Shy", the human body is *only the vehicle* of the soul and is *not* conterminous with the soul. True individuality need rest only within the soul. There is no reason why we should not all "drive" Cadillac, Mercedes, and Rolls Royce "bodies" if we can develop the technology that will enable us to do this. Within a century or so there should be no need for any human being to ever have to die of cancer again, to suffer high blood pressure, or sickle cell anemia, or potentially fatal diseases of the heart, Altzheimer's disease, etc., or to be born nonbeautiful or low on intelligence, to have the depression gene, the schizophrenia gene, *or the shyness genes*! More specifically, within a century it should be possible through the gains that are made on research into gene splicing, to abolish severe love-shyness through abolishing (1) the inhibition gene, (2) the low anxiety threshold gene, and (3) low levels of physical attractiveness.

Again, such genetic research will most assuredly not result in our all being the same! Instead, it will provide a much better chance than that which currently exists, for the *true uniqueness* of each individual soul to manifest itself via the incarnate body. If the inhibition gene is abolished, people can be accorded the *driver's seat* of their own lives. They can take charge of their own lives and enjoy the free choice and self-determination which severe shyness obviates. Diseases and malfunctionings of the mind and the body serve to impede the manifestation of man's true uniqueness *and goodness*. Rather than taking our individuality and uniqueness away from us, advances in genetic research (e.g., gene splicing, cloning, etc.) will restore these things to us. Such research results will ultimately accord each and every human being the happiness and productivity which he/she deserves.

Bullying

Bullying is a form of child abuse. It differs from what is ordinarily thought of as "child abuse" only in that it victimizes male children only, and it is perpetuated by children themselves rather than by parents and other adult figures. The data presented in this book strongly support the premise that a history of chronic victimization by bullies exists in the childhood backgrounds of a very large majority of severely love-shy adults. Thus, bullying causes inhibited boys to fear and to avoid their fellow human beings. It forces inhibited males to grow up as inadequately socialized isolates. And it is my contention that unless and until all forms of bullying behavior are stopped, chronic and severe love-shyness will continue to plague a significant minority of America's male adults. Bullying is a prime cause of lifelong people-phobia in males.

Psychologist Howard Kaplan's work on aggression has revealed that arbitrary and capricious victimization by aggression is much more likely if the victimized individual is perceived by the perpetrator as being either unable and/or unwilling to retaliate. Pre-love-shy elementary school boys develop a reputation very early in life for being both unwilling and unable to fight back and to defend themselves. The large majority of the love-shy men studied for this book had been pacifists (both ideologically *and* out of fear) throughout the entirety of their formative years. Moreover, any suggestion that they ought to take lessons on learning how to defend themselves had been reacted to by these men as constituting a form of cruel discrimination against the male sex—inasmuch as girls are never told that they must learn how to defend themselves against physical forms of abuse. To phrase the question quite directly, why indeed should pacifists be constrained to give up being pacifists? In a supposedly free society, why shouldn't a male child have a *right* (1) to remain a pacifist, and (2) to remain free from both physical and psychological harassment and persecution by bullies?!

Up to now American educators and community leaders have approached the problem of bullying with an incredibly permissive set of attitudes. Many people assume the validity of such cliches as "boys will be boys" and "all male children are naturally cruel;" and that all little boys had better learn to defend themselves. Many educators believe that since chronic bullies come from problem families, it is best to deal with the child bully as more of a victim of circumstances himself than as a creator of what is often a lifetime of unhappy circumstances for the quiet, fearful and pacifistic boys upon whom he picks.

The past several decades of anthropological research have proved beyond any shadow of a doubt that all male children are *NOT* "naturally cruel". Indeed, there are scores of societies all over the world wherein violent, highly aggressive contact play among male children is simply non-existent. The large number of bullying-prone children in the United States at *all* socioeconomic levels is a natural byproduct of our culturally based tendency to aggressively encourage our children to compete vis-a-vis each other in all things instead of to cooperate. It is also caused by the way we glorify and glamorize football both in the mass media as well as in our schools.

A problematical home life can and does function to increase the chances that a particular child will gravitate towards finding satisfaction in hazing and bullying other children. But a problematical home life is never a sufficient cause by itself to assure that a child will bully and harass others. Indeed, most male children who come from disturbing or less-than-happy homes do *not* bully or haze others. In all probability most bullies doubtless possess the *choleric* sort of inborn temperament (see page 00).

In criminology today there is an increasing and much welcomed trend towards the assuring and protecting of the *victim's rights* . Bullies cause emotional scars and ruin lives by creating "people-phobes" and social isolates. Moreover, in not being swiftly, consistently, and severely punished for their mindless cruelty, bullies' tendencies to treat their fellow human beings as *things* (without feelings, or with feelings that do not count) *rather than as people*, are strongly reinforced and rewarded.

To be sure, "swift and severe punishment" must *NEVER* under *ANY* circumstances entail corporal punishment. Actions speak louder than words, and corporal punishment has been shown in study after study to teach violence as a normal response to frustration, and to promote violence, bullying, and other forms of physical aggression. In essence, corporal punishment is itself a *prime cause* of bullying. The upshot of the best research that has come out of the social sciences in recent years is that WE MUST TEACH PARENTS AND TEACHERS NEVER TO USE PHYSICAL FORMS OF DISCIPLINE AT ANY TIME OR FOR ANY REASON.

I would recommend immediate suspension from school for any and all bullying behavior. Such action should be taken with respect to bullies of *ALL* age levels from kindergarten through the twelfth grade. Each suspension should be for a minimum of at least one full day. Serious and chronic violators should be suspended for two and three days or even a week for each offense. Furthermore, all boys who have lost more than five days of school within a year's time for bullying their age-mates, should be placed in special schools. I believe there is a serious price to be paid for America's insistence upon educating all kinds of personalities in the same classroom.

I strongly oppose all forms of racial and sexual segregation. But as an educator I *very strongly support* segregation of elementary school aged children on the basis of *native temperament*. Highly aggressive, bullying-prone male children *must not* take classes in the same classroom or play on the same playgrounds as naturally inhibited, low anxiety threshold male children. Wolves are not kept in the same pen as lambs, and

Chihuahuas and Miniature Poodles are not housed with Dobermans. Most shy children do not need to be educated exclusively with other shy children. But they certainly must not be made to regularly interface with those whose native temperaments are poles apart from their own, and whose very presence represents noxious stimuli.[4]

The Perils of Competition

Anthropologists have documented the fact that bullying among male children is almost unknown in societies that do not glorify competition. With proper safeguards, competition can bring the best out of people, and can assure high quality products and services. In stark contrast, competition involving *physical* activities almost always invites and causes a very great deal of conflict and wastage of human resources. Simply put, competition is far less effective than cooperation at inspiring mutually gratifying interaction and friendly sociability. Indeed, competition (especially in physical activities) is almost always antithetical to effective cooperation and to the ability of people to work together peacefully, harmoniously and productively.

It is important to note that many persons simply withdraw from competition whenever they lose too regularly.

"In singing the praises of competition, many people overlook the important fact that although competition stimulates those who win fairly often, it discourages those who nearly always lose. The slow learner in the classroom, the athletic dub on the playground, *the adolescent who fails to draw the interest of the opposite sex* (italics mine)— such persons usually quit trying, for the pain of repeated failure becomes unendurable. They withdraw from competition in these areas, having decided that the activity isn't worthwhile. There is even experimental evidence that repeated failures not only dampen one's willingness to compete, but may even impair one's actual ability to compete . . . . It appears that repeated failures will fill people with such a sense of incompetence and such an overwhelming expectation of failure that they are unable to use their abilities to good advantage. Success or failure becomes self-perpetuating. There is ample experimental evidence that feelings of self-confidence and expectations of success will improve performance . . . Even the expectations of other people have been found to affect one's ability to perform well . . . . It is not surprising that repeated failures destroy both the willingness and the ability to compete. It may be that for every genius whom competition has stimulated to great achievement, there are a hundred or a thousand shiftless failures whom competition has demoralized . . . . Competition seems to be stimulating only in some kinds of activity. Where the task is simple and routeine, competition is followed by the greatest gains in output. As the task becomes more intricate and the quality of work more important, competition is less helpful . . . . Indeed, competition often degenerates into conflict and harassment." (Horton, Paul B., and Chester L. Hunt 4th Edition, 1976, p. 296)

A Non-Punitive Antidote for Bullying

Sociologist Urie Bronfenbrenner (1970) has done some extensive researching of the Soviet system of education. In his studies of a large number of elementary schools in the Ukraine, he took full advantage of many opportunities to observe children engaged in spontaneous play. And he noted that there was never any bullying or rough horse play of the sort which is so commonplace here in the United States. He further learned that any sort of peer bullying is very much against Russian norms.

Russian schools foster upon their pupils a very interesting social arrangement from which we here in America could stand to learn a very great deal. To be sure, Russia is doubtless a far less desirable country for lifetime residence than is the United States. Nevertheless, there are a good many things which we could do well to learn from the Russians— just as there are a great many things which they would do well to learn from us. Lately most educated Americans have recognized the benefits of learning certain business philosophies and approaches from the Japanese. There is not a person or a group alive from whom we could not learn something—and derive substantial benefits as a result.

Beginning with the fourth grade (9-year olds), every child is assigned to another child of his/her own gender, who is *three years younger* than he/she is. Thus, every child from the fourth grade through the twelfth grade is assigned to and is responsible for a charge. If that charge falls behind in his/her school work, the elder child is viewed as responsible, and that elder child (along with his/her entire classroom) loses valued points. Similarly, if someone's younger child is mistreated or teased, it is considered the hard, fast responsibility of the child three years his senior to stop the teasing and to do the necessary protecting.

Most Russian children spend a great deal of their after-school playtime with the child three years younger than themselves to whom they had been assigned. They engage in a great deal of recreation with this child, they instruct and tutor him/her in both academic and social skills, and they are extremely protective in a fatherly or motherly way towards that child. Moreover, they revel in their charge's every victory and accomplishment. When the younger child successfully masters some learning task with which he/she had been experiencing difficulty, the older "big brother" or "big sister" very often enjoys the victory even more than the younger child himself/herself does.

Along with obviating the sort of bullying and hazing which prevails in almost all elementary schools here in the United States, Bronfenbrenner asserts that this pairing up of older child with younger child teaches (*through the actual living of roles*) a great deal about social responsibility and compassion. For example, the age-grade groupings which dominate life here in the United States are largely unknown in the Soviet Union. Children of all ages have ample opportunities for enjoying interaction with and getting to know and appreciate people of all ages, *including the elderly*.

In a highly competitive society such as our own, the virtue of compassion is seldom taught. The rewards and benefits of compassion are typically lost sight of by adults in their unabashed quest for ego aggrandizement. And as a result, valuable human resources are lost or sacrificed.

As Bronfenbrenner's work made clear, there *is* competition in the Soviet Union. But it is invariably a matter of groups of people competing against groups of people, rather than having individuals compete against individuals, as we do here in the United States. The advantage of group-based competition is that children learn early in life to care about the propitious growth and development of other people besides just themselves. In a painless and often enjoyable way, they learn to want to help one another instead of bullying and harassing individuals who are less competitive or less competent than they are. Simply put, Russian children are taught to care about their age-mates, and especially about the "charge" three years younger than they, to whom each Soviet child is assigned and for whom they are responsible.

It seems to me that peer group avoidance and quite possibly love-shyness itself could be almost totally prevented through the adopting of a plan similar to the foregoing. Indeed, such a plan could be extended to include all people in society up to the age of 25. Hence, each 25-year old would be assigned to a college or university senior; and each university senior would be assigned to a university freshman; and each university freshman would be assigned to a high school sophomore, etc. With this sort of benign regimen, cases of incipient long-term love-shyness could be nipped in the bud. Every young man and women in college and in high school would have ample opportunities for dating members of the opposite sex because every high school and college student's "big brother" or "big sister" would see to it that he/she did—

and that he/she was actively involved in gaining the necessary social self-confidence and interpersonal finesse vis-a-vis the opposite sex for effective adjustment throughout adult life.

Lest the reader suspect that this sort of regimen might undermine academic mastery, it should be stated in no uncertain terms that Russian students at all education levels tend to be much more serious and much more accomplished than their American counterparts. For example, chronic cases of underachievement and truancy are very seldom seen in the Soviet Union.

In sum, bullying and hazing, and quite possibly love-shyness itself, can be prevented through assigning every child to a "big brother" or "big sister" three years his/her senior. Besides enabling children to achieve better grades in school, such a procedure could well eliminate pathological shyness through helping children in an enjoyable and benign way to develop strong interpersonal skills and social self-confidence.

The Cruelest Bully of All

Mindless patriotism and religious fundamentalism can and do inspire bullying as well as a host of other forms of violence. What happened in Vietnam, in Jonestown, Guyana, and during the Nazi Holocaust, etc., along with what is currently happening in Iran, well illustrates this point.

Throughout the history of man, patriotism and religious fundamentalism have both been responsible for the cruelest, most mindless, and most relentless forms of bullying. Politically and religiously conservative people have often been characterized by a highly uncompassionate intolerance for any kind of weakness, and by an ideology which often views the victim as fully responsible for his plight. It is therefore not surprising that love-shy men tend to have little sympathy for the viewpoints of conservative political and religious officials. Indeed, love-shy men endeavor to avoid the clutches of such officials at all costs. And this is reflected in their attitudes toward the draft and towards the military establishment.

It is also reflected in their attitudes toward patriotism generally. Patriotism is a form of mindless, uncritical "*groupthink*". Children from kindergarten age onward are required to stand and recite the flag salute every morning until the day they graduate high school. They are encouraged to develop feelings of uncritical emotionalism surrounding the idea of "love of country", and to associate political directives (*whatever* these might be) with highly charged emotional feelings.

In Iran this *patriotic "groupthink"* is reflected in the mindless chanting of such slogans as "death to America" which young people of all ages are required to do. It is similarly reflected in the zealous chanting of "Jesus this" and "Jesus that" by various fundamentalistic religious groups, and in the group violence that went on in Germany during the Nazi era.

Abundant examples of similarly intolerant and highly uncompassionate groupthink occurred in the United States during the Vietnam War era. For example, James Mitchner pointed out in his book on the KENT STATE tragedy (wherein four students were shot by the National Guard in 1970) that almost half of the locals believed that the students *"deserved to die"* for their part in protesting the war, and that "more of them should be shot".

Some examples of how the groupthink of mindless patriotism can and does cause the most heinous and extremely cruel manifestations of bullying can be seen in how draft resisters were treated in the United States during the Civil War and during World War I. Then as during the Vietnam era there was a tremendous amount of bullying of pacifists which was done in the name of patriotism—as though patriotism justifies cruelty against those who are temperamentally and/or morally incapable of handling either the giving or the taking of extreme forms of physical aggression. However, the level of overt cruelty during these earlier times was far worse than that which prevailed during the worst of the Vietnam years. For example, hundreds of pacifist-oriented young men were incarcerated, tortured, and murdered in prison by guards and by other prisoners. And many other pacifists were tortured and murdered before anyone had ever even arrested them or charged them with draft evasion. In essence, those least capable from a psychoemotional standpoint of defending themselves have always received the most bullying and cruelty from sadistic individuals. And down through human history a very great deal of this cruelty has been wrought in the name and interest of *"patriotism"*.

Given their life-long feminine interest patterns and penchants, it is not surprising that most love-shy men sustain very hostile attitudes toward both the draft and the military. In fact, many of them casually refer to the draft as "selective slavery", and almost all of them speak bitterly and disparagingly about a political establishment that could permit a system of conscription to exist which "forces young men to become dispensable pawns" and which insists upon spending 40 or more percent of all tax dollars on the accutraments of military defense.

Yet *all* of the older love-shys had managed to successfully find ways of keeping out of the military. Specifically, 62 percent had obtained either a psychiatric "4-F" or a "1-Y"; and a surprisingly high 31 percent had successfully gotten away with never having registered. This is especially interesting as many of these 35 to 50-year old men had grown up during the Vietnam War era. The remaining 7 percent had had "1-A" or "2-S" classifications, and had never been called. This latter group had fantasies about pursuing "conscientious objector" status if they were called. (Parenthetically, almost a third of the psychiatric "4-Fs" were *homosexual* 4-Fs"; thus, these men had feigned homosexuality vis-a-vis the required two psychiatrists so that they could be assured of never having to have anything to do with the military.)

Many Americans perceive attitudes such as these as "unAmerican". But as one love-shy man pointed out, the government provides little or no choice of service activity to the young men it conscripts.

> "Shit, I don't have any objection to the idea of being of service to my country during a time of real and genuine crisis. What I could not accept for myself was the possibility of being placed in a situation that I know I could never adjust to—not even in the remotest way. Ever since I was a very young kid I've avoided all contact sports and anything aggressive. I knew there was no way I could ever be of service to anybody in any kind of combat capacity. If the government had some way of assuring people like me of clerical jobs and of no basic training of any physical kind, I would have no objection to entering the service. I mean they guarantee women those kinds of jobs. Even in World War II they didn't force women to fight. I mean, they put them in different kinds of clerical jobs. Well, I don't feel that I'm any different from any woman that way. I could never be of service in combat because it's against my nature to have anything to do with aggression. And it's always been that way for me. But I'm sure there are lots of things I could do well that would be of help—just so long as they didn't require me to live in the same building with a bunch of guys who would bother and annoy me." (35-year old love-shy man.)

Thus, the government has a tendency to want to *force square pegs into round holes*. It operates under a set of untested assumptions concerning what "men" are like and about what their capacities are. And just as not all boys fit the junior high school physical education teacher's preconceptions about what all 12 to 15 year old boys are like or should be like, it is similarly true that not all 19–24 year olds can or do fit the government's notions of what a "man" in that age group should be like.

Forcing square pegs into round holes can prove dangerous to more than just one person. The presence of a shell-shock-prone soldier in a fighting unit can easily cause the mortal endangerment of all the other men in his battalion. In addition to the necessity of coping with their severe fearfulness and hypervigilance (and this may be impossible given their earlier tendency to run away from any involvement in touch football!), love-shy males are not used to cooperative interaction. As the data of this book have demonstrated, most love-shys grow up as friend-less isolates. Unlike shy girls, most severely shy boys experience few if any friendships during the course of their formative years. An effective combat unit must necessarily be dependent upon a "group mind", and upon a deep and abiding sense of group loyalty. Severe fearfulness and daydream-proneness will block this from happening in a combat unit just as surely as it will obviate effective team spirit among a group of 14-year olds put together for touch football by a physical education teacher.

The shy, inhibited, football-hating 14-year old with feminine inter-est patterns will behave in a football context just like the proverbial "duck out of water". And he may unintentionally sabotage his so-called "team's" efforts and game plan. The same applies to the using of a highly fearful, socially avoidant person in a combat situation. The net result could very well prove catastrophic! Thus, any rigid insistence that all types of personalities owning male bodies must "serve" in combat could seriously undermine military effectiveness and needlessly cause the loss of many lives.

Simply put, the love-shy would constitute a serious *liability* in any combat situation. Their innate fearfulness and shell-shock-prone dis-positions could easily cause the lives of their fellow soldiers to be need-lessly endangered. As the shy and inhibited naturally avoid anxiety-provoking situations (instead of fighting or confronting them), there is no logical way their presence in a military context could be viewed as representing an *"asset"*. Love-shy men are not emotionally capable of physically defending anybody or anything. They are men who had sim-ply not been born with the tools that are indispensable for fighting and killing. Even among successful sportsmen, there are some people who cannot function rationally under conditions of extreme stress, and who could never bring themselves to kill. With the love-shy, either the giving or the taking of such aggression would be a total impossibility. Emo-tionally sensitive cowards could never, in all common sense, be expected to make a constructive contribution on the combat battlefield.

In addition, combat experience would doubtless be the worst con-ceivable thing for a love-shy person's mental health and eventual chances for stability. To be sure, this statement doubtless holds validity for the majority of different kinds of personalities. *Combat is extremely bad for mental health*, period! And the many psychiatric "basket cases" to accrue from combat exercises in the Vietnam War represent ample testimony to that fact. But on the basis of all the data presented and discussed in this book, it would appear to be *especially* true for the inhibited, severely love-shy person.

Yale University psychologist Stanley Milgram has collected some very fascinating data that are particularly germane to the issue of forcing all manner of male personalities into combat situations. In his celebrated study of obedience to authority, Milgram found women to be as likely as men to obey authority when such obedience required the severe hurting of another human being. However, the women took a much, much longer period of time than the men to obey this authority. They hemmed and hawed, perspired and vehemently protested before engaging in the required cruelty. They suffered a great deal more than the men did before engaging in the cruel action. However, the key point is that they were ultimately responsible for as much aggressive cruelty vis-a-vis their victims as were the men. They were merely much slower and far less efficient in the delivery of this cruelty.

As the data presented in this book clearly document, love-shy males are temperamentally very much like women. Indeed, their biologically based temperament appears to be far more similar to that which is typical for women than it is to what is typical for men. The net conclusion, of course, is that all of the reasons usually cited for keeping women out of combat situations are at the very least *equally applicable* to love-shy men, or to any men with inborn inhibition and low inborn anxiety thresholds. If such men would shoot to kill at all, they could be predicted from Milgram's data to take much longer to respond than "normal" men, thus endangering their own lives as well as the lives of their peers.

Today with the reinstitution of draft registration we see the United States Government spending many millions of the taxpayers' dollars on trying to seek out and enforce the cooperation of what are probably *the very least appropriate* sorts of personalities for potential combat situations! Indeed, they are probably the least appropriate sort of personalities for *any* type of military activity that purports to prove effective. In this sense, the frenetic effort to "force square pegs into round holes" can only lead to a host of socially deleterious, counterproductive consequences. Thus, the military is doubtless the only sort of employer *in existence* that spends vastly more money for the recruitment of the *very least appropriate job candidates* than it does upon the recruitment of the *most* suitably qualified and appropriate ones!

On the basis of the findings reported in this book, there are several obvious steps which the government could take to assure that men with inappropriate native temperaments for military activity are screened out. Some of this "screening" is now being done on a self-initiated basis as is witnessed by the large number of "4-Fs" among the sample of older love-shys studied for this book. However, some additional steps that the government could and should take include the following:

1. Exclude anyone who can document a fear of and an unwillingness to partake in any contact sports throughout the formative
   years of childhood and adolescence. It is most unlikely that any
   "goldbricking" could occur here because most boys find great
   joy in contact sports, and meet (as well as keep) most of their
   closest friends through such participation.
2. Exclude anyone who has not had the experience of being an
   integral part of a network of friends. Again, it seems very unlikely
   that anyone would "fake" this as for most people it is quite
   painful not to have friends.
3. Exclude anyone whose interest patterns do not include any of
   the traditionally prescribed male participant/spectator sports of
   football, basketball, baseball, hockey, rugged calesthenics, etc.,
   or rock music.
4. Exclude any man whose native temperament places him high
   up in the melancholic quadrant of the Eysenck Cross (see
   Figure 1, page 41).

Thus, under conditions of all-out war, men who are "doubtful"
could be conscripted for non-combat duties. On the other hand, men
with any or all of the four above characteristics could and should be left
out entirely from the military without in any way endangering an efficient and effective national defense.

Cowardice

The term "coward" has been applied to people throughout history
in a very derogatory and disparaging manner. The implicit assumption,
of course, is that these people *choose* to be the way they are. And because
of that they should be punished and/or treated as morally inferior.

First we need to note that *female* human beings are *almost NEVER*
labeled "cowards"; and they are certainly never punished for being part
of this noncomformist category. Secondly, the evidence presented in
this book strongly suggests that cowardice is to a far greater extent a
function of inborn temperament than it is of gender. People do not and
cannot select the temperament with which they are born, anymore than
they can select the color of skin or the relative degree of handsomeness
or beauty with which they will be born.

The upshot is that punishing cowardice is tantamount to punishing
an inborn, native trait or characteristic such as that of race or sex, over
which an individual has no control. It seems to me that any reasonable
person would have to agree that this is *immoral*. You cannot reduce the
prevalence of black people by punishing black people. You cannot reduce

the prevalence of homosexuality by punishing homosexuals. And similarly, you cannot reduce the prevalence of cowardice by punishing those who possess that inborn characteristic. And, of course, the same applies to love-shyness as well.

Thus, punishing cowardice can never help to win wars or to effect any other constructive accomplishment. Indeed, we might even do well to recognize that cowardice may even have its positive side: If by some magical quirk everyone on the face of the earth could suddenly be turned into a coward, there would be no such thing as war, and all the taxpayers' monies throughout the world could be freed at last to create a better life and world for everyone!

Finally, inasmuch as cowardice does appear to be inborn, it can be assumed that the incidence of *true* cowardice is the same in all countries. Thus, America doubtless possesses no higher a percent of true cowards than any other country. And this represents a prime reason as to why American can well afford to be kind and compassionate towards its cowards. Again, punishing the phenonmenon will never serve to reduce its incidence![1]

Corporal Punishment Needs to be Outlawed

Many of the love-shys had been frequently traumatized as children as a result of the corporal punishment that they had received from their parents. In addition, the bullies who had so frequently victimized the love-shys had also (according to the best available data on child bullies) received a great deal of corporal punishment at the hands of their parents. As per my discussion in Chapter 8, a huge amount of empirical research evidence overwhelmingly contraindicates *any* use of physical punishment upon human beings. Simply put, we know *as fact* that corporal punishment gives rise to a large host of very deleterious consequences.

Accordingly, I would recommend getting laws passed at the federal, state and local levels which clearly prohibit any use at all of corporal punishment in the private home and in the school. (A teacher defending himself/herself vis-a-vis a delinquent youth would not be considered guilty of violating the law.) Sweden passed such a law in 1979. And in their nation of some 8.5 million inhabitants, their law seems to be working out quite well.

We must get over the idea that parents "own" their children. No human being can ever "own" another. It is definitely counterproductive for any society to allow the private home to be so "private" that within its confines parents can be permitted to screw up the minds and lives of their children. Society has a vested interest in the propitious growth and development of *all* its children. And child-rearing philosophies and approaches which are *known* to contribute to undesirable outcomes cannot reasonably be considered justifiable or permissible simply because "a man's home is his castle"!

Such a law against corporal punishment could be assiduously enforced merely by frequently (e.g., daily) reminding children at school of its existence and of its importance from the standpoint of their welfare. Very few violators of this law would ever be either jailed or fined as a penalty for its violation. Instead, it would be made clear to both parents and children alike that the penalties would be essentially three-fold, and would, in time, serve to drastically upgrade the quality of American family life:

1. All violators would be required to take (and attend regularly) an intensive 20-week "Parent-Effectiveness Training" seminar. Such seminars were founded in the 1960s by Dr. Thomas Gordon, and are based upon his books titled PARENT-EFFECTIVENESS TRAINING, P.E.T. IN ACTION, TEACHER-EFFECTIVENESS TRAINING, and LEADERSHIP EFFECTIVE-NESS TRAINING. The Gordon approach has been found to give rise to far better results than any other method. It is an approach rooted in the principles of participatory democracy; and in it the needs and feelings of *both* parents *and* child are respected. Some parents might well require a repeated exposure to these seminars, whereas others might satisfactorily master the techniques after having learned them once. The "ONE MINUTE FATHER" and "ONE MINUTE MOTHER" works of Dr. Spencer Johnson (1983) should also be integrated into these seminars.
2. All violators would be required to join a "Parents Anonymous" support group (composed of other parents who have also been found guilty of "spanking" their children) which would meet twice per week for one hour each time. This lay group would act to support "P.E.T." goals and methods; each member would be helped in a whole host of ways by fellow parents.
3. All violators would be visited on a regular basis by a social worker who is highly trained in methods of effective parenting. He/she would be charged with the responsibility of tactfully teaching parents quality child-rearing methods. The social worker would also be responsible for following up each family to make

sure that there is no reversion to corporal punishment or to any other form of psychoemotionally abusive parenting.

Some Recommendations Concerning Dogs

Most love-shy men seem to have an unusually strong affinity for dogs. They very much like them, and they interact with them far better and more successfully than they do with human beings. I believe that this special penchant can and should be capitalized upon in both therapeutic and preventive efforts with regard to love-shyness. And I would like to offer two suggestions in this regard.

First, instead of banning dogs from dormitories and other campus facilities, university administrators should establish a kennel on each campus under their care. All students found through testing to be shy and/or lonely and/or depressed would be encouraged to take advantage of kennel programs and facilities, although such facilities would be open and freely available to all interested students.

Upon going away to college each interested student could either bring his/her dog with him/her; or he/she could purchase one of his/her preferred breed at the kennel. Dogs could be kept either at the kennel, or they could be housed inside of the regular student housing. In the latter case, each dog owner would have another dog owner as a room mate.

Through the operation of such university-based kennels, love-shy students would be accorded an excellent opportunity for meeting and interacting with opposite-sexed people of similar interests. Special programs could be instituted that require dog owners to work together and to cooperate with each other. Earlier in this book I introduced the concept of *"superordinate goals"*. Simply put, when a boy and a girl have to work together in order to successfully attain some mutually desired goal, they grow closer together both socially and emotionally. Thus, they are forced in a very pleasant, benevolent way to interact with each other for the attainment of their mutually desired goal. And as a result they both grow in terms of interpersonal skills and social self-confidence.

It is a fairly well known fact that dogs represent an excellent way for people of opposite sexes to meet each other.[2] Given the penchant that the love-shy have for dogs, I believe that this presents a therapeutic modus operandi that should be capitalized upon. Today virtually hundreds of psychotherapists are very successfully treating people (especially children and the elderly) through dog-oriented psychotherapy. Dogs are enormously valuable therapeutic aids and growth facilitators.

And their value in treating love-shy, lonely and depressed people for too long now has remained ignored and neglected.

My second suggestion is that we need to launch the development of singles' apartment buildings containing appropriately staffed kennels. Most love-shy people would very much like to own a dog. But many of them feel that they cannot do so (1) because it is often very difficult for a person of limited funds to locate an apartment building where dogs are permitted, and (2) because most love-shys have to work and/or attend school, and the dog would have to be left alone all day.

There are already a good many singles apartment complexes around. However, most of these cater to the extroverted, outgoing, financially well-off individual who is able to pretty much take care of his/her own needs. And none of the singles apartment complexes that I have heard about contain dog kennels.

It seems to me that a great selling point for the renting of furnished apartments for singles would be something like the following: "This apartment building caters to unmarried dog lovers of both sexes. You don't have to worry about having to leave your dog alone in your apartment all day long while you are at work or on vacation. In lieu of a swimming pool, our entire central courtyard is given over to a professionally staffed and supervised dog kennel. When you go to work in the morning you simply drop your dog behind the appropriate dog fence, and he/she will have plenty of canine companionship as well as room to romp and play all day long. When you come home from work you simply pick up your dog and take him/her to your apartment with you. We have three large doggie playgrounds: one for large dogs, one for medium-sized dogs, and one for small dogs. All dogs are welcomed excepting attack-trained animals of the German Shepherd, Doberman, Rottweiler genre. We merely require proof of spaying, neutering, and of anti-rabies and distemper inoculations."

This type of "day care center for dogs" arrangement, if it could be made sufficiently widespread to meet the demand, could greatly facilitate and expand opportunities for meaningful heterosexual interaction. Of course, social programs could also be offered. Some of these could involve dogs (e.g., discussion groups concerning grooming, dog contests, etc.), and some could involve dances and parties—featuring "middle-of-the-road" piano music by such greats as Richard Rodgers, Cole Porter, Jerome Kern, George Gershwin, Jule Styne, Frank Loesser, etc.

Love-shys (and indeed all singles) have long had to deal with an unnaturally antiseptic attitude among landlords. There are still far too many apartment buildings wherein people with dogs *and with human children* are not welcomed. People who don't want dogs or children should not be forced to live with them. But the proportion of buildings not permitting dogs and/or children is *at least three times greater* than the number of apartment renters who do not wish to reside in a building with dogs and/or human children. Because apartment owners and land-lords command financial wherewithall, they have for too long been permitted to have the last word. Segregation of the age groups and of animals from man is known not to be good for optimal mental health. In a mentally healthy society money would never be permitted to be the determining factor in courts of law as to what is good, right, best, etc.

I believe that universities could take a lead role here in developing communities which the rest of society could emulate. For comparatively little money, virtually all large universities could set aside a fenced in area for dogs. Thus, by expanding opportunities in areas wherein the love-shy have always maintained strong interests (e.g., dogs, psychic and occult subjects, Broadway show music, motion pictures and dra-matics, travel, love ballad music, etc.), university and community leaders can do much to both prevent and cure severe love-shyness. This is especially true if some benevolent coercion (tactfully effected) is employed to involve love-shy males, and if concerted efforts are made to assure *at least* a 50-50 sex ratio at all events. (Ideally, there should always be at least a few more girls on hand than young men.)

As a final point, the following dog breeds are particularly recom-mended for the love-shy. Thus, it may not be feasible for interested universities to breed all the different kinds of dogs. My experience has taught me that the following *12* breeds represent the most prudent selections from the standpoint of the love-shy: Standard Poodles; Golden Retrievers; Laborador Retrievers; Airedale Terriors; Irish Terriers; Irish Setters; Afgan Hounds; Collies; Old English Sheepdogs; Siberian Huskies; Dalmations; and Wirehaired Fox Terriers. To be avoided are the toy breeds, the superlarge breeds, the aggressive "guard dog" breeds, and breeds of all sizes with asymmetrical body proportions (e.g., overly short legs; turned-in snouts; overly large heads, etc.), and other ugly, unesth-etic characteristics. In general, the more conspicuously attractive and exuberant a breed is, the better that breed is likely to be for the love-shy.

Universities might also consider breeding pygmy chimpanzees, wooley monkeys, capuchin monkeys, and spider monkeys, as these animals also seem to hold considerable appeal for the love-shy. As recent segments on the CBS news magazine "60 Minutes" have demonstrated, some of these species of monkeys are extremely intelligent. They can be taught to spoon feed the elderly and paraplegic patients, do minor household chores, fetch things, etc.

Coeducational Dormitories: Their Limitations

The research literature published up to now on the subject of coeducational dormitories is bound to be perceived by a majority of love-shy men as highly demoralizing and disheartening. Only 15 percent of university students resident in coed dorms ever develop love relationships with opposite sexed residents of their own dorms. And this 15 percent represents a figure worth remembering because it has cropped up in several different studies. In essence, the lion's share of coed dorm residents do not fall in love with fellow dorm residents. If a dormitory resident falls in love at all while he/she is residing in a dormitory, it will usually be with someone who lives outside of his/her dorm. Dormitory residents come to perceive their opposed-sexed fellows in "brother-sister" terms. Thus, there appears to be a transfer of the incest taboo. And strangely enough, this "transfer" is quite often supported by the informal norms which develop among the young people themselves.

This quite formidable limitation of coed dormitory life must be recognized at the outset by both love-shys and psychotherapists alike. Love-shyness is an excruciatingly painful condition, and there is no room for delusions when it comes to matters pertinent to its treatment. My data make it very clear that *all* love-shy men desperately want just one emotionally close companion of the opposite sex; and they want this more strongly than they want anything else. And I believe that attaining this goal for them represents the *first and most important* therpaeutic goal *of the immediate moment.*

The coed dormitory will not secure for the love-shys what they most strongly need and crave. However, I believe that a coeducational dorm living experience can and usually will serve some other very useful therapeutic purposes. And I believe that these purposes can be served without in any way slowing down the speed with which the love-shy man can be helped to obtain a meaningful love relationship in which he can enmesh himself. We are living in a coeducational world. And there is evidence that men need coeducation a great deal more than women do. There clearly would be no useful purpose served by returning to the days of the gender-segregated type of dormitory.

One of the major findings of the research upon which this book is based was that the self-confident non-shys were *five times as likely as the love-shys* to have grown up in homes with female siblings. Simply put, merely having an opposite-sexed sibling appears to operate as a major deterrent to the development of chronic and intractable love-shyness. Inasmuch as fellow residents of coeducational dormitories are commonly perceived in brother-sister terms, the experience of living in a coed dormitory and of eating in coeducational situations may facilitate (1) the ability to feel at ease around the opposite sex, and (2) it may facilitate relaxed, informal, cross-sexed communication. It doesn't always work out this way. In many coeducational dorms the men and women still seem to gravitate towards eating at gender-segregated tables. Nevertheless, the available research evidence on coed dorms indicates that things are improving, and that casual heterosexual interaction is facilitated by the experience.

On the other hand, there is one thing which residence in a coeducational dorm will *not* do: it will not solve the love-shy man's problem of inability to initiate conversations with members of the opposite sex (or with *anybody*, for that matter); it will not enable a love-shy man to suddenly become assertive in a friendly, cordial and congenial sort of way. And it will not stop him from perceiving friendliness as "requiring a great deal of nerve".

It is possible for a person to spend four years in a coeducational dormitory and never informally socialize with members of the opposite sex. Fully 54 percent of the younger love-shys had resided in coeducational dormitories. And all preferred coed dorms to the gender segregated option. But not a single one of this 54 percent had ever even "come close" to making any opposite-sexed friends throughout the entirety of their residence in coed dorms. And most of the time they just ate alone at a table off somewhere in an isolated corner of the dining hall.

Hence, love-shy men absolutely require a series of strong catalysts for the facilitation of frequent, informal heterosexual interaction. Dormitories do not provide such catalysts; and without them the love-shy will make no therapeutic gains at all. In essence, therapists must engineer ways of catalyzing informal heterosexual interaction. Again, I believe that practice-dating therapy offers by far the best promise in this regard. Love-shy men should be strongly encouraged to live in coeducational housing while they are involved in practice-dating therapy. But this coeducational housing should be regarded as *a very minor therapeutic adjunct*, and nothing more. The *real and central* therapeutic modality must be that of practice-dating therapy acting in concert with membership in a coeducational Shys Anonymous mutual support and self-help group.

The "Harrad" Dormitory Option

Within the next 200 to 300 years, I believe that all incoming freshmen college students will be routeinely paired up with a coeducational roommate. In 1966, Robert H. Rimmer published a pedagogic novel entitled THE HARRAD EXPERIMENT, which sold somewhere in excess of five million copies. In addition, two motion pictures were made which were based rather loosely on the novel.

Today the idea of routinely pairing young people off with opposite-sexed roommates whom they've never met before appears inordinately controversial to most people. However, insofar as our world is a *coeducational* one, the idea of opposite sexed roommates may actually be far more "natural" than the idea of same-sexed roommates—except, of course, for true homosexuals who would certainly do far better living with other true homosexuals as roommates. Further, there is no reason to assume that any particular pair of male/female roommates will necessarily decide to have sex; they might in time decide to have it, and then again they might not.

Personally, I cannot think of any better way to prevent severe and chronic love-shyness from developing in the first place than to provide a program of coeducational roommates for all college and university students—excepting homosexuals and religious fundamentalists. As is the case now with same-sexed roommates, incompatible roommates would be separated, and each would be assigned to a new, more suitable roommate. Over the course of a four-year college career, the typical student might experience living with as many as six or seven different opposite-sexed roommates. And many romances as well as many marriages might well develop from these relationships. But most importantly, I believe that some genuine, life-long *friendships* would develop from them. Right now cross-sexed friendships are very rare in our society. I think that with the onset of widespread "Harrad-type" dormitories, such friendships would become far more prevalent.

Like the experience of growing up in the same house with a sister, I think that having an opposite-sexed roommate would (1) remove the aura of mystery and anxiety surrounding the other sex, and (2) it would enable each young person to more easily perceive the other sex as just regular human beings like themselves. Some people don't seem to like the idea of "removing the aura of mystery". I very much approve of the idea because wherever you find an "aura of mystery", you also find fear, social distance, misunderstandings, and deficits of communication. I think we can all do without such "auras of mystery". Indeed, I think we can all do a whole lot better without them!

The "Harrad-styled" coeducational roommate approach is fundamentally very different from the notion of premarital cohabitation. In premarital cohabitation a young man and woman with an already established love-relationship "live together" as an integral part of their courtship. (Remember, courtship is a screening device for marriage and the family. Thus, premarital cohabitation is in no way competitive with the institutions of marriage and the family.) With "Harrad-styled" coed room mates, there is no romantic or sexual interest *at the outset*. Such might develop in many cases; and when it does the couple might be deemed to be "premaritally cohabitating"—which is fine. But until each young man or woman finds "that special someone", the experience of residing with an opposite-sexed roommate is bound to be far more educational than the traditional experience of residing with a same-sexed roommate.

As happened with most of the roommate pairs in Rimmer's THE HARRAD EXPERIMENT, sexual intimacy (including coitus) was experienced within the context of friendship (i.e., non-romantic) relationships. Most of the couples required between six and eight weeks of living together as roommates before they became involved sexually. As birth control was effectively practiced by all—as per the Harrad regulations, no harm and only good came out of these sexual liaisons. For example, through having sex on many occasions with different roommates of the opposite sex, each person (1) developed an increasingly favorable social self-confidence, (2) gained increasing self-knowledge; (3) became increasingly realistic about male-female relationships; (4) developed a significantly better understanding of the opposite sex; and (5) became a far better lover than he/she would have been without having had the coed roommate experience. Thus, as in preliterate societies, as a result of having had a series of opposite-sexed roommates, each young man and woman becomes a far better partner and lover vis-a-vis his/her selected love-mate, than he/she would have been without the experience.

Would the "Harrad-styled" dormitory breed life-long promiscuity? I have heard it said that whereas the love-shy might benefit enormously from this approach, more outgoing young people might well find it difficult to remain faithful to one life-long partner. However, the evidence from hundreds of societies around the world suggests that *most* human beings become quite psychoemotionally monogamous after they reach the age of 24 or 25. In point of fact, adultery is a great deal more rare in sexually permissive (re: *premarital* sex) societies than it is here in the United States. And the evidence at our disposal strongly suggests that better than 85 percent of all young people would gravitate in due course towards a life-long commitment to just one lover and marriage partner. Indeed, many anthropologists believe that when the Harrad-styled dormitory becomes fully institutionalized in American society we will enjoy a much more stable marriage and family life than we enjoy today. Again, the sexes will *understand* both themselves and each other a great deal better than they do today.

Of course, none of this is likely to commence happening with any rate of speed until approximately the year 2200. On the other hand, in the year 1950 no one would have dreamed that the decades of the 1960s and 1970s would bring forth as much social change as indeed happened during those decades. Harrad-styled dormitories under private auspices could be developed *now*, especially near campuses with top quality students from stable, upper-middle class, professional homes. And I would strongly recommend that this be done. The present trend in religion is away from the more fundamentalistic Christian approach, and towards a more spiritualistic philosophy and approach. This can be seen in the burgeoning popularity of such subjects as "life after life", the work of such people as Raymond Moody, Jr., and Elizabeth Kubler-Ross, "out-of-the-body" experiences, extra-sensory (psi) perception, apparitions, psychic healing, psychic surgery, Kirlian photography, acupuncture, the human aura, reincarnation, the effects of meditation and biofeedback upon the body, etc. If this trend continues, and I very definitely believe that it will, then by the year 2200 (and possibly a great deal sooner) there will be a religious basis for *in good conscience* supporting Harrad-styled dormitories as well as premarital cohabitation generally.

The Psychic Healing of Important Enzymes

It is likely that most chronic illness and pathology is at least partially rooted in malfunctioning enzymes. And as I suggested earlier in this book, this appears to be as true for chronic shyness and inhibition as it is for various forms of cancer, heart disease, arthritis, Altzheimer's disease, and hundreds of other scourges of mankind. What is more, there appears to be a vicious cycle operating here. Just as a malfunctioning enzyme may cause severe inhibition, the *anxiety-ridden states of mind* which are associated with chronic people-phobia may themselves operate to "neutralize and disorder" certain crucial enzymes. For example, we know that people who recover from cancer possess much more optimism, much more of a *"will to live"*, than those who do not recover. We also know that not having any purely selfish personal goals similarly predisposes people to come down with cases of terminal cancer. In short, psychoemotional states of mind do have a profound impact upon the body. And much of this impact is upon enzyme activity which is indispensable for catalyzing a whole host of metabolic activities.

Dr. Justa Smith, a biochemist at Rosery Hill College, has found that enzymes react very strongly to the "laying on of hands" by *quality* psychic healers. More importantly, she found that formerly disordered or malfunctioning enzymes are quite quickly rendered fully healthy and functional in this way. Dr. Smith's findings have been strongly corroborated by Dr. Bernard Grad and his staff of the biochemistry department at McGill University in Montreal.

At this point there is no way of knowing whether the "laying on of hands" (psi healing) would work effectively upon the love-shy. However, some careful research efforts along these lines are definitely warrented. A most promising line of research might be to systematically apply psychic healing (*by reputable healers*) to the heads of 3- to 7-year old male children who withdraw from "rough and tumble" play. If that works with any degree of success, similar psychic healing could be performed on young adult love-shys. Scientists in East Germany have achieved considerable success in the masculinizing of socially withdrawn young boys; but they have relied primarily upon hormone therapy. Instead of injecting young boys with masculinizing hormones, the curing of malfunctioning enzymes (thus permitting hormones already in the blood stream to work) via psychic healing might well prove to be an easier and far more "natural" solution.

It should be remembered that a neutralized or disordered enzyme is one which is effectively prevented from enabling a hormone to do its job upon appropriate tissues in the brain. As I pointed out in chapter six, there is evidence that a pregnant mother's state of mind can serve to effectively disable certain masculinizing hormones in a male fetus.

A key shortcoming of contemporary empirical science has been its aversion to research on psychic and occult subjects. To be sure, not all scientists are biased against this area of scholarly inquiry. Indeed, an ever increasing number of scholars, especially in quantum physics, are becoming quite actively involved with the researching of occult subjects. Nevertheless, a sufficiently high proportion of university scientists who are in charge of (1) funding, and (2) promotion and tenure decisions, are irrationally and blindly biased against research in this field. I believe that these reactionary academics have served to greatly impede the evolution of knowledge, of effective treatment programs, and of a better way of life for all people.

Simply put, I believe that these biased scholars are guilty of ignoring one of the most important of all scientific laws: namely, that an *open mind* must be sustained until facts are presented which contraindicate a particular principle. These scientists and their pig-headed attitudes must be fought hard. And it is my hope that within the next few decades all major universities throughout the United States will have initiated a separate academic department which will be called "department of psychic and occult studies".

The Effect of Increasing Social Interaction

Any increase in activity will almost always serve to stave off depression. Many therapists believe that shy people must be prodded to increase their activity level and their amount and frequency of informal social interaction. They believe that shy people ought to be distracted as strongly as possible from their enormously strong need and preoccupation about finding an intimate—an emotionally close friend and confidant of the opposite sex.

Sociologists Marjorie Lowenthal and Clayton Haven (1968) collected some fascinating data which have a strong bearing upon this issue. They divided a large sample of elderly people (63 years of age and older) into two different groups: (1) those who had *increased* their amount and frequency of informal social interaction, and (2) those whose rate of informal social interaction had *decreased*. They then in turn divided *both* of these groups by whether the person did or did not have a *confidant*. A "confidant" was defined as any person upon whom the individual could depend for close, intimate friendship and emotionally meaningful psychological support. For most people a "confidant" is normally represented by a spouse or an opposite-sexed lover/friend.

Lowenthal and Haven's findings revealed that the presence or absence of a confidant in a person's life makes far greater difference from the standpoint of depression, psychoemotional health, and *medical symptomology*, than does the fact of merely increasing the amount or frequency of informal social interaction. In short, having a lot of casual friends and acquaintances can benefit a person's morale. But such interaction will not make anywhere nearly as much of a positive impact upon a person's physical or mental health as will the sheer fact of having an emotionally close friend and intimate upon whom he can count for love and psychological support.

> "It is clear that if you have a confidant, you can decrease your social interaction and run no greater risk of becoming depressed than if you had increased it. Further, if you have no confidant, you may increase your social activities and yet be far more likely to be depressed than the individual who has a confidant but has *lowered* his interaction level. Finally, if you have no confidant and retrench in your social life, the odds for depression become overwhelming." (Lowenthal and Haven, 1968, p. 26)

Lowenthal and Haven further found that *single, never married men* were the least likely to have a confidant of all major categories of people. Only 36 percent of them were classified as having a confidant, compared to 74 percent of married men, 50 percent of separated, divorced and widowed men, 67 percent of "single, never married" women, and 81 percent of married women. "Single, never married" males are a good deal less likely than other groups to have a normally healthy capacity for intimacy. Because of their "trained incapacity" for intimacy, they are much more vulnerable than other groups to a wide variety of health problems and to a short longevity. Having a confidant and a viable capacity for intimacy has been found to very significantly buffer all of the stresses and strains, trials and tribulations of everyday living. In addition, there is mounting evidence that *not* having a confidant is itself a very major life stressor that can ultimately cause the development of a wide variety of chronic diseases and disorders.

I believe that Lowenthal and Haven's data support my basic premise that the first and primary task of any therapist treating love-shy men is to promote (1) the finding of an opposite-sexed lover and confidant, and (2) to promote a capacity for intimacy. And I believe that these two goals can only be successfully pursued through practice-dating therapy. To be sure, helping a person to expand his network of friendships *is* a desirable goal. But it should not be pursued until *after* the far more important *presenting problem* of the need for an opposite-sexed lover and confidant has been solved.

A man cannot truly *become himself* with another man unless and until he has a woman. In that sense, a love-shy man cannot and will not commence working upon the expansion of his friendship network unless and until he has found his female confidant and lover. To place friendships before opposite-sexed confidants is tantamount to placing the cart before the horse. Most love-shy men realize this. And that is one reason why few of them will cooperate with a therapist who arrogantly tries to tell his/her client what he/she ought to want, and what he/she ought to begin working on before the presenting problem of a need for a lover can be taken seriously.

Lowenthal and Haven's findings hold some important implications from the standpoint of prevention. For example, the having of a genuine intimate/confidant throughout one's formative years can probably do more to prevent the development of severe love-shyness than having a large network of same-sexed friends. During the years of childhood that intimate/confidant might usually be the mother. This is especially true for boys from psychologically healthy families. As the person moves through the years of adolescence, to an increasing extent the field of significant confidantes would include girlfriends. The key point is that to the extent a male child or adolescent has these intimates and confidantes throughout his years of growing up, to that extent he is never likely to become severely love-shy. It should be noted that a caring mother is *not necessarily* going to be an intimate/confidant to her son. In order for her to qualify as an intimate and true confidant vis-a-vis her son she must have a warm and meaningful relationship with her son. She must be perceived by him as being (1) approachable, and (2) always emotionally relaxing and enjoyable to be with.

The High School Curriculum

Most American high schools maintain a very rigid curriculum. A rigid educational philosophy is almost always counterproductive inasmuch as it is fundamentally insensitive to basic human needs and differences. Worst of all, it results in the wasting of a great deal of valuable time. By the time children reach their junior high school years, cases of incipient, chronic love-shyness are virtually always conspicuously evident. There is much that public education can do to reverse the development of love-shyness.

Foreign Languages

Many educators strongly defend the view that all high school students should take two years of a foreign language. I would suggest that for those students who are too shy to assert themselves in a friendly, relaxed, sociable way *in their native English language*, it is downright ludicrous and absurd in the extreme to require the cognitive mastery of some other language. The ability to enjoy normal social intercourse *in one's own tongue* should precede any foreign language study. If a child is too shy to properly assert himself in the English language, how the hell can he logically be expected to do so in some other language!?

To a greater extent than the large majority of young people, the shy and inhibited require education *which they can use* both now and in the future. They require an education that is germane to the *developmental tasks* which, compared to their age-mates, they are exceptionally slow in even attempting to accomplish. Foreign languages are of relevance to neither the socioemotional nor the vocational developmental tasks of the love-shy.

History and Civics

The ostensible purpose of requiring history and civics courses is that of cultivating in young people a sense of responsibility for participating in the affairs of their respective communities. Civics, in particular, is intended to foster a deep sense of appreciation for America's democratic heritage. And it is intended to assure that all young people will want to study the issues that affect the community *and vote.*

It is a curious paradox that very few of the love-shy men I interviewed had received grades lower than "*A*" or "*B*" in their high school and college civics/history courses. Yet as my research data show, very few love-shy males ever vote. Moreover, very few of the love-shy males I studied felt themselves to be a part of the respective communities in which they resided.

More succinctly, for love-shy males neither the taking of history/civics courses nor the attaining of high grades in such courses seems to be associated with voting or with any kind of meaningful civic participation. On the other hand, (1) *NON-SHYNESS*, (2) *social self-confidence, and* (3) active involvement and participation in a network of meaningful friendships, have all been found to be HIGHLY ASSOCIATED with VOTING and with responsible participation in the democratic governance of community affairs.

Therefore, if a school district wishes to maximize the chances that its students will vote when they come of age, they would do far better to (1) teach interpersonal skills, (2) cure all cases of love-shyness, and (3) make sure that all of their students enjoy respected and meaningful participation within peer groups composed of trusted, well-liked friends of both sexes. The cognative, intellectual skills/knowledge which might be accumulated through the study of academic history and civics courses simply will not accomplish this goal.

Academic courses in history and civics may be all well and good for the majority of non-shy young people who already enjoy a respected place amid a network of friends. For the shy and inhibited, on the other hand, I recommend practice-dating therapy and interpersonal skills building classes in lieu of academic work in history and civics. Such would represent a far more prudent and judicious use of school time and of psychointellectual energies. Further, there is a copious abundance of time at the college and university level during which academic courses in history and civics can be taken by the shy.

Literature Courses

I believe that all students need to be taught how to competently and effectively express themselves in both the spoken and the written word. However, there is no way that requiring all students to read and master such books as THE SCARLET LETTER, IVANHOE, THE RED BADGE OF COURAGE, GIANTS IN THE EARTH, SILAS MARNER, TREASURE ISLAND, etc., can logically be considered germane to the effective attainment of this end. Such fictional works as the foregoing have for some inexplicable reason remained intractably welded to high school curricula for well over a century. No one has ever empirically demonstrated (through a controlled research study) the benefit of these works for normal high school young people, much less for the highly inhibited, love-shy ones. Moreover, such literary works could not be more irrelevant to the necessary, highly pressing developmental tasks and psychoemotional needs of youths with deficits in interpersonal skills and social self-confidence.

Such traditional literary works as the foregoing can also give students a misguided idea of their writing ability. For example, how can a love-shy boy compose a theme about IVANHOE when every page of such a war mongering work bores him to tears?! How can a love-shy person write about a book that contains absolutely no characters with whom he can identify?! Most love-shy boys want to read love stories. Works such as ROMEO AND JULIET, LORNA DOONE, TRISTAN AND ISAULD, and TOM SAWYER, go over well with love-shys because there is a boy/girl romance in each of these works. Until such time as a love-shy male acquires a meaningful boy/girl romance of his own, I strongly suspect that boy/girl romances are likely to constitute the *only* type of fiction upon which he will be able to concentrate for any length of time. Just as boy/girl romance represents a major fixture of a love-shy boy's wish-fulfillment daydreams, a love-shy boy is likely to relish any novel, short story or motion picture which deals with a boy/girl love affair.

A forced exposure to such works as IVANHOE, THE SCARLET LETTER, etc., may further cause many young people (especially the love-shy) to associate the idea of reading *any* work of fiction with feelings of intense displeasure. For the duller students it may cause *reading itself* to become associated with feelings of displeasure. Parenthetically, most of the love-shys I studied for this book did a great deal of reading. But their reading was confined—almost exclusively to non-fiction. However, I noticed that many of them had popular romance novels strewn about their apartments. Thus, a significant minority of love-shy men would appear to spend quite a bit of their time reading popular love and romance novels.

In sum, if the hours which high school students are required to be involved in the study of foreign languages, history, civics, literary works, and physical education, were to be tallied up, the sum total would doubtless be remarkably high. To be sure, most of these activities may well prove at least somewhat beneficial for a majority of high school aged young people. But for students who are love-shy social isolates, these many hundreds of school and homework hours should be used for what is of far, far greater importance.

Simply put, the love-shy should be involved in practice-dating therapy programs, assertiveness training programs, interpersonal skills development programs, and other related endeavors. Such activities will not only benefit love-shy young people far, far more pervasively than the less-than-indispensable academic courses and the enormously loathed "rough and tumble" physical education, but they will also assure that the love-shy will acquire the skills and the psychoemotional set that they need to become integrated members of their local communities.

Ballroom Dancing

At one time or another, several of the love-shys studied for this book had gotten up enough nerve to try ballroom dance lessons as a possible means to meeting eligible young women. Major commercial dance schools such as Arthur Murray's and Fred Astaire Studios, often run sales promotional schemes which permit a new customer to receive a dozen lessons for under $100. The fact that organizations teaching ballroom dance typically operate parties and socials for their paying students tended to serve as an especially strong lure for the older love-shy men, as did the sort of music which is customarily associated with ballroom dance. Thus, most love-shys very much enjoy "big band" music, as well as the usual fox trots, romantic love ballads, waltzes, tangos, etc., which are usually associated with ballroom dance.

There is no question about the fact that ballroom dance *could* serve as an extremely helpful adjunct to practice-dating therapy. (So indeed could square dancing.) But unfortunately, ballroom dance lessons *which are administered by commercial firms* CANNOT BE RECOMMENDED for love-shy men. Here is why:

First, to a love-shy man dancing ability (and some of them already knew how to dance before they took the lessons) *is only a MEANS to an END, and NOT the end itself.* To those administering the teaching, *dancing IS the end in itself.* Moreover, many if not most women who are enrolled in dance studio classes are primarily interested in learning dance as an end goal in itself, and NOT as a means to meeting eligible men. This can be observed in what happens when a male student dances with a female student at one of the studio-managed sociables. The female partner will typically focus her entire attention upon doing the dance steps correctly. Virtually *none* of her attention will be upon either her male partner or upon the idea of involving herself in a meaningful conversation with him.

This sort of scenario is obviously tantamount to placing the cart before the horse as far as love-shy males are concerned. Love-shy males want to meet women (potential mates), and they want to polish up their conversational skills. They invariably perceive dancing as only a *means* toward this end. And they quite often bitterly resent any intimation that learning how to dance well ought to be the end in itself. They don't mind cooperating by endeavoring to dance satisfactorily. But they both want and demand a program which will accentuate meeting and informally conversing with eligible members of the opposite sex.

The concept of *"eligible partners"* represents another big problem as far as ballroom dance lessons are concerned. Ballroom dance studios quite commonly attract women in their middle and late middle ages. In fact, it is not uncommon to find quite elderly people in attendance at ballroom dance socials. Most of these women are divorced, and virtually all of them are well beyond the childbearing ages.

Almost all love-shy men are interested in finding a woman who is still young enough for going through the pregnancy experience, and who is pretty enough to visually turn them on. Ballroom dance clientele include almost no women who fit this description. And this represents a major disappointment to love-shy, never married men who naively give ballroom dance lessons a try.

In essence, ballroom dance lessons have no effect at all upon ameliorating the love-shyness problem for afflicted men. At best after the lessons are over the love-shy client will simply end up a love-shy man who just happens to know how to dance well. And since he will be too shy to *use* or practice these skills, the skills will rapidly fade away as a consequence of disuse.

Social self-confidence and at least a normal ability to deal with interpersonal anxiety *must* be gained *first* BEFORE the acquiring of such specific technical skills as ballroom dancing ability will do any good. This fact is well illustrated by the following quite poignant comment:

> "One time when I was about 26, I noticed an ad for a singles dance in the *New York Times*. It was supposed to be held on a Sunday evening at this hotel on the corner of 8th and 34th; and it was supposed to feature romantic band music. I knew how to dance pretty well at that time. And since the ad said the dance was intended only for single men between 21 and 35, and for single women between 18 and 30, my heart started beating kind of hard. Anyway, I thought I should try to gather up enough courage to go to it. Well, I got all dressed up really nicely, and I went. But when I arrived within about a block of the hotel I froze. I mean I really broke out into a cold sweat. I just didn't have the nerve to go in. I remember I walked around and around that hotel—it must have been 25 or 30 times. And each time I walked around it I tried to sneak a glance through the lobby doors to see if I could see anything. I mean I didn't even have the nerve to go into the lobby because I was dressed too well to just make believe I had to phone somebody. Anyway, after I walked around the block about 25 times my mind started drifting to

less anxiety-provoking subjects. I noticed that the area around the hotel was awfully quiet, even for a Sunday night. So maybe not too many people went to the dance. I mean I didn't see any really attractive girls go in. So after about two hours of just pacing around and around the hotel I just got tired and depressed and went home." (36-year old love-shy man.)

Dancing *may* serve as a catalixt to the further development of already existent interpersonal skills and social self-confidence. But these very important psychoemotional attributes obviously need to be present at a certain minimum level before dance lessons can rationally commence— unless the dance lessons are a concomitant adjunct to a practice-dating therapy program. Simply put, the love-shys studied for this book who knew how to dance were unable to derive any profit therefrom.

Religion

The situation with regard to religion is directly analogous to that of ballroom dancing. The goal or *"end"* of religious organizations is to disseminate and indoctrinate a religious ideology, NOT to find lovers and/or marriage partners for love-shy men. Thus we are again faced with a means/end conflict. For the love-shy man, meeting an appropriate single girl represents the all-important "end". And as I made clear in Chapter 20, when he endeavors to use religious organization as a *means* to that end, he is highly likely to end up disappointed and frustrated.

Encounter Groups

Quite a few of the love-shys studied for this book had tried participating in encounter groups. For a good many years encounter groups had been very popular on the west coast. Thus, it is not surprising that most of the love-shys who had experimented with encounter group participation were California residents.

An encounter group is very similar to group psychotherapy. A major difference, of course, is that the facilitator is seldom a professionally trained person. He or she is usually a layperson with a special knack for handling and motivating people. Another difference is that encounter group participants are usually required to sit on the floor or on pillows. Ordinary chairs are seldom used by most encounter group organizations.

The basic goal of encounter groups is to encourage participants to share their feelings and experiences. No one is forced into talking, and no one is prodded into sharing any information about themselves. The atmosphere is largely permissive. And each session lasts between 90 and 120 minutes. The cost seldom exceeds $5 per person per session.

As with ballroom dancing, a good many of the love-shys interviewed for this book had approached their initial encounter group experiences with an attitude of considerable optimism. And as with ballroom dancing this optimism was shattered. Attractive, single, never married women in the 18–25 age range are almost never found at encounter groups. And the majority of encounter groups have the problem of an extremely poorly balanced sex ratio. A typical scenario might entail 20 people in attendance, including 16 males and only 4 females; the 4 females will *all* be in the divorced, 35 to 55 year old age category. In fact, several of the love-shys had found no females at all present at some of the encounter group meetings they had attended.

Of course, encounter group facilitators commonly champion other alleged rewards such as the chance to get away from one's lonely apartment for an evening, the chance to make same-sexed friends, the chance to learn how to open up and share feelings, the chance to observe that one's own problems are not unique, etc. The problem, however, is that love-shy males are seldom psychoemotionally capable of *accepting* even a *willing* male friend unless and until some progress has been made towards meaningful heterosexual interaction. Further, most love-shy men emerge from their encounter group experiences with the distinct impression that their problems *are indeed* more unusual and more severe than those of *anybody* whom they might have encountered.

Further, most love-shy men seem to find sitting on the floor for 90 minutes to be exceedingly uncomfortable and often physically painful as well. The ostensible purpose of not having chairs is to facilitate sociable relaxation and the lowering of defenses. For most love-shy men the absence of chairs seems to create the very opposite effect; it makes them even more tense and less relaxed than they usually are. The data which I obtained from the love-shys indicated that 73 percent of them objected to sitting on the floor. In contrast, just 27 percent of the *non-shy* male population appears to dislike sitting on the floor.

Most of the love-shy men with encounter group experience claimed that sitting on the floor provoked (usually after about twenty minutes) leg cramps, arm discomforts, and aches in the hands. Getting comfortable on the floor with only a soft pillow upon which to sit is evidently something which a significant fraction of the population is ill equipped to do. Hypochondriasis was another problem which evidenced itself among a good many of the love-shys with whom I talked. Thus, several of these men confessed that they found it disconcerting and emotionally uncomfortable to touch any surface (such as a floor or carpet) upon which people walk. These men felt that floors are dirty and unsanitary;

and as a result several of them while in attendance at an encounter group had tried to sit for as long as they could without permitting their hands to touch the rug. Quite understandably, this behavior created aches and other discomforts in the torso and throughout the legs. And the fact that many of these men could hardly wait to get to a sink where they could wash their hands, further served to make concentration upon the encounter group proceedings quite difficult for them.

Most of the love-shy men did not return twice to the same encounter group organization. Several of them went to as many as four or five different encounter group organizations, each time hoping and expecting to find young, attactive women, *and chairs* upon which to sit. However, each time they were disappointed on both counts. Being too shy to simply leave, they reluctantly paid the required $5, and remained throughout the physically uncomfortable ordeal of a 90-minute session.

In sum, most of the love-shys studied for this book had tried a number of indirect ways of meeting women. Ballroom dance instruction, church groups, encounter groups, attendance at various advertised lectures, etc., had all been tried by the love-shy as a *means* to the *end goal* of meeting eligible women. Interestingly (and quite significantly), some of the love-shys even attributed their choice of a major field of study at the university to their need to be around young women. One young man had started out majoring in accounting, and had performed satisfactorily in all of his business courses. But he found it necessary to switch to psychology "because I was too depressed about the fact that there were practically no girls in any of my classes." Another man with whom I spoke had switched from electrical engineering (in which he had been averaging "*B*" grades) to English literature. And now at age 37 he sorely regrets having made the switch. His *only* reason for changing fields was that he had deeply wanted to increase his chances of meeting attractive girls. Yet the taking of a lot of coursework in the company of female students failed to help him in this regard—as it had indeed failed to benefit all 300 of the love-shy men studied for this book. Simply put, sitting adjacent to women in a lot of university classes cannot be of any help to a love-shy man until and unless he develops the capacity to "open up" and relate.

Each organization has its basic, major manifest purpose. The key purpose of a university is to foster and encourage academic (intellectual) learning. The purpose of a ballroom dance studio is to teach ballroom dancing, and to make lots of money for the owner-managers. The purpose of religious organizations is to disseminate and indoctrinate religious ideologies, etc., etc., etc. Thus, every organization has its purpose. And whereas people occasionally do meet their lifemates while participating in such organizational activities, the accomplishment of such a purpose requires a degree of social finesse and social self-confidence which the love-shy sorely lack. This is why the love-shy absolutely require active participation and involvement on a daily basis in an organization whose *exclusive* purpose is the facilitation of heterosexual interaction among those sincerely desirous of emotionally intimate, meaningful boy/girl type companionship. And in regard to this, practice-dating therapy quite clearly fills the bill far better than anything else.

Might Fraternity Membership Help?

Some people have suggested that university love-shy men ought to be benevolently goaded into signing up with a fraternity. The theory here is that fraternities are socializing agents. They operate to train their members in interpersonal skills; and they inspire the development of lifelong friendships. Fraternities are often viewed as social support systems which do much to involve their members in comfortable, casual and friendly interaction with members of the opposite sex. This is particularly so inasmuch as most fraternities are directly associated with one or more sorority groups with which they exchange frequent parties and informal get-togethers.

I have no doubt that fraternities and sororities entail an enormous *potential* for remedying the plight of the love-shy. But as of right now, *potential* is all that Greek organizations can offer. Fraternities and sororities do engage in a great many charitable activities. But they are *NOT* in and of themselves charitable organizations. In fact, more than anything else, they are *status placement* organizations. And individuals who do not "measure up" are simply not pledged or accorded continued membership.

Fraternities *do* provide some valuable socialization for interpersonal skills and social self-confidence. However, the problem for the love-shy is that a young man must have *already* attained a certain *minimum level* of interpersonal skills *BEFORE* any fraternity will pledge him. To be sure, love-shys are often outstanding students. But from the standpoint of interpersonal skills they embark upon their college and university educations *seriously retarded*. And no fraternity will accept a young man who is conspicuously retarded from the standpoint of social self-confidence and interpersonal skills. And this is true no matter how good a student he might be.

A further problem is that the love-shy would have to be (literally) *taken by the hand* into a fraternity house. Simply put, love-shys simply do not have the nerve to enter and ask about how to pledge. Of course, most students lack a well-structured social support system when they first enter a college or university. But entering college with a satisfactory level of interpersonal self-confidence picked up in high school and earlier, most freshmen take little time in establishing new networks of mean-ingful friendships. The love-shy cannot do this. They remain social iso-lates just as they had been in high school. And as long as there is no one around to take a personal interest in their well-being and to involve them directly in social activities, the love-shy can be fully expected to remain far too inhibited to assert themselves socially and to solicit the opportunity to pledge a fraternity.

Of course, an equally difficult problem is the sort of personality which characteristically chooses to become involved with fraternities and sororities. Generally speaking, Greek organizations both attract and pledge the most highly competitive, social status striving young people. Most such young people are highly outgoing with very few introspective tendencies. Most are already (as entering freshmen) well above average in social self-confidence; and most are very strict and authoritarian when it comes to insisting upon conformity among fellow members. They are psychologically capable of giving as well as taking hazing and other forms of bullying, and of enjoying the process of such oppressive activ-ities. Like the typical fundamentalistic religious group, fraternity and sorority people are fully amenable to what psychologists call *"group-think"*. (See chapter twenty.) Virtually all love-shys are highly individ-ualistic; and as such they are highly averse to anything which smacks of *"groupthink"*.

Moreover, whereas fraternity and sorority students love to asso-ciate with the opposite sex, most of them enjoy associating with their own gender a good deal more. And the general thrust of their norms is to discourage strong, romantic pair-bonding prior to the senior year of college. Inasmuch as the love-shy crave strong pair-bonding from the earliest years of elementary school onward, the general attitude towards love and romance prevalent among Greek organization leaders would be highly refractory to the needs of love-shy men. And indeed so would the chauvinistic norm which stipulates that love interests must only be formed with members of Greek organizations, and *not* with non-affiliated "outsiders".

Finally, the general attitude towards life which currently prevails in virtually all college and university fraternities is drastically "out of sync" with what love-shy men are emotionally capable of tolerating. Continued membership in a fraternity absolutely requires the following:

(1) A willingness to interrupt one's studies at any hour of the day or night, in order to partake in singing or some other raucous, all-male activity.
(2) A willingness to participate in a variety of self-degradation activities, particularly during the so-called "pledge period".

Many fraternities still permit hazing; and each year there are at least a half-dozen deaths caused by this and related forms of hypermasculine bullying. Even in places where hazing is not permitted, milder forms of hazing (which may *not* be "mild" to the love-shy) continue to be ubiquotous throughout the world of Greek organizations. In addition, no love-shy man would ever want to haze or bully others.

(3) Fraternity membership absolutely requires the psychoemotional predisposition to enter into the flow of *"groupthink"*. Again, any form of *"groupthink"* tends to make love-shy men extremely nervous and uncomfortable.

(4) Even though most love-shys drink, they drink only in moderation. Love-shy men reject the idea of drinking for the sake of drinking, or for purposes of proving their masculinity. Refusal to "conform" in this regard would soon result in the ejection of any love-shy person from the midst of any group of fraternity men. It would further result in the public doubting of the love-shy man's masculinity.

(5) Love-shy men tend to prefer peace and quiet. They desperately want female companionship and premarital erotic sexuality. But they want even these amenities to be available to them under peaceful and quiet, loving and monogamous circumstances. Even the love-shys' musical tastes tend to be at dramatic variance with those which are *prescribed and enforced* upon fraternity men. Love-shy men hate "rock" as well as the kinds of traditional, highly repetitive beer-drinking songs that are sung in unison by fraternity men.

(6) Fraternity men are expected to like sports, and to be ready to participate in "rough and tumble" activities at any time of the day or night.

(7) Most love-shy men are far from being at their best vis-a-vis authoritarian leadership. Love-shys have a stronger than average need to make their own day-to-day decisions. They are *not* "team players". As serious-minded individuals, they are ready to willingly cooperate with others *only when* it appears *rational* to do so. Most of what goes on in a fraternity or sorority house is far from "rational".

(8) Fraternity membership requires a natural ability to find great pleasure in all-male interaction. The love-shy flourish best in situations which are pervasively coeducational through and through—with preferably more females than males about.

(9) Fraternity membership requires an ability to accept a socially and politically conservative ideology. Most love-shys are liberal in their social and political beliefs.

(10) Most love-shy men sustain a negative attitude towards tradition. Tradition and related rituals are very important to Greek organizations. As serious-minded individuals, the love-shy are inclined to look first towards empirical science to decide what is right for them. If a tradition seems tangental or refractory to their personal needs and interests, the love-shy will behave very indifferently towards it. Simply put, love-shy men do not perceive any of the traditions which they encounter as being in consonance with their vested interests. (Traditions had never done anything from the standpoint of correcting their love-shyness problems.)

Use of Sorority Girls

On large university campuses which contain a copious abundance of so-called Greek organizations, the help of sorority girls could be enlisted in dealing with severely love-shy males. Sorority organizations pride themselves upon motivating their girls to take an active role in the provision of charitable services to their local communities. What more worthwhile charity can there be but to help their own male age-mates who have not yet even begun to live their adult lives! *Charity begins at home*, as the old cliche tells us. It would seem to me that to the extent that sorority girls help the socially deprived males on their own university campuses, to that extent they would truly be practicing "charity at home".

In this regard I asked each of my respondents to answer the following question:

> Which of the following two types of social service activities do you view as being the more socially desirable and useful for a group of college sorority girls to engage in?
> —Spend a couple of hours each week providing companionship in a home for the elderly.
> —Spend a couple of hours each week helping severely shy college men of their own age get started dating.

Fully 84 percent of the older love-shy men together with 72 percent of the university love-shys checked the *second* alternative. In fact, I found it quite gratifying to learn that 55 percent of even the self-confident non-shys would rather see the sorority girls help love-shy males commence dating than see them simply provide companionship in a home for the aging.

To be sure, I am not arguing here that the elderly are not also entitled to help, caring and concern. In truth, *all* human beings are. And of all human groups it is clear that *very few* have heretofore been more severely neglected than that of severely love-shy university males. Studies on the elderly have shown that most old people (1) want to be able to do things for themselves, (2) do *not* want anyone around who is going to be feeling sorry for them, and (3) benefit best from being given a pet dog or cat. Many aging people have enjoyed visitations by sorority girls; but many more have been found to view the girls' attitudes as being patronizing and condescending.

In point of fact, the best group of people to spend blocks of time around the elderly are *very young children* in the *age 3 to age 7 group*— certainly not college girls. Next to that the elderly appear to benefit enormously from being permitted to keep pet dogs. Visitations to nursing homes have long been among the most frequent charitable activities engaged in by sorority girls. I strongly recommend that this custom be changed forthwith!

For numerous reasons sorority girls could prove to be a tremendously potent source of and impetus for constructive growth and change among love-shy males. Further, some of the girls might find that in spite of themselves they actually grow to *like* the love-shy males—that "still waters run very deep", and that there is far more to the love-shy than meets the eye.

Several university researchers have found sorority women to be at least somewhat more physically attractive than non-sorority women. In addition, sorority women tend to be above average for their age group in interpersonal skills and finesse. With such personality assets at their command, the services of sorority girls could do much to increase the social self-confidence of love-shy males. For example, each sorority girl could agree to spend one evening per fortnight with a love-shy male. If that were deemed too much, then one evening per month might well prove extremely helpful if a large number of girls assumed an active role in the program. Love-shy males interested in taking part could simply leave their names, addresses and telephone numbers in some central office, such as the university counseling clinic. And each participating girl would simply draw one name card per each two or four-week period.

Contests could be developed out of this. Sorority girls, like fraternity men, are known to be well above average in competitive drive. Quite socially constructive use could be made of their competitive spirit and drive by offering prizes to those women who successfully integrate the largest number of love-shy men into the mainstream of college social life. In other words, those women who do the most to free the intractable inhibitions of the greatest number of love-shy men (thus permitting these men for the first time in their lives to commence dating women of their choosing), would be awarded such items as $200 prizes, clothing, metals of various sorts, write-ups in the university newspaper, etc.

Of course, some of this prize money could come from a fund established by the love-shy men themselves. Each participating love-shy man might be required to contribute $25 to the prize and award fund. In an effort to sustain a high level of excitement and enthusiasm, at least a dozen girls could be awarded prizes at the end of each five-week period of the 30-week academic year.

What Can Be Done:

Even though membership in conventional fraternities appears to be "out" as an option for love-shy men, it may be feasible to initiate the development of fraternities and sororities just for the shy. Simply put, if the proper organizations existed, students commencing higher education retarded from an interpersonal skills/social self-confidence standpoint would have someplace to go. And they would have an appropriate environment in which to live. They would have a support group at the very outset of their educational experience that would undertake to socialize them for reasonable competence and effectiveness in the social world.

A System of Coed Roommates

Unfortunately, the world may not be quite ready for it yet. However, what I expect to see happen within the next two or three centuries is that love-shy students of both genders will be assigned opposite sexed roommates immediately upon entrance into a college or university. The best and most sensible preparation for competent and effective interaction in a coeducational world is coeducational living—with *everything* that this might entail. There is no better way to extinguish a person's anxieties pertinent to the other gender than to place him or her in the same bedroom with a roommate of that other gender—in a situation wherein everyone else is *also* placed in a bedroom with a roommate of the other gender. Simply put, this is one way to speed the time when love-shy individuals can commence viewing the opposite sex as feeling human beings like themselves, and not as some mysterious entity to fear and to avoid. It is a way to speed the time when all young people of both sexes can truly feel free to "let down their hair" and bare their innermost secrets just as easily in the company of members of the opposite sex as they might be able to do in the company of members of their own sex.

If a particular young man or woman could not get along with his or her roommate, that roommate could be changed. This is what happens now anyway with regard to same-sexed roommates. So why worry about room mate shifting just because the roommates happen to be of opposite as opposed to similar genders?! In his THE HARRAD EXPERIMENT, Robert H. Rimmer recommended that it might be best to restrict college students to a maximum of one roommate change every ten-week quarter. Such a restriction may be a good idea because it might provide for some constructive learning experiences. Moreover, during a student's years as an upperclassman he or she could choose his or her opposite sexed roommates if he or she wished to do so—or he or she could be assigned. Both approaches would be satisfactory depending upon the needs and situation of the individual student.

The Courtship System Versus Marriage and the Family

Many Americans continue to view premarital cohabitation as competitive with marriage and family life. Today it is becoming increasingly clear to the social scientists who study it that cohabitation is competitive with marriage and the family *if and only if* it continues to be practiced by a couple *after* the onset of parenthood. Down through the history of man the key purpose of legal marriage has always been (1) to legitimate parenthood, and (2) to assure a stable, orderly and predictable environment for the socialization and propitious growth and development of new offspring. In order to survive with any degree of success, every society must be concerned about the favorable socialization, growth and development of its new generation of offspring. And this is the *only* reason why all societies the world over invented systems of marriage and the family.

Courtship is a *screening device* for marriage and family relationships. Courtship represents a system of norms which *precedes* marriage. And since courtship precedes marriage, it can never reasonably be construed as being competitive with it. Indeed, rather than being competitive with marriage and family life, a good system of courtship is fully supportive of the highest quality of marriage and family life, and should lead to same in the majority of instances. In short, premarital cohabitation is a *courtship custom* and is *NOT* in any way competitive with marriage and family institutions. Premarital cohabitation and premarital sexmaking must never be interpreted as being "alternatives" to marriage. Like any attribute of the courtship system, premarital cohabitation should be construed as being part of the preparation and screening for the eventual development of happy, fulfilling, lifelong marriages, and for the development of happy adulthood lives.

Unless a young person is very lucky and happens to meet very early in life with a person who is virtually ideal for him/her, I believe that young people should have the experience of cohabiting one at a time with several different opposite sexed roommates before they finally decide upon a permanent one for the marriage and family phases of their lives. Indeed, there are probably few if any groups for whom the experience of premarital cohabitation would be more thoroughly beneficial than that of the love-shy—of *both* genders.

Use of Autistic Adolescent Girls

One of the especially interesting (if somewhat bizarre) characteristics of autistic children is that they tend to be unusually beautiful/handsome. Indeed, most autistic people tend to be quite far above average on looks. Moreover, they are quite probably the *only* beautiful people lacking in a strong aura. Virtually all beautiful girls/women tend to be highly sociable, status striving and dominant. Simply put, their general ambiance and demeanor tends to be perceived by love-shy men as highly threatening.

Yet as this book has shown, love-shy males seem to have an unusually strong and uncompromising need for a girl with beauty—with long hair, pretty, youthful face, and trim figure. Love-shys also seem to be turned on by women who are beautiful enough not to wear any make-up—whose beauty is natural and not in any way artificial.

It seems to me that the foregoing facts suggest the desirability of therapeutic experimentation with autistic teenaged and young adult girls. Dr. Theodore Issac Rubin's charming story of DAVID AND LISA clearly illustrated how an inhibited, highly neurotic high school boy could be greatly healed of his problems as a result of his love relationship with a beautiful, autistic girl. And, of course, the same true story also documented how the autistic girl was also able to substantially improve as a result of her love relationship with the inhibited, neurotic boy. *Love* is inherently therapeutic, and is the "universal solvent" for all psycho-emotional problems, including ones like love-shyness that are rooted in *genetic* attributes which (in males) are not appreciated in our highly competitive, aggressive world.

Again, the typical beautiful girl here in America does not act as though she needs any protection or nurturance. Similarly, the typical beautiful girl does not act as though she has any interest at all in being nurturant towards any young man, or in being impressed by his intellectual or educational accomplishments. If some experiments were done in which severely love-shy males were introduced to beautiful autistic girls (e.g., in university psychotherapy centers), a very great deal of good might be accomplished for everyone involved. To be sure, the love-shy man and the autistic girl would have to be assigned to a series of activities that would require them to work together on some task on a day-after-day basis. And on a semi-supervised basis they would need to be given a good deal of time alone together. For example, each couple could be assigned to take care of one or two pet dogs; these might serve as a catalyst for facilitating rapid, therapeutic interaction. However such an experiment might be managed, I think it would yield some particularly fascinating and immediately usable data.

Changing the Norms

One of the most obvious ways of preventing the development of severe love-shyness is simply that of changing certain social norms. After all, if love-shyness is indeed primarily due to a poorness of fit between social expectations and inborn temperament, then it stands to reason that love-shyness will rapidly diminish to the extent that the norms are restructured to be in greater harmony with man's nature.

The major norm in need of changing is the one which stipulates that the male, *not the female*, must *always* be the one to make the first move in initiating cross-sexed friendships and conversations. I would suggest that NATIVE TEMPERAMENT and *NOT* gender should be the prime determinant in any given situation as to which sex should make the first move towards the initiation of a friendship. There is no evidence that the native temperaments of males and females differ substantially regarding the natural proclivity to be assertive. Women who are naturally assertive should be both permitted and encouraged to make the first move. And corollatively, men who are naturally passive should be both allowed and encouraged to play the passive role—without any cost to them in social respect, honor or esteem. No one should be penalized for attributes that accrue from native temperament.

Accordingly, we must stop socializing (hypnotizing) our little girls into believing that they should never ask boys for dates. Elementary school children at all levels from kindergarten through the eighth grade should be exposed to learning experiences which make it very clear that gender should never have anything whatsoever to do with the issue of who should assume the socially assertive role in any given cross-sexed situation. Parents need to be helped towards an understanding as to why the traditional norm prescribing social assertiveness for males but proscribing it for females is destructive and highly deleterious to mental health and self-actualization. They should be helped to understand why this norm needs to be thrown away forever into the trash can and replaced with a normative system that is compassionate and congruent with the needs and natures of human beings. Inasmuch as the family is the prime socializer of all children, it is quite clear that adults must be won over as to the belief and conviction that certain traditional norms promote love-shyness, loneliness, and poor mental health. Lectures and discussions at PTA meetings might well be a good place at which to commence this effort.

The "Sadie Hawkins" Type Event

In Hamburg, Berlin, Frankfurt, Munich, and several other German cities, there are some very popular establishments at which the women (*only the women*) ask the men for dances—and if a man refuses a given woman he is asked to leave.[3] Similarly in America the "Sadie Hawkins" dance is a social event to which the girls are expected to ask the boys. If a program of social change is ultimately to prove successful in reducing the incidence of love-shyness, I believe that it must make copious use of so-called "Sadie Hawkins" type events. And these should commence from a very early point onward in the lives of our children. Certainly by the time of junior and senior high school, fully *fifty percent* of all cross-sexed social events should be designated as being of "the girl asks the boy" variety. Over time I believe that this approach might effectively teach young people that whichever gender group a person belongs to has no bearing at all upon who should make the first move in informal social situations. In this way our sexist social norms *can* in time be made to undergo sweeping reform.

One way of assuring full participation at all cross-sexed social events (by those who truly wish to participate) is to make up a list of all persons in a school who indicate on a questionnaire that they would like to attend a specific event with an opposite sexed partner. A few weeks before the social event, this list would be posted in some central location, such as on a bulletin board just outside the principal's office. Each time a girl asks a boy (or a boy asks a girl) to the event, the name of both students would be crossed off the list. On the final Friday before the social event, all remaining names on the list would be placed into a hat. And the principal or school counselor would pair up each of the remaining names so that everyone who wished to attend the event with an opposite sexed partner would be able to do so. Again, students not wishing to attend the event would not have their names on the list in the first place.

NOTES

1. In chapters 2 and 3 I explained how each of us is born with a set of *elastic* limits. Since these limits are elastic, people *can* work towards forms of personal change that are in consonance with their goals. However, just as every elastic band has its own "breaking

point", *people* similarly have different "breaking points". This represents a key reason why it is counterproductive as well as highly uncompassionate to require all males to face either military or any other type of situation entailing or necessitating physical aggression.

2. During the past several years numerous experiments have been conducted in this regard. In a representative study conducted in London (see Fogle, 1984), a large sample of men and women were asked to take a two-mile walk along a particular route. After each man or woman completed the walk by himself/herself, he/she was asked to take the same walk—only this time with his/her dog. Each experimental subject was closely followed and observed from behind by a professionally trained scientist. And note was systematically taken of all interactions, eye contacts, etc., vis-a-vis strangers.

In sum, whereas the experimental subjects averaged *zero* conversations with strangers when they took the two-mile walk by themselves, these same men and women averaged *three* conversations when they took the same walk with their dog. It should be noted that the men as well as the women ended up talking to significantly more people when they walked with their dogs than when they walked alone. And whereas unusually beautiful and ornate breeds tended to attract the most attention, *any dog* was found to constitute a powerful catalyst for facilitating *human* interaction. Indeed, even those male adults walking mongrels averaged more conversations than those walking alone.

3. So far as I am aware, there has never been an establishment anywhere where a *woman* is asked to leave if she refuses a man's request for a dance. Herein lies testimony as to the second class status of the male sex throughout the western world.

4. For the best research heretofore published on the bullying-whipping boy phenomenon the reader is referred to the work of Dan Olweus which is cited in the bibliography. See especially his 1984 paper.

Chapter 25

Some Final Thoughts

In psychological circles whenever recommendations are made regarding the practical issue of how to help a shy person, the focus has almost always been upon how to motivate that person to help himself/ herself. Almost never does a psychiatrist or psychologist endeavor to even think about engineering ways of trouble-shooting the problem for the shyness victim. Thus, psychology and psychiatry are both very much unlike conventional medicine wherein the practice has always been to engineer viable ways of permanently curing the patient's presenting problem.

A major thesis of this book is that conventional psychological and psychiatric approaches cannot and will not work for cases of prolonged and intractable love-shyness. Indeed, for most cases of love-shyness I believe that all the usual psychotherapeutic approaches are fundamentally wrong, inappropriate, misleading, and counterproductive. I believe that this is so for three key reasons:

(1) As this book has clearly documented, severe love-shyness is rooted in a range of *genetic* and *congenital* factors over which the victim never had any control or responsibility. Being born with a strongly dominant *inhibition gene* constitutes a key basis for the development of intractable love-shyness *in males*. As such, shyness is *not* a "psychological problem" in the first instance unless and until society (especially peer group and family) defines it as one, reacts to it as one, and makes it one.

(2) All the available evidence quite clearly demonstrates that love-shy men absolutely require very strong catalysts. Left to their own devices they will do nothing to help themselves. A love-shy man could dine every night for a year in a university dining hall composed of 70 percent young women and only 30 percent young men. Yet unless someone actually took a personal interest in that love-shy man and consistently saw to it *on a day after day basis* that he ate with and interacted with women, he would be just as badly off (most probably *worse* off) at the end of the

613

year as he had been at the beginning of it. To be sure, none of the young women would take it upon themselves to assert themselves in a friendly manner vis-a-vis such a love-shy, conspicuously isolated young man. In essence, victims of intractable love-shyness *cannot and must not* be expected to "help themselves out", to "solve their own problems", to "grab the bull by the horns" (when the bull hasn't got any horns), etc. I believe that society has an ethical responsibility to find and get love-shy men situated with appropriately suitable female love-partners.

(3) Conventional psychotherapeutic approaches *waste time*. And time is an extremely valuable resource when it comes to helping severely love-shy people. As love-shy men become increasingly older they become *decreasingly* confident vis-a-vis attractive, eligible young women. It becomes increasingly difficult for love-shy men as to an increasing extent they inevitably grow too old for women who have never given birth to a child. Time is of the essence in treating love-shyness. As more and more time passes in the absence of *appropriate* treatment, the problem becomes more and more overwhelming in its level of difficulty. For a love-shy man there is no catalyst more powerfully therapeutic than a copious abundance each and every day of informal heterosexual interaction among genuinely eligible young women. Such heterosexual interaction must be guaranteed and assured all severely love-shy men.

To be sure, conservative minds decry the idea of providing love-shy males with a "crutch". In psychotherapy "crutches" are commonly thought to foster dependency. Yet in medicine crutches are known to speed the day when a person can function on his or her own unencumbered. Crutches also permit self-sufficiency, even as the healing is going on.

For example, if subsequent to a skiing accident the victim were not supplied with suitable and appropriate crutches, he or she would be constrained to remain indoors. He or she would not be able to get around and to pursue a normal life. And what is perhaps of even greater importance, he or she would require *much more time* to recuperate from the skiing injury. In short, crutches not only permit a person to lead some semblance of a normal life while they are recovering; but crutches also facilitate a maximally speedy and propitious recovery.

As I have stressed throughout this book, dependency is a prerequisite for socialization and for growth. *Therapeutic crutches* in psychotherapy as well as in medicine permit the person to venture forth and to develop his/her incapacitated muscles. A crutch permits a person with a broken leg to develop and strengthen his/her incapacitated muscles by using them in as near-normal a manner as possible. The *"therapeutic crutch"* that is intrinsic in practice-dating therapy, in match-making services, in "Shys Anonymous", in "Coed Scouting", etc., similarly permits the person incapacitated by severe love-shyness to exercise what limited interpersonal skills he might have, and to thereby slowly but surely develop increasingly strong social self-confidence. Without the "crutch" the love-shy person cannot "go out" at all. What few positive attributes he might have are thereby condemned to wither and undergo severe atrophy through disuse—just as a leg muscle would undergo severe atrophy if the accident victim failed to receive a "crutch" which would *permit* him to exercise that muscle.

Just as a seriously crippled person would never be expected to go out and prematurely fend for himself, this should not be expected of a love-shy person either. Further, no orthopedic physician in his/her right mind would allow a patient to depend upon a mere set of instructions that would, if followed, permit a full recovery. It is the orthopedic surgeon who first places the cast on the broken leg. The surgeon *never* requires his/her patient to do this for himself/herself. A competent physician further takes his/her patient by the hand and gets him started on certain regular exercises. Eventually the patient will do these on his/her own. But at the outset (and sometimes for a long time after the outset) the physician and his/her assistants accompanies the patient and helps him/her through each exercise. And so it is with practice-dating therapy.

Thus, love-shy men are cripples, every bit as much as a person born with a twisted leg is a cripple. In essence, neither the love-shy male nor the person born with a twisted leg managed to enter the world with the properties which American society deems "desirable" and "normal". A dominant inhibition gene gives rise to effects that are every bit as "undesirable" (in terms of public reaction) as does a twisted leg. Close, personalized attention together with good *therapeutic crutches* (and the dependency which these entail) will effectively remedy both kinds of problems—at least to the point of permitting the victims of these problems to lead normal, productive lives. On the other hand, deny a "crutch" and temporary dependency to *either* person and you deny him/her the chance to become a normal, happy, productive citizen.

A Different Philosophy

On the basis of the foregoing it is clear that this book reflects a philosophy that is very different from that which prevails in contemporary psychotherapeutic circles. However, it is not my purpose to be "different" just for the sake of being "different". In order for therapeutic recommendations to be of any real use they must harmonize with the facts concerning what love-shyness is and how it develops. Up to now none of the books and articles pretending to make recommendations pertinent to therapeutic modalities that might be suitable for love-shyness have any kind of an empirical research basis at all. Simply put, the book which you have just finished reading is the first to provide a fully comprehensive, interdisciplinary, research-based explanation as to what love-shyness is and of how it develops and worsens over time.

I believe that the recommendations contained in this book jibe with the facts on love-shyness that are now known. The recommendations contained in other works are based to a greater extent upon wishful thinking than on facts. They are based on the idea that *all* human beings can be successfully motivated to "pick themselves up by their own boots-traps" on the basis of mere exposure to one or another of the myriad "talking cures", which is all that the vast majority of clinical psychologists and psychiatrists ever endeavor to offer. As I have demonstrated in this book, a person without "bootstraps" cannot pick himself up by these! You cannot force square pegs into round holes. Conventional psychotherapeutic approaches are simply inappropriate for love-shy men because each of these is premised upon the assumption that the love-shy client already possesses certain necessary "bootstraps" which all the best available data quite clearly indicate he does *not* possess.

To be sure, the philosophy of therapy recommended by this book has been criticized for discouraging the development among love-shys of proper adult levels of self-sufficiency. However, throughout this book I have tried to show that meaningful female companionship represents the most powerful catalyst for growth and adult masculine self-sufficiency. As far as adult male love-shys are concerned, I can think of nothing that holds a stronger potential for promoting growth and psychological health (including self-sufficiency) than meaningful involvement with a suitable female companion and lover.

Furthermore, dependency is a prerequisite for socialization (which is what psychotherapy is) and for full-fledged adult self-sufficiency. Most contemporary psychotherapists approach the concept of dependency and "crutches" with irrational levels of trepidation and lack of understanding.

What Is Needed

For the love-shy man the central problem of life is that of how to find an opposite sexed confidant and fall in love. A number of anthropologists have suggested that this problem may be much greater for

Americans than for members of certain other cultures in which there is less freedom of choice about social relations. Brain (1976), for example, discussed cultures in which arranged marriages and even arranged same-sexed friendships guarantee that *everyone* has those social ties that are considered essential by the culture. He commented:

> "We have overrated the necessity of choosing our friends and wives. We decry arranged marriages . . . Choice is the thing! However, this freedom of choice often means that it is never made—hence the frustrated spinsters, the friendless and the lonely." (Brain, 1976, p. 19)

Doubtless the forcing of everyone to accept arranged marriages would never be workable or even desirable. However, for those wishing to accept the idea of having their dates and their ultimate marriages arranged for them, I believe that this option needs to become freely and easily available. It is perfectly possible for a person to go all the way through life without *ever* being able to start a conversation with a stranger in a purely social (*non*-impersonal) situational context and *still* be happy and fulfilled. For the large majority of the male population, on the other hand, it is most assuredly NOT possible for a person to go through life without a marriage partner or an intimate confidant, and *still* be happy, well adjusted and productive.

Except for those who are violent, I believe that *every man* should have the right, guaranteed and assured *by law*, to be married by the age of 28, and to be actively involved in heterosexual dating and courtship by the age of 18. Again, no one would ever be forced to take advantage of such a law. However, such a law and social policy needs to exist for the protection of the many love-shy men who *do* very much want to date and to court and to marry, but who haven't got the requisite nerve to be able to lift a finger for purposes of helping themselves in this regard. We have employment agencies which get people jobs which they could very easily get for themselves if they had the psychoemotional "gumption". We have travel agencies which make travel arrangements for people—arrangements which they could easily make for themselves, often at considerably less cost. And we have dog grooming centers for people who for one reason or another are "too damned lazy" to learn how to groom their own pooch. We even have professional housecleaners for people who do not want or are not able to clean their own homes or apartments. I would contend that there is similarly no reason at all as to why analogous organizations ought not to become available for tending to the far more important needs of those who want and need heterosexual companionship but are incapable due to love-shyness of obtaining it for themselves.

One young man told me that he would be willing to pay $20,000 up front to a yenta (Jewish matchmaker) who could guarantee that within one year of the time he affixed his signature to the contract he would be married. His only stipulation was that he would have to have reasonable veto power over the selections made.

This attitude towards yentas and other matchmakers was not unlike that of most of the severely love-shy men who were studied for this book. Love-shys want to avoid having to suffer what they commonly refer to as the "indignity" of going through the regular dating and courtship process. Yet they still very much want to get married and to experience a normal family life. A fear of rejection and of risk-taking may well be an integral component of most love-shyness cases. But why should all people be forced into suffering rejection simply because they want to have a wife and family? As the old cliche stipulates, "one man's meat is another man's poison". Many men actually *enjoy* the chase (the *process* of finding and winning a girl) far more than they enjoy the ultimate victory or conquest. The love-shy are just the opposite of this; and they wish to avoid "the chase" to the maximum extent possible.

In a highly competitive society such as the United States, we tend to "put down" such love-shyness-related attitudes. And yet it is not difficult to see how an "anti-chase" type of man might stand a far better chance than most men of being fully faithful to his wife—if the fates allow him to ever end up getting one! If a man does not enjoy "the chase", he can most probably be counted upon to remain at home nights and weekends with his wife and children. Contrariwise, who is to say that a man who thoroughly enjoyed "the chase" *before* marriage is going to be able to quite suddenly *stop* enjoying "the chase" the minute he finds himself married?! In this respect the love-shy may well be more adaptable to the demands and expectations of stable family life than the socially well-skilled charmer of great finesse whom everyone likes and with whom everyone wants to go to bed.

In fact, one of the questions I asked of each of my respondents has an interesting bearing upon this issue. I asked: "Should people try to continue their marriage if one or both of them becomes dissatisfied?" And 47 percent of the older love-shys together with 38 percent of the younger ones said "yes", compared to only 20 percent of the self-confident, non-shy men. These differences certainly suggest that love-shy people are probably a good deal more likely than the non-shy to exercise patience and tolerance in marriage. At the very least, it would certainly appear that the love-shy would be much more difficult than most people to provoke into divorce.

From the standpoint of therapy for the love-shy, I believe that a nationwide network of practice-dating clinics needs to be established.

In addition, I believe that a network of professionally staffed marriage-arranging organizations is sorely needed. The kinds of dating services which currently prevail in our cities are of very little help to severely love-shy men. What is needed is a marriage-arranging organization that will stick to the job until "the job" has been properly accomplished for each love-shy client.

In traditional times the "yenta" (Jewish matchmaker) took a deep and abiding *personal interest* in each one of her clients. She took it upon herself to quite closely follow up each male and female client until each was appropriately suited and married. Thus, in contrast to the contemporary dating service, the yenta did not follow the model of disinterested big business. She made it her business never to forget a client until he/she finally married.

It seems quite likely that most young Americans would not want any yentas "on their backs". However, love-shy men are *not* typical young Americans. And indeed, most severely love-shy men would welcome a deeply dedicated yenta with open arms and with the utmost enthusiasm. Like the Jewish aunt in the small Polish community of a century ago, a good yenta would be expected to work very closely with and very closely follow up upon each one of her clients until each one is suitably married.

For the severely love-shy man some extremely important functions are served through a well coordinated institution of arranged marriages. Getting a wife for oneself without the benefit of a marriage arrangement option requires the ability to function in unstructured social situations where there is no "script" or "role" to play. As we have seen, love-shy males cannot handle such unstructured situational contexts.

For most people dating and courtship fulfills a *screening* function. Thus, most young men and women are psychoemotionally capable of screening each other. The love-shy person is not capable of doing this because his native anxiety threshold is too low; he experiences painful anxiety too easily, too frequently, and too strongly compared to most people. In doing the screening for the love-shy man, the yenta would be screening out any woman who might be conspicuously wrong for the love-shy man, or who might be viewed by him as cold and indifferent. Thus, the matchmaker saves the love-shy man the kind of psychoemotional pain and embarrassment of which he is so strongly afraid.

At what juncture in time should love-shy men be encouraged to pursue the yenta option? I believe that the love-shy should be strongly encouraged to regularly attend and participate in the activities of a practice-dating clinic. Such clinics should be available to all love-shy males from the age of 15 onward. Those who continue to remain single and unattached beyond their 28th birthday would be encouraged to retain the deeply dedicated services of a professional matchmaker.

In no case would a man or woman ever be required to accept a matchmaker's selection. As commonly prevailed in traditional times, a man or woman could veto the yenta's selection after according that selection the benefit of a few lengthy conversations. The important virtue of having a deeply dedicated matchmaker at one's disposal is that in a very caring, professional way she continues to search out an opposite sexed partner who will prove fully suitable and acceptable.

There is, of course, a great deal of sham and pretense inherent in the courtship role. In America most young people relish this sham and pretense—at least for a few years during late adolescence and early adulthood. It is part of the "*game* of love". And most young people have been socialized (programmed; hypnotized) in such a way as to relish "*games*" of all types. In contrast, severely love-shy men are highly romantic. And like romantic people generally, they thoroughly dislike and wish to completely avoid this sham and pretense (game aspect) of dating and courtship activity. They don't want to "role play". They want to get right to the heart of things by finding and fully committing themselves to their one lifelong "soulmate"—that girl with the long hair, pretty face, trim, youthful figure, and noncompetitive, nurturing personality. In short, many men cannot psychoemotionally deal with the sham and pretense "role playing" that is integral to dating and courtship. Love-shys simply don't like to play games!

Thus, love-shy men are *results oriented* rather than *process oriented*. Most young people are capable to at least some extent of enjoying the "*process*" of screening many opposite sexed partners before committing themselves on a deep, psychoemotional level to just one. In fact, many young people are quite capable of relishing the many embarrassing moments that are an inevitable component of heavy involvement in dating and courtship activity. Because of their low anxiety thresholds, their inhibition genes, and their low social self-confidence, love-shy men are not capable of "laughing off" embarrassing moments. Indeed, embarrassing moments often cause love-shys to emotionally shudder for weeks and sometimes months after the event had taken place. Of course, their lack of male friendships and their situational status as "loners" further serve to make it very difficult for love-shys to forget psychological pains, insults, embarrassing moments, misunderstood signals, etc.

To the extrovert, the *process* of doing something (winning a girl, developing a musical talent, a vocational competence, etc.), is usually more important than the end result of finally getting what he/she wants. Thus, to the extrovert the real enjoyment of life rests in the *process* with all of its embarrassing moments, failures, setbacks, turbulence and minor victories which are experienced along the way. To the highly inhibited person, on the other hand, successfully (and rapidly) attaining the desired end result is the only thing that matters. The love-shys' constant need is to attain their goals *without* experiencing any embarrassing moments and with the least amount of psychoemotional turbulence (anxiety) possible.

A key problem here is that those providing psychotherapeutic services often pursue a quite moralistic stance with regard to this issue. They often expect severely love-shy men to become as *"process oriented"* as the average extrovert. And such "therapists" imply vis-a-vis their love-shy clients that they (the love-shys) are not entitled to a woman unless and until they (the love-shys) become as fully process oriented as the average extrovert.

To be sure, this quite prevalent attitude among "psychotherapists" serves as a strong roadblock to meaningful communication. And it represents a key reason why few love-shy men remain in conventional psychotherapy for very long. Many therapists assume a similar attitude with respect to risk-taking. Their attitude seems to be that unless a love-shy man becomes willing to risk-take, to become a gambler, then he is not entitled to emotionally close female companionship.

In short, the attitude of such therapists is that the unwillingness to risk-take and the unwillingness to become "process oriented" should receive the therapeutic emphasis, *not* the need to engineer a viable way of getting the client a suitable female lover. Indeed, the love-shys' need for a girlfriend should be all but forgotten in therapy, according to these therapists. Again, this attitude represents a powerful roadblock to meaningful and effective communication. And it all but guarantees that love-shy men will steer themselves very clear of all conventional psychotherapy.

Hence, moralistic attitudes serve as roadblocks to therapeutic communication. There is a kind of *tyranny* here too, which should be quite evident to most readers. After all, why shouldn't a shy man be free to choose to concern himself primarily with the *"process"* of sustaining a good marriage (or premarital cohabitation relationship) instead of with the sham and pretense (game playing) process of conventional dating and courtship?! To the love-shy man it is far better to get right to the person with whom he is likely to spend the balance of his life. Rather than being "fun", playing the field is very frightening and anxiety provoking to shy men. They dream of having their "fun" exclusively with just one female lover.

Finally, the thought seldom crosses the minds of most conventional therapists that female companionship might serve as a powerful catalyst causing the love-shy to begin taking some risks and to begin deriving some enjoyment out of the *"process"* of life and of living. Thus, for some people meaningful female companionship may have to *precede* an ability to take risks rather than the other way around.

Interpersonal Skills versus Interpersonal Anxiety

During the past few years a number of researchers have challenged the assumption that love-shy people are deficient in interpersonal skills. For example, in some studies the love-shy have been found to be no less *knowledgeable* of interpersonal skills than the socially self-confident non-shys. Of course, the key word here is "knowledgeable". The love-shy often *"know"* as much as the non-shy. But their inhibition and low interpersonal anxiety thresholds serve to effectively keep them from applying this knowledge.

Many psychologists perceive such interpersonal anxiety fears as being rooted in a "fear of rejection". And in some important respects such psychologists are correct. However, the problem for severely love-shy people is that anxiety fears (e.g., the fear of an anxiety attack) override rational, intellectual considerations. It is comparatively easy to get many love-shy men to agree that the anxiety fears motivating their social withdrawal tendencies are rooted to a major extent in a fear of rejection. But accepting and/or agreeing with that fact is almost never enough to motivate a change in behavior. It is never enough to cause a severely love-shy man to start a friendly conversation with a girl, and thus risk rejection.

Rationally and intellectually the love-shy man *"knows"* that there are plenty of other "fishes in the sea"; and that if he is rejected (even if this is done crudely and callously) the consequences for his ultimate social success need be nothing more than nil. But that fear of a painful anxiety attack ensuing from either (1) the fact of being rejected, or (2) from being lost for words or from not handling a conversation adequately, determines his behavior. In short, it determines that he will abstain from all attempts at trying.

Most lay people and, indeed, most clinical psychologists have great difficulty understanding the enormous potency of these anxiety fears. And I think the main reason for that fact is that fortunately most people are born with reasonably high anxiety thresholds. As I clearly documented in the first part of this book, people with low native thresholds tend to experience anxiety feelings (1) *sooner* than most people do in any given situation which they have learned to associate with anxiety, (2) *more frequently* than most people—as a result of learning to associate a wider variety of different sorts of stimuli and experiences with anxiety feelings, and (3) *more intensely and painfully* than most people.

The third (#3) factor is doubtless the most important and significant one from the standpoint of arriving at a proper understanding of the behavior and behavioral inaction of the severely and intractably love-shy. It is virtually impossible for a severely love-shy person to communicate to a less shy person how excruciatingly painful an anxiety attack really is. The vast majority of people have never experienced such a thing and doubtless never could experience it. And this is because most people had had the good fortune to have been born with *normally high* anxiety thresholds.

During the years I spent interviewing for this book, I was told time and time again that *anxiety is a thing that is more fearsome than death itself*. To be sure, love-shy men use different words and expressions to convey this view. But always there is a clear message to the effect that severely love-shy people are incapable of handling or constructively coping with anxiety attacks, or with the fear of same. Thus, the severely love-shy will do virtually anything to prevent anxiety feelings from happening.

Moreover, the love-shy tend to *remember* their multitudinous anxiety attacks of the past. Virtually all such past attacks had involved *social situations* of one sort or another, thus explaining how the love-shys had learned to associate anxiety feelings with people. And the word *"past"* here can mean as much as 40 or more years ago. For example, one 48-year old love-shy man could be hurled into a severe fit of anxiety simply by remembering embarrassing situations that had befallen him during his earliest years of elementary school. Love-shy people seem to have a difficult time forgetting, even when they strongly wish to forget. And events of many years ago can cause them very painful anxiety spells.

Of course, such spells are doubtless exacerbated by the absence of anyone in the love-shys' lives to distract them. Presumably if someone were around, love-shy people would not have to deal with quite so many foul memories entering into their conscious minds on an uninvited basis.

In addition, many love-shys seem to worry that their private reactions to anxiety (i.e., how they react to anxiety when they are in private) may become uncontrollably manifest in public places, and thus compound the intensely severe and prolonged painfulness of the anxiety itself. For example, when in private many love-shys fly off into a spate of uncontrolled neoglogisms (the uttering of words that are not words in any known language). A great many of them run outside even during the dark, early hours of the morning—if the early morning happens to be the occasion for an anxiety attack. Still others display a spate of spastic-like facial, hand and arm movements whenever they experience painful anxiety feelings while alone. Thus, many love-shys fear such loss of control while in public.

Some Final Thoughts on Prevention

Throughout this book I have underscored the importance of preventive efforts with respect to love-shyness. Whereas it is true that the underlying basis for love-shyness *is inborn*, the problem itself is learned as I clearly documented in chapters two and three. Because society reacts in very nasty ways to little boys who persistently display behaviors brought about by the inhibition and low anxiety threshold genes, painful "people-phobias" tend to develop. And when such boys are required to grow up in families which do not contain sisters, severe and intractable love-shyness is highly likely to develop. This is especially true when (1) the parents are incompetent from the standpoint of adequately managing, understanding and accepting a highly inhibited boy, and (2) when the parents are comparatively isolated from any kind of meaningful, extended kin network including uncles, aunts, cousins, etc.

With respect to the first point, it is widely accepted today in psychological circles that a child is free to change only to the extent that he/she is accepted and respected *as he/she is*—highly inhibited or otherwise. As the data presented in this book quite clearly demonstrated, the love-shys' parents had always sustained a deep and abiding preoccupation with their children's weaknesses, shortcomings, inadequacies, etc. Yet it is well-known in psychological research circles today that *focusing on weaknesses serves to block communication and meaningful growth;* and that concentrating on strengths vis-a-vis a child tends to open up meaningful communication, encourage participation and positive change. Further, concentrating upon weaknesses tends to *strengthen and enhance* those very weaknesses.

In this regard it is worth repeating Alexander Thomas' key conclusion inasmuch as it has a strong bearing upon how severe shyness develops: *Behavior disorders* (including intractable shyness) *are caused by a bad fit between a child's inborn temperament on the one hand, and parental, teacher and peer expectations on the other.*

As Thomas and others have been able to demonstrate, being born high on introversion (inhibition) *and* high on emotionality is NEVER ENOUGH by itself to create a "people-phobia". Thus, when an introvert with a low anxiety threshold is accorded (1) a plentiful abundance of pleasurable play experiences with peers, and (2) genuine acceptance (*as he is*) from his parents, he invariably develops a healthy sociability and social self-confidence. As an introvert he will ordinarily prefer just a few very close friends in lieu of many less close ones; and he will usually prefer play and recreation that is more or less on the quiet side. *But he will* (and this is the important point) *be normally sociable*; he will be able to genuinely enjoy the companionship of others.

Hence, my position is that people entering the world with high inhibition and low anxiety thresholds are *not* entering the world "sick". I believe they are made "sick" by a sick society. And it is high time that we started to think seriously about ways of constructively changing this sick society instead of trying all the time to force the individual with difficulties to do all the changing. A person with high inhibition and a low anxiety threshold can, under propitious circumstances, become fully healthy from a psychoemotional standpoint. Females with this combination of genetic characteristics *usually* develop reasonably healthy levels of self-esteem and social self-confidence, and they almost always manage to date and to marry at normally early ages. The only reason why *males* with these characteristics do *NOT* develop strong self-esteem and social self-confidence is that their native characteristics are met with misapprobation by the "powers that be". The "powers that be" define these native characteristics as being the boy's "own fault", and as being in need of fast changing. In girls these characteristics are usually accepted and respected.

It is instructive to note that our society tends to be a great deal more friendly and helpful towards various forms of maladaptive behavior that are not associated with psychoemotional states of mind. Thus, children with learning disabilities are accorded all manner of special attention. Even normally intelligent children who are very slow in learning to read are given special classes along with quite a bit of one-on-one attention, all of which is aimed at remediating these problems.

We don't tell slow readers: "If we put you in a special class we would be doing you a disservice. This is a competitive world, and the only way you're going to be able to cope with it as an adult is to learn how to cope with it now." Instead we realize that it is only through special training and special attention to specific learning problems that a child will eventually become capable of catching up. (And many slow readers do possess normal-to-above-normal native intelligence.) The same logic applies to the inhibited boy. We need to appreciate the fact that being born inhibited and "slow to warm up" to people socially is directly analogous to being born with some sort of minor learning disability. We don't bully and disparage slow learners the way we disparage shy and inhibited boys. Instead we provide special classrooms and specially trained teachers to handle all the various forms of major and minor learning disabilities.

The inhibited boy similarly requires special attention. He requires a coeducational learning environment that is gentle, accepting, non-threatening and noncompetitive. If and when he is accorded this he will stand a reasonable chance of one day being able to compete effectively within the mainstream of society.

The Family Structure Factor

The data uncovered by the research reported in this book also served to emphasize the importance of family composition as a cause of severe love-shyness. First, love-shyness appears to be closely associated with isolation from kin networks. Family kin networks (extended families) that are emotionally close appear to provide very important help services which effectively reduce the probability of severe shyness ever developing among any of their members. Secondly, love-shy men appear to be more likely than most people to have grown up as "only children". Actually most only children do slighty better in life than children who grow up with siblings; and this is especially true for boys. However, an incompetent and nonaccepting parent can emotionally damage an only child (*especially* if it is a boy) to a far worse extent than he or she could in most cases damage a child with siblings. And that is what the data reported in this book seemed to show.

But the most important finding about family structure concerns *sisters*. Simply put, severely love-shy men appear to have grown up in isolation from girls in their age range. The non-shys studied for this book were fully five times as likely as the love-shys to have grown up with sisters in the home.

I would suggest that all boys need to see girls as regular, non-mysterious human beings. And in this regard I strongly feel that we need to take our cue from Swedish, Danish, Icelandic, and Israeli approaches to socializing young children. In particular, boys from families without sisters need to be accorded a copious abundance of opportunity throughout early and middle childhood (to say nothing of adolescence) to pleasurably and very informally interact with girls in a wide variety of different settings and circumstances. And in regard to this I believe that we need to drop our unhealthy preoccupation with sex and nudity. Religious fundamentalists have wrought a great deal of damage upon our culture in this regard. Sweden, Iceland and Denmark all enjoy greater harmony, stability and security than America does. Some amount of casual nudity and sex play among children is clearly not going to destroy a society! Indeed, it is likely to help our society to become stronger through fostering happier, more relaxed, higher quality interpersonal relationships between the sexes.

Towards this end I have recommended the nationwide development of a new recreational organization for children to be called the *Coed Scouts*. This organization, at least at the outset, would not in any way take the place of the YMCA, YWCA, Boy Scouts, Girl Scouts, Boys Club of America, Brownies, Campfire Girls, etc. Instead, it would be offered as a forward-looking alternative to liberal-minded people and to those who have the responsibility for caring for socially isolated, highly inhibited children. Regular, daily participation in the activities of a Coed Scouting group would serve as a great boon to boys from families without sisters. Simply put, it would foster the kind of social growth that would assure psychoemotional health and possibly even a competitive edge in the dating, courtship and marriage marketplace. (After all, boys who grow up with sisters in their homes seem to enjoy such a competitive edge.)

The Abuse Factor

Another matter of crucial significance from a preventive standpoint is that of properly dealing with school bullies. Up to now the enormously deleterious impact that school bullies have upon the psychoemotional and social growth of inhibited boys has received almost no attention at all from psychologists and educators. Even though bullies may be children, I believe that strong action must be taken in regard to their behavior.

When an adult in our society is arbitrarily and capriciously punched or knocked down he is accorded legal recourse; he can sue for damages on an assault and battery charge. The question naturally arises as to why children (especially *male* children) must be forced to suffer physical pain just because they are children and boys! Male children are human beings, and they have feelings the same as any other human being. And yet as a culture we encourage "spanking" by parents as a mode of so-called "discipline", and we overlook and forgive the rank cruelty of the capricious acts taken by classroom bullies. And, of course, we expect our males to become pieces of metal (dispensable pawns) from the standpoint of feelings and emotions when it comes to the "selective slavery" system and military activity.

As I pointed out in Chapter 24, *bullying hurts*. Among highly inhibited boys it commonly creates life-long scars, and a life-long people-avoidance ("people-phobia"). Legal recourse needs to be made available to all male children. And they need to be shown in easy-to-understand language how to bring charges against age-mates who assault them. Some people argue that all boys need to get used to "handling bullies", and that they need to learn how to defend themselves. And yet bullies (except in criminal muggings) do not single *adults* out for such physical abuse. An adult "defends himself" against bullies by consulting with an attorney. *That* is the way defense is supposed to be handled in the United States, *not* by using violence to counteract violence! I believe that our little boys should similarly be taught how to defend themselves by seeking out and employing the coercive power of the law through a licensed attorney.

To summarize my other major recommendations with respect to this issue, I believe that elementary education in the United States must (1) being employing *long-term suspensions* for boys who bully; and (2) highly extroverted, hyperactive boys should *not* be educated in the same classroom as inhibited boys. Again, lions must not be kept in the same cage with sheep! This is only common sense! Especially in elementary education, teachers often misperceive inhibited boys as being a great deal less intelligent than they actually are. Such counterproductive misconstruals are bound to become less commonplace as teachers become used to dealing with whole classrooms filled with inhibited children.

Finally, I believe that we need to pass laws similar to those in Sweden, which ban all uses of corporal punishment (at home and in school) in "disciplining" children. There are over a score of research based arguments contraindicating the use of physical punishment on human beings. And yet the tradition of corporal punishment continues to be blythly passed on from generation to generation. The Civil Rights laws of the 1960s put a stop to most forms of racial discrimination being passed on from generation to generation. I believe that the law can and should be used with respect to the corporal punishment issue as well.

People still rationalize their demonstrably *physical* approaches to "discipline" by saying that "spanking" is the "only way" they can express to the child their caring and concern. Yet an absolute prerequisite for expressing genuine caring and concern is awareness of and sensitivity to the emotional needs and feelings of the child. And, of course, respecting and recognizing a child's needs and feelings does not entail always "giving in".

Many scientists today are beginning to operationalize the very concept of *love* as representing the genuine, mutual caring and sensitivity to the feelings and needs of the other person expressed through ongoing, unimpeded communication. Quite clearly, you cannot cause pain to another person and still be sensitive to that person's feelings. Further, such hurtful actions serve to *block* meaningful communication and thus *reduce* actual influence. To be sure, children's behaviors are occasionally exasperating. But in order to erase such behaviors a parent must first overtly recognize and respect the need systems which precipitated such outlandish behaviors in the first place.

Judging a Person By His Actions

It is almost axiomatic in our society that people are to be judged by their actions. Throughout this book I have stressed the fact that this axiom cannot be used at all in properly dealing with or in understanding the love-shy. Expressed more succinctly, *you cannot assume that an introvert does not want to do something simply because he is never observed doing it!*

To be sure, some young people are truly disinterested in heterosexual interaction. And some are very slow in developing any noteworthy heterosexual interests. Love-shy males, however, are definitely *not* among the ranks of those who tend to be disinterested in informal boy-girl interaction. As the data for this book demonstrated, love-shy males become strongly interested in girls substantially earlier in life than non-shy boys do. But unlike the non-shy, love-shy boys spend much of their time and psychoemotional energies (at school and at home) off in a world of wish-fulfillment fantasies and daydreams. Thus, because they do not enjoy the free choice and self-determination necessary to have a girlfriend *in reality*, they create one in fantasy. As this book demonstrated, this tends to be as true for five-year old love-shys as it is for those in their twenties and thirties.

Parents, teachers and relatives often think that they are doing a favor for the inhibited boy (who only *"appears"* to be disinterested in girls) by saying things like "Oh, leave him alone; he's still got plenty of time!" In point of fact, such well-meaning adults are doing a very grave disservice as a result of their *laissez-faire* posture. Unless a child presents clear and irrefutable evidence that he is not interested in the opposite sex, ways need to be engineered which effectively facilitate relaxed, comfortable boy-girl interaction. And towards this end I strongly recommend making practice-dating clinics freely and easily available to all children 15-years of age and older. Inhibited boys of younger ages should be tactfully introduced to the non-threatening "fun" activities of a Coed Scouting group and/or of a Shys Anonymous group.

One point here is completely certain: love-shys *do not* have "plenty of time". Time is of the essence in dealing with love-shy males. As this book clearly documented, love-shy males become increasingly worse off as time passes, *never better*! A boy who is love-shy at the *seemingly* "youthful" age of 15 will become ten times more severely and intractably love-shy by the time he reaches the age of 30—unless someone intervenes quite decisively towards the end of doing something definitive about his problem.

Again, "helping him to help himself" *just won't work*! Decisive action must be taken to involve love-shy males in informal activities with girls, *and to keep them involved* on a daily basis. There must never be any let up in this regard. The love-shy boy must not be left alone until he has arrived at the point wherein he is actually asserting himself in a friendly way vis-a-vis girls and participating fully in the social life of his community.

Misreading Actions and Inactions

It is very interesting to note that up until now homosexuals have received a very great deal more research attention than love-shy heterosexuals. It would appear that a major reason for this is that homosexuals have been widely perceived (incorrectly so) as constituting a threat to the traditional moral order and normative structure. In contrast, love-shys have never been perceived as constituting a threat to anything. From the time they are small boys in elementary school, love-shys just sit and suffer in silence. Since no one considers them to be a threat, it has not been particularly easy for researchers interested in shyness to secure very much governmental funding for their projects. On the other hand, projects of pertinence to homosexuality have been rather generously funded.

One point which came up again and again in this research was the tendency for love-shy males to complain about being misperceived as homosexuals. Most love-shy men tend to be misperceived by all manner of different kinds of people (women and men alike, and homosexuals and heterosexuals alike) as being homosexuals. In fact, quite a few of the love-shys interviewed for this study had reason to believe that even their parents and other major relatives tended to view them as being probable homosexuals.

Extreme care was taken in drawing up the samples for this research to make sure that all of the men studied were of *genuinely heterosexual orientation*. Thus, it can be said that love-shy heterosexual men have a very difficult time *commanding their performance* on the stage of everyday life. In essence, they do not possess a normal capacity for controlling their behaviors in accordance with their wishes, desires, value systems and goals. As I have expressed it throughout this book, love-shy men lack free choice and self-determination when it comes to friendly assertiveness in most types of informal, unstructured, social situations where there is no purpose apart from pure sociability, and where there is no preordained script or role to play.

Herein lies the real tragedy of love-shyness. The fear of anxiety combined with strong inhibition keeps the love-shy man from developing and expressing his humanity. It keeps the love-shy man confined to a kind of prison which inevitably becomes more and more fully and completely escape-proof with each passing year.

Elementary School Children

For the present moment, I strongly recommend that all conspicuously shy, timid, socially inhibited elementary school boys be singled out for experimentation with the monoamine oxidase inhibitors and/or the tricyclic antidepressant drugs. At the very least, these drugs will operate (most probably in 75 to 85 percent of all cases) to take away the anxiety and fears. Once the social anxieties and "rough and tumble" fears are removed, the child is free to learn interpersonal skills and at least normal levels of social self-confidence. It should always be remembered that the peer group is one of the two most powerfully important socializing agents. With a mind-state that is free from social fears and timidity, interpersonal interaction in the full-range of children's activities becomes permitted. Once a child is accorded full participation in the mainstream of childish play, he can be assured (as this book has demonstrated) full access to the pleasures of dating, courtship and heterosexual interaction—once his fellow same-sexed buddies become involved in such activities.

Among high school and university students the MAO Inhibitors and tricyclics may also prove helpful as an accompanyment to practice-dating therapy. But for a smooth sail, high school (and especially college) age is far too late for such psychopharmacological medication. At such advanced ages the young person (1) must be helped to overcome long established habits of social inertia, and (2) must be put through often very difficult interpersonal skills/social self-confidence training—training to arrive at a level of performance and affect that his age-mates (competitors) had arrived at years before. I think that drug treatment should be used as an *accompanyment* to therapy for high school and college males; but such treatment may now represent a *real boon* to boys in the age 3 through 12 age bracket.

Postscript

This book was written during the early 1980s. As a futurist I would like to say a few words about how I believe shyness will be cured three or four centuries from now.

In essence, I believe that the sort of severe shyness dealt with in this book has as its basic origin a disturbance in the electromagnetic energy field which suffuses the body. This electromagnetic energy force field can also be called the "aura" or the bioplasmic body.

In the severely shy person this electromagnetic energy (aura) field does not intersperse well with the electromagnetic energy fields (auras) of other people. Indeed, it repels other auras to some extent. This is the essence of why from a very early age in life very shy people do not feel comfortable around other people, including age-mates (*people-phobia*). And it is for this reason that the shy child can be singled out very easily in the kindergarten, nursery school, or elementary school classroom.

This disturbance in the individual's electromagnetic energy force field (which makes convivial sociability *feel* unnatural and foreign) is probably rooted in karmic debts; and it is probably created by psycho-emotional disturbances inherent in the mother during her pregnancy. There is always a strong, karmic link between a mother and her child; and the karmic debts of mother and child are likely to be intertwined. Of course, as discussed in chapter 6, boys are far more vulnerable than girls are to the plentitude of things which can go wrong during pregnancy.

I believe that treatment for severe shyness five centuries from now will entail acupuncture techniques as well as a certain form of body massage incorporating a special type of quartz crystal. Shyness will be nipped in the bud because afflicted kindergarten five-year olds will be accorded the intensive anti-shyness treatments which they require. Integral to therapeutic treatment will be the taking of frequent Kirlian photographs and movies of the afflicted person's aura. This will serve to closely and effectively monitor therapeutic changes. Changes in the health of a person's aura should accompany and directly parallel changes in the health of overt behavior.

As Florin Dumetresco's work at the University of Bucharest has shown that acupuncture points usually light up in a person's Kirlian aura when there is a physiologically based problem, various techniques of acupuncture may thus eventually prove serviceable for the treating of such anxiety-based problems as love-shyness. (See especially the Thelma Moss and Lee Steiner works which are listed in the bibliography.)

POSTSCRIPT

Developments While Going to Press

As of July 1985, extreme shyness and behavioral inhibition constitutes an area of research activity that is beginning to expand fast. This is particularly true concerning research into the genetics, biochemistry and physiology of severe shyness and social timidity. And doubtless that is how it should be because if there is to be a final answer to the ultimate *prevention* of shyness it is sure to come from such research areas as genetic engineering and engineering of the intrauterine environment of the developing fetus.

First, Nicholas Zill has just completed a fascinating study that was reported on by Jeff Meer (1985) in a *Psychology Today* article. Zill found that 9 percent of 2,279 children between the ages of 7 and 11 whom he interviewed said that they often "felt lonely and wished that they had more friends." By the time *these same children* had reached the ages of 12 to 16, fully 10 percent reported being lonely "a lot." Most importantly, almost all of the *same children* who were lonely and shy at the ages of 7 through 11, were *still* lonely and shy at the ages of 12 through 16, *five years later*. Thus, the conditions of debilitating shyness, inhibition and social timidity tend to be quite stable over time.

And in his just published book THE NATURE OF THE CHILD, Jerome Kagan (1984) cites a remarkably similar statistic. He points out that *about 10 percent* of American two-year-olds *consistently* display an extreme degree of inhibition to nonthreatening but unfamiliar social stimuli involving people.

An inhibited but physically healthy child may recover from his social fright (upon the introduction of a stranger into an experimental room) after ten or fifteen minutes. And at that point he might talk and play with the stranger with considerable zeal. This is why Alexander Thomas called this sort of child "slow to warm up to other people" (see chapter 2 of this book). But even though the inhibition is temporary, it is a realiable reaction during the second and third years of life. Among a group of children selected by Garcia-Cole (1984) as extremely inhibited at twenty-one months, fully three-fourths had retained this quality through their fourth birthday. Among the group selected as extremely *un*inhibited, *not one* had become inhibited by age four.

When each four year old child in Garcia-Coll's experiment played with an unfamiliar child of the same age and sex, the inhibited children rarely approached the peer and typically were passive to attack from the other child. In contrast, the uninhibited children made frequent overtures, occasionally seized toys, and were generally very gleeful and exuberantly active.

When tested by an unfamiliar woman, the inhibited children rarely made interrupting comments. They looked at the examiner frequently and spoke in soft, hesitant voices. In contrast, the uninhibited children interrupted the examiner with questions and irrelevant comments, laughed frequently, and spoke with confident, vital voices.

To unfamiliar or challenging situations, inhibited children (even at pre-school ages) display physiological reactions indicating that they are very easily aroused by mild stress. One of these reactions involves the heart. About half of the inhibited children in a study by Kagan (1984), but only 10 percent of the uninhibited ones, manifested higher and more stable heart rates when they were looking at pictures or listening to stories that were a little difficult for them to comprehend.

When a person is relaxed the heart rate displays a cycling that is in phase with his/her breathing. As a person breathes in the heart rate rises; as he/she expires the heart rate normally drops off a bit. This decrease in the heart rate is mediated by the vagus nerve which is under parasympathetic control. However, when a person of any age becomes involved in a task that is perceived as somewhat stressful, the physiological arousal that ensues can inhibit vagal control of the heart rate. And as a result, the heart rate rises slightly and becomes much more stable.

This fact suggests that children who usually have higher and more stable heart rates when in new and potentially competitive social situations are (as a result of a genetic basis) more physiologically arousable than the majority of people. Thus, if such afflicted children become aroused in unexpected, unfamiliar, or difficult-to-understand situations, they might well be expected to display an initial and conspicuous degree of caution upon finding themselves in social situations not involving family.

This tendency to become easily aroused by the stresses of daily life was also found in a study by Kagan (1984) to be present in inhibited children during the first year of life. As infants Kagan found inhibited children to have been more irritable than those who later populated the uninhibited, sociable group of children. Also, compared to the uninhibited, the inhibited children as infants displayed a large number of *allergic reactions*. More succinctly, allergic reactions including an unusually large number of bodily itches can be viewed as constituting symptoms which reflect a much higher than normal level of physiological arousal to harmless stimuli and to everyday events. As I clearly documented in chapter 15 of this book, love-shys are far more likely than non-shys to suffer from a host of allergic sensitivities. Thus, allergic sensitivities may well be precipitated by the same gene as severe shyness. In any case, like behavioral inhibition, allergic reactions appear to represent a behavioral quality that for about 10 percent of the population remains stable across entire liftimes.

Kagan (1984) studied one group of children from birth to age fourteen, and again as young adults. This group included seven boys who had been extremely inhibited throughout the first three years of their lives. They remained different from the extremely uninhibited boys throughout childhood, adolescence, and adulthood. The inhibited males avoided (because of severe shyness) traditional masculine sexual activities, they selected less masculine occupations in adulthood, and as adults were found to be highly introverted and very anxious in new social situations (see also Kagan and Moss, 1983).

An initial behavioral tendency favoring inhibition or lack of inhibition is also believed by Scarr (1969) to be one of the few behavioral dispositions that persists over the long haul of life—because it has a strong basis in genetics and body biochemistry. And this body biochemistry impacts the cerebral neurotransmitters in a whole host of ways.

One of the basic principles of physiology is that each animal species is characterized by a few complementary systems that compete for dominance. The competition between the sympathetic and the parasympathetic nervous systems is a good example of competing systems. And it is quite possible that genetic or prenatal influences create conditions which, in some children, promote the sympathetic nervous system to a position of dominance over the parasympathetic nervous system. Such children would be prone towards becoming extremely inhibited, especially if their early environments were somewhat stressful, and if the social norms impacting them prescribe competitive, "rough and tumble" activity.

Identical twins were found by Plomin and Rowe (1979) to be much more similar in their tendencies to be inhibited or uninhibited than a sample of fraternal twins. This and the many similar findings reported earlier in this book strongly imply genetic imfluence. See also Scarr (1969) for further strong evidence in this regard. On the other hand, Kagan (1984) believes that a biological susceptibility to inhibition may not be actualized in any sort of severe way if the home environment is unusually benevolent—if the child has sensitive, accepting parents and is somehow protected from peer bullying (the most overlooked of all forms of child abuse).

The Energyzing Body Biochemistry of Feeling Good about Oneself

During the past fifteen years several researchers have emphasized the point that feeling good about oneself is *energyzing* from a biochemical and physiological standpoint. See especially the work of Norman Cousins (1984), and Spencer Johnson (1983) in this regard. It appears that there are chemical concomitants of high self-esteem which serve to promote high and continuing levels of productive activity. By way of contrast, virtually all of the data presented in this book clearly and incisively document the point that love-shy teenagers, young adults and middle-agers tend to be lethargic and very low on physical energy.

In chapter one I discussed an experiment which powerfully documents the energyzing affects of heterosexual love. Simply put, love makes people (and especially males) feel good—and strongly energized—because it makes them feel good about themselves. Being loved in return by someone whom one deeply and sincerely loves is a powerful reinforcer, and it doubtless underlies the popular cliche that there is a woman behind every successful man. The powerfully energyzing properties of heterosexual love constitute a very strong reason for the "powers that be" in society to take action to get severely love-shy males (of all ages) involved in informal heterosexual interaction so that they can find somebody to love—so that they can become energyzed and perform at their "peak" best.

The Impact of Testosterone on Intrauterine Brain Development of the Fetus

During the past several years mounting research evidence has come to the fore which provides strong support for the principles that I delineated in chapter six of this book. Much of this evidence is clearly presented in the first fourteen chapters of a new book titled SEX AND THE BRAIN, by Jo Durden-Smith and Diane deSimone (1983), which I strongly recommend (together with Wender and Klein's book MIND, MOOD AND MEDICINE) as "must" reading for anyone genuinely desirous of a full understanding of the root causes of intractable love-shyness.

Durden-Smith and deSimone place particular emphasis upon the work of East German researcher Gunter Dorner. Simply put, it appears that testosterone has a profound effect upon the brain's three major neurotransmitters, serotonin, dopamine, and norepinephrine. These are the three neurotransmitters discussed at length in chapter two, as having a profound impact upon mood and upon relative proneness to anxiety (anxiety threshold).

The sex hormones, and particularly testosterone, profoundly influence brain development, brain structure, and ultimate behavior. Bruce McEwen, a neurobiologist at Rockefeller University, has discovered sex hormone receptors during the critical period of *intrauterine development* in precisely those areas of the brain which are now believed to organize differences in behavior (between males and females) *other than the sexual*, such as the tendency to run away and avoid stress (a "female" response), the tendency to be assertive, competitive and aggressive ("male" response), etc. Most importantly, *the genetic sex of body tissue is relatively unimportant in terms of ultimate social behavior and preferences. It is the operation of the sex hormones (especially before birth) that is of enormous importance.*

Durden-Smith and deSimone (1983) discuss at considerable length the work of Anke A. Ehrhardt and Heino Meyer-Bahlburg of Columbia University. In their in-depth studies of the hormonal environment of the womb, these researchers have focused their attention upon children whose mothers had been given hormones for purposes of pregnancy maintenance. Beginning in the 1950s science developed an increasing ability to manipulate natural hormones and to synthesize new ones. And over a period of thirty years various versions of these hormones were routeinely dispensed, not only to women at risk for spontaneous abortion or miscarriage, but also to many women who had no reason to need science's help at all. Burgeoning malpractice insurance rates have been one of the key forces behind the increased tendency to employ these hormones on pregnant women, and to require them for giving birth via Cesarean section.

The children born after their mothers had been treated with these hormones differ from controls *only in the circulating sex hormones they were exposed to in the womb*. Ehrhardt and Meyer-Bahlburg along with June Reinisch of the Kinsey Institute (Indiana University), and Richard Green of State University of New York at Stony Brook, have tried to tease out the intrauterine effects of these hormones. The case is clearest for the progestogens. Girls who had been exposed intrautero to androgen-based progestogens tended to become a great deal *more tomboyish and energetic* than the large majority of unaffected girls; and many of them had been born with subtly masculinized genitals. The affected boys were also found to be much more energetic and aggressive than their peers.

The reverse of these findings, however, was found to obtain with respect to children affected intrautero by *progesterone*-based progestogens—whether administered alone or in combination with estrogens. These hormones had a demonstrably demasculinizing effect. Boys exposed to them as fetuses were found as children to be demonstrably less aggressive and assertive than their male peers. Further, they were found to display poorer athletic coordination and *"lowered masculine interests"*. The picture was found to be similar for girls whose mothers had been treated with progesterone-based progestogens. They too were found as children to be less active, less verbally aggressive, and less given to energetic play than their peers. Further, the affected *boys* and girls were found during the elementary school years to display a preference for female as opposed to male friends.

All of the evidence that is in to date clearly indicates that in humans as well as in monkeys the sex hormones operating in the uterus upon the developing brain are responsible for what might be called *a pretuning of the personality*. In essence, the sex hormones organize the social demeanor of the sexes, their orientation to the problems of life and the way they go about solving them.

As I have clearly shown, love-shy men are not homosexual. However, a feminization of sexual orientation appears to be *just one* of the things that can go wrong for male children while they are still in the intrauterine environment. Evidently, only some of the sex hormone receptors in the hypothalamus relate to ultimate sexual preference—as I suggested in chapter six of this book. Other receptors relate to sex-appropriate behaviors and interests. And evidently, in some male fetuses these can be adversely impacted without the sexual preference receptors being adversely affected (feminized).

We are still a long way from understanding how all of these processes work. However, numerous interesting hints have been issuing from the work of Gunter Dorner. Dorner observed that rats could be rendered homosexual if deprived intrautero of testosterone during the critical period of brain differentiation. Dorner injected a sample of such homosexual rats (as adults) with estrogen. His argument was that if the brains of these rats had indeed been feminized in the intrauterine environment, then their brains would respond as if to a signal from a non-existent ovary, with a surge of ovulation-inducing hormone—the so-called luteinizing hormone (LH). *And they did so.* Their brains were indeed feminized.

Dorner then applied this technique to human male homosexuals and he found the same thing. Their brains responded with this delayed hormonal surge *whereas the brains of a sample of heterosexual males did not.*

During this time Ingeborg Ward at Villanova University had been showing that if you subjected pregnant female rats to stress, then their male offspring would have extremely low levels of testosterone at birth and would exhibit feminized and demasculinized sexual behavior in adulthood. In essence, they would become bisexual or homosexual. Dorner repeated her experiment and then looked at the human population to see if there might be a connection between prenatal stress and male homosexuality.

First he looked at the records to see whether more male homosexuals had been born during the stressful period of World War II than had been born either before or after it. And he found that there was indeed a very high peak during 1944 and 1945 with regard to homosexuals being born. After having done this, Dorner interviewed a sample of 100 homosexual and bisexual men that was matched with a sample of 100 heterosexual men. And he found that more than two-thirds of the mothers of the homosexuals and bisexuals had been under moderate to quite severe stress during the period that they had been pregnant. In contrast, only about 10 percent of the mothers of the heterosexual men had been under some stress, and most of their stress was reported as having been quite mild.

On the basis of these and other data (some of which was reported in chapter six of this book), Dorner concluded that male homosexuality is the result of permanent neurochemical changes in the hypothalamus effected by reduced levels of testosterone during fetal life. This produces a feminization of the brain which is activated, as far as sexual behavior is concerned, at puberty. The data indicate that *stress in the mother* is a major risk factor—which causes the production of substances in the adrenal gland which depress testosterone levels in the male fetus. This and other related factors operate to permanently alter the neural circuitry of the brain, the nerve pathways that are controlled by the local brain hormones, the neurotransmitters (serotonin, dopamine, and norepinephrine). These three brain hormones are among the major substances by which individual nerve cells in different parts of the brain communicate with one another across the tiny gap between them (i.e., the *synapse*). And this particular group of three brain hormones seem to be the local mediators of the effects the sex hormones (particularly testosterone) have on brain cells, and on behavior, throughout life.

Of course, one clear way in which heterosexual love-shyness differs from male homosexuality is that the activated sexual interests in love-shys *at puberty* are exclusively *heterosexual* in nature. However, both before as well as after puberty male love-shys much prefer the idea of playing with girls as opposed to playing with boys; and their recreational interests are (as demonstrated in chapter 10) demonstrably "feminine" as far as our cultural definitions are concerned. Further, heterosexual love-shys (as per the data presented in chapter 11) appear to have *always* been deeply romantically oriented both *before* as well as after pubescence. This strong, preadolescent need for pair-bonding with a romantic lover does not appear to be a consistent earmark of homosexual males.

This is why it is prudent to speculate upon the existence of *different* sex hormone receptors in the brain which respond to these chemicals during intrauterine life.

Evidently, the impact of the sex hormones *at puberty* is quite different for male homosexuals than it is for male heterosexual love-shys. This is because certain sex hormone receptors in homosexuals had been pretuned well before birth, whereas in the latter these same sex hormone receptors had not been pretuned.

On the other hand, male homosexual and heterosexual love-shys appear to have numerous important traits in common. And an attribute of the most important sort which they appear to have in common is the history of having been feminized intrautero by the subjectivity perceived prenatal stress of a hypertensive mother.

It is now possible to demonstrate that the levels of serotonin, dopamine, and norepinephrine are quite dramatically altered in different areas of the brain as a result of prenatal stress in both male and female rats. In fact, it has recently been shown that not only the male but also the female offspring of prenatally stressed mothers have (1) altered levels as adults of these neurotransmitters, and (2) a poor reproductive capacity. The latter is manifested by irregular estrus cycle, low sexual receptivity, difficulty becoming pregnant, tendency to spontaneously abort, and failure to produce sufficient milk for offspring. To be sure, extrapolating from rats to humans is always risky. But these research results must be viewed as strongly suggestive.

Testosterone in humans gives rise to a number of behavioral effects quite in addition to that of merely increasing level of aggression and assertiveness. A number of studies have suggested that testosterone increases behavioral reactivity—the opposite of the inhibition which love-shys display. But more importantly, it has also been found to alleviate fatigue. As I have indicated in chapter 15, severely shy men tend to be quite lacking in energy; they suffer from frequent periods of fatigue which get in the way of their ability to show persistent effort even in activities they enjoy, much less in those wherein there is opposition requiring some degree of competition. The fact that love-shys tend to have an above average amount of difficulty getting up out of bed in the morning can be seen as further illustrative of low energy and perhaps a diminished sensitivity to testosterone in areas of the brain that should react to testosterone but cannot do so because they were inadequately primed for it before birth.

Bob Goy of the primate lab at University of Wisconsin, Madison, has provided some further data which has a suggestive bearing upon the development of love-shyness in males. Goy has studied dominance patterns among rhesus monkeys, and he has shown that females whose mothers were given testosterone during pregnancy are much more likely to be the dominant members of a mixed troup as adults than are other, untreated females.

Goy has highlighted four major ways in which male rhesus monkeys at young ages differ in their behavior from females: (1) they initiate play more often, (2) they roughhouse more often, (3) they mount peers of both sexes more often, and (4) they mount their mothers more often than females do. But interestingly, Goy has been able to produce a male-typical frequency of all of these behaviors in young females by giving their pregnant mothers thigh injections of testosterone for various periods of time during the critical period of development which in rhesus monkeys as in humans is before birth. As a result of such treatment the young females will play rough and will act assertively.

Many of Goy's testosterone-treated female monkeys tend to be born with somewhat masculinized genitals. Thus, there is clearly a critical prenatal period for the formation of genitals. But far more interesting is the fact that there also appears to be a *critical period* for every one of the four sex-specific behaviors delineated above. In essence, there is a critical period in intrauterine development during which the sex hormones affect every single one of these "sex-appropriate" behaviors. Given the many similarities between rhesus monkeys and man (both primates), these findings may well hold considerable implications for the intractable passivity which male (human) love-shys display. Further, these findings suggest that the individual traits which comprise masculinity are separately controlled, *over time*, by the sex hormones. The masculinization of the brain which takes place before birth is thus a slow, complicated, "more-or-less" type process. Hence, you can get some males which are born with highly aggressive play tendencies, and you get others that are born less "masculine".

Hence, there are two biological forces which conspire in a synergistic way with the environment to give rise to severe shyness: (1) genes, and (2) congenital forces operating before birth. The genes can be seen as constituting interlocking sets of potentials and predispositions. The congenital variables highlight the importance of the hormonal and immune environment of the womb. Once born, of course, the feminized male child exudes (through no "free choice" fault of his own) and becomes a victim of an adverse *social stimulus value*—as per my detailed discussion in chapter three.

It's Time to Take the Problem of Shyness Seriously

In the July 1985, issue of PSYCHOLOGY TODAY, British psychologist Peter Harris (of University of Nottingham) emphasizes that a key reason some people experience so much trouble and unhappiness in overcoming their shyness is that most people simply do not take the shyness problem seriously. Indeed, shyness (*especially in males*) vis-a-vis the opposite sex fails to excite feelings of sympathy and compassion, except in very few people. It is deeply and sincerely hoped that this book will begin to greatly change all that. Through reading and studying the numerous case reports presented in this book it is hoped that the public (and particularly those involved as teachers and administrators at *all levels* of education) will at long last begin to appreciate how enormously and excruciatingly painful and life-debilitating shyness, and especially "*love-shyness*" can be. Once the seriousness of the problem is fully realized by people of some influence, the effective modes of therapy and prevention discussed in this book can begin to be aggressively pursued on behalf of the victims.

Bibliography

A.B.C. Television. 1982.
"Depression." TWENTY/TWENTY. Thursday, January 28, 1982.
A.B.C. Television. 1983.
"There But for the Grace of God." TWENTY/TWENTY. Thursday, April 28, 1983.
A.B.C. Television. 1985.
"Anxiety Disease." TWENTY/TWENTY. Thursday, May 2, 1985.
Achterberg, Jeanne. 1976.
"Philosophical and Ethical Considerations in the Research of Cancer," In Simonton, O. Carl, and Stephanie Matthews Simonton (Eds.), PSYCHOLOGICAL FACTORS, STRESS, AND CANCER, Fort Worth, Texas: Cancer Counseling and Research Center.
Adinolfi, Allen A. 1970.
"Characteristics of Highly Accepted, Highly Rejected, and Relatively Unknown University Freshmen." JOURNAL OF COUNSELING PSYCHOLOGY 17 (No. 5): 456–464.
Anderson, Rosemarie, and Steve A. Nida. 1978.
"Effect of Physical Attractiveness on Opposite and Same-Sex Evaluations." JOURNAL OF PERSONALITY 46 (No. 3):401–413.
Arkowitz, Hal, et. al. 1975.
"The Behavioral Assessment of Social Competence in Males." BEHAVIOR THERAPY 6: 3–13.
Arkowitz, Hal. 1977.
"Measurement and Modification of Minimal Dating Behavior," In Hersen, M., et. al. (Ed.), PROGRESS IN BEHAVIORAL MODIFICATION (Vol. 5), New York: Academic Press, pp. 1–61.
Avery, Arthur W., et. al. 1981.
"Teaching Shy Students: The Role of the Family Life Educator." FAMILY RELATIONS 30 (January):39–43.
Azrin, Nathan. 1979.
THE PSYCHOLOGY OF JOB HUNTING. New York: Ziff-Davis.
Beatty, Michael J., et. al. 1978.
"Situational Determinants of Communication Apprehension." COMMUNICATION MONOGRAPHS 45 (August):187–191.
Beck, Alan, and Aaron Katcher. 1983.
BETWEEN PETS AND PEOPLE: THE IMPORTANCE OF ANIMAL COMPANIONSHIP. New York: G. P. Putnam's Sons.
Becker, Ernest. 1968.
"Socialization, Command of Performance, and Mental Illness," In Spitzer, Stephan P., and Norman K. Denzin (Eds.), THE MENTAL PATIENT: STUDIES IN THE SOCIOLOGY OF DEVIANCE. New York: McGraw-Hill.
Bell, Sanford. 1902.
"A Preliminary Study of the Emotion of Love Between the Sexes." AMERICAN JOURNAL OF PSYCHOLOGY 13, 325–354.

Bermann, Eric, and Daniel R. Miller. 1967.
"The Matching of Mates," In Jessor, Richard, and Seymour Feshbach (Eds.), COG-NITION, PERSONALITY, AND CLINICAL PSYCHOLOGY. San Francisco: Jossey-Bass, pp. 90–111.

Bernstein, Morey. 1956.
THE SEARCH FOR BRIDEY MURPHY. New York: Bantam Books.

Berscheid, Ellen, and Karen Dion. 1971.
"Physical Attractiveness and Dating Choice: A Test of the Matching Hypothesis." JOURNAL OF EXPERIMENTAL SOCIAL PSYCHOLOGY 7, pp. 173–189.

Berscheid, Ellen, and Elaine Walster. 1974.
"Physical Attractiveness," In Berkowitz, L. (Ed.), ADVANCES IN EXPERIMENTAL SOCIAL PSYCHOLOGY (Vol. 7), New York: Academic Press, pp. 157–215.

Block, Michael. 1979.
LETTERS TO MICHAEL. New York: Coward, McCann & Geoghegan.

Borkovec, Thomas D., et. al. 1974.
"Evaluation of a Clinically Relevant Target Behavior for Analog Outcome Research." BEHAVIOR THERAPY 5, pp. 503–513.

Bradburn, Norman. 1969.
THE STRUCTURE OF PSYCHOLOGICAL WELL-BEING. Chicago: Aldine Publishing.

Braginsky, Dorothea and Ben. 1976.
SURPLUS PEOPLE. New York: Ziff-Davis.

Brain, Robert. 1976.
FRIENDS AND LOVERS. New York: Basic Books.

Brennan, Tim. 1982.
"Loneliness at Adolescence," In Peplau, Letitia Anne, and Daniel Perlman (Eds.), LONELINESS. New York: John Wiley & Sons, pp. 269–290.

Brim, J. 1974.
"Social Network Correlates of Avowed Happiness." JOURNAL OF NERVOUS AND MENTAL DISEASE 158, pp. 432–439.

Bristol, Claude M. 1948.
THE MAGIC OF BELIEVING. Englewood Cliffs, New Jersey: Prentice-Hall.

Broderick, Carlfred B., and Stanley Fowler. 1961.
"New Patterns of Relationships Between the Sexes Among Preadolescents." JOURNAL OF MARRIAGE AND THE FAMILY 23 (February):27–30.

Broderick, Carlfred B. 1966.
"Socio-Sexual Development in a Suburban Community." JOURNAL OF SEX RESEARCH 2 (April):1–24.

Broderick, Carlfred B. 1972.
"Children's Romances." SEXUAL BEHAVIOR 2 (May):16–21.

Brody, Eugene B. 1977.
"Research in Reincarnation and Editorial Responsibility." JOURNAL OF NERVOUS AND MENTAL DISEASE 165 (September):151.

Bronfenbrenner, Urie. 1970.
TWO WORLDS OF CHILDHOOD: U.S. AND U.S.S.R. New York: Russell Sage Foundation.

Brown, D. 1955.
"Helping Adolescents Win Social Acceptance." HIGH SCHOOL JOURNAL 38, pp. 157–162.

Bryant, Bridget, and P. E.Trower. 1974.
"Social Difficulty in a Student Sample." BRITISH JOURNAL OF EDUCATIONAL PSYCHOLOGY 44, pp. 13–21.

Burk, Michael P. 1978.
"Coming Out: The Gay Identity Process," In Murstein, Bernard I. (Ed.), EX-PLORING INTIMATE LIFE STYLES. New York: Springer Publishing, pp. 257–272.

Burns, David D. 1985.
    INTIMATE CONNECTIONS. New York: William Morrow & Company.
Byrne, Charles E. 1981.
    "Diabetics in the Classroom." M.T.A. TODAY 11 (March 15):11.
Cameron, C., et. al. 1977.
    "Courtship American Style: Newspaper Ads." THE FAMILY COORDINATOR 26
    (January):27–30.
Carducci, Bernardo J., and Arthur W. Webber. 1979.
    "Shyness as a Determinant of Interpersonal Distance." PSYCHOLOGICAL REPORTS
    44, pp. 1075–1078.
Cargan, Leonard, and Matthew Melko. 1982.
    SINGLES: MYTHS AND REALITIES. Beverly Hills, CA: Sage Publishers.
Cassill, Kay. 1982.
    TWINS: NATURE'S AMAZING MYSTERY. New York: Atheneum.
Cerminara, Gina. 1950.
    MANY MANSIONS. New York: New American Library.
Chen, E., and Sidney Cobb. 1960.
    "Family Structure in Relation to Health and Disease." JOURNAL OF CHRONIC
    DISEASES 12, pp. 544–567.
Christensen, Andrew, and Hal Arkowitz. 1974.
    "Preliminary Report on Practice Dating and Feedback as Treatment for College
    Dating Problems." JOURNAL OF COUNSELING PSYCHOLOGY 21 (No. 2):
    92–95.
Christensen, Andrew, et. al. 1975.
    "Practice Dating as Treatment for College Dating Inhibitions." BEHAVIOR
    RESEARCH AND THERAPY 13, pp. 321–331.
Christensen, Harold T., and Christina F. Gregg. 1970.
    "Changing Sex Norms in America and Scandinavia." JOURNAL OF MARRIAGE
    AND THE FAMILY 32 (November):616–627.
Cobb, Sidney. 1976.
    "Social Support as a Moderator of Life Stress." PSYCHOSOMATIC MEDICINE 38,
    pp. 300–314.
Coombs, Robert H. 1966.
    "Value Consensus and Partner Satisfaction Among Dating Couples." JOURNAL
    OF MARRIAGE AND THE FAMILY 28 (May):166–173.
Coombs, Robert H. 1969.
    "Social Participation, Self-Concept and Interpersonal Valuation." SOCIOMETRY 32
    (No. 3):273–286.
Coopersmith, Stanley. 1967.
    THE ANTECEDENTS OF SELF-ESTEEM. San Francisco: W. Freeman.
Coser, Lewis. 1956.
    THE FUNCTIONS OF SOCIAL CONFLICT. New York: The Free Press of Glencoe.
Cousins, Norman. 1984.
    MIND OVER ILLNESS: THIS I BELIEVE. Chicago: Nightengale-Conant Corporation.
Curran, James P., et. al. 1976.
    "A Comparison Between Behavioral Replication Training and Sensitivity Training
    Approaches to Heterosexual Dating Anxiety." JOURNAL OF COUNSELING PSY-
    CHOLOGY 23 (No. 3):190–196.
Curran, James P. 1977.
    "Skills Training as an Approach to the Treatment of Heterosexual-Social Anxiety:
    A Review." PSYCHOLOGICAL BULLETIN 84, pp. 140–157.
Cutright, Phillips. 1970.
    "Income and Family Events: Getting Married." JOURNAL OF MARRIAGE AND
    THE FAMILY 32 (November): 628–637.
Cutrona, Carolyn E. 1982.
    "Transition to College: Loneliness and the Process of Social Adjustment," In Peplau,

Letitia Anne, and Daniel Perlman (Eds.), LONELINESS. New York: John Wiley and Sons, pp. 291–309.

Daly, John A. 1978.
"The Assessment of Social-Communication Anxiety via Self-Reports: A Comparison of Measures." COMMUNICATION MONOGRAPHS 45 (August):204–218.

Daniels, Denise, and Robert Plomin. 1985.
"Shy Baby Genes." PSYCHOLOGY TODAY 19 (June):16–17.

DeVore, Steven. 1982.
THE NEUROPSYCHOLOGY OF ACHIEVEMENT. San Leandro, CA (2450 Washington Avenue; zip: 94577): Sybervision Systems, Inc.

Dion, Karen, et. al. 1972.
"What is Beautiful is Good." JOURNAL OF PERSONALITY AND SOCIAL PSYCHOLOGY 24 (No. 3):285–290.

Dixon, James J., et. al. 1957.
"Patterns of Anxiety: An Analysis of Social Anxieties." BRITISH JOURNAL OF MEDICAL PSYCHOLOGY 30, pp. 107–112.

Durden-Smith, Jo, and Diane DeSimone. 1983.
SEX AND THE BRAIN. New York: Arbor House Publishing Company.

Durkheim, Emile. 1961.
SUICIDE. New York: The Free Press of Glencoe.

Dworkin, Robert H., et. al. 1976.
"A Longitudinal Study of the Genetics of Personality." JOURNAL OF PERSONALITY AND SOCIAL PSYCHOLOGY 34, 510–518.

Eaves, Lindon, and Hans J. Eysenck. 1975.
"The Nature of Extroversion: A Genetic Analysis." JOURNAL OF PERSONALITY AND SOCIAL PSYCHOLOGY 32 (No. 1):102–112.

Elliott, Jane, and William Peters. 1971.
A CLASS DIVIDED. New York: Ballantine Books.

Ellis, Albert. 1978.
DEALING WITH SEXUALITY AND INTIMACY. New York: Biomonitoring Applications, Inc.

Ellis, Robert A., and W. Clayton Lane. 1967.
"Social Mobility and Social Isolation." AMERICAN SOCIOLOGICAL REVIEW 32 (June):237–256.

Erikson, Kai T. 1962.
"Notes on the Sociology of Deviance." SOCIAL PROBLEMS 8 (Spring):307–314.

Eysenck, Hans J. 1967.
THE BIOLOGICAL BASIS OF PERSONALITY. Springfield, Illinois: Charles C. Thomas Publishers.

Eysenck, Hans J. 1971.
"Personality and Sexual Adjustment." BRITISH JOURNAL OF PSYCHIATRY 118, pp. 593–608.

Eysenck, Hans J. 1973.
THE INEQUALITY OF MAN. San Diego: EdITS Publishers.

Eysenck, Hans J. 1974.
"Personality, Premarital Sexual Permissiveness, and Assortive Mating." JOURNAL OF SEX RESEARCH 10 (February):47–51.

Eysenck, Hans J., and Sybil B. G. Eysenck. 1975.
MANUAL FOR THE EYSENCK PERSONALITY QUESTIONNAIRE. San Diego: EdITS Publishers.

Eysenck, Hans J. 1976.
"Genetic Factors in Personality Development," In Kaplan, A. R. (Ed.), HUMAN BEHAVIOR GENETICS. Springfield, Illinois: Charles C. Thomas Publishers, pp. 198–229.

Eysenck, Hans J., and Sybil B. G. Eysenck. 1976.
PSYCHOTICISM AS A DIMENSION OF PERSONALITY. New York: Crane, Russak & Company.

Eysenck, Hans J. 1976.
    SEX AND PERSONALITY. Austin: University of Texas Press.
Farber, Susan L. 1981.
    IDENTICAL TWINS REARED APART. New York: Basic Books.
Feinberg, M. R. 1953.
    "Relation of Background Experience to Social Acceptance." JOURNAL OF ABNOR-
    MAL AND SOCIAL PSYCHOLOGY 48, pp. 206–214.
Fischer, Claude S., and Susan L. Phillips. 1982.
    "Who Is Alone? Social Characteristics of People with Small Networks," In Peplau,
    Letitia Anne, and Daniel Perlman (Eds.), LONELINESS. New York: John Wiley and
    Sons, pp. 21–39.
Fishman, Scott M., and David V. Sheehan. 1985.
    "Anxiety and Panic: Their Cause and Treatment." PSYCHOLOGY TODAY 19
    (April):26–32.
Fogle, Bruce. 1984.
    PETS AND THEIR PEOPLE. New York: Viking Books.
Freedman, Jonathan, and Anthony N. Doob. 1968.
    DEVIANCY: THE PSYCHOLOGY OF BEING DIFFERENT. New York: Academic
    Press.
Freedman, Jonathan. 1978.
    HAPPY PEOPLE: WHAT HAPPINESS IS, WHO HAS IT, AND WHY. New York:
    Harcourt Brace Jovanovich.
Fromm, Erich. 1956.
    THE ART OF LOVING. New York: Harper & Row.
Garcia-Coll, Cynthia. 1981.
    "Psychophysiological Correlates of a Tendency toward Inhibition in Infants."
    Unpublished Doctoral Dissertation. Cambridge, MA: Harvard University.
Garcia-Coll, Cynthia, and Jerome Kagan. 1984.
    "Behavioral Inhibition to the Unfamiliar." CHILD DEVELOPMENT 55 (December):
    2212–2225.
Garrison, John P., and Karen R. Garrison. 1979.
    "Measurement of Oral Communication Apprehension Among Children." COM-
    MUNICATION EDUCATION 28 (May):119–128.
Gaylin, Jody. 1979.
    "What Girls Really Look for in Boys." SEVENTEEN (March):131–137.
Gil, David G. 1971.
    "Violence Against Children." JOURNAL OF MARRIAGE AND THE FAMILY 33
    (November): 637–648.
Gilmartin, Brian G. 1965.
    "Relationship of Traits Measured by the California Psychological Inventory to Pre-
    marital Sexual Standards and Behaviors." Unpublished Masters Thesis. Salt Lake
    City: University of Utah.
Gilmartin, Brian G. 1968.
    "Social Antecedents of Psychoneurotic Disorders: Inadequate Socialization or Socie-
    tal Intolerance?" Unpublished Manuscript. Iowa City: University of Iowa.
Gilmartin, Brian G. 1974.
    "Sexual Deviance and Social Networks," In Smith, James R. and Lynn G. (Eds.),
    BEYOND   MONOGAMY.   Baltimore: Johns   Hopkins   University   Press.
    pp. 291–323.
Gilmartin, Brian G. 1975.
    "That Swinging Couple Down the Block." PSYCHOLOGY TODAY 8 (February):54–
    58.
Gilmartin, Brian G. 1976.
    "The Social Antecedents and Correlates of Comarital Sexual Behavior." Unpublished
    Doctoral Dissertation. Iowa City: University of Iowa.
Gilmartin, Brian G. 1977.
    "Swinging: Who Gets Involved and How?" In Libby, Roger W., and Robert N.

Whitehurst (Eds.), MARRIAGE AND ALTERNATIVES. Chicago: Scott, Foresman, pp. 161–185.

Gilmartin, Brian G. 1978.
THE GILMARTIN REPORT: INSIDE SWINGING FAMILIES. Secaucus, New Jersey: Citadel Press.

Gilmartin, Brian G. 1979.
"Corporal Punishment: A Research Update." HUMAN BEHAVIOR 8 (February): 18–25.

Gilmartin, Brian G. 1985.
"Some Family Antecedents of Severe Shyness in Males." FAMILY RELATIONS 34 (July): 429–438.

Gilmartin, Brian G. 1987.
"Peer Group Antecedents of Severe Love-Shyness in Males." JOURNAL OF PERSONALITY 55 (May).

Ginzberg, Eli. 1969.
MEN, MONEY AND MEDICINE. New York: Columbia University Press.

Girodo, Michel. 1978.
SHY? YOU DON'T HAVE TO BE! New York: Pocket Books.

Gittelman-Klein, Rachel, and Donald F. Klein. 1971.
"Controlled Imipramine Treatment of School Phobia." ARCHIVES OF GENERAL PSYCHIATRY 25, 204–214.

Goldberg, Herb. 1976.
THE HAZARDS OF BEING MALE. New York: Nash Publishing.

Gordon, Thomas. 1970.
PARENT EFFECTIVENESS TRAINING. New York: Wyden Books.

Gordon, Thomas. 1974.
TEACHER EFFECTIVENESS TRAINING. New York: Wyden Books.

Gordon, Thomas. 1976.
P.E.T. IN ACTION. New York: Wyden Books.

Gore, Susan. 1978.
"The Effect of Social Support in Moderating the Health Consequences of Unemployment." JOURNAL OF HEALTH AND SOCIAL BEHAVIOR 19 (June):157–165.

Gottesman, Irving I. 1966.
"Genetic Variance in Adaptive Personality Traits." JOURNAL OF CHILD PSYCHOLOGY AND PSYCHIATRY 7, pp. 199–208.

Grant, Vernon W. 1976.
FALLING IN LOVE: THE PSYCHOLOGY OF THE ROMANTIC EMOTION. New York: Springer.

Gray, J. A. 1972.
"The Psychophysiological Nature of Introversion-Extroversion: A Modification of Eysenck's Theory." In Nebylitsyn, V. D., and J. A. Gray (Eds.), BIOLOGICAL BASES OF INDIVIDUAL BEHAVIOR. New York: Academic Press, pp. 167–198.

Greeley, Andrew. 1971.
THE SOCIOLOGY OF THE PARANORMAL. Beverly Hills: Sage Publishers.

Gronlund, Norman E. 1959.
SOCIOMETRY IN THE CLASSROOM. New York: Harper and Row.

Gutman, E. Michael. 1982.
"The Shyness Disorder: Should It Be Included in the DSM-IV?" Paper Presented at the Annual Meeting of the FLORIDA PSYCHIATRIC SOCIETY, Tampa, Florida, November 20.

Haley, Jay. 1959.
"The Control of Fear with Hypnosis." AMERICAN JOURNAL OF CLINICAL HYPNOSIS 2, pp. 109–115.

Harlow, Harry F., and Margaret K. Harlow. 1962.
"Social Deprivation in Monkeys." SCIENTIFIC AMERICAN 207 (November):136–146.

Harper, Lawrence V., and Karen M. Sanders. 1978.
    "Sex Differences in Preschool Children's Social Interactions and Use of Space: An Evolutionary Perspective," In McGill, Thomas E., et. al. (Eds.), SEX AND BEHAVIOR: STATUS AND PROSPECTS. New York: Plenum Press, pp. 61–81.
Harris, Peter. 1985.
    "Serious Shyness." PSYCHOLOGY TODAY 19 (July):12.
Havighurst, Robert J. 1952.
    DEVELOPMENTAL TASKS AND EDUCATION. New York: Longmans, Green.
Hedquist, Francis J., and Barry K. Weinhold. 1970.
    "Behavioral Group Counseling with Socially Anxious and Unassertive College Students." JOURNAL OF COUNSELING PSYCHOLOGY 17 (No. 3):237–242.
Helfer, Ray E. 1974.
    CHILD ABUSE AND NEGLECT: THE DIAGNOSTIC PROCESS AND TREATMENT PROGRAMS. Washington, D.C.: DHEW Publication #(OHD)75-69.
Helmstetter, Shad. 1982.
    WINNING FROM WITHIN. Chicago: Nightengale-Conant Corporation.
Hendrick, Clyde and Susan. 1983.
    LIKING, LOVING, AND RELATING. Monterey, CA: Brooks/Cole Publishing Company.
Hill, Charles T., et. al. 1976.
    "Breakups Before Marriage: The End of 103 Affairs," JOURNAL OF SOCIAL ISSUES, 32 (No. 1):147–168.
Hill, Napolean. 1960.
    THINK AND GROW RICH. New York: Fawcett Crest.
Himadi, William G., et. al. 1980.
    "Minimal Dating and its Relationship to Other Social Problems and General Adjustment," BEHAVIOR THERAPY 11, pp. 345–352.
Himmelweit, Hilda. 1947.
    "A Comparative Study of the Level of Aspiration of Normal and Neurotic Persons," BRITISH JOURNAL OF PSYCHOLOGY 37 (January):41–59.
Homans, George. 1950.
    THE HUMAN GROUP. New York: Harcourt, Brace & World.
Hoover, Stephanie, et. al. 1979.
    "Correlates of College Students' Loneliness," PSYCHOLOGICAL REPORTS 44, p. 1116.
Horowitz, Leonard M., et. al. 1982.
    "The Prototype of a Lonely Person," In Peplau, Letitia Anne, and Daniel Perlman (Eds.), LONELINESS. New York: John Wiley & Sons, pp. 183–205.
Horton, Paul B., and Chester L. Hunt. 1976.
    SOCIOLOGY (4th edition), New York: McGraw-Hill.
House, James S. 1974.
    "Occupational Stress and Coronary Heart Disease: A Review and Theoretical Integration," JOURNAL OF HEALTH AND SOCIAL BEHAVIOR 15, pp. 12–27.
House, James S. 1981.
    WORK STRESS AND SOCIAL SUPPORT. Reading, MA: Addison-Wesley.
Jackson, David, and Ted Huston. 1976.
    "Physical Attractiveness and Assertiveness," JOURNAL OF SOCIAL PSYCHOLOGY 98, pp. 79–83.
Jedlicka, Davor. 1978.
    "Sex Inequality, Aging and Innovation in Preferential Mate Selection," THE FAMILY COORDINATOR 23, pp. 137–140.
Jedlicka, Davor. 1980.
    "Formal Mate Selection Networks in the United States," FAMILY RELATIONS 29 (April):199–203.
Jencks, Christopher, et. al. 1977.
    WHO GETS AHEAD: THE DETERMINANTS OF ECONOMIC SUCCESS IN AMERICA. New York: Basic Books.

Jesser, Clinton J. 1978.
"Male Responses to Direct Verbal Sexual Initiatives of Females," JOURNAL OF SEX RESEARCH *14* (May):118–128.

Johnson, Spencer. 1983.
THE ONE MINUTE FATHER. New York: William Morrow & Company, Inc.

Johnson, Spencer, 1983.
THE ONE MINUTE MOTHER. New York: William Morrow & Company, Inc.

Jones, Warren H. 1982.
"Loneliness and Social Behavior," In Peplau, Letitia Anne, and Daniel Perlman (Eds.), LONELINESS. New York: John Wiley & Sons, pp. 238–252.

Kagan, Jerome. 1978.
THE GROWTH OF THE CHILD. New York: Norton.

Kagan, Jerome. 1981.
THE SECOND YEAR. Cambridge, MA: Harvard University Press.

Kagan, Jerome. 1982.
"The Fearful Child's Hidden Talents." PSYCHOLOGY TODAY *16* (July):50–59.

Kagan, Jerome, and Howard A. Moss. 1983.
BIRTH TO MATURITY. New Haven: Yale University Press.

Kagan, Jerome. 1984.
THE NATURE OF THE CHILD. New York: Basic Books.

Kagan, Jerome. 1984.
"Behavioral Inhibition in the Young Child." CHILD DEVELOPMENT *55* (June):1005–1014.

Kandel, Denise, and Gerald S. Lesser. 1969.
"Parent-Adolescent Relationships and Adolescent Independence in the United States and Denmark." JOURNAL OF MARRIAGE AND THE FAMILY *31* (May): 348–358.

Kaplan, Howard B. 1980.
DEVIANT BEHAVIOR IN DEFENSE OF SELF. New York: Academic Press.

Klein, Donald F., et. al. 1980.
DIAGNOSIS AND DRUG TREATMENT OF PSYCHIATRIC DISORDERS: ADULTS AND CHILDREN. Baltimore: Williams and Wilkins.

Klein, Donald F., and Judith G. Rabkin. 1981.
ANXIETY: NEW RESEARCH AND CHANGING CONCEPTS. New York: Raven Press.

Kleiner, Robert J., and Seymour Parker. 1963.
"Goal-Striving, Social Status, and Mental Disorder: A Research Review." AMERICAN SOCIOLOGICAL REVIEW *28* (April):169–203.

Knox, David, and Kenneth Wilson. 1981.
"Dating Behaviors of University Students." FAMILY RELATIONS *30* (April):255–258.

Knox, David, and Kenneth Wilson. 1983.
"Dating Problems of University Students." COLLEGE STUDENT JOURNAL *17*, 225–228.

Knupfer, Genevieve, et. al. 1966.
"The Mental Health of the Unmarried." AMERICAN JOURNAL OF PSYCHIATRY *122*, 841–851.

Kohn, Melvin L., and John A. Clausen. 1955.
"Social Isolation and Schizophrenia." AMERICAN SOCIOLOGICAL REVIEW *20* (June):265–273.

Komarovsky, Mirra. 1976.
DILEMMAS OF MASCULINITY: A STUDY OF COLLEGE YOUTH. New York: Norton.

Kopmeyer, M. R. 1982.
KOP'S KEYS TO SUCCESS AND HAPPINESS. Chicago: Nightengale-Conant Corporation.

Krebs, Dennis, and Allen A. Adinolfi. 1975.
"Physical Attractiveness, Social Relations, and Personality Style." JOURNAL OF PERSONALITY AND SOCIAL PSYCHOLOGY 31 (No. 2):245–253.

Landis, Judson T., and Mary G. Landis. 1973.
BUILDING A SUCCESSFUL MARRIAGE. Englewood Cliffs, New Jersey: Prentice-Hall.

Lane, Robert E. 1959.
"Fathers and Sons: Foundations of Political Beliefs." AMERICAN SOCIOLOGICAL REVIEW 24 (August):502–511.

Larson, Reed, and Mihaly Csikszentmihalyi. 1978.
"Experiential Correlates of Time Alone in Adolescence." JOURNAL OF PERSONALITY 46 (No. 4):677–693.

Lawson, J. J., et. al. 1977.
SOCIAL SELF-ESTEEM INVENTORY. Washington, D.C.: American Psychological Association.

Lazarus, Arnold. 1977.
IN THE MIND'S EYE. New York: Rawson Associates Publishers.

LeShan, Lawrence. 1977.
EMOTIONS AND CANCER. New York: Ziff-Davis Publishing.

LeShan, Lawrence. 1982.
THE MEDIUM, THE MYSTIC, AND THE PHYSICIST. New York: Ballantine Books.

Lester, David. 1974.
A PHYSIOLOGICAL BASIS FOR PERSONALITY TRAITS. Springfield, Illinois: Charles C. Thomas Publishers.

Leventhal, D. B., et. al. 1968.
"Effects of Sex-Role Adjustment Upon the Expression of Aggression," JOURNAL OF PERSONALITY AND SOCIAL PSYCHOLOGY 8 (No. 4):393–396.

Libby, Roger W. 1977.
"Creative Singlehood as a Sexual Life-Style," In Libby, Roger W., and Robert N. Whitehurst (Eds.), MARRIAGE AND ALTERNATIVES. Glenview, Illinois: Scott, Foresman.

Liem, Ramsay and Joan. 1978.
"Social Class and Mental Illness Reconsidered: The Role of Economic Stress and Social Support," JOURNAL OF HEALTH AND SOCIAL BEHAVIOR 19, pp. 139–156.

Loesser, Frank. 1950.
GUYS AND DOLLS. New York: Frank Music Corporation.

Lowenthal, Majorie F. 1964.
"Social Isolation and Mental Illness in Old Age," AMERICAN SOCIOLOGICAL REVIEW 29 (February):54–70.

Lowenthal, Majorie F., and C. Haven. 1968.
"Interaction and Adaptation: Intimacy as a Critical Variable," AMERICAN SOCIOLOGICAL REVIEW 33, pp. 20–30.

Lu, Yi-chuang. 1962.
"Contradictory Parental Expectations in Schizophrenia: Dependence and Responsibilities," ARCHIVES OF GENERAL PSYCHIATRY 6 (March):219–235.

Lynch, James J. 1977.
THE BROKEN HEART: THE MEDICAL CONSEQUENCES OF LONELINESS. New York: Basic Books.

MacDonald, Marian L., et. al. 1975.
"Social Skills Training: Behavior Rehearsal in Groups and Dating Skills," JOURNAL OF COUNSELING PSYCHOLOGY 22 (No. 3):224–230.

Macklin, Eleanor. 1974.
"Living Together Unmarried," PSYCHOLOGY TODAY 8 (November): 32–40.

Macklin, Eleanor. 1974.
"Unmarried Heterosexual Cohabitation on the University Campus," In Wiseman,

Jacqueline P. (Ed.), THE SOCIAL PSYCHOLOGY OF SEX. New York: Harper & Row, pp. 108–142.

Macklin, Eleanor. 1978.
"Review of Research on Nonmarital Cohabitation in the United States," in Murstein, Bernard I. (Ed.), EXPLORING INTIMATE LIFE STYLES. New York: Springer Publishing, pp. 196–243.

Maltz, Maxwell. 1960.
PSYCHO-CYBERNETICS. Englewood Cliffs, New Jersey: Prentice-Hall.

Maltz, Maxwell. 1964.
THE MAGIC POWER OF SELF-IMAGE PSYCHOLOGY. Englewood Cliffs, New Jersey: Prentice-Hall.

Mantell, David M. 1974.
"Doves vs. Hawks: Guess Who Had the Authoritarian Parents?" PSYCHOLOGY TODAY 7 (September) 56–62.

Martin, R. M., and F. L. Marcuse. 1957.
"Characteristics of Volunteers and Nonvolunteers for Hypnosis," JOURNAL OF CLINICAL AND EXPERIMENTAL HYPNOSIS 5 (October):176–179.

Martinson, William D., and James P. Zerface. 1970.
"Comparison of Individual Counseling and a Social Program with Nondaters," JOURNAL OF COUNSELING PSYCHOLOGY 17 (No. 1):36–40.

Marzillier, J. S., et. al. 1976.
"A Controlled Evaluation of Systematic Desensitization and Social Skills Training for Socially Inadequate Psychiatric Patients," BEHAVIOR RESEARCH AND THERAPY 14, pp. 225–238.

Mayo, J., et. al. 1978.
"An Empirical Study of the Relation Between Astrological Factors and Personality," JOURNAL OF SOCIAL PSYCHOLOGY 105 (August):229–236.

McCaffrey, Mike. 1982.
FOCUS: HOW TO USE THE POWER OF SELF-IMAGE PSYCHOLOGY. Chicago: Nightengale-Conant.

McClosky, H., and J. H. Scharr. 1965.
"Psychological Dimensions of Anomie," AMERICAN SOCIOLOGICAL REVIEW 30 (February): 14–40.

McCroskey, James C. 1977.
"Oral Communication Apprehension: A Summary of Recent Theory and Research," HUMAN COMMUNICATION RESEARCH 4 (Fall):78–96.

McCroskey, James C. 1978.
"Validity of the PRCA as an Index of Oral Communication Apprehension," COMMUNICATION MONOGRAPHS 45 (August):192–203.

McCroskey, James C., and Virginia P. Richmond. 1979.
"The Quiet Ones." Unpublished Manuscript, Morgantown, West Virginia: West Virginia University.

McGovern, Kevin B., et. al. 1975.
"Evaluation of Social Skill Training Programs for College Dating Inhibitions," JOURNAL OF COUNSELING PSYCHOLOGY 22 (No. 6):505–512.

McGovern, Leslie P. 1976.
"Dispositional Social Anxiety and Helping Behavior Under Three Conditions of Threat," JOURNAL OF PERSONALITY 44 (No. 1):84–97.

McKeown, James E. 1950.
"The Behavior of Parents of Schizophrenic, Neurotic, and Normal Children," AMERICAN JOURNAL OF SOCIOLOGY 56 (September):175–179.

Meer, Jeff. 1985.
"Loneliness." PSYCHOLOGY TODAY 19 (July):28–33.

Melnick, Joseph. 1973.
"A Comparison of Replication Techniques in the Modification of Minimal Dating Behavior," JOURNAL OF ABNORMAL PSYCHOLOGY 81 (No. 1): 51–59.

Michener, James A. 1971.
    KENT STATE. New York: Random House.
Milgram, Stanley. 1974.
    OBEDIENCE TO AUTHORITY. New York: Harper & Row.
Monahan, Evelyn M. 1975.
    THE MIRACLE OF METAPHYSICAL HEALING. West Nyack, New York: Parker
    Publishing.
Montagu, Ashley. 1971.
    TOUCHING: HUMAN SIGNIFICANCE OF THE SKIN. New York: Harper and
    Row.
Morse, Mary. 1965.
    THE UNATTACHED. Baltimore: Pelican Books.
Moss, Thelma. 1979.
    THE BODY ELECTRIC. Los Angeles: J. P. Tarcher, Inc.
Myers, Jerome K., et. al. 1975.
    "Life Events, Social Integration, and Psychiatric Symptomatology." JOURNAL OF
    HEALTH AND SOCIAL BEHAVIOR 16, pp. 121–127.
Nass, Gilbert D., and Roger W. Libby. 1981.
    SEXUAL CHOICES. Monterey, CA: Wadsworth.
Nedelsky, R. 1952.
    "The Teacher's Role in the Peer Group During Middle Childhood." ELEMENTARY
    SCHOOL JOURNAL 52, pp. 325–334.
Netherton, Morris, and Nancy Shiffrin. 1978.
    PAST LIVES THERAPY. New York: William Morrow.
Nightengale, Earl. 1972.
    THE STRANGEST SECRET. Chicago: Nightengale-Conant Corporation.
Nightengale, Earl. 1981.
    LEAD THE FIELD. Chicago: Nightengale-Conant Corporation.
Olweus, Dan. 1977.
    "Aggression and Peer Acceptance in Adolescent Boys: Two Short-Term Longitu-
    dinal Studies of Ratings." CHILD DEVELOPMENT, 48, pp. 978–987.
Olweus, Dan. 1978.
    AGGRESSION IN THE SCHOOLS: BULLIES AND WHIPPING BOYS. Washington,
    D.C.: Hemisphere Publishers.
Olweus, Dan. 1979.
    "Stability of Aggressive Reaction Patterns in Males: A Review." PSYCHOLOGICAL
    BULLETIN, 84, pp. 852–875.
Olweus, Dan. 1984.
    "Aggressors and their Victims: Bullying at School." In Frude, Neil, and Hugh Gault
    (Eds.), DISRUPTIVE BEHAVIOR IN SCHOOLS. New York: John Wiley & Sons.
Ostrander, Shiela, and Lynn Schroeder. 1972.
    ASTROLOGICAL BIRTH CONTROL. Englewood Cliffs, New Jersey: Prentice-Hall.
Oyle, Irving. 1975.
    THE HEALING MIND. New York: Pocket Books.
Parks, Malcolm R. 1977.
    "Anomia and Close Friendship Communication Networks." HUMAN COMMU-
    NICATION RESEARCH 4 (Fall):48–57.
Pelletier, Kenneth R. 1977.
    MIND AS HEALER; MIND AS SLAYER. New York: Delta.
Peplau, Letitia Anne, et. al. 1977.
    "Sexual Intimacy in Dating Relationships." JOURNAL OF SOCIAL ISSUES 33
    (No. 2):86–109.
Peplau, Letitia Anne. 1979.
    UNDERSTANDING AND OVERCOMING LONELINESS. New York: Ziff-Davis.
Peplau, Letitia Anne, and Daniel Perlman. 1982.
    LONELINESS: A SOURCEBOOK OF CURRENT THEORY, RESEARCH AND
    THERAPY. New York: John Wiley & Sons.

Phillips, Derek L. 1963.
"Rejection: A Possible Consequence of Seeking Help for Mental Disorders." AMER-
ICAN SOCIOLOGICAL REVIEW 28, pp. 963–972.

Phillips, Derek L. 1966.
"Deferred Gratification in a College Setting: Some Costs and Gains." SOCIAL PROB-
LEMS 13, pp. 333–343.

Phillips, Derek L. 1967.
"Mental Health Status, Social Participation, and Happiness." JOURNAL OF HEALTH
AND SOCIAL BEHAVIOR 8 (December):285–291.

Phillips, Gerald M. 1981.
HELP FOR SHY PEOPLE. Englewood Cliffs, New Jersey: Prentice-Hall.

Pilkonis, Paul A. 1977.
"Shyness, Public and Private, and its Relationship to Other Measures of Social
Behavior." JOURNAL OF PERSONALITY 45 (No. 4):585–595.

Pilkonis, Paul A. 1977.
"The Behavioral Consequences of Shyness." JOURNAL OF PERSONALITY 45
(No. 4):596–611.

Pines, Maya. 1979.
"Superkids." PSYCHOLOGY TODAY 12 (January):53–63.

Plomin, Robert, and D. C. Rowe. 1979.
"Genetic and Environmental Etiology of Social Behavior in Infancy." DEVELOP-
MENTAL PSYCHOLOGY 15, 62–72.

Rainwater, Lee. 1960.
AND THE POOR GET CHILDREN. Chicago: Quadrangle Books.

Raschke, Helen J., and Vernon J. Raschke. 1979.
"Family Conflict and Children's Self-Concepts: A Comparison of Intact and
Single-Parent Families." JOURNAL OF MARRIAGE AND THE FAMILY 41 (May):367–
374.

Rehm, Lynn P., and Albert R. Marston. 1968.
"Reduction of Social Anxiety Through Modification of Self-Reinforcement: An Insti-
gation Therapy Technique." JOURNAL OF CONSULTING AND CLINICAL PSY-
CHOLOGY 32 (No. 5):565–574.

Reiss, Ira L. 1980.
FAMILY SYSTEMS IN AMERICAN (3rd edition). New York: Holt, Rinehart &
Winston.

Renne, Karen S. 1970.
"Correlates of Dissatisfaction in Marriage." JOURNAL OF MARRIAGE AND THE
FAMILY 32 (February):54–67.

Rimmer, Robert H. 1966.
THE HARRAD EXPERIMENT. Los Angeles: Sherbourne Press.

Roberts, Jane. 1972.
SETH SPEAKS. New York: Bantam Books.

Roberts, Jane. 1978.
THE NATURE OF PERSONAL REALITY. New York: Bantam Books.

Roberts, J. D. 1952.
"Improving the Status of Isolates." NATIONAL ELEMENTARY PRINCIPAL 32,
pp. 183–188.

Rogo, D. Scott. 1985.
THE SEARCH FOR YESTERDAY: A CRITICAL EXAMINATION OF THE EVI-
DENCE FOR REINCARNATION. Englewood Cliffs, New Jersey: Prentice-Hall.

Rollins, Boyd C., and Darwin L. Thomas. 1979.
"Parental Support, Power, and Control Techniques in the Socialization of Children,"
In Burr, Wesley R. et. al. (Eds.), CONTEMPORARY THEORIES ABOUT THE FAM-
ILY (Vol. 1). New York: The Free Press of Glencoe, pp. 317–364.

Rook, Karen S., and Letitia Anne Peplau. 1982.
"Perspectives on Helping the Lonely," In Peplau, Letitia Anne, and Daniel Perlman
(Eds.), LONELINESS. New York: John Wiley & Sons, pp. 351–378.

Rorvik, David. 1977.
    IN HIS IMAGE: THE CLONING OF A MAN. Philadelphia: J. B. Lippincott.
Rose, Arnold M. 1955.
    MENTAL HEALTH AND MENTAL DISORDERS. New York: Norton.
Rose, Arnold M. 1968.
    "A Social-Psychological Theory of Neurosis," In Spitzer, Stephan P., and Norman
    K. Denzin (Eds.), THE MENTAL PATIENT: STUDIES IN THE SOCIOLOGY OF
    DEVIANCE. New York: McGraw-Hill, pp. 52–59.
Rosenberg, Morris. 1963.
    SOCIETY AND THE ADOLESCENT SELF-IMAGE. Princeton: Princeton University
    Press.
Rosenfeld, Anne H. 1985.
    "Depression: Dispelling Despair." PSYCHOLOGY TODAY 19 (June):28–34.
Rothbart, Mary K., and Eleanor E. Maccoby. 1966.
    "Parents' Differential Reactions to Sons and Daughters." JOURNAL OF PERSON-
    ALITY AND SOCIAL PSYCHOLOGY 4 (No. 3):237–243.
Rubenstein, Carin M., and Phillip Shaver. 1982.
    "The Experience of Loneliness," In Peplau, Letitia Anne, and Daniel Perlman (Eds.),
    LONELINESS. New York: John Wiley & Sons, pp. 206–223.
Rubin, Zick. 1973.
    LIKING AND LOVING: AN INVITATION TO SOCIAL PSYCHOLOGY. New York:
    Holt, Rinehart & Winston.
Rubin, Zick. 1982.
    "Children Without Friends," In Peplau, Letitia Anne, and Daniel Perlman (Eds.),
    LONELINESS. New York: John Wiley & Sons, pp. 255–268.
Samuels, Mike and Nancy. 1975.
    SEEING WITH THE MIND'S EYE: THE HISTORY, TECHNIQUES AND USES OF
    VISUALIZATION. New York: Random House.
Sarnoff, I., and Philip G. 1961.
    "Anxiety, Fear, and Social Affiliation." JOURNAL OF ABNORMAL AND SOCIAL
    PSYCHOLOGY 62, pp. 356–363.
Scarr, S. 1969.
    "Social Introversion-Extroversion as a Heritable Response." CHILD DEVELOP-
    MENT 40, 823–832.
Schachter, Stanley. 1959.
    THE PSYCHOLOGY OF AFFILIATION. Stanford: Stanford University Press.
Scheff, Thomas J. 1963.
    "The Role of the Mentally Ill and the Dynamics of Mental Disorder: A Research
    Framework." SOCIOMETRY 26, pp. 436–453.
Scott, William A. 1958.
    "Social Psychological Correlates of Mental Illness and Mental Health." PSYCHO-
    LOGICAL BULLETIN 55 (March):72–87.
Sears, Robert. 1957.
    PATTERNS OF CHILD REARING. Stanford: Stanford University Press.
Sheehan, David V. 1982.
    "Panic Attacks and Phobias." NEW ENGLAND JOURNAL OF MEDICINE 307, 156–
    158.
Sheehan, David V. 1983.
    ANXIETY DISEASE. New York: Charles Scribner & Company.
Sheehan, David V., and J. B. Claycomb. 1984.
    "The Use of MAO Inhibitors in Clinical Practice." In Manschreck, J. C. (Ed.), PSY-
    CHIATRIC MEDICINE UPDATE. New York: Elsevier, pp. 45–60.
Sherif, Muzafer. 1956.
    "Experiments in Group Conflict." SCIENTIFIC AMERICAN 195 (November):54–58.
Sherman, A. Robert. 1972.
    "Real-Life Exposure as a Primary Therapeutic Factor in the Desensitization Treat-
    ment of Fear." JOURNAL OF ABNORMAL PSYCHOLOGY 79 (No. 1):19–28.

Sherman, Clay. 1984.
    STRESS FREE LIVING. Chicago: Nightengale Conant Corporation.
Shettles, Landrum B., and David Rorvik. 1970.
    YOUR BABY'S SEX; NOW YOU CAN CHOOSE. New York: Dodd, Mead.
Simonton, O. Carl, and Stephanie Simonton. 1976.
    PSYCHOLOGICAL FACTORS, STRESS, AND CANCER. Fort Worth, Texas: Cancer
    Counseling and Research Center.
Simonton, O. Carl, et. al. 1978.
    GETTING WELL AGAIN. Los Angeles: J. B. Tarcher.
Smithers, A. G., and H. J. Cooper. 1978.
    "Personality and Season of Birth." JOURNAL OF SOCIAL PSYCHOLOGY 105
    (August):237–241.
Sother, Ann. 1982.
    "The Effect of Meditation Upon Prisoner Recidivism." SCIENCE FOR TODAY'S
    SOCIETY. Vancouver, British Columbia: Canadian Broadcasting Company.
Steffan, John J., and Joan Redden. 1977.
    "Assessment of Social Competence in an Evaluation-Interaction Analogue." HUMAN
    COMMUNICATION RESEARCH 4 (Fall):30–37.
Stein, Peter J., et. al. 1981.
    SINGLE LIFE: UNMARRIED ADULTS IN SOCIAL CONTEXT. New York: St. Mar-
    tin's Press.
Steiner, Lee R. 1977.
    PSYCHIC SELF-HEALING FOR PSYCHOLOGICAL PROBLEMS. Englewood Cliffs,
    New Jersey: Prentice-Hall.
Stevenson, Ian. 1974.
    TWENTY CASES SUGGESTIVE OF REINCARNATION. Charlottesville, Virginia:
    University of Virginia Press.
Stevenson, Ian. 1977.
    "The Explanatory Value of the Idea of Reincarnation." JOURNAL OF NERVOUS
    AND MENTAL DISEASE 164, pp. 305–326.
Stevenson, Ian. 1977.
    "The Southeast Asian Interpretation of Gender Dysphoria: An Illustrative Case
    Report." JOURNAL OF NERVOUS AND MENTAL DISEASE 165 (No. 3):201–208.
Stone, Carol I. 1960.
    "Some Family Characteristics of Socially Active and Inactive Teenagers." THE FAM-
    ILY COORDINATOR 5 (March):53–57.
Sutphen, Dick. 1976.
    YOU WERE BORN AGAIN TO BE TOGETHER. New York: Pocket Books.
Sutphen, Dick. 1978.
    PAST LIVES, FUTURE LOVES. New York: Pocket Books.
Tec, Nechama. 1970.
    "Family and Differential Involvement with Marijuana: A Study of Suburban Teen-
    agers." JOURNAL OF MARRIAGE AND THE FAMILY 32 (November):656–664.
Thomas, Alexander, et. al. 1968.
    TEMPERAMENT AND BEHAVIOR DISORDERS IN CHILDREN. New York: New
    York University Press.
Thomas, Alexander, et. al. 1970.
    "The Origin of Personality." SCIENTIFIC AMERICAN 223 (August):102–109.
Thomas, Alexander. 1976.
    "Behavioral Individuality in Childhood," In Kaplan, A. R. (Ed.), HUMAN BEHAV-
    IOR GENETICS. Springfield, Illinois: Charles C. Thomas Publishers, pp. 151–163.
Thomas, Alexander, and Stella Chess. 1982.
    "The Reality of Different Temperaments." MERRILL-PALMER QUARTERLY 28, 1–
    28.
Thomas, William I., and Florian Znaniecki. 1920.
    THE POLISH PEASANT IN AMERICA. Chicago: University of Chicago Press.

Timnick, Lois. 1982.
"Now You Can Learn to be Likable, Confident, Socially Successful for Only the Cost of Your Present Education." PSYCHOLOGY TODAY 16 (August):42–49.

Tracy, Brian. 1984.
THE PSYCHOLOGY OF ACHIEVEMENT. Chicago: Nightengale-Conant Corporation.

Twentyman, Craig T., and Richard M. McFall. 1975.
"Behavioral Training of Social Skills in Shy Males." JOURNAL OF CONSULTING AND CLINICAL PSYCHOLOGY 43 (No. 3):384–395.

Vandenberg, S. G. 1967.
"Hereditary Factors in Normal Personality Traits as Measured by Inventories," In Wortis, John (Ed.), RECENT ADVANCES IN BIOLOGICAL PSYCHIATRY (Vol. 9). New York: Plenum Press, 1967.

Vane, Andrew R. 1977.
THE CAUSES OF SOCIAL SUCCESS. Ottawa, Ontario: Social Relations Program Press.

Verbrugge, Lois M. 1979.
"Marital Status and Health," JOURNAL OF MARRIAGE AND THE FAMILY 41 (May):267–286.

Waitley, Denis. 1978.
THE PSYCHOLOGY OF WINNING. Chicago: Nightengale-Conant Corporation.

Wallace, K. M. 1972.
"An Experiment in Scientific Matchmaking," In Albrecht, R. E., and E. W. Bock (Eds.), ENCOUNTER: LOVE, MARRIAGE, AND FAMILY. Boston: Holbrook, pp. 127–148.

Walster, Elaine, et. al. 1966.
"Importance of Physical Attractiveness in Dating Behavior," JOURNAL OF PERSONALITY AND SOCIAL PSYCHOLOGY 4 (No. 5):508–516.

Wambach, Helen. 1978.
RELIVING PAST LIVES: THE EVIDENCE UNDER HYPNOSIS. New York: Harper and Row.

Wambach, Helen. 1979.
LIFE BEFORE LIFE. New York: Bantam Books.

Ward, Ingeborg. 1972.
"Prenatal Stress Feminizes and Demasculinizes the Behavior of Males," SCIENCE 175 #4017 (January):82–84.

Watson, David, and Ronald Friend. 1969.
"Measurement of Social-Evaluative Anxiety," JOURNAL OF CONSULTING AND CLINICAL PSYCHOLOGY 33, pp. 448–457.

Weber, Eric. 1980.
HOW TO TALK TO WOMEN. Tenafly, New Jersey: Symphony Press.

Weber, Eric. 1981.
THE SHY MAN'S GUIDE TO A HAPPIER LOVE LIFE. Tenafly, New Jersey: Symphony Press.

Weinberg, S. Kirson. 1967.
"Social Psychological Aspects of Disordered Behavior," In Weinberg, S. Kirson (Ed.), THE SOCIOLOGY OF MENTAL DISORDERS. Chicago: Aldine, pp. 133–142.

Weinberg, S. Kirson. 1967.
"Social Psychological Aspects of Neurotic Anxiety," In Weinberg, S. Kirson (Ed.), THE SOCIOLOGY OF MENTAL DISORDERS. Chicago: Aldine, pp. 143–149.

Weinstein, Eugene A. 1969.
"The Development of Interpersonal Competence," In Goslin, David A. (Ed.), HANDBOOK OF SOCIALIZATION THEORY AND RESEARCH. Chicago: Rand McNally, pp. 753–775.

Weintraub, Pamela. 1981.
"The Brain: His and Hers," DISCOVER 2 (April):15–20.

Weiss, Robert S. 1973.
    LONELINESS: THE EXPERIENCE OF EMOTIONAL AND SOCIAL ISOLATION.
    Cambridge, Massachusetts: M.I.T. Press.
Weiss, Robert S. 1975.
    MARITAL SEPARATION. New York: Basic Books.
Weiss, Robert S. 1982.
    "Issues in the Study of Loneliness," In Peplau, Letitia Anne, and Daniel Perlman
    (Eds.), LONELINESS. New York: John Wiley & Sons, pp. 71–80.
Wells, Brian W. P. 1980.
    PERSONALITY AND HEREDITY: AN INTRODUCTION TO PSYCHOGENETICS.
    London: Longman.
Wender, Paul H., and Donald F. Klein. 1981.
    MIND, MOOD AND MEDICINE. New York: Farrar, Straus, Giroux.
Wendt, H. W. 1978.
    "Season of Birth, Introversion, and Astrology: A Chronobiological Alternative."
    JOURNAL OF SOCIAL PSYCHOLOGY 105 (August):243–247.
Whelan, Elizabeth M. 1977.
    BOY OR GIRL? New York: Pocket Books.
White, Betty, and Thomas J. Watson. 1983.
    PET LOVE. New York: William Morrow.
Wolpe, Joseph, and Arnold A. Lazarus. 1966.
    BEHAVIOR THERAPY TECHNIQUES. London: Pergamon Press.
Wolpe, Joseph. 1979.
    BEHAVIOR THERAPY. New York: Ziff-Davis.
Young, Jeffrey E. 1982.
    "Loneliness, Depression and Cognitive Therapy: Theory and Application," In Peplau,
    Letitia Anne, and Daniel Perlman (Eds.), LONELINESS. New York: John Wiley &
    Sons, pp. 379–406.
Young, Perry Deane. 1982.
    GOD'S BULLIES. New York: Holt, Rinehart & Winston.
Zimbardo, Philip G. 1972.
    PRISON REFORM. New York: Ziff-Davis.
Zimbardo, Philip G. 1977.
    SHYNESS: WHAT IT IS; WHAT TO DO ABOUT IT. Reading, Masachusetts: Addison-
    Wesley.
Zimbardo, Philip G. 1978.
    SHYNESS CLINIC. New York: Biomonitoring Applications, Inc.

Appendix I

The Survey of Heterosexual Interactions ("SHI Questionnaire")

This scale was employed for determining eligibility for inclusion in the *non-shy* sample. It has the benefit of national statistical norms, and it has been used in many different research studies. It was originally designed by psychologists Craig T. Twentyman and Richard M. McFall of the University of Wisconsin at Madison.

> *INSTRUCTIONS*: Please circle the appropriate number in the following situations. Try to respond as if you were actually in that situation.

1. You want to call a girl up for a date. This is the first time you are calling her up as you only know her slightly. When you get ready to make the call, your roommate comes into the room, sits down on his bed, and begins reading a magazine. In this situation you would:

1	2	3	4	5	6	7
be unable to call in every case		be able to call in some cases			be able to call in every case	

2. You are at a dance. You see a very attractive girl whom you do not know. She is standing *alone* and you would like to dance with her. You would:

1	2	3	4	5	6	7
be unable to ask her in every case		be able to ask her in some cases			be able to ask her in every case	

3. You are at a party and you see two girls talking. You do not know

these girls but you would like to know one of them better. In this situation you would:

1	2	3	4	5	6	7

be unable to initi-
ate a conversation

be able to initiate a conversation in some cases

be able to initiate
a conversation in
every case

4. You are at a bar where there is also dancing. You see a couple of girls sitting in a booth. One, whom you do not know, is talking with a fellow who is standing by the booth. These two go over to dance leaving the other girl sitting alone. You have seen this girl around, but do not really know her. You would like to go over and talk to her (but you wouldn't like to dance). In this situation you would:

1	2	3	4	5	6	7

be unable to go
over and talk to
her

be able to go over and talk
to her in some cases

be able to go over
and talk to her in
every case

5. On a work break at your job you see a girl who also works there and is about your age. You would like to talk to her, but you do not know her. You would:

1	2	3	4	5	6	7

be unable to talk
to her in every
case

be able to talk to her in
some cases

be able to talk to
her in every case

6. You are on a crowded bus, a girl you know *only slightly* is sitting in front of you. You would like to talk to her but you notice that the fellow sitting next to her is watching you. You would:

1	2	3	4	5	6	7

be unable to talk
to her in every
case

be able to talk to her in
some cases

be able to talk to
her in every case

7. You are at a dance. You see an attractive girl whom you do not know, standing *in a group* of four girls. You would like to dance. In this situation you would:

1	2	3	4	5	6	7

be unable to ask
in every case

be able to ask in some cases

be able to ask in
every case

8. You are at a drugstore counter eating lunch. A girl whom you do not know sits down beside you. You would like to talk to her. After

her meal comes she asks you to pass the sugar. In this situation you would pass the sugar:

1	2	3	4	5	6	7
but be unable to initiate a conversation with her		and in some cases be able to initiate a conversation			and be able to initiate a conversation	

9. A friend of yours is going out with his girlfriend this weekend. He wants you to come along and gives you the name and phone number of a girl he says would be a good date. You are not doing anything this weekend. In this situation you would:

1	2	3	4	5	6	7
be unable to call in every case		be able to call her in some cases			be able to call in every case	

10. You are at the library. You decide to take a break, and as you walk down the hall you see a girl whom you know only casually. She is sitting at a table and appears to be studying. You decide that you would like to ask her to get a coke with you. In this situation you would:

1	2	3	4	5	6	7
be unable to ask her in every case		be able to ask her in some cases			be able to ask her in every case	

11. You want to call a girl up for a date. You find this girl attractive but you do not know her. You would:

1	2	3	4	5	6	7
be unable to call in every case		be able to call in some cases			be able to call in every case	

12. You are taking a class at the university. After one of your classes you see a girl whom you know. You would like to talk to her; however, she is walking with a couple of other girls you do not know. You would:

1	2	3	4	5	6	7
be unable to talk to her in every case		be able to talk to her in some cases			be able to talk to her in every case	

13. You have been working on a committee for the past year. There is a banquet at which you are assigned a particular seat. On one side of you there is a girl you do not know; on the other side is a guy you do not know. In this situation you would:

1	2	3	4	5	6	7

be unable to initiate a conversation with the girl and talk only with the guy

be able to initiate a conversation with the girl in some cases but talk mostly to the guy

be able to initiate a conversation in every case and be able to talk equally as freely with the girl as with the guy

14. You are in the lobby of a large apartment complex waiting for a friend. As you are waiting for him to come down, a girl whom you know well walks by with another girl whom you have never seen before. The girl you know says hello and begins to talk to you. Suddenly she remembers that she left something in her room. Just before she leaves you she tells you the other girl's name. In this situation you would:

1	2	3	4	5	6	7

find it very difficult to initiate and continue a conversation with the other girl

find it only slightly difficult

find it easy to initiate and continue a conversation

15. You are at a party in a friend's apartment. You see a girl who has come alone. You don't know her, but you would like to talk to her. In this situation you would:

1	2	3	4	5	6	7

be unable to go over and talk to her

be able to go over and talk to her in some cases

be able to go over and talk to her in every case

16. You are walking to your mailbox in the large apartment building where you live. When you get there you notice that two girls are putting their names on the mailbox of the vacant apartment beneath yours. In this situation you would:

1	2	3	4	5	6	7

be unable to go over and initiate a conversation

be able to go over and initiate a conversation in some cases

be able to go over and initiate a conversation in every case

17. You are at a record store and see a girl that you once were introduced

to. That was several months ago and now you have forgotten her name. You would like to talk to her. In this situation you would:

1	2	3	4	5	6	7

be unable to start a conversation with her in every case

be able to start a conversation with her in some cases

be able to start a conversation with her in every case

18. You are at the student union or local cafeteria where friends your age eat lunch. You have gotten your meal and are now looking for a place to sit down. Unfortunately, there are no empty tables. At one table, however, there is a girl sitting alone. In this situation you would:

1	2	3	4	5	6	7

wait until another place was empty and then sit down

ask the girl if you could sit at the table but not say anything more to her

ask the girl if you could sit at the table and then initiate a conversation

19. A couple of weeks ago you had a first-date with a girl you now see walking on the street towards you. For some reason you haven't seen each other since then. You would like to talk to her but aren't sure of what she thinks of you. In this situation you would:

1	2	3	4	5	6	7

walk by without saying anything

walk up to her and say something in some cases

walk up to her and say something in every case

20. Generally, in most social situations involving girls whom I do not know, I would:

1	2	3	4	5	6	7

be unable to initiate a conversation

be able to initiate a conversation in some cases

be able to initiate a conversation in every case

SCORING: The foregoing twenty items comprise the "SHI Questionnaire." It is scored by simply adding up the circled numbers for each one of the twenty items. Scores can range from a low of 20 to a high of 140. The *lower* a man's score is, the more *love-shy* he is likely to be. See Chapter 5, page 137, for a fuller discussion.

Appendix II

The Gilmartin Love-Shyness Scale

This scale is included here for the benefit of researchers who might want to use it in their own work. The numbers which are indicated underneath each item are for purposes of *coding*. The *higher* a man's score, the more severely love-shy he is. The *lower* a person's score is, the more self-confident and *non*-shy he is likely to be in friendly, casual encounters vis-a-vis the opposite sex. Whereas the scale ("GLSS") was intended for males only, it can be used for women if the items containing an asterisk (*) are first removed.

1. I feel relaxed even in unfamiliar social situations.
    0 True;   1 False.
2. I try to avoid situations which force me to be very sociable.
    1 True;   0 False.
3. It is easy for me to relax when I am with strangers.
    0 True;   1 False.
4. I have no particular desire to avoid people.
    0 True;   1 False.
5. I often find social situations upsetting.
    1 True;   0 False.
6. I usually feel calm and comfortable at social occasions.
    0 True;   1 False.
7. I am usually at ease when talking to someone of the opposite sex.
    0 True;   1 False.
8. I try to avoid talking to people unless I know them well.
    1 True;   0 False.
9. If the chance comes to meet new people, I often take it.
    0 True;   1 False.
10. I often feel nervous or tense in casual get-togethers in which both sexes are present.
    1 True;   0 False.
11. I am usually nervous with people unless I know them well.
    1 True;   0 False.

12. I usually feel relaxed when I am with a group of people
    0 True;   1 False.
13. I often want to get away from people.
    1 True;   0 False.
14. I usually feel uncomfortable when I am in a group of people
    I don't know.
    1 True;   0 False.
15. I usually feel relaxed when I meet someone for the first time.
    0 True;   1 False.
16. Being introduced to people makes me tense and nervous.
    1 True;   0 False.
17. I find it very difficult to display emotion and feeling.
    1 True;   0 False.
18. I would avoid walking up and joining a large group of people.
    1 True;   0 False.
19. After I was about 13 or so I usually tried not to sing out loud
    whenever anyone was around.
    1 True;   0 False.
20. I tend to withdraw from people.
    1 True;   0 False.
21. I often feel on edge when I am with a group of people.
    1 True;   0 False.
22. I find it easy to start conversations with people of the opposite
    sex in informal social situations.
    0 True;   1 False.
23. I sometimes take the responsibility for introducing people to
    each other.
    0 True;   1 False.
24. When I like someone I am able to let them know it without
    difficulty.
    0 True;   1 False.
25. I find it easy to relax with other people.
    0 True;   1 False.
26. I often feel that I don't know what to say in certain types of
    informal social situations.
    1 True;   0 False.
27. When I would like to be friendly with someone, I often feel
    that I know what to say but I just haven't got the nerve to
    say it.
    1 True;   0 False.
28. It requires a tremendous amount of nerve to be friendly with
    the opposite sex.
    4 Strongly agree.

3 Agree.

2 Uncertain.

1 Disagree.

0 Strongly disagree.

*29. I am proficient at making friendly overtures to the opposite sex.

    0 Very true of me.

    1 On the most part true of me.

    2 Slightly true of me.

    3 Not true of me.

    4 Very untrue of me.

30. It wouldn't bother me at all if I had no friends of my own sex. Just so long as I had friends of the opposite sex I'd be alright.

    4 Strongly agree.

    3 Agree.

    2 Uncertain.

    1 Disagree.

    0 Strongly disagree.

31. The idea of starting a conversation with someone of the opposite sex whom I do not know and in whom I have a secret romantic interest is very frightening to me.

    2 True;   0 False.

32. How optimistic are you that you will be able to overcome a sufficient amount of your shyness to enable you to find a partner and get married?

    0 I am *NOT* shy.

    1 Very optimistic.

    2 Somewhat optimistic.

    3 Slightly optimistic.

    4 Not optimistic.

33. I am sure that it would do me a very great deal of good if I had one or two really close friends who would (figuratively speaking) take me by the hand and help me get involved with the opposite sex.

    4 Strongly agree.

    3 Agree.

    2 Uncertain.

    1 Disagree.

    0 Strongly disagree.

*34. How confident are you right now about *initiating* love-making (not necessarily sexual) with someone of the opposite sex with whom you would like to make love?

0 Very confident.

1 Confident.

2 Fairly confident.

3 Not too confident.

4 Lacking in confidence.

35. I have hesitated to make or to accept dates because of shyness.

2 True;   0 False.

*36. Do you envy women for the passive role they are permitted to play in dating and courtship?

3 Frequently.

2 Sometimes.

1 Rarely.

0 Never.

*37. I would like to see arranged marriages available as an option in our society so that I could get married without having to suffer the indignity of having to ask women for dates.

2 True;   0 False.

38. How satisfied are you with your current dating frequency?

5 Very dissatisfied.

4 Dissatisfied.

3 Slightly dissatisfied.

2 Slightly satisfied.

1 Moderately satisfied.

0 Very satisfied.

39. How satisfied are you with the amount of informal boy/girl interaction you are currently engaging in these days?

5 Very dissatisfied.

4 Dissatisfied.

3 Slightly dissatisfied.

2 Slightly satisfied.

1 Moderately satisfied.

0 Very satisfied.

40. *Before* you were 13 years old, did you ever experience loneliness for the close, emotionally meaningful companionship of an age-mate *of the opposite sex*?

2 Yes;   0 No.

41. I would much rather not date at all than date someone whose face is insufficiently attractive to please my aesthetic and romantic sensibilities.

2 True.

1 Uncertain.

0 False.

42. I would not want to date anyone to whom I could not visualize (fantasize) myself as being married.

2 True.

1 Uncertain.

0 False.

43. I have never made love (not necessarily sexual love) in my life.

2 True;   0 False.

44. Would you be too shy to ask the clerk in a drug store for a package of condoms or vaginal foam?

2 Yes;   0 No.

45. There have been times when I have stared for long periods at a person of the opposite sex whom I have found attractive. But as soon as she/he would look in my direction I would immediately look away.

3 True.

2 True; but I've only done this once or twice.

1 False; but I have had the urge to do this.

0 False.

46. There have been times when I have *followed* a person of the opposite sex whom I have found attractive. But as soon as she/he would look in my direction I would immediately look away.

3 True.

2 True; but I've only done this once or twice.

1 False; but I have had the urge to do this.

0 False.

47. Sometimes I get the feeling that society does everything in its power to keep the two sexes separated from each other.

2 True;   0 False.

48. How confident are you at present in associating with the other sex?

0 Very confident.

1 Confident.

2 Fairly confident.

3 Not too confident.

4 Lacking in confidence.

*49. When I was a child of about 10 or 11, there was nothing I used to spend more time daydreaming about than little girls of my age or younger.

2 True;   0 False.

50. I have been in love with a number of people of the opposite sex who were not even aware of my existence.

1 True;   0 False.

51. On a 10-point scale with "10" representing the extremely handsome or beautiful end and "0" representing the ugly end,

how would you rate your own *current* physical attractiveness?
Give number: . (*Coding*: 0=10; 1=9; 2=8; 3=7; 4=6;
                      5=5; 6=4; 7=3; 8=2; 9=1; 10=0.)

52. It requires a tremendous amount of nerve to be friendly with people.
    4 Strongly agree.
    3 Agree.
    2 Uncertain.
    1 Disagree.
    0 Strongly disagree.

53. There is little if anything in life more frightening or overwhelming to me than the thought of experiencing anxiety.
    4 Strongly agree.
    3 Agree.
    2 Uncertain.
    1 Disagree.
    0 Strongly disagree.

54. How often do you worry about having things to talk about with people?
    4 Very frequently.
    3 Frequently.
    2 Sometimes.
    1 Seldom.
    0 Never.

55. I am far less friendly with people than I would really like to be.
    2 True;   0 False.

56. It would overwhelm me with extremely painful feelings of anxiety to accidentally say "hello" to someone on the street who, upon closer examination, turned out to be a total stranger instead of the person to whom I thought I had said "hello".
    3 True.
    2 I'd be upset, but it wouldn't unruffle me *that* much.
    1 Uncertain.
    0 False.

57. People often misunderstand, misinterpret, or "misread" the way I act or fail to act.
    4 Very true.
    3 Somewhat true.
    2 Slightly true.
    1 Not true.
    0 Very untrue.

58. I often feel that I lack free choice and self-determination because of my shyness.

      4 Very true of me.

      3 Somewhat true of me.

      2 Slightly true of me.

      1 Not true of me.

      0 Very untrue of me.

59. My shyness has caused me to be incorrectly seen by some people as a homosexual.

      4 Very true of me.

      3 Somewhat true of me.

      2 Slightly true of me.

      1 Not true of me.

      0 Very untrue of me.

60. How severe a problem is shyness for your life at this time?

      4 Very severe.

      3 Somewhat severe.

      2 A moderate problem.

      1 A slight problem.

      0 Not a problem.

NOTE: This scale assumes that the person taking it is (1) single, never married; and (2) heterosexual.

APPENDIX III

TABLE 1

SUMMARY OF MEAN SCORES ON EYSENCK PERSONALITY QUESTIONNAIRE FOR FIVE SAMPLES

Scale	Older Love-Shys N = 100	Younger Love-Shys N = 200	Non-Shys N = 200	Norms for Men Aged 20–29* N = 649	Norms for Men Aged 40–49* N = 126
E (Extroversion) (21 items)	2.96	5.38	17.70	13.72	12.38
N (Neuroticism) (23 items)	18.86	15.96	6.15	9.81	9.17
P (Psychoticism) (25 items)	2.88	3.43	4.20	4.19	3.09
L (Lie scale) (21 items)	4.53	5.94	7.52	6.50	8.07

*Taken from the Manual for the Eysenck Personality Questionnaire (1975, p. 9).

Name Index

A.B.C. Television, 643
Achterberg, Jeanne, 643
Adinolfi, Allen A., 643, 651
Albrecht, R. E., 657
Anderson, Rosemarie, 643
Arkowitz, Hal, 493, 643, 645
Avery, Arthur W., 643
Azrin, Nathan, 643

Bagley, Ben, 487
Beatty, Michael J., 643
Beck, Alan, 643
Becker, Ernest, 643
Bell, Sanford, 267, 643
Berkowitz, L., 644
Bermann, Eric, 644
Bernstein, Morey, 112, 644
Berscheid, Ellen, 644
Block, Michael, 644
Bock, E. W., 657
Borkovec, Thomas D., 644
Bouchard, Thomas J., Jr., 38, 55
Bradburn, Norman, 644
Braginsky, Dorothea, 644
Braginsky, Ben, 644
Brain, Robert, 617, 644
Brennan, Tim, 644
Bresler, David, 537
Brim, J., 644
Bristol, Claude M., 434, 644
Broderick, Carlfred B., 266–267, 282, 644
Brody, Eugene B., 644
Bronfenbrenner, Urie, 572–574, 644
Brothers, Joyce, 429

Brown, D., 644
Bryant, Bridget, 644
Burk, Michael P., 644
Burns, David D., 645
Burr, Wesley R., 654
Byrne, Charles E., 645

Cameron, C., 645
Carducci, Bernardo J., 645
Cargan, Leonard, 645
Carson, Johnny, 429
Cassill, Key, 645
Cerminara, Gina, 645
Chayefsky, Paddy, 485
Chen, E., 645
Chess, Stella, 656
Christensen, Andrew, 493, 645
Christensen, Harold T., 645
Clausen, John A., 650
Claycomb, J. B., 655
Clemens, Samuel (Mark Twain), 267
Cobb, Sidney, 645
Cooley, Charles Horton, 88
Coombs, Robert H., 645
Cooper, H. J., 656
Coopersmith, Stanley, 645
Coser, Lewis, 645
Cousins, Norman, 635, 645
Csiksyentmihalyi, Mihaly, 651
Curran, James P., 645
Cutright, Phillips, 645
Cutrona, Carolyn, 645
Cytryus, Leon, 62

Daly, John A., 646
Daniels, Denise, 80, 646
Denzin, Norman K., 643, 655
DeSimone, Diane, 636–637, 646
DeVore, Steven, 533, 558, 646
Dion, Karen, 644, 646
Dixon, James J., 646
Donahue, Phil, 294
Doob, Anthony N., 425, 647
Dorner, Gunter, 636, 638–639
Durden-Smith, Jo, 636–637, 646
Durkheim, Emile, 646
Dumitresko, Florin, 367, 632
Dworkin, Robert H., 80, 646

Eaves, Lindon, 646
Ehrhardt, Anke A., 637
Eikerenkoetter, Frederick (Rev. Ike), 533
Elliott, Jane, 92–97, 646
Ellis, Albert, 37, 646
Ellis, Robert A., 33, 646
Erikson, Kai T., 646
Eysenck, Hans J., 38, 40, 47, 53, 56, 62,
    103–104, 214, 235, 325, 350, 352, 388,
    646
Eysenck, Sybil B. G., 646

Farber, Susan L., 647
Feinberg, Michael, 63
Feinberg, M. R., 647
Feshbach, Seymour, 644
Fischer, Claude S., 647
Fishman, Scott M., 647
Fogle, Bruce, 611, 647
Fossey, Bridget, 293, 474, 481
Fowler, Stanley, 644
Freedman, Daniel, 53
Freedman, Jonathan, 29, 425, 647
Freud, Sigmund, 105
Friend, Ronald, 657
Fromm, Erich, 182–184, 441, 647
Frude, Neil, 653

Garcia-Coll, Cynthia, 54, 633, 647
Garrison, John P., 647
Garrison, Karen R., 647
Gault, Hugh, 653
Gaylin, Jody, 647
Gershwin, George, 583
Gil, David G., 647

Gilmartin, Brian G., 219, 647–648, 665
Ginzberg, Eli, 11–12, 648
Girodo, Michel, 648
Gittelman-Klein, Rachel, 66, 648
Goldberg, Herb, 648
Gordon, Thomas, 160, 221, 581, 648
Gore, Susan, 648
Goslin, David A., 657
Gottesman, Irving I., 80, 648
Goy, Bob, 640–641
Grad, Bernard, 590
Grant, Vernon W., 282, 299, 648
Gray, J. A., 648
Greeley, Andrew, 472, 648
Green, Richard, 637
Gregg, Christina F., 645
Gronlund, Norman E., 648
Gutman, E. Michael, 648

Haley, Jay, 648
Harlow, Harry F., 228–229, 648
Harlow, Margaret K., 648
Harper, Lawrence V., 649
Harris, Peter, 641, 649
Haven, Clayton, 591–592, 651
Havighurst, Robert J., 649
Hawn, Goldie, 474–476
Hedquist, Francis J., 649
Helfer, Ray E., 649
Helmstetter, Shad, 533, 558, 649
Hendrick, Clyde, 649
Hendrick, Susan, 649
Herbart, George, 98–101
Hersen, M., 643
Hill, Charles T., 6, 649
Hill, Napolean, 534, 649
Himadi, William G., 649
Himmelweit, Hilda, 649
Homans, George, 649
Hoover, Stephanie, 649
Horowitz, Leonard M., 649
Horton, Paul B., 571–572, 649
House, James S., 649
Hunt, Chester L., 571–572, 649
Huston, Ted, 649

Jackson, David, 649
Jedlicka, Davor, 649
Jencks, Christopher, 9, 12, 51, 649
Jesser, Clinton J., 650

Jessor, Richard, 644
Johnson, Spencer, 160, 208, 221, 224, 581, 635, 650
Johnson, Virginia, 528
Jonas, Eugen, 438–440
Jones, Warren H., 650
Jung, Carl, 105

Kagan, Jerome, 38, 50–55, 633–635, 647, 650
Kandel, Denise, 650
Kaplan, A. R., 646, 656
Kaplan, Howard B., 85, 569, 650
Katcher, Aaron, 643
Kern, Jerome, 485, 487, 583
Kety, Seymour, 406
King, Martin Luther, 92
Kinney, Dennis, 406
Klein, Donald F., 65–66, 74, 80, 149, 263, 406, 636, 648, 650, 658
Kleiner, Robert J., 650
Knox, David, 6, 650
Knupfer, Genevieve, 650
Kohn, Melvin L., 650
Komarovsky, Mirra, 15, 163, 171, 178, 650
Kopmeyer, M. R., 458, 533, 650
Krebs, Dennis, 651
Kubler-Ross, Elizabeth, 589
Kupfer, David, 61–62

Laing, Robert, 367
Landers, Ann, 33
Landis, Judson T., 33, 651
Landis, Mary G., 33, 651
Lane, Robert E., 179, 651
Lane, W. Clayton, 33, 646
Larson, Reed, 651
Lawson, J. J., 651
Lazarus, Arnold, 534, 559, 651, 658
LeShan, Lawrence, 651
Lesser, Gerald S., 650
Lester, David, 651
Leventhal, D. B., 651
Lewin, Kurt, 179
Lewis, Jerry, 291
Libby, Roger W., 647, 651, 653
Liddy, Gordon, 551
Liem, Joan, 651
Liem, Ramsay, 651

Locke, John, 98
Loesser, Frank, 372, 484–485, 583, 651
Lowenthal, Marjorie F., 591–592, 651
Lu, Yi-chuang, 651
Lynch, James J., 208, 651

Maccoby, Eleanor E., 655
MacDonald, Marian L., 651
Macklin, Eleanor, 651–652
Maltz, Maxwell, 548, 652
Manschreck, J. C., 655
Mantell, David M., 652
Marcuse, F. L., 652
Margolin, Janet, 474, 482
Marston, Albert R., 654
Martin, R. M., 652
Martinson, William D., 652
Marzillier, J. S., 652
Masters, William, 528
Mastorakos, Paul Leon, 459
Mayer-Bahlburg, Heino, 637
Mayo, James 103–104, 106, 652
McCaffrey, Mike, 533, 652
McCloskey, H., 652
McCroskey, James C., 652
McEwen, Bruce, 636
McFall, Richard M., 137, 657, 659
McGill, Thomas E., 649
McGovern, George, 463
McGovern, Kevin B., 652
McGovern, Leslie P., 652
McKeown, James E., 652
McKnew, Donald, 62–63
Meer, Jeff, 633, 652
Melko, Matthew, 645
Melnick, Joseph, 493, 652
Michener, James A., 575, 653
Milgram, Stanley, 578, 653
Miller, Daniel R., 644
Monahan, Evelyn M., 559, 653
Montagu, Ashley, 188, 653
Moody, Raymond, Jr., 589
Morgan, Robin, 293
Morse, Mary, 653
Moss, Howard A., 635, 650
Moss, Thelma, 14, 534, 632, 653
Murphy, Bridey, 112
Murstein, Bernard I., 652, 644
Myers, Jerome K., 653

Nass, Gilbert D., 653
Nebylitsyn, V. D., 648
Nedelsky, R., 653
Netherton, Morris, 111–112, 653
Nida, Steve A., 643
Nightengale, Earl, 533, 653

O'Connor, Glynnis, 474, 483
Olweus, Dan, 653
Ostrander, Shiela, 440, 653
Oyle, Irving, 653

Parkes, Seymour, 650
Parks, Malcolm R., 653
Pelletier, Kenneth R., 653
Peplau, Letitia Anne, 6, 259–261, 419–
    421, 644–647, 649–650, 653–655, 658
Perlman, David, 644, 646–647, 649–650,
    653–655, 658
Peters, William, 646
Phillips, Derek L., 29, 654
Phillips, Gerald M., 654
Phillips, Susan L., 647
Pilkonis, Paul A., 5, 79, 654
Pines, Maya, 654
Pitts, Ferris, 72
Plomin, Robert, 54, 80, 635, 646, 654
Porter, Cole, 583

Rabkin, Judith G., 650
Rainwater, Lee, 439–440, 654
Raschke, Helen J., 654
Raschke, Vernon J., 654
Redden, Joan, 656
Redmond, Eugene, 73
Rehm, Lynn P., 654
Reinisch, Jane, 637
Reiss, Ira L., 654
Renee, Karen S., 654
Richmond, Virginia P., 652
Rimmer, Robert H., 586–589, 607, 654
Roberts, Jane, 654
Roberts, J. D., 654
Rodgers, Richard, 485, 487, 583
Rogo, D. Scott, 654
Rollins, Boyd C., 173, 654
Rook, Karen S., 259–261, 654
Roosevelt, Theodore, 82
Rorvik, David, 314, 655–656
Rose, Arnold M., 655

Rosenberg, Morris, 655
Rosenblatt, Steven, 391
Rosenfeld, Anne H., 655
Rothbart, Mary K., 655
Rowe, D. C., 54, 635, 654
Rubenstein, Carin M., 655
Rubin, Theodore Issac, 608
Rubin, Zick, 6, 655

Samuels, Mike, 655
Samuels, Nancy, 655
Sanders, Karen M., 649
Sarnoff, I., 423–424, 655
Sarnoff, Philip G., 655
Scarr, S., 635, 655
Schachter, Stanley, 423, 655
Scharr, J. H., 652
Scheff, Thomas J., 655
Schroeder, Lynn, 440, 653
Schwartz, Jack, 551
Scott, William A., 655
Sears, Robert, 187–189, 655
Shaver, Phillip, 655
Shaw, George Bernard, 456
Sheehan, David V., 38, 67, 73, 160, 534,
    647, 655
Sherif, Muzafer, 89, 655
Sherman, A. Robert, 655
Sherman, Clay, 392, 656
Shettles, Landrum B., 656
Shiffrin, Nancy, 653
Simmons, Ruth, 112–113
Simonton, O. Carl, 534, 537, 559, 656
Simonton, Stephanie, 534, 537, 559, 656
Smith, James R., 647
Smith, Justa, 56–57, 589
Smith, Lynn G., 647
Smithers, A. G., 656
Sother, Ann, 656
Spitzer, Stephan P., 643, 655
Steffan, John J., 656
Stein, Peter J., 656
Steiner, Lee R., 113–114, 632, 656
Stevenson, Ian, 110–112, 656
Stone, Carol I., 656
Styne, Jule, 583
Sutphen, Dick, 111–112, 656

Tec, Nechama, 656
Thomas, Alexander, 38, 47–49, 52, 55,
    62, 83, 395, 624, 633, 656

Thomas, Darwin L., 173, 654
Thomas, William I., 229, 656
Timnick, Lois, 657
Tracy, Brian, 533, 558, 657
Trower, P. E., 644
Twentyman, Craig T., 137, 657, 659

Vandenberg, S. G., 80, 657
Vane, Andrew R., 657
Verbrugge, Lois M., 657

Waitley, Denis, 533, 558, 657
Wallace, K. M., 545–546, 657
Walster, Elaine, 644, 657
Wambach, Helen, 111–113, 657
Ward, Ingeborg, 638, 657
Watson, David, 657
Watson, Thomas J., 658
Webber, Arthur W., 645
Weber, Eric, 657
Weinberg, S. Kirson, 657
Weinhold, Barry K., 649
Weinstein, Eugene A., 657
Weintraub, Pamela, 657

Weiss, Robert S., 658
Wells, Brian W. P., 658
Wells, H. G., 485–486
Wender, Paul H., 65–66, 74, 80, 149, 263, 406, 636, 658
Wendt, H. W., 658
Whelan, Elizabeth M., 437–438, 658
White, Betty, 658
Whitehurst, Robert N., 648, 651
Wilson, Kenneth, 6, 650
Wiseman, Jacqueline P., 651–652
Wolpe, Joseph, 658
Wortis, John, 657

Yeko, Bruce, 487
Young, Jeffrey E., 658
Young, Perry Deane, 658

Zill, Nicholas, 633
Zimbardo, Philip G., 21–26, 33, 37, 79, 131, 343, 423–424, 499, 501, 506, 518, 520, 658
Znaniecki, Florian, 229, 656

Subject Index

abortion, 437
abreaction, 111
academic majors, 442–443, 452
academic performance, 461
acid stomach, 379
acne, 387–389
action orientation, 252
active listening, 564
activity level, 43
acupuncture, 589, 632
acupuncture points, 367–368, 391
adaptability, 398
addiction (to brain biochemistry), 295–296
"Adelade's Lament", 372–373
adjustment to oppression/injustice, 521–522, 524
adjustment, stress upon, 519–520
advice calls, 447–448
advice re: higher education, 452–455
affiliation, 424–426
affirmation making, 555–556, 559
Affirmative Action, 10
aggression, 43, 52, 74, 85–86, 99, 219, 248, 253–256, 569, 636–637, 640–641
aggressive extroverts, 263
aging (among love-shys), 309–310
agnosticism, 464
agoraphobia, 66
alcohol, 350–353
alcoholics, 26, 28, 63, 350, 352–353
Alcoholics Anonymous, 26, 28, 319, 516, 563
alienation, 463–464
  from siblings, 202

alignment of nature, 105
allergies, 72–73, 368, 371, 382, 391–393, 399, 406, 634
all-girl peer group (attraction to), 127
aloneness vs. loneliness, 426
aloofness, 150, 165
alprazolam, 71
ambiguity, fear of, 3, 51, 53, 141, 467, 469–470, 543–545, 563
ambiverts, 42, 224, 295
American Medical Association, 318, 523
American Psychiatric Association, 523
American Psychological Association, 318, 521, 523
amniocentesis, 437
amphetamines (brain), 295–298
androgens, 56–57, 59, 388–389, 422
anger, 152–153, 211, 272, 279, 381, 422, 426
anhedonia, 65
animal research, 39
anthropology, 569, 571, 616–617
anti-anxiety drugs, 160
anticipatory anxiety, 2, 73, 120, 265, 401–402, 411, 413, 453, 511, 622–623, 631
anti-depressant activity, 248
anti-depressant drugs, 65–67, 80
anxiety, 47, 52, 60, 71–74, 111, 118–120, 142, 165, 226, 265, 277, 284, 307, 411–413, 423–426, 467, 505, 553–554, 562, 565, 621, 623–624
  and enzyme neutralization, 59
  endogenous vs. exogenous, 68–70
  vs. fear, 423–424

681

anxiety disease, 38, 67, 71, 160
anxiety proneness, 80, 111, 118, 133, 211, 454, 589
anxiety threshold, 40, 43–45, 47, 53, 72–73, 75, 91, 96, 217, 222, 224, 235, 244, 248, 262, 308, 350, 352, 454–455, 464, 540, 552, 570, 578, 619–620, 622–625, 636
apartment buildings for singles, 583
apocrine sweat glands, 382
apperceptive mass, 98–101
approach/avoidance, 277, 597
aptitudes (native), 46, 105
archery, 247
arranged marriages, 208, 278, 617–619
arthritis, 28
ascending reticular formation, 295
ascetic moralists, 453
assertion phobia, 412–413
assertiveness, 39, 58–59, 118, 157, 412, 453, 586, 609, 630, 640
    fear of, 120, 142
    norms, 5, 57, 118
assertiveness training, 513, 516, 520, 522
asthmatics, 28
astigmatism, 386
astrological gender selection, 438–440
astrological theory, 104–105
astrology, 55, 103–109
atheism, 464
athletics, 143–144
attitudes vs. behavior, 8, 409–410, 506
attractiveness (see physical attractiveness; also see beauty)
audio-cassette programs, 532–534, 557
aura (Kirlian), 14–15, 83, 113–114, 367–368, 391, 410, 589, 608, 632
auric health, 113–114
autistic girls (use of), 608–609
autonomic nervous system, 42, 49
aventyl, 62
avoidance (see social avoidance)

backaches, 364
ballroom dancing, 247, 596–598
band music, 247
barbie doll case, 332–333
baseball, 46, 195, 197, 237–244, 246, 248–249, 251, 258, 285, 432–434, 436, 579
bashfulness, 286
basketball, 46, 237–238, 241–244, 246, 248–249, 251–252, 258, 285

basketball free throw study, 558–559
beatings (also see corporal punishment), 213–217
beauty (also see physical attractiveness), 299–321, 476–477, 483, 485–486, 500–501, 528, 546, 579, 608
    need among love-shys for beauty, 122
    tastes in beauty, 313
bedwetting (see enuresis)
beer drinking, 351
behavior disorders, 47
    behavior therapy, 67, 79, 383, 491, 493, 501–509
    behavior vs. attitudes, 8, 409–410, 506
belittlement, persistent, 153, 186, 215–218, 220–223, 435
benevolent coercion, 252
Bible, 96, 202, 466, 551
bibliotherapy, 453, 533–534
bicycle riding, 191, 195, 199, 247
big brother (need for among shys), 466
billiards, 246, 251
biochemical imbalances, 60–64, 71, 75, 144
biochemistry, 37, 57, 59, 374, 635–636
    of romantic love feelings, 294–298
    of shyness, 632
biogenic amines, 65–67
biological considerations, 37, 55, 394, 398, 453, 631–641
bioplasmic body (also see aura), 551, 632
birth control (hot water), 527
birthdate data, 106
bisexuality, 58, 121, 297
bitterness, 271–272
bizarre maternal behavior, 153, 167, 178, 216
"black sheep", 201–202, 204
blaming the victim, 625
blood tests, 61–63
boccie, 248
body build, 231–232
"bootstraps", 616
"born again" religionists, 464, 466
bowel movements (fascination with), 333, 390
bowling, 49, 238, 242, 244–245, 249, 251
boxing, 255
"boyish" preference patterns, 284
Boys Club of America, 166, 283, 627
Boy Scouts of America, 166, 194, 254, 283, 627

'boy" stereotypes, 237
brag (parents' need to), 203
brain biochemistry, 61–64, 66–67, 71, 73–
    76, 144, 218, 294–298, 631–641
brain development (intrauterine), 631–
    641
brain masculinization, 57, 144–147, 631–
    641
brain neurology, 61, 67, 73, 631–641
brain (oxygen needs of), 370
brain vs. mind, 470
breakfast cereal, 406
breakfast food and fatigue, 376, 406
breaking points, 610–611
breakups in courtship, 6
breast size preferences, 305–306
breathing (nasal) difficulty, 367–369
bridge, 251
Brigadoon, 477, 480, 485–486
Briquet's syndrome, 151
Broadway show music, 254, 477, 480,
    484–488
brooding, 256
brothers, 161–163, 167, 170
Brownies, 166, 234, 627
buck teeth, 390
buddy system, 195–196
bullying, 47, 49, 62–64, 83, 85–87, 89–93,
    97–98, 146, 150, 159, 191, 195–199,
    218–219, 230–231, 237, 242, 244, 252–
    256, 258, 263, 291, 317, 331, 335–336,
    344–346, 385, 399–400, 402, 427–428,
    432–434, 468, 472, 552, 568–580, 602–
    603, 627–629, 635
Butterflies Are Free, 475–477

Caesarean section, 150, 637
calisthenics/gymnastics, 240–249
camp (summer), 80, 193–199, 254
Campfire Girls, 166, 284, 627
Candid Camera, 423
cantankerousness (maternal), 145, 147,
    167
Capture the Flag, 198
capuchin monkeys, 584
Caput Algol, 109
careers,
    goals, 452
    choice, 51, 113, 201, 635
    effectiveness, 30, 52, 140, 219, 445–461
    instability of, 444
    opportunities, 452
    search for, 445–461

catecholamines, 71
catharsis, 111
causation (probable), 128, 131, 161
celibacy, 124, 201
central nervous system, 79
change, disruptive effects of, 27–28
chanting (repetitious), 196, 575
characterological flaws, 60, 91
chemical additives, 393
chess, 251
child abusers, 168, 211, 214, 219, 229,
    346, 635
childbirth-related pain, 149–150, 153
childhood, importance of, 229–230
chimpanzees (pigmy), 584
Chinese-American children, 52–53
chocolate (craving for), 296
choleric native temperament, 570
cholesterol in blood, 28
Christianity, 472
Chronicle of Higher Education, 521
citrus fruits (predilections for), 406, 429
Civil War (American), 575
classical music, 486–488
clay glob (metaphor for mind), 99–101
clergyman psychotherapists, 465
client-centered psychotherapy, 522, 564–
    565
climate, 395–397
cloning, 311–318, 568
closet heterosexuals, 123–124, 142, 429,
    523–524
closet homosexuality, 123–124
clothing (and love-shyness), 182, 184,
    221, 310–311
cloudy days (and shyness), 197
clowning behavior in school, 86–87, 90,
    93–94, 291
coeducation (desire among shys for),
    239, 260, 287, 510
coeducational dormitories, 585–589
coeducational peer groups, 49, 80, 83,
    166
coeducational play (importance of for
    shys), 244, 249, 251, 260, 287, 510
coeducational play preferences, 58, 166,
    249–250, 260
coed roommates, 586–589, 606
Coed Scouts, 166, 260, 285, 320, 510,
    524, 556, 615, 627, 629
coed sports, 244–248
coercion, 255, 435

cohabitation (premarital), 136–137, 324–
325, 607
    attitudes toward, 328
cold water, sensitivity to, 403
combat, wartime, 577–578
comedies (avoidance of), 418
"coming out", 124
commission sales work, 454
common cold, (see headcolds)
communication,
    apprehension (see speech reticence)
    as *love* indicator, 180, 628
    disordered, 207
    importance of, 462, 628–629
    intrafamilial, 179, 184–185
comparison group (non-shy sample),
    128, 135, 142
compassion, 86, 97, 209, 253, 255–256,
    417, 462, 513, 573–575, 580, 609, 611,
    641
competition (perils of), 564, 571–573
competitive effectiveness, 6, 51, 57–59,
    109, 165, 197, 221, 248, 450, 547, 605,
    636
compulsions, 76–78, 353–360
compulsive staring/following behavior,
    353–360
computer dating services, 492
computer tape (as metaphor for subcon-
    scious mind), 101
concentration difficulties (internal dis-
    tractions), 14, 77, 119–120, 122, 124,
    140, 392, 421–422
conditioning, 217, 224
confidants, importance of having, 28–29,
    591–593
conflict, fear of, 192–193, 434–436
conflict resolution skills, 192
conformity (overemphasis upon), 254,
    464
congenital factors (in etiology of love-
    shyness), 60, 106–107, 223, 613, 631–
    641
conservatism (attitudes toward social/
    political), 297, 305
conspicuousness (of love-shyness behav-
    ior), 85–90
constipation, 365
contact lenses, 386
contact sports (fear and avoidance of),
    56, 242, 249, 251, 255, 577, 579

contracepting (and shyness), 439–440
control,
    fear of losing, 311, 353
    over personal life, 29, 222, 419, 510
conversation,
    initiation of, 416
    skills, 273, 417, 530
coordination (at play), 239, 247
"cop out", 520
coprophilia, 333
corporal punishment, 173–174, 213–217,
    345, 570, 580–582, 627–628
    age at cessation of use, 217
    frequency of, 215
    implements used, 215–217
    negative consequences of, 218–220
    vs. discipline, 219
correspondence clubs (foreign), 309–310
cortisol, 63
coughing (frequent), 384–385
courtesy, 211
courtship institution, 607–608
cowardice, 426, 577, 579–580
    as inborn attribute, 580
craft shop activity (summer camp), 197
creativity, 505
criminality and shyness, 343
critical periods, 458, 641
croquet, 49, 245
crutches (therapeutic), 614–615
Cub Scouts, 166, 254, 283
curriculum, high school, 593–596
cynicism, 138, 426

darts, 248
dating,
    and happiness, 12
    as a socializer, 10
    dislike of among love-shys, 208, 302
    inability to participate in, 131, 133,
    142, 163
dating services, 132, 138–140, 531–532,
    539–547, 619
daughters, procreational preference for,
    431–432
David and Lisa, 474–475, 477, 479, 481–
    483, 608
day care center for dogs, 583
daydreaming (also see fantasy), 14, 93,
    108, 121–122, 133, 191, 196–197, 199,
    256–257, 266–267, 274, 276–277, 282–

daydreaming (*cont.*)
  285, 288, 291–292, 300–301, 303, 314,
  354, 389, 509, 572, 629
  need for, 287
  content, 257, 266, 282, 412, 595
defense mechanisms, 78–79, 87
defense systems,
  love-shys' bodily, 371–372
  love-shys' psychoemotional, 60, 185,
  219, 318, 352
defensiveness (of love-shys' mothers),
  158–159, 164
deferral of gratification, 459
definition of the situation, 96
degradation ceremonies, 428, 602–603
dehumanization, 256
democracy (in family governance), 179–
  180
Democratic Party, 464
demonstrativeness (paternal), 187
deodorants, difficulty using, 382–383
dependency, 80, 519, 552, 614–616
  as prerequisite for growth/socializa-
  tion, 467, 514, 562–563
  fear of among psychotherapists, 563
depersonalized treatment, 96
depression, 28, 57, 60–67, 75, 140, 145–
  147, 152, 221, 272, 276, 279, 370, 383,
  392, 421–422, 426, 462, 591
  in children, 62–63, 277–279
  vital (endogenous) vs. exogenous, 64–
  65
developmental tasks, 50, 514, 593
deviancy (shyness as), 425–426, 505–506
deviant role (recruitment for), 53, 88–90,
  98, 102
deviated septum (nose), 368–369, 373,
  380, 392
dexamethasone suppression test, 62–63
diagnostic tools, 109, 113, 123, 125, 137–
  138, 142
diarrhea, 365
"different" (feeling of being), 127, 423–
  426
difficult children, 48, 101, 221
dinner table conversation, 176, 179
discarnate spirits, 471
discarnations, 105
discipline,
  fear among love-shys of using, 434–
  436

in love-shys' families of orientation,
  173–224
discomfort thresholds, 395, 404
discouragement, 165
discrimination, 93–97, 428
dislike of own gender/same-sexed peers,
  127, 431–432
distractions, internal (also see concentration difficulties; obsessions), 77, 119–
  120, 140, 462
divorce, 169–171, 618
divorced women (and love-shys), 541
doctor (medical) visitations, 400
dogs, 39–40, 54–55, 246, 277–278, 290,
  299–300, 332, 582–584, 605, 609, 611,
  617
  and frisbee throwing, 246
  as catalysts for *human* social interaction, 299–300, 377, 611
  as sexual love objects, 332
  day care center for, 583
dolls as toys, 236, 332–333
domestic orientation (among love-shys),
  262
dominance patterns, 640
door knob handling (phobia), 390
dopamine, 74, 263, 636, 639–640
double jeopardy, 177
doubles (coed tennis), 246–247
downward social mobility, 444
draft, military, 428, 574–576, 578, 627
draft resistance, 575
dramatics, 252
dress habits (among love-shys), 311, 319
drinking (alcohol) alone, 352
drives, long automobile, 191
drug abusers, 63
drug treatment (also see psychopharmacological treatment), 65, 566, 631
dry mouth, 371–372, 380

"early bloomers", 271
East German researchers, 143–146, 152,
  154, 157, 590, 636
"easy children", 48, 101
education,
  advanced, 187, 451–460
  level attained, 442, 546–547
  limits of, 51, 451–455
  perils of higher, (for shys), 451–460
effeminacy, 58

ego deflating talk, 153, 215, 220–223, 435
ego strength, 469, 556–557
ejaculations, sexual (average number/
    week), 324
elastic limits, 24, 55, 79, 81–82, 102, 105,
    224, 553–554, 610
electroencephalograph (EEG), 42
electromagnetic energy force field, 317–
    318, 391, 632
elementary school,
    environment, 227, 261, 273, 280, 289,
        312, 632, 637
    romances, 265–298, 629
    teachers, 158–159, 166, 240, 286, 628,
        631
embarrassing situations (fear of), 566,
    620–621, 623
emotion vs. intellect, 167–168, 553, 562
emotional demonstrativeness, 414, 418,
    475
emotional dependency, 563
emotional health (of unattached gradu-
    ate students), 124
emotionality (native), 24, 40, 42–43, 45,
    79, 82, 96, 103–104, 325, 350, 624
emotional support, 55, 168–169, 171,
    173–174, 176–177, 181, 348
emotional support networks (see sup-
    port groups)
employment,
    and love-shyness, 9–10, 12, 221, 441–
        452, 510–511
    attitudes, 450–451
    ineffectiveness, 450–451, 460
    of love-shys' mothers, 155–157
    of love-shys' mothers while pregnant,
        155
    opportunities, 227–228
    physical attractiveness and, 311–312
    terminations, 356, 359, 458
encounter group therapy, 403, 496, 598–
    601
    sex ratio in, 599
endurance, 109, 637
energy,
    and hypoglycemia, 375–383
    from being loved, 13–15
    low level of, 62, 65, 72, 80, 108–109,
        176, 222, 274, 282, 295, 371, 375, 377–
        378, 635, 640
    thought, 555

enuresis (bedwetting), 364–365
envy,
    of female privilege, 125, 427–429
    of homosexuals, 339–340
enzymes,
    malfunctioning, 56–59, 71, 73, 106,
        146, 152, 156, 418, 589–590
    neutralization of by anxiety, 59–60
Episcopalian denomination, 468
Equal Opportunity Employment, 10
erection (ability to have an), 324–325,
    341
erotic directionality, 234
Escalan, 526
esthetic,
    attributes of love-shys, 306–309
    needs of love-shys, 122, 281, 301–302,
        305, 317, 320, 474, 477
estrogens, 56, 637
etheric body (also see aura), 318
exceptional children, 211, 244
executive search services, 448–449
exercise, need for, 49, 241, 244–249
expectorate (frequent need to), 381
experimental research group (of love-
    shys), 128
experimental social psychology, 423–426
extinguishing anxiety, 208, 491, 493,
    511, 513, 517, 520, 522, 528–529, 562,
    565–566, 606
extra-sensory perception (ESP or psi),
    112–113
    belief in, 471
extroversion-introversion dimension of
    native temperament, 40, 43, 79–80,
    103–104, 214, 217, 295, 306, 325
extroverts, 263, 620–621, 628
eye color,
    and shyness, 405–406
    as criterion for discrimination, 92–97
eyeglasses, 385–387
eye itch, 403
Eysenck Cross of Inborn Temperament,
    40–41, 45, 51, 79, 84, 91, 95, 579
Eysenck Personality Questionnaire (mean
    scores), 673

facial beauty, 302–304
family,
    atmosphere and love-shyness, 175–179
    background of love-shys, 173–224

family (*Cont.*)
  formation, 131
  governance, 180
  happiness (recalled) during formative
    years, 175–176
  networks (see kinship networks)
  size preferences of love-shys, 431–432
  structure and composition, 161–171,
    626–627
fantasy (also see daydreaming), 14, 93,
  108, 121–122, 133, 191, 248–249, 267,
  273–274, 277, 284–285, 296, 300–302,
  304–305, 354, 469, 473, 500, 595, 629
fastidiousness, 190
fatalistic attitudes, 426, 560
father-son relationships, 178
fathers (perceived shyness of love-
  shys'), 189
fatigue (chronic), 113, 375–377, 380
  alleviation of, 640
fear,
  of anxiety (see anticipatory anxiety)
  of catching headcold germs, 380, 390
  of pain in medical settings, 400–402
  vs. anxiety, 423–424
fearfulness, 39, 51, 98, 232
feeling loved vs. being loved, 180–181,
  208, 224
feelings (ability to express), 7, 414, 418,
  547, 627
feelings, importance of, 256, 475
felt deprivation, 119–120, 140, 259, 267,
  326, 389
female privilege, envy of, 125, 427–429
feminine interest patterns, 72, 236
feminizing male offspring, 58–60, 145–
  148, 151–152, 154, 174, 187–189, 631–
  641
fetal growth and development, 57–59,
  143–160, 631–641
fetishes, 331–333
fidelity in marriage, 618
field of roses metaphor, 271–278
figurines, attraction to, 236
financial,
  costs of shyness, 27, 30
  dependence on parents, 221
  success, 52, 444–460
fire-setting fantasies, 345
fire walkers, 549–550
first date, 33

first grade (elementary school), 158–159,
  166, 204, 261, 266, 274, 276–277
first impressions (importance of), 232
5-HIAA, 64
flag salute, 574
following behavior (compulsive), 353–
  360
food allergies, 377, 380, 393, 406
football, 46, 195, 235, 237–238, 241–244,
  246, 248–249, 251–256, 258, 285, 351,
  432–434, 436, 570, 577, 579
  as an *illegal* sport, 252–256
  consciousness, 254
foot fetish case, 334–335
Forbidden Games, 293, 474–475, 477, 480–
  483
foreign correspondence clubs, 209–210
foreign language study, 593
forgetting (difficulty in), 192, 212, 214,
  235, 620, 623
frailness of body, 231–232
fraternal (dizygotic) twins, 54
fraternities, 601–604
free choice, 1, 55, 105, 136, 139, 201,
  205, 265, 269, 273, 341, 374, 509, 521–
  522, 561, 629–630, 641
freedom, sense of, 367–368, 371
friendliness (sociability)
friends (importance of), 250, 262
friendship-making ability, 244
friendship networks, 8–9, 28–29, 44–45,
  157, 227, 256, 259–260, 262–263, 349,
  447, 455, 485, 507, 516, 543–544, 547,
  563, 592, 594
friendships,
  same-sexed during formative years,
    225–263, 420
  current, 256–261
"frills" in education, 457–458
frisbee throwing, 246, 249
fruit preferences (and native temperament), 429
fundamentalist churches/beliefs, 330,
  464–466, 468, 519, 574–579, 587, 589,
  626
funding difficulties (for love-shyness
  research), 630

"game" of dating, 20–21
gas problems, 385

gender,
preferences (re: future children), 431
ratio imbalance, 229, 539–542
role expectations, 45–46, 56, 58, 106–107
segregated peer groups (also see segregation of sexes), 239, 249, 283–284
selection, 158, 165, 436–439
generosity (financial) of parents, 181–182
gene splicing research, 567–568
genetic engineering, 633
genetics, 37, 54, 60, 63–64, 71, 75–76, 80, 101, 106–107, 149, 223–224, 281, 397–399, 404, 406, 608, 613, 625, 632, 634–641
gentle life, preference for, 435
geographic mobility, 461–462
Gestalt therapists, 565
getting up out of bed, 378–379
Gilmartin Love-Shyness Scale, 665–671
Girl Scouts of America, 166, 284, 627
"going steady", 267
golf, 238, 245
good impression (need to create a), 159–160
"goose" case study, 205–207
grade-point average, 14, 124, 452, 458
graduate students (celibacy among), 124
grandchildren (parents' deprivation of), 200–202, 209
"Greek" organizations, 601–606
group therapy (conventional), 522
groupthink, 574–579, 602–603
group visualization, 536
guidance counselors, 194
grooming, 311, 319
Guys and Dolls, 372
gynecologists, 158

hair length preferences, 303–306
halitosis, 317, 372, 379–380
handsomeness (and employment), 312
handwashing, 390–391
happiness, 13, 418, 617
correlates of, 29, 113, 119, 140, 158, 226, 250, 441, 444–445, 452
dating and, 12
Harrad Experiment, The, 586–589, 607
Harrad-styled dormitories, 586–589
Harvey Milk High School, 263

hazing (see bullying)
headaches, 151, 364
headcolds, 60, 369, 371–375, 390, 392
and sun's angularity to earth, 392
health, medical, 250, 417–418
heart disease, 28
heart rate patterns and inhibition, 52–54, 634
hermaphroditism (gender dysphoria), 148
heterosexuality (of love-shys), 118, 120–123
heterosexuals (as distinguished from homosexuals), 120–123
high blood pressure, 28
high school (difficulties with), 378–379
"high strung" nature, 152, 158, 167, 217
hiking, 285
Hinkley case, 360–361
hobbies (solitary), 195–199
holistic medicine, 146
home and family orientation, 262
homesickness, 66, 198–199
homogeneous peer groups, 90
homophobia, 297
homosexual, being misperceived/mislabeled as, 234, 254, 258, 330–339, 409, 425–426, 505, 510, 630
homosexuality, 1, 57–58, 87, 118, 122, 131, 144–145, 234–235, 297, 335–340, 519, 523, 580, 587, 630, 638
as distinguished from heterosexuality, 120–123
as distinguished from male lesbianism, 126
feigning of, 576
intrauterine development of, 638–639
parental (unintentional) encouragement of, 297
homosexual rights, 121
homosexuals, 263, 396–397, 426, 523–524
friendships with, 338–339
unwanted overtures from, 334–335
Hopi Indians, 552
hopscotch, 247
hormonal abnormalities, 61, 146, 631–641
hormones, 56–57, 59, 106, 144, 148, 294, 388, 422, 590, 637–641
horseback riding, 247

horseshoes, 49, 245
housing of love-shys, 443
human physiology, 37
humidity, 395–396
humiliation, use of, 216
humor, sense of, 165, 308–309, 417–418, 547
hyperarousability, 42
hyperperspiration, 311, 381–383, 396
hypersalivation, 380–381
hyperseriousness of parents, 185–187, 190
hypnosis, 110–113, 291, 318–319, 352, 550, 552, 566
hypnotherapy, 318–319, 561
hypnotic age regression, 110–113
hypnotizability, 318, 551
hypochondria, 390, 403, 599–600
hypocrisy, disdain of, 468
hypoglycemia (reactive idiopathic), 62, 113, 147, 371–372, 375–383
hypothalamus, 294–296, 638–639
    sex hormone receptors in, 638
hysterical disorders, 151
hysterical laughter (uncontrolled), 220

identity, sense of, 547
ideology,
    intellectual, 143
    psychotherapeutic, 38, 143
identical (monozygotic) twins, 54–55, 80, 635
    reared apart, 55
ignoring,
    by parents, 177, 181, 207
    by peers, 86–87, 89, 91–92, 146, 159
illegitimacy, 155
immortality, 470–472
impersonal social situations, 3, 141, 523
impotence, 341
impulse control problems (of mothers), 152–160, 216
inadequate socialization, 562
inborn factors, 31, 38–80, 146, 157, 231, 369, 375, 377, 380, 453, 503–504, 523, 538, 553–554, 566, 631
inborn temperament (see temperament)
incarnations (past), 105, 110–113
incest taboo (transfer of), 585
income of love-shys, 443–444, 546

incompetent parenting, 167, 175–224
inertia (behavioral), 58, 108, 140, 170, 218, 350, 367–368
infant mortality, 148–149
infatuation, 13–14, 267, 274, 276, 280, 282, 286–287, 292–293, 296, 354, 358–359, 422, 474–475, 499, 515
inferiority complex, 88
infidelity proneness, 262
influence,
    general social, 219, 435
    parental, 184–185
inheritance from parents, 199–203
inhibition, 40, 42–43, 45, 47, 50–54, 56, 74, 79–80, 82, 90–91, 96, 98, 100, 103–104, 108, 113–114, 120, 133–134, 166, 187, 192, 194, 198–199, 211, 214, 244, 262–263, 295, 318, 406, 429, 440, 461, 469, 516, 543, 545–546, 552, 568, 570, 578, 589, 600, 602, 605, 613, 615, 620, 624, 626–629, 633–635
inhibition gene, 24, 40, 42–54, 167, 222, 224, 405, 461–462, 506, 510, 520, 540, 622, 624, 627, 634–635
injuries (sports), 255
innate sensitivities, 393–407
insecurity, 158, 160
insensitivity of parents, 186–187, 194, 198–199
insight, 66, 111, 452–453, 561–562
insomnia, 389
intact homes, 169–171
intellectual,
    awareness, 562
    ideology, 143
    maturity, 459
    orientation, 51
    skills, 458
intellect vs. emotion, 553, 562
intelligence, 46, 105–107, 149, 453, 456, 458, 546–547, 553
interest patterns (of love-shys), 58, 195, 637–638
internalization of ideas, 88, 101, 224
internalized controls (self-control), 219
interpersonal anxiety, 2, 120, 319, 453, 597, 622–624
interpersonal skills, 8–9, 46, 49–50, 83–87, 89, 91, 157, 241, 247, 249, 268, 308, 319, 371, 392, 444, 452–453, 455, 458,

interpersonal skills (*cont.*)
  460–461, 505, 511, 513, 574, 582, 595,
  601, 605–606, 615, 622–624, 631
interpersonal skills training, 247, 249,
  268, 457, 460, 513, 572, 574, 594, 596
interpretative function of mind, 100–101
interviews (for this research), 134–140
intimacy, importance of, 592
intrauterine factors, 143–160, 631–641
  and brain development, 636–641
introduction services (see dating
  services)
introduction (to women) arranging, 272–
  273, 286
introspectiveness, 17, 235, 256, 409, 428,
  565
introversion (introverts), 42–43, 45, 74,
  80, 82, 96, 98, 104, 108, 217, 235, 306,
  325, 350, 352, 406, 461, 624–625, 629,
  635
invisibility (social) of love-shyness, 340,
  412
iproniazid, 61
irascibility (maternal), 57, 145, 147, 152,
  154, 158, 167, 212, 218
J Remember Mama, 293
irritability,
  infant, 634
  maternal, 145–147, 167
isolates, 150, 158, 250, 274, 287, 524,
  602, 614
isolation (social), 168, 252
  from *women* in particular, 195
isoproterenol, 73
itches (bodily), 394–395, 398, 403, 634

jacuzzi baths (therapeutic use of), 525–
  527, 530
jazz, 247
Jeremy, 474, 477, 482–483
job search, 445–450
job prestige levels, 546
joining (aversion to), 331, 464–465, 467–
  468, 488

karma, 55, 105–107, 223, 317, 632
kidney dialysis, 74
kindergarten, 158–159, 166, 261, 268,
  274, 276–277, 632
kinship networks, 28–29, 157, 168–169,

  225–226, 263, 347–348, 455, 485, 516,
  543–544, 547–548, 624, 626
Kirlian aura (see aura)
Kirlian photography, 113–114, 589, 632
kleenex, excessive use of, 366, 370–371,
  380
kleptomania, 348–349
knocked down, fear of being, 234
labeling theory, 56, 58, 79, 96, 101–102,
  220, 224, 335–336, 553–554, 560
lactate sensitivity, 71–73
"late bloomers", 265, 271
latent functions, 516–517
"latent homosexual" labeling, 505, 510
Latter-Day Saints, 468–470
laughter, 417, 475
law of least resistance, 452
leadership capacity, 16
learning,
  as *cause*, 37, 39, 74, 76, 91, 101, 106,
    143, 157, 554
  negative, 88, 143
  problems, 77
lecturing by parents, 184–185
"left out" position, 240–241
left out syndrome, 240–241
legal changes, 194, 617
legal recourse, 627–628
leg cramps (morning), 79
lesbians, 263
lethargy, 635
letter writing, 20, 133, 135, 291, 310,
  358–359, 412, 465–466, 484, 541, 544
liberal arts (perils of for shys), 453, 461–
  462
liberality (social-political), 97, 463–464
"life after life", 470, 589
life purposes, 105
life scripts, 287
lifetime sports, 238, 244–249
locus ceruleus, 73–74, 295
loneliness, 201, 208, 234, 260, 419–426,
  633
long hair/pretty face, 20–21, 265–321
"looking-glass self" concept, 88
Los Angeles, 132, 138–139, 142
love,
  as an elixir of life, 15, 282
  as a *causal* force, 17–18, 224, 482, 565
  and communication, 462

love (*cont.*)
  as a game, 620–621
  as healer, 19
  operational definition of, 180–184, 222, 628
love ballads, 247, 254, 486, 584
love chemicals, 294
love feelings,
  biochemical basis of, 294–298
  prepubescent, 265–298
love laboratory (U.C.L.A.), 13
love letters, 358–359
lovelorn periods, 268, 270, 272
love needs, 208, 274
love needs vs. sexual needs, 281
"love nucleus" of hypothalamus, 295
love roles (importance of), 441
love-shyness,
  and astrological factors, 103–110
  and auric health, 114
  and the criminal mind, 343–362
  and the need for a beautiful lover, 299–321
  as a lifetime script, 269–270, 287
  as deviance/nonconformity, 5, 425
  biological underpinnings of, 35–79
  careers and, 441–462
  creation of, 156–157
  definition of, 1, 4, 117–118, 131
  education and, 447–461
  family composition and, 161–171
  gender and, 5
  importance of, 140–141
  in females, 5
  innate sensitivities and, 393–407
  intrauterine antecedents of, 143–156, 631–641
  karma and, 103–107
  medical symptoms and, 363–392
  model for explaining, 106–107
  money and, 444–445
  parenting antecedents, 173–224
  peer group antecedents, 225–263
  political beliefs and, 463–464
  prepubescent infatuations and, 265–298
  prevalence of, 6, 23, 33, 102, 131–132
  prevention of, 157–160, 243–251, 567–611

  psychological characteristics of, 117–118, 409–429
  reincarnation and, 110–113
  religion and, 464–472
  sexual history/attitudes and, 323–341
  sisters and, 161–162
  therapy for, 493–566
love-shy research samples, 132–140
Love-Shys Anonymous, 502, 524, 556
love stories, predilection for, 474
lower brain stem, 294–296
lymbic system, 42

"male lesbian" concept, 125–127, 142, 273, 429, 523–524
mannequins (sex with), 333
maps, interest in, 277
marijuana, use of, 349–350
marital happiness, correlates of, 262, 417
marriage bureaus, 531–532, 619
marriage,
  attitudes toward, 618
  career success and, 11–12
married women (as easier to talk to than single women), 164–165
Marty, 484–485
masculinizing the brain, 57, 146, 162, 631–641
mask (facade) wearing, 20–21, 164–165
massage, 530
masturbation, 121, 131, 323–325, 327, 389, 528
  personality correlates of frequent, 326
matchmakers, 618–620
maturity (emotional), 459, 461
May-December romances, 483–484
media,
  inspired love infatuations, 292–294
  need for attention from (re: love-shyness), 523
  starlets, 292
  use of, 232, 523–524
medical examinations, fear of, 401
medical symptoms, 27–29, 209, 363–392, 591–592
meditation, 530, 534–538, 555, 557, 589
melancholic quadrant (Eysenck Cross), 42, 47, 49, 51, 75, 79, 82, 84, 91, 95–96, 192, 244, 352, 529

melody in music (love-shys' emphasis upon), 486–487
memory (acuity of in love-shys), 235, 273
menopause (painful), 150
menstruation, 160
mental attitude, 43, 219
mental health, 250, 417–418, 584
  of unattached graduate students, 124
mental rehearsal (also see visualization), 301, 502–503, 558–560
mental retardation, 90–92
metaphysics, 503
methodology (research), 132–140
microbiology, 57
military establishment, 464, 574–575, 627
military treatment of male sex, 428
milk allergy, 72, 380–381
"milk" vs. "honey", 182–184
mindless patriotism, 574–580
mind's eye, 301
mind vs. brain, 470
miniature golf, 49, 242, 245, 249, 251
Minnesota Multiphasic Personality Inventory (MMPI), 124
misbehavior in siblings, 202, 213
miscarriages, 147–148, 637
misinterpreting of shy behavior, 1, 120, 142
mislabeling (as "homosexual"), 58, 87, 120, 142, 200, 202
missionary work, 469–470
modeling, 170, 185, 189, 192
mode of standardization, 162–166
money (as an aphrodisiac), 444
monoamine oxidase inhibitors (MAO Inhibitors), 43, 72, 102, 263, 631
monogamous premarital coitus, 16, 136–137
monogamy, 287
  discouraging (unintentional) of, 297
  psychoemotional vs. sexual, 588
monozygotic (identical) twins, 54–55, 80
mood control, 65
moralistic psychotherapists, 18, 26, 91, 183, 564
moralistic summer camp administrators, 194
moralists, 530–532, 553, 564, 621
moralizing (of parents), 187, 191

moral liberality/conservatism, 305, 329–330
mosquitoes, 198, 398–399
Most Happy Fella, The, 484
mothers,
  as primary punishing agents, 163, 216–217, 229
  mental state of, 57, 60, 590
  personalities of, 144–146, 152–160
  pregnancies of, 143–160, 632, 637–641
  relationships with love-shy sons, 178–180
motion pictures (attendance at), 418, 473–486
movie starlets (infatuation for), 287, 292–293
moving, 461–462
musical comedy, 485
musical tastes/interests, 254, 256, 285, 299, 473, 486–488
My Fair Lady, 277
myopia, 386
mystical significance, 290

name calling, 335–336
nardil, 67, 72, 160
nasal itches, 392
nasal polyps, 368–369, 371, 373, 380, 392
nasal problems, 365–371, 373
natal charts (horoscopes), 104, 108–109
native talents/aptitudes, 81–82
nature/nurture debate, 54, 56, 101, 156
Nazi holocaust, 574–575
neatness (compulsion for), 190
need for people, 421
negative attention, 86–87, 90
negative control, 427
negative healers, 112
negative mental attitude, 157
negativity, 410, 417
neologisms, 623
"nerve" to be friendly, 409–410, 412, 445–449, 456
nervousness, 217, 273, 371, 401, 415–416, 547
nervous system, 61, 65, 71, 75, 294
neurologists, 566
neurosis (creation of), 42–43, 113, 119, 234–235, 481–482

neurotransmitters, 61, 65, 71, 75, 635–636, 639
never married status, 1
New Testament, 551
New York, 132, 138–139, 142
nightmares, 67
nonbehaving, 218
nonconformity (involuntary), 234, 261, 425
nondaters, 265
non-shy research sample, 134–137
norepinephrine, 73–74, 634–640
normative change, 609–610
normative expectations, 46–48
normative stereotypy, 235
nose picking behavior, 392
nude beaches, 330
nude jacuzzi therapy, 524–527
nudity (attitudes toward), 109, 626–627

obedience (mindless), 578
objective vs. subjective reality, 120
obsessions, 75–78, 267, 282, 326, 474, 476
obsessive-compulsive disorders, 75–78
obstetrical complications, 149
obstetricians, 150, 158
occult interests/issues, 24–25, 103, 256, 290, 470–472, 478, 503, 584, 590
occupational choice, 441–461, 635
older love-shys (research sample), 138–139
older vs. younger love-shys, 18, 129–130, 138
Olympic Games, 143
one-minute parenting, 160, 208, 221, 224, 581
only child status, 166–168, 171, 199, 626
"On the Street Where You Live", 277
"oozie-goozie" case, 333
open-mindedness, 38
optimism, 301
options, 235, 238, 244
orgasms, 325
sexual satisfaction and, 327
out-of-body experiences, 471, 550, 589
overprotectiveness (of parents), 191
overt behavior vs. attitudes/values, 409–410
oxygen deprivation, 149

oxygen needs of brain, 370

pacifists, 569, 575
pain, 226
in childbirth, 149–150
sensitivity, 398–402
threshold, 147, 220, 386
panacea (love as a), 17, 19
parahippocampal gyrus, 71–72
parasympathetic nervous system (dominance of), 635
parental friendships, 203–205
parental support groups, 48
Parent-Effectiveness Training, 158, 160, 221, 581
parenthood aspirations (of love-shys), 431–440
parenting education, need for, 221, 457
parenting,
incompetent, 167, 171, 173–224, 272
responsibilities (fear of assuming), 431–437
skills, 461
Parents Anonymous, 158, 516, 563, 581
parents' marriages (quality of), 169–170
Parents of Gay and Lesbian Children, 209
Parents of Love-Shy Heterosexuals, 209
parents of shy and inhibited children support groups, 158
passive-aggressive behavior, 205–208, 276
passivity, 50, 58, 106, 109, 146–147, 158–159, 174, 194, 219, 427, 609, 641
paternal dominance, 174
paternal sex anxiety, 187–189
patience,
among love-shys, 494, 618
among love-shys' mothers, 153, 222–223
patriotism (mindless), 574–580
pecking order, 89
pediatrics, 158
peer environment (as a cause of love-shyness), 173–224, 272
peer group (same-sexed), 6, 44, 62, 82, 122, 127, 175, 221, 224–263
as major socializing agent, 50, 86
attitudes of, 47, 144
pressures, 144, 613

peer group (*cont.*)
    treatment by, 47, 144, 150, 157
peer interaction (currently as adults), 256–262
Penthouse magazine, 326
People Are Funny, 423
people-phobia, 44, 47, 49, 319, 348, 351, 393, 412, 453–454, 569–570, 589, 624, 627, 632
Peplau Loneliness Scale, 420–421
personality,
    defined, 38
    in dating partners, 302, 306, 313
    of love-shys' mothers, 152–160
    of love-shys' mothers during pregnancy, 145–146
person-orientation, 181
perversions (sexual), 331–335
pessimism, 138, 503
pharmacological treatment, 61, 66, 73, 566
pharmacologists, 566
phenylethylamine, 295–296
phobias, 111
physical affection inhibitions, 505, 512
physical appearance, 299–321, 387
physical attractiveness (also see beauty), 46, 79, 84, 87–88, 99, 105–107, 118, 122, 299–321, 455–456, 483, 515, 546
    self-ratings of, 307
physical coercion (see corporal punishment)
physical education, 240–241
physical education enthusiasts, 250, 254
physical exercise, 72, 230–251
physical fitness, 250
physical weakness, 82, 232
physiology, human, 40, 53, 73, 144, 146, 453, 633–635
physiological psychology, 553
piano playing, 81–82, 252, 488
pineal gland, 56
ping pong, 49, 242, 245, 251
pituitary gland, 56, 294
play-acting, 20
Playboy magazine, 326
play (importance of), 50, 229–230
play therapy, 67, 158
pleasuring (physical) skills, 530
"plenty of time" myth, 205

Polish peasant, 229
political involvement, 180
political power base (love shys' need for), 522–523
politics, 463–464
popularity, 250
population explosion, 431–432
positive mental attitude, 43, 319, 411, 454–458
positive mind science, 81, 587
post-hypnotic suggestions, 566
powerlessness feelings, 222
practice-dating therapy, 32, 208, 259, 262, 383, 469, 491–524, 531–535, 537–538, 547, 555–556, 559–562, 564–566, 586, 592, 594, 598, 601, 615, 618–619, 629, 631
    absences from meetings, 501, 506–508
    Alcoholics Anonymous ("AA") model 501–502
    as behavior therapy, 492–493, 495, 502–503, 511, 513, 520
    as socialization, 514
    beauty as a problem in, 499–501
    chair usage, 494–495
    chronological age and speed of therapeutic progress, 509–510
    coping with rejection, 511
    dances, 497
    dating activities permitted, 495
    emotionally detached attitudes in, 500
    enthusiasm for living, 501
    falling in love in, 499–501
    for elementary school children, 509
    for high school aged young people, 508–511
    gender and commitment to therapy, 506–508
    grooming patterns, 496, 501
    ground rules, 495–496
    high school usage in recruitment, 508
    incipient romances within the therapy group, 515–516
    interpersonal skills training in, 496
    length of therapeutic treatment, 495
    marrying of assigned dates, 516–517
    meditation in, 496, 503
    meeting frequency, 494–496
    militancy re: soliciting therapy (need for), 522–524

practice-dating therapy (*cont.*)
  physical affection inhibitions, 505, 512
  psychodrama use in, 496, 512–513
  recruitment of female participants,
    507–508
  relaxation, 496, 504
  role playing in, 496, 512–513
  role taking, 513
  screening for, 498–499, 507
  seating arrangements, 494
  "second plateau" in, 504–506, 511
  sex ratio in, 494, 497, 507–508
  structure within, 496
  support groups within, 501–503
  termination of therapy, 511–512
  time limits for therapy, 513–515
  visualization and mental rehearsal,
    502–504
  waiting lists in, 494, 507–509, 518
prayer groups, 465
preadolescent infatuations (see prepubescent romantic love interests)
precociousness of romantic love interests and desires, 265–298
preferences (sexual), 121–123
pregnancy,
  bashfulness during, 154–155
  management, 147, 152, 632, 637
prejudice among academics, 38, 537
preliterate societies, 282, 588
premarital cohabitation, 136–137, 305,
  587–589, 607–608, 621
premarital sexual intercourse, 178, 304–
  305, 324, 326, 588, 607
  attitudes regarding, 328, 350, 384
premature births, 150
premenstrual stress syndrome ("PMS"),
  73, 160
prenatal development, 56–58, 631–641
prenatal stress, 143–160, 639–641
  and homosexuality development, 143–
    147, 638
preoccupations, 119–120, 122, 389
prepubescent romantic fantasies, 126,
  204
prepubescent romantic love interests
  and desires, 261, 265–298, 566, 629,
  639
perspiration (excessive), 381–383
pretenses in dating, 165, 620–622

prevention (of love-shyness), 128–129,
  131, 133, 142, 157–160, 165–166, 276,
  311, 509–510, 566–611, 624–629, 633
prisoners and meditation, 535
prison (shyness as a), 631
privacy (invasion of), 186, 400
problem drinking patterns, 352–353
process orientation, 618, 620–622
procreational preferences (of love-shys),
  127, 431–440
prodding by parents, 205–208
progesterone, 73, 160, 637
progestogens, 637
programming of minds, 552
promiscuity, 588
proselytising work, 469
prostaglandins, 71
psi phenomena, 256, 470–472, 584, 589–
  590
psychiatric,
  diagnosis, 63
  "4-F", 575–576, 578
  treatment, 291–292, 519–520, 522
psychiatry, 291, 516, 519, 522
psychic (psi) healing abilities, 112–113,
  589–590
psychic (psi) variables, 103
psychoanalysis, 111, 522, 561
psychodormia, 113–114
psychodrama, 95–96, 220, 319, 512–513
psychoemotional abuse, 152–160, 211,
  214–215, 220–223
psychoemotional energy consumption,
  274
psychokenesis ("PK"), 503, 537
psychological characteristics (of love-
  shys), 409–429
psychological pressure (use of), 144
psychopathic attitudes/behavior, 219,
  343, 347–348
psychopharmacological treatment (also
  see drug treatment), 61, 66, 73, 566,
  631
psychosomatic medicine, 146, 148
psychosomatic symptoms, 150, 363–392
  as a false diagnosis, 363, 369
psychotherapists, 481, 504, 519–520, 563,
  613–616, 621
psychotherapy, 291–292, 465, 516, 519–
  520, 522

psychotherapy (*cont.*)
  dissatisfaction of love-shys with, 78–79, 261, 391, 481
  socialization method (as a), 616
psychoticism, 40
PTA meetings, 610
pubescence, onset of, 387
public speaking, 141, 469, 523
punching bags, 237
punching by bullies, 231
punishment (public), 192
punitiveness, 213
puppies, 39
"puppy love", 280, 296

quality (vs. quantity) time, 156
quantum physics, 590
quartz crystal massage, 632
quasi-kinship support groups, 501–502, 514
questionnaire (self-administered), 134
quiet babies (love-shys as), 151–152

racial discrimination, 92–97
racquetball, 247
rage, 272
rational-emotive therapy, 522, 553
rat research, 39
reading (as recreational pastime), 348
reading problems, 77
reality, subjective nature of, 555
recall (accuracy of), 152, 188, 223
recognition, need for, 252, 254
recreational play interests, 127, 234, 273, 639
recycled fathers, 436
regression, 98
reincarnation, 103, 110–113, 470, 589
rejection,
  as a love-shyness generator, 7, 47, 106, 159
  coping with, 511
  fear of, 2, 271, 618, 622
  women's role in, 6
relatives, importance of, 169, 171
relax (inability to), 163, 190, 411, 415–417, 454–455, 459
reliability, 130–131, 180
religion, 97, 331, 464–472, 598
religious meetings, 196

Religious Mind Science, 468
religious values, 136
reliving of past events (in psychotherapy), 111
resocialization, 143
respect, need for, 252, 254
respondent selection, 132–140
responsibility,
  assuming, 60, 75, 136, 564–565
  disclaiming of, 2
  for others, 514
  teaching of, 573
restlessness, 422
retaliation (willingness to seek), 86
Rhesus monkeys, 228–229
rhinologists, 369, 371, 373
"rich get richer", 83–87, 417
right wing politics, 555
risk taking, 7, 218, 350, 410, 412–413, 427, 445, 618, 621–622
roadblocks to communication, 621, 624, 628–629
rock music, 247, 254, 405, 486–487, 579, 603
role (as unambiguous "script"), 141, 619
role flexibility, 56, 619
role models, 189, 435
role playing, 95, 164–165, 220, 512–513
role/situation (as independent variable), 97–98
role taking, 513
romance novels, 595
romantic attraction, 299
romantic directionality, 234
romantic love (felt need for), 21, 113, 282, 474–475, 508, 541, 620, 639
romantic preoccupations/fantasies, 268, 274, 281, 301, 474, 484
romantic vs. sexual love (need for), 121–122, 281
rope jumping, 247
rosy colored smokescreen, 296, 313
rough and tumble play, 45–49, 56, 72, 85, 122, 144–146, 157, 191, 195, 197, 222, 233–234, 237, 239–244, 246, 248–249, 251, 254, 261, 284, 552, 590, 596, 603, 631, 635, 640
"R" rated films, 191, 197
rugged individualism, 27, 60
rules (family), 180

running behavior, 422
running as sport, 248–249
"Sadie Hawkins" type social events, 610
saliva problems, 72, 371
salivary glands (hyperactive), 371
salivation (excessive), 380–381
salt shaker passing, 392, 412
same-sexed friendships, 122, 225–263,
    420, 424
sample (research) heterogeneity/homo-
    geneity, 129–130
samples (research) studied, 127–131
Saturn (influence of in astrology), 108–
    109
scapegoating, 167
schizoid neurotic tendencies, 75, 124,
    149, 218
schizoid personality, 406
schizophrenia, 74–75, 80, 149, 174
school letter awards, 251–252
school phobias, 66–67
scratching, 392, 395
screening for summer camps, 194
script learning, 3, 141, 164, 469–470, 619
secondary gain, 151
"second plateau" in therapy, 504, 526,
    532, 544–545
secretaries, 164–165
segregation of the sexes, 166, 283, 470
self-acceptance, 178
self-awareness, 453–454
self-centeredness, 260
self-confidence norms, 16
self-confidence (social), 49–51, 84–87, 90,
    108, 113, 128, 136–137, 157, 162–163,
    165, 167, 174, 178, 192, 241, 243, 249–
    250, 271, 276, 305, 308–309, 314, 317,
    357, 440, 444–445, 449, 452–454, 458–
    459, 461, 467, 470, 494, 511–514, 529,
    547, 562, 574, 582, 594–595, 597, 600–
    602, 605–606, 615, 620, 625
self-consciousness, 370, 380, 382, 388–
    389, 392, 410–411
self-defense, 231
self-determination (also see free choice),
    509, 629
self-discipline, 201, 469, 556–557
self-disclosure reticence, 133–135, 180,
    187, 288–292, 382, 440
self-esteem, 43, 46–47, 66, 81–82, 87–88,
    94, 96, 106–107, 114, 167, 174, 178,
    191, 219, 241, 252, 263, 307–309, 317,
    341, 444–445, 456, 469, 554, 557, 625,
    635
self-fulfilling prophecy, 96, 312, 435,
    560–561
self-image (self-definition), 55, 87–88, 94,
    121, 143, 157, 178, 186, 188, 191–192,
    219, 222, 308, 319, 456, 546
    crystallization of, 157
    psychologists, 553–555
    psychology, 548–561
    therapy, 555–561
self-knowledge, 454
self-love, 13, 97
self-preoccupation, 260
self-revelation norms, 19–21
self-sufficiency (low), 108, 514, 516, 519,
    563, 614, 616
self-talk (positive), 504, 555–557, 559–560
senility, 62
sensate focus, 530–532
sensitivity threshold, 386
separation anxiety, 66–67, 80
separation (marital), 169–171
seriousness, 165, 185–187, 547
serotonin, 64, 636, 639–640
sex discussions in home, 188–189
sex drive, 389
sexist norms, 610
sex play as children,
    actual experience, 123
    with boys (same-sexed peers), 122–123
    with girls, 122–123
sex role norms, 125–126, 235
sex role orientation, 174
sexual anxieties, 529
sexual attitudes and values, 327–329
sexual desires (love-shys'), 324–326
sexual experience,
    need for, 281
    premarital, 136–137
sexual fidelity, 516
sexual harassment, 356
sexual interests, 122
sexual lives of love-shys, 323–341
sexual love-making (initiation of), 118
sexual obsessions, 326
sexual satisfaction, 326–327
sexual surrogate therapy, 524, 527–533

sham in dating, 19–21, 620
shell shock proneness, 576–577
shoplifting, 348–349
shortness of stature, 387
Show Boat, 477, 480
showers, 203–205
show (theatre) music, 254, 584
shuffle board, 49, 245, 251
shyness,
    auric health and, 114
    definition, 2
    deviance and, 5
    in women, 5
    milder forms, 131
    preoccupation and, 12
    prevalence, 33
    vs. self-control, 7
shyness-generating situations, 243
Shys Anonymous (also see Love-Shys
    Anonymous), 209, 319–320, 502, 524,
    556, 615, 629
siblings, 161–162, 167, 170–171, 211–212
significant others, 88, 101–102, 111
singing, 252, 415, 427–428
single life style, 201
single-never-married status (prevalence
    of), 1, 129
singles apartment buildings, 583
sinus arrhythmia, 52
sisters, 161–167, 170–171, 189, 237, 249,
    481, 510, 585, 624, 626
    desire for as youngsters, 285–286
situational shyness, 83
"60 Minutes", 253, 584
size of body, 232
sleep (and being loved), 14
sleep disturbance, 62
sleep needs (and learning), 379
sleep test, 61
"slow-to-warm-up" child, 48–49, 52–53,
    55, 653
small talk, 244, 249
sociability, 16, 39, 43, 55, 80, 136, 178,
    188, 244, 350, 406, 409, 411, 440, 447,
    454–455, 546, 625, 632
social ambiguity (fear of), 563–564
social avoidance, 64, 72, 192, 226, 230–
    231, 380, 383, 388–389, 410, 573
    of mothers, 155
social competence, 173–174
social connections, 205

social control (as a function of religion),
    472
social dancing, 247
social desirability valence, 176, 378
social distance, 219
social engineering (need for), 227, 252
social facilitation, 349
social finesse, 307
social isolation (chronic), 124, 150, 157,
    159–160, 166, 171, 225, 229, 234, 274,
    287, 347
socialization, 562, 614, 616, 631
    and dependency, 552
    as hypnosis, 550
    as mental programming, 550
    function of peer group, 4, 157, 159
social learning, 223–224
socially handicapped children, 244
social mobility, 219
social participation, 176–177, 503–504,
    507, 514, 516, 586
social phobias (also see people phobia),
    566
social situations classified, 2, 141
social skills (also see interpersonal
    skills), 243, 250, 562
social stimulus value, 40, 45–47, 62, 79,
    83–88, 99, 102, 106–107, 145–146, 223–
    224, 231–232, 313, 392, 552–554, 641
social support networks, 27, 29, 44, 157,
    168, 171, 228, 260, 268–271, 422, 447,
    455, 503, 516, 524
societal expectations, 233, 609
societal reaction, 37, 79, 81, 88, 102, 106
society (responsibility of), 133
socioeconomic status (in childhood),
    443–444
sociological perspective, 88
sodium lactate, 72
softball, 285
solitary activities, 191
solitary confinement, 226
sorority girls, 604–606
"soul" concept, 316–318, 471, 568
sounding board, 564
Soviet education 572–574
spanking (see corporal punishment)
Special Olympics, 90
speech making (also see public speak-
    ing), 469, 523
speech reticence, 140–141

spider monkeys, 584
spinal fluid, 64
spinsters, 119
spirit mind, 113
Spiritualists/Spiritualism, 106, 367, 459, 468, 470–472, 478, 550–551, 589
spirit vs. body, 316
"spoiled" children, 183–184
spontaneity, 547
spontaneous remission, 131
sports,
    attitudes toward, 237–243
    effectiveness at, 250
    participation in, 241
square dancing, 247
square pegs in round holes, 576, 578, 616
squeaking sounds (painful aversion to), 402
stability, need for, 452
standardization of personality, 234
staring behavior, 195, 228–229, 269, 277, 353–360, 450, 462
"stars" at school, 83–85
status consciousness, 159–160
status inconsistency, 444, 546
stereotypes (traditional), 211
stillbirths, 147–148
stomach aches, 379
strength (physical), 232
stress, 59–60, 147, 149, 168, 171, 214, 218, 347, 372, 386, 423, 592, 634–636, 638
    in mothers during pregnancy, 143–152, 638–639
structure, need for, 141, 469–472, 563–564, 619
stuttering, 390
subconscious mind, 101, 548–549, 553, 555, 557, 560–561
subjective vs. objective reality, 120, 555
sugary diet, 376, 389, 392
suggestibility, 552
suicide, 63–64, 153, 213
summer camps, 181, 193–199, 214, 254, 278–279, 344–345
    administrators of, 194
    screening for, 194
sunlight (aversion to intense), 197, 239, 397–398
sun signs (astrological), 103–109

superordinate goals, 286, 582
support groups, 17, 25, 27, 29, 48, 158, 171, 209, 259, 268–271, 319, 339–340, 422–423, 535, 556–557, 560, 563, 606
Survey of Heterosexual Interaction (SHI), 137–138, 659–663
swearing and cursing, 212
sweets, craving for, 147, 376–377
swimming, 49, 195, 246, 249, 251, 285, 403
sympathetic nervous system (subordination of), 635
symptom displacement hypothesis, 561
symptom need hypothesis, 78, 561
synchronicity, 105–106

"tableau rasa", 98
tactile contact, 188, 530–531
"talking cure", 60, 66–67, 208, 518–522, 616
task orientation, 181
team sports, 248
technical knowledge/training, 452–457, 461–462
teenage love stories (penchant for), 483
telekenetic power, 555
telephones, 132–135, 140, 411–412, 445, 447, 450, 544
television starlets (infatuation with), 287, 292–293
temperament (inborn), 38–40, 46–48, 53, 56, 75, 79, 81–84, 86–88, 90–91, 98, 101–103, 105–107, 113, 125, 231, 244, 248, 254–255, 258, 271, 273, 284–285, 317, 350, 393, 429, 454, 561, 570–571, 578–579, 609, 624, 631–641
    defined, 38, 46–48
temper of mothers, 152–160, 212–213
temper tantrums (of mothers), 153, 212, 218, 220
tennis, 239, 246–247, 251
tenseness, 145–146, 152, 167, 186, 411, 415–416, 496, 505, 547, 551
testosterones (blood), 57, 59, 144–147, 152, 156, 388, 422, 636–641
testosterone shots, 157–158, 160
tetherball, 247
theatre arts, 252
therapeutic forces, 482
therapeutic ideology, 38, 561–565
thinking style, 409

throat clearing, 384–385
tics, 76–77
time,
    consciousness, 494, 508
    importance of, 614
    misjudging of limits, 272–273
    rapidly passing, 272–273, 629
    required for childbirthing, 149
time limits (see critical periods, and
    developmental tasks)
timetables (preconceived), 283
timidity (social), 52, 113, 406, 631–633
tiredness (see fatigue)
tolerance, 55, 60, 121
touch (see tactile contact)
"touch" football, 238, 242, 255
toy preferences, 235–237
toys, 182
"trained incapacity", 250, 417–418, 459,
    547
transfer of anxiety, 284
transfer of behavior, 218
transsexualism, 125–126, 429
transvestite tendencies, 126
trauma, 454
traumas (past life), 111
travel (penchant for), 413–414
tricyclic antidepressants, 72, 631
truculent abrasiveness (in mothers), 145,
    153, 158, 167, 218
trust, 513
tunnel vision, 411
two-facedness, 159

ulcers, 379
unconditional acceptance (importance
    of), 48, 55, 222
underachievement, 78, 119, 443, 450,
    521, 546
underemployment, 221, 442, 456, 458
unemployability, 453, 458
unemployment, 442, 458
unfavorable comparisons (by parents),
    191–192
unhappiness, 140, 417
universal cosmic consciousness ("God-
    mind"), 106
unpopularity (chronic), 144, 159–160
unrealistic expectations, 305, 318

unrequited love, 13, 274, 282, 287, 296
unstructured, purely sociable situations,
    3, 141
unwanted pregnancy (causes of), 297
urban centers, 132
urine tests, 61

validity, 180
values, 299, 425, 506
values (inferring from overt behavior),
    8, 409–410
verbal abuse and hazing, 199, 335–336,
    341, 385
verbal reasoning, 173–174
vested interests, 194, 202, 315, 422, 457,
    463, 520, 604
vicarious gratification, 473–475, 479
victim (blaming of), 133
victims' rights, 570
video tape machines, use of, 512
Vietnam War, 574–577
violence,
    family, 168
    fantasies of, 344–345
    societal, 255, 263
    television, 253–256
violent tendencies (learning of), 219
virginity, premarital, 15, 117, 121, 133,
    136, 138, 142, 171, 178, 279, 323, 529
virus (schizoid-inducing), 406
visitation (of love-shys with parents/
    kin), 201, 203, 221
visualization (mental rehearsal), 301,
    304–305, 320, 452, 492, 502–504, 535–
    538, 549, 551, 553, 555, 558–560, 566
visual needs, 21
vital depression, 65–66
volleyball, 49, 240, 245–246, 248–249, 251
voting behavior, 179, 463, 594

walks, long, 191, 195, 199
waltzes, penchant for, 247
wedding presents, 203–205
weight (bodily), 232, 365
wheat allergies, 406
wheat and rye consumption, 406
wife batterers, 346
wishes (three, case of), 289
witchcraft, 502, 536
withdrawal (from drugs), 296

withdrawal (social), 48–49, 53, 106, 123–124, 146–147, 149, 156–157, 166, 218, 249–250, 263, 406, 415–416, 622
    reasons for, 284
withholding of behavior, 218
"wish bone effect", 83–89, 98
wish-fulfillment fantasies, 267, 300, 629
women and love-shyness, 4–5
women's liberation movement, 56, 118, 201
wooley monkeys, 584
wool, sensitivity to, 398
work roles, importance of, 441
World War I, 575
World War II, 638

xenoglossy, 110

yentas, 618–620
yohimbine, 73
younger love-shys (research samples), 132–134
younger vs. older love-shys, 18, 129–130
Young Men's Christian Association, 166, 194, 246, 254, 284, 627
Young *People's* Christian Association, 246
Young Women's Christian Association, 166, 184, 627

zero population growth, 431
Zuni Indians, 552